Berry's Greek-English New Testament Lexicon with Synonyms

Berry's Greek-English New Testament Lexicon with Synonyms

NUMERICALLY CODED TO
STRONG'S EXHAUSTIVE CONCORDANCE

George Ricker Berry

KING JAMES VERSION

BAKER BOOK HOUSE
Grand Rapids, Michigan 49506

Reprinted by Baker Book House
from the original edition issued by
Handy Book Company, Reading, Pennsylvania
Copyright 1897 by Hinds & Noble

ISBN: 0-8010-0791-7

Numerical coding copyright 1980
by Baker Book House Company

PHOTOLITHOPRINTED BY CUSHING - MALLOY, INC.
ANN ARBOR, MICHIGAN, UNITED STATES OF AMERICA

PUBLISHER'S INTRODUCTION

This new edition of George Ricker Berry's *Greek-English New Testament Lexicon* has numerous features that in days to come will make it more popularly useful than any other lexicon in its class. A brief perusal of *Berry's Greek-English New Testament Lexicon with Synonyms: Numerically Coded to Strong's Exhaustive Concordance* will instantly commend it to three classes of students. First, college and seminary students of New Testament Greek will recognize it as a portable lexicon for the briefcase, with succinct, pointed definitions and grammatical information that will make it a valuable constant companion. It is a perfect aid to the mastery of New Testament Greek vocabulary. Second, busy pastors will welcome it as a ready tool for maintaining and improving their grasp of Greek. Finally, the student of New Testament Greek words, who has had no opportunity for formal Greek study, will find it to be the perfect traveling companion for *Strong's Exhaustive Concordance*. It can be easily taken along on vacations, to retreats, to Sunday school, to home Bible-study meetings. It is primarily to this third class of students that this Introduction is addressed.

Since this handy lexicon's definitions are much clearer and more easily grasped than those of the "Greek Dictionary of the New Testament" in the back of *Strong's Exhaustive Concordance*, it is ideal for quick reference in personal study and group discussions. It is important to realize, however, that neither George Ricker Berry nor the publisher of this edition intended this little reference volume to be used for exploring or arguing the finer points of grammar or biblical interpretation. For that purpose one must consult larger and more detailed reference works (to be mentioned later).

Let us suppose, now, that you are reading a verse in the New Testament, and you realize that there is a certain word in the verse upon which the meaning of that verse hinges. It occurs to you that unless you can find out the meaning of the original Greek word behind that English word, you will not be able to comprehend the thrust of the verse, or perhaps even the thrust of the passage. At this point it is most important to be sure that the version of the New Testament you are using for study is a *translation* (that is, as far as is possible, a word-for-word rendering of the Greek into English) and *not a paraphrase* (an attempt at rephrasing and interpreting in English the thoughts of the original Greek as perceived by the paraphraser). Now read the verse in the King James Version (KJV), picking out the key word (or words) in question. Look up this word in *Strong's Exhaustive Concordance*. This work provides a bridge between the English text of the KJV and the original Greek of the New Testament (as well as the Hebrew and Aramaic of the Old Testament). Having found in *Strong's* the word in question, locate under it the Scripture reference of the verse you are studying. Beside it you will find a contextual extract from the verse with the word itself abbreviated. On the right you will discover a *code number*. Write this code number down. Now you may use this code number to look up in the Greek Dictionary in the back of *Strong's* the Greek word behind the English word being considered. There you will find after the code number the actual Greek word in Greek letters, the word transliterated into our own familiar (Latin) alphabet, the pronunciation, and the way(s) it is translated in the KJV. Study Strong's definition(s) if you wish (if you do, be sure that you understand his abbreviations and symbols as explained at the beginning of the Greek Dictionary).

Now that you know the code number of the Greek word, its pronunciation, and some of the ways it is translated into English, use the code number to look it up in this handy lexicon. Here you will find one or more definitions of the word, one of which may fit in the context that you are studying. It is most important to know, and to remember, that *Berry's Greek-English New Testament Lexicon* is *not* a detailed reference work that differentiates all the various nuances and subtle shades of meaning of any particular Greek word. For that you should obtain our numerically coded edition of Thayer's *Greek-English Lexicon of the New Testament*. This handy lexicon *will* serve to keep a Greek word's most common and basic meanings at your fingertips.

If you desire to delve into a Greek word's derivation, use the code number to look it up in Strong's Greek Dictionary. There you will find (if it is indeed derived from some other Greek word or words) one or more code numbers. Look these up also in Strong's Greek Dictionary or Thayer's *Greek-English Lexicon*.

It may be that you will want to discover all the Greek words which are translated by a single English word in various contexts in the KJV

New Testament. Find the word in *Strong's Exhaustive Concordance.* Then note on paper the various code numbers found next to the New Testament occurrences of the word. By studying each of the Greek words corresponding to those code numbers you will become aware of distinctions that were previously hidden since the same English word was employed to translate them. Since something is lost in any translation from one language to another, no matter how good the translation may be, you will find such study enlightening and most rewarding. Through prayer for enlightenment and diligent application many difficulties will be cleared up, and the way of salvation, which is a way of truth and holiness, will grow progressively clearer (Prov. 2).

In the numerically coded editions of Thayer's *Greek-English Lexicon* and *Englishman's Greek Concordance* published by Baker, you will find valuable introductory articles on the proper method of doing New Testament word studies. By consulting those volumes and Louis Berkhof's *Principles of Biblical Interpretation,* you may find that you have been enabled to avoid the dangerous pitfalls of hastily drawn conclusions and erroneous private interpretations.

Please take note of the special section entitled "New Testament Synonyms" that begins on page 165. Two hundred ninety-two words are listed in the Index at the beginning of the section, some of which are treated only in the "New Testament Synonyms" section, some of which are treated only in the body of the lexicon, and some of which are dealt with in both places. Please read Berry's Introduction to the section and his explanation of the Index before using the materials for research.

TABLE OF SYMBOLS AND ABBREVIATIONS PERTAINING TO THE NUMERICAL APPARATUS

•	The accompanying word is for one reason or another not in the exact order in which it is found in Strong's Greek Dictionary. Therefore, its code number is not in proper numerical sequence even though the word is properly alphabetized in the lexicon.
□	Two or more entries with the code number appear on the same page, though not consecutively. Be sure to study each entry.
* or **	Look for omitted entries to be referred to in a footnote.
St	The number referred to can be found only in (or ought to be examined in) Strong's Greek Dictionary
see [000] St	The bracketed number referred to is to be found in Strong's Hebrew and Chaldee Dictionary.
see Strong	The word is listed separately in Strong's Greek Dictionary but not in this lexicon.
cf 000St	The word's spelling or form is considerably different in Strong's Greek Dictionary.
see 000	This word is (1) a variant spelling or reading of the word to be consulted, or (2) a synonym. In case a word has one or more synonyms that are referred to in the text of the definition but there is no cross reference, look up the word by its code number in

the Index to New Testament Synonyms on page 167.

L-S. p. 000A or p. 000B The word so noted does not appear in the Greek New Testament and thus was assigned no code number by Strong. It may be found on the indicated page and column (A or B) in *A Greek-English Lexicon* by Henry George Liddell and Robert Scott, revised and augmented throughout by Sir Henry Stuart Jones with the assistance of Roderick McKenzie, with a Supplement (Oxford: At the Clarendon Press, 1968).

INTRODUCTION TO NEW TESTAMENT LEXICON

A S a result of their wide experience as sellers of text-books of all kinds, extending over many years, the publishers have become aware that clergymen, theological students, and New Testament students generally, possess the conviction that none of the smaller New Testament Lexicons is entirely satisfactory. There are several essential and entirely practical features, not embodied in any of the smaller New Testament Lexicons, which should be incorporated in a work intended to fulfill all necessary requirements. It is with the definite intention of supplying this need that the publishers nave undertaken the preparation of this new Lexicon. It aims to retain all the desirable features of the best small Lexicons in use, and also to present the several additional points demanded, while keeping within the compass of a volume of convenient size.

This Lexicon endeavors to put into a brief and compact form as much as possible of the material found in the larger New Testament Lexicons. The fact has been remembered that in nine cases out of ten the object in consulting a Lexicon is to refer quickly to the standard meanings of a word, rather than to study an exhaustive treatment of it. Hence, while every clergyman would like to possess one of the larger New Testament Lexicons, he still needs the small one for convenience in ordinary use. So it is assumed that this small New Testament Lexicon will be needed both for use independently, and also by those who have one of the larger Lexicons. It is hoped that in this volume the publishers' intention has been realized of producing a volume that better than any other so far published will serve this purpose quickly and well.

It may be desirable to point out a few features which have been made prominent. It will be at once apparent that some of these are not ordinarily found in the smaller New Testament Lexicons:

The inflection of nouns, adjectives, and verbs has been indicated with all the fullness which was considered practically necessary. In nouns, the ending of the genitive case has regularly been given, being omitted only with indeclinable nouns. The article indicating the gender regularly follows the genitive ending. Other cases have been given only rarely, when they are irregular or peculiar. In adjectives, the endings of the nominative have been given. In verbs, a different form for the present tense, such as a contracted form, has regularly been given, and ordinarily the ending of the future. The endings of the other tenses have only been given in some special cases when they are peculiar, or irregular. Of course the inflection in general has considered only the forms occurring in the New Testament; it is only rarely that classical forms not occurring in the New Testament have been given, since they would be of little practical value in ordinary New Testament study.

The hyphen, to separate the parts of compound words, has been used with considerable freedom, but in general accordance with the following principles. It has been used of course to separate the parts of words which are actually compounded of the two or more portions which appear in the word. Words derived from a compound word would not usually have the hyphen, but sometimes it has been inserted, especially when otherwise the derivation would not be obvious. So, too, the hyphen has been used with derivatives of a compound word, in cases where the original compound word does not occur in the New Testament, as otherwise the character of the word would not appear. The hyphen has also been used in many cases where the compound word is slightly changed in form from the parts of which it is composed, where this variation is not very great. Such a wide use of the hyphen has been for the purpose of increasing the practical value of this feature.

The original plan in reference to Synonyms was to give in the Lexicon itself definitions of a few of the most important ones. After most of the Lexicon was in type, however, it was decided, in view of the importance of the subject, that a very helpful feature would be a special section devoted to Synonyms. This has accordingly been prepared. The result is, of course, that a few words already treated in the Lexicon have here been given a fuller treatment.

The Index to the Synonyms includes all the nouns treated in the Lexicon proper, as well as those in the Synonyms, and this double treatment will always be found to be expressly indicated by its appropriate sign.

Some indications of the history of a word will surely be serviceable to the average student. Consequently, the words whose first known occurrence is in **the Septuagint, in the Apocrypha, and in the New Testament, are indicated by** the respective abbreviations at the end of the articles. Where the usage is in doubt, no indication has been given. The material for this has been drawn chiefly from Thayer. The other classifications which Thayer gives, it was thought would not be of sufficient practical use to the average student to be incorporated.

In the case of words from foreign languages, the language has been indicated in every instance, except with a part of the proper names, chiefly from the Hebrew, where the origin would be readily inferred. It has been the aim to make this feature accurate and up to date. In this matter, considerable help has been received from E. Kautzsch, *Grammatik des Biblisch-Aramäischen.*

The grammatical references given are to the three grammars which are probably in the most common use, viz.: S. G. Green, *Handbook to the Grammar of the Greek Testament*, Revised and Improved Edition; G. B. Winer, *A Grammar of the Idiom of the New Testament*, Seventh Edition, Translated by J. H. Thayer; and Alexander Buttman, *A Grammar of the New Testament Greek*, Translated by J. H. Thayer. These have been indicated respectively by the abbreviations Gr., Wi., and Bu., the references in the first two being by sections, in the last, for convenience, by pages.

The usual custom has been followed of making the received text, the so-called *Textus Receptus*, the basis of this Lexicon, except that sometimes another accentuation has been adopted, which seemed preferable. All the variations of any importance of the text of Westcott and Hort have been given. This does not include all the minor variations in spelling and accentuation. It was thought that to indicate the variants of other editors would occupy more space than it would be profitable to give. For the same reason no mention has been made of variant readings of the *Textus Receptus* itself.

The asterisk * at the end of many articles indicates that all the passages in which the word occurs in the New Testament have been given.

Besides other works which have already been mentioned, much material has been drawn from R. C. Trench, *Synonyms of the New Testament*, and from the New Testament Lexicons of Thayer and Cremer, as well as from the small ones of Green and Hickie.

The New Testament books have been indicated by the shortest abbreviations that would be easily intelligible. It is thought that they will be understood without explanation. The list of other abbreviations which is here added includes only those which might not be recognized without express indication.

ABBREVIATIONS

Ap.   = Apocrypha (of the Old Testament).
A. V. = Authorized Version.
Bu.   = Alexander Buttman (*Grammar of New Testament Greek*).
dim. = diminutive.
fig. = figurative.
Gr.   = S. G. Green (*Handbook to the Grammar of the Greek Testament*).
i.e. = that is.
lit. = literally.
met. = metaphorically.
mrg. = margin.
N. T. = New Testament.
orig. = originally.

O. T. = Old Testament.
Rec. = Textus Receptus.
R. V. = Revised Version.
S.   = Septuagint.
sc.   = namely, to wit.
sq.   = following.
W. H. = Westcott and Hort (*The New Testament in the Original Greek*).
Wi.   = G. B. Winer (*Grammar of the Idiom of the New Testament*).
- hyphen, see Introduction.
* indicates that all the passages in which a word occurs in the New Testament have been given.

Concerning the abbreviations for the Books of the New Testament, see last paragraph of Introduction.

GREEK-ENGLISH NEW TESTAMENT LEXICON

1 Α, α, ἄλφα, *alpha*, *a*, the first letter. Numerally, α' = 1; ,α = 1000. For α in composition, see Gr. § 147*b*, *c*. Fig., τὸ Α, or τὸ Ἄλφα (W. H.), *the first principle of all things;* of the Father, Rev. i. 8, xxi. 6; the Son, i. 11 (W. H. omit), xxii. 13.*

2 Ἀαρών (Heb.), *Aaron*, Lu. i. 5; Ac. vii. 40; Heb. v. 4, vii. 11, ix. 4.*

3 Ἀβαδδών, ὁ (Heb. "destruction"), *Abaddon*, Rev. ix. 11. (S.)*

4 ἀ-βαρής, ές (from βάρος), *without weight;* hence, *not burdensome*, 2 Cor. xi. 9.*

5 Ἀββᾶ, or Ἀββά (W. H.), (Aram), *Father!* only as an invocation, Mar. xiv. 36; Ro. viii. 15; Gal. iv. 6. (N. T.)*

6 Ἄβελ, ὁ (W. H." Ἀβελ), (Heb.), *Abel*, Mat. xxiii. 35; Lu. xi. 51; Heb. xi. 4, xii. 24.*

7 Ἀβιά, ὁ (Heb.), *Abia* or *Abijah*, the king, Mat. i. 7; the priest, Lu. i. 5.*

8 Ἀβιάθαρ, ὁ (Heb.), *Abiathar*, Mar. ii. 26.*

9 Ἀβιληνή, ῆς, ἡ, *Abilene*, a district between Lebanon and Hermon towards Phœnicia, named from Abila, its chief city, Lu. iii. 1.*

10 Ἀβιούδ, ὁ (Heb.), *Abiud*, Mat.

11
12

13

14

15

16

17

18

i. 13.*
Ἀβραάμ, ὁ (Heb.), *Abraham*, Mat. i. 1, 2; Ro. iv. 1, 2, 3.

ἄ-βυσσος, ου, ἡ (originally adj. *bottomless*), *abyss*, Lu. viii. 31; Ro. x. 7; Rev. ix. 1, 2, 11, xi. 7, xvii. 8, xx. 1, 3.*

Ἄγαβος, ου, ὁ, *Agabus*, Ac. xi. 28, xxi. 10.*

ἀγαθο-εργέω, ῶ (or ἀγαθουργέω), *to be beneficent*, 1 Tim. vi. 18; Ac. xiv. 17 (W. H.). (N. T.)*

ἀγαθο-ποιέω, ῶ, (1) *to do good to*, acc. of pers., Lu. vi. 33; (2) *to act well*, 1 Pet. ii. 15, 20. (S.)

ἀγαθο-ποιΐα, ας, ἡ, *well-doing*, in sense (2) of preceding, 1 Pet. iv. 19. (N. T.)*

ἀγαθο-ποιός, οῦ, ὁ (originally adj), *well-doer*, 1 Pet. ii. 14.*

ἀγαθός, ή, όν (κρείσσων, κράτιστος), *good* in general, in various senses, in itself or its effects, physically or morally, used of both persons and things, Mat. vii. 18; Lu. vi. 45; 1 Pet. ii. 18; Phil. i. 6. τὸ ἀγαθόν, *the Good*, Mat. xix. 17 (W. H.); τὰ ἀγαθά, *goods, wealth, blessings*, Lu. i. 53; Ro. x. 15.

19 ἀγαθωσύνη, ης, ἡ, *goodness*, 2 Th. i. 11. (S.) *Syn.*: ἀγαθωσύνη emphasizes the *zeal for goodness;* χρηστότης, *kindness, benignity.*

20 ἀγαλλίασις, εως, ἡ, *exultation,*

21 *gladness*, Lu. i. 14, 44. (S.)

ἀγαλλιάω, ῶ, ασω, *to leap for joy;* hence, *exult, rejoice;* generally deponent. Followed by ἵνα (subj.), Jn. viii. 56; ἐπί (dat.), Lu. i. 47; or ἐν (dat.), Jn. v. 35. (S.)

22 **ἄ-γαμος, ον,** adj., *unmarried,* 1 Cor. vii. 8, 11, 32, 34.*

23 **ἀγανακτέω, ῶ, ήσω,** *to be indignant,angry.* With περί (gen.), Mat. xx. 24; or ὅτι, Lu. xiii. 14.

24 **ἀγανάκτησις, εως, ἡ,** *indignation,* 2 Cor. vii. 11.*

25 **ἀγαπάω, ῶ, ήσω,** *to love,* Lu. vii. 47; *to wish well to,* Mat. v. 43, xix. 19; *to take pleasure in,* Heb. i. 9; *to long for,* 2 Tim. iv. 8. *Syn.:* ἀγαπάω denotes the love of the reason, esteem; φιλέω, the love of the feelings, warm instinctive affection.

26 **ἀγάπη, ης, ἡ,** *love, benevolence.* Object with εἰς, ἐν, or genitive, Gr. § 269, Wi. § 30a, Bu. 329. ἀγάπαι (Ju. 12), *love-feasts.* (S.)

27 **ἀγαπητός, ἡ, όν,** *beloved,* Mat. iii. 17.

28 **Ἄγαρ, ἡ** (W. H. Ἅγαρ), (Heb.), *Hagar,* Gal. iv. 24, 25 (W. H.).*

29 **ἀγγαρεύω, σω** (from the Persian), *to impress* into the public service; hence, *to compel to perform any service,* Mat. v. 41, xxvii. 32; Mar. xv. 21.*

30 **ἀγγεῖον, ου, τό,** *vessel, utensil,* Mat. xiii. 48 (Rec.), xxv. 4.*

31 **ἀγγελία, ας, ἡ,** *message,* 1 Jn. i. 5 (W. H.), iii. 11.*

32 **ἄγγελος, ου, ὁ,** *messenger,* Mat. xi. 10; spec. of God's messengers to men, *angel,* Mat. iv. 6. So of fallen spirits, Ju. 6. "Angel of a church" (Rev. i. 20, ii., iii.), either *messenger,* or *elder,* or *an angel* who watches over the church.

see 30 **ἄγγος, εος, τό,** *vessel,* Mat. xiii. 48 (W. H.).*

33 **ἄγε,** interj. (properly impv. of ἄγω), *come now!* Ja. iv. 13, v. 1.*

34 **ἀγέλη, ης, ἡ,** *a flock* or *herd,* Mat. viii. 30.

35 **ἀ-γενεα-λόγητος, ου,** adj., *of unrecorded genealogy,* Heb. vii. 3. (N. T.)*

36 **ἀ-γενής, ές** (from γένος), *low-born, base,* 1 Cor. i. 28.*

37 **ἁγιάζω, σω** (from ἅγιος), *to set apart* from common use. Hence, *to hallow,* or regard with religious reverence, Mat. vi. 9; *to consecrate* to religious service, whether persons or things, Mat. xxiii. 17; Jn. xvii. 19; *to cleanse* for such consecration, Heb. ix. 13; so *to purify, sanctify,* 1 Cor. vi. 11. οἱ ἁγιαζόμενοι, *those who are being sanctified;* οἱ ἡγιασμένοι, *those who are sanctified,* Ac. xx. 32.

38 **ἁγιασμός, οῦ, ὁ,** *sanctification, holiness,* 1 Cor. i. 30; 1 Th. iv. 7. (S.)

●40. 39 **ἅγιος, α, ον,** *hallowed, worthy of veneration, holy, consecrated,* whether persons, places, or things. οἱ ἅγιοι, *"the Saints";* τὸ ἅγιον, *the Temple;* τὰ ἅγια, *the Sanctuary;* ἅγια ἁγίων, *the Holy of Holies;* πνεῦμα ἅγιον, *the Holy Spirit. Syn.:* see Trench, § lxxxviii.

41 **ἁγιότης, τητος, ἡ,** *holiness,* Heb. xii. 10; 2 Cor. i. 12 (W. H.). (Ap.)*

42 **ἁγιωσύνη, ης, ἡ,** *holiness,* Ro. i. 4; 2 Cor. vii. 1; 1 Th. iii. 13. (S.)*

43 **ἀγκάλη, ης, ἡ,** *the* (curve of the) *arm,* Lu. ii. 28.*

44 **ἄγκιστρον, ου, τό,** *fishhook,* Mat. xvii. 27.*

45 **ἄγκυρα, ας, ἡ,** *an anchor,* Ac. xxvii. 29, 30, 40; Heb. vi. 19.

46 **ἄ-γναφος, ον,** adj., *unfulled, undressed,* Mat. ix. 16; Mar. ii. 21. (N. T.)*

47 **ἁγνεία, ας, ἡ,** *purity,* 1 Tim. iv. 12, v. 2.*

48 **ἁγνίζω, σω,** *to cleanse,, purify;* ceremonially, Jn. xi. 55; morally, Ja. iv. 8.

49 **ἁγνισμός, οῦ, ὁ,** ceremonial *purification,* Ac. xxi. 26.*

50 **ἀ-γνοέω, ῶ, ήσω** (see γιγνώσκω), (1) *not to know, to be ignorant,* 1 Tim. i. 13; ἀγνοῶν, *ignorant;* ἀγνοούμενος, *unknown,* Gal. i. 22; *ignored, disregarded,* 1 Cor. xiv. 38 (W. H.); (2) *not to understand,* Mar. ix. 32; Lu. ix. 45.

51 **ἀγνόημα, ατος, τό,** *a sin of ignorance, error,* Heb. ix. 7.* *Syn.:* see Trench, § lxvi.

52 **ἄγνοια, ας, ἡ,** *ignorance,* Ac. iii.

2

17, xvii. 30; Ep. iv. 18; 1 Pet. i. 14.*

53 ἀγνός, ή, όν, *pure*, 2 Cor. vii. 11; *chaste*, Tit. ii. 5. *Syn.:* see ἅγιος.

54 ἀγνότης, τητος, ή, *purity*, 2 Cor. vi. 6, xi. 3 (W. H.).*

55 ἀγνῶς, adv., *purely, sincerely*, Phil. i. 17.*

56 ἀγνωσία, ας, ή, *ignorance*, spec. willful ignorance, 1 Cor. xv. 34; 1 Pet. ii. 15.*

57 ἄγνωστος, ον, *unknown*, Ac. xvii. 23.*

58 ἀγορά, ᾶς, ή (ἀγείρω), *a place of public resort, forum, market place*, Ac. xvii. 17; used for the market, Mar. vii. 4; as the place of public assemblies, trials, etc., Ac. xvi. 19.

59 ἀγοράζω, σω, *to purchase, buy*, with gen. of price, Mar. vi. 37, or ἐκ, Mat. xxvii. 7, once ἐν, Rev. v. 9; fig., *to redeem, ransom*, Rev. v. 9, xiv. 3.

60 ἀγοραῖος, ον, *belonging to the forum;* hence (sc. ἡμέραι) *court days*, Ac. xix. 38; (sc. ἄνθρωποι) *idlers*, xvii. 5.*

61 ἄγρα, ας, ή, *a catching*, Lu. v. 4; *the thing caught, a catch* of fish, v. 9.*

62 ἀ-γράμματος, ον, *unlearned*, *i.e.*, in Rabbinical lore, Ac. iv. 13.* *Syn.:* ἀγράμματος means *illiterate*, without knowledge gained by study; ἰδιώτης, not a specialist, or without knowledge gained by mingling in public life.

63 ἀγρ-αυλέω, ῶ, *to live in the fields*, Lu. ii. 8.*

64 ἀγρεύω, σω (to take in hunting), fig., *to ensnare*, Mar. xii. 13.*

65 ἀγρι-έλαιος, ον, ή, *wild olive*, Ro. xi. 17, 24.*

66 ἄγριος, ία, ιον, *wild*, of honey, Mat. iii. 4; Mar. i. 6; *fierce*, of waves, Ju. 13.*

67 Ἀγρίππας, α, ὁ, *Agrippa, i.e.*, Herod Agrippa II. See Ἡρώδης.

68 ἀγρός, οῦ, ὁ, *field*, spec. *the country*, Mat. vi. 28; plur., *country districts, hamlets*, Mar. v. 14.

69 ἀγρυπνέω, ῶ (ὕπνος), *to be sleepless;* hence, met., *to watch, to be vigilant*, Mar. xiii. 33; Lu. xxi. 36; Ep. vi. 18; Heb. xiii. 17.*

70 ἀγρυπνία, ας, ή, *sleeplessness*,

watching, 2 Cc᷄. vⁱ. 5, xi. 27.*

71 ἄγω, ξω, 2 a., ἤγαγον, trans., *to lead, bring;* with πρός (acc.), ἕως, εἰς, of destination; with ἐπί (acc.)., of purpose, as Ac. viii. 32; *to bring before*, for trial, Ac. xxv. 17. Also *to spend*, as of time; *to keep*, as a particular day, Mat. xiv. 6 (not W. H.); Lu. xxiv. 21 (impers.). Fig., *to lead the inclination, induce*, Lu. iv. 1. Mid., *to go, depart;* subj., ἄγωμεν, *let us go!* Mat. xxvi. 46.

72 ἀγωγή, ῆς, ή (ἄγω), *a leading, course of life*, 2 Tim. iii. 10.*

73 ἀγών, ῶνος, ὁ, *contest, conflict;* fig., of the Christian life, as Heb. xii. 1; *solicitude, anxiety*, Col. ii. 1.

74 ἀγωνία, ας, ή, *contest, agony*, Lu. xxii. 44 (not W. H.).*

75 ἀγωνίζομαι, *to strive*, as in the public games, 1 Cor. ix. 25; *to contend* with an adversary, Jn. xviii. 36; fig., of Christian effort and endurance, Col. i. 29.

76 Ἀδάμ, ὁ (Heb.), *Adam.*

77 ἀ-δάπανος, ον, *free of charge, gratuitous*, 1 Cor. ix. 18.*

78 Ἀδδί, ὁ, *Addi*, Lu. iii. 28 (not mentioned in O. T.).*

79 ἀδελφή, ῆς, ή, *a sister*, (1) lit., Mat. xix. 29; (2) fig. of Christian friendship, 1 Cor. vii. 15.

80 ἀδελφός, οῦ, ὁ, *a brother*, (1) lit. (see Gr. § 256), Mat. i. 2; (2) of more general relations, *a fellow-countryman*, Mat. v. 47; *a fellow-Christian*, Mat. xxiii. 8; *a fellow-man*, Mat. v. 22–24; also expressing the relation between Christ and believers, Mat. xxv. 40. The "brethren of Jesus" (Mat. xiii. 55; Jn. vii. 3; Ac. i. 14; Gal. i. 19) are probably to be understood literally.

81 ἀδελφότης, τητος, ή, *the brotherhood, i.e.*, the Christian community, 1 Pet. ii. 17, v. 9. (Ap.)*

82 ἄ-δηλος, ον, *not manifest, uncertain*, Lu. xi. 44; 1 Cor. xiv. 8.*

83 ἀ-δηλότης, τητος, *uncertainty.* 1 Tim. vi. 17.*

84 ἀδήλως, adv., *uncertainly*, 1 Cor. ix. 26.*

85 ἀδημονέω, ῶ, *to be troubled, distressed*, Mar. xiv. 33.

86 ᾅδης, ου, ὁ (ἀ priv. and ἰδεῖν), *the invisible world, Hades,* Lu. xvi. 23; fig., of deep degradation, Mat. xi. 23. See πύλη.

87 ἀ-διά-κριτος, ον, *without uncertainty, unambiguous,* Ja. iii. 17.*

88 ἀ-διά-λειπτος, ον, *without intermission, unceasing,* Ro. ix. 2; 2 Tim. i. 3.*

89 ἀδιαλείπτως, adv., *without intermission, incessantly,* Ro. i. 9; 1 Th. i. 2, ii. 13, v. 17.*

90 ἀ-δια-φθορία, ας, ἡ, *incorruptibility, soundness,* Tit. ii. 7 (not W. H.). (N. T.)*

91 ἀδικέω, ῶ, ήσω (ἄδικος), intrans., *to act unjustly, commit a crime,* Ac. xxv. 11; trans., *to wrong, injure,* Mat. xx. 13; hence, *to hurt,* without any notion of wrong, Lu. x. 19, and Rev. often; pass., *to be wronged,* 2 Cor. vii. 12; mid., *to suffer wrong,* 1 Cor. vi. 7.

92 ἀδίκημα, ατος, τό, *a wrong, misdeed,* Ac. xviii. 14, xxiv. 20; Rev. xviii. 5.*

93 ἀδικία, ας, ἡ, *wrong* (towards man or God); hence, *injustice,* Lu. xviii. 6; Ro. ix. 14; *unrighteousness,* Ro. i. 18, 29; *act of unrighteousness,* 1 Jn. v. 17; Heb. viii. 12.

94 ἄ-δικος, ον, *unjust, unrighteous,* generally, opposed to δίκαιος, as Mat. v. 45, to εὐσεβής, as 2 Pet. ii. 9, or to πιστός, as Lu. xvi. 10.

95 ἀδίκως, adv., *unjustly, undeservedly,* 1 Pet. ii. 19.*

96 ἀ-δόκιμος, ον (tested, but not approved), *reprobate, rejected,* Ro. i. 28; 1 Cor. ix. 27; 2 Cor. xiii. 5, 6, 7; 2 Tim. iii. 8; Tit. i. 16; Heb. vi. 8.*

97 ἄ-δολος, ον, *without fraud, unadulterated,* 1 Pet. ii. 2.* *Syn.:* see Trench, § lvi.

98 Ἀδραμυττηνός, ή, όν, *of Adramyttium,* a seaport of Mysia, Ac. xxvii. 2.*

99 Ἀδρίας, ου, ὁ, *the Adriatic,* the sea between Greece and Italy, Ac. xxvii. 27.*

100 ἁδρότης, τητος, ἡ, *abundance, liberality,* 2 Cor. viii. 20.*

101 ἀδυνατέω, ῶ, ήσω, *to be impossible,* with dat. of pers., Mat. xvii. 20; or παρά (dat., W. II. gen.), Lu. i. 37.*

102 ἀ-δύνατος, ον, (1) of persons, act., *powerless,* Ac. xiv. 8; (2) of things, pass., *impossible,* Ro. viii. 3.

103 ᾄδω, ᾄσω (contr. from ἀείδω), *to sing,* with cognate acc., ᾠδήν, *a song,* Rev. v. 9, xiv. 3, xv. 3; with dat., *to sing* (praise) *to,* Ep. v. 19; Col. iii. 16.*

104 ἀεί, adv., *always;* of continuous time, *unceasingly,* Ac. vii. 51; of successive intervals, *from time to time, on every occasion,* 1 Pet. iii. 15.

105 ἀετός, οῦ, ὁ, *an eagle,* Rev. iv. 7; gen. *bird of prey,* as Mat. xxiv. 28.

106 ἄ-ζυμος, ον, *unleavened,* only in plur., sc. λάγανα, *cakes,* or ἄρτοι, *loaves;* met., *the paschal feast,* Lu. xxii. 1; fig., *uncorrupted, sincere,* 1 Cor. v. 7, 8.

107 Ἀζώρ, indecl. (Heb.), *Azor,* Mat. i. 13, 14; not mentioned in O. T.*

108 Ἄζωτος, ου ἡ, *Azotus* or *Ashdod,* Ac. viii. 40.*

109 ἀήρ, ἀέρος, ὁ, *the air, atmosphere,* Ac. xxii. 23; Ep. ii. 2.

110 ἀ-θανασία, ας, ἡ (see θάνατος), *immortality,* 1 Cor. xv. 53, 54; 1 Tim. vi. 16.*

111 ἀ-θέμιτος, ον (θέμις, *law*), *unlawful, criminal,* Ac. x. 28; 1 Pet. iv. 3.*

112 ἄ-θεος, ον, *without God,* Ep. ii. 12.*

113 ἄ-θεσμος, ον (θεσμός, *statute*), *lawless,* 2 Pet. ii. 7, iii. 17.*

114 ἀ-θετέω, ῶ, ήσω (θε- as in τίθημι), *to make void, invalid;* of things, *to nullify,* Lu. vii. 30; chiefly of persons, *to slight, reject,* Lu. x. 16.

115 ἀ-θέτησις, εως, ἡ, *nullification, abrogation,* Heb. vii. 18, ix. 26.*

116 Ἀθῆναι, ῶν, αἱ, *Athens,* Ac. xvii. 15.

117 Ἀθηναῖος, α, ον, *Athenian,* Ac. xvii. 21, 22.*

118 ἀθλέω, ῶ (ἆθλος, *a contest*), *to contend* in the public games, 2 Tim. ii. 5.*

119 ἄθλησις, εως, ἡ, *contest,* as in the public games; only fig. Heb. x. 32.*

see 4867 ἀθροίζω, *to gather together,* Lu. xxiv. 33 (W. H.).*

4

120 ἀ-θυμέω, ω, *to lose heart, despond*, Col. iii. 21.*

121 ἀθῷος, ον, *unpunished, innocent*, Mat. xxvii. 4 (not W. H.); with ἀπό, of the crime, ver. 24.*

122 αἴγειος, η, ον (αἴξ, *goat*), *of or belonging to a goat*, Heb. xi. 37.*

123 αἰγιαλός, οῦ, ὁ, *the shore, beach; used of Gennesaret*, Mat. xiii. 2, 48; Jn. xxi. 4; of the Mediterranean, Ac. xxi. 5, xxvii. 39, 40.*

124 Αἰγύπτιος, α, ον, *Egyptian*, Ac. vii. 22.

125 Αἴγυπτος, ου, ἡ, *Egypt*, Mat. ii. 13.

126 ἀΐδιος, ον, adj. (ἀεί), *eternal, everlasting*, Ro. i. 20; Ju. 6.*

127 αἰδώς, οῦς, ἡ, *modesty*, 1 Tim. ii. 9; *reverence*, Heb. xii. 28 (not W. H.).* *Syn.:* see Trench, § xix; Thayer, p. 14.

128 Αἰθίοψ, οπος, ὁ, *an Ethiopian*, Ac. viii. 27.*

129 αἶμα, ατος, τό, *blood*, (1) in general, Jn. xix. 34; (2) *natural life*, which was believed to reside in the blood, especially with σάρξ, 1 Cor. xv. 20; so *human nature* generally; hence, (3) *natural relationship*, Jn. i. 13; (4) blood *shed* of sacrificial victims, Heb. ix. 7, 12; (5) hence, *the blood of Christ, his atoning death*, 1 Cor. x. 16; Rev. vii. 14; (6) *violent death, bloodshed, murder*, Lu. xiii. 1; Mat. xxiii. 30, 35; (7) in Ac. ii. 20, etc., the reference is to the *color of blood*.

130 αἱματ-εκ-χυσία, ας, ἡ, *shedding of blood*, Heb. ix. 22. (N.T.)*

131 αἱμορροέω, ῶ, *to suffer from a flow of blood*, Mat. ix. 20.*

132 Αἰνέας, α, ὁ, *Aeneas*, Ac. ix. 33, 34.*

133 αἴνεσις, εως, ἡ, *praise*, Heb. xiii. 15. (S.)*

134 αἰνέω, ῶ, ἐσω and ἤσω, *to praise*, only of praise to God, Lu. ii. 13, 20.

135 αἴνιγμα, ατος, τό, *an enigma, an obscure thing*, 1 Cor. xiii. 12.*

136 αἶνος, ου, ὁ, *praise* to God, Mat. xxi. 16; Lu. xviii. 43.*

137 Αἰνών, ἡ (Heb.), *Aenon*, Jn. iii. 23.*

●139 αἵρεσις, εως, ἡ (αἱρέω), *choice*, its act or result; hence, *a*

tenet, heresy, 2 Pet. ii. 1; *a sect*, Ac. v. 17; *dissension*, Gal. v. 20.

●140 αἱρετίζω, σω, *to choose*, Mat. xii. 18.*

●141 αἱρετικός, ἡ, όν, *schismatic, factious*, Tit. iii. 10.*

138 αἱρέω (irreg., Gr. § 103, 1, Wi. § 15, Bu. 53), *to take*, only in mid. in N. T., *to choose, prefer*, Phil. i. 22; 2 Th. ii. 13; Heb. xi. 25.*

142 αἴρω (Gr. § 92), (1) *to raise, lift up*, Mar. xvi. 18; Jn. xi. 41; (2) *to bear, carry*, Mat. iv. 6; Lu. ix. 23; (3) *to bear away, carry off*, in general, Mat. xxi. 21; Jn. xix. 31; *to take away* sin, of the redeeming work of Christ, Jn. i. 29; 1 Jn. iii. 5; *to remove by death*, Jn. xvii. 15; Mat. xxiv. 39.

143 αἰσθάνομαι, 2 a. ἠσθόμην, dep., *to perceive, understand*, Lu. ix. 45.*

144 αἴσθησις, εως, ἡ, *perception, discernment*, Phil. i. 9.*

145 αἰσθητήριον, ου, τό, *organ of perception, faculty of judgment*, Heb. v. 14.*

146 αἰσχρο-κερδής, ες, *eager for base gain, sordid*, 1 Tim. iii. 3 (not W. H.), 8; Tit. i. 7.*

147 αἰσχροκερδῶς, *from eagerness for base gain*, 1 Pet. v. 2. (N. T.)*

148 αἰσχρο-λογία, ας, ἡ, *foul language, scurrility*, Col. iii. 8.*

●150, 149 αἰσχρός, ά, όν, *base, disgraceful*, 1 Cor. xi. 6.

151 αἰσχρότης, τητος, ἡ, *baseness, dishonor*, Ep. v. 4.*

152 αἰσχύνη, ης, ἡ, *shame*, in personal feeling, Lu. xiv. 9; or in the estimation of others, Heb. xii. 2; *a shameful thing*, Ju. 13. *Syn.:* see αἰδώς.

153 αἰσχύνομαι, οῦμαι, in N. T. only pass., *to be put to shame, made ashamed*, 2 Cor. x. 8; Phil. i. 20.

154 αἰτέω, ῶ, ἤσω, *to ask, pray, require*, Ja. i. 6; usually with two accs., or acc. of thing and ἀπό or παρά (gen.) of person; mid., *to ask for one's self, beg*, Jn. xvi. 26. *Syn.:* αἰτέω is to ask a favor, as a suppliant; ἐρωτάω, to ask a question, or as an equal; πυνθάνομαι, to ask for infor-

5

mation. But see Thayer, p. 18.

155 αἴτημα, ατος, τό, *petition, request*, Lu. xxiii. 24; Phil. iv. 6; I Jn. v. 15. *Syn.:* see Trench, § li.

156 αἰτία, as, ἡ, *cause*, (1) as the *reason* or *ground* of anything, Ac. x. 21; (2) in Mat. xix. 10, *the state of the case;* (3) forensically, *a crime*, Ac. xiii. 28; *a charge of crime, accusation*, Ac. xxv. 18, 27.

157 αἰτίαμα, ατος, τό, *accusation, charge*, Ac. xxv. 7 (W. H. read αἰτίωμα).*

●159, 158 αἴτιος, ία, ιον, *causative of*, used as subst., in masc., *the cause, author*, only Heb. v. 9; in neut., *a cause, reason*, espec. of punishment, Ac. xix. 40; *a fault, crime*, like αἰτία, Lu. xxiii. 4, 14, 22.*

see 157 αἰτίωμα. See αἰτίαμα. (N. T.)*

160 αἰφνίδιος, ον, *unexpected, sudden*, Lu. xxi. 34 (W. H. ἐφνίδιος); I Th. v. 3.*

161 αἰχμ-αλωσία, as, ἡ, *captivity*, Rev. xiii. 10; abstract for concrete, Ep. iv. 8.*

162 αἰχμ-αλωτεύω, σω, *to make prisoners of, to take captive*, Ep. iv. 8; 2 Tim. iii. 6 (W. H. read the following). (S.)*

163 αἰχμ-αλωτίζω, σω, *to lead captive*, Lu. xxi. 24.

164 αἰχμ-άλωτος, ου, ὁ, ἡ, *captive*, Lu. iv. 18 (from Is. lxi. 1).*

165 αἰών, ῶνος, ὁ (ἀεί), originally *an indefinitely long period of time, an age;* hence, (1) *an unbroken age, eternity*, past, as Ac. xv. 18; future, 2 Pet. iii. 18, especially in the following phrases : εἰς τὸν αἰῶνα, *for ever*, with negative adv. *never;* εἰς τοὺς αἰῶνας, a stronger expression, *for evermore;* εἰς τοὺς αἰῶνας τῶν αἰώνων, stronger still (see Gr. § 327, ii, Wi. § 36, 2), *for ever and ever*. Phrase slightly varied, Ep. iii. 21 ; Heb. i. 8; 2 Pet. iii. 18; Ju. 25; Rev. xiv. 11; (2) in plur., *the worlds, the universe*, Heb. i. 2, xi. 3; (3) *the present age* (ὁ αἰὼν οὗτος, ὁ ἐνεστὼς αἰών, ὁ νῦν αἰών), Gal. i. 4; 1 Tim. vi. 17, in contrast with the time after the second coming of Christ, *the coming age* (ὁ αἰων ἐκεῖνος, αἰὼν μέλλων, ὁ

αἰὼν ὁ ἐρχόμενος, οἱ αἰῶνες οἱ ἐπερχόμενοι), Lu. xx. 35, xviii. 30; Ep. ii. 7; Mat. xii. 32. *Syn.:* αἰών is the world under the aspect of *time;* κόσμος, under that of *space*. See Thayer, p. 19.

166 αἰώνιος (ία, only in 2 Th. ii. 16; Heb. ix. 12; or ιος), ιον, (1) *without beginning or end, eternal*, Ro. xvi. 26; Heb. ix. 14; (2) *without beginning*, Ro. xvi. 25; 2 Tim. i. 9; (3) *without end, everlasting;* often with ζωή, *eternal life*, denoting life which in its character is essentially eternal, see Jn. v. 24, vi. 47, xvii. 3. Neut., used as adv., *for ever*, Philem. 15.

167 ἀ-καθαρσία, as, ἡ (καθαίρω), *uncleanness, impurity*, usually in a moral sense, Ro. i. 24; 2 Cor. xii. 21.

168 ἀ-καθάρτης, τητος, ἡ, *impurity*, Rev. xvii. 4 (W. H. read the following). (N. T.)*

169 ἀ-κάθαρτος, ον, *unclean, impure*, (1) of ceremonial defilement, Ac. x. 14; I Cor. vii. 14; (2) of evil spirits, with πνεῦμα, Gospels, Acts, Rev.; (3) of human beings, *impure, lewd*, Ep. v. 5.

170 ἀ-καιρέομαι, οῦμαι, dep., *to lack opportunity*, Phil. iv. 10.*

171 ἀ-καίρως, adv., *unseasonably*, 2 Tim. iv. 2, opp. to εὐκαίρως.*

172 ἄ-κακος, ον, *guileless*, Ro. xvi. 18; Heb. vii. 26.*

173 ἄκανθα, ης, ἡ, *thorn, briar*, Mat. vii. 16.

174 ἀκάνθινος, ον, *made of thorns*, Mar. xv. 17; Jn. xix. 5.*

175 ἄ-καρπος, ον, *unfruitful, barren*, generally fig., Mat. xiii. 22; Tit. iii. 14.

176 ἀ-κατά-γνωστος, ον, *not to be condemned*, Tit. ii. 8.*

177 ἀ-κατα-κάλυπτος, ον, *unveiled*, I Cor. xi. 5, 13.*

178 ἀ-κατά-κριτος, ον, *uncondemned*, Ac. xvi. 37, xxii. 25. (N. T.)*

179 ἀ-κατά-λυτος, ον, *indissoluble*, Heb. vii. 16.*

see 180 ἀ-κατά-παστος, ον, *unfed, hungry for* (gen.), 2 Pet. ii. 14 (W. H. for the following). (N. T.)*

180 ἀ-κατά-παυστος, ον, *not to be restrained*, with gen., 2 Pet. ii. 14 (see preceding).*

181 ἀ-κατα-στασία, as, ἡ, *instabil-*

ity; hence, *sedition, tumult, disorder,* Ja. iii. 16, 2 Cor. vi. 5.

ά-κατά-στατος, ον, *inconstant, unstable,* Ja. i. 8, iii. 8 (W. H.).*

ά-κατά-σχετος, ον, *that cannot be restrained,* Ja. iii. 8 (W. H. read preceding). (S.)*

'Ακελ-δαμά (Aram., *field of blood*), *Aceldama,* Ac. i. 19 (W. H. read 'Ακελδαμάχ). (N. T.)*

ά-κέραιος, ον (κεράννυμι), *unmixed;* hence, fig., *simple, innocent, guileless,* Mat. x. 16; Ro. xvi. 19; Phil. ii. 15.*

ά-κλινής, έs, *unbending;* hence, *firm, steadfast,* Heb. x. 23.*

άκμάζω, σω, *to reach the point of perfection;* so, of fruit, *to be fully ripe,* Rev. xiv. 18.*

άκμήν, acc. of άκμή as adv., *even now, even yet,* Mat. xv. 16.*

άκοή, ῆs, ἡ (άκούω), *hearing,* (1) *the sense of hearing,* 2 Pet. ii. 8; (2) *the organ of hearing, the ear,* 2 Tim. iv. 3, 4; (3) *the thing heard, a report, speech, doctrine,* Jn. xii. 38; Mar. i. 28. άκοῇ άκούειν, "to hear with hearing," *i.e,* attentively (a Hebraism), Mat. xiii. 14.

άκολουθέω, ῶ, ήσω, (1) *to accompany, follow,* or *attend,* with dat., or μετά (gen.), or ὀπίσω (gen.), espec. of the disciples of Christ; so, met., *to obey* and *imitate,* Mat. iv. 25; Mar. ix. 38.

άκούω, σω or σομαι, pf., άκήκοα, *to hear,* (1) without object, Mar. iv. 3, vii. 37; (2) with object (acc. or gen., Gr. § 249a, 1, Wi. § 30, 7c, Bu. 165 sq., 301), *to hear, listen to, heed, understand,* Mat. xii. 19; Lu. i. 41. οἱ άκούοντες, *hearers* or *disciples.* In pass., *to be noised abroad,* Ac. xi. 22.

ά-κρασία, αs, ἡ, *intemperance, incontinence,* Mat. xxiii. 25; 1 Cor. vii. 5.*

ά-κρατής, έs (κράτος), *powerless, without self-control,* 2 Tim. iii. 3.*

ά-κρατος, ον (κεράννυμι), *unmixed, undiluted* (of strong wine), Rev. xiv. 10.*

άκρίβεια, αs, ἡ, *exactness, strictness,* Ac. xxii. 3.*

---

196. 197

198

199

200

201

202

203

204

205

206

207

208

209

210

211

212

213

214

215

216

217

218

άκριβής, έs, *exact, strict,* Ac. xxvi. 5.

άκριβόω, ῶ, ώσω, *to inquire closely, learn carefully* (R. V.), Mat. ii. 7, 16.*

άκριβῶς, adv., *exactly, diligently,* Ac. xviii. 25.

άκρίς, ίδος, ἡ, *a locust,* Mat. iii. 4.

άκροατήριον, ίου, τό (άκροάομαι, *to hear*), *the place of* (judicial) *hearing,* Ac. xxv. 23.*

άκροατής, οῦ, ὁ, *a hearer,* Ro. ii. 13; Ja. i. 22, 23, 25.*

άκροβυστία, αs, ἡ, *the foreskin,* Ac. xi. 3; *uncircumcision,* Ro. iv. 10; met., *an uncircumcised Gentile,* Ep. ii. 11. (S.)

άκρο-γωνιαῖος, α, ον (with λίθος expressed or understood), *a corner foundation stone,* ref. to Christ, Ep. ii. 20; 1 Pet. ii. 6. (S.)*

άκρο-θίνιον, ίου, τό, *first-fruits, i.e,* the best of the produce, applied (plur.) to spoils taken in battle, Heb. vii. 4.*

άκρος, α, ον, *outermost, pointed;* neut., τὸ άκρον, *the end, extremity,* Lu. xvi. 24.

'Ακύλας, ου, ὁ (Latin), *Aquila,* Ac. xviii. 2.

ά-κυρόω, ῶ, *to deprive of power, set aside* (a law), Mat. xv. 6; Mar. vii. 13; Gal. iii. 17.

ά-κωλύτως, adv., *freely, without hindrance,* Ac. xxviii. 31.*

άκων, ουσα, ον (ά, ἔκων), *unwilling,* 1 Cor. ix. 17.*

άλάβαστρον, ου, τό, *a box made of alabaster, a vessel for perfume,* Mat. xxvi. 7; Mar. xiv. 3; Lu. vii. 37.*

άλαζονία, αs, ἡ, *boasting, show, ostentation,* Ja. iv. 16; 1 Jn. ii. 16.*

άλαζών, όνος, ὁ, *a boaster,* Ro. i. 30; 2 Tim. iii. 2.*

άλαλάζω, άσω, *to raise a cry* or loud sound; in mourning, Mar. v. 38; of cymbals, 1 Cor. xiii. 1.*

ά-λάλητος, ον, *not to be uttered in words,* Ro. viii. 26.*

ά-λαλος, ον, *dumb, making dumb,* Mar. vii. 37, ix. 17, 25.*

άλας, ατος, τό, *salt,* lit. and fig., as Mat. v. 13.

άλείφω, ψω, *to anoint,* festally, or in homage, also medicinally, or in embalming the

dead, Mar. xvi. 1, Lu. vii.
46. *Syn.:* χρίω has always
a religious and symbolical
force, which is absent in
ἀλείφω.

219   ἀλεκτορο-φωνία, as, ἡ, *the cock-
crowing,* the third watch of
the night, between midnight
and dawn, Mar. xiii. 35.*

220   ἀλέκτωρ, ορος, ὁ, *a cock,* Mat.
xxvi. 34; Jn. xiii. 38.

221   Ἀλεξανδρεύς, έως, ὁ, *an Alexandrian,* Ac. vi. 9, xviii. 24.*

222   Ἀλεξανδρινός, ή, όν, *Alexandrian,* Ac. xxvii. 6, xxviii.
11.*

223   Ἀλέξανδρος, ου, ὁ, *Alexander.*
Four of this name are mentioned, Mar. xv. 21; Ac. iv.
6; Ac. xix. 33; 1 Tim. i. 20;
2 Tim. iv. 14.*

224   ἄλευρον, ου, τό, *wheaten flour,*
Mat. xiii. 33; Lu. xiii. 21.*

225   ἀλήθεια, ας, ἡ, *truth;* generally,
as Mar. v. 33; espec., (1)
*freedom from error, exact-
ness,* as (2) the Truth, or
Word of God; Jesus is called
the Truth, Jn. xiv. 6; (3)
*truthfulness, veracity, sincer-
ity, integrity,* opposed to ἀδικία, Ro. ii. 8; 1 Cor. xiii. 6.

226   ἀληθεύω, *to speak the truth,* Gal.
iv. 16; Ep. iv. 15.*

227   ἀληθής, ές (ἀ, λαθ- in λανθάνω),
unconcealed, true, Ac. xii. 9;
Jn. iv. 18; *truthful,* Mat.
xxii. 16; Mar. xii. 14. *Syn.:*
ἀληθής means true *morally,
faithful;* ἀληθινός, *genuine,*
in contrast either with the
false or the *imperfect.*

228   ἀληθινός, ή, όν, *real, genuine,*
contrasted with the ficti-
tious, as Lu. xvi. 11; Jn. i. 9;
with the typical, as Jn. vi.
32; Heb. viii. 2, ix. 24. *Syn.:*
see ἀληθής.

229   ἀλήθω, ήσω, *to grind* with a
handmill, Mat. xxiv. 41; Lu.
xvii. 35.*

230   ἀληθῶς, adv., *truly, really, certainly,* Ac. xii. 11.

231   ἁλιεύς (W. H. ἁλεεύς), έως, ὁ, *a
fisherman,* Mat. iv. 18.

232   ἁλιεύω, εύσω, *to fish,* Jn. xxi. 3.
(S.)*

233   ἁλίζω, ίσω, *to salt, season with
salt,* Mat. v. 13; Mar. ix. 49

234   ἁλίσγημα, ατος, τό, *pollution*
Ac. xv. 20. (N. T.)*

235   ἀλλά (prop. n. plur. of ἄλλος),
but, an adversative particle.

See Gr. § 404, Wi. § 53, 7,
Bu. 369 sq.

236   ἀλλάσσω, άξω, *to change,* Ac.
vi. 14; *to exchange,* Ro. i. 23;
to transform, 1 Cor. xv. 51.

237   ἀλλαχόθεν, adv., *from elsewhere,* Jn. x. 1.*

see 237   ἀλλαχοῦ, adv., *elsewhere,* Mar.
i. 38 (W. H.).*

238   ἀλλ-ηγορέω, ῶ, *to speak allegor-
ically;* pass. part., Gal. iv.
24.*

239   Ἀλληλούϊα (W. H. Ἀλ-),
(Heb.), Hallelujah, *Praise
ye Jehovah,* Rev. xix, 1, 3,
4, 6. (S.)*

240   ἀλλήλων, reciprocal pron., gen.
plur. (Gr. § 61c), *one another, each other,* Ro. i. 12.

241   ἀλλο-γενής, ές, *of another nation, a foreigner,* Lu. xvii. 18.
(S.)*

242   ἄλλομαι (dep.), ἀλοῦμαι, ἡλάμην,
to leap, Ac. iii. 8, xiv. 10; *to
bubble up,* as water, Jn. iv.
14.*

243   ἄλλος, η, ο, *other, another,* Mar.
vi. 15; ὁ ἄλλος, *the other,*
Mat. v. 39; οἱ ἄλλοι, *the
others, the rest. Syn.:* ἄλλος
indicates that which is simply *numerically* distinct; ἕτερος, that which is generically
distinct, *different.*

244   ἀλλοτριο-επίσκοπος, ου, ὁ, *one
who looks at* or *busies himself in the things of another,
a busybody,* 1 Pet. iv. 15
(W. H. ἀλλοτριεπίσκοπος).
(N. T.)*

245   ἀλλότριος, ία, ιον, *belonging to
another,* Heb. ix. 25; *foreign,
strange,* Ac. vii. 6; *not of
one's own family,* Mat. xvii.
25; *hostile,* Heb. xi. 34.

246   ἀλλό-φυλος, ου, adj., *foreign,
of another tribe* or *race,* Ac.
x. 28.*

247   ἄλλως, adv., *otherwise,* 1 Tim.
v. 25.*

248   ἀλοάω, ῶ, ήσω, *to beat* or *thresh,*
as grain, 1 Cor. ix. 9, 10;
1 Tim. v. 18.*

249   ἄ-λογος, ον, (1) *without speech*
or *reason, irrational,* 2 Pet.
ii. 12, Ju. 10; (2) *unreason-
able, absurd,* Ac. xxv. 27.*

250   ἀλόη, ης, ἡ, *the aloe,* Jn. xix. 39.
(S.)*

251   ἅλς, ἁλός, ὁ, *salt.* Rec. only in
Mar. ix. 49 (dat.), W. H.
only in ix. 50 (acc.). See
ἅλας.*

252   ἀλυκός, ή, όν (ἅλς), salt, brackish, Ja. iii. 12.*

253   ἄ-λυπος, ον, free from sorrow, Phil. ii. 28.*

254   ἅλυσις, εως, ή, a chain or manacle, Mar. v. 3; Ac. xxi. 33.

255   ἀ-λυσιτελής, ές, without gain, unprofitable, Heb. xiii. 17.*

256   ἄλφα, το, see Α.
'Αλφαῖος, ον, ὁ, Alphæus. Two of the name are mentioned, Mar. ii. 14, iii. 18 (the latter being called Κλωπᾶς, Jn. xix. 25; another form of the orig. Hebrew name).

257   ἅλων, ωνος, ὁ, ή, a threshing-floor; met., the grain of the threshing-floor, Mat. iii. 12; Lu. iii. 17.

258   ἀλώπηξ, εκος, ή, a fox, Mat. viii. 20; Lu. ix. 58; applied to Herod, Lu. xiii. 32.*

259   ἅλωσις, εως, ή, a taking or catching, 2 Pet. ii. 12.*

260   ἅμα, adv., at the same time, Ac. xxiv. 26; prep., with or to-gether with (dat.), Mat. xiii. 29; ἅμα πρωΐ, with the dawn, Mat. xx. 1.

261   ἀ-μαθής, ές, unlearned, ignorant, 2 Pet. iii. 16.*

262   ἀμαράντινος, ον, adj., composed of amaranth, i.e., everlasting, 1 Pet. v. 4.*

263   ἀ-μάραντος, ον, adj. (μαραίνο-μαι), unfading, 1 Pet. i. 4.*

264   ἁμαρτάνω, τήσω, to miss a mark, to err, to sin, Mat. xxvii. 4; Jn. v. 14; with cogn. acc., ἁμαρτίαν, to sin a sin, 1 Jn. v. 16; with εἰς, to sin against, Lu. xv. 18, 21.

265   ἁμάρτημα, ατος, τό, a sin, evil deed. Syn.: see ἀγνόημα.

266   ἁμαρτία, ας, ή, (1) a sinning (= τὸ ἁμαρτάνειν), Ro. v. 12, 13; 2 Cor. v. 21; (2) a sin, sing., as Ac. vii. 60; plur. (more freq.), spec. in the phrase ἀφιέναι τὰς ἁμαρτίας, to forgive sins, Mat. ix. 2, 5, 6. In Heb. x. 6, 8, 18, περὶ ἁμαρτίας is sin-offering. Syn.: see ἀγνόημα.

267   ἀ-μάρτυρος, ον, without witness, Ac. xiv. 17.*

268   ἁμαρτωλός, ον, sinful, or sub-stantively, a sinner, espec. habitually and notoriously, 1 Tim. i. 19; Lu. xv. 2. The Jews used the word for idolaters, i.e., Gentiles, Mar. xiv. 41.

269   ἄ-μαχος, ον, not quarrelsome, 1 Tim. iii. 3; Tit. iii. 2.*

270   ἀμάω, ῶ, ήσω, to reap, Ja. v. 4.*

271   ἀμέθυστος, ον, ή, an amethyst (supposed to be an antidote against drunkenness. Hence the name, from ἀ, μεθύω), Rev. xxi. 20.*

272   ἀμελέω, ῶ, ήσω, not to care for, to disregard, neglect, with gen. or inf., Heb. ii. 3; 2 Pet. i. 12 (not W. H.).

273   ἄ-μεμπτος, ον, blameless, Phil. ii. 15; Heb. viii. 7.

274   ἀ-μέμπτως, adv., blamelessly, 1 Th. ii. 10, iii. 13 (W. H. mrg.).

275   ἀ-μέριμνος, ον, free from solici-tude or anxiety, Mat. xxviii. 14; 1 Cor. vii. 32.*

276   ἀ-μετά-θετος, ον, unchangeable, Heb. vi. 18; τὸ ἀμετάθετον, immutability, Heb. vi. 17.*

277   ἀ-μετα-κίνητος, ον, adj., immov-able, firm, 1 Cor. xv. 58.*

278   ἀ-μετα-μέλητος, ον, not to be regretted or repented of, Ro. xi. 29; hence, unchangeable, 2 Cor. vii. 10.*

279   ἀ-μετα-νόητος, ον, adj., unre-pentant, impenitent, Ro. ii. 5.*

280   ἄ-μετρος, ον, beyond measure, immoderate, 2 Cor. x. 13, 15.*

281   ἀμήν, Amen, a Hebrew adjec-tive, true, faithful, used (1) as an adverb, at the begin-ning of a sentence, verily, truly, indeed; (2) at the end of ascriptions of praise, etc., optatively, as γένοιτο, so be it; (3) substantively, 2 Cor. i. 20, as a name of Christ, the Amen, the faithful wit-ness, Rev. iii. 14. (S.)

282   ἀ-μήτωρ, ορος, ὁ, ή (μήτηρ), without mother, i.e., in the genealogies, Heb. vii. 3.*

283   ἀ-μίαντος, ον (μιαίνω), undefiled, sincere, pure, Heb. vii. 26, xiii. 4; 1 Pet. i. 4; Ja. i. 27.*

284   'Αμιναδάβ, ὁ (Heb.), Aminadal, Mat. i. 4; Lu. iii. 33 (not W. H.).*

285   ἄμμος, ον, ή, sand, Ro. ix. 27; Heb. xi. 12.

286   ἀμνός, οῦ, ὁ, a lamb; fig., of Christ, Jn. i. 29, 36; Ac. viii. 32; 1 Pet. i. 19.*

287   ἀμοιβή, ῆς, ἡ (ἀμείβω), *requital*, 1 Tim. v. 4.*

288   ἄμπελος, ου, ἡ, *a vine*, (1) lit., Mat. xxvi. 29; (2) fig., as Jn. xv. 1.

289   ἀμπελ-ουργός, οῦ, ὁ, ἡ, *a vine-dresser*, Lu. xiii. 7.*

290   ἀμπελών, ῶνος, ὁ, *a vineyard*, Lu. xx. 9; 1 Cor. ix. 7.

291   Ἀμπλίας, ίου, ὁ, *Amplias*, Ro. xvi. 8.*

see 292 St   ἀμύνω, ῶ, in N. T. only in mid., *to defend from*, *take vengeance on*, Ac. vii. 24.*

see 294   ἀμφιάζω, *to clothe*, Lu. xii. 28 (W. H.).*

see 293   ἀμφιβάλλω, *to cast around*, Mar. i. 16 (W. H.).*

293   ἀμφί-βληστρον, ου, τό, *a fishing net*, Mat. iv. 18; Mar. i. 16 (not W. H.).* *Syn.:* σαγήνη is the *drag-net*, much larger than ἀμφίβληστρον, the *casting net;* δίκτυον is general, a net of any kind.

294   ἀμφι-έννυμι, έσω, *to put on, to clothe*, Lu. vii. 25.

295   Ἀμφίπολις, εως, ἡ, *Amphipolis*, a city in the S. of Macedonia, Ac. xvii. 1.*

296   ἄμφ-οδον, ου, τό, *a street*, Mar. xi. 4.*

297   ἀμφότεροι, αι, α, *both*, Ac. xxiii. 8.

298   ἀ-μώμητος, ον, *without blame* or *fault*, Phil. ii. 15 (W. H. ἀμεμπτοι); 2 Pet. iii. 14.*

see 2368   ἄμωμον, ου, τό, *amomum, a spice plant*, Rev. xviii. 13 (not Rec.).*

299   ἄ-μωμος, ον, *without blemish*, 1 Pet. i. 19; Heb. ix. 14; fig., *blameless*, Eph. i. 4; Ju. 24.

300   Ἀμών, ὁ (Heb.), *Amon*, Mat. i. 10 (W. H. Ἀμώς).*

301   Ἀμώς, ὁ (Heb.), *Amos*, Lu. iii. 25.*

302   ἄν, a particle, expressing *possibility, uncertainty*, or *conditionality*. At the beginning of a sentence it is a contraction of ἐάν. See Gr. §§ 378b, 380, 383δ, Wi. § 42, Bu. 216 sq.

303   ἀνά, prep., lit., *upon* (acc.); in composition, *up, again;* used in many phrases. See Gr. §§ 297 and 147a, Wi. §§ 49b, 52, 4, 2), Bu. 331, 332.

304   ἀνα-βαθμός, οῦ, ὁ (βαίνω), *means of ascent, steps, stairs*, Ac. xxi. 35, 40.*

305   ἀνα-βαίνω, βήσομαι, 2 a. ἀνέβην, (1) *to ascend*, espec. to Jerusalem, Mat. xx. 17; on board ship, Mar. vi. 51; to heaven, Ro. x. 6; (2) *to spring up*, as plants, etc., used of a rumor, Ac. xxi. 31; of thoughts coming into mind, Lu. xxiv. 38.

306   ἀνα-βάλλω, mid., *to postpone, defer*, Ac. xxiv. 22.*

307   ἀνα-βιβάζω, *to draw up*, as a net to shore, Mat. xiii. 48.*

308   ἀνα-βλέπω, (1) *to look up*, as Mar. viii. 24; (2) *to look again, to recover sight*, as Mat. xi. 5.

309   ἀνά-βλεψις, εως, ἡ, *recovery of sight*, Lu. iv. 18.*

310   ἀνα-βοάω, ῶ, *to exclaim, cry aloud* (not in W. H.), Mat. xxvii. 46, Mar. xv. 8, Lu. ix. 38.*

311   ἀνα-βολή, ῆς, ἡ, *putting off, delay*, Ac. xxv. 17.*

see 508 St   ἀνάγαιον, ου, τό, *upper room*, W. H. in Mar. xiv. 15; Lu. xxii. 12, for Rec. ἀνώγεον.*

312   ἀν-αγγέλλω, *to announce, make known*, Ac. xiv. 27, xix. 18; *to report*, 2 Cor. vii. 7.

313   ἀνα-γεννάω, ῶ, *to beget again*, 1 Pet. i. 3, 23.*

314   ἀνα-γινώσκω, *to know again, to know well*. N. T., *to read*, Jn. xix. 20; 2 Cor. iii. 15.

315   ἀναγκάζω, άσω, *to force, to compel* by force or persuasion, Ac. xxvi. 11; 2 Cor. xii. 11.

316   ἀναγκαῖος, αία, αῖον, *necessary, fit*, Tit. iii. 14; Phil. i. 24; also *close* or *near*, as friends, Ac. x. 24.

317   ἀναγκαστῶς, adv., *necessarily* or *by constraint*, 1 Pet. v. 2.*

318   ἀνάγκη, ης, ἡ, (1) *necessity*, Philem. 14; 1 Cor. vii. 37; followed by inf. (with ἐστι understood), *there is need to*, Mat. xviii. 7; (2) *distress*, Lu. xxi. 23.

319   ἀνα-γνωρίζω, *to make known*, aor. pass., Ac. vii. 13 (Rec.).*

320   ἀνά-γνωσις, εως, ἡ, *reading*, Ac. xiii. 15; 2 Cor. iii. 14; 1 Tim. iv. 13.*

321   ἀν-άγω, *to bring, lead*, or *take up*, Lu. ii. 22; Ac. ix. 39; *to offer up*, as sacrifices, Ac. vii. 41; pass., *to put to sea, to set sail*, Lu. viii. 22; Ac. xiii. 13.

322   ἀνα-δείκνυμι, *to show*, as by uplifting, *to show plainly*, Ac.

i. 24; *to appoint, announce,*
Lu. x. 1.*

323 ἀνά-δειξις, εως, ἡ, *a showing* or *public announcing,* Lu. i. 80.*

324 ἀνα-δέχομαι, dep., *to receive* with a welcome, guests, Ac. xxviii. 7; promises, Heb. xi. 17.*

325 ἀνα-δίδωμι, *to give up, deliver,* as by messengers, Ac. xxiii. 33.*

326 ἀνα-ζάω, ῶ, *to live again, revive* (W. H. only in Ro. vii. 9, and doubtfully Lu. xv. 24).

327 ἀνα-ζητέω, ῶ, *to seek* with diligence, Lu. ii. 44, 45 (W. H.); Ac. xi. 25.*

328 ἀνα-ζώννυμι, *to gird* or *bind up,* as a loose dress is girded about the loins; mid. fig., 1 Pet. i. 13. (S.)*

329 ἀνα-ζωπυρέω, ῶ (πῦρ), *to re-kindle* or *rouse up;* fig., 2 Tim. i. 6.*

330 ἀνα-θάλλω, *to thrive* or *flourish again,* Phil. iv. 10.*

331 ἀνά-θεμα, ατος, τό, *a person* or *thing accursed,* Gal. i. 8; 1 Cor. xvi. 22; *an execration* or *curse,* Ac. xxiii. 14. *Syn.*: ἀνάθημα is a thing *devoted in honor of God, consecrated;* ἀνάθεμα, simply a later form of ἀνάθημα, has come to mean *a thing devoted to destruction.*

332 ἀναθεματίζω, ίσω, *to bind* (one's self) *by a curse,* Ac. xxiii. 12, 14, 21; *to affirm with curses,* Mar. xiv. 71.*

333 ἀνα-θεωρέω, ῶ, *to look at attentively, to consider,* Ac. xvi. 031 Heb. xiii. 7.*

334 ἀνά-θημα, ατος, τό, *anything consecrated and laid by, a votive offering,* Lu. xxi. 5 (W. H.).* *Syn.:* see ἀνάθεμα.

335 ἀν-αιδεία, ας, ἡ, *shamelessness, impudence,* Lu. xi. 8.*

336 ἀναίρεσις, εως, ἡ, *a taking away. i.e.,* by a violent death; Ac. viii. 1, xxii. 20 (Rec.).*

337 ἀν-αίρεω, ῶ (see Gr. § 103, 1, Wi. § 15, Bu. 53), *to take away, to abolish,* Heb. x. 9; *to take off, to kill,* Mat. ii. 16; mid., *to take up,* Ac. vii. 21.

338 ἀν-αίτιος, ον, *guiltless,* Mat. xii. 5, 7.*

339 ἀνα-καθίζω, *to sit up* (properly trans. with ἑαυτόν under

stood), Lu. vii. 15; Ac. ix. 40.*

340 ἀνα-καινίζω, *to renew, restore to a former condition,* Heb. vi. 6.*

341 ἀνα-καινόω, ῶ, *to renew, amend, to change* the life, 2 Cor. iv. 16; Col. iii. 10. (N. T.)*

342 ἀνα-καίνωσις, εως, ἡ, *a renewal* or *change* of heart and life, Ro. xii. 2: Tit. iii. 5. (N. T.)* *Syn.:* see Trench, § xviii.

343 ἀνα-καλύπτω, *to unveil, make manifest;* pass., 2 Cor. iii. 14, 18.*

344 ἀνα-κάμπτω, *to bend* or *turn back, return,* Heb. xi. 15.

345 ἀνά-κειμαι, dep., *to recline* at a meal, Mat. ix. 10; ὁ ἀνακείμενος, one who reclines at table, *a guest,* Mat. xxii. 10, 11 (W. H. omit in Mar. v. 40).

346 ἀνα-κεφαλαιόω, ῶ, *to gather together into one. to sum up under one head;* pass., Ro. xiii. 9; mid., Ep. i. 10.*

347 ἀνα-κλίνω, *to lay down* an infant, Lu. ii. 7; *to make to recline* at table, Mar. vi. 39; pass., *to recline,* as at a feast, like ἀνάκειμαι, Lu. xiii. 29.

348 ἀνα-κόπτω, *to check* (lit., *beat back*), Gal. v. 7 (W. H. ἐγκόπτω).*

349 ἀνα-κράζω, *to cry out, to shout aloud,* Mar. i. 23, vi. 49.

350 ἀνα-κρίνω, *to investigate, inquire, examine* (judicially), *to judge of.* Only in Lu., Ac., and 1 Cor.

351 ἀνά-κρισις, εως, ἡ, *judicial examination,* Ac. xxv. 26.*

see 617 St ἀνα-κυλίω, *to roll back,* Mar. xvi. 4 (W. H. for ἀποκ.).*

352 ἀνα-κύπτω, *to raise one's self up,* Lu. xiii. 11; Jn. viii. 7, 10; fig., *to be elated,* Lu. xxi. 28.*

353 ἀνα-λαμβάνω, *to take up,* Ac. vii. 43; pass., of Christ's being taken up to heaven, Mar. xvi. 19.

354 ἀνά-ληψις (W. H. -λημψις), εως, ἡ, *a being taken up, i.e.,* into heaven, Lu. ix. 51.*

355 ἀν-αλίσκω, λώσω, *to consume, destroy,* Lu. ix. 54; Gal. v. 15; 2 Th. ii. 8 (not W. H.).*

356 ἀνα-λογία, ας, ἡ, *proportion, analogy,* Ro. xii. 6.*

357 ἀνα-λογίζομαι, *to think upon, consider attentively,* Heb. xii. 3.*

358   ἄν-αλος, ον, *without saltness, insipid*, Mar. ix. 50.*

359   ἀνά-λυσις, εως, ἡ, *a loosening* of a ship from her moorings, *departure*, 2 Tim. iv. 6.*

360   ἀνα-λύω, *to depart*, Phil. i. 23; *to return*, Lu. xii. 36.*

361   ἀν-αμάρτητος, ον, *without blame, faultless*, Jn. viii. 7 (W. H. omit).*

362   ἀνα-μένω, *to await*, 1 Th. i. 10.*

363   ἀνα-μιμνήσκω, *to remind, admonish*, two accs., or acc. and inf., 1 Cor. iv. 17; pass., *to remember, to call to mind*, gen. or acc., 2 Cor. vii. 15.

364   ἀνά-μνησις, εως, ἡ, *remembrance, a memorial*, Heb. x. 3.

365   ἀνα-νεόω, ῶ, *to renew;* mid., *to renew one's self, to be renewed*, Ep. iv. 23.*

366   ἀνα-νήφω, *to recover soberness*, 2 Tim. ii. 26.*

367   Ἀνανίας, α, ὁ (from Heb.), *Ananias.* Three of the name are mentioned, Ac. v. 1–5, ix. 10, xxiii. 2.

368   ἀν-αντι-ρρήτος, ον, *indisputable, not to be contradicted*, Ac. xix. 36.*

369   ἀναντιρρήτως, adv., *without contradiction*, Ac. x. 29.*

370   ἀν-άξιος, ον, *unworthy, inadequate*, 1 Cor. vi. 2.*

371   ἀναξίως, adv., *unworthily, unbecomingly*, 1 Cor. xi. 27 (not in ver. 29, W. H.).*

372   ἀνά-παυσις, εως, ἡ, *rest, cessation from labor, refreshment*, Rev. iv. 8; Mat. xii. 43.

373   ἀνα-παύω, *to give rest* or *refreshment*, Mat. xi. 28; mid., *to take rest*, Mar. vi. 31 (W. H. read in Rev. xiv. 13, ἀναπαήσονται, 2 fut. pass.).

374   ἀνα-πείθω, σω, *to persuade*, in a bad sense, *seduce, mislead*, Ac. xviii. 13.*

375   ἀνα-πέμπω, *to remit, send back*, Lu. xxiii. 11.

see 450   ἀνα-πηδάω, *leap up* (W. H., in Mar. x. 50, for Rec. ἀνίστημι).*

376   ἀνά-πηρος, ον, *maimed, having lost a member*, Lu. xiv. 13, 21 (W. H. ἀνάπειρος).*

377   ἀνα-πίπτω, *to fall down, lie down*, Mat. xv. 35; N. T., *to recline* at table, Lu. xi. 37, xiv. 10.

378   ἀνα-πληρόω, ῶ, *to fill up*, 1 Th. ii. 16; *to fulfill*, as a prophecy,

Mat. xiii. 14; *to perform*, as a precept, Gal. vi. 2; *to occupy* or *fill* a place, 1 Cor. xiv. 16; *to supply* a deficiency, Phil. ii. 30.

379   ἀν-απο-λόγητος, ον, adj., *inexcusable*, Ro. i. 20, ii. 1.*

380   ἀνα-πτύσσω, *to unroll*, as a volume, Lu. iv. 17 (not W. H.).*

381   ἀν-άπτω, *to kindle, set on fire*, Lu. xii. 49; Ac. xxviii. 2 (not W. H.); Ja. iii. 5.*

382   ἀν-αρίθμητος, ον, *innumerable*, Heb. xi. 12.*

383   ἀνα-σείω, *to stir up, move, instigate*, Mar. xv. 11; Lu. xxiii. 5.*

384   ἀνα-σκευάζω, *to pervert, unsettle, destroy*, Ac. xv. 24.*

385   ἀνα-σπάω, *to draw up*, Lu. xiv. 5; Ac. xi. 10.*

386   ἀνά-στασις, εως, ἡ, *a rising up*, as opposed to falling, Lu. ii. 34; *rising*, as from death or the grave, *resurrection, the future state*, Ro. i. 4, vi. 5.

387   ἀνα-στατόω, ῶ, *to unsettle, put in commotion*, Ac. xvii. 6, xxi. 38; Gal. v. 12.*

388   ἀνα-σταυρόω, ῶ, *to crucify afresh*, Heb. vi. 6.*

389   ἀνα-στενάζω, *to groan* or *sigh deeply*, Mar. viii. 12.*

390   ἀνα-στρέφω, *to turn up, overturn*, Jn. ii. 15; intrans., *to return*, Ac. v. 22; mid. (as Lat. *versari*), *to be* or *to live in* a place or state, *to move among, to pass one's time* or *be conversant with* persons; generally, *to conduct one's self*, 2 Cor. i. 12; 1 Tim. iii. 15.

391   ἀνα-στροφή, ῆς, ἡ, *behavior, manner of life*, Gal. i. 13; Ep. iv. 22.

392   ἀνα-τάσσομαι, *to arrange, compose* a narrative, Lu. i. 1.*

393   ἀνα-τέλλω, *to spring up* or *rise*, as the sun, a star, a cloud, Mat. xiii. 6; Lu. xii. 54; of the Messiah, Heb. vii. 14; trans., *to cause to rise*, Mat v. 45.

394   ἀνα-τίθημι, mid., *to set forth, declare*, Ac. xxv. 14; Gal. ii. 2.*

395   ἀνατολή, ῆς, ἡ, *the dawn, dayspring*, Lu. i. 78; generally, *the east*, where the sun rises, Mat. ii. 2, 9; sing. and plur., see Gr. § 240 a.

396 **ἀνα-τρέπω,** *to subvert, overthrow,* 2 Tim. ii. 18; Tit. i. 11.*

397 **ἀνα-τρέφω,** *to nurse, bring up, educate,* Lu. iv. 16 (W. H. mrg.); Ac. vii. 20, 21, xxii. 3.*

398 **ἀνα-φαίνω,** mid., *to appear,* Lu. xix. 11; pass., *to be shown a thing* (acc.), Ac. xxi. 3 (W. H. read act., in sense *to come in sight of*).*

399 **ἀνα-φέρω,** οἴσω, *to bear* or *lead, to offer,* as sacrifice, Heb. vii. 27; *to bear,* as sin, 1 Pet. ii. 24.

400 **ἀνα-φωνέω,** ῶ, *to cry out aloud,* Lu. i. 42.*

401 **ἀνά-χυσις,** εως, ἡ, *a pouring out;* hence, *excess,* 1 Pet. iv. 4.*

402 **ἀνα-χωρέω,** ῶ, *to depart, withdraw,* Mat. ix. 24; Mar. iii. 7.

403 **ἀνά-ψυξις,** εως, ἡ, *a refreshing,* Ac. iii. 20.*

404 **ἀνα-ψύχω,** *to refresh, to revive,* 2 Tim. i. 16.*

405 **ἀνδραποδιστής,** οῦ, ὁ, *a man-stealer,* 1 Tim. i. 10.*

406 **Ἀνδρέας,** ου, ὁ, *Andrew,* Jn. i. 40.

407 **ἀνδρίζω,** ίσω, mid., *to act like a man, to be brave,* 1 Cor. xvi. 13.*

408 **Ἀνδρόνικος,** ου, ὁ, *Andronicus,* Ro. xvi. 7.*

409 **ἀνδρό-φονος,** ου, ὁ, *a man-slayer,* 1 Tim. i. 9.*

410 **ἀν-έγκλητος,** ον, *not open to accusation, unblamable,* 1 Cor. i. 8; Col. i. 22.

411 **ἀν-εκ-διήγητος,** ον, *not to be spoken, inexpressible,* 2 Cor. ix. 15. (N. T.)*

412 **ἀν-εκ-λάλητος,** *unspeakable,* 1 Pet. 1. 8. (N. T.)*

413 **ἀν-έκ-λειπτος,** ον, *unfailing,* Lu. xii. 33.*

414 **ἀνεκτός,** ή, όν, *tolerable, supportable;* only in comp., Mat. x. 15, xi. 22, 24.

415 **ἀν-ελεήμων,** ον, *without compassion, cruel,* Ro. i. 31.*

416 **ἀνεμίζω,** *to agitate* or *drive with wind;* pass., Ja. i. 6. (N.T.)*

417 **ἄνεμος,** ου, ὁ, *the wind,* Mat. xi. 7; fig., applied to empty doctrines, Ep. iv. 14.

418 **ἀν-ένδεκτος,** ον (ἐνδέχομαι), adj., *impossible,* Lu. xvii. 1. (N. T.)*

419 **ἀν-εξ-ερεύνητος** (W. H. -ραύ-), ον, adj., *unsearchable,* Ro. xi. 33.*

420 **ἀνεξί-κακος,** ον, *patient of injury,* 2 Tim. ii. 24. (N. T.)*

421 **ἀν-εξ-ιχνίαστος,** ον, *that cannot be explored, incomprehensible,* Ro. xi. 33; Ep. iii. 8. (S.)*

422 **ἀν-επ-αίσχυντος,** ον, *having no cause to be ashamed,* 2 Tim. ii. 15.*

423 **ἀν-επί-ληπτος** (W. H. -λημπ-), ον, adj., *never caught doing wrong, irreproachable,* 1 Tim. iii. 2, v. 7, vi. 14.*

424 **ἀν-έρχομαι,** *to come* or *go up,* Jn. vi. 3; Gal. i. 17, 18.*

425 **ἄνεσις,** εως, ἡ (ἀνίημι), *relaxation, remission,* as from bonds, burden, etc., Ac. xxiv. 23; 2 Th. i. 7.

426 **ἀν-ετάζω,** *to examine judicially,* Ac. xxii. 24, 29. (S.)*

427 **ἄνευ,** adv. as prep., with gen., *without,* 1 Pet. iii. 1.

428 **ἀν-εύθετος,** ον, *inconvenient,* Ac. xxvii. 12. (N. T.)*

429 **ἀν-ευρίσκω,** *to find by searching for,* Lu. ii. 16; Ac. xxi. 4.*

430 **ἀν-έχω,** mid., *to bear with, forbear, have patience with, endure,* Mat. xvii. 17; Lu. ix. 41; gen. of pers. or thing.

431 **ἀνεψιός,** οῦ, ὁ, *a cousin,* Col. iv. 10.*

432 **ἄνηθον,** ου, τό, *anise, dill,* Mat. xxiii. 23.*

433 **ἀνήκει,** impers., *it is fit* or *proper;* part., τὸ ἀνῆκον, τὰ ἀνήκοντα, *the becoming,* Philem. 8.

434 **ἀν-ήμερος,** ον, adj., *not tame, fierce,* 2 Tim. iii. 3.*

435 **ἀνήρ,** ἀνδρός, ὁ, (1) *a man,* in sex and age (Lat. *vir*), Ac. viii. 12; hence, (2) *a husband,* Ro. vii. 2, 3; (3) *a person* generally, Lu. vii. 41; plur. voc., ἄνδρες, Sirs!; often in apposition with adjectives and nouns, as ἀνὴρ ἁμαρτωλός, ἀνὴρ προφήτης, Lu. v. 8, xxiv. 19.

436 **ἀνθ-ίστημι,** *to oppose, withstand, resist,* with dat., Ro. ix. 19, Mat. v. 39.

437 **ἀνθ-ομολογέομαι,** οῦμαι, *to confess, give thanks to,* dat., Lu. ii. 38.*

438 **ἄνθος,** ους, τό, *a flower,* Ja. i. 10, 11; 1 Pet. i. 24.*

439 **ἀνθρακιά,** ᾶς, ἡ, *a heap of burning coals,* Jn. xviii. 18, xxi. 9.*

440 **ἄνθραξ,** ακος, ὁ, *a coal,* Ro. xii. 20.*

441 ἀνθρωπ-άρεσκος, ον, *desirous of pleasing men*, Ep. vi. 6; Col iii. 22. (S.)*

442 ἀνθρώπινος, ίνη, ινον, *human. belonging to man*, Ja. iii. 7; I Cor. x. 13.

443 ἀνθρωπο-κτόνος, ου, ὁ, ἡ, *a homicide, a manslayer*, Jn. viii. 44; I Jn. iii. 15.*

444 ἄνθρωπος, ου, ὁ, *a man, one of the human race* (Lat. *homo*). Like ἀνήρ, joined in apposition with substantives, as Mat. xviii. 23, xxi. 33.

445 ἀνθ-υπατεύω, *to be proconsul*, Ac. xviii. 12 (not W. H.).*

446 ἀνθ-ύπατος, ου, ὁ, *a proconsul*, Ac. xiii. 7, 8, 12.

447 ἀν-ίημι, *to unloose, let go*, Ac. xvi. 26, xxvii. 40; *to give up*, Ep. vi. 9; *to leave, neglect*, Heb. xiii. 5.*

448 ἀν-ίλεως, ων, *without mercy*, Ja. ii. 13 (W. H. read ἀνέλεος). (N. T.)*

449 ἄ-νιπτος, ον, adj., *unwashed*, Mat. xv. 20; Mar. vii. 2, 5 (Rec.).*

450 ἀν-ίστημι, *to raise up* one lying or dead, Ac. ix. 41; Jn. vi. 39, 40; intrans. (in 2 a., pf. and mid.), *to rise* from a recumbent posture, Mar. i. 35; *to rise again* from the dead, Lu. xvi. 31; aor. part., often combined with other verbs, as "rising (ἀναστάς) he went."

451 Ἄννα, ας, ἡ, *Anna*, Lu. ii. 36.*

452 Ἅννας, α, ὁ, *Annas*, Lu. iii. 2; Jn. xviii. 13, 24; Ac. iv. 6.*

453 ἀ-νόητος, ον, *foolish, thoughtless,* Ro. i. 14; I Tim. vi. 9.

454 ἄνοια, ας, ἡ, *folly, madness*, Lu. vi. 11; 2 Tim. iii. 9.*

455 ἀνοίγω, ξω, *to open*, Ac. v. 19, xii. 10, 14; intrans. in 2 perf., ἀνέῳγα, *to be open*, 2 Cor. vi. 11; I Cor. xvi. 9.

456 ἀν-οικο-δομέω, ῶ, *to build up again*, Ac. xv. 16.*

457 ἄνοιξις, εως, ἡ, *opening* (the act of), Ep. vi. 19.*

458 ἀ-νομία, ας, ἡ, *lawlessness, iniquity*, Mat. xxiii. 28; Tit. ii. 14; αἱ ἀνομίαι, *iniquities, evil deeds*, Ro. iv. 7. *Syn.:* see ἀγνόημα.

459 ἄ-νομος, ον, (1) *without law*, not subject to the law, used of Gentiles, I Cor. ix. 21; (2) *lawless;* as subst., *a male-*

factor; ὁ ἄνομος, *the lawless one*, 2 Th. ii. 8.

460 ἀνόμως, adv., *without law*, Ro. ii. 12.

461 ἀν-ορθόω, ῶ, *to make upright* or *straight again, to rebuild, make strong*, Lu. xiii. 13; Ac. xv. 16; Heb. xii. 12.*

462 ἀν-όσιος, ον, *unholy*, I Tim. i. 9; 2 Tim. iii. 2.*

463 ἀνοχή, ῆς, ἡ, *forbearance, toleration*, Ro. ii. 4, iii. 25.* *Syn.:* ὑπομονή is patience under trials, referring to *things;* μακροθυμία, patience under provocation, referring to *persons;* ἀνοχή is a forbearance *temporary* in its nature.

464 ἀντ-αγωνίζομαι, *to resist, strive against*, Heb. xii. 4.*

465 ἀντ-άλλαγμα, ατος, τό, *an equivalent, price*, Mat. xvi. 26; Mar. viii. 37.*

466 ἀντ-ανα-πληρόω, ῶ, *to fill up in turn*, Col. i. 24.*

467 ἀντ-απο-δίδωμι, *to recompense, requite*, Lu. xiv. 14; Ro. xii. 19.

468 ἀντ-από-δομα, ατος, τό, *a recompense, requital*, Lu. xiv. 12; Ro. xi. 9. (S.)*

469 ἀντ-από-δοσις, εως, ἡ, *a reward, recompense*, Col. iii. 24.*

470 ἀντ-απο-κρίνομαι, *to reply against, contradict*, Lu. xiv. 6; Ro. ix. 20.*

471 ἀντ-εῖπον (used as 2 aor. of ἀντιλέγω, see φημί), *to contradict, to gainsay*, Lu. xxi. 15; Ac. iv. 14.*

472 ἀντ-έχω, mid., *to hold fast, to adhere to* (gen.), Mat. vi. 24; Lu. xvi. 13; I Th. v. 14; Tit. i. 9.*

473 ἀντί, prep., gen., *instead of, for.* See Gr. §§ 291, 147 a, Wi. §§ 47 a, 52, 4, 3), Bu. 321.

474 ἀντι-βάλλω, *to throw in turn, exchange words*, Lu. xxiv. 17.*

see 475 St   ἀντι-δια-τίθημι, mid., *to set one's self against, oppose*, 2 Tim. ii. 25.*

476 ἀντί-δικος, ου, ὁ (orig. adj.), *an opponent at law*, Mat. v. 25; Lu. xii. 58, xviii. 3; *an adversary*, I Pet. v. 8.*

477 ἀντί-θεσις, εως, ἡ, *opposition*, I Tim. vi. 20.*

478 ἀντι-καθ-ίστημι, *to resist*, Heb. xii. 4.*

479 ἀντι-καλέω, *to call* or *invite in turn*, Lu. xiv. 12.*

480 ἀντί-κειμαι, *to oppose, resist*

(dat.), Lu. xiii. 17, xxi. 15;
ὁ ἀντικείμενος, an adversary,
1 Cor. xvi. 9; Phil. i. 28.

481 ἀντικρύ (W. H. ἄντικρ•ι), adv.,
over against, Ac. xx. 15.*

482 ἀντι-λαμβάνω, mid., to take hold
of, help, share in (gen.), Lu.
i. 54; Ac. xx. 35; 1 Tim.
vi. 2.

483 ἀντι-λέγω, to speak against, contradict (dat.), Ac. xiii. 45;
to oppose, deny, Jn. xix. 12.

484 ἀντί-ληψις (W. H. -λημψ-), εως,
help, ministration, 1 Cor. xii.
28.*

485 ἀντι-λογία, ας, ἡ, contradiction,
contention, rebellion, Heb. vi.
16, vii. 7, xii. 3; Ju. 11.*

486 ἀντι-λοιδορέω, to revile or reproach again, 1 Pet. ii. 23.*

487 ἀντί-λυτρον, ου, τό, a ransom-
price, 1 Tim. ii. 16.*

488 ἀντι-μετρέω, ῶ, to measure in
return, Mat. vii. 2 (not W.
H.); Lu. vi. 38. (N. T.)*

489 ἀντι-μισθία, ας, ἡ, recompense,
Ro. i. 27; 2 Cor. vi. 13. (N.
T.)*

490 Ἀντιόχεια, ας, ἡ, Antioch. Two
places of the name are mentioned, Ac. xi. 26, xiii. 14.

491 Ἀντιοχεύς, έως, ὁ, a citizen of
Antioch, Ac. vi. 5.*

492 ἀντι-παρ-έρχομαι, to pass by opposite to, Lu. x. 31, 32.*

493 Ἀντίπας, α, ὁ, Antipas, Rev.
ii. 13.*

494 Ἀντιπατρίς, ίδος, ἡ, Antipatris,
Ac. xxiii. 31.*

495 ἀντι-πέραν (W. H. ἀντιπερα),
adv., on the opposite side or
shore, Lu. viii. 26.*

496 ἀντι-πίπτω, to fall against, resist, Ac. vii. 51.*

497 ἀντι-στρατεύομαι, dep., to make
war against, Ro. vii. 23.*

498 ἀντι-τάσσω, mid., to set one's
self against, resist (dat.), Ro.
xiii. 2; Ja. iv. 6, v. 6; 1 Pet.
v. 5; Ac. xviii. 6.*

499 ἀντί-τυπος, ον, like in pattern,
Heb. ix. 24; τὸ ἀντίτυπον,
corresponding in form, as
wax to the seal, antitype, 1
Pet. iii. 21.*

500 Ἀντί-χριστος, ου, ὁ, opposer
of Christ, Antichrist, 1 Jn.
ii. 18, 22, iv. 3; 2 Jn. 7.
(N. T.)*

501 ἀντλέω, ῶ, to draw from a vessel, Jn. ii. 8, 9, iv. 7, 15.*

502 ἄντλημα, ατος, τό, a bucket, Jn.
iv. 11.*

503 ἀντ-οφθαλμέω, ῶ, to look in the
face; so to meet the wind,
Ac. xxvii. 15.*

504 ἄν-υδρος, ον, without water, dry.
Mat. xii. 43; Lu. xi. 24.

505 ἀν-υπό-κριτος, ον, adj., without
hypocrisy, unfeigned, Ro. xii.
9; 2 Cor. vi. 6. (Ap.)

506 ἀν-υπό-τακτος, ον, not subject to
rule, of things, Heb. ii. 8;
unruly, of persons, 1 Tim. i.
9; Tit. i. 6, 10.*

507 ἄνω, adv. (ἀνά), up, above, up-
wards; τὰ ἄνω, heaven or
heavenly things, as Jn. viii. 23.

508 ἀνώγεον, ου, τό, an upper chamber. See ἀνάγαιον.*

509 ἄνωθεν, adv. (ἄνω), (1) of place,
from above, as Jn. iii. 31, xix.
11; with prepp. ἀπό, ἐκ, from
the top, as Mar. xv. 38; Jn.
xix. 23; (2) of time, from the
first, only Lu. i. 3; Ac. xxvi.
5. In Jn. iii. 4, 7, again (see
Gal. iv. 9); or, perhaps here
also, from above.

510 ἀνωτερικός, ή, όν, upper, higher,
Ac. xix. 1.*

511 ἀνώτερος, α, ον (compar. of ἄνω;
only neut. as adv.), higher, to
a higher place, Lu. xiv. 10;
above, before, Heb. x. 8.*

512 ἀν-ωφελής, ές, unprofitable, Tit.
iii. 9; Heb. vii. 18.*

513 ἀξίνη, ης, ἡ, an axe, Mat. iii.
10; Lu. iii. 9.*

514 ἄξιος, ία, ιον, adj., worthy, de-
serving of, suitable to (gen.),
Heb. xi. 38; Lu. xii. 48; Ac.
xxvi. 20.

515 ἀξιόω, ῶ, to deem worthy (acc.
and gen., or inf.), Lu. vii. 7;
2 Th. i. 11; think fit, Ac. xv.
38, xxviii. 22.

516 ἀξίως, adv., worthily, suitably
(with gen.), Ro. xvi. 2; Phil.
i. 27.

517 ἀ-όρατος, ον. invisible, unseen,
Col. i. 16; 1 Tim. i. 17.

518 ἀπ-αγγέλλω, to report, relate,
make known, declare, Ac. iv.
23; 1 Th. i. 9.

519 ἀπ-άγχω, mid., to hang or
strangle one's self, Mat. xxvii.
5.*

520 ἀπ-άγω, to lead, carry, or take
away, Lu. xiii. 15; to lead
away to execution, Mat. xxvi.
57; Mar. xiv. 44, 53; to lead
or tend, as a way, Mat. vii.
13, 14.

521 ἀ-παίδευτος, ον, adj., uninstruct-
ed, ignorant, 2 Tim. ii. 23.*

15

522   ἀπ-αίρω, *to take away;* in N.T. only 1 a. pass., Mat. ix. 15; Mar. ii. 20; Lu. v. 35.*

523   ἀπ-αιτέω, *to ask back, require, reclaim,* Lu. vi. 30, xii. 20.*

524   ἀπ-αλγέω, *to be past feeling,* Ep. iv. 19.*

525   ἀπ-αλλάσσω, pass., *to be removed from, to depart,* Ac. xix. 12; pass., *to be set free* (with ἀπό), Lu. xii. 58; *to deliver,* Heb. ii. 15.*

526   ἀπ-αλλοτριόω, *to estrange, alienate* (gen.), Ep. ii. 12, iv. 18; Col. i. 21.*

527   ἀπαλός, ή, όν, *tender,* as a shoot of a tree, Mat. xxiv. 32; Mar. xiii. 28.*

528   ἀπ-αντάω, ῶ, *to meet, to encounter* (dat.), Mar. xiv. 13.

529   ἀπ-άντησις, εως, ή, *a meeting, an encountering;* εἰς ἀπάντησιν (gen. or dat.), *to meet* any one, Ac. xxviii. 15.

530   ἅπαξ, adv., of time, *once,* 1 Th. ii. 18; *once for all,* Heb. vi. 4, x. 2.

531   ἀ-παρά-βατος, ον, *inviolable, unchangeable,* Heb. vii. 24.*

532   ἀ-παρα-σκεύαστος, ον, adj., *unprepared,* 2 Cor. ix. 4.*

533   ἀπ-αρνέομαι, οῦμαι, *to deny, disown,* Mat. xxvi. 34, 35; *to disregard,* Mar. viii. 34.

534   ἀπ-άρτι, adv., of time (see ἄρτι), *henceforth,* Rev. xiv. 13. (W. H. read ἀπ' ἄρτι.)*

535   ἀπ-αρτισμός, οῦ, ὁ, *completion,* Lu. xiv. 28.*

536   ἀπ-αρχή, ῆς, ή, *the first-fruits,* consecrated to God (see W H., 2 Th. ii. 13).

537   ἅ-πας, ασα, αν (like πᾶς, Gr. § 37), *all, all together, the whole.*

see 782   ἀπασπάζομαι, see ἀσπάζομαι. (N. T.)*

538   ἀπατάω, ῶ, ήσω, *to deceive, lead into error,* Ja. i. 26; Ep. v. 6; 1 Tim. ii. 14 (W. H. ἐξαπ-).* (The stronger form ἐξαπατάω is more freq.)

539   ἀπάτη, ης, ή, *deceit, deceitfulness,* Col. ii. 8; Heb. iii. 13.

540   ἀ-πάτωρ, ορος, ὁ, ή (πατήρ), *without father, i.e.,* in the genealogies, Heb. vii. 3.*

541   ἀπ-αύγασμα, ατος, τό, *reflected brightness,* Heb. i. 3.*

542   ἀπ-εῖδον (W H. ἀφεῖδον), 2 aor. οἱ ἀφοράω, which see.

543   ἀ-πείθεια, ας, ή, *willful unbelief,*

obstinacy, disobedience, Heb. iv. 6, 11.

544   ἀ-πειθέω ῶ, *to refuse belief, be disobedient,* Jn. iii. 36; Ro. ii. 8.

545   ἀ-πειθής, ές, *unbelieving, disobedient,* Lu. i. 17; 2 Tim. iii. 2.

546   ἀπειλέω, ῶ, ήσω, *to threaten, forbid by threatening,* Ac. iv. 17; 1 Pet. ii. 23.*

547   ἀπειλή, ῆς, ή, *a threatening, threat,* Ac. iv. 17 (W. H. omit), 29, ix. 1; Ep. vi. 9.*

548   ἄπ-ειμι (εἰμί, *to be*), *to be absent,* as 1 Cor. v. 3.

549   ἄπ-ειμι (εἶμι, *to go*), *to go away, to depart,* Ac. xvii. 10.*

550   ἀπ-εῖπον (see εἶπον), mid., *to renounce, disown,* 2 Cor. iv. 2.*

551   ἀ-πείραστος, ον, adj., *incapable of being tempted,* Ja. i. 13.*

552   ἄ-πειρος, ον, adj., *inexperienced, unskillful* in (gen.), Heb. v. 13.*

553   ἀπ-εκ-δέχομαι, *to wait for, expect earnestly or patiently,* Ro. viii. 19, 23, 25; Heb. ix. 28. (N. T.)

554   ἀπ-εκ-δύομαι, *to strip, divest, renounce,* Col. ii. 15, iii. 9.*

555   ἀπέκδυσις, εως, ή, *a putting or stripping off, renouncing,* Col. ii. 11. (N. T.)*

556   ἀπ-ελαύνω, *to drive away,* Ac. xviii. 16.*

557   ἀπ-ελεγμός, οῦ, ὁ (ἐλέγχω), *repudiation, censure, disrepute,* Ac. xix. 27. (N. T.)*

558   ἀπ-ελεύθερος, ον, ὁ, ή, *a freedman,* 1 Cor. vii. 22.*

559   Ἀπελλῆς, οῦ, ὁ, *Apelles,* Ro. xvi. 10.*

560   ἀπ-ελπίζω, σω, *to despair,* Lu. vi. 35; R.V. "never despairing" (see R.V. mrg.).*

561   ἀπ-έναντι, adv. (gen.), *over against, in the presence of, in opposition to.*

562   ἀ-πέραντος, ον (περαίνω), *interminable,* 1 Tim. i. 4.*

563   ἀ-περισπάστως, adv. (περισπάω), *without distraction,* 1 Cor. vii. 35.*

564   ἀ-περί-τμητος, ον, *uncircumcised;* fig., Ac. vii. 51. (S.)*

565   ἀπ-έρχομαι, *to go or come from* one place to another, *to go away, depart; to go apart; to go back, to return; to go forth,* as a rumor.

566, 567, 568   ἀπ-έχω, *to have in full,* Mat.

16

vi. 2; *to be far* (abs., or ἀπό),
Lu. vii. 6; impers., ἀπέχει,
it is enough, Mar. xiv. 41;
mid., *to abstain from* (gen.,
or ἀπό), 1 Th. iv. 3.

569   ἀπιστέω, ῶ, *to disbelieve* (dat.),
Mar. xvi. 11; *to be unfaith-
ful*, Ro. iii. 3.

570   ἀπιστία, as, ἡ, *unbelief, dis-
trust, a state of unbelief*, 1
Tim. i. 13; Heb. iii. 12, 19:
unfaithfulness, Ro. iii. 3.

571   ἄ-πιστος, ον, *not believing, in-
credulous*, Jn. xx. 27; hence,
an unbeliever or *infidel*, 2
Cor. iv. 4; *unfaithful*, Lu.
xii. 46; Rev. xxi. 8; pass.,
incredible, only Ac. xxvi. 8.

•573   ἀπλόος, οῦς, ἡ, οῦν, *simple,
sound*, Mat. vi. 22; Lu. xi.
34.*

572   ἀπλότης, τητος, ἡ, *simplicity,
sincerity, purity*, 2 Cor. i. 12;
Col. iii. 22.

574   ἀπλῶς, adv., *simply, sincerely*,
Ja. i. 5.*

575   ἀπό, prep. gen., *from.* See Gr.
§ 292, Wi. § 47 *b*, Bu. 321 sq.;
and for the force of the prep.
in composition, Gr. § 147 *a*,
Wi. § 52, 4, Bu. 344.

576   ἀπο-βαίνω (for βαίνω, see Gr.
§ 94, I., 6 *d*; fut., -βήσομαι), *to
go* or *come out of*, as from a
ship, Lu. v. 2; Jn. xxi. 9; *to
turn out, result*, Lu. xxi. 13;
Phil. i. 19.*

577   ἀπο-βάλλω, *to throw away*, Mar.
x. 50; Heb. x. 35.*

578   ἀπο-βλέπω, *to look away from
all besides*; hence, *to look
earnestly at* (εἰς), Heb. xi.
26.*

579   ἀπό-βλητος, ον, verbal adj., *to
be thrown away, rejected*, 1
Tim. iv. 4.*

580   ἀπο-βολή, ῆς, ἡ, *a casting away,
rejection, loss*, Ac. xxvii. 22;
Ro. xi. 15.*

581   ἀπο-γίνομαι, *to die*, 1 Pet. ii.
24.*

582   ἀπο-γραφή, ῆς, ἡ, *a record,
register, enrolment*, Lu. ii. 2;
Ac. v. 37.*

583   ἀπο-γράφω, *to enrol, inscribe in
a register*, Lu. ii. 1, 3, 5;
Heb. xii. 23.*

584   ἀπο-δείκνυμι, *to show by proof,
demonstrate, set forth*, Ac. ii.
22, xxv. 7; 1 Cor. iv. 9; 2
Th. ii. 4.*

585   ἀπό-δειξις, εως, ἡ, *demonstra-
tion, proof*, 1 Cor. ii. 4.*

586   ἀπο-δεκατόω, ῶ, (1) *to pay the
tenth* or *tithe*, Mat. xxiii. 23;
(2) *to levy tithes on*, acc.,
Heb. vii. 5. (S.)

587   ἀπό-δεκτος, ον, verbal adj., *acceptable*, 1 Tim. ii. 3, v. 4.*

588   ἀπο-δέχομαι, *to receive with
pleasure, to welcome*, Ac.
xviii. 27, xxviii. 30.

589   ἀπο-δημέω, ῶ, *to go from one's
own people, to go into another
country;* only in the parables
of our Lord, as Mat. xxi. 33;
Lu. xv. 13.

590   ἀπό-δημος, ον, *gone abroad, sojourning in another country*
(R. V.), Mar. xiii. 34.*

591   ἀπο-δίδωμι, *to give from one's
self, to deliver*, Mat. xxvii.
58; in mid., *to sell*, Ac. v. 8;
to pay off, discharge what is
due, Mat. v. 26; Lu. xvi. 2;
to restore, Lu. iv. 20; *to requite, recompense*, Ro. ii. 6;
Rev. xviii. 6.

592   ἀπο-δι-ορίζω, *to separate off, i.e.*,
into parties, Ju. 19.*

593   ἀπο-δοκιμάζω, *to reject*, as dis-
approved or worthless, Mar.
viii. 31; Heb. xii. 17.

594   ἀπο-δοχή, ῆς, ἡ, *acceptance, ap-
probation*, 1 Tim. i. 15, iv.
9.*

595   ἀπό-θεσις, εως, ἡ, *a putting
away*, 1 Pet. iii. 21; 2 Pet.
i. 14.*

596   ἀπο-θήκη, ης, ἡ, *a repository,
granary, storehouse*, Mat. iii.
12; Lu. iii. 17.

597   ἀπο-θησαυρίζω, *to treasure up,
lay by in store*, 1 Tim. vi. 19.*

598   ἀπο-θλίβω, *to press closely*, Lu.
viii. 45.*

599   ἀπο-θνήσκω (ἀπό, intensive;
the simple θνήσκω is rare),
to die, (1) of natural death,
human, animal, or vegetable,
Mat. ix. 24; (2) of spiritual
death, Ro. vii. 10; Rev. iii.
2; (3) in Epp. of Paul, *to die
to* (dat.), as Ro. vi. 2; also
in other shades of meaning.
For tenses see θνήσκω.

600   ἀπο-καθ-ίστημι, ἀποκαταστήσω
(also -καθιστάω and -άνω, see
Mar. ix. 12; Ac. i. 6), *to restore, e.g.*, to health, or as a
state or kingdom, Lu. vi. 10,
Ac. i. 6.

601   ἀπο-καλύπτω, *to uncover, bring
to light, reveal*, Mat. x. 26;
Lu. x. 21; 1 Cor. ii. 10. See
Thayer, p. 62.

602 ἀπο-κάλυψις, εως, ἡ, *revelation, manifestation, enlightenment,* 1 Cor. xiv. 26; Ep. iii. 3; 2 Th. i. 7. (S.) *Syn.:* see Trench, § xciv.

603 ἀπο-καρα-δοκία, . . as, ἡ (κάρα, *head;* ἀπό, intensive), *earnest expectation,* as if looking for with the head outstretched, Ro. viii. 19; Phil. i. 20.*

604 ἀπο-κατ-αλλάσσω, *to reconcile, change from one state of feeling to another,* Ep. ii. 16; Col. i. 20, 22. (N. T.)*

605 ἀπο-κατά-στασις, εως, ἡ, *restitution, restoration,* Ac. iii. 21.*

606 ἀπό-κειμαι, *to be laid away, to be reserved for* (dat.), Lu. xix. 20; Col. i. 5; 2 Tim. iv. 8; Heb. ix. 27.*

607 ἀπο-κεφαλίζω (κεφαλή), *to behead,* Mat. xiv. 10; Mar. vi. 16, 27; Lu. ix. 9. (S.)*

608 ἀπο-κλείω, *to shut close,* as a door, Lu. xiii. 25.*

609 ἀπο-κόπτω, *to smite* or *cut off,* Mar. ix. 43, 45; Jn. xviii 10, 26; Ac. xxvii. 32; mid., Gal. v. 12 (see R. V.).*

610 ἀπό-κριμα, ατος, τό, *an answer,* 2 Cor. i. 9.*

611 ἀπο-κρίνομαι (for aor., see Gr. § 100, Wi. § 39, 2), *to answer,* Mar. xii. 28; Col. iv. 6; often used (like the corresponding Hebrew verb) where the "answer" is not to a distinct question, but to some suggestion of the accompanying circumstances; so especially in the phrase ἀποκριθεὶς εἶπεν, *answered and said,* as Mat. xi. 25; Lu. i. 60.

612 ἀπό-κρισις, εως, ἡ, *an answer, reply,* Lu. ii. 47.

613 ἀπο-κρύπτω, *to hide, conceal,* 1 Cor. ii. 7; Ep. iii. 9.

614 ἀπό-κρυφος, ον, *hidden, concealed,* Mar. iv. 22; Lu. viii. 17; *stored up,* Col. ii. 3.

615 ἀπο-κτείνω, ενῶ, *to put to death, kill,* Mat. xvi. 21; Rev. ii. 13; fig., *to abolish,* Ep. ii. 16.

616 ἀπο-κυέω, ῶ, *to bring forth;* fig., Ja. i. 15, 18.*

617 ἀπο-κυλίω, ίσω, *to roll away,* Mat. xxviii. 2; Mar. xvi. 3; Lu. xxiv. 2. (S.)*

618 ἀπο-λαμβάνω, *to receive from* any one, Gal. iv. 5· *to receive back, recover,* Lu. xv. 27;

mid., *to take aside* with one's self, Mar. vii. 33.

619 ἀπό-λαυσις, εως, ἡ (λαύω, *to enjoy*), *enjoyment,* 1 Tim. vi. 17; Heb. xi. 25.*

620 ἀπο-λείπω, *to leave, to leave behind,* 2 Tim. iv. 13, 20; *to desert,* Ju. 6; pass., *to be reserved,* Heb. iv. 9.

621 ἀπο-λείχω, *to lick,* as a dog, Lu. xvi. 21 (W. H. ἐπιλείχω).*

622 ἀπ-όλλυμι (see Gr. § 116, 2, Wi. § 15, Bu. 64), *to destroy, to bring to nought, to put to death,* Mar. i. 24; Ro. xiv. 15; *to lose,* Mat. x. 42; Jn. vi. 39; mid., pass. (and 2d perf.), *to perish, die,* Mat. viii. 25; *to be lost,* Lu. xxi. 18.

623 Ἀπολλύων, οντος, ὁ (prop. part of ἀπολλύω, *Destroyer*), *Apollyon,* Rev. ix. 11. (N. T.)*

624 Ἀπολλωνία, ας, ἡ, *Apollonia,* a city of Macedonia, Ac. xvii. 1.*

625 Ἀπολλώς, ώ, ὁ, *Apollos,* Ac. xviii. 24.

626 ἀπο-λογέομαι, οῦμαι (λόγος), *to defend one's self by speech,* Lu. xxi. 14; Ac. xxvi. 24; *to defend, excuse,* Ro. ii. 15.

627 ἀπο-λογία, ας, ἡ, *a verbal defense,* "apology," Ac. xxv. 16; 1 Cor. ix. 3.

628 ἀπο-λούω, mid., *to wash away,* as sins, Ac. xxii. 16; 1 Cor. vi. 11.*

629 ἀπο-λύτρωσις, εως, ἡ, *redemption, deliverance,* Ro. iii. 24; Heb. ix. 15, xi. 35. *Syn.:* see Trench, § lxxvii.

630 ἀπο-λύω, *to release, let go, to send away,* Ac. xxviii. 18; Mat. xv. 23; spec., *to put away* a wife, *divorce,* Mat. i. 19; Lu. xvi. 18; mid., *to depart,* Ac. xxviii. 25.

631 ἀπο-μάσσω, ξω, *to wipe off,* as dust from the feet; mid., Lu. x. 11.*

632 ἀπο-νέμω, *to assign to, apportion,* 1 Pet. iii. 7.*

633 ἀπο-νίπτω, mid., *to wash one's self,* Mat. xxvii. 24.*

634 ἀπο-πίπτω, *to fall from,* Ac. ix. 18.*

635 ἀπο-πλανάω, ῶ, *to lead astray,* Mar. xiii. 22; 1 Tim. vi. 10.*

636 ἀπο-πλέω, εύσω, *to sail away,* Ac. xiii. 4, xiv. 26, xx. 15, xxvii. 1.*

18

637 ἀπο-πλύνω, to wash or rinse, as nets, Lu. v. 2 (W. H. πλύνω).*

638 ἀπο-πνίγω, to suffocate, choke, Mat. xiii. 7; Lu. viii. 7, 33.*

639 ἀ-πορέω, ῶ (πόρος, resource), except Mar. vi. 20 (W. H.), only mid. in N. T., to be in doubt, to be perplexed, Jn. xiii. 22; 2 Cor. iv. 8.

640 ἀπορία, as, ἡ, perplexity, disquiet, Lu. xxi. 25.*

641 ἀπο-ρρίπτω, to throw or cast down or off, Ac. xxvii. 43; ἑαυτούς understood.*

642 ἀπ-ορφανίζω (ὀρφανος), "to make orphans of"; to bereave, pass., 1 Th. ii. 17.*

643 ἀπο-σκευάζομαι, to pack away, pack up, Ac. xxi. 15 (W. H. ἐπισκευάζομαι).*

644 ἀπο-σκίασμα, ατος, τό (σκιάζω), a shade, a shadow, Ja. i. 17. (N. T.)*

645 ἀπο-σπάω, ῶ, άσω, to draw out, unsheathe, Mat. xxvi. 51; to withdraw, to draw away, Ac. xxi. 1.

646 ἀπο-στασία, as, ἡ, defection, apostasy, Ac. xxi. 21; 2 Th. ii. 3.*

647 ἀπο-στάσιον, ου, τό, repudiation, divorce, Mat. xix. 7; Mar. x. 4; met., bill of divorce, as Mat. v. 31.*

648 ἀπο-στεγάζω (στέγη), to unroof, Mar. ii. 4.*

649 ἀπο-στέλλω, to send forth, send, as a messenger, commission, etc., spoken of prophets, teachers, and other messengers, Mat. x. 40, Lu. vii. 3; Ac. x. 36; to send away, dismiss, Lu. iv. 18; Mar. v. 10, viii. 26.

650 ἀπο-υστερέω, ῶ, ήσω, to defraud, abs., as Mar. x. 19; deprive of by fraud, acc. and gen., 1 Tim. vi. 5.

651 ἀπο-στολή, ῆς, ἡ, apostleship, Ac. i. 25; Ro. i. 5; 1 Cor. ix. 2; Gal. ii. 8.*

652 ἀπό-στολος, ου, ὁ, (1) a messenger, 2 Cor. viii. 23; Heb. iii. 1; (2) an apostle, i.e., a messenger of Christ to the world, Lu. vi. 13; Gal. i. 1; used of others besides Paul and the Twelve, Ac. xiv. 14; 1 Th. ii. 6; 2 Cor. viii. 23.

653 ἀπο-στοματίζω (στόμα), to entice to speak off-hand, Lu. xi. 53.*

654 ἀπο-στρέφω, to turn away, trans.

655 (with ἀπό, as Ac. iii. 26); restore, replace, Mat. xxvi. 52; mid., to desert, reject, acc., Mat. v. 42.

655 ἀπο-στυγέω, ῶ, to detest, to abhor, Ro. xii. 9.*

656 ἀπο-συνάγωγος, ον, excluded from the synagogue, excommunicated, Jn. ix. 22, xii. 42, xvi. 2. (N. T.)*

657 ἀπο-τάσσω, ξω, mid., to separate one's self from, withdraw from (dat.), Mar. vi. 46; to take leave of, renounce, send away (dat.), Lu. xiv. 33.

658 ἀπο-τελέω, ῶ, έσω, to perfect, Ja. i. 15; Lu. xiii. 32 (W. H.).*

659 ἀπο-τίθημι, mid., to lay off or aside, Ac. vii. 58; to renounce, Ro. xiii. 12.

660 ἀπο-τίνασσω, to shake off, Lu. ix. 5; Ac. xxviii. 5.*

661 ἀπο-τίνω (or -τίω), τίσω, to repay, Philem. 19.*

662 ἀπο-τολμάω, ῶ, to assume boldness, Ro. x. 20.*

663 ἀπο-τομία, as, ἡ (τέμνω, to cut), severity, Ro. xi. 22.*

664 ἀπο-τόμως, adv., severely, sharply, 2 Cor. xiii. 10; Tit. i. 13.*

665 ἀπο-τρέπω, mid., to turn away from, shun, acc., 2 Tim. iii. 5.*

666 ἀπ-ουσία, as (ἄπειμι), absence, Phil. ii. 12.*

667 ἀπο-φέρω, to bear away from one place to another, Mar. xv. 1; Rev. xvii. 3.

668 ἀπο-φεύγω, to escape, 2 Pet. i. 4, ii. 18, 20.*

669 ἀπο-φθέγγομαι, to speak out, declare, Ac. ii. 4, 14, xxvi. 25. (S.)*

670 ἀπο-φορτίζομαι (φόρτος, a burden), to unload, discharge, Ac. xxi. 3.*

671 ἀπό-χρησις, εως, ἡ (ἀπό, intens.), abuse, misuse, Col. ii. 22.*

672 ἀπο-χωρέω, ῶ, to go away, depart, Mat. vii. 23; Lu. ix. 39; Ac. xiii. 13.*

673 ἀπο-χωρίζω, to part asunder, Ac. xv. 39; Rev. vi. 14.*

674 ἀπο-ψύχω, to breathe out life, to faint, Lu. xxi. 26.*

675 Ἄππιος, ου, ὁ, Appius; Ἀππίου φόρον, the Forum of Appius, a town in Italy, situated on the Appian Way, Ac. xxviii. 15.*

676 ἀ-πρός-ιτος, ον (προς, εἶμι), not to be approached, 1 Tim. vi. 16.*

677   ά-πρός-κοπος, ον (κόπτω), act., not causing to stumble, 1 Cor. x. 32; pass., not caused to stumble, blameless, without offense, Ac. xxiv. 16; Phil. i. 10. (Ap.)*

678   ά-προσωπο-λήπτως (W. H. -λήμπτ-), adv., without respect of persons, impartially, 1 Pet. i. 17. (N. T.)*

679   ἄ-πταιστος, ον (πταίω, to fall), without stumbling or falling, Ju. 24.*

680, 681   ἅπτω, ψω, to kindle, as light or fire, Lu. viii. 16, xi. 33; mid., to touch, Mat viii. 3; 1 Cor. vii. 1. Syn.: ἅπτομαι is to touch or handle; θιγγάνω, a lighter touch; ψηλαφάω, to feel or feel after.

682   ᾿Απφία, ας, ἡ, Apphia, Philem. 2.*

683   ἀπ-ωθέω, ῶ, ἀπώσω, mid., to repulse, to reject, Ac. vii. 27, 39.

684   ἀπώλεια, ας, ἡ (ἀπόλλυμι), destroying, waste, of things, Ro. ix. 22; Mar. xiv. 4; destruction, in general, Ac. viii. 20; perdition, 2 Th. ii. 3; Rev. xvii. 8, 11.

685   ἀρά, ᾶς, ἡ, curse, imprecation, Ro. iii. 14.*

686   ἄρα, conj., illative, therefore, thence, since. See Gr. § 406, Wi. § 53, 8, Bu. 371.

687   ἆρα, adv. interrogative, usually where the answer is negative, Lu. xviii. 8; Ac. viii. 30; Gal. ii. 17.*

688   ᾿Αραβία, ας, ἡ, Arabia, Gal. i. 17, iv. 25.*

689   ῍Αραμ, ὁ (Heb.), Aram, Mat. i. 3, 4; Lu. iii. 33 (not W. H.).*

690   ῍Αραψ, αβος, ὁ, an Arabian, Ac. ii. 11.*

691   ἀργέω, ῶ, to linger, to delay, 2 Pet. ii. 3.*

692   ἀργός, όν (ά, ἔργον), idle, lazy, Mat. xx. 3; Tit. i. 12.

693   ἀργύρεος, οῦς, ᾶ, οῦν, made of silver, Ac. xix. 24; 2 Tim. ii. 20; Rev. ix. 20.*

694   ἀργύριον, ου, τό, silver, Ac. iii. 6; a piece of silver, a shekel, Mat. xvi. 15; money in general, Mar. xiv. 11.

695   ἀργυρο-κόπος, ου, ὁ, a silversmith, Ac. xix. 24.*

696   ἄργυρος, ου, ὁ, silver, Ac. xvii. 29; Ja. v. 3.

697   ῍Αρειος πάγος, ου, ὁ, Areopagus, or Mars' Hill, an open space on a hill in Athens, where the supreme court was held, Ac. xvii. 19, 22.* (῍Αρειος is an adj. from῍Αρης, Mars.)

698   ᾿Αρεοπαγίτης, ου, ὁ, a judge of the Areopagite court, Ac. xvii. 34.*

699   ἀρέσκεια, ας, ἡ, a pleasing, a desire of pleasing, Col. i. 10.*

700   ἀρέσκω, ἀρέσω, to be pleasing to, Mat. xiv. 6; Gal. i. 10; to seek to please or gratify, to accommodate one's self to (dat.), 1 Cor. x. 33; 1 Th. ii. 4.

701   ἀρεστός, ή, όν, acceptable, pleasing to, Jn. viii. 29; Ac. xii. 3.

702   ᾿Αρέτας, α, ὁ, Aretas, a king of Arabia Petræa, 2 Cor. xi. 32.*

703   ἀρετή, ῆς, ἡ, virtue, 2 Pet. i. 5; any moral excellence, perfection, Phil. iv. 8; 1 Pet. ii. 9; 2 Pet. i. 3.*

704   (ἄρην), gen. ἀρνός, a lamb, Lu. x. 3.*

705   ἀριθμέω, ῶ, to number, Mat. x. 30; Lu. xii. 7; Rev. vii. 9.*

706   ἀριθμός, οῦ, ὁ, a number, Jn. vi. 10; Ac. vi. 7.

707   ᾿Αριμαθαία, ας, ἡ, Arimathæa, a city of Palestine, Mat. xxvii. 57; Mar. xv. 43.

708   ᾿Αρίσταρχος, ου, ὁ, Aristarchus, Ac. xix. 29; Col. iv. 10.

709   ἀρνστάω, ῶ, ἤσω (ἄριστον), to breakfast, Jn. xxi. 12, 15; to dine, Lu xi. 37.

710   ἀριστερός, ά, όν, left; ἡ ἀριστερά (χείρ), the left hand, Mat. vi. 3; ἐξ ἀριστερῶν, on the left, Mar. x. 37 (W. H.); Lu. xxiii. 33, without ἐξ; 2 Cor. vi. 7. (The more common word is εὐώνυμος.)*

711   ᾿Αριστόβουλος, ου, ὁ, Aristobulus, Ro. xvi. 10.*

712   ἄριστον, ου, τό, dinner, Mat. xxii. 4; Lu. xi. 38, xiv. 12.* See δεῖπνον.

713   ἀρκετός, ή, όν, sufficient, Mat. vi. 34, x. 25; 1 Pet. iv. 3.*

714   ἀρκέω, ῶ, to be sufficient for, Mat. xxv. 9; 2 Cor. xii. 9; pass., to be satisfied with, Lu. iii. 14; Heb. xiii. 5.

715   ἄρκτος (W. H. ἄρκος), ου, ὁ, ἡ, a bear, Rev. xiii. 2.*

716   ἅρμα, ατος, τό, a chariot, Ac. viii. 28, 29, 38; Rev. ix. 9.*

717   ᾿Αρμαγεδδών (Heb. or Aram., der. disputed), (W. H. ᾿Αρ Μαγεδών), Harmageddon, Rev. xvi. 16. (N. T.)*

718 ἁρμόζω, σω, *to fit together;* mid., *to espouse, to betroth,* 2 Cor. xi. 2.*

719 ἁρμός, οῦ, ὁ, *a joint, i.e.,* of limbs in a body, Heb. iv. 12.*

720 ἀρνέομαι, οῦμαι, *to deny,* Mat. xxvi. 70; Jn. i. 20; 2 Tim. ii. 12; *to renounce,* Tit. ii. 12; *to reject,* Ac. iii. 14.*

721 ἀρνίον, ου, τό (dimin. of ἀρήν), *a little lamb,* Jn. xxi. 15; freq. in Rev., of Christ.

722 ἀροτριάω, ῶ, άσω, *to plow,* Lu. xvii. 7; 1 Cor. ix. 10.*

723 ἄροτρον, ου, τό, *a plow,* Lu. ix. 62.*

724 ἁρπαγή, ῆς, ἡ (ἁρπάζω), *the act of plundering,* Heb. x. 34; *plunder, spoil,* Mat. xxiii. 25; Lu. xi. 39.*

725 ἁρπαγμός, οῦ, ὁ, *spoil, an object of eager desire, a prize,* Phil. ii. 6.*

726 ἁρπάζω, άσω (2 aor. pass., ἡρπάγην), *to snatch, seize violently, take by force,* Jn. x. 12; *to carry off suddenly,* Jn. vi. 15; Ac. xxiii. 10.

727 ἅρπαξ, αγος, adj., *rapacious, ravenous,* Mat. vii. 15; Lu. xviii. 11; *a robber, an extortioner,* 1 Cor. v. 10, 11, vi. 10.*

728 ἀρραβών, ῶνος, ὁ (from Heb.), *a pledge, an earnest,* ratifying a contract, 2 Cor. i. 22, v. 5; Ep. i. 14.*

729 ἄρραφος (W. H. ἄραφος), ον, *not seamed* or *sewn,* Jn. xix. 23. (N. T.)*

730□ ἄρρην, εν (W. H. ἄρσην, εν), *of the male sex,* Ro. i. 27; Rev. xii. 5, 13.*

731 ἄρρητος, ον, adj., *unspoken, unspeakable,* 2 Cor. xii. 4.*

732 ἄρρωστος, ον, adj. (ῥώννυμι), *infirm, sick,* Mat. xiv. 14; 1 Cor. xi. 30.

733 ἀρσενο-κοίτης, ου, ὁ (ἄρσην κοίτη), *a sodomite,* 1 Cor. vi. 9; 1 Tim. i. 10.*

730□ ἄρσην, εν, *male,* Mat. xix. 4; Gal. iii. 28.

734 Ἀρτεμᾶς, ᾶ, ὁ, *Artemas,* Tit. iii. 12.*

735 Ἄρτεμις, ιδος or ιος, ἡ, *Artemis,* the Persian or Ephesian Artemis, to be distinguished from the Artemis of the Greeks, the sister of Apollo, Ac. xix. 24, 27, 28, 34, 35.*

736 ἀρτέμων, ονος ὁ (ἀρτάω, *to sus-*

pend'), prob. *the foresail,* Ac. xxvii. 40.*

737 ἄρτι, adv. of time, *now, just now, at this moment;* with other particles, as ἕως ἄρτι, *till now;* ἀπ᾽ ἄρτι, *from now* or *henceforward.*

738 ἀρτι-γέννητος, ον, *newly* or *recently born,* 1 Pet. ii. 2. (N. T.)*

739 ἄρτιος, ου, adj., *perfect, complete,* wanting in nothing, 2 Tim. iii. 17.* *Syn.:* ἄρτιος means fully adapted for its purpose; ὁλόκληρος, entire, having lost nothing; τέλειος, fully developed, complete.

740 ἄρτος, ου, ὁ, *bread, loaf, food;* fig., *spiritual nutriment;* ἄρτοι τῆς προθέσεως, *show-bread,* Mat. xii. 4; Mar. ii. 26.

741 ἀρτύω (ἄρω, *to fit*), *to season, to flavor,* as with salt, Mar. ix. 50; Lu. xiv. 34; fig., Col. iv. 6.*

742 Ἀρφαξάδ, ὁ (Heb.), *Arphaxad,* Lu. iii. 36.*

743 ἀρχ-άγγελος, ου, ὁ, *an arch-* or *chief-angel,* 1 Th. iv. 16; Ju. 9. (N. T.)*

744 ἀρχαῖος, α, ον, *old, ancient,* Lu. ix. 8, 19; 2 Pet. ii. 5.

745 Ἀρχέλαος, ου, ὁ, *Archelaus,* Mat. ii. 22.*

746 ἀρχή, ῆς, ἡ, (1) *a beginning,* of time, space, or series, Jn. i. 1; 2 Pet. iii. 4; *the outermost point,* Ac. x. 11. Used of Christ, *the leader,* Col. i. 18; Rev. iii. 14, xxi. 6, xxii. 13. Adv. phrases: ἀπ᾽ ἀρχῆς, *from the beginning;* ἐν ἀρχῇ, *in the beginning;* ἐξ ἀρχῆς, *from the beginning* or *from the first;* κατ᾽ ἀρχάς, *at the beginning;* τὴν ἀρχήν, *originally.* (2) *rule, preeminence, principality* (see ἄρχω): espec. in pl., ἀρχαί, *rulers, magistrates,* as Lu. xii. 11; of supramundane powers, *principalities,* as Ep. iii. 10.

747 ἀρχ-ηγός, οῦ, ὁ (ἀρχή, ἄγω), *the beginner, author, prince,* Ac. iii. 15, v. 31; Heb. ii. 10, xii. 2.*

748 ἀρχ-ιερατικός, ή, όν, *belonging to the office of the high-priest, pontifical,* Ac. iv. 6.*

749 ἀρχ-ιερεύς, έως, ὁ, (1) *the high-priest,* Mat. xxvi. 3; Heb. ix. 7, 25; so of Christ only in

Heb., as ii. 17, iii. 1, etc.;
(2) in pl. used more widely to include high-priestly
families and deposed high-
priests, Mat. ii. 4; Lu. xix.
47; Ac. iv. 23.

750 ἀρχι-ποίμην, ενος, ὁ, *the chief
shepherd*, a title of Christ,
1 Pet. v. 4. (N. T.)*

751 Ἄρχιππος, ου, ὁ, *Archippus*,
Col. iv. 17; Philem. 2.*

752 ἀρχι-συνάγωγος, ου, ὁ, *presid-
ing officer* or *ruler of a synagogue* Lu. viii. 49; Ac. xiii.
15.

753 ἀρχι-τέκτων, ονος, ὁ, *a master-
builder, an architect*, 1 Cor.
iii. 10.*

754 ἀρχι-τελώνης, ου, ὁ, *a chief collector of taxes, a chief pub-
lican*, Lu. xix. 2. (N. T.)*

755 ἀρχι-τρίκλινος, ου, ὁ, *a super-
intendent of a dining room*,
Jn. ii. 8, 9. (N. T.)*

756, 757 ἄρχω, *to reign, to rule* (gen.),
only Mar. x. 42; Ro. xv. 12;
mid., *to begin*, often with
infin.; ἀρξάμενος ἀπό, *beginning from* (see Gr. § 287).

758 ἄρχων, οντος, ὁ, prop. particip.,
ruler, prince, leader, Ac. xvi.
19; Ro. xiii. 3.

759 ἄρωμα, ατος, τό, *spice, perfume*,
Mar. xvi. 1; Lu. xxiii. 56,
xxiv. 1; Jn. xix. 40.*

760 Ἀσά, ὁ (Heb.), *Asa*, Mat. i. 7, 8.*

761 ἀ-σάλευτος, ον, *unshaken, im-
movable*, Ac. xxvii. 41; Heb.
xii. 28.*

762 ἄ-σβεστος, ον, adj. (σβέννυμι),
*not to be quenched, inextin-
guishable*, Mat. iii. 12; Lu.
iii. 17; Mar. ix. 43, 45 (W.
H. omit).*

763 ἀσέβεια, ας, ἡ, *impiety, ungodliness, wickedness*, Ro. i. 18;
Ju. 15, 18. *Syn.*: see ἀγνόημα.

764 ἀσεβέω, ῶ, ήσω, *to be ungodly,
act impiously*, 2 Pet. ii. 6;
Ju. 15.*

765 ἀ-σεβής, ές (σέβομαι), *impious,
ungodly, wicked*, Ro. iv. 5;
Ju. 4, 15.

766 ἀ-σέλγεια, ας, ἡ, *excess, wanton-
ness, lasciviousness*, Mar. vii.
22; Ep. iv. 19.

767 ἄ-σημος, ον, *not remarkable, obscure, ignoble*, Ac. xxi. 39.*

768 Ἀσήρ, ὁ, *Asher*, Lu. ii. 36;
Rev. vii. 6.*

769 ἀσθένεια, ας, ἡ, *weakness, bodily
infirmity, sickness*, 1 Cor. xv.
43; Heb. xi. 34; fig., *mental

weakness, distress, Ro. vi. 19;
Heb. v. 2.

770 ἀσθενέω, ῶ, *to be weak*, Ro. viii.
3; 2 Cor. xiii. 4; *to be sick*,
Lu. iv. 40; Ac. ix. 37.

771 ἀσθένημα, ατος, τό, *weakness,
infirmity*; fig., Ro. xv. 1.*

772 ἀ-σθενής, ές (σθένος, *strength*),
"without strength," *weak,
infirm*, Mat. xxvi. 41; Ro.
v. 6; 1 Cor. iv. 10; *sick*, Lu.
x. 9; Ac. iv. 9; 1 Cor. xi.
30.

773 Ἀσία, ας, ἡ, *Asia proper* or
Proconsular Asia, a district
in the west of Asia Minor,
Ac. vi. 9; 1 Pet. i. 1; Rev. i.
4; *a part of Proconsular Asia*,
Ac. ii. 9.

774 Ἀσιανός, οῦ, ὁ, *belonging to
Asia*, Ac. xx. 4.*

775 Ἀσιάρχης, ου, ὁ, *an Asiarch,
a president of Asia*, a citizen
appointed annually to preside over the worship and
celebrations in honor of the
gods, Ac. xix. 31.*

776 ἀσιτία, ας, ἡ (σῖτος, *corn*), *ab-
stinence, a fast*, Ac. xxvii.
21.*

777 ἄ-σιτος, ον, *fasting*, Ac. xxvii.
33.*

778 ἀσκέω, ῶ, ήσω, *to exercise one's
self, use diligence in*, Ac.
xxiv. 16.*

779 ἀσκός, οῦ, ὁ, *a bottle* of skin,
Mat. ix. 17; Mar. ii. 22; Lu.
v. 37, 38.*

780 ἀσμένως, adv. (from part. of
ἥδομαι), *with joy, gladly*, Ac.
ii. 41 (W. H. omit); Ac. xxi.
17.*

781 ἄ-σοφος, ον, *not wise*, Ep. v.
15.*

782 ἀσπάζομαι, dep., *to embrace,
salute, to greet* (actually or
by letter), Mat. x. 2; 1 Cor.
xvi. 19, 20; always of persons, except Heb. xi. 13,
"having embraced (R. V.
greeted) the promises"; *to
take leave of* (only Ac. xx. 1;
in xxi. 6, W. H. read ἀπασπάζομαι).

783 ἀσπασμός, οῦ, ὁ, *salutation,
greeting*, Mat. xxiii. 7; Col.
iv. 18.

784 ἄ-σπιλος, ον (σπῖλος), *without
spot, unblemished*, 1 Tim. vi.
14; 1 Pet. i. 19.

785 ἀσπίς, ίδος, ἡ, *an asp, a venom-
ous serpent*, Ro. iii. 13.*

786 ἄ-σπονδος, ον (σπονδή), "not

to be bound by truce," *implacable*, 2 Tim. iii. 3; Ro. i. 31 (not W. H.).*

787   ἀσσάριον, ίου, τό, *a small coin equal to the tenth part of a drachma, an assarium*, Mat. x. 29; Lu. xii. 6. See Gr. § 154a.

788   ᾶσσον, adv. (compar. of ᾶγχι), *nearer, close by*, Ac. xxvii.13.*

789   Ἄσσος, ου, ἡ, *Assos*, Ac. xx. 13, 14.*

790   ἀ-στατέω, ῶ, ήσω, *to be unsettled, to have no fixed abode*, 1 Cor. iv. 11.*

791   ἀστεῖος, ον (ἄστυ, *city*, see urbane), *fair, beautiful*, Ac. vii. 20; Heb. xi. 23.*

792   ἀστήρ, έρος, ὁ, *a star*, Mar. xiii. 25; 1 Cor. xv. 41; Rev. vi. 13.

793   ἀ-στήρικτος, ον (στηρίζω), *unsettled, unstable*, 2 Pet. ii. 14, iii. 16.*

794   ἄ-στοργος, ον (στοργή), *without natural affection*, Ro. i. 31; 2 Tim. iii. 3.*

795   ἀ-στοχέω, ῶ (στόχος), *to miss in aim, swerve from*, 1 Tim. i. 6, vi. 21; 2 Tim. ii. 18.*

796   ἀστραπή, ῆς, ἡ, *lightning*, Lu. x. 18; Rev. iv. 5; vivid *brightness, lustre*, Lu. xi. 36.

797   ἀστράπτω, *to flash*, as lightning, Lu. xvii. 24; *to be lustrous*, xxiv. 4.*

798   ἄστρον, ου, τό, *a star* (orig. *constellation*), Lu. xxi. 25; Ac. vii. 43, xxvii. 20; Heb. xi. 12.*

799   Ἀσύγκριτος, ου, ὁ, *Asyncritus*, Ro. xvi. 14.*

800   ἀ-σύμφωνος, ον, *dissonant, discordant*, Ac xxviii. 25.*

801   ἀ-σύνετος, ον, *without understanding, foolish*, Mat. xv. 16; Ro. x. 19.

802   ἀ-σύνθετος, ον, *covenant-breaking, treacherous*, Ro. i. 31.*

803   ἀσφάλεια, ας, ἡ, *security*, Ac. v. 23; 1 Th. v. 3; *certainty*, Lu. i. 4.*

804   ἀ-σφαλής, ές (σφάλλω, *fallo*), *safe*, Phil. iii. 1; *secure, firm*, Heb. vi. 19; *certain*, Ac. xxv. 26; τὸ ἀσφαλές, *the certainty*, Ac. xxi. 34, xxii. 30.*

805   ἀσφαλίζω, σω (mid.), *to make fast, to secure*, Mat. xxvii. 65, 66; Ac. xvi. 24; pass., *to be made secure*, Mat. xxvii. 64.*

806   ἀσφαλῶς, adv., *safely*, Mar. xiv.

---

807   44; Ac. xvi. 23; *assuredly*, Ac. ii. 36.*

808   ἀσχημονέω, ῶ, *to act improperly* or *unseemly*, 1 Cor. vii. 36, xiii. 5.*

ἀσχημοσύνη, ης, ἡ, *unseemliness*, Ro. i. 27; *shame, nakedness*, Rev. xvi. 15.*

809   ἀ-σχήμων, ον (σχῆμα), *uncomely, unseemly*, 1 Cor. xii. 23.*

810   ἀ-σωτία, ας, ἡ (σώζω), *an abandoned course, profligacy*, Ep. v. 18; Tit. i. 6; 1 Pet. iv. 4.*

811   ἀ-σώτως, adv., *profligately, dissolutely*, Lu. xv. 13.*

812   ἀτακτέω, ῶ, *to behave disorderly*, 2 Th. iii. 7.*

813   ἄ-τακτος, ον (τάσσω), *irregular, disorderly*, 1 Th. v. 14.*

814   ἀτάκτως, adv., *disorderly, irregularly*, 2 Th. iii. 6, 11.*

815   ἄ-τεκνος, ου, ὁ, ἡ (τέκνον), *childless*, Lu. xx. 28, 29.*

816   ἀτενίζω, σω, *to look intently upon* (dat. or εἰς), Lu. iv. 20; Ac. i. 10; 2 Cor. iii. 7, 13.

817   ἄτερ, adv., as prep. with gen., *without, in the absence of*, Lu. xxii. 6, 35.*

818   ἀτιμάζω, σω, *to dishonor, contemn*, whether persons or things, by word or by deed, Lu. xx. 11; Jn. viii. 49; Ja. ii. 6.

819   ἀτιμία, ας, ἡ, *dishonor, ignominy, disgrace, ignoble use*, 1 Cor. xi. 14; Ro. i. 26, ix. 21.

820   ἄ-τιμος, ον (τιμή), *without honor, despised*, Mat. xiii. 57; Mar. vi. 4; 1 Cor. iv. 10, xii. 23.*

821   ἀτιμόω, ῶ, *to dishonor, treat with indignity*, Mar. xii. 4 (not W. H.).*

822   ἀτμίς, ίδος, ἡ, *a vapor*, Ac. ii. 19; Ja. iv. 14.

823   ἄ-τομον, ου, τό (τέμνω), *an atom* of time, *moment*, 1 Cor. xv. 52.*

824   ἄ-τοπος, ον (τόπος), *misplaced, unbecoming, mischievous*, Lu. xxiii. 41; Ac. xxviii. 6.

825   Ἀττάλεια, ας, ἡ, *Attalia*, Ac. xiv. 25.*

826   αὐγάζω, *to shine forth*, 2 Cor. iv. 4.*

827   αὐγή, ῆς, ἡ, *brightness, daylight*, Ac. xx. 11.*

828   Αὔγουστος, ου, ὁ (Lat.), *Augustus*, Lu. ii. 1.* Compare Σεβαστός.

829   αὐθάδης, ες (αὐτός, ἥδομαι), *self-*

23

pleasing, arrogant, Tit. i. 7 ;
2 Pet. ii. 10.*

830 αὐθαίρετος, ον (αὐτός, αἱρέομαι),
of one's own accord, 2 Cor.
viii. 3, 17.*

831 αὐθεντέω, ῶ, to exercise authority over (gen.), 1 Tim. ii. 12.
(N. T.)*

832 αὐλέω, ῶ, ήσω, to play on a flute,
to pipe, Mat. xi. 17 ; Lu. vii.
32 ; 1 Cor. xiv. 7.

833 αὐλή, ῆς, ἡ (ἄω, to blow), an
open space, uncovered court
or hall of a house, as Lu. xi.
21, xxii. 55 ; a sheepfold, Jn.
x. 1, 16.

834 αὐλητής, οῦ, ὁ, a flute-player,
Mat. ix. 23 ; Rev. xviii. 22.*

835 αὐλίζομαι (to lodge in the open
air), to lodge, pass the night,
Mat. xxi. 17 ; Lu. xxi. 37.*

836 αὐλός, οῦ, ὁ (ἄω), a flute, pipe,
1 Cor. xiv. 7.*

837 αὐξάνω (also αὔξω), αὐξήσω,
trans., to make to grow, as
1 Cor. iii. 6, 7 ; pass., to grow,
increase, become greater, Mat.
xiii. 32 ; Col. i. 10 ; generally
intrans., to grow, increase, as
Mat. vi. 28.

838 αὔξησις, εως, ἡ, growth, increase,
Ep. iv. 16 ; Col. ii. 19.*

839 αὔριον, adv. (αὔρα, morning
breeze, ἄω), to-morrow, Mat.
vi. 30 ; Lu. xiii. 32, 33 ; ἡ (sc.
ἡμέρα) αὔριον, the morrow,
Mat. vi. 34 ; Ac. iv. 3.

840 αὐστηρός, ά, όν (dry), harsh,
austere, Lu. xix. 21, 22.*

841 αὐτάρκεια, ας, ἡ, sufficiency, 2
Cor. ix. 8 ; contentment, 1 Tim.
vi. 6.*

842 αὐτ-άρκης, ες (ἀρκέω, sufficient
for self), content, satisfied,
Phil. iv. 11.*

843 αὐτο-κατά-κριτος, ον, self-con-
demned, Tit. iii. 11. (N. T.)*

844 αὐτόματος, ον, spontaneous, of
its own accord, Mar. iv. 28 ;
Ac. xii. 10.*

845 αὐτ-όπτης, ου, ὁ, an eye-witness,
Lu. i. 2.*

846 αὐτός, ή, ό, pron., he, she, it ;
in nom. nearly always em-
phatic. Properly demonstrative, self, very ; joined with
each of the persons of the
verb, with or without a pers.
pron., I myself, thou thyself,
etc. ; with the article, the
same ; the same with (dat.), 1
Cor. xi. 5 ; ἐπὶ τὸ αὐτό, at the
same place or time, together ;

κατὰ τὸ αὐτό, together, only
Ac. xiv. 1. See Gr. § 335, WL
§ 22, 3, 4, Bu. 105 sq.

847 αὐτοῦ, adv. of place, here, there,
Mat. xxvi. 36 ; Ac. xviii. 19,
xxi. 4.

848 αὐτοῦ, ῆς, οῦ, pron. reflex. (contr
for ἑαυτοῦ), of himself, her-
self, etc. (W. H. in the majority of cases read αὐτοῦ,
αὐτῷ, etc., but retain αὑτοῦ,
etc., in some, as Mat. vi. 34 ;
Jn. ii. 24 ; Ac. xiv. 17, etc.).

see 1888 αὐτό-φωρος, ον (φώρ, a thief),
in the very act, Jn. viii. 4,
neut. dat. with ἐπί (W. H.
omit).

849 αὐτό-χειρ, ρος, ὁ, with one's own
hand, Ac. xxvii. 19.*

850 αὐχμηρός, ά, όν, dark, dismal,
2 Pet. i. 19.*

851 ἀφ-αιρέω, to take away, as Lu.
x. 42 ; to take away sin, only
Ro. xi. 27 ; Heb. x. 4 ; to
smite off, as Mat. xxvi. 51,
and parallel passages.

852 ἀ-φανής, ές (φαίνω), not appear-
ing, hidden, Heb. iv. 13.*

853 ἀ-φανίζω, to put out of sight,
destroy, Mat. vi. 19, 20 ; to
disfigure, Mat. vi. 16 ; pass.,
to vanish, perish, Ac. xiii.
41 ; Ja. iv. 14.*

854 ἀ-φανισμός, οῦ, ὁ, a disappearing, destruction, Heb. viii.
13.*

855 ἄ-φαντος, ον, disappearing, not
seen, Lu. xxiv. 31.*

856 ἀφεδρών, ῶνος, ὁ, draught, privy,
Mat. xv. 17 · Mar. vii. 19.
(N. T.)*

857 ἀ-φειδία, ας, ἡ (φείδομαι), severity, Col. ii. 23.*

858 ἀφελότης, τ ητος, simplicity, sincerity, Ac. ii. 46. (N. T.)*

859 ἄφ-εσις, εως, ἡ (ἀφίημι), deliverance ; lit., only Lu. iv.
18 ; elsewhere always of deliverance from sin, remission, forgiveness, Mat. xxvi.
28 ; Lu. i. 77 ; Ep. i. 7. Syn.:
πάρεσις is a simple suspen-
sion of punishment for sin,
in contrast with ἄφεσις, complete forgiveness.

860 ἀφή, ῆς, ἡ (ἅπτω, to fit), that
which connects, a joint, Ep.
iv. 16 ; Col. ii. 19.*

861 ἀφθαρσία, ας, ἡ, incorruption,
immortality, 1 Cor. xv., Ro.
ii. 7 ; 2 Tim. i. 10 ; Ep. vi. 24,
incorruptness, Tit. ii. 7 (W.
H. ἀφθορία).*

24

862 ἄ-φθαρτος, ον (φθείρω), *incorruptible, imperishable*, Ro. i. 23; I Cor. ix. 25, xv. 52; I Tim. i. 17; I Pet. i. 4, 23, iii. 4.*

see 90 ἀ-φθορία, ας, ἡ, *incorruptness*, Tit. ii. 7 (W. H.). (N. T.)*

863 ἀφ-ίημι (see Gr. § 112, Wi. § 14, 3), *to send away*, as (1) *to let go, emit*, Mat. xxvii. 50; Mar. xv. 37; *dismiss*, in senses varying according to the obj.; spec., *to disregard, pass by, send away, divorce*, Mat. xv. 14; Heb. vi. 1; I Cor. vii. 11, 12, 13; hence, (2) *to forgive* (dat. pers.), very often, Mat. xviii. 27; Mar. ii. 5, 7; (3) *to permit, concede*, abs., or with inf., as Mar. x. 14; or acc., as Mat. iii. 15 (dat., Mat. v. 40); or ἵνα, subj., Mar. xi. 6; or subj. alone, Lu. vi. 42; (4) *to leave, depart from, abandon, leave behind*, Mat. xxii. 22; Mar. i. 31; Lu. v. 11, xvii. 34, 35.

864 ἀφικνέομαι, οῦμαι (2 aor., ἀφικόμην), *to arrive at, to reach*, Ro. xvi. 19.*

865 ἀ-φιλ-άγαθος, ον, *not loving goodness and good men*, 2 Tim. iii. 3. (N. T.)*

866 ἀ-φιλ-άργυρος, ον, *not loving money, not avaricious*, I Tim. iii. 3; Heb. xiii. 5. (N. T.)*

867 ἄφιξις, εως, ἡ, orig. arrival; *departure*, Ac. xx. 29.*

868 ἀφ-ίστημι, ἀποστήσω, trans. in pres., imperf., 1 aor., fut., *to lead away, to seduce*; intrans. in perf., plup., 2 aor., *to go away, depart, avoid, withdraw from* (often with ἀπό); mid., *to fail, abstain from, absent one's self*.

869 ἄφνω, adv., *suddenly*, Ac. ii. 2, xvi. 26, xxviii. 6.*

870 ἀ-φόβως, adv., *without fear*, Lu. i. 74; Phil. i. 14; I Cor. xvi. 10; Ju. 12.*

871 ἀφ-ομοιόω, ῶ, *to make like*, in pass., Heb. vii. 3.*

872 ἀφ-οράω, ῶ (2 a., ἀπ- or ἀφεῖδον), *to look away from* others *at* (εἰς) one, *to regard earnestly*, Heb. xii. 2; *to see*, Phil. ii. 23.*

873 ἀφ-ορίζω, fut. ιῶ, trans., *to separate from* (ἐκ or ἀπό), Mat. xiii. 49, xxv. 32; *to separate for a purpose* (εἰς, Ac. xiii. 2; Ro. i. 1; or inf.,

Gal. i. 15); *to excommunicate*, Lu. vi. 22.

874 ἀφ-ορμή, ῆς, ἡ, *an occasion, opportunity*, Ro. vii. 8, 11; 2 Cor. v. 12.

875 ἀφρίζω, *to foam at the mouth*, Mar. ix. 18, 20.*

876 ἀφρός, οῦ, ὁ, *foam, froth*, Lu. ix. 39.*

877 ἀ-φροσύνη, ης, ἡ, *foolishness*, Mar. vii. 22; 2 Cor. xi. 1, 17, 22.*

878 ἄ-φρων, ονος, ὁ, ἡ (φρήν), *inconsiderate, foolish, rash*, Lu. xi. 40; Ro. ii. 20.

879 ἀφ-υπνόω, ῶ (ἀπό, intensive), *to fall asleep*, Lu. viii. 23.*

see 650 ἀφυστερέω, ῶ, *to keep back by fraud*, Ja. v. 4 (W. H.).*

880 ἄ-φωνος, ον, *dumb, without the faculty of speech :* of animals, Ac. viii. 32; 2 Pet. ii. 16; of idols, I Cor. xii. 2. In I Cor. xiv. 10 the R. V. mrg. is probably the correct rendering.*

881 Ἄχαζ, ὁ (Heb.), *Ahaz*, Mat. i. 9.*

882 Ἀχαΐα, ας, ἡ, *Achaia*, a Roman province including all Greece except Thessaly, Ac. xix. 21; I Cor. xvi. 15.

883 Ἀχαϊκός, οῦ, ὁ, *Achaicus*, I Cor. xvi. 17.*

884 ἀ-χάριστος, ον, *unthankful*, Lu. vi. 35; 2 Tim. iii. 2.*

885 Ἀχείμ, ὁ (Heb.), *Achim*, Mat. i. 14.*

886 ἀ-χειρο-ποίητος, ον, *not made with hands*, Mar. xiv. 58; 2 Cor. v. 1; Col. ii. 11. (N. T.)*

887 ἀχλύς, ύος, ἡ, *a mist, dimness*, Ac. xiii. 11.*

888 ἀ-χρεῖος, ον, *useless, good for nothing, unprofitable*, Mat. xxv. 30; Lu. xvii. 10.*

889 ἀ-χρειόω (W. H. ἀχρεόω), pass., *to be made useless*, Ro. iii. 12.*

890 ἄ-χρηστος, ον, *useless, unprofitable*, Philem. 11.*

891 ἄχρι and ἄχρις, adv. as prep., with gen., *even to, until*, as *far as*, whether of place, time, or degree; ἄχρις οὗ or ἄχρις alone, with the force of a conjunction, *until*. See μέχρι.

892 ἄχυρον, ου, τό, *chaff*, Mat. iii. 12; Lu. iii. 17.*

893 ἀ-ψευδής, ές, *free from falsehood, truthful*, Tit. i. 2.*

894 ἄψινθος, ου, ὁ and ἡ, *worm-wood*, Rev. viii. 11.*

895 ἄ-ψυχος, ου, *without life, in-animate*, 1 Cor. xiv. 7.*

B

B, β, βῆτα, *beta, b*, the second letter. Numerally, β′ = 2 ; ‚β = 2000.

896 Βαάλ (W. H. Βάαλ), ὁ, ἡ (Heb. *Master*), *Baal*, chief deity ot the Phœnicians and other Semitic nations, Ro. xi. 4 (fem.), from 1 Kings xix. 18 (S.)*

897 Βαβυλών, ῶνος, ἡ, *Babylon*, lit., Mat. i. 11, 12, 17 ; Ac. vii. 43, and prob. 1 Pet. v. 13 ; mystically, in Rev. xiv. 8, xvi. 19, xvii. 5, xviii. 2, 10, 21.*

898 βαθμός, οῦ, ὁ (βαίνω, *to step*), *a step* or *degree* in dignity, 1 Tim. iii. 13. (S.)*

899 βάθος, ους, τό, *depth*, lit. or fig. Mat. xiii. 5 ; 1 Cor. ii. 10 ; 2 Cor. viii. 2 (ἡ κατὰ βάθους πτωχεία, *their deep poverty*).

900 βαθύνω, υνῶ, *to make deep*, Lu. vi. 48 *

901 βαθύς, εῖα, ύ, *deep*, Jn. iv. 11 ; in Lu. xxiv. 1, ὄρθρου βαθέος, in the early dawn (W. H. βαθέως, probably a genit. form).

902 βαΐον, ου, τό (Egyptian), *a palm branch*, Jn. xii. 13.*

903 Βαλαάμ, ὁ (Heb.), *Balaam*. A name emblematic of seduc-ing teachers, 2 Pet. ii. 15 ; Ju. 11 ; Rev. ii. 14.*

904 Βαλάκ, ὁ (Heb.), *Balak*, Rev. ii. 14.*

905 βαλάντιον (W. H. -λλ-), ου, τό, *a money-bag, purse*, Lu. x. 4, xii. 33, xxii. 35, 36.*

906 βάλλω, βαλῶ, βέβληκα, ἔβαλον, *to throw, cast, put* (with more or less force, as modified by the context) ; of liquids, *to pour*. Pass. perf., with in-trans. force, as Mat. viii. 6 ("has been cast"), *lies*. The verb is intrans., Ac. xxvii. 14, *rushed*. In Mar. xiv. 65 the true reading is prob. ἔλα-βον. Generally trans. with acc. and dat., or ἐπί (acc., sometimes gen.), εἰς, ἀπό, ἐκ, and other prepp. or advv.

907 βαπτίζω, σω (in form a fre-quentative of βάπτω, see Gr

§ 144 b), (1) mid. or pass., reflex., *to bathe* one's self, only in Mar. vii. 4 ; Lu. xi. 38 ; (2) of the Christian ordi-nance, *to immerse, submerge, to baptize*. The material (wa-ter, fire, the Holy Spirit) is expressed by dat., εἰς or ἐν ; the purpose or result by εἰς. Pass. or. mid., *to be baptized, to receive baptism ;* (3) fig., of overwhelming woe, Mar. x. 38, 39 ; Lu. xii. 50.

908 βάπτισμα, ατος, τό, *the rite* or *ceremony of baptism*, Mat. iii. 7 ; Ep. iv. 5 ; fig., for over-whelming afflictions, Mar. x. 38, 39 ; Lu. xii. 50. (N. T.)

909 βαπτισμός, οῦ, ὁ, *the act of cleansing*, as vessels, Mar. vii. 4, 8 (W. H. omit) ; of Jewish lustrations, *washings* (pl.), Heb. ix. 10. For Heb. vi. 2, see Gr. § 260 b, 2 (b).*

910 βαπτιστής, οῦ, ὁ, *one who bap-tizes ;* the surname of Johr., Christ's forerunner, Mat. iii. 1 ; Mar. viii. 28.

911 βάπτω, βάψω, *to dip*, Lu. xvi. 24 ; Jn. xiii. 26 ; *to dye, color*, Rev. xix. 13.*

see [1247] St βάρ (Aram.), *son*, only Mat. xvi. 17 (βὰρ Ἰωνᾶ, W. H. βαριωνᾶ). Also prefix to many surnames, meaning *son of*. (N. T.)

912 Βαρ-αββᾶς, ᾶ, ὁ, *Barabbas*, Mat. xxvii. 16, 17 ; Jn. xviii. 40.

913 Βαράκ, ὁ, *Barak*, Heb. xi. 32.*

914 Βαραχίας, ου, ὁ, *Barachiah*, Mat. xxiii. 35.*

915 βάρβαρος, ου, ὁ (prob. onoma-top., descriptive of unintel-ligible sounds), properly adj., *a foreigner, barbarian*, as 1 Cor. xiv. 11 ; used of all foreigners not Greeks, Ac. xxviii. 2, 4 ; Col. iii. 11 ; Ro. i. 14.*

916 βαρέω, ῶ (see βάρος), in N. T. only pass. βαρέομαι, οῦμαι, *to be weighed down, to be op-pressed*, as by sleep, Lu. ix. 32 ; mental troubles, 2 Cor. i. 8, v. 4.

917 βαρέως, adv., *heavily, with dif-ficulty*, Mat. xiii. 15 ; Ac. xxviii. 27.*

918 Βαρ-θολομαῖος, ου, ὁ, *Bartholo-mew*, surname (prob.) of Nathanael, Mat. x. 3.

919 Βαρ-ιησοῦς, οῦ, ὁ, *Bar-Jesus*, Ac. xiii. 6.*

920 Βαρ-ιωνᾶs, ᾶ, ὁ, *Bar-Jonas*, surname of Peter, Mat. xvi. 17 (W. H.).*

921 Βαρ-νάβαs, a, ὁ, *Barnabas* (perhaps "son of comfort," see παράκλησιs), Ac. ix. 27; Col. iv. 10.

922 βάροs, ουs, τό, *weight, burden*, only fig., Ac. xv. 28; Rev. ii. 24.

923 Βαρ-σαβᾶs, ᾶ, ὁ, *Barsabas.* Two are mentioned, Ac. i. 23, xv. 22.*

924 Βαρ-τίμαιοs, ου, ὁ, *Bartimæus*, Mar. x. 46.*

925 βαρύνω, *to weigh down*, Lu. xxi. 34 (Rec.).*

926 βαρύs, εῖα, ύ (see βάροs), (1) *heavy*, Mat. xxiii. 4; (2) *weighty, important*, Mat. xxiii. 23; Ac. xxv. 7; 2 Cor. x. 10; (3) *oppressive* or *grievous*, Ac. xx. 29; 1 Jn. v. 3.*

927 βαρύ-τιμοs, ον, *of great price*, Mat. xxvi. 7.*

928 βασανίζω (see βάσανοs), *to examine*, as by torture; hence, *to torment, vex*, Mar. v. 7; Rev. xi. 10, xii. 2; of waves, *to buffet*, Mat. xiv. 24; Mar. vi. 48.

929 βασανισμόs, οῦ, ὁ, *torture, torment*, Rev. ix. 5, xiv. 11, xviii. 7, 10, 15.*

930 βασανιστήs, οῦ, ὁ, *one who tortures, a tormentor, jailer*, Mat. xviii. 34.*

931 βάσανοs, ου, ἡ (lit., *a touchstone*), *torture, torment*, Mat. iv. 24; Lu. xvi. 23, 28.*

932 βασιλεία, αs, ἡ, *a kingdom, royal power* or *dignity, reign*; ἡ βασιλεία τοῦ θεοῦ, τοῦ χριστοῦ, τῶν οὐρανῶν (the last form only in Mat.), *the divine, spiritual kingdom*, or *reign* of Messiah, in the world, in the individual, or in the future state; υἱοὶ τῆs βασιλείαs, *sons of the kingdom*, Jews, its original possessors, Mat. viii. 12; true believers, Mat. xiii. 38. In Rev. i. 6, v. 10, for βασιλεῖs καὶ, W. H. read βασιλείαν, *a kingdom* consisting of priests (R. V.).

•934, 933 βασίλειοs, ον, *royal, regal*, 1 Pet. ii. 9, from Exod. xix. 6; τὰ βασίλεια, as subst., *a regal mansion, palace*, Lu. vii. 25.*

935 βασιλεύs, έωs, ὁ, *a leader, ruler,*

king, sometimes subordinate to higher authority, as the Herods. Applied to God, always with distinguishing epithets, Mat. v. 35; 1 Tim. i. 17, vi. 15; Rev. xv. 3; to Christ, Mat. ii. 2; Jn. i. 49, etc.; to Christians, Rev. i. 6, v. 10 (Rec., but see under βασιλεία).

936 βασιλεύω, εύσω, *to have authority, to reign*, or *to possess* or *exercise dominion; to be* βασιλεύs generally. With gen. or ἐπί (gen.), of the kingdom; ἐπί (acc.), of the persons governed.

937 βασιλικόs, ή, όν, *belonging to a king, royal*, Jn. iv. 46, 49; Ac. xii. 20, 21; Ja. ii. 8.*

938 βασίλισσα, ηs, ἡ, *a queen*, Mat. xii. 42; Lu. xi. 31; Ac. viii. 27; Rev. xviii. 7.*

939 βάσιs, εωs, ἡ (βαίνω), prop. *a going*, hence, *the foot*, Ac. iii. 7.*

940 βασκαίνω, ανῶ, *to bewitch, bring under malign influence*, Gal. iii. 1.*

941 βαστάζω, άσω, *to lift, lift up; often with the sense of bearing away*. Thus, (1) *to carry*, a burden, as Lu. xiv. 27; (2) *tidings*, as Ac. ix. 15; (3) *to take on one's self*, as disease or weakness, Ro. xv. 1; condemnation, Gal. v. 10; reproach, Gal. vi. 17; (3) *to bear with* or *endure*, Rev. ii. 2; (4) *to take away*, Mat. viii. 17; Jn. xii. 6.

942 βάτοs, ου, ὁ, ἡ, *a thorn-bush* or *bramble*, Lu. vi. 44; Ac. vii. 30, 35. "The Bush," Mar. xii. 26; Lu. xx. 37 denotes the section of the O. T. so called (Exod. iii.).*

943 βάτοs, ου, ὁ (Heb.), *a bath*, or Jewish measure for liquids containing 8 or 9 gallons, Lu. xvi. 6. (Ap.)*

944 βάτραχοs, ου, ὁ, *a frog*, Rev. xvi. 13.*

945 βαττο-λογέω, ῶ (prob. from βατ, an unmeaning sound; see βάρβαροs), *to babble, talk to no purpose*, Mat. vi. 7. (N. T.)*

946 βδέλυγμα, ατοs, τό (see βδελύσσω), *something unclean and abominable, an object of moral repugnance*, Lu. xvi. 15; spec. (as often in O.T.) *idol-*

atry, Rev. xvii. 4, 5, xxi. 27.
"Abomination of desolation," Mat. xxiv. 15; Mar.
xiii. 14 (from Dan. ix. 27)
refers to the pollution of
the temple by some idolatrous symbol. (S.)*

947 βδελυκτός, ή, όν, *disgusting,
abominable,* Tit. i. 16. (S.)*

948 βδελύσσω, ξω, *to defile,* only
mid.; *to loathe,* Ro. ii. 22;
and pass. perf. part., *defiled,*
Rev. xxi. 8.*

949 βέβαιος, a, ov, *steadfast, constant,
firm,* Heb. vi. 19; Ro. iv. 16.

950 βεβαιόω, ῶ, *to confirm, to establish,* whether of persons or
things, Mar. xvi. 20; Ro.
xv. 8; Heb. xiii. 9.

951 βεβαίωσις, εως, ή, *confirmation,*
Phil. i. 7; Heb. vi. 16.*

952 βέβηλος, ov (βα- in βαίνω,
"that on which any one
may step"), *common, unsanctified, profane,* of things
or persons, 1 Tim. iv. 7;
Heb. xii. 16.

953 βεβηλόω, ῶ, *to make common,
to profane,* the Sabbath, Mat.
xii. 5; the temple, Ac. xxiv.
6. (S.)*

954 Βεελ-ζεβούλ (W. H. Βεεζεβούλ),
ὁ (Heb.), *Beelzebul,* a name
of *Satan,* Mat. x. 25; Lu. xi.
15, 18, 19. (N. T.)

955 Βελίαλ, ὁ (Heb. *worthlessness*),
or Βελίαρ (W. H.), derivation
doubtful, a name for *Satan,*
2 Cor. vi. 15. (N. T.)*

see 956 βελόνη, ης, ή, *a needle,* Lu.
xviii. 25 (W. H.).*

956 βέλος, ους, τό (βάλλω), *a missile,*
such as *a javelin* or *dart,* Ep.
vi. 16.*

957 βελτίων, ov, ovos (a compar. of
ἀγαθός), *better;* neut. as adv.,
2 Tim. i. 18.*

958 Βεν-ιαμίν, ὁ (Heb. *Ben* = son),
Benjamin, Ac. xiii. 21; Rev.
vii. 8.

959 Βερνίκη, ης, ή, *Bernice,* Ac.
xxv. 13, 23, xxvi. 30.*

960 Βέροια, ας, ή, *Berœa,* Ac. xvii.
10, 13.*

961 Βεροιαῖος, a, ov, *Berœan,* Ac.
xx. 4.*

**see
[1004]St** Βηθ-, a Hebrew and Aramaic
prefix to many local names,
meaning *house* or *abode of.*

962 Βηθ-αβαρά, ᾶς, ή, *Bethabara,*
"house of the ford," Jn. i.
28 (W. H. read Βηθανία).*

963 Βηθ-ανία, ας, ή, *Bethany,* "house

of misery." There were two
places of the name: (1) Jn.
xi. 1, etc.; (2) on the Jordan,
Jn. i. 28 (W. H.). See Βηθαβαρά.

964 Βηθ-εσδά, ή, *Bethesda,* "house
of compassion," Jn. v. 2 (W.
H. Βηθζαθά).*

965 Βηθ-λεέμ, ή, *Bethlehem,* "house
of bread," Lu. ii. 4, 15.

966 Βηθ-σαϊδά, ή, *Bethsaida,* "house
of hunting" or "fishing."
There were two places of
the name: one in Galilee,
Jn. xii. 21; the other on the
east of the Jordan, Lu. ix.
10.

967 Βηθ-φαγή, ή, *Bethphage,* "house
of figs," Mat. xxi. 1; Mar.
xi. 1; Lu. xix. 29.*

968 βήμα, ατος, τό (βα- in βαίνω), *a
step, a space; βῆμα ποδός,* a
space for the foot, Ac. vii. 5;
a raised space or *bench, tribunal, judgment-seat,* Jn. xix.
13; 2 Cor. v. 10.

969 βήρυλλος, ου, ὁ, ή, *a beryl,* a
gem of greenish hue, Rev.
xxi. 20.*

970 βία, ας, ή, *force, violence,* Ac.
v. 26, xxi. 35, xxiv. 7 (W. H.
omit), xxvii. 41.*

971 βιάζω, *to use violence;* mid., *to
enter forcibly,* with εἰς, Lu.
xvi. 16; pass., *to suffer violence, to be assaulted,* Mat. xi.
12.*

**972
973** βίαιος, a, ov, *violent,* Ac. ii. 2.*
βιαστής, οῦ, ὁ, *one who employs
force, a man of violence,* Mat.
xi. 12.*

974 βιβλαρίδιον, ου, τό, *a little book,*
Rev. x. 2, 8 (not W. H.), 9,
10. (N. T.)*

975 βιβλίον, ου, τό (dim. of following), *a small book, a scroll,*
as Lu. iv. 17; Rev. v. 1;
βιβλίον ἀποστασίου, a bill of
divorcement, Mat. xix. 7;
Mar. x. 4.

976 βίβλος, ου, ὁ, *a written book,
roll* or *volume,* Mat. i. 1;
Phil. iv. 3. The word means
papyrus, from which ancient
books were made.

977 βιβρώσκω (βρο-), perf. βέβρωκα,
to eat, Jn. vi. 13.*

978 Βιθυνία, ας, ή, *Bithynia,* Ac.
xvi. 7; 1 Pet. i. 1.*

979 βίος, ου, ὁ, (1) *life,* as Lu. viii.
14; (2) *means of life, livelihood,* as Lu. viii. 43; (3)
goods or *property,* as Lu. xv.

12; 1 Jn. iii. 17. *Syn.*: ζωή is life in its *principle*, and used for spiritual and immortal life; βίος is life in its *manifestations*, denoting the manner of life.

980 βιόω, ῶ, *to pass one's life*, 1 Pet. iv. 2.*

981 βίωσις, εως, ἡ, *manner* or *habit of life*, Ac. xxvi. 4. (Ap.)*

982 βιωτικός ἡ, όν, *of* or *belonging to* (this) *life*, Lu. xxi. 34; 1 Cor. vi. 3, 4.*

983 βλαβερός, ά, όν, *hurtful*, 1 Tim. vi. 9.*

984 βλάπτω (βλαβ-), βλάψω, *to hurt* or *injure*, Mar. xvi. 18 (W. H. omit); Lu. iv. 35.*

985 βλαστάνω (or βλαστάω, Mar. iv. 27, W. H.), βλαστήσω, intrans., *to sprout, to spring up, to put forth buds*, Mat. xiii. 26; Mar. iv. 27; Heb. ix. 4; trans., *to bring forth* (καρπόν), Ja. v. 18.*

986 Βλάστος, ου, ὁ, *Blastus*, Ac. xii. 20.*

987 βλασφημέω, ῶ. *to speak abusively, to rail*, abs., as Ac. xiii. 45; *to calumniate, speak evil of, blaspheme*, with acc., rarely εἰς; often of men or things. Spec. of God, Rev. xvi. 11; the Holy Spirit, Lu. xii. 10; the divine name or doctrine, 1 Tim. vi. 1.

988 βλασφημία, ας, ἡ, *evil-speaking, reviling, blasphemy*, Mat. xii. 31; Mar. xiv. 64.

989 βλάσφημος, ον, *slanderous*, Ac. vi. 11; subst., *a blasphemer*, 1 Tim. i. 13; 2 Tim. iii. 2.

990 βλέμμα, ατος, τό, *a look, glance*, 2 Pet. ii. 8.*

991 βλέπω, ψω, *to see, to have the power of seeing, to look at, behold;* with εἰς, *to look to*, Mat. xxii. 16; Mar. xii. 14; with ἵνα or μή, *to take care* (once without, Mar. xiii. 9) with ἀπό, *to beware of;* once with κατά (acc.), geographically, *to look towards*, Ac. xxvii. 12.

992 βλητέος, έα, έον, a verbal adj. (βάλλω), *that ought to be put*, Mar. ii. 22 (W. H. omit); Lu. v. 38. (N. T.)*

993 Βοανεργές (W. H. -ηρ-), (Heb.), *Boanerges*, "sons of thunder," Mar. iii. 17. (N. T.)*

994 βοάω, ῶ (βοή), *to shout* for joy, Gal. iv. 27; *to cry* for grief,

Ac. viii. 7; *to publish openly, to cry aloud*, Mar. xv. 34; Ac. xvii. 6; with πρός (acc.), *to appeal to*, Lu. xviii. 7, 38.

995 βοή, ῆς, ἡ, *a loud cry*, Ja. v. 4.*

996 βοήθεια, ας, ἡ, *help*, Ac. xxvii. 17; Heb. iv. 16.*

997 βοηθέω, ῶ, *to go to the help of, to succor* (dat.), Mat. xv. 25; Rev. xii. 16.

998 βοηθός, οῦ, ὁ, ἡ (properly adj.), *a helper*, Heb. xiii. 6.*

999 βόθυνος, ου, ὁ, *a pit, ditch*, Mat. xii. 11, xv. 14; Lu. vi. 39.*

1000 βολή, ῆς, ἡ, *a throwing;* λίθου βολή, *a stone's throw*, Lu. xxii. 41.*

1001 βολίζω, σω, *to heave the lead, take soundings*, Ac. xxvii. 28. (N. T.)*

1002 βολίς, ίδος, ἡ, *a weapon thrown*, as *a dart* or *javelin*, Heb. xii. 20 (W. H. omit).*

1003 Βοόζ, ὁ (Heb.), *Booz* or *Boaz*, Mat. i. 5 (W. H. Βοές); Lu. iii. 32 (W. H. Βοός).*

1004 βόρβορος, ου, ὁ, *mire, filth*, 2 Pet. ii. 22.*

1005 Βορρᾶς, ᾶ, ὁ (*Boreas*, the north wind), *the North*, Lu. xiii. 29; Rev. xxi. 13.*

1006 βόσκω, ήσω, *to feed*, as Mat. viii. 33; Jn. xxi. 15, 17; mid., *to feed, graze*, as Mar. v. 11. *Syn.*: ποιμαίνω is the broader word, to act as shepherd, literally or spiritually; βόσκω, simply to *feed* the flock.

1007 Βοσόρ, ὁ (Heb. *Beor*), *Bosor*, 2 Pet. ii. 15 (W. H. Βεώρ).*

1008 βοτάνη, ης, ἡ (βόσκω), *herbage, pasturage*, Heb. vi. 7.*

1009 βότρυς, υος, ὁ, *a cluster of grapes*, Rev. xiv. 18.*

1010 βουλευτής, οῦ, ὁ, *a councilor, a senator*, Mar. xv. 43; Lu. xxiii. 50.*

1011 βουλεύω, σω, *to advise*, N. T. mid. only; (1) *to consult, to deliberate*, with εἰ, Lu. xiv. 31; (2) *to resolve on* or *purpose*, with inf., Ac. v. 33, xv. 37 (W. H. in both passages read βούλομαι), xxvii. 39; ἵνα, Jn. xi. 53 (W. H.), xii. 10; acc., 2 Cor. i. 17.*

1012 βουλή, ῆς, ἡ, *a design, purpose, plan*, Lu. xxiii. 51; Ac. v. 38; Ep. i. 11.

1013 βούλημα, ατος, τό (βούλομαι), *will, counsel, purpose*, Ac. xxvii. 43; Ro. ix. 19; 1 Pet. iv. 3 (W. H.).*

1014 βούλομαι, 2d pers. sing. βούλει, aug. with ἐ or ἠ, *to will,* as (1) *to be willing, to incline to,* Mar. xv. 15; (2) *to intend,* Mat. i. 19; (3) *to desire,* 1 Tim. vi. 9. Generally with inf., sometimes understood, as Ja. i. 18; with subj., Jn. xviii. 39.

1015 βουνός, οῦ, ὁ, *a hill, rising ground,* Lu. iii. 5; xxiii. 30.*

1016 βοῦς, βοός, ὁ, ἡ, *an animal of the ox kind,* male or female, Lu. xiii. 15; 1 Tim. v. 18.

1017 βραβεῖον, ου, τό, *the prize,* in the games, 1 Cor. ix. 24; Phil. iii. 14.*

1018 βραβεύω (lit., to act as arbiter in the games), *to rule, arbitrate,* Col. iii. 15.*

1019 βραδύνω, νῶ (βραδύς), *to be slow, to linger,* 1 Tim. iii. 15; 2 Pet. iii. 9 (gen.).*

1020 βραδυ-πλοέω, ῶ, *to sail slowly,* Ac. xxvii. 7. (N.T.)*

1021 βραδύς, εῖα, ύ, *slow;* dat. of sphere, Lu. xxiv. 25; εἰς, Ja. i. 19.*

1022 βραδυτής, τῆτος, ἡ, *slowness,* 2 Pet. iii. 9.*

1023 βραχίων, ονος, ὁ, *the arm;* met., *strength,* Lu. i. 51; Jn. xii. 38; Ac. xiii. 17.*

1024 βραχύς, εῖα, ύ, *short, little,* only neut.; of time, Lu. xxii. 58; Ac. v. 34; Heb. ii. 7, 9; place, Ac. xxvii. 28; διὰ βραχέων, Heb. xiii. 22, *in few words;* βραχύ τι, Jn. vi. 7, of quantity, *a little.**

1025 βρέφος, ους, τό, *a child unborn,* Lu. i. 41, 44; *a babe,* as Lu. ii. 12, 16; 2 Tim. iii. 15.

1026 βρέχω, ξω, *to moisten,* Lu. vii. 38, 44; *to rain, to send rain,* Mat. v. 45; Lu. xvii. 29; impers., Ja. v. 17; intrans., Rev. xi. 6.*

1027 βροντή, ῆς, ἡ, *thunder,* Jn. xii. 29; Rev. iv. 5.

1028 βροχή, ῆς, ἡ (βρέχω), *a heavy rain,* Mat. vii. 25, 27. (S.)*

1029 βρόχος, ου, ὁ, *a noose* or *snare,* 1 Cor. vii. 35.*

1030 βρυγμός, οῦ, ὁ, *a grinding* or *gnashing,* as Mat. viii. 12.

1031 βρύχω, ξω, *to grind* or *gnash,* as the teeth, for rage or pain, Ac. vii. 54.*

1032 βρύω, σω, *to send forth abundantly,* as a fountain, Ja. iii. 11.*

1033 βρῶμα, ατος, τό (see βιβρώσκω), *food* of any kind, Mat. xiv. 15; Jn. iv. 34; 1 Cor. viii. 8, 13.

1034 βρώσιμος, ον, *eatable,* Lu. xxiv 41.*

1035 βρῶσις, εως, ἡ, (1) *the act of eating,* as 1 Cor. viii. 4; (2) *corrosion,* Mat. vi. 19, 20; (3) *food,* Jn. iv. 32; Heb. xii. 16.

1036 βυθίζω, σω, *to cause to sink,* fig., 1 Tim. vi. 9; mid., *to sink,* Lu. v. 7.*

1037 βυθός, οῦ, ὁ, *the deep, the sea,* 2 Cor. xi. 25.*

1038 βυρσεύς, έως, ὁ, *a tanner,* Ac. ix. 43, x. 6, 32.*

1039 βύσσινος, η, ον, *made of byssus, fine linen,* Rev. xviii. 12 (W. H.), 16, xix. 8, 14.*

1040 βύσσος, ου, ἡ, *byssus,* a species of flax, and of linen manufactured from it, highly prized for its softness, whiteness, and delicacy, Lu. xvi. 19; Rev. xviii. 12 (Rec.).*

1041 βωμός, οῦ, ὁ, *an altar,* Ac. xvii. 23.* *Syn.:* βωμός is a heathen altar; θυσιαστήριον, the altar of the true God.

Τ

Τ, τ, γάμμα, *gamma,* g hard, the third letter of the Greek alphabet. In numeral value, γ´ = 3; ͵γ = 3000.

1042 Γαββαθά (W. H.-θά), ἡ (Aram.), *Gabbatha; an elevated place* or *tribunal,* Jn. xix. 13. See λιθόστρωτον. (N. T.)*

1043 Γαβριήλ, ὁ (Heb. *man of God*), the archangel *Gabriel,* Lu. i. 19, 26.*

1044 γάγγραινα, ης, ἡ, *a gangrene, mortification,* 2 Tim. ii. 17.*

1045 Γάδ, ὁ (Heb.), *Gad,* Rev. vii. 5.*

1046 Γαδαρηνός, ἡ, όν, *belonging to Gadara,* Mar. v. 1 (Rec.); Mat. viii. 28 (W. H.). See Γεργεσηνός.

1047 γάζα, ης, ἡ (Persian), *treasure,* as of a government, Ac. viii. 27.*

1048 Γάζα, ης, ἡ (Heb.), *Gaza,* a strong city of the ancient Philistines in the W. of Palestine, Ac. viii. 26. (The adj., ἔρημος, *desert,* refers to ὁδός.)*

1049 γαζο-φυλάκιον, ου, τό, *a place*

1050

for the guardianship of treasure, treasury; a part of the temple so called, Mar. xii. 41, 43; Lu. xxi. 1; Jn. viii. 20. (S.)*

1050 Γάϊος, ου, ὁ (Lat.), Gaius, or Caius. There are four of the name in N. T., Ac. xix. 29, xx. 4; 1 Cor. i. 14, and Ro. xvi. 23; 3 Jn. 1.*

1051 γάλα, ακτος, τό, milk, lit., 1 Cor. ix. 7; fig., for the elements of Christian knowledge, 1 Cor. iii. 2; Heb. v. 12, 13; 1 Pet. ii. 2.*

1052 Γαλάτης, ου, ὁ, a Galatian, Gal. iii. 1.*

1053 Γαλατία, ας, ἡ, Galatia, or Gallogræcia, a province of Asia Minor, Gal. i. 2; 1 Cor. xvi. 1; 2 Tim. iv. 10; 1 Pet. i. 1.*

1054 Γαλατικός, ή, όν, belonging to Galatia, Ac. xvi. 6, xviii. 23.*

1055 γαλήνη, ης, ἡ, a calm, Mat. viii. 26, Mar. iv. 39; Lu. viii. 24.*

1056 Γαλιλαία, ας, ἡ (from Heb.), Galilee, the N. division of Palestine, Mat. iv. 15.

1057 Γαλιλαῖος, αία, αῖον, of or belonging to Galilee, Mat. xxvi. 69; Ac. i. 11.

1058 Γαλλίων, ωνος, ὁ, Gallio, a proconsul of Achaia, Ac. xviii. 12, 14, 17.*

1059 Γαμαλιήλ, ὁ (Heb.), Gamaliel, Ac. v. 34, xxii. 3.*

1060 γαμέω, ῶ, ήσω, 1st aor. ἐγάμησα and ἔγημα, abs. or trans. (with acc.), to marry; active properly of the man; pass. and mid. of the woman, with dat., 1 Cor. vii. 39; Mar. x. 12 (W. H. ἄλλον für Rec. ἄλλῳ); but in N. T. the act. also is used of the woman, as 1 Cor. vii. 28, 34.

see 1547 γαμίζω, to give in marriage (a daughter), Rec. only Mar. xii. 25; Lu. xvii. 27, xx. 35; W. H. add Mat. xxii. 30, xxiv. 38; 1 Cor. vii. 38. (N. T.)*

1061 γαμίσκω = γαμίζω, Mar. xii. 25 (Rec.); Lu. xx. 34 (W. H.).*

1062 γάμος, ου, ὁ, marriage, spec. a marriage feast, sing. or plur., Heb. xiii. 4; Rev. xix. 7. See Gr. § 240, Wi. § 27, 3, Bu. 23.

1063 γάρ (γε ἄρα), "truly then," a causal postpositive particle

or conjunction, for, introducing a reason for the thing previously said. Used in questions to intensify the inquiry; often with other particles. For the special uses of γάρ, see Gr. § 407, Wi. § 53, 8, Bu. 370.

1064 γαστήρ, τρός (sync.), ἡ, (1) the womb, as Mat. i. 18; (2) the stomach, only Tit. i. 12, from Epimenides, "idle bellies," gluttons.

1065 γέ, an enclitic particle indicating emphasis, at least, indeed. Sometimes used alone, as Ro. viii. 32; 1 Cor. iv. 8; generally in connection with other particles, as ἀλλά, ἄρα, εἴ; εἰ δὲ μήγε, stronger than εἰ δὲ μή, if otherwise indeed; καίγε, and at least, and even; καίτοιγε, though indeed; μενοῦνγε, yea, indeed; μήτιγε, "to say nothing of," 1 Cor. vi. 3.

1066 Γεδεών, ὁ (Heb.), Gideon, Heb. xi. 32.*

1067 γέ-εννα, ης, ἡ (Heb. valley of Hinnom), met., Gehenna, place of punishment in the future world, Mat. x. 28, etc. Sometimes with τοῦ πυρός, as Mat. v. 22. Compare 2 Kings xxiii. 10. (S.)

1068 Γεθ-σημανῆ, or -νεί (W. H.), ἡ (Heb. oil-press), Gethsemane, a small field at the foot of the Mount of Olives, over the brook Kidron, Mat. xxvi. 36; Mar. xiv. 32.*

1069 γείτων, ονος, ὁ, ἡ, a neighbor, Lu. xiv. 12, xv. 6, 9; Jn. ix. 8.*

1070 γελάω, ῶ, άσω, to laugh, Lu. vi. 21, 25.*

1071 γέλως, ωτος, ὁ, laughter, Ja. iv. 9.*

1072 γεμίζω, σω, to fill, with acc. and gen. (also ἀπό or ἐκ), Mar. xv. 36; Rev. viii. 5; pass. abs., to be full, Mar. iv. 37; Lu. xiv. 23.

1073 γέμω, to be full of, with gen. (ἐκ, Mat. xxiii. 25; perhaps acc., Rev. xvii. 3).

1074 γενεά, ᾶς, ἡ, generation, as (1) offspring, race, descent, Mat. i. 17; Lu. ix. 41; (2) the people of any given time; (3) an age of the world's duration, Mat. xxiv. 34; Ac. xiii. 36; εἰς γενεὰς καὶ γενεάς (W.

1075

H.), *unto generations and generations* (R. V.), Lu. i. 50
γενεα-λογέω, ῶ, *to reckon a genealogy* or *pedigree*, pass. with ἐκ, Heb. vii. 6.*

1076

γενεα-λογία, ας, ἡ, *genealogy*, N. T. plur., 1 Tim. i. 4 ; Tit. iii. 9 ; prob. of Gnostic speculations on the origin of being.*

1077

γενέσια, ων, τά, *a birthday celebration*, Mat. xiv. 6 ; Mar. vi. 21.*

1078

γένεσις, εως, ἡ, *birth, lineage*, Mat. i. 1 (W. H. add Mat. i. 18 ; Lu. i. 14, for Rec. γέννησις); Ja. i. 23, τὸ πρόσωπον τῆς γενέσεως αὐτοῦ, *the countenance of his birth*, or, as A. V., R. V., "his natural face"; Ja. iii. 6, τὸν τροχὸν τῆς γενέσεως, *the wheel of nature* (R. V.).*

1079
see 1081

γενετή, ῆς, ἡ, *birth*, Jn. ix. 1.*
γένημα, ατος, τό. See γέννημα.

1080

γεννάω, ῶ, ἡσω, *to beget, give birth to, produce, effect*, Mat. i. 3, 5, 6 ; Lu. i. 13, 57 ; Ac. vii. 8, 29 ; pass., *to be begotten, born* (often in John, of spiritual renewal), Mat. i. 20 ; Jn. i. 13 ; 1 Jn. v. 1.

1081

γέννημα, ατος, τό, (1) *progeny, generation*, as Mat. iii. 7 ; (2) *produce* generally, as Mat. xxvi. 29 ; fig., *fruit, result*, as 2 Cor. ix. 10. In sense (2) W. H. always read γένημα, and sometimes elsewhere.

1082

Γεννησαρέτ (Aram.), *Gennesaret* (*Chinnereth* or Chinneroth, in O. T.), a region of Galilee, with village or town of the same name, Mat. xiv. 34. Used of the adjacent lake, as Lu. v. 1.

1083
1084

γέννησις, εως, ἡ. See γένεσις.*
γεννητός, ἡ, όν, verb. adj., *begotten, born*, Mat. xi. 11 ; Lu. vii. 28.*

1085

γένος, ους, τό, (1) *offspring*, Ac. xvii. 28, 29 ; (2) *family*, Ac. xiii. 26 ; (3) *stock, race*, Ac. vii. 19 ; Gal. i. 14 ; (4) *nation* Mar. vii. 26 ; (5) *kind* or *species*, Mar. ix. 29 ; 1 Cor. xiv. 10.

1086

Γεργεσηνός, ἡ, όν, or Γερασηνός, *Gergesene, belonging to Gergesa* or *Gerasa*. The copies vary between these forms and Γαδαρηνός, Mat. viii. 28 ; Mar. v. 1 ; Lu. viii. 26, 37.*

1087

γερουσία, ας, ἡ (γέρων), *an assembly of elders, senate*, Ac. v. 21.*

1088

γέρων, οντος, ὁ, *an old man*, Jn. iii. 4.*

1089

γεύω, *to make to taste*, only mid. in N. T.; *to taste*, as abs., *to take food*, Ac. x. 10 ; or with obj. gen., or acc. See Gr. § 249 a, (2), Wi. §§ 3, p. 33, 30, 7 c, Bu. 167. Fig., *to experience*, as Mat. xvi. 28 ; once with ὅτι, 1 Pet. ii. 3.

1090
1091
1092

γεωργέω, ῶ, *to cultivate* or *till the earth*, Heb. vi. 7.*
γεώργιον, ου, τό, *a tilled field*, fig., 1 Cor. iii. 9. (3.)*
γεωργός, οῦ, ὁ, *one who tills the ground, a husbandman*, 2 Tim. ii. 6 ; Ja. v. 7 : *a vinedresser*, Lu. xx. 9, 10, 14, 16.

1093

γῆ, γῆς, ἡ, contr. for γέα or γαῖα, *land* or *earth*, as (1) *the material soil*; (2) *the producing soil, the ground*; (3) *land*, as opposed to sea; (4) *earth*, as opposed to heaven, often involving suggestions of human weakness and sin; (5) *region* or *territory*.

1094

γῆρας, (αος) ως, τό, *old age*, Lu. i. 36 (dat., Rec. γήρᾳ, W. H. γήρει).*

1095

γηράσκω, or γηράω, ἀσω, *to become old*, Jn. xxi. 18 ; Heb. viii. 13.*

1096

γίνομαι, for γίγνομαι. See Gr. § 94, 8 a. γενήσομαι, ἐγενόμην and ἐγενήθην, γέγονα (with pres. force) and γεγένημαι, *to become*, as (1) *to begin to be*, used of persons, *to be born*, Jn. viii. 58 ; of the works of creation, *to be made*, Jn. i. 3, 10 ; and of other works, *to be wrought* or *performed*; so, *to pass out of one state into another*, *to grow into, to be changed into*, Jn. ii. 9 ; often with εἰς, Lu. xiii. 19 ; (2) of ordinary or extraordinary occurrences, *to happen, to take place, to be done;* of the day, the night, Mar. vi. 2 ; of thunder, earthquake, calm, etc. ; of feasts or public solemnities, *to be held* or *celebrated;* frequently in the phrase καὶ ἐγένετο, *and it came to pass* (with καί, or following verb, or inf.) ; also, μὴ γένοιτο, *let it never happen!* or *God forbid!*; (3) with

adj. or predicative subst., *to
become*, where quality, character, or condition is speci-
fied; often in prohibitions,
μὴ γίνου, μὴ γίνεσθε, *become
not*, as Mat vi. 16; (4) with
the cases of substantives and
the prepositions, the verb
forms many phrases, to be
interpreted according to the
meaning of the case or prep.

1097 **γινώσκω,** or γιγνώσκω (see Gr.
§ 94, 8*b*, Wi. § 39, 3, note 2,
Bu. 55), γνώσομαι, 2d aor.
ἔγνων (imper. γνῶθι), perf.
ἔγνωκα, (1) *to become aware
of*, *to perceive*, with acc.; (2)
to know, *to perceive*, *understand*, with acc. or ὅτι, or
acc. and inf., or τί interrog.;
Ἑλληνιστὶ γ., *to understand*
Greek, Ac. xxi. 37; *to be conscious of*, by experience, as
2 Cor. v. 21; (3) *to know
carnally* (a Hebraistic euphe-
mism), Mat. i. 25; Lu. i. 34;
(4) specially of the fellowship between Christians and
God or Christ, 1 Cor. viii. 3;
Mat. vii. 23 (negatively); Jn.
xvii. 3; Heb. viii. 11; Phil.
iii. 10, etc.

1098 **γλεῦκος,** ους, τό, *sweet* or *new
wine*, Ac. ii. 13.*

1099 **γλυκύς,** εἶα, ύ, *sweet*, Ja. iii. 11,
12; Rev. x. 9, 10.*

1100 **γλῶσσα,** ης, ἡ, (1) *the tongue*,
Mar. vii. 33, 35; 1 Jn. iii. 18
(2) *a language*, Ac. ii. 11;
(3) *a nation* or *people* distinguished by their language,
Rev. v. 9, vii. 9.

1101 **γλωσσό-κομον,** ου, τό, *a little
box* or *case for money*, Jn.
xii. 6, xiii. 29 (orig. from
holding the "tongue-pieces"
of flutes, etc.).*

1102 **γναφεύς,** έως, ὁ, *a fuller, cloth-
dresser*, Mar. ix. 3.*

1103 **γνήσιος,** α, ον (sync. from γενή-
σιος), *legitimate, genuine, true*,
1 Tim. i. 2; Tit. i. 4; Phil.
iv. 3; τὸ γνήσιον, *sincerity*,
2 Cor. viii. 8.*

1104 **γνησίως,** adv., *genuinely, sincerely*, Phil. ii. 20.*

1105 **γνόφος,** ου, ὁ, *darkness, gloom*,
Heb. xii. 18.*

1106 **γνώμη,** ης, ἡ, (γνο- in γινώσκω),
opinion, judgment, intention,
1 Cor. i. 10; 2 Cor. viii. 10.

1107 **γνωρίζω,** ίσω, or ιῶ, (1) *to make
known, to declare* (with acc.

and dat., ὅτι or τί, interrog.,
Col. i. 27); (2) intrans., *to
know*, only Phil. i. 22.

1108 **γνῶσις,** εως, ἡ, (1) subj., *knowledge*, with gen. of obj. (gen.
subj., Ro. xi. 33); (2) obj.,
science, doctrine, wisdom, as
Lu. xi. 52. *Syn.*: see Trench,
§ lxxv.

1109 **γνώστης,** ου, ὁ, *one who knows,
an expert*, Ac. xxvi. 3. (S.)*

1110 **γνωστός,** ή, όν, verb. adj.,
known, as Ac. ii. 14, iv. 10;
knowable, Ro. i. 19; *notable*,
Ac. iv. 16; οἱ γνωστοί, *one's
acquaintance*, Lu. ii. 44.

1111 **γογγύζω,** ύσω, *to murmur* in a
low voice, Jn. vii. 32; dis-
contentedly, *to grumble*, as
1 Cor. x. 10, with acc., or
περί, gen., πρός, acc., κατά,
gen. (S.)

1112 **γογγυσμός,** οῦ, ὁ, *muttering*, Jn.
vii. 12; *murmuring*, Ac. vi.
1; Phil. ii. 14; 1 Pet. iv. 9.
(S.)*

1113 **γογγυστής,** οῦ, ὁ, *a murmurer,
complainer*, Ju. 16. (N. T.)*

1114 **γόης,** ητος, ὁ (γοάω, *to moan*),
an enchanter, an impostor, 2
Tim. iii. 13.*

1115 **Γολγοθά** (W. H., some -θᾶ),
(Aram.), *Golgotha*, "the place
of a skull" (prob. from its
shape), *Calvary*, Mat. xxvii.
33; Mar. xv. 22; Jn. xix. 17.
See κρανίον. (N. T.)*

1116 **Γόμορρα,** ας, ἡ, and ων, τά, *Go-
morrha*, Ro. ix. 29.

1117 **γόμος,** ου, ὁ (γέμω), (1) *a burden, e.g.*, of a ship, Ac. xxi.
3; (2) *wares* or *merchandise*,
Rev. xviii. 11, 12.*

1118 **γονεύς,** έως, ὁ (γεν- in γίγνομαι),
a parent, only in plural, Lu.
ii. 41, Ep. vi. 1.

1119 **γόνυ,** ατος, τό, *the knee*; often
in plur. after τιθέναι or κάμπ-
τειν, *to put* or *bend the knees,
to kneel*, in devotion, Lu. xxii.
41; Ro. xi. 4.

1120 **γονυ-πετέω,** ῶ (πίπτω), *to fall
on the knees, to kneel to* (acc.),
Mar. x. 17.

1121 **γράμμα,** ατος, τό (γράφω), (1) *a
letter of the alphabet*, Gal.
vi. 11, *in what large letters*,
perhaps noting emphasis;
letter, as opposed to spirit,
Ro. ii. 29, etc.; (2) *a writing*,
such as *a bill* or *an epistle*,
as Lu. xvi. 6, 7; Ac. xxviii.
21; τὰ ἱερὰ γράμματα, 2 Tim.

iii. 15, *the holy writings*, or *the Scriptures*; (3) plur., *literature*, *learning* generally, Jn. vii. 15.

1122 γραμματεύς, έως, ὁ, (1) *a clerk*, *secretary*, *a scribe*, Ac. xix. 35; (2) *one of that class among the Jews who copied and interpreted the O. T. Scriptures* (see νομικός), Mat. xxiii. 34; (3) met., *a man of learning generally*, Mat. xiii. 52.

1123 γραπτός, ή, όν, verb. adj., *written*, Ro. ii. 15.*

1124 γραφή, ῆs, ή, (1) *a writing;* (2) spec., ή γραφή or αl γραφαί, *the Scriptures, writings* of the O. T., 2 Pet. iii. 16; (3) a particular *passage*, Mar. xii. 10.

1125 γράφω, ψω, γέγραφα, *to grave, write, inscribe;* έγράφη, γέγραπται, or γεγραμμένον έστί, a formula of quotation, *It is written;* often with dat. of pers., as Mar. x. 5.

1126 γραώδης, ες (γραῦς, εἶδος), *old-womanish, foolish*, 1 Tim. iv. 7.*

1127 γρηγορέω, ῶ (from έγρήγορα, perf. of έγείρω), *to keep awake, watch, be vigilant*, Mar. xiii. 35, 37; Rev. xvi. 15.

1128 γυμνάζω (γυμνός), *to exercise, train*, 1 Tim. iv. 7; Heb. v. 14, xii. 11; 2 Pet. ii. 14.*

1129 γυμνασία, as, ή, *exercise, training*, 1 Tim. iv. 8.*

1130 γυμνητεύω, or ιτεύω (W. H.), *to be naked* or *poorly clad*, 1 Cor. iv. 11.*

1131 γυμνός, ή, όν, (1) *naked*, Mar. xiv. 52; Rev. iii. 17; *ill-clad*, Mat. xxv. 36, 48; *having only an inner garment*, Jn. xxi. 7; (2) *bare, i.e., open* or *manifest*, Heb. iv. 13; (3) *mere*, 1 Cor. xv. 37.

1132 γυμνότης, τητος, ή, (1) *nakedness*, Rev. iii. 18; (2) *scanty clothing*, Ro. viii. 35; 2 Cor. xi. 27. (N. T.)*

1133 γυναικάριον, ου, τό (dim.), *a silly woman*, 2 Tim. iii. 6.*

1134 γυναικεῖος, a, ον, *womanish, female;* 1 Pet. iii. 7, the *weaker* vessel.*

1135 γυνή, γυναικός, voc. γύναι, ή, (1) *a woman*, Mat. ix. 20; Ro. vii. 2; (2) *a wife*, Ac. v. 1, 7; Ep. v. 28. The voc. is the form of ordinary address,

often used in reverence and honor; compare Jn. ii. 4 and xix. 26.

1136 Γώγ, ὁ, a proper name, *Gog.* In Ezek. xxxviii. 2, king of Magog, a land of the remote north; hence, in Rev. xx. 8, of a people far remote from Palestine.*

1137 γωνία, as, ή, *a corner*, as Mat. vi. 5, xxi. 42 (from S.); met., *a secret place*, Ac. xxvi. 26.

Δ

Δ, δ, δέλτα, *delta, d*, the fourth letter of the Greek alphabet. As a numeral, δ′ = 4; ͵δ = 4000.

1138 Δαβίδ, also Δαυΐδ, Δαυείδ (W. H.), ὁ (Heb.), *David*, king of Israel; ὁ υἱὸς Δ., *the Son of David*, an appellation of the Messiah; έν Δ., *in David*, i.e., in the Psalms, Heb. iv. 7.

1139 δαιμονίζομαι (see δαίμων), 1st aor. part., δαιμονισθείς, *to be possessed by a demon*, Mat. iv. 24; Mar. i. 32.

1140 δαιμόνιον, ου, τό (orig. adj.), *a deity*, Ac. xvii. 18; *a demon* or *evil spirit;* δαιμόνιον έχειν, *to have a demon* or *to be a demoniac*, Lu. iv. 33; Jn. vii. 20.

1141 δαιμονιώδης, ες, *resembling a demon, demoniacal*, Ja. iii. 15. (N. T.)*

1142 δαίμων, ονος, ὁ, ή, in classic Greek, any spirit superior to man; hence often of the inferior deities; in N. T., *an evil spirit, a demon* (W. H. have the word only in one passage, Mat. viii. 31); δαιμόνιον is generally used.

1143 δάκνω, *to bite*, met., Gal. v. 15.*

1144 δάκρυ, υος, or δάκρυον, ου, τό, *a tear*, Ac. xx. 19, 31: Heb. v. 7.

1145 **1146** δακρύω, σω, *to weep*, Jn. xi. 35.*

δακτύλιος, ου, ὁ (δάκτυλος), *a ring*, Lu. xv. 22.*

1147 δάκτυλος, ου, ὁ, *a finger;* έν δακτύλῳ θεοῦ, met., *by the power of God*, Lu. xi. 20, comp. Mat. xii. 28.

1148 Δαλμανουθά, ή, *Dalmanutha*, a town or village near Magdala, Mar. viii. 10.*

1149 Δαλματία, as, ή, *Dalmatia*, a

part of Illyricum near Macedonia, 2 Tim. iv. 10.*

1150 δαμάζω, σω, *to subdue, tame*, Mar. v. 4; Ja. iii. 7, 8.*

1151 δάμαλις, εως, ἡ, *a heifer*, Heb. ix. 13.*

1152 Δάμαρις, ιδος, ἡ, *Damaris*, Ac. xvii. 34.*

1153 Δαμασκηνός, ή, όν, *belonging to Damascus*, 2 Cor. xi. 32.*

1154 Δαμασκός, οῦ, ἡ, *Damascus*, Ac. ix. 2, 3.

1155 δανείζω, *to lend* money, Lu. vi. 34, 35; mid., *to borrow*, Mat. v. 42.*

1156 δάνειον, ου, τό, *a loan, a debt*, Mat. xviii. 27.*

1157 δανειστής, οῦ, ὁ, *a money-lender, a creditor*, Lu. vii. 41.*

1158 Δανιήλ, ὁ (Heb.), *Daniel*, Mat. xxiv. 15; Mar. xiii. 14 (not W. H.).*

1159 δαπανάω, ῶ, ήσω, *to spend*, Mar. v. 26; trans., *to bear expense* for (ἐπί, dat.), Ac. xxi. 24; (ὑπέρ, gen.), 2 Cor. xii. 15; *to consume in luxury, to waste*, Lu. xv. 14; Ja. iv. 3.*

1160 δαπάνη, ης, ἡ, *expense, cost*, Lu. xiv. 28.*

1161 δέ, an adversative and distinctive particle, *but, now, moreover*, etc. See Gr. § 404, ii, Wi. § 53, 7, Bu. 364 sq., and μέν.

1162 δέησις, εως, ἡ, *supplication, prayer*, Ep. vi. 18; Ja. v. 16. *Syn.:* see αἴτημα.

1163; see also on p. 36 δεῖ, impers., see Gr. § 101, Wi. § 58, 9b, Bu. 147, 164, *it is necessary, one must, it ought, it is right* or *proper*, with inf. (expressed or implied), as Mat. xvi. 21; Ac. iv. 12; Mar. xiii. 14.

1164 δεῖγμα, ατος, τό (δείκνυμι), *an example, a specimen*, Ju. 7.*

1165 δειγματίζω, σω, *to make an example* or *spectacle of* (as disgrace), Col. ii. 15; Mat. i. 19 (W. H.). (N. T.)*

1166 δείκνυμι and δεικνύω (see Gr. § 114, Bu. 45), (1) *to present to sight, to show, to teach* (acc and dat.), Mat. iv. 18; 1 Cor xii. 31; Rev. xvii. 1; (2) *to prove* (acc. and ἐκ), Ja. ii. 18, iii. 13; *to show by words* (ὅτι), Mat. xvi. 21 inf., Ac. x. 28.

1167 δειλία, ας, ἡ, *timidity, cowardice*, 2 Tim. i. 7.* *Syn.:* δειλία is always used in a bad sense; εὐλάβεια, regularly in a good

sense, *pious* fear; φόβος is general, denoting either bad or good.

1168 δειλιάω, ῶ, *to be timid, fearful*, Jn. xiv. 27. (S.)*

1169 δειλός, ή, όν, *timid, cowardly*, Mat. viii. 26; Mar. iv. 40; Rev. xxi. 8.*

1170 δεῖνα, ὁ, ἡ, τό, gen. δεῖνος, pron., *a certain person, such a one*, Mat. xxvi. 18.*

1171 δεινῶς, adv. (δεινός, *vehement*), *vehemently, terribly*, Mat. viii. 6; Lu. xi. 53.*

1172 δειπνέω, ῶ, *to take the* δεῖπνον, *to sup*, Lu. xvii. 8, xxii. 20; 1 Cor. xi. 25; met., of familiar intercourse, Rev. iii. 20.*

1173 δεῖπνον, ου, τό, *the chief or evening meal, supper* (see ἄριστον), Lu. xiv. 17, 24; Jn. xiii. 2, 4; κυριακὸν δεῖπνον, *the Lord's Supper*, 1 Cor. xi. 20.

•1175 δεισιδαιμονία, ας, ἡ, *religion*, in general, Ac. xxv. 19.*

cf 1174St δεισι-δαίμων, ον (δείδω, *to fear*), *devoutly disposed, addicted to worship*, Ac. xvii. 22. See Gr. § 323 c.* *Syn.:* see Trench, § xlviii.

1176 δέκα, οἱ, αἱ, τά, *ten*; in Rev. ii. 10, *a ten days' tribulation*, *i.e.*, brief.

1177 δεκα-δύο (W. H. δώδεκα), *twelve*, Ac. xix. 7, xxiv. 11. (S.)*

1178 δεκα-πέντε, *fifteen*, Jn. xi. 18; Ac. xxvii. 28, Gal. i. 18.*

1179 Δεκά-πολις, εως, ἡ, *Decapolis*, a district E. of Jordan comprising ten towns. It is uncertain what they all were, but they included Gadara, Hippo, Pella, and Scythopolis, Mat. iv. 25; Mar. v. 20, vii. 31.*

1180 δεκα-τέσσαρες, ων, οἱ, αἱ, -σαρα, τά, *fourteen*, Mat. i. 17; 2 Cor. xii. 2; Gal. ii. 1.*

1181 δεκάτη, ης, ἡ, *a tenth part, a tithe*, Heb. vii. 2, 4, 8, 9.*

1182 δέκατος, η, ον, ordinal, *tenth*, Jn. i. 39; Rev. xxi. 20; τὸ δέκατον, Rev. xi. 13, *the tenth part.*

1183 δεκατόω, ῶ, *to receive tithe of*, acc., Heb. vii. 6; pass., *to pay tithe*, Heb. vii. 9. (S.)*

1184 δεκτός, ή, όν (verbal adj. from δέχομαι), *accepted, acceptable*, Lu. iv. 19, 24; Ac. x. 35; 2 Cor. vi. 2; Phil. iv. 18. (S.)*

1185 δελεάζω (δέλεαρ, *a bait*), *to take*

or *entice*, as with a bait, Ja.
i. 14; 2 Pet. ii. 14, 18.*

1186   δένδρον, ου, τό, *a tree*, Mat. vii.
1187   17; Lu. xiii. 19.
δεξιό-λαβος, ου, ὁ, "holding in
the right hand"; plur., *spear-
men*, Ac. xxiii. 23. (N. T.)*

1188   δεξιός, ά, όν, *the right*, opp. to
ἀριστερός, *the left;* ἡ δεξιά,
the right hand; τὰ δεξιά, *the
right-hand side;* ἐκ δεξιῶν, *on
the right* (see Gr. § 293, 1,
Wi. § 19, 1 a); δεξιὰς διδόναι,
*to give the right hand, i.e., to
receive to friendship* or *fellowship.*

1189   δέομαι, 1st aor. ἐδεήθην, *to have
need of* (gen.), as mid. of δέω
(see δεῖ); *to make request of*
(gen.); *to beseech, pray*, abs.,
or with εἰ, ἵνα, or ὅπως, of
purpose.

**1163; see
also on
p. 35**   δέον, οντος, τό (particip. of δεῖ,
as subst.), *the becoming* or
needful; with ἐστί = δεῖ, 1
Pet. i. 6; Ac. xix. 36; plur.,
1 Tim. v. 13.*

**see 127,
2124&5401**   δέος, ους, τό (W. H.), *fear, awe,*
Heb. xii. 28.*

1190   Δερβαῖος, ου, ὁ, *of Derbe*, Ac.
xx. 4.*

1191   Δέρβη, ης, ἡ, *Derbe*, a city of
Lycaonia, Ac. xiv. 6, 20,
xvi. 1.*

1192   δέρμα, ατος, τό (δέρω), *an animal's skin*, Heb. xi. 37.*

1193   δερμάτινος, η, ον, *made of skin,
leathern*, Mat. iii. 4; Mar.
i. 6.*

1194   δέρω, 1st aor. ἔδειρα, 2d fut. pass.
δαρήσομαι, *to scourge, to beat*,
so as to flay off the skin;
ἀέρα δέρων, 1 Cor. ix. 26,
beating air.

1195   δεσμεύω, σω, *to bind, put in
chains* as a prisoner, Lu.
viii. 29 (W. H.); Ac. xxii. 4;
to bind as a bundle, Mat.
xxiii. 4.*

1196   δεσμέω, ῶ, *to bind*, Lu. viii. 29
(Rec.).*

1197   δέσμη, ης, ἡ, *a bundle*, Mat.
xiii. 30.*

1198   δέσμιος, ίου, ὁ, *one bound, a
prisoner*, Ac. xvi. 25, 27 ; Ep.
iii. 1.

1199   δεσμός, οῦ, ὁ (δέω), *a bond*, sing.
only in Mar. vii. 35, ὁ δεσμὸς
τῆς γλώσσης, and Lu. xiii.
16; plur., δεσμοὶ or (τὰ)
δεσμά, *bonds* or *imprisonment*, Lu. viii. 29; Phil. i.
13.

1200   δεσμο-φύλαξ, ακος, ὁ, *a jailer,*
Ac. xvi. 23, 27, 36.*

1201   δεσμωτήριον, ίου, τό, *a prison*,
Mat. xi. 2; Ac. v. 21, 23,
xvi. 26.*

1202   δεσμώτης, ου, ὁ, *a prisoner*, Ac.
xxvii. 1, 42.

1203   δεσπότης, ου, ὁ, *a lord* or *prince,
a master*, as 1 Tim. vi. 1;
applied to God, Lu. ii. 29;
Ac. iv. 24; Ju. 4; to Christ,
2 Pet. ii. 1; Rev. vi. 10. *Syn.:*
δεσπότης indicates more ab-
solute and unlimited authority than κύριος.

1204   δεῦρο, adv., (1) of place, *here,
hither;* used only as an im-
perative, *come hither*, as Mat.
xix. 21; (2) of time, *hitherto*,
only Ro. i. 13.

1205   δεῦτε, adv., as if plur. of δεῦρο
(or contr. from δεῦρ' ἴτε),
come, come hither, as Mat
iv. 19, xi. 28.

1206   δευτεραῖος, αία, αῖον, *on the
second day*, Ac. xxviii. 13.
See Gr. § 319.*

1207   δευτερό-πρωτος, ον, *the second-
first*, Lu. vi. 1 (W. H. omit).
See Gr. § 148, Wi. § 16, 4,
and note. (N. T.)*

1208   δεύτερος, α, ον, ordinal, *second*
in number, as Mat. xxii. 26;
in order, Mat. xxii. 39; τὸ
δεύτερον or δεύτερον, adverbially, *the second time, again*,
as 2 Cor. xiii. 2; so ἐκ δευτέ-
ρου, as Mar. xiv. 72; ἐν τῷ
δευτέρῳ, Ac. vii. 13.

1209   δέχομαι, 1st aor. ἐδεξάμην, dep.,
*to take, receive, accept, to re-
ceive* kindly, *to welcome*, persons, as Mar. vi. 11; things
(a doctrine, the kingdom of
heaven), as Mar. x. 15; 2 Cor.
xi. 4.

**see 1163
&1189**
1210   δέω, *to want*. See δεῖ and δέομαι.
δέω, 1st aor., ἔδησα; perf.,
δέδεκα; pass., δέδεμαι; 1st
aor. pass. inf., δεθῆναι, *to bind
together*, bundles, as Ac. x.
11; *to swathe* dead bodies
for burial, as Jn. xi. 44; *to
bind* persons in bondage, as
Mat. xxii. 13; Mar. vi. 17;
2 Tim. ii. 9; fig., Mat. xviii.
18; δεδεμένος τῷ πνεύματι,
Ac. xx. 22, *bound in the
spirit*, under an irresistible
impulse.

1211   δή, a particle indicating *certainty* or *reality*, and so aug-
menting the vivacity of a

1212
clause or sentence; *truly, indeed, by all means, therefore.* Used with other particles, δήποτε, δήπου, which see.
δῆλος, η, ον, *manifest, evident,* Mat. xxvi. 73; neut., sc. ἐστί, *it is evident,* with ὅτι, 1 Cor. xv. 27; Gal. iii. 11; 1 Tim. vi. 7 (W. H., R. V. omit).*

1213
δηλόω, ῶ, *to manifest, to reveal, to bring to light, to imply* or *signify,* 1 Cor. i. 11, iii. 13; Col. i. 8; Heb. ix. 8, xii. 27; 1 Pet. i. 11; 2 Pet. i. 14.*

1214
Δημᾶς, ᾶ, ὁ, *Demas,* Col. iv. 14; Philem. 24; 2 Tim. iv. 10.*

1215
δημ-ηγορέω, ῶ, *to deliver a public oration;* with πρός, Ac. xii. 21.*

1216
Δημήτριος, ου, ὁ, *Demetrius.* Two of the name are mentioned, Ac. xix. 24, 38; 3 Jn. 12.*

1217
δημι-ουργός, οῦ, ὁ ("a public worker"), *an artisan, a builder,* Heb. xi. 10.* *Syn.:* δημιουργός emphasizes more the idea of *power;* τεχνίτης, that of *wisdom.*

1218
δῆμος, ου, ὁ, *the people,* an organized multitude publicly convened, Ac. xii. 22, xvii. 5, xix. 30, 33.*

1219
δημόσιος, α, ον, *belonging to the people, public,* Ac. v. 18; dat. fem., as adv., δημοσίᾳ, *publicly,* Ac. xvi. 37, xviii. 28, xx. 20.*

1220
δηνάριον, ίου, τό, *properly a Latin word* (see Gr. § 154 a), *denarius,* Mat. xviii. 28; Rev. vi. 6.

1221
δή-ποτε, adv. with ᾧ, *whatsoever,* giving a generalizing force, Jn. v. 4 (W. H. omit).*

1222
δή-που, adv., *indeed, perhaps, verily,* Heb. ii. 16.*

1223
διά, prep. (cognate with δύο, *two;* δίς, *twice), through;* (1) with gen., *through, during, by means of;* (2) with acc., *through, on account of, for the sake of.* See Gr. §§ 147 a, 299, Wi. § 47 i, Bu. 182, 183, 187.

1224
δια-βαίνω, *to pass through,* trans., Heb. xi. 29; or intrans., with πρός (person), Lu. xvi. 26; εἰς (place), Ac. xvi. 9.*

1225
δια-βάλλω, *to slander, accuse,* Lu. xvi. 1.*

1226
δια-βεβαιόω, ῶ, in mid., *to affirm, assert strongly,* 1 Tim. i. 7; Tit. iii. 8.*

1227
δια-βλέπω, *to see through, to see clearly,* Mat. vii. 5; Lu. vi. 42; Mar. viii. 25 (W. H.).*

1228
διάβολος, ον (διαβάλλω), *prone to slander, slanderous,* 1 Tim. iii. 11; 2 Tim. iii. 3; Tit. ii. 3; ὁ διάβολος, *the accuser, the devil,* equivalent to the Hebrew *Satan,* Mat. iv. 1, 5; 2 Tim. ii. 26.

1229
δι-αγγέλλω, *to announce everywhere, publish abroad,* Lu. ix. 60; Ac. xxi. 26; Ro. ix. 17.*

see 1065
διά-γε, or διά γε (W. H.), *yet on account of.* Lu. xi. 8.*

1230
δια-γίνομαι, *to pass, elapse,* of time; in N. T. only 2d aor. part., gen. abs., *having elapsed,* Mar. xvi. 1; Ac. xxv. 13, xxvii. 9.*

1231
δια-γινώσκω, *to distinguish, know accurately,* Ac. xxiii. 15; *to examine, decide,* Ac. xxiv. 22.*

1232
δια-γνωρίζω, *to publish abroad,* Lu. ii. 17 (W. H. γνωρίζω).*

1233
διά-γνωσις, εως, ἡ, *judicial examination, decision,* Ac. xxv. 21.*

1234
δια-γογγύζω, *to murmur greatly,* Lu. xv. 2, xix. 7. (S.)*

1235
δια-γρηγορέω, ῶ, *to remain awake* or *to be fully awake,* Lu. ix. 32. (N. T.)*

1236
δι-άγω, *to lead* or *pass,* as time, life, 1 Tim. ii. 2 (βίον); Tit. iii. 3 (βίον omitted).*

1237
δια-δέχομαι, *to succeed to,* Ac. vii. 45.*

1238
διά-δημα, ατος, τό (δέω), *a diadem, crown,* Rev. xii. 3, xiii. 1, xix. 12.* *Syn.:* διάδημα always indicates the fillet, the symbol of royalty; στέφανος is the festal *garland* of victory.

1239
δια-δίδωμι, *to distribute, divide,* Lu. xi. 22, xviii. 22; Jn. vi. 11; Ac. iv. 35; Rev. xvii. 13 (W. H. δίδωμι).*

1240
διά-δοχος, ου, ὁ, ἡ, *a successor,* Ac. xxiv. 27.*

1241
δια-ζώννυμι, *to gird,* Jn. xiii. 4, 5, xxi. 7.*

1242
δια-θήκη, ης, ἡ (διατίθημι), (1) *a will* or *testament, a disposition,* as of property, Gal. iii. 15; Heb. ix. 16, 17; (2) *a compact* or *covenant* between God and man (see Gen. vi,

37

ix, xv, xvii; Exod. xxiv; Deut. v, xxviii). The two covenants mentioned, Gal. iv. 24; that of the O. T. is termed ἡ πρῶτη δ., Heb. ix. 15; that of the N. T., ἡ καινὴ δ., Lu. xxii. 20. The O. T. itself (ἡ παλαιὰ δ., 2 Cor. iii. 14) as containing the first, and the N. T. as containing the second, are each called διαθήκη.

1243 δι-αίρεσις, εως, ἡ, *difference, distinction*, as the result of distribution, 1 Cor. xii. 4, 5, 6.*

1244 δι-αιρέω, ῶ, *to divide, distribute,* Lu. xv. 12; 1 Cor. xii. 11.*

1245 δια-καθαρίζω, ιῶ, *to cleanse thoroughly*, Mat. iii. 12; Lu. iii. 17 (W. H. διακαθαίρω). (N. T.)*

1246 δια-κατ-ελέγχομαι, *to confute entirely*, Ac. xviii. 28. (N. T.)*

1247 διακονέω, ῶ, *to serve* or *wait upon*, especially at table, Jn. xii. 26; Lu. iv. 39; *to supply wants, to administer* or *distribute alms*, etc. (dat., person; acc., thing; occasionally abs.), Mat. xxv. 44; Ro. xv. 25; specially, *to serve as a deacon*, 1 Tim. iii. 10, 13, of prophets and apostles who *ministered* the divine will, 1 Pet. i. 12; 2 Cor. iii. 3.

1248 διακονία, ας, ἡ, *service, ministry*, in various senses, especially for Christ, 2 Cor. iii. 7; Ro. xi. 13; Ac. vi. 4; *relief*, Ac. xi. 29; *a serving*, Lu. x. 40; *the office of deacon*, Ro. xii. 7.

1249 διάκονος, ου, ὁ, ἡ, *a servant*, viewed in relation to his *work*, specially at table, as Mat. xxiii. 11; Mar. x. 43; one in God's service, *a minister*, as Ro. xiii. 4, xv. 8; *one who serves in the church, deacon* or *deaconess*, Phil. i. 1; 1 Tim. iii. 8, 12; Ro. xvi. 1.

1250 διακόσιοι, αι, α, card. num., *two hundred*, Mar. vi. 37; Jn. vi. 7.

1251 δι-ακούω, *to hear thoroughly*, Ac. xxiii. 35.*

1252 δια-κρίνω, *to discern, to distinguish, make a distinction*, as Ac. xv. 9; 1 Cor. xi. 29. Mid. (aor pass.), (1) *to doubt, to*

hesitate, as Mat. xxi. 21; Ja. i. 6; (2) *to dispute with*, Ac. xi. 2; Ju. 9.

1253 διά-κρισις, εως, ἡ, *the act of distinction, discrimination*, Ro. xiv. 1; 1 Cor. xii. 10; Heb. v. 14.*

1254 δια-κωλύω, *to hinder*, Mat. iii. 14.*

1255 δια-λαλέω, ῶ, *to converse together*, Lu. vi. 11; *to talk of*, Lu. i. 65.*

1256 δια-λέγω, in mid., *to reason, to discuss, to dispute*, as Mar. ix. 34; Ac. xx. 7; Ju. 9.

1257 δια-λείπω, *to leave off, to cease*, Lu. vii. 45.*

1258 διά-λεκτος, ου, ἡ, *speech, dialect, language*, Ac. i. 19, ii. 6, 8, xxi. 40, xxii. 2, xxvi. 14.*

1259 δι-αλλάσσω, *to change*, as the disposition; pass., *to be reconciled to*, Mat. v. 24.*

1260 δια-λογίζομαι, *to reason, to deliberate, to debate*, as Mar. ii. 6, 8, viii. 16, ix. 33.

1261 διαλογισμός, οῦ, ὁ, *reflection, thought*, as Lu. ii. 35; *reasoning, opinion*, as Ro. i. 21; *hesitation, doubt*, Lu. xxiv. 38; *dispute, debate*, as Phil. ii. 14; 1 Tim. ii. 8.

1262 δια-λύω, *to disperse, to break up*, Ac. v. 36.*

1263 δια-μαρτύρομαι, dep. mid., *to testify, solemnly charge*, as Ac. ii. 40; 1 Tim. v. 21; *to testify to, solemnly affirm*, Ac. viii. 25; Heb. ii. 6.

1264 δια-μάχομαι, dep. mid., *to contend* or *dispute fiercely*, Ac. xxiii. 9.*

1265 δια-μένω, *to remain, continue*, Lu. i. 22, xxii. 28; Gal. ii. 5; Heb. i. 11; 2 Pet. iii. 4.*

1266 δια-μερίζω, (1) *to divide* or *separate into parts*, as Mat. xxvii. 35, etc.; *to distribute*, as Lu. xxii. 17; (2) pass. with ἐπὶ, *to be divided* against, *be at discord* with; acc., Lu. xi. 17; dat., xii. 52.

1267 δια-μερισμός, οῦ, ὁ, *dissension*, Lu. xii. 51.*

1268 δια-νέμω, *to disseminate, to spread abroad*, Ac. iv. 17.*

1269 δια-νεύω, *to make signs*, prob. by nodding, Lu. i. 22.*

1270 δια-νόημα, ατος, τό, *a thought*, Lu. xi. 17.*

1271 διά-νοια, ας, ἡ, *the mind, the intellect*, or *thinking faculty*, as Mar. xii. 30; *the under-standing,* 1 Jn. v. 20; *the feelings, disposition, affec-tions,* as Col. i. 21; plur., *the thoughts,* as willful, depraved, Ep. ii. 3 (in Ep. i. 18, A. V., *the eyes of your understand-ing* (διανοίας), W. H. and R. V. read καρδίας, *the eyes of your heart*).

1272 δι-αν-οίγω, *to open fully, i.e.,* the ears, Mar. vii. 34; the eyes, Lu. xxiv. 31; the heart, Ac. xvi. 14; the Scriptures, Lu. xxiv. 32.

1273 δια-νυκτερεύω, *to pass the whole night,* Lu. vi. 12.*

1274 δι-ανύω, *to perform to the end, complete,* Ac. xxi. 7.*

1275 δια-παντός, adv., *always, con-tinually* (W. H. always read διὰ παντός).

see 3859 δια-παρα-τριβή, ῆς, ἡ, *conten-tion, incessant wrangling,* 1 Tim. vi. 5 (W. H., Rec. has παραδιατριβή). (N. T.)*

1276 δια-περάω, ῶ, άσω, *to cross over,* as Mat. ix. 1.

1277 δια-πλέω, εύσω, *to sail across,* Ac. xxvii. 5.*

1278 δια-πονέω, ῶ, mid., aor. pass., *to grieve one's self, to be vexed,* Ac. iv. 2, xvi. 18.*

1279 δια-πορεύομαι, pass., *to go* or *pass through,* as Lu. xiii. 22.

1280 δι-απορέω, ῶ, *to be in great doubt* or *perplexity,* Lu. ix. 7, xxiv. 4 (W. H. ἀπορέω); Ac. ii. 12, v. 24, x. 17.*

1281 δια-πραγματεύομαι, *to gain by business* or *trading,* Lu. xix. 15.*

1282 δια-πρίω (πρίω, *to saw*), in pass., *to be sawn through;* fig., *to be greatly moved with anger,* Ac. v. 33, vii. 54.*

1283 δι-αρπάζω, άσω, *to plunder,* Mat. xii. 29; Mar. iii. 27.*

1284 δια-ρρήγνυμι and διαρρήσσω, ξω, *to tear,* as garments, in grief or indignation, Mat. xxvi. 65; Mar. xiv. 63; Ac. xiv 14; *to break asunder,* as a net, Lu. v. 6; as bonds, Lu. viii. 29.*

1285 δια-σαφέω, ῶ, *to make clear, to declare,* Mat. xiii. 36 (W. H.), xviii. 31.

1286 δια-σείω, *to treat with violence, so as to extort anything,* Lu. iii. 14.*

1287 δια-σκορπίζω, *to scatter, to win-now,* as Mat. xxv. 24; *to dis-perse* in conquest, as Lu. i. 51; *to waste* or *squander,* Lu. xv. 13, xvi. 1.

1288 δια-σπάω, 1st aor. pass. διεσπά-σθην, *to break asunder,* Mar. v. 4; *to tear in pieces,* Ac. xxiii. 10.*

1289 δια-σπείρω, 2d aor. pass. διεσπά-ρην, *to scatter abroad, disperse,* Ac. viii. 1, 4, xi. 19.*

1290 δια-σπορά, ᾶς, ἡ, *dispersion, state of being dispersed;* used of the Jews as scattered among the Gentiles, Jn. vii. 35; Ja. i. 1; 1 Pet. i. 1. (Ap.)*

1291 δια-στέλλω, in mid., *to give a command* or *injunction,* Mar. viii. 15; Ac. xv. 24; foll. by ἵνα, Mat. xvi. 20 (W. H. mrg.); Mar. v. 43, vii. 36, ix. 9; pass. part., τὸ διαστελ-λόμενον, Heb. xii. 20, *the command.**

1292 διά-στημα, ατος, τό, *an inter-val* of time, Ac. v. 7.*

1293 δια-στολή, ῆς, ἡ, *distinction, difference,* Ro. iii. 22, x. 12; 1 Cor. xiv. 7.*

1294 δια-στρέφω, *to seduce, turn a-way,* Lu. xxiii. 2; Ac. xiii. 8; *to pervert, oppose,* Ac. xiii. 10; perf. part. pass., διε-στραμμένος, *perverse, corrupt,* Mat. xvii. 17; Lu. ix. 41; Ac. xx. 30; Phil. ii. 15.*

1295 διασώζω, σω, *to save, to convey safe through,* Ac. xxiii. 24, xxvii. 43; 1 Pet. iii. 20; pass., *to reach a place in safety,* Ac. xxvii. 44, xxviii. 1, 4; *to heal perfectly,* Mat. xiv. 36; Lu. vii. 3.*

1296 δια-ταγή, ῆς, ἡ, *a disposition, arrangement, ordinance,* Ac. vii. 53; Ro. xiii. 2.*

1297 διά-ταγμα, ατος, τό, *a mandate, a decree,* Heb. xi. 23.*

1298 δια-ταράσσω, *to trouble greatly, to agitate,* Lu. i. 29.*

1299 δια-τάσσω, *to give orders to* (dat.), *arrange, prescribe,* Mat. xi. 1; Lu. viii. 55; 1 Cor. xvi. 1; mid., *to appoint, to ordain,* as 1 Cor. vii. 17 (also with dat. person; acc., thing).

1300 δια-τελέω, ῶ, *to continue,* Ac. xxvii. 33.*

1301 δια-τηρέω, ῶ, *to guard* or *keep with care,* Lu. ii. 51; with ἑαυτόν, etc., *to guard one's self from, to abstain* (ἐκ or ἀπό), Ac. xv. 29.*

1302　δια-τί or διὰ τί (W. H.), *where-fore?*

1303　δια-τίθημι, only mid. in N. T., *to dispose*, as (1) *to assign*, Lu. xxii. 29; (2) with cog. acc., διαθήκην, *make* a covenant with (dat. or πρός, acc.), Ac. iii. 25; Heb. viii. 10, x. 16; *make* a will, Heb. ix. 16, 17. See διαθήκη.*

1304　δια-τρίβω, *to spend* or *pass* (χρόνον or ἡμέρας), as Ac. xiv. 3, 28; abs., *to stay*, as Jn. iii. 22.

1305　δια-τροφή, ῆς, ἡ, *food, nourishment*, 1 Tim. vi. 8.*

1306　δι-αυγάζω, *to shine through, to dawn*, 2 Pet. i. 19.*

1307　δια-φανής, ές, *transparent*, Rev. xxi. 21 (W. H. διαυγής in same signif.).*

1308　δια-φέρω, (1) *to carry through*, Mar. xi. 16; (2) *to spread abroad*, Ac. xiii. 49; (3) *to carry hither and thither*, Ac. xxvii. 27; (4) *to differ from* (gen.), 1 Cor. xv. 41; Gal. iv. 1; hence, (5) *to excel, surpass*, as Mat. vi. 26; (6) impers., διαφέρει, with οὐδέν, *it makes no difference* to (dat.), *matters nothing* to, Gal. ii. 6.

1309　δια-φεύγω, *to escape by flight*, Ac. xxvii. 42.*

1310　δια-φημίζω, *to report, publish abroad*, Mat. ix. 31, xxviii. 15; Mar. i. 45.*

1311　δια-φθείρω, *to corrupt*, 1 Tim. vi. 5; Rev. xi. 18; *to destroy utterly*, Lu. xii. 33; Rev. viii. 9, xi. 18; pass., *to decay. to perish*, 2 Cor. iv. 16; opp. to ἀνακαινόω, *to renew*.*

1312　δια-φθορά, ᾶς, ἡ, *decay, corruption, i.e.*, of the grave, Ac. ii. 27, 31, xiii. 34–37 (from S.).*

1313　διά-φορος, ον, (1) *diverse, of different kinds*, Ro. xii. 6; Heb. ix. 10; (2) compar., *more excellent* than, Heb. i. 4, viii. 6.*

1314　δια-φυλάσσω, *to guard carefully, protect, defend*, Lu. iv. 10 (from S.).*

1315　δια-χειρίζω, mid. N. T., *to lay hands on, put to death*, Ac. v. 30, xxvi. 21.*

see 5512　δια-χλευάζω, see χλευάζω.

1316　δια-χωρίζω, pass. N. T., "to be separated," *to depart from* (ἀπό), Lu. ix. 33.*

1317　διδακτικός, ή. όν. *apt in teach-*

---

ing, 1 Tim. iii. 2; 2 Tim. ii. 24.*

1318　διδακτός, ή, όν, *taught, instructed*, Jn. vi. 45; 1 Cor. ii. 13.*

1319　διδασκαλία, ας, ἡ, *instruction, teaching*, as Ro. xii. 7; *the doctrine taught, precept, instruction*, as Mat. xv. 9, etc.

1320　διδάσκαλος, ου, ὁ, *a teacher*, especially of the Jewish law, *master, doctor*, as Lu. ii. 46; often in voc. as a title of address to Christ, *Master, Teacher*.

1321　διδάσκω, διδάξω, *to teach, to be a teacher*, abs., Ro. xii. 7; *to teach*, with acc. of person, generally also acc. of thing; also with inf. or ὅτι, Mat. v. 2; Ac. iv. 2.

1322　διδαχή, ῆς, ἡ, *the act of teaching*, Ac. ii. 42; 2 Tim. iv. 2; *that which is taught*, doctrine, Mar. i. 27; Ac. xvii. 19; Rev. ii. 24; with obj. gen., perhaps in Heb. vi. 2, see Gr. § 260 b, note, Wi. § 30, 1 a.

1323　δί-δραχμον, ου, τό (prop. adj., sc. νόμισμα, *coin*), *a double drachma*, or silver half-shekel (in S. often *the shekel*), Mat. xvii. 24. (S.)*

1324　Δίδυμος, η, ον, *double*, or *twin; a surname of Thomas* the apostle, Jn. xi. 16, xx. 24, xxi. 2.*

1325　δίδωμι, *to give* (acc. and dat.); hence, in various connections, *to yield, deliver, supply, commit*, etc. When used in a general sense, the dat. of person may be omitted, as Mat. xiii. 8. The thing given may be expressed by ἐκ or ἀπό, with gen. in a partitive sense instead of acc.; so Mat. xxv. 8; Lu. xx. 10. The purpose of a gift may be expressed by inf., as Mat. xiv. 16; Jn. iv. 7; Lu. i. 73.

1326　δι-εγείρω, *to wake up thoroughly*, as Lu. viii. 24; *to excite*, Jn. vi. 18; fig., *to stir up, arouse*, 2 Pet. i. 13.

see 1760　δι-ενθυμέομαι, οῦμαι (W. H.), *to reflect*, Ac. x. 19. (N. T.)*

1327　δι-έξ-οδος, ου, ἡ, *a meeting-place of roads, a public spot* in a city, Mat. xxii. 9.*

1328　δι-ερμηνευτής, οῦ, ὁ, *an interpreter*, 1 Cor. xiv. 28. (N. T.)*

1329 δι-ερμηνεύω, *to interpret*, Lu.
xxiv. 27; 1 Cor. xii. 30, xiv.
5, 13, 27; *to translate*, Ac. ix.
36.*

1330 δι-έρχομαι, *to pass through*, acc.
or διά (gen.), destination ex
pressed by εἰς or ἕως; *to pass
over* or *travel*, abs., Ac. viii.
4; *to spread*, as a report, Lu.
v. 15.

1331 δι-ερωτάω, ῶ, *to find by inquiry*,
Ac. x. 17.*

1332 δι-ετής, ές (δίς), *of two years*,
Mat. ii. 16.*

1333 διετία, ας, ἡ, *the space of two
years*, Ac. xxiv. 27, xxviii.
30.*

1334 δι-ηγέομαι, οῦμαι, *to relate in
full, describe*, Mar. v. 16; Ac.
viii. 33, ix. 27.

1335 διήγησις, εως, ἡ, *a narrative*,
Lu. i. 1.*

1336 δι-ηνεκής, ές, *continuous; εἰς τὸ
διηνεκές, continually*, Heb
vii. 3, x. 1, 12, 14.*

1337 δι-θάλασσος, ον (δίς), *lying between two seas*, Ac. xxvii.
41.*

1338 δι-ϊκνέομαι, οῦμαι, *to pass
through, pierce*, Heb. iv.
12.*

1339 δι-ΐστημι, *to put apart, proceed*,
Ac. xxvii. 28; 2 aor., intrans.,
Lu. xxii. 59, *one hour having intervened; * xxiv. 51, *he
parted* from them.*

1340 δι-ϊσχυρίζομαι, *to affirm con-
fidently*, Lu. xxii. 59; Ac. xii.
15.*

1341 δικαιο-κρισία, ας, ἡ, *just judgment*, Ro. ii. 5. (S.)*

1342 δίκαιος, α, ον, *just, right, upright, righteous, impartial; *
applied to things, to persons,
to Christ, to God, Mat. i. 19;
Heb. xi. 4; Ac. x. 22.

1343 δικαιοσύνη, ης, ἡ, *righteousness,
justice, rectitude*, Mat. iii. 15;
Jn. xvi. 8, 10; Ro. v. 17, 21.

1344 δικαιόω, ῶ, *to show to be righteous*, 1 Tim. iii. 16; Ro. iii. 4;
usually in N. T. in the de-
clarative sense, *to hold guiltless, to justify, to pronounce*
or *treat as righteous*, as Mat.
xii. 37; 1 Cor. iv. 4.

1345 δικαίωμα, ατος, τό, *a righteous
statute, an ordinance*, Lu. i.
6; Ro. i. 32, ii. 26; Heb. ix.
1, 10; especially *a judicial
decree*, of acquittal (opp. to
κατάκριμα, *condemnation*),
Ro. v. 16; *of condemnation*,

Rev. xv. 4; *a righteous act*,
Ro. v. 18; Rev. xix. 8.*

1346 δικαίως, adv., *justly*, 1 Pet. ii.
23; Lu. xxiii. 41; *properly*,
1 Cor. xv. 34; *uprightly*, 1 Th.
ii. 10; Tit. ii. 12.*

1347 δικαίωσις, εως, ἡ, *acquittal, jus-
tification*, Ro. iv. 25, v. 18.*

1348 δικαστής, οῦ, ὁ, *a judge*, Lu.
xii. 14 (W. H. κριτής); Ac.
vii. 27, 35.*

1349 δίκη, ης, ἡ, *a judicial sentence*,
Ac.xxv. 15 (W. H. καταδίκη);
τίνω or ὑπέχω δίκην, *to suffer
punishment*, 2 Th. i. 9; Ju. 7;
*Justice, the name of a heathen
deity*, Ac. xxviii. 4.*

**1350; see
293** δίκτυον, ου, τό, *a fishing-net*, Jn.
xxi. 6, 8, 11. *Syn.*: see ἀμφί-
βληστρον.

1351 δι-λόγος, ον (δίς), *double-tongued,
deceitful*, 1 Tim. iii. 8. (N.T.)*

1352 διό, conj. (διά and δ), *on which
account, wherefore*.

1353 δι-οδεύω, *to journey through*,
Ac. xvii. 1; *to go about*, Lu.
viii. 1.*

1354 Διονύσιος, ου, ὁ, *Dionysius*, Ac.
xvii. 34.*

1355 διό-περ, conj., *for which very
reason*, 1 Cor. viii. 13, x. 14,
xiv. 13 (W. H. διό).*

1356 Διο-πετής, ές, *fallen from Zeus*,
i.e., from heaven, Ac. xix.35.*

see 2735 δι-όρθωμα, see κατόρθωμα.

1357 δι-όρθωσις, εως, ἡ, *reformation*,
Heb. ix. 10.*

1358 δι-ορύσσω, ξω, *to dig through*,
Mat. vi. 19, 20, xxiv. 43; Lu.
xii. 39.*

1359 Διόσ-κουροι, ων, οἱ (children of
Zeus), *Castor* and *Pollux*, Ac.
xxviii. 11.*

1360 δι-ότι, conj. (= διὰ τοῦτο, ὅτι),
on this account, because, for.

1361 Διο-τρεφής, οῦς, ὁ, *Diotrephes*,
3 Jn. 9.*

1362 διπλόος, οῦς, ῆ, οῦν, *double, twofold*, 1 Tim. v. 17; Rev. xviii.
6; comp., διπλότερος with
gen., *twofold more than*, Mat.
xxiii. 15.*

1363 διπλόω, ῶ, *to double*, Rev. xviii.
6.*

1364 δίς, adv., *twice*, Lu. xviii. 12.
(Δίς), obsolete nom. for Ζεύς,
gen. Διός, acc. Δία, Zeus or
Jupiter, see Ζεύς.

1365 διστάζω, σω (δίς), *to waver, to
doubt*, Mat. xiv. 31, xxviii.
17.*

1366 δί-στομος, ον (δίς), *two-edged*,
Heb. iv. 12; Rev. i. 16, ii. 12.*

41

1367   δισ-χίλιοι, αι, α, num., *two thousand*, Mar. v. 13.

1368   δι-υλίζω, *to strain off, filter through*, Mat. xxiii. 24.*

1369   διχάζω, σω, *to set at variance, divide*, Mat. x. 35.*

1370   διχο-στασία, ας, ἡ, *division, dissension*, Ro. xvi. 17; 1 Cor. iii. 3 (not W. H.); Gal. v. 20.*

1371   διχο-τομέω, ῶ, ήσω, *to cut in two*, perhaps meaning *to scourge severely*, Mat. xxiv. 51; Lu. xii. 46.*

1372   διψάω, ῶ, ήσω, *to thirst for, to desire earnestly*, acc., Mat. v. 6; or abs., *to thirst*, Jn. iv. 15; 1 Cor. iv. 11.

1373   δίψος, ους, τό, *thirst*, 2 Cor. xi. 27.*

1374   δί-ψυχος, ον (δίς), *double-minded*, Ja. i. 8, iv. 8.*

1375   διωγμός, οῦ, ὁ, *persecution*, Mat. xiii. 21; Ro. viii. 35.

1376   διώκτης, ου, ὁ, *a persecutor*, 1 Tim. i. 13. (N. T.)*

1377   διώκω, ξω, *to pursue*, in various senses according to context; *to follow, follow after, press forward, to persecute.*

1378   δόγμα, ατος, τό (δοκέω), *a decree, edict, ordinance*, Lu. ii. 1; Ac. xvi. 4, xvii. 7; Ep. ii. 15; Col. ii. 14.*

1379   δογματίζω, σω, *to impose an ordinance;* mid., *to submit to ordinances*, Col. ii. 20.*

1380   δοκέω, ῶ, δόξω, (1) *to think*, acc. and inf., Lu. viii. 18; 2 Cor. xi. 16; (2) *to seem, appear*, Lu. x. 36; Ac. xvii. 18; (3) δοκεῖ, impers., *it seems*, Mat. xvii. 25; *it seems good to* or *pleases*, dat., Lu. i. 3; Ac. xv. 22. *Syn.:* φαίνομαι means to appear *on the outside;* δοκέω, to appear *to an individual* to be true.

1381   δοκιμάζω, σω, *to try, scrutinize, prove*, as 2 Cor. viii. 22; Lu. xii. 56; *to judge fit, approve*, as 1 Cor. xvi. 3. *Syn.:* δοκιμάζω means to test anything with the expectation of finding it good; πειράζω, either with no expectation, or of finding it bad.

see 1381   δοκιμασία, ας, ἡ, the act of *proving*, Heb. iii. 9 (W. H.).*

1382   δοκιμή, ῆς, ἡ, *a trial*, 2 Cor. viii. 2; *a proof*, 2 Cor. xiii. 3; *tried, approved character*, Ro. v. 4; 2 Cor. ix. 13. (N. T.)

1383   δοκίμιον, ου, τό, *a test, trial*, 1 Pet. i. 7; Ja. i. 3.*

1384   δόκιμος, ον (δέχομαι), *approved, acceptable*, as Ro. xiv. 18, xvi. 10.

1385   δοκός, οῦ, ἡ, *a beam*, Mat. vii. 3, 4, 5; Lu. vi. 41, 42.*

1386   δόλιος, ία, ιον, *deceitful*, 2 Cor. xi. 13.*

1387   δολιόω, ῶ, *to deceive*, impf., 3d pers. plur., ἐδολιοῦσαν, an Alexandrian form from S., Ro. iii. 13. (S.)*

1388   δόλος, ου, ὁ, *fraud, deceit, craft*, Mat. xxvi. 4; 2 Cor. xii. 16.

1389   δολόω, ῶ, *to adulterate, corrupt*, 2 Cor. iv. 2.*

1390   δόμα, ατος, τό (δίδωμι), *a gift*, Mat. vii. 11; Lu. xi. 13; Ep. iv. 8; Phil. iv. 17.*

1391   δόξα, ης, ἡ, from δοκέω, in two main significations: (1) *favorable recognition* or *estimation, honor, renown*, as Jn. v. 41, 44; 2 Cor. vi. 8; Lu. xvii. 18; and very frequently (2) *the appearance, the manifestation of that which calls forth praise;* so especially in the freq. phrase ἡ δόξα τοῦ θεοῦ, *glory, splendor.* Concrete plur. δόξαι, in 2 Pet. ii. 10; Ju. 8, *dignities*, angelic powers.

1392   δοξάζω, σω, *to ascribe glory to, to honor, glorify*, Ro. xi. 13; 1 Cor. vi. 20.

1393   Δορκάς, άδος, ἡ, *Dorcas*, Ac. iv. 36, 39.*

1394   δόσις, εως, ἡ, *a giving*, Phil. iv. 15; *a gift*, Ja. i. 17.*

1395   δότης, ου, ὁ, *a giver*, 2 Cor. ix. 7. (S.)*

1396   δουλ-αγωγέω, ῶ, *to bring into subjection*, 1 Cor. ix. 27.*

1397   δουλεία, ας, ἡ, *slavery, bondage*, Ro. viii. 15, 21; Heb. ii. 15.

1398   δουλεύω, σω, (1) *to be a slave*, absolutely, Ep. vi. 7; Ro. ix. 12; (2) *to be subject to, to obey*, dat., Ro. vii. 6; Gal. iv. 8.

•1401, 1399, 1400   δοῦλος, η, ον, adj. only Ro. vi. 19; as subst. ἡ δούλη, *a female slave*, Lu. i. 38, 48; ὁ δοῦλος, *a slave, bondman*, the lowest word for this idea (opp. to ἐλεύθερος); *a servant* (opp. to κύριος, δεσπότης), so in the freq. phrases δοῦλος τοῦ θεοῦ, δοῦλος Χριστοῦ.

1402   δουλόω, ῶ, ώσω, *to reduce to*

1403
δοχή, ῆς, ἡ (δέχομαι), *a receiving* of guests, *a banquet*, Lu. v. 29, xiv. 13.*

1404
δράκων, οντος, ὁ, *a dragon* or *huge serpent ;* syrab. for Satan, Rev.

see 5143
δράμω, obs., *to run*, see τρέχω.

1405
δράσσομαι, dep., *to grasp, take ;* acc., 1 Cor. iii. 19.*

1406
δραχμή, ῆς, ἡ, *a drachma*, an Attic silver coin nearly equal to the Roman denarius, or worth about sixteen cents of our money, Lu. xv. 8, 9.*

1407
δρέπανον, ου, τό, *a sickle* or *pruning-hook*, Mar. iv. 29 ; Rev. xiv. 14–19.*

1408
δρόμος, ου, ὁ, *a running;* fig., *course, career*, Ac. xiii. 25, xx. 24 ; 2 Tim. iv. 7.*

1409
Δρούσιλλα, ης, ἡ, *Drusilla*, Ac. xxiv. 24.*

1410
δύναμαι, dep. (see Gr. § 109*b*, 1), *to be able*, abs., or with inf. (sometimes omitted) or acc.: *to have a capacity for ; to be strong*, as 1 Cor. iii. 2 ; *to have power to do*, whether through ability, disposition, permission, or opportunity.

1411
δύναμις, εως, ἡ, (1) *power, might*, absolutely or as an attribute, Lu. i. 17 ; Ac. iii. 12 ; (2) *power* over, expressed by εἰς or ἐπί (acc.), *ability to do ;* (3) *exercise of power, mighty work, miracle*, as Mat. xi. 20; (4) *forces*, as of an army, spoken of the heavenly hosts, as Mat. xxiv. 29 ; (5) *force*, as of a word, *i.e., significance*, 1 Cor. xiv. 11. *Syn.:* τέρας indicates a miracle as a wonderful portent or prodigy ; σημεῖον, as a sign, authenticating the divine mission of the doer ; δύναμις, as an exhibition of divine power.

1412
δυναμόω, ῶ, *to strengthen, confirm*, Col. i. 11 ; Heb. xi. 34 (W. H.). (S.)*

1413
δυνάστης, ου, ὁ, (1) *a potentate, prince*, Lu. i. 52 ; 1 Tim. vi. 15; (2) *one in authority*, Ac. viii. 27.*

1414
δυνατέω, ῶ, *to be powerful, have power*, 2 Cor. xiii. 3 ; (inf.),

Ro. xiv. 4 (W. H.) ; 2 Cor. ix. 8 (W. H.). (N. T.)*

1415
δυνατός, ή, όν, *able, having power, mighty*, Lu. xiv. 31 ; 1 Cor. i. 26 ; ὁ δυνατός, *the Almighty*, Lu. i. 49; δυνατόν, *possible*, Ro. xii. 18; Gal. iv. 15.

1416
δύνω or δύω, 2d aor. ἔδυν, *to sink ; to set*, as the sun, Mar. i. 32 ; Lu. iv. 40.*

1417
δύο, indecl. num., except dat. δυσί, *two*.

1418
δυσ-, an inseparable prefix, implying *adverse, difficult*, or *grievous*.

1419
δυσ-βάστακτος, ον, *hard to be borne*, Mat. xxiii. 4 (not W. H.) ; Lu. xi. 46. (S.)*

1420
δυσ-εντερία, ας, ἡ (W. H. ιον, τό), *dysentery*, Ac. xxviii. 8.*

1421
δυσ-ερμήνευτος, ον, *hard to explain*, Heb. v. 11.*

1422
δύσ-κολος, ον (lit., "difficult about food"), *difficult*, Mar. x. 24.*

1423
δυσκόλως, adv., *with difficulty, hardly*, Mat. xix. 23 ; Mar. x. 23 ; Lu. xviii. 24.*

1424
δυσμή, ῆς, ἡ (only plur., δυσμαί), *the setting of the sun, the west*, Rev. xxi. 13; Mat. viii. 11.

1425
δυσ-νόητος, ον, *hard* or *difficult to be understood*, 2 Pet. iii. 16.*

see 987
δυσ-φημέω, ῶ, *to speak evil, defame*, 1 Cor. iv. 13 (W. H.).*

1426
δυσ-φημία, ας, ἡ, *evil report, defamation*, 2 Cor. vi. 8.*

1427
δώδεκα, indecl. num., *twelve ;* οἱ δώδεκα, *the twelve, i.e., the Apostles*.

1428
δωδέκατος, η, ον, ord. num., *twelfth*, Rev. xxi. 20.*

1429
δωδεκά-φυλον, ου, τό, *the twelve tribes, Israel*, Ac. xxvi. 7.*

1430
δῶμα, ατος, τό, *a house, a housetop*, Mat. xxiv. 17; Ac. x. 9.

1431
δωρεά, ᾶς, ἡ, *a gift*, Jn. iv. 10; Ro. v. 15 ; Ep. iv. 7.

1432
δωρεάν, accus. of preced., as an adv., *freely*, as 2 Cor. xi. 7 ; *without cause, groundlessly*, Jn. xv. 25 ; Gal. ii. 21.

1433
δωρέομαι, οῦμαι, *to present, bestow*, Mar. xv. 45 ; pass., 2 Pet. i. 3, 4.*

1434
δώρημα, ατος, τό, *a gift, bounty*, Ro. v. 16; Ja. i. 17.*

1435
δῶρον, ου, τό, *a gift, present*, Ep. ii. 8 ; Rev. xi. 10.

E

E, ε, ἐψῖλον, *epsilon, e,* the fifth
letter. As a numeral, ε' = 5;
,ε = 5000.

1436   ἔα, interj., expressing surprise
or indignation, *ha! ah!* Mar.
i. 24 (W. H. omit) ; Lu. iv.
34.*

1437   ἐάν or ἄν, conj. (for εἰ ἄν), *if,*
usually construed with sub-
junctive verb. See Gr. § 383,
Wi. § 41 *b*, 2, Bu. 221 sq.
W. H. have the indic. fut.
in Lu. xix. 40; Ac. viii. 31 ;
pres. in 1 Th. iii. 8 ; 1 Jn. v.
15 (Rec. also). Sometimes
equivalent to a particle of
time, *when,* Jn. xii. 32 ; after
the relative, with an indefinite force, ὃς ἐάν, who*soever,*
as Mat. v. 19, viii. 19 ; 1 Cor.
xvi. 6 ; ἐὰν δὲ καί, *and if also ;*
ἐὰν μή, *except, unless,* Mat.
v. 20 ; *but that,* Mar. iv. 22 ;
ἐὰν πέρ, *if indeed,* Heb. vi. 3.

1438   ἑαυτοῦ, ῆς, οῦ, pron., reflex., 3d
pers., *of one's self ;* used also
in 1st and 2d persons.   See
Gr. § 335, Wi. §§ 22, 5, 38, 6,
Bu. 111 sq.   Genitive often
for possess. pron.   λέγειν or
εἰπεῖν ἐν ἑαυτῷ, *to say within
one's self ;* γίνεσθαι or ἔρ-
χεσθαι ἐν ἑαυτῷ, *to come to
one's self ;* πρὸς ἑαυτόν, *to
one's home,* Jn. xx. 10, or
privately, as Lu. xviii. 11 ; ἐν
ἑαυτοῖς, *among yourselves,*
i.e., one with another ; καθ'
ἑαυτόν, *apart ;* παρ' ἑαυτόν,
at home.

1439   ἐάω, ῶ, ἐάσω ; impf., εἴων ; 1st
aor., εἴασα, (1) *to permit,* inf.,
or acc. and inf., Mat. xxiv.
33 ; Lu. iv. 41 ; (2) *to leave,*
Ac. xxvii. 40.

1440   ἑβδομήκοντα, indecl. num., *sev-
enty ;* οἱ ἑβδομήκοντα, *the sev-
enty* disciples, Lu. x. 1, 17.

1441   ἑβδομηκοντάκις, num. adv., *sev-
enty times,* Mat. xviii. 22.
(S.)*

1442   ἕβδομος, η, ον, ord. num., *seventh,*
Jn. iv. 52 ; Heb. iv. 4.

1443   Ἔβερ, ὁ, *Eber* or *Heber,* Lu. iii.
35.*

1444   Ἑβραϊκός, ή, όν (from Heb.),
Hebrew, Lu. xxiii. 38 (W. H.
omit). (N. T.)*

1445   Ἑβραῖος (W. H. 'E-), αία, αῖον
(from Heb.), also subst., ὁ, ἡ, *a
Hebrew ;* designating (1) any

Jew, 2 Cor. xi. 22; Phil. iii. 5;
(2) a Jew of Palestine, in distinction from οἱ Ἑλληνισταί,
or Jews born out of Palestine,
and using the Greek lan-
guage, Ac. vi. 1; (3) any Jewish Christian, Heb. (head-
ing). (S.)* *Syn. :* Ἑβραῖος
denotes a Jew who spoke
Aramaic or Hebrew, in distinction from Ἑλληνιστής, a
Greek-speaking Jew ; Ἰου-
δαῖος, a Jew in distinction
from other nations ; Ἰσραηλίτης, one of the chosen
people.

1446   Ἑβραΐς (W. H. 'E-), (from
Heb.), ίδος, ἡ, *Hebrew, i.e.,*
the Aramaic language, ver-
nacular in the time of Christ
and the Apostles, Ac. xxi.
40, xxii. 2, xxvi. 14.   See
Gr. § 150, Wi. § 3 *a*. (Ap.)*

1447   Ἑβραϊστί (W. H. 'E-), (from
Heb.), adv., *in the Hebrew
language, i.e., in Aramaic,*
Jn. v. 2 ; Rev. ix. 11. (Ap.)

1448   ἐγγίζω, fut. att., ἐγγιῶ ; pf.,
ἤγγικα, *to approach, to draw
near, to be near,* abs., or with
dat. or εἰς, or ἐπί (acc.), Lu.
xviii. 40; Ac. ix. 3; Mar. xi. 1.

1449   ἐγ-γράφω (W. H. ἐνγ-), *to inscribe, engrave,* 2 Cor. iii. 2 ;
Lu. x. 20 (W. H.).*

1450   ἔγγυος, ον, ὁ, ἡ, *a surety,* Heb.
vii. 22.*

1451   ἐγγύς, adv., *near ;* used of both
place and time, with gen. or
dat.

1452   ἐγγύτερον, comp. of preceding,
nearer, Ro. xiii. 11.*

1453   ἐγείρω, ἐγερῶ, pass. perf., ἐγή-
γερμαι, *to arouse, to awaken,*
Ac. xii. 7 ; *to raise up,* as a
Savior, Ac. xiii. 23 (Rec.);
to erect, as a building, Jn. ii.
19, 20 ; mid., *to rise up,* as
from sleep, or from a re-
cumbent posture, as at table,
Jn. xi. 29, xiii. 4 ; applied to
raising the dead, Jn. v. 21 ;
used also of *rising up against,*
as an adversary, or in judgment, Mat. xxiv. 7.

1454   ἔγερσις, εως, ἡ, *a rousing up ;*
of the resurrection, Mat.
xxvii. 53.*

1455   ἐγκ-. In words beginning thus,
W. H. generally write ἐνκ-.

1455   ἐγ-κάθ-ετος, ον, ὁ, ἡ (ἐγκαθίημι),
a spy, Lu. xx. 20.*

1456   ἐγκαίνια, ίων, τά, *a dedication,*

Jn. x. 22 ; of the feast commemorating the dedicating or purifying of the temple, after its pollution by Antiochus Epiphanes, 25 Chisleu, answering to mid-December. (S.)*

1457 ἐγ-καινίζω, *to dedicate*, Heb. ix. 18, x. 20. (S.)*

see 1573 ἐγ-κακέω, ῶ, and ἐνκακέω, *to grow weary, to faint* (W. H. in many passages for Rec. ἐκκακέω).

1458 ἐγ-καλέω, ῶ, ἐσω, impf., ἐνεκάλουν, *to bring a charge against, accuse*, pers. dat., or κατά (gen.), *crime in gen.*, Ac. xix. 38, 40; Ro. viii. 33.

1459 ἐγ-κατα-λείπω, ψω, (1) *to desert, to abandon*, Mat. xxvii. 46; 2 Tim. iv. 10, 16; (2) *to leave remaining*, Ro. ix. 29.

1460 ἐγ-κατ-οικέω, ῶ, *to dwell among* (ἐν), 2 Pet. ii. 8.*

see 2744 ἐγ-καυχάομαι, *to boast in*, 2 Th. i. 4 (W. H.).*

1461 ἐγ-κεντρίζω, *to insert*, as a bud or graft, *to graft in;* fig., Ro. xi. 17, 19, 23, 24.*

1462 ἔγ-κλημα, ατος, τό, *a charge* or *accusation*, Ac. xxiii. 29, xxv. 16.*

1463 ἐγ-κομβόομαι,οῦμαι,*to gird on*,as an outer garment, the badge of slavery, 1 Pet. v. 5. (N. T.)*

1464 ἐγ-κοπή, ῆς, ἡ (W. H. ἐνκ-), *a hindrance*, 1 Cor. ix. 12.*

1465 ἐγ-κόπτω, ψω, *to impede, to hinder* (acc., or inf. with τοῦ), Ro. xv. 22 ; 1 Th. ii. 18.

1466 ἐγκράτεια, ας, ἡ, *self-control, continence*, Ac. xxiv. 25; Gal. v. 23; 2 Pet. i. 6.*

1467 ἐγκρατεύομαι, dep., *to be self-controlled, continent*, especially in sensual pleasures, 1 Cor. vii. 9, ix. 25.*

1468 ἐγ-κρατής, ές, *self-controlled, continent*, Tit. i. 8.*

1469 ἐγ-κρίνω, *to adjudge* or *reckon*, to a particular rank (acc. and dat.), 2 Cor. x. 12.*

1470 ἐγ-κρύπτω, *to hide in, to mix with*, Mat. xiii. 33; Lu. xiii. 21 (W. H. κρύπτω).*

1471 ἔγ-κυος, ον, *pregnant*, Lu. ii. 5.*

1472 ἐγ-χρίω, *to rub in, anoint*, Rev. iii. 18.*

1473 ἐγώ, pers. pron., *I;* plur., ἡμεῖς, *we.* See Gr. § 53.

1474 ἐδαφίζω, fut. (attic), ιῶ, *to throw to the ground, to raze*, Lu. xix. 44.*

1475 ἔδαφος, ους, τό, *the base, the ground*, Ac xxii. 7.*

1476 ἑδραῖος, αία, αῖον, *steadfast, firm*, 1 Cor. vii. 37, xv. 58; Col. i. 23.*

1477 ἑδραίωμα, ατος, τό, *a stay, support*, 1 Tim. iii. 15. (N. T.)*

1478 Ἐζεκίας, ου, ὁ, *Hezekiah*, Mat. i. 9, 10.*

1479 ἐθελο-θρησκεία, ας, ἡ, *voluntary, arbitrary worship*, Col. ii. 23. (N. T.)*

see 2309 ἐθέλω, see θέλω.

1480 ἐθίζω, *to accustom ;* pass., perf. part., neut., τὸ εἰθισμένον, *the custom*, Lu. ii. 27.*

1481 ἐθνάρχης, ου, ὁ, *a prefect, ethnarch*, 2 Cor. xi. 32.*

1482 ἐθνικός, ή, όν, *of Gentile race, heathen*, as subst. ὁ ἐθνικός, *the pagan, the Gentile*, Mat. v. 47 (W. H.), vi. 7, xviii. 17; 3 Jn. 7 (W. H.).*

1483 ἐθνικῶς, adv., *like the Gentiles*, Gal. ii. 14. (N. T.)*

1484 ἔθνος, ους, τό, *a race, a nation*, Lu. xxii. 25 ; Ac. x. 35; τὰ ἔθνη, *the nations, the heathen world, the Gentiles*, Mat. iv. 15; Ro. iii. 29; by Paul, even *Gentile Christians*, Ro. xi. 13; Gal. ii. 12.

1485 ἔθος, ους, τό, *a usage, custom*, Lu. i. 9; Ac. xxv. 16.

1486 ἔθω, obs., pf. εἴωθα in pres. signif., *to be accustomed*, Mat. xxvii. 15; Mar. x. 1; τὸ εἰωθὸς αὐτῷ, *his custom*, Lu. iv. 16; Ac. xvii. 2.*

1487 εἰ, a conditional conjunction (see Gr. § 383), *if, since, though*. After verbs indicating emotion, εἰ is equivalent to ὅτι, Mar. xv. 44. As an interrogative particle, εἰ occurs in both indirect and direct questions, Mar. xv. 45; Ac. i. 6. In oaths and solemn assertions, it may be rendered by *that ... not.* εἰ μή and εἰ μήτι, *unless, except;* εἰ δὲ μή, *but if not, otherwise*, Jn. xiv. 2 ; εἰ περ, *if so be ;* εἴ πως, *if possibly ;* εἴτε ... εἴτε, *whether ... or.*

see 3708 εἶδον, see ὁράω, οἶδα.

1491 εἶδος, ους, τό, *outward appearance, form*, Lu. iii. 22, ix. 29; Jn. v. 37; 2 Cor. v. 7; ★ *species, kind*, 1 Th. v. 22.*⁹*

45

★ For **1488** see **1510**; **1489**, **1490**, & **1492** see Strong.

1493 εἰδωλεῖον, ου, τό, *an idol-temple,*
1 Cor. viii. 10. (Ap.)*

1494 εἰδωλό-θυτος, ον, *sacrificed to
idols ;* used of meats, as Ac.
xv. 29. (Ap.)

1495 εἰδωλο-λατρεία, ας, ἡ, *idolatry,*
1 Cor. x. 14; Gal. v. 20; Col.
iii. 5 ; 1 Pet. iv. 3. (N. T.)*

1496 εἰδωλο-λάτρης, ου, ὁ, *an idolater,*
1 Cor. x. 7; Rev. xxi. 8. (N.
T.)

1497 εἴδωλον, ου, τό, *an idol, a false
★   god* worshipped in an image,
Ac. vii. 41 ; Ro. ii. 22.

1500 εἰκῆ or εἰκῇ (W. H.), adv., *without purpose,* as Ro. xiii. 4 ;
in vain, 1 Cor. xv. 2 (W. H.
and R. V. omit in Mat. v.
22).

1501 εἴκοσι, indecl. num., *twenty.*

1502 εἴκω, *to give way, to yield,* Gal.
ii. 5.*

1503 εἴκω, obs., whence 2d perf.
ἔοικα, *to be like ;* with dat.,
Ja. i. 6, 23.*

1504 εἰκών, όνος, ἡ, *an image, likeness,* Mar. xii. 16; 1 Cor. xi.
7. *Syn.:* see Trench, § xv.

1505 εἰλικρίνεια, ας, ἡ, *clearness, sincerity,* 1 Cor. v. 8 ; 2 Cor. i.
12, ii. 17.*

1506 εἰλικρινής, ές (derivation doubtful), *sincere, pure,* Phil. i. 10 ;
2 Pet. iii. 1.*

1507 εἰλίσσω (W. H. ἐλίσσω), *to roll
★   together,* as a scroll, Rev. vi.
14.*

1510, 1511 εἰμί (see Gr. § 110, Wi. § 14, 2,
Bu. 49, 50), a verb of exist-
ence, (1) used as a predicate,
*to be, to exist, to happen, to
come to pass ;* with an infin.
following, ἔστι, *it is convenient, proper,* etc., as Heb.
ix. 5 ; (2) as the copula of
subject and predicate, simply
to be, or in the sense of *to be
like, to represent,* Jn. vi. 35 ;
Mat. xxvi. 26 ; 1 Cor. x. 4.
With participles, it is used
to form the periphrastic
tenses, as Lu. i. 22, iv. 16;
Mat. xvi. 19, etc. With gen.,
as predicate, it marks quality, possession, participation,
etc.; with dat., property, possession, destination, etc. The
verb, when copula, is often
omitted. Participle, ὤν, *be-*
see 548, 549, *ing ;* τὸ ὄν, *that which is ;* οἱ
1524, 1826 ὄντες, τὰ ὄντα, persons or
& 4896 things *that are.*
εἶμι, *to go,* in some copies for

εἰμί, in Jn. vii. 34, 36 (not
W. H.).*

see 1752 εἵνεκα, εν, see ἕνεκα, εν.
1512 ★ εἴπερ, εἴπως, see under εἰ.
see 2036 St εἶπον (see Gr. § 103, 7, Wi.
§ 15, Bu. 57), (W. H. εἶπα),
from obs. ἔπω, or εἴπω, *to
say ;* in reply, *to answer ;* in
narration, *to tell ;* in authoritative directions, *to bid* or
command, as Lu. vii. 7.

1514 εἰρηνεύω, *to have peace, to be at
peace,* Mar. ix. 50; Ro. xii.
18; 2 Cor. xiii. 11 ; 1 Th. v.
13.*

1515 εἰρήνη, ης, ἡ, *peace,* the opposite
of strife; *peace of mind,* aris-
ing from reconciliation with
God. In N. T. (like the corresponding Heb. word in
O. T.), εἰρήνη generally denotes *a perfect well-being.*
Often employed in saluta-
tions, as in Hebrew.

1516 εἰρηνικός, ή, όν, *peaceable,* Ja.
iii. 17 ; *peaceful,* Heb. xii.
11.*

1517 εἰρηνο-ποιέω, ῶ, *to make peace,
reconcile,* Col. i. 20. (S.)*

1518 εἰρηνο-ποιός, όν, *pacific, loving
peace,* Mat. v. 9.*

1519 εἰς, prep. governing acc., *into,
to* (the interior). See Gr.
§§ 124, 298. In composition,
it implies motion into or towards.

1520 εἷς, μία, ἕν, a card. num., *one ;*
used distributively, as Mat.
xx. 21 ; by way of emphasis,
as Mar. ii. 7 ; and indefinitely, as Mat. viii. 19; Mar. xii.
42. As an ordinal, *the first,*
Mat. xxviii. 1 ; Rev. ix. 12.

1521 εἰσ-άγω, 2d aor. εἰσήγαγον, *to
lead in, bring in,* Lu. xxii.
54; Ac. viii. 45.

1522 εἰσ-ακούω, *to listen to, to hear
prayer,* Mat. vi. 7 ; Lu. i. 13;
Ac. x. 31; Heb. v. 7 ; *to hear
so as to obey* (gen.), 1 Cor.
xiv. 21.*

1523 εἰσ-δέχομαι, ἔξομαι, *to receive
with favor* (acc.), 2 Cor. vi.
17, from S.*

1524 εἴσ-ειμι, impf. εἰσῄειν. inf. εἰσιέ-
ναι (εἶμι), *to go in, to enter* (with
εἰς), Ac. iii. 3, xxi. 18, 26 ;
Heb. ix. 6.*

1525 εἰσ-έρχομαι, 2d aor. εἰσῆλθον,
to come in, to enter (chiefly
with εἰς), Ac. xxiii. 16, 33 ;
εἰσέρχομαι καὶ ἐξέρχομαι, *to
come and go in and out,*

46

★For 1498, 1499, 1508 & 1509 see
Strong.

★For 1513 see Strong.

spoken of daily life and intercourse, Ac. i. 21; fig., of entrance into any state or condition, Mat. xix. 17; Heb. iii. 11, 18.

*
1528 εἰσ-καλέω, ῶ, only mid. in N.T., *to call* or *invite in,* Ac. x. 23.*

1529 εἴσ-οδος, ου, ἡ, *an entrance, the act of entering,* Heb. x. 19; 2 Pet. i. 11.

1530 εἰσ-πηδάω, ῶ, *to spring in,* Ac. xiv. 14 (W. H. ἐκπ-), xvi. 29.*

1531 εἰσ-πορεύομαι, dep., *to go in, to enter;* spoken of persons, as Mar. i. 21; of things, as Mat. xv. 17; εἰσπορεύομαι καὶ ἐκπορεύομαι, *to go in and out* in daily duties, Ac. ix. 28.

1532 εἰσ-τρέχω, 2d aor. εἰσέδραμον, *to run in,* Ac. xii. 14.*

1533 εἰσ-φέρω (see Gr. § 103, 6, Wi. § 15, Bu. 68), *to lead into* (with εἰς), *e.g.,* temptation, as Lu. xi. 4; *to bring in,* Ac. xvii. 20; 1 Tim. vi. 7.

1534 εἶτα, adv., *then, afterwards.*

1535; see εἴτε, conj., see εἰ.

1487 & 5037 ἐκ, or, before a vowel, ἐξ, a prep. gov. gen., *from, out of* (the interior), used of place, time, and source. See Gr. § 293, Wi. § 47 b, Bu. 326 sq. In composition, ἐκ implies *egress, removal, origin, publicity, unfolding,* or is of *intensive force.*

*
1537

1538 ἕκαστος, η, ον, *each, every one* (with partitive gen.); εἰς ἕκαστος, *every one.*

1539 ἑκάστοτε, adv., *at every time, always,* 2 Pet. i. 15.*

1540 ἑκατόν, card. num., *a hundred,* Mat. xiii. 8, xviii. 12.

1541 ἑκατοντα-έτης, ες, *a hundred years old,* Ro. iv. 9.*

1542 ἑκατονταπλασίων, ου, acc. ονα, *a hundredfold,* Mat. xix. 29 (not W. H.); Mar. x. 30; Lu. viii. 8.*

1543 ἑκατοντάρχης, ου, ὁ, *captain over a hundred men, a centurion,* Ac. x. 1, 22, xxiv. 23.

1543 ἑκατόνταρχος, ου, ὁ = preceding, Mat. viii. 5, 8, 13. In many passages a variant for preceding.

see 1831 ἐκ-βαίνω, 2d aor. ἐξέβην, *to go out,* Heb. xi. 15 (W. H.).*

1544 ἐκ-βάλλω, βαλῶ, *to cast out,* Jn. vi. 37; *to drive out,* Mat. xxi. 12; *to expel,* Gal. iv. 30; *to send away, dismiss, reject,*

1545 Mar. i. 43; Lu. vi. 22; *to extract, draw out,* Lu. vi. 42; Mat. xii. 35.

ἔκ-βασις, εως, ἡ, *a way of escape,* 1 Cor. x. 13; *end, issue,* Heb. xiii. 7.*

1546 ἐκ-βολή, ῆς, ἡ, *a throwing out,* Ac. xxvii. 18.*

1547 ἐκ-γαμίζω (W. H. γαμίζω), *to give in marriage,* Mat. xxiv. 38 (Rec.); 1 Cor. vii. 38 (Rec.). (N. T.)

1548 ἐκ-γαμίσκω = preceding, Lu. xx. 34, 35 (Rec.). (N. T.)*

1549 ἔκ-γονος, ον, *sprung from;* neut. plur., *descendants,* 1 Tim. v. 4.*

1550 ἐκ-δαπανάω, ῶ, *to spend entirely;* pass. reflex., *to expend one's energies* for (ὑπέρ), 2 Cor. xii. 15.*

1551 ἐκ-δέχομαι, *to expect* (ἕως), *to wait for* (acc. or ἕως), Ja. v. 7; Heb. x. 13.

1552 ἔκ-δηλος, ον, *conspicuous, manifest,* 2 Tim. iii. 9.*

1553 ἐκ-δημέω, ῶ, *to go abroad, to be absent,* 2 Cor. v. 6, 8, 9.*

1554 ἐκ-δίδωμι, N. T. mid., *to let out for one's advantage,* Mat. xxi. 33, 41; Mar. xii. 1; Lu. xx. 9.*

1555 ἐκ-δι-ηγέομαι, οῦμαι, dep. mid., *to narrate at length, to declare,* Ac. xiii. 41, xv. 3.*

1556 ἐκ-δικέω, ῶ, *to do justice to, defend, avenge* a person (acc. and ἀπό), Lu. xviii. 3, 5; Ro. xii. 19; *to demand requital for, avenge* a deed (acc.), 2 Cor. x. 6; Rev. vi. 10, xix. 2.*

1557 ἐκ-δίκησις, εως, ἡ, *an avenging, vindication, punishment,* Ac. vii. 24; Ro. xii. 19; 1 Pet. ii. 14.

1558 ἔκ-δικος, ου, ὁ, ἡ, *an avenger, one who adjudges* a culprit (dat.) *to punishment* for (περὶ) a crime, Ro. xiii. 4; 1 Th. iv. 6.*

1559 ἐκ-διώκω, ώξω, *to persecute, to expel by persecuting,* Lu. xi. 49 (not W. H.); 1 Th. ii. 15.*

1560 ἔκ-δοτος, ον, *delivered up,* Ac. ii. 23.*

1561 ἐκ-δοχή, ῆς, ἡ, *a waiting for, expectation,* Heb. x. 27.*

1562 ἐκ-δύω, *to unclothe, to strip off* (two accs.), Mat. xxvii. 31; 2 Cor. v. 4.

1563 ἐκεῖ, adv., *there, thither.*

47

*For 1526, 1527 & 1536 see Strong.

1564   ἐκεῖθεν, adv., *from that place, thence.*

1565   ἐκεῖνος, η, ο, pron., demonst., *that, that one there;* used antithetically, Mar. xvi. 20; and by way of emphasis, Mat. xxii. 23. See Gr. §§ 338, 340, Wi. §§ 18, 4, 23, 1, Bu. 104, 120.

1566   ἐκεῖσε, adv., *thither*, Ac. xxi. 3; in const. præg., Ac. xxii. 5.*

1567   ἐκ-ζητέω, ῶ, *to seek out* with diligence, Heb. xii. 17; 1 Pet. i. 10; *to seek after* God, Ac. xv. 17; Ro. iii. 11; Heb. xi. 6; *to require,* judicially, Lu. xi. 50, 51. (S.)*

see 1567 & 2214   ἐκ-ζήτησις, εως, ἡ, *a subject of inquiry,* 1 Tim. i. 4 (W. H.).*

1568   ἐκ-θαμβέω, ῶ, N. T. pass., *to be amazed, greatly astonished,* Mar. ix. 15, xiv. 33, xvi. 5, 6.*

1569   ἔκ-θαμβος, ον, *greatly astonished, amazed,* Ac. iii. 11.*

see 2296   ἐκ-θαυμάζω, *to wonder greatly,* Mar. xii. 17 (W. H.).*

1570   ἔκ-θετος, ον, *cast out, exposed* to perish, Ac. vii. 19.*

1571   ἐκ-καθαίρω, 1st aor. ἐξεκάθαρα, *to cleanse thoroughly,* 1 Cor. v. 7; 2 Tim. ii. 4.*

1572   ἐκ-καίω, N. T. pass., *to burn vehemently,* as with lust, Ro. i. 27.*

1573   ἐκ-κακέω, ῶ, *to faint, to despond through fear* (Rec., for which W. H. have ἐγκ- and ἐνκ-).

1574   ἐκ-κεντέω, ῶ, *to pierce through, to transfix,* Jn. xix. 37; Rev. i. 7.*

1575   ἐκ-κλάω, *to break off,* Ro. xi. 17, 19, 20 (W. H.).*

1576   ἐκ-κλείω, σω, *to shut out,* Gal. iv. 17; *to exclude,* Ro. iii. 27.*

1577   ἐκκλησία, ας, ἡ (ἐκκαλέω), *an assembly,* Ac. xix. 32, 39, 41; usually legally, sometimes tumultuously gathered. Espec. in N. T., *an assembly of Christian believers, a church* in one place, Ac. xi. 26; often plural, as Ac. xv. 41; *the whole body of believers* on earth, 1 Cor. xii. 28; Ep. i. 22; or in heaven, Heb. xii. 23. *Syn.:* see Trench, § 1.

1578   ἐκ-κλίνω, *to turn away from* (ἀπό), Ro. iii. 12, xvi. 17; 1 Pet. iii. 11.*

1579   ἐκ-κολυμβάω, ῶ, *to swim out,* Ac. xxvii. 42.*

1580   ἐκ-κομίζω, *to carry out* for burial, Lu. vii. 12.*

1581   ἐκ-κόπτω, κόψω, *to cut off,* Mat. iii. 10, v. 30; 2 Cor. xi. 12 (in 1 Pet. iii. 7, W. H. read ἐνκόπτω, *to hinder*).

1582   ἐκ-κρέμαμαι (mid. of ἐκκρεμάννυμι), *to hang upon,* of earnest attention, Lu. xix. 48.*

1583   ἐκ-λαλέω, ῶ, *to speak out, to disclose,* Ac. xxiii. 22.*

1584   ἐκ-λάμπω, *to shine forth,* Mat. xiii. 43.*

1585   ἐκ-λανθάνω, in mid., *to forget entirely,* Heb. xii. 5.*

1586   ἐκ-λέγω, mid. in N. T., 1st aor. ἐξελεξάμην, *to choose out* for one's self, *to elect,* Lu. x. 42; Ac. vi. 5, xiii. 17; 1 Cor. i. 27, 28.

1587   ἐκ-λείπω, 2d aor. ἐξέλιπον, *to fail, to cease, to die,* Lu. xvi. 9, xxii. 32, xxiii. 45 (W. H.); Heb. i. 12.*

1588   ἐκλεκτός, ή, όν, (1) *chosen, elect,* Lu. xviii. 7, xxiii. 35; 1 Tim. v. 21; Ro. viii. 33; Rev. xvii. 14; (2) *choice, select,* 2 Jn. i. 13; 1 Pet. ii. 4.

1589   ἐκλογή, ῆς, ἡ, *a choice, selection,* Ro. ix. 11; 1 Th. i. 4; Ac. ix. 15 (*a vessel of choice, i.e., a chosen vessel*); concr., *the chosen ones,* Ro. xi. 7

1590   ἐκ-λύω, in pass., *to become weary* in body, or *despondent* in mind, Mar. viii. 3; Gal. vi. 9; Heb. xii. 5.

1591   ἐκ-μάσσω, ξω, *to wipe, to wipe off,* Lu. vii. 38, 44; Jn. xi. 2, xii. 3, xiii. 5.*

1592   ἐκ-μυκτηρίζω, *to deride, scoff at* (acc.), Lu. xvi. 14, xxiii. 35. (S.)*

1593   ἐκ-νέω (lit., swim out), or ἐκνεύω (lit., turn by a side motion), *to withdraw,* Jn. v. 13.*

1594   ἐκ-νήφω, *to return to soberness* of mind, 1 Cor. xv. 34.*

1595   ἑκούσιος, ον (ἑκών), *voluntary, spontaneous,* Philem. 14.*

1596   ἑκουσίως, adv., *voluntarily, of one's own accord,* Heb. x. 26; 1 Pet. v. 2.*

1597   ἔκ-παλαι, adv., *from of old,* 2 Pet. ii. 3, iii. 5.*

1598   ἐκ-πειράζω, σω, *to put to the test, to make trial of, to tempt,* Mat. iv. 7; Lu. iv. 12, x. 25; 1 Cor. x. 9. (S.)*

1599	ἐκ-πέμπω, *to send forth*, Ac. xiii. 4, xvii. 10.*
see 1537 & 4053	ἐκ-περισσῶς, adv., *exceedingly*, Mar. xiv. 31 (W. H.). (N.T.)*
1600	ἐκ-πετάννυμι, 1st aor. ἐξεπέτασα, *to stretch forth*, Ro. x. 21.*
see 1530	ἐκ-πηδάω, ῶ, 1st aor. ἐξεπήδησα (W. H.), *to spring forth*, Ac. xiv. 14.*
1601	ἐκ-πίπτω, *to fall from* (ἐκ), Ac. xii. 7; abs., *to fall*, Ja. i. 11; of a ship driven from its course, Ac. xxvii. 17; of love, *to fail*, 1 Cor. xiii. 8; of moral lapse, Gal. v. 4.
1602	ἐκ-πλέω, εύσω, *to sail away*, Ac. xv. 39, xviii. 18, xx. 6.*
1603	ἐκ-πληρόω, ῶ, *to fill entirely*, *fulfill*, Ac. xiii. 32.*
1604	ἐκ-πλήρωσις, εως, ἡ, *fulfillment*, Ac. xxi. 26.*
1605	ἐκ-πλήσσω, 2d aor. pass. ἐξεπλάγην, *to strike with astonishment*, Mat. xiii. 54; Ac. xiii. 12.
1606	ἐκ-πνέω, εύσω, *to breathe out, to expire*, Mar. xv. 37, 39; Lu. xxiii. 46.*
1607	ἐκ-πορεύομαι, dep., *to go out* (ἀπό, ἐκ, παρά, and εἰς, ἐπί, πρός); *to proceed from*, as from the heart; or as a river from its source, etc.
1608	ἐκ-πορνεύω, *to be given up to fornication*, Ju. 7. (S.)*
1609	ἐκ-πτύω, *to reject, to loathe*, Gal. iv. 14.*
1610	ἐκ-ριζόω, ῶ, *to root out, root up*, Mat. xiii. 29, xv. 13; Lu. xvii. 6; Ju. 12.*
1611	ἔκ-στασις, εως, ἡ, *trance*, Ac. x. 10; *amazement*, Mar. v. 42.
1612	ἐκ-στρέφω, perf. pass. ἐξέστραμμαι, *to change for the worse, to corrupt*, Tit. iii. 11.*
1613	ἐκ-ταράσσω, ξω, *to agitate greatly*, Ac. xvi. 20.*
1614	ἐκ-τείνω, νῶ, 1st aor. ἐξέτεινα, *to stretch out* the hand, as Lu. v. 13; *to cast out*, as anchors, Ac. xxvii. 30.
1615	ἐκ-τελέω, ῶ, έσω, *to complete*, Lu. xiv. 29, 30.*
1616	ἐκτένεια, ας, ἡ, *intentness*, Ac. xxvi. 7.*
•1618, 1617	ἐκ-τενής, ές, *intense, fervent, intent*, 1 Pet. iv. 8; Ac. xii. 5 (W. H. -ῶς); ἐκτενέστερον, comp. as adv., *more earnestly*, Lu. xxii. 44 (W. H. omit).*
1619	ἐκτενῶς, adv., *intently, earnestly*, 1 Pet. i. 22; Ac. xii. 5 (W. H.).*
1620	ἐκ-τίθημι (see Gr. § 107, Wi. § 14, 1 b, Bu. 45 sq.), (1) *to put out, expose* an infant, Ac. vii. 21; (2) *to expound*, Ac. xi. 4, xviii. 26, xxviii. 23.*
1621	ἐκ-τινάσσω, ξω, *to shake off*, Mat. x. 14; Mar. vi. 11; Ac. xiii. 51; *to shake out*, Ac. xviii. 6.*
•1623	ἕκτος, η, ον, ord. num., *sixth*.
1622	ἐκτός, adv., generally as prep., with gen., *without, besides, except*, 1 Cor. vi. 18; Ac. xxvi. 22; ἐκτὸς εἰ μή, *except*, 1 Cor. xiv. 5; τὸ ἐκτός, *the outside*, Mat. xxiii. 26.
1624	ἐκ-τρέπω, pass. in mid. sense, *to turn from, to forsake*, 1 Tim. i. 6, v. 15, vi. 20; 2 Tim. iv. 4; Heb. xii. 13.*
1625	ἐκ-τρέφω, *to nourish*, Ep. v. 29; *to bring up*, Ep. vi. 4.*
1626	ἔκ-τρωμα, ατος, τό, *an abortive birth, an abortion*, 1 Cor. xv. 8.*
1627	ἐκ-φέρω, ἐξοίσω, *to bring forth, carry out;* espec. to burial, Ac. v. 6, 9; *to produce*, of the earth, Heb. vi. 8.
1628	ἐκ-φεύγω, *to flee out* (abs., or with ἐκ), Ac. xvi. 27, xix. 16; *to escape*, 1 Th. v. 3; Ro. ii. 3.
1629	ἐκ-φοβέω, ῶ, *to terrify greatly*, 2 Cor. x. 9.*
1630	ἔκ-φοβος, ον, *greatly terrified*, Mar. ix. 6; Heb. xii. 21.*
1631	ἐκ-φύω, 2d aor. pass. ἐξεφύην, *to put forth*, as a tree its leaves, Mat. xxiv. 32; Mar. xiii. 28.*
1632	ἐκ-χέω, also ἐκχύνω; fut. ἐκχεῶ, 1st aor. ἐξέχεα (see Gr. § 96 c, Wi. § 13, 3 a, Bu. 68), *to pour out*, as Rev. xvi. 1–17; money, Jn. ii. 15; *to shed* blood, Lu. xi. 50; fig., *to shed abroad*, love, Ro. v. 5; pass., *to be wholly given up to*, Ju. 11.
1633	ἐκ-χωρέω, ῶ, *to depart from*, Lu. xxi. 21.*
1634	ἐκ-ψύχω, *to expire*, Ac. v. 5, 10, xii. 23.*
1635	ἑκών, οῦσα, όν, *voluntary, willing;* used adverbially, Ro. viii. 20; 1 Cor. ix. 17.*
1636	ἐλαία, ας, ἡ, *an olive tree*, Ro. xi. 17, 24; its fruit, *the olive*, Ja. iii. 12; τὸ ὄρος τῶν ἐλαιῶν, *the Mount of Olives*, Mar. xi. 1.

1637 ἔλαιον, ου, τό, *olive oil*, Mat.
xxv. 3; Rev. vi. 6.

1638 ἐλαιών, ῶνος, ὁ, *an olive orchard*,
i.e., the Mount of Olives, Ac.
i. 12. (S.)*

1639 Ἐλαμίτης, ου, ὁ, *an Elamite*,
i.e., inhabitant of the province of Elymais, Ac. ii. 9.*

1640 ἐλάσσων or -ττων, ον, compar.
of ἐλαχύς for μικρός, *less;*
in excellence, Jn. ii. 10; in
age, Ro. ix. 12; in rank, Heb.
vii. 7; ἔλαττον, as adv., *less*,
1 Tim. v. 9.*

1641 ἐλαττονέω, ῶ, *to have less, to
lack*, 2 Cor. viii. 15.*

1642 ἐλαττόω, ῶ, *to make less* or *inferior*, Heb. ii. 7, 9; pass.,
to decrease, Jn. iii. 30.*

1643 ἐλαύνω, perf. part. ἐληλακώς, *to
drive*, Lu. viii. 29; Ja. iii. 4;
2 Pet. ii. 17; *to drive a ship,
to row*, Mar. vi. 48; Jn. vi.
19.*

1644 ἐλαφρία, ας, ἡ, *levity, incon-
stancy*, 2 Cor. i. 17.*

1645 ἐλαφρός, ά, όν, *light*, as a burden, Mat. xi. 30; 2 Cor. iv.
17.*

1646 ἐλάχιστος, η, ον (superl. of ἐλαχύς for μικρός), *smallest, least*,
in size, amount, or importance, Ja. iii. 4; Lu. xvi. 10;
1 Cor. vi. 2.

1647 ἐλαχιστότερος, α, ον, a double
comparison, *less than the
least*, Ep. iii. 8. (N. T.)*

see 1643 ἐλάω, see ἐλαύνω.

1648 Ἐλεάζαρ, ὁ, *Eleazar*, Mat. i.
15.*

see 1653 ἐλεάω (W. H., Rec. ἐλεέω), Ro.
ix. 16; Ju. 22, 23.*

see 1650 ἐλεγμός, οῦ, ὁ, *reproof*, 2 Tim.
iii. 16 (W. H.). (S.)*

1649 ἔλεγξις, εως, ἡ, *refutation, rebuke*, 2 Pet. ii. 16. (S.)*

1650 ἔλεγχος, ου, ὁ, *evident demon-
stration, proof*, Heb. xi. 1;
2 Tim. iii. 16 (not W. H.).*

1651 ἐλέγχω, ξω, *to convict, refute,
reprove*, 1 Cor. xiv. 24; Jn.
iii. 20; 1 Tim. v. 20.

1652 ἐλεεινός, ή, όν, *pitiable, miserable*, 1 Cor. xv. 19; Rev. iii.
17.*

1653 ἐλεέω, ῶ, *to have mercy on, succor* (acc.), Mat. ix. 27; Lu.
xvi. 24; pass., *to obtain mercy*,
Mat. v. 7.

1654 ἐλεημοσύνη, ης, ἡ, *mercy, pity*;
in N. T., *alms*, sometimes
plur., Mat. vi. 4; Lu. xi. 41;
Ac. ix. 36.

1655 ἐλεήμων, ον, *full of pity, merciful*, Mat. v. 7; Heb. ii. 17.*

1656 ἔλεος, ους, τό (and ου, ὁ, see Gr.
§ 32a, Wi. § 9, note 2, Bu.
22), *mercy, pity*, especially
on account of misery, Tit.
iii. 5; Mat. ix. 13.

1657 ἐλευθερία, ας, ἡ, *liberty, freedom*,
from the Mosaic yoke, as 1
Cor. x. 29; Gal. ii. 4; from
evil, as Ja. ii. 12; Ro. viii.
21; *license*, 2 Pet. ii. 19.

1658 ἐλεύθερος, α, ον, *free*, as opposed
to the condition of a slave;
delivered from obligation
(often with ἐκ, ἀπό); *at
liberty to* (inf.); once with
dat. of reference, Ro. vi.
20.

1659 ἐλευθερόω, ῶ, *to set free* (generally with acc. and ἀπό); with
modal dative, Gal. v. 1.

1660 ἔλευσις, εως, ἡ (ἔρχομαι), *a coming, an advent*, Ac. vii. 52.*

1661 ἐλεφάντινος, η, ον, *made of
ivory*, Rev. xviii. 12.*

1662 Ἐλιακείμ, ὁ (Heb.), *Eliakim*,
Mat. i. 13; Lu. iii. 30.*

**see 1667
& 3395** ἕλιγμα, ατος, τό, *a roll*, Jn. xix.
39 (W. H. for Rec. μίγμα).*

1663 Ἐλιέζερ, ὁ (Heb.), *Eliezer*, Lu.
iii. 29.*

1664 Ἐλιούδ, ὁ (Heb.), *Eliud*, Mat.
i. 14, 15.*

1665 Ἐλισάβετ, ἡ (Heb. *Elisheba*),
Elisabeth, Lu. i. 5, etc.

1666 Ἐλισσαῖος, ου, ὁ, *Elisha*, Lu.
iv. 27.*

1667 ἑλίσσω, ίξω, as εἱλίσσω, *to roll
up*, Heb. i. 12; Rev. vi. 14
(W. H.).*

1668 ἕλκος, ους, τό, *a wound, an ulcer*,
a sore, Lu. xvi. 21; Rev. xvi.
2, 11.*

1669 ἑλκόω, ῶ, *to make a sore;* pass.,
to be full of sores, Lu. xvi.
20.*

1670 ἑλκύω, σω, *to drag*, Ac. xvi. 19;
to draw, a net, Jn. xxi. 6, 11;
a sword, Jn. xviii. 10; *to
draw over, to persuade*, Jn.
vi. 44, xii. 32.* *Syn.:* σύρω
always means to drag *by
force;* ἑλκύω only *sometimes*
involves force, often not.

1670 ἕλκω (old form of foregoing),
impf. εἷλκον, Ja. ii. 6; Ac.
xxi. 30.*

1671 Ἑλλάς, άδος, ἡ, *Hellas, Greece*,
= Ἀχαΐα, Ac. xx. 2.*

1672 Ἕλλην, ηνος, ὁ, *a Greek*, as distinguished (1) from βάρβαρος,
barbarian, Ro. i. 14, and (2)

from Ἰουδαῖος, *Jew*, as Jn. vii. 35. Used for Greek proselytes to Judaism, Jn. xii. 20; Ac. xvii. 4.

1673 Ἑλληνικός, ή, όν, *Grecian*, Lu. xxiii. 38 (W. H. omit); Rev. ix. 11.*

1674 Ἑλληνίς, ίδος, ή, *a Greek* or *Gentile woman*, Mar. vii. 26; Ac. xvii. 12.*

1675 Ἑλληνιστής, οῦ, ὁ (ἑλληνίζω, to *Hellenize*, or *adopt Greek manners and language*), a *Hellenist, Grecian Jew* (R. V.); a Jew by parentage and religion, but born in a Gentile country and speaking Greek, Ac. vi. 1, ix. 29, xi. 20.*

1676 Ἑλληνιστί, adv., *in the Greek language*, Jn. xix. 20; Ac. xxi. 37.*

1677 ἐλ-λογέω (ἐν; W. H. -άω), to *charge to*, to *put to one's account*, Ro. v. 13; Philem. 18. (N. T.)*

1678 Ἐλμωδάμ (W. H. -μα-), ὁ, *Elmodam*, Lu. iii. 28.*

1679 ἐλπίζω, att. fut. ἐλπιῶ, 1st aor. ἤλπισα, to *expect* (acc. or inf., or ὅτι); to *hope for* (acc.); to *trust in* (ἐπί, dat.; ἐν, once dat. only); to *direct hope towards* (εἰς, ἐπί, acc.).

1680 ἐλπίς, ίδος, ή, *expectation, hope;* especially of the Christian *hope*. Met., (1) the *author*, as 1 Tim. i. 1; (2) the *object of hope*, as Tit. ii. 13 (in Ro. viii. 20 W. H. read ἐφ' ἐλπίδι).

1681 Ἐλύμας, α, ὁ (from Aram.), *Elymas*, Ac. xiii. 8.*

1682 ἐλωΐ (prob. Aram. = Heb. ἠλί), *my God!* Mar. xv. 34; Mat. xxvii. 46 (W. H.); see ἠλί. (N. T.)*

1683 ἐμαυτοῦ, ῆς, οῦ, *of myself*, a reflexive pron., found only in the gen., dat., and acc. cases; ἀπ' ἐμαυτοῦ, *from myself*, Jn. v. 30.

1684 ἐμ-βαίνω, 2d aor. ἐνέβην, part. ἐμβάς, to *go upon, into* (εἰς), always of entering a ship except Jn. v. 4 (W. H. omit).

1685 ἐμ-βάλλω, to *cast into*, Lu. xii. 5.*

1686 ἐμ-βάπτω, to *dip into*, Mat. xxvi. 23; Mar. xiv. 20; Jn. xiii. 26 (W. H. βάπτω).*

1687 ἐμ-βατεύω, to *enter*, to *intrude*, to *pry into*, Col. ii. 18.*

1688 **1689** ἐμ-βιβάζω, to *cause to enter*, to *put on board*, Ac. xxvii. 6.* ἐμ-βλέπω, to *direct the eyes to* anything, to *look fixedly*, to *consider*, to *know by inspection* (acc., dat., or εἰς), Mar. viii. 25; Mat. xix. 26; Ac. xxii. 11.

1690 ἐμ-βριμάομαι, ῶμαι, dep., to *snort*, to *be very angry*, Mar. xiv. 5; Jn. xi. 33, 38; to *charge sternly* (dat.), Mat. ix. 30; Mar. i. 43.*

1692 ἐμέω, ῶ, 1st aor. inf. ἐμέσαι, to *vomit forth*, Rev. iii. 16.*

1693 ἐμ-μαίνομαι, to *rage against* (dat.), Ac. xxvi. 11.*

1694 Ἐμμανουήλ, ὁ (Heb. *God with us*), *Immanuel*, a name of Christ, Mat. i. 23. (S.)*

1695 Ἐμμαούς, ή, *Emmaus*, a village a short distance from Jerusalem, Lu. xxiv. 13.*

1696 ἐμ-μένω, to *remain* or *persevere in* (dat. or ἐν), Ac. xxviii. 30 (W. H.); Gal. iii. 10.

1697 Ἐμμόρ, ὁ, *Emmor*, or *Hamor*, Ac. vii. 16.*

1699 ἐμός, ή, όν, *mine*, denoting possession, power over, authorship, right, etc. See Gr. § 336, Wi. § 22, 7, Bu. 115 sq.

see 1702 & 1703 ἐμπαιγμονή, ῆς, ή, *mockery*, 2 Pet. iii. 3 (W. H.). (N. T.)*

1701 ἐμπαιγμός, οῦ, ὁ, a *mocking, scoffing*, Heb. xi. 36. (S.)*

1702 ἐμ-παίζω, ξω, to *mock* (abs. or dat.), Mar. x. 34, xv. 20; to *delude*, Mat. ii. 16.

1703 ἐμπαίκτης, ου, ὁ, a *mocker*, 2 Pet. iii. 13; Ju. 18. (S.)*

1704 ἐμ-περιπατέω, ῶ, ήσω, to *walk about in* (ἐν), 2 Cor. vi. 16. (S.)*

1705 ἐμ-πίπλημι and -πλάω, ἐμπλήσω, ἐνέπλησα, part. pres. ἐμπιπλῶν, to *fill up*, to *satisfy*, as with food, etc. (gen.), Lu. i. 53; Ro. xv. 24.

1706 ἐμ-πίπτω, to *fall into* or *among* (εἰς), Lu. x. 36; fig., to *incur*, as condemnation or punishment, 1 Tim. iii. 6; Heb. x. 31.

1707 ἐμ-πλέκω, 2d aor. pass. ἐνεπλάκην, to *entangle, involve in*, 2 Tim. ii. 4; 2 Pet. ii. 20 (dat. of thing).*

1708 ἐμ-πλοκή, ῆς, ή, a *plaiting, braiding*, of hair, 1 Pet. iii. 3.*

1709 ἐμ-πνέω (W. H. ἐνπ-), to *breathe in, inhale* (gen.), Ac. ix. 1.*

51

*For 1691, 1698 & 1700 **see** Strong.

1710   **ἐμ-πορεύομαι,** dep., *to go about;* hence, *to trade, to traffic,* abs., Ja. iv. 13; *to use for gain* (acc.), 2 Pet. ii. 3.*

1711   **ἐμ-πορία,** ας, ἡ, *trade, merchandise,* Mat. xxii. 5.*

1712   **ἐμ-πόριον,** ου, τό, *emporium, a place for trading,* Jn. ii. 16.*

1713   **ἔμ-πορος,** ου, ὁ, *a traveler, merchant, trader,* Mat. xiii. 45; Rev. xviii. 3, 11, 15, 23.*

1714   **ἐμ-πρήθω,** σω, *to set on fire, to burn,* Mat. xxii. 7.*

1715   **ἔμ-προσθεν,** adv., *before* (ἔμπροσθεν καὶ ὄπισθεν, *in front and behind,* Rev. iv. 6); as prep. (gen.), *before,* in presence of, Mat. x. 32; *before,* in rank, Jn. i. 15, 30.

1716   **ἐμ-πτύω,** σω, *to spit upon* (dat. or εἰς), Mat. xxvii. 30; Mar. x. 34.

1717   **ἐμ-φανής,** ές, *manifest* (dat.), Ac. x. 40; Ro. x. 20.*

1718   **ἐμφανίζω,** ίσω, *to make manifest* (acc. and dat.), Jn. xiv. 22; Heb. ix. 24; *to disclose, make known* (ὅτι, or prepp. πρός, περί, etc.), Heb. xi. 14; Ac. xxv. 15.

1719   **ἔμ-φοβος,** ον, *terrified, afraid,* Ac. x. 4, xxiv. 25.

1720   **ἐμ-φυσάω,** ῶ, *to breathe upon,* acc., Jn. xx. 22.*

1721   **ἔμ-φυτος,** ον, *implanted,* Ja. i. 21.*

1722   **ἐν,** prep. gov. dat., *in,* generally as being or resting in; *within, among.* See Gr. § 295, Wi. § 48 a, Bu. 328 sq. *ἐν-* in composition has the force of *in, upon, into.* It is changed before γ, κ, ξ, and χ, into ἐγ-; before β, π, φ, ψ, and μ, into ἐμ-; and before λ, into ἐλ- (but W. H. prefer the unassimilated forms). The ν is, however, restored before the augment in verbs.

1723   **ἐν-αγκαλίζομαι,** *to take into the arms,* Mar. ix. 36, x. 16.*

1724   **ἐν-άλιος,** ον (ἅλς), *marine,* plur., *marine* animals, Ja. iii. 7.*

1725   **ἔν-αντι,** adv., as prep. with gen., *in the presence of, before,* Lu. i. 8; Ac. viii. 21 (W. H.). (S.)*

1726, 1727   **ἐν-αντίος,** α, ον, *over against, contrary,* of the wind, as Ac. xxvii. 4; *adverse, hostile,* as Ac. xxvi. 9; ἐξ ἐναντίας, *over against,* Mar. xv. 39. Neut., *ἐναντίον,* adv. as prep. with

   gen., *in the presence of,* as Lu. xx. 26; Ac. vii. 10.

1728   **ἐν-άρχομαι,** *to begin,* Gal. iii. 3; Phil. i. 6.*

see 1766

1729   **ἔνατος,** see ἔννατος.

1729   **ἐν-δεής,** ές, *in want, destitute,* Ac. iv. 34.*

1730   **ἔν-δειγμα,** ατος, τό, *proof, token,* 2 Th. i. 5.*

1731   **ἐν-δείκνυμι,** N. T. mid., *to show, to manifest,* Ro. ix. 22; 2 Tim. iv. 14.

1732   **ἔνδειξις,** εως, ἡ, *a proof, manifestation,* Ro. iii. 25, 26; 2 Cor. viii. 24; *a sign, token,* Phil. i. 28.*

1733   **ἔν-δεκα,** οἱ, αἱ, τά, *eleven;* οἱ ἔνδεκα, *the eleven, i.e.,* apostles, Mat. xxviii. 16; Ac. i. 26.

1734   **ἐν-δέκατος,** η, ον, *eleventh,* Mat. xx. 6, 9; Rev. xxi. 20.*

1735   **ἐν-δέχομαι,** dep., *to allow;* only impersonally, οὐκ ἐνδέχεται, *it is not admissible* or *possible,* Lu. xiii. 33.*

1736   **ἐν-δημέω,** ῶ, *to be at home,* 2 Cor. v. 6, 8, 9.*

1737   **ἐν-διδύσκω,** *to put on, clothe,* Mar. xv. 17 (W. H.); mid., *to clothe one's self with* (acc.), Lu. viii. 27 (not W. H.), xvi. 19; Mar. xv. 17 (W. H.); see ἐνδύω. (S.)*

1738   **ἔν-δικος,** ον, *righteous, just,* Ro. iii. 8; Heb. ii. 2.*

1739   **ἐν-δόμησις,** εως, ἡ, *the material of a building, a structure,* Rev. xxi. 18.*

1740   **ἐν-δοξάζω,** σω, N. T. pass., *to be glorified in,* 2 Th. i. 10, 12. (S.)*

1741   **ἔν-δοξος,** ον, *highly esteemed,* 1 Cor. iv. 10; *splendid, glorious,* Lu. xiii. 17; *of external appearance, splendid,* Lu. vii. 25; fig., *free from sin,* Ep. v. 27.*

1742   **ἔνδυμα,** ατος, τό, *a garment, raiment,* Mat. iii. 4, xxviii. 3. (S.)

1743   **ἐν-δυναμόω,** ῶ, *to strengthen,* Phil. iv. 13; 1 Tim. i. 12; pass., *to acquire strength, be strengthened,* Ac. ix. 22; Ro. iv. 20. (S.)

1744, •1746   **ἐν-δύνω** (2 Tim. iii. 6) and ἐνδύω, *to clothe* or *to invest with* (two accs.); mid., *to enter, insinuate one's self into* (2 Tim. iii. 6), *to put on, clothe one's self with* (acc.); often fig., *to invest with.*

1745   ἔν-δυσις, εως, ἡ, *a putting on of clothing*, 1 Pet. iii. 3.*

1747   ἐν-έδρα, ας, ἡ, *an ambush*, Ac. xxiii. 16 (W. H.), xxv. 3.*

1748   ἐν-εδρεύω, *to lie in ambush for* (acc.), Lu. xi. 54; Ac. xxiii. 21.*

★

1750   ἐν-ειλέω, ῶ, 1st aor. ἐνείλησα, *to roll up, wrap in* (acc. and dat.), Mar. xv. 46.*

1751   ἔν-ειμι, *to be in*, Lu. xi. 41, τὰ ἐνόντα, *such things as are in* (the platter, ver. 39), or *the things within your power.* For ἔνεστι, impers., see ἔνι.*

1752   ἕνεκα or ἕνεκεν, sometimes εἵνεκεν, prep. with gen., *because of, by reason of, on account of*; οὗ ἕνεκεν, *because*, Lu. iv. 18; τίνος ἕνεκεν, *for what cause?* Ac. xix. 32.

1753   ἐν-έργεια, ας, ἡ, *working, efficiency*, Ep. i. 19, 20, iv. 16; 2 Th. ii. 9.

1754   ἐν-εργέω, ῶ, *to be operative, to work*, as Gal. ii. 8; trans., *to accomplish*, as 1 Cor. xii. 11; mid., *to work, to display activity*, 2 Cor. i. 6; 1 Th. ii. 13; part., ἐνεργουμένη, Ja. v. 16 (see R. V.).

1755   ἐν-έργημα, ατος, τό, *working, effect*; plur., 1 Cor. xii. 6, 10.*

1756   ἐν-εργής, ές, *active, effectual*, 1 Cor. xvi. 9; Heb. iv. 12; Philem. 6.*

see 1764   ἐν-εστώς, perf. participle of ἐνίστημι.

1757   ἐν-ευ-λογέω, ῶ, *to bless, to confer benefits on*, Ac. iii. 25 (W. H. εὐλ-); Gal. iii. 8. (S.)*

1758   ἐν-έχω, (1) *to hold in, entangle*, only in pass. (dat.), Gal. v. 1; (2) *to set one's self against* (dat.), Mar. vi. 19; Lu. xi. 53.*

1759   ἐνθά-δε, adv., *here*, Lu. xxiv. 41; Ac. xvii. 6; *hither*, Jn. iv. 15; Ac. xxv. 17.

1760   ἐν-θυμέομαι, οῦμαι, dep. pass., *to revolve in mind, to think upon*, Mat. i. 20, ix. 4; Ac. x. 19 (W. H. διεν-).*

1761   ἐν-θύμησις, εως, ἡ, *thought, reflection*, Mat. ix. 4, xii. 25; Ac. xvii. 29; Heb. iv. 12.*

1762   ἔνι, perhaps contracted from ἔνεστι, impers., *there is in, is present*, 1 Cor. vi. 5 (W. H.); Gal. iii. 28; Col. iii. 11; Ja. i. 17.*

1763   ἐνιαυτός, οῦ, ὁ, *a year*, Ac. xi. 26; Ja. iv. 13.

1764   ἐν-ίστημι, *to place in*; in pf., plpf., and 2d aor., *to be at hand, to threaten*, 2 Th. ii. 2; 2 Tim. iii. 1; perf. part. ἐνεστηκώς, sync. ἐνεστώς, *impending*, or *present*, 1 Cor. vii. 26; Gal. i. 4; Heb. ix. 9; τὰ ἐνεστῶτα, *present things*, opp. to τὰ μέλλοντα, *things to come*, Ro. viii. 38; 1 Cor. iii. 22.*

1765   ἐν-ισχύω, *to invigorate, to strengthen*, Lu. xxii. 43 (W. H. omit); Ac. ix. 19 (see W. H.).*

1766   ἔννατος, η, ον (W. H. ἔνατος), *ninth*, Lu. xxiii. 44; Rev. xxi. 20.

1767   ἐννέα, οἱ, αἱ, τά, *nine*, Lu. xvii. 17.*

1768   ἐννενηκοντα-εννέα (W. H. as two words), *ninety-nine*, Mat. xviii. 12, 13; Lu. xv. 4, 7. (N. T.)*

1769   ἐννεός, ά, όν (W. H. ἐνεός), *dumb, speechless*, as with amazement, Ac. ix. 7.*

1770   ἐν-νεύω, *to signify by a nod* or *sign* (dat.), Lu. i. 62.*

1771   ἔν-νοια, ας, ἡ (νοῦς), *way of thinking, purpose*, Heb. iv. 12; 1 Pet. iv. 1.*

1772   ἔν-νομος, ον, *bound by the law*, 1 Cor. ix. 21; *lawful, regular*, Ac. xix. 39.*

1773   ἔν-νυχος, ον (νύξ), *in the night*, neut. as adv., Mar. i. 35 (W. H. ἔννυχα).*

1774   ἐν-οικέω, ῶ, ήσω, *to dwell in* (ἐν), Ro. viii. 11; Col. iii. 16.

1775   ἑνότης, τητος, ἡ (εἷς), *unity, unanimity*, Ep. iv. 3, 13.*

1776   ἐν-οχλέω, ῶ, *to disturb, to occasion tumult*, Heb. xii. 15; Lu. vi. 18 (W. H.).*

1777   ἔν-οχος, ον, *guilty of* (gen. of the crime, or of that which is violated), 1 Cor. xi. 27; Mar. iii. 29; *liable to* (dat. of court, gen. of punishment, εἰς of the place of punishment), Mat. v. 21, 22; Mar. xiv. 64.

1778   ἔν-ταλμα, ατος, τό, *a precept*, Mat. xv. 9; Mar. vii. 7; Col. ii. 22. (S.)*

1779   ἐν-ταφιάζω, *to prepare for burial*, as by washing, swathing, adorning, anointing the body, Mat. xxvi. 12; Jn. xix. 40.*

1780   ἐνταφιασμός, οῦ, ὁ, *preparation*

★For 1749 see Strong.

of a body for burial, Mar. xiv.
8, Jn. xii. 7. (N. T.)*

1781 ἐν-τέλλω, in N. T. only mid.
and pass.; fut. mid. ἐντελοῦ-
μαι; perf., ἐντέταλμαι, to
command, to enjoin (dat. of
pers., or πρός with acc.), Ac.
i. 2; Heb. ix 20.

1782 ἐντεῦθεν, adv., hence; from this
place or cause; repeated Jn.
xix. 18, on this side and that.

1783 ἔν-τευξις, εως, ἡ, prayer, inter-
cession, 1 Tim. ii. 1, iv. 5.*
Syn.: see αἴτημα.

1784 ἔν-τιμος, ον, held in honor; precious, highly esteemed, Lu.
vii. 2, xiv. 8; Phil. ii. 29; 1
Pet. ii. 4, 6.*

1785 ἐντολή, ῆς, ἡ, a command or
prohibition: of God's commands, 1 Cor. vii. 19; Christ's
precepts or teachings, 1 Cor.
xiv. 37; 1 Tim. vi. 14; tradi-
tions of the Rabbis, Tit. i.
14; αἱ ἐντολαί, the command-
ments, i.e., the ten.

1786 ἐν-τόπιος, ον, ὁ (prop. adj.), a
resident, Ac. xxi. 12.*

1787 ἐντός, adv. as prep., with gen.,
within, Lu. xvii. 21; τὸ ἐντός,
the inside, Mat. xxiii. 26.*

1788 ἐν-τρέπω, ψω, 2d fut. pass., ἐν-
τραπήσομαι; 2d aor. pass.,
ἐνετράπην; to put to shame,
as 1 Cor. iv. 14; Tit. ii. 8;
mid., to reverence, as Mat.
xxi. 37.

1789 ἐν-τρέφω, to nourish in (dat.);
pass., fig., to be educated in,
1 Tim. iv. 6.*

1790 ἔν-τρομος, ον, trembling through
fear, Ac. vii. 32, xvi. 29;
Heb. xii. 21.*

1791 ἐν-τροπή, ῆς, η, shame, 1 Cor.
vi. 5, xv. 34.* Syn.: see
αἰδώς.

1792 ἐν-τρυφάω, ῶ, to live luxuriously, to revel (with ἐν), 2 Pet.
ii. 13.*

1793 ἐν-τυγχάνω, to meet with, to address, Ac. xxv. 24; with ὑπέρ
(gen.), to intercede for, Ro.
viii. 27, 34; Heb. vii. 25;
with κατά (gen.), to plead
against, Ro. xi. 2.*

1794 ἐν-τυλίσσω, ξω, to wrap in, to
wrap up, Mat. xxvii. 59; Lu.
xxiii. 53; Jn. xx. 7.*

1795 ἐν-τυπόω, ῶ, to engrave, 2 Cor.
iii. 7.*

1796 ἐν-υβρίζω, σω, to treat contempt-
uously, Heb. x. 29.*

1797 ἐν-υπνιάζομαι, dep. pass., to

1798

1799

dream (cognate acc.), Ac.
ii. 17; to conceive impure
thoughts, Ju. 8.*

ἐν-ύπνιον, ον, τό, a dream, Ac.
ii. 17.*

ἐνώπιον (neut. of ἐνώπιος, from
ἐν ὠπί, in view), as prep.,
with gen., before, in sight or
presence of, Lu. i. 17; Rev.
iii. 9; ἐνώπιον τοῦ θεοῦ, in the
sight of God, Ro. xiv. 22;
used in adjuration, 1 Tim. v.
21; χάρις ἐνώπιον τοῦ θεοῦ
(Ac. vii. 4), favor with God.

1800   Ἐνώς, ὁ, Enos, Lu. iii. 38.*
1801   ἐν-ωτίζομαι, dep. mid. (ἐν ὠτίοις,
in the ears), to listen to, Ac.
ii. 14. (S.)*

1802   Ἐνώχ, ὁ, Enoch, Lu. iii. 37;
Ju. 14.*

see 1537 ἐξ, prep., see ἐκ.
1803   ἔξ, οἱ, αἱ, τά, card. num., six.
1804   ἐξ-αγγέλλω, to declare abroad,
celebrate, 1 Pet. ii. 9.*

1805   ἐξ-αγοράζω, to redeem, Gal. iii.
13 (ἐκ), iv. 5; τὸν καιρόν, to
buy up, redeem the opportunity from being lost, Ep. v. 16;
Col. iv. 5.*

1806   ἐξ-άγω, 2d aor. ἐξήγαγον, to
lead out (with ἔξω, ἐκ, εἰς).

1807   ἐξ-αιρέω, ῶ (see Gr. § 103, 1,
Wi. § 15, Bu. 53), to take out,
pluck out, Mat. v. 29, xviii.
9; mid., to rescue, deliver,
Ac. vii. 10, 34, xii. 11, xxiii.
27, xxvi. 17; Gal. i. 4.*

1808   ἐξ-αίρω (see Gr. § 92), to lift up;
to remove, 1 Cor. v. 2 (W. H.
αἴρω), 13.*

1809   ἐξ-αιτέω, ῶ, N. T., mid., to demand of; to ask for, Lu.
xxii. 31.*

1810   ἐξ-αίφνης (W. H. ἐξέφ-, except
in Ac. xxii. 6), adv., suddenly, unexpectedly, Mar. xiii. 36.

1811   ἐξ-ακολουθέω, ῶ, to follow after,
to imitate, 2 Pet. i. 16, ii. 2,
15.*

1812   ἐξακόσιοι, αι, α, six hundred,
Rev. xiii. 18, xiv. 20.*

1813   ἐξ-αλείφω, to wipe out, obliterate,
Rev. iii. 5; Col. ii. 14; Ac.
iii. 19; to wipe away (ἀπό or
ἐκ), Rev. vii. 17, xxi. 4.*

1814   ἐξ-άλλομαι, to leap up, Ac. iii. 8.*
1815   ἐξ-ανά-στασις, εως, ἡ, a resurrection, Phil. iii. 11 (followed
by ἐκ, W. H.).*

1816   ἐξ-ανα-τέλλω, to spring up, as
plants or corn, Mat. xiii. 5
Mar. iv. 5.*

1817   ἐξ-αν-ίστημι, (1) trans., to raise

up offspring, Mar. xii. 19; Lu. xx. 28; (2) 2d aor. intrans., *to rise up*, Ac. xv. 5.*

1818   ἐξ-απατάω, ῶ, *to deceive thoroughly*, Ro. vii. 11 ; 2 Th. ii. 3.

1819   ἐξάπινα, adv. (= ἐξαίφνης), *suddenly*, Mar. ix. 8. (S.)*

1820   ἐξ-απορέομαι, οῦμαι, dep., *to be utterly without resource, to be in despair*, 2 Cor. i. 8, iv. 8.*

1821   ἐξ-απο-στέλλω, *to send forth, send away*, Ac. vii. 12, xi. 12, xvii. 14.

1822   ἐξ-αρτίζω, (1) *to completely furnish* (πρός, acc.), 2 Tim. iii. 17; (2) *to complete*, Ac. xxi. 5.*

1823   ἐξ-αστράπτω, *to shine*, as lightning; of raiment, Lu. ix. 29. (S.)*

1824   ἐξ-αυτῆς, adv. (sc. ὥρας), *from that very time, instantly*, as Mar. vi. 25; Ac. x. 33.

1825   ἐξ-εγείρω, *to raise up*, Ro. ix. 17 ; 1 Cor. vi. 14.*

1826   ἔξ-ειμι (εἶμι, see Gr. § 111, Bu. 50), *to go out*, Ac. xiii. 42, xvii. 15, xx. 7, xxvii. 43.*

see 1832   ἔξ-ειμι (εἰμί), see ἔξεστι.

1827   ἐξ-ελέγχω, *to convict, to rebuke sternly, to punish*, Ju. 15 (W. H. ἐλέγχω).*

1828   ἐξ-έλκω, *to draw out* from the right way, Ja. i. 14.*

1829   ἐξ-έραμα, ατος, τό, *vomit*, 2 Pet. ii. 22.*

1830   ἐξερευνάω (W. H. -ραν-), ῶ, *to search diligently*, 1 Pet. i. 10.*

1831   ἐξ-έρχομαι (see Gr. § 103, 2, Wi. p. 33, § 15, Bu. 58), *to go* or *to come out of* (with gen. or ἐκ, ἀπό, ἔξω, παρά) ; *to go away, to depart, to issue* or *to spring from ; to go forth ;* of a rumor, *to be divulged* or *spread abroad; to emanate*, as thoughts from the heart, healing power from the Savior ; *to go out, i.e.*, vanish, as expiring hope, Ac. xvi. 19.

1832   ἔξ-εστι, part. neut. ἐξόν (impers. from ἔξειμι), *it is lawful*, as Mat. xiv. 4; *it is becoming*, as Ac. xvi. 21 ; *it is possible*, as Mat. xx. 15. The part. is used in the same sense, with or without subst. verb, Mat. xii. 4; 2 Cor. xii. 4 (dat. and inf.).

1833   ἐξ-ετάζω, *to search out, to examine strictly*, Mat. ii. 8, x. 11 ; Jn. xxi. 12.*

1834   ἐξ-ηγέομαι, οῦμαι, dep. mid., *to narrate fully*, as Lu. xxiv. 35; *to declare*, as a teacher, as Jn. i. 18.

1835   ἐξήκοντα, οἱ, αἱ, τά, *sixty*.

1836   ἑξῆς, adv. (ἔχω), *next in order*, only in the phrase τῇ ἑξῆς (sc. ἡμέρᾳ), *on the next day* (ἡμέρᾳ is expressed, Lu. ix. 37).

1837   ἐξ-ηχέω, ῶ, N. T. only in pass., *to be sounded forth, promulgated widely*, 1 Th. i. 8.*

1838   ἕξις, εως, ἡ (ἔχω), *habit, use*, Heb. v. 14.*

1839   ἐξ-ίστημι, -ιστάω and -ιστάνω (see Gr. § 107, Wi. § 14, 1, Bu. 44 sq.), *to displace;* (1) trans., *to astonish*, Lu. xxiv. 22; Ac. viii. 9, 11 ; (2) 2d aor., perf. and mid., intrans., *to be astonished*, Mat. xii. 23 ; *to be insane*, 2 Cor. v. 13.

1840   ἐξ-ισχύω, *to be perfectly able*, Ep. iii. 18.*

1841   ἔξ-οδος, ον, ἡ, *an exit, departure*, Heb. xi. 22; *departure*, as from life, Lu. ix. 31 ; 2 Pet. i. 15.*

1842   ἐξ-ολοθρεύω, *to destroy utterly*, Ac. iii. 23. (S.)*

1843   ἐξ-ομολογέω, ῶ, *to confess fully, to make acknowledgment of*, as of sins, etc.; in mid., *to acknowledge benefits conferred, to praise* (with dat.). Once, *to promise*, Lu. xxii. 6. (S.)

1844   ἐξ-ορκίζω, *to adjure, put to oath*, Mat. xxvi. 63.*

1845   ἐξ-ορκιστής, οῦ, ὁ, *an exorcist*, one who expels demons by conjuration, Ac. xix. 13.*

1846   ἐξ-ορύσσω, ξω, *to dig out*, Gal. iv. 15; *to dig through*, Mar. ii. 4.*

see 1848   ἐξ-ουδενέω = ἐξουθενέω, ῶ (οὐδείς), Mar. ix. 12 (W. H.).*

1847   ἐξ-ουδενόω, ῶ = preceding, Mar. ix. 12 (Rec.).*

1848   ἐξουθενέω, ῶ, *to make of no account, to despise utterly*, Lu. xviii. 9; Gal. iv. 14; perf. pass. part. ἐξουθενημένος, *contemned, despised*, 1 Cor. i. 28, vi. 4. (S.)

1849   ἐξ-ουσία, ας, ἡ (ἔξεστι), (1) *power, ability*, as Jn. xix. 11 ; (2) *liberty, license, privilege, right*, as Ro. ix. 21; (3) *commission, authority*, as Mat. xxi. 23; (4) αἱ ἐξουσίαι, *the powers, i.e., rulers, magis-*

55

trates, Lu. xii. 11; *angels,
good and bad*, Ep. i. 21, vi.
12. In 1 Cor. xi. 10, ἐξουσίαν,
*a sign of the authority of a
husband over his wife, i.e.,
the veil.*

1850   ἐξ-ουσιάζω, *to exercise authority
over* (gen.), Lu. xxii. 25; 1
Cor. vii. 4; pass., *to be under
the power of* (ὑπό), 1 Cor. vi.
12.*

1851   ἐξ-οχή, ῆς, ἡ, *eminence, distinction;* only in the phrase κατ'
ἐξοχήν, *by way of distinction,*
Ac. xxv. 23 (Gr. § 300β,
5).*

1852   ἐξ-υπνίζω, σω, *to wake from
sleep,* Jn. xi. 11. (S.)*

1853   ἔξ-υπνος, ον, *roused out of sleep,*
Ac. xvi. 27.*

1854   ἔξω, adv., *abs.,* or as prep. with
gen., *without, outside;* οἱ ἔξω,
those without, as Mar. iv. 11;
1 Cor. v. 12, 13. Used often
after verbs of motion compounded with ἐκ.

1855   ἔξωθεν, adv. of place, *from without;* τὸ ἔξωθεν, *the outside,* as
Lu. xi. 39; οἱ ἔξωθεν, *those
from without,* as 1 Tim. iii.
7; as prep. gen., Mar. vii.
15; Rev. xi. 2.

1856   ἐξ-ωθέω, ῶ, *to drive out, expel,*
Ac. vii. 45; *to propel,* as a
vessel, Ac. xxvii. 39 (not W.
H. text).*

1857   ἐξώτερος, α, ον (comp. of ἔξω),
outer, in the phrase "outer
darkness," Mat. viii. 12, xxii.
13, xxv. 30. (S.)*

see 1503   ἔοικα, see εἴκω.

1858   ἑορτάζω, *to keep* or *celebrate a
feast,* 1 Cor. v. 8.*

1859   ἑορτή, ῆς, ἡ, *a feast, a festival;*
used of Jewish feasts, es-
pecially of the Passover, as
Lu. ii. 41, xxii. 1.

1860   ἐπ-αγγελία, ας, ἡ, (1) *a promise,*
as 2 Cor. i. 20; Ac. xxiii. 21,
generally plur.; *the promises,*
specially, *e.g.,* to Abraham,
or those of the Gospel, as 2
Tim. i. 1; (2) met., *the thing
promised,* as Ac. ii. 33; Heb.
xi. 13, 33, 39.

1861   ἐπ-αγγέλλω, mid. in N. T., except pass., Gal. iii. 19, (1) *to
promise,* with dat., or acc.
and dat., or inf., once cognate acc., 1 Jn. ii. 25; (2) *to
make profession* or *avowal
of* (acc.), 1 Tim. ii. 10, vi.
21.

1862   ἐπ-άγγελμα, ατος, τό, *a promise,*
2 Pet. i. 4, iii. 13.*

1863   ἐπ-άγω, *to bring upon,* Ac. v.
28; 2 Pet. ii. 1, 5.*

1864   ἐπ-αγωνίζομαι, *to contend earnestly for* (dat.), Ju. 3.*

1865   ἐπ-αθροίζω, pass., *to gather together,* Lu. xi. 29.*

1866   Ἐπ-αίνετος, ον, ὁ, *Epænetus,*
Ro. xvi. 5.*

1867   ἐπ-αινέω, ῶ, ἔσω, 1st aor. ἐπῄ-
νεσα, *to commend, to praise,*
Lu. xvi. 8; Ro. xv. 11; 1 Cor.
xi. 2, 17, 22.*

1868   ἔπ-αινος, ον, ὁ, *commendation,
praise,* Ro. ii. 29; Ep. i. 6,
12, 14; Phil. i. 11.

1869   ἐπ-αίρω (see Gr. § 92), *to raise
up,* as hoisting a sail, Ac.
xxvii. 40; *to lift up,* as the
eyes, the hands in prayer,
the head in courage, the
heel against, or in opposition; pass., *to be lifted up*
2 Cor. xi. 20, of the ascen-
sion of Christ, Ac. i. 9.

1870   ἐπ-αισχύνομαι, *to be ashamed,*
abs., 2 Tim. i. 12; *to be a-
shamed of* (acc. or ἐπί, dat.),
Mar. viii. 38; Ro. vi. 21.

1871   ἐπ-αιτέω, ῶ, *to beg, to ask alms,*
Lu. xvi. 3, xviii. 35 (W. H.).*

1872   ἐπ-ακολουθέω, ῶ, *to follow after*
(dat.); fig., 1 Tim. v. 10, 24;
1 Pet. ii. 21; Mar. xvi. 20
(see W. H.).*

1873   ἐπ-ακούω, *to hearken to favor-
ably* (gen. pers.), 2 Cor. vi.
2.*

1874   ἐπ-ακροάομαι, ῶμαι, *to hear,
listen to* (gen. pers.), Ac. xvi.
25.*

1875   ἐπάν, conj. (ἐπεὶ ἄν), *after, when*
(subj.), Mat. ii. 8; Lu. xi. 22,
34.*

1876   ἐπ-άναγκες, adv., *necessarily*
(with art.), Ac. xv. 28.*

1877   ἐπ-αν-άγω, trans., *to put* a vessel
out to sea, Lu. v. 3, 4; in-
trans., *to return,* Mat. xxi.
18.*

1878   ἐν-ανα-μιμνῄσκω, *to remind* one
again (acc.), Ro. xv. 15.*

1879   ἐπ-ανα-παύομαι, *to rest upon*
(ἐπί, acc.), Lu. x. 6; *to rely,
to trust in* (dat.), Ro. ii. 17.
(S.)*

1880   ἐπ-αν-έρχομαι, *to come back
again,* Lu. x. 35, xix. 15.*

1881   ἐπ-αν-ίστημι, N. T. mid., *to rise
up against* (ἐπί, acc.), Mat.
x. 21; Mar. xiii. 12.*

1882   ἐπ-αν-όρθωσις, εως, ἡ, *correc-*

tion, reformation, 2 Tim. iii. 16.*

1883 ἐπ-άνω, adv., *also used as prep.* gen., *above, upon; more than,* in price or number; *superior to,* in authority.

see 1944 ἐπ-άρατος, ον, *accursed,* Jn. vii. 49 (W. H.).*

1884 ἐπ-αρκέω, ῶ, ἐσω, *to aid, to relieve* (dat.), 1 Tim. v. 10, 16.*

1885 ἐπ-αρχία, ας, ἡ, *a province,* a region subject to a prefect, Ac. xxiii. 34, xxv. 1.*

1886 ἔπ-αυλις, εως, ἡ, *a dwelling,* Ac. i. 20.*

1887 ἐπ-αύριον, adv., *on the morrow,* τῇ ἐπαύριον (ἡμέρᾳ), *on the next day,* Mar. xi. 12. (S.)

1888;
see Strong ἐπ-αυτο-φώρῳ = ἐπ᾿ αὐτὸ-φώρῳ.

1889 ----- Ἐπαφρᾶς, ᾶ, ὁ, *Epaphras of* Colossæ, Col. i. 7, iv. 12; Philem. 23.*

1890 ἐπ-αφρίζω, *to foam up* or *out* (acc.), Ju. 13.*

1891 Ἐπαφρόδιτος, ου, ὁ, *Epaphroditus,* a Macedonian, Phil. ii. 25, iv. 18.*

1892 ἐπ-εγείρω, *to raise up, to excite against* (ἐπί, acc., or κατά, gen.), Ac. xiii. 50, xiv. 2.*

1893 ἐπεί, conj., (1) *of time, after,* only Lu. vii. 1 (W. H. ἐπειδή); (2) *of reason, since, because, seeing that,* Lu. i. 34; Jn. xiii. 29.

1894 ἐπει-δή, conj., *since, inasmuch as,* Lu. xi. 6; Phil. ii. 26; *of time, after that,* only Lu. vii. 1 (W. H.).

1895 ἐπει-δή-περ, conj., *since verily, forasmuch as,* Lu. i. 1.*

1896 ἐπ-εῖδον, see ἐφοράω.

see 1966 ἔπ-ειμι (εἶμι, Gr. § 111, Bu. 50), *to come after, to follow;* only in part., ἐπιών, οὖσα, ὄν, *following,* Ac. vii. 26, xxiii. 11; τῇ ἐπιούσῃ (sc. ἡμέρᾳ), *on the following day,* Ac. xvi. 11, xx. 15, xxi. 18.*

1897 ἐπεί-περ, conj., *since indeed,* Ro. iii. 30 (W. H. εἴπερ).*

1898 ἐπ-εισ-αγωγή, ῆς, ἡ, *a bringing in besides,* Heb. vii. 19.*

1899 ἔπ-ειτα, adv., *thereupon, thereafter;* marking succession of time, as Gal. i. 18; also of order, as 1 Cor. xv. 46; 1 Th. iv. 17.

1900 ἐπ-έκεινα (sc. μέρη), adv. with gen., *beyond,* Ac. vii. 43.*

1901 ἐπ-εκ-τείνω, in mid., *to stretch forward to* (dat.), Phil. iii. 14.*

●1903 ἐπενδύτης, ου, ὁ, *an upper garment,* Jn. xxi. 7.*

1902 ἐπ-εν-δύω, in mid., *to put on over,* as an upper garment, 2 Cor. v. 2, 4.*

1904 ἐπ-έρχομαι, *to come on, approach, overtake, impend,* Ep. ii. 7; Ac. viii. 24; *to attack,* Lu. xi. 22; τὰ ἐπερχόμενα, *the things that are coming on* (dat.), Lu. xxi. 26.

1905 ἐπ-ερωτάω, ῶ, (1) *to interrogate, to question* (two accs., or acc. and περί, gen., or with εἰ, τίς, etc.), Mat. xii. 10; Lu. ii. 46; Ac. xxiii. 34; *to inquire after* God, Ro. x. 20; (2) *to demand of* (acc. and inf.), Mat. xvi. 1.

1906 ἐπ-ερώτημα, ατος, τό, probably *inquiry,* or *earnest desire,* 1 Pet. iii. 21; see R. V.*

1907 ἐπ-έχω, (1) *to apply* (the mind) *to* (dat.), *give attention to,* Lu. xiv. 7; Ac. iii. 5; 1 Tim. iv. 16; (2) *to hold out, to exhibit,* Phil. ii. 16; (3) *to delay, tarry,* Ac. xix. 22.*

1908 ἐπηρεάζω, *to insult, to treat abusively,* Mat. v. 44 (not W. H.); Lu. vi. 28; *to accuse falsely* (acc. of charge), 1 Pet. iii. 16.*

1909 ἐπί, a preposition governing gen., dat., or acc.; general signification, *upon.* For its various applications, see Gr. § 305, Wi. §§ 47g, 48c, 49l, 52, 4, 7), Bu. 336 sq. ἐπί-, in composition, signifies *motion upon, towards,* or *against; rest on, over,* or *at; addition, succession, repetition, renewal;* and it is often intensive.

1910 ἐπι-βαίνω, *to go upon* a ship, *to mount* a horse or ass, *to come to* or *into* a country (ἐπί, acc., εἰς, or simple dat.), Mat. xxi. 5; Ac. xx. 18, xxi. 2, 4 (W. H.), 6 (W. H. ἐμβ-), xxv. 1, xxvii. 2.*

1911 ἐπι-βάλλω, (1) trans., *to cast upon,* as Mar. xi. 7; *to put on,* as a patch on a garment, Lu. v. 36; *to lay upon,* Lu. xx. 19; Jn. vii. 30; (2) intrans., *to rush upon,* Mar. iv. 37; *to fix the mind steadfastly on* (dat.), Mar. xiv. 72; (3) part., ἐπιβάλλων, *falling to* his share, Lu. xv. 12.

1912 ἐπι-βαρέω, ῶ, *to burden;* fig., ?

Cor. ii. 5; 1 Th. ii. 9; 2 Th.
iii. 8.*

1913 **ἐπι-βιβάζω**, *to cause to mount,
to place upon*, Lu. x. 34, xix.
35; Ac. xxiii. 24.*

1914 **ἐπι-βλέπω**, *to look upon* with
favor (with ἐπί), Lu. i. 48,
ix. 38; Ja. ii. 3.*

1915 **ἐπί-βλημα**, ατος, τό, *a patch* on
a garment, Mat. ix. 16; Mar.
ii. 21; Lu. v. 36.*

1916 **ἐπι-βοάω**, ῶ, *to cry out*, Ac. xxv.
24 (W. H. βοάω).*

1917 **ἐπι-βουλή**, ῆς, ἡ, *a design a-
gainst, a plot*, Ac. ix. 24, xx.
3, 19 (plur.), xxiii. 30.*

1918 **ἐπι-γαμβρεύω**, *to marry a de-
ceased brother's wife* (acc.),
Mat. xxii. 24. (S.)*

1919 **ἐπί-γειος**, ον, *earthly, belonging
to the earth*, 2 Cor. v. 1; Phil.
ii. 10; τὰ ἐπίγεια, *earthly
things*, Phil. iii. 19.

1920 **ἐπι-γίνομαι**, *to arise, spring up,*
as a wind, Ac. xxviii. 13.*

1921 **ἐπι-γινώσκω**, (1) *to know clearly, understand, discern;* (2)
to acknowledge; (3) *to recognize;* (4) *to learn* (ὅτι), *become acquainted with* (2cc.).

1922 **ἐπί-γνωσις**, εως, ἡ, *accurate
knowledge*, Ro. x. 2; Ep. i.
17; Heb. x. 26. *Syn.:* see
γνῶσις.

1923 **ἐπι-γραφή**, ῆς, ἡ, *an inscription,
a title*, as Lu. xx. 24, xxiii. 38.

1924 **ἐπι-γράφω**, ψω, *to inscribe, write
upon*, as Mar. xv. 26; Rev.
xxi. 12.

1925 **ἐπι-δείκνυμι** (see Gr. § 114, Bu.
45), (1) *to show, exhibit*, Mat.
xxiv. 1; Lu. xvii. 14; (2) *to
demonstrate, prove* by argument, Ac. xviii. 28; Heb. vi.
17.

1926 **ἐπι-δέχομαι**, *to receive hospitably*, 3 Jn. 10; *to accept, ad-
mit*, 3 Jn. 9.*

1927 **ἐπι-δημέω**, ῶ, *to sojourn*, as
foreigners in a country, Ac.
ii. 10, xvii. 21.*

1928 **ἐπι-δια-τάσσομαι**, *to ordain besides*, Gal. iii. 15. (N.T.)*

1929 **ἐπι-δίδωμι**, *to deliver, to give
up* (acc. and dat.), as Mat.
vii. 9; Ac. xv. 30; *to give
way* to the wind, Ac. xxvii.
15.

1930 **ἐπι-δι-ορθόω**, *to set in order besides*, Tit. i. 5.*

1931 **ἐπι-δύω**, *to set*, as the sun, Ep.
iv. 26.*

1932 **ἐπιείκεια**, ας, ἡ, *clemency, gen-*

tleness, Ac. xxiv. 4; 2 Cor.
x. 1.*

1933 **ἐπι-εικής**, ές, *gentle, mild*, Phil.
iv. 5; 1 Tim. iii. 3; Tit. iii.
2; Ja. iii. 17; 1 Pet. ii.
18.*

1934 **ἐπι-ζητέω**, ῶ, *to seek for, search
for*, Ac. xii. 19; *to desire*,
Mat. vi. 32; Ac. xiii. 7; *to
demand*, Mat. xii. 39, xvi.
4.

1935 **ἐπι-θανάτιος**, ον, *condemned to
death*, 1 Cor. iv. 9.*

1936 **ἐπί-θεσις**, εως, ἡ, *a laying on* of
hands, Ac. viii. 18; 1 Tim.
iv. 14; 2 Tim. i. 6; Heb. vi.
2.*

1937 **ἐπι-θυμέω**, ῶ, *to long for, to
covet, to lust after*, Ja. iv. 2;
Ro. vii. 7; Ac. xx. 33. (On
Lu. xxii. 15, see Gr. § 280*b*,
Wi. § 54, 3, Bu. 184.)

1938 **ἐπι-θυμητής**, οῦ, ὁ, *an eager de-
sirer of*, 1 Cor. x. 6.*

1939 **ἐπι-θυμία**, ας, ἡ, *desire, eagerness for*, 1 Th. ii. 17; gener-
ally in a bad sense, *inordi-
nate desire, lust, cupidity*, Ja.
i. 14, 15; 2 Pet. ii. 10.

1940 **ἐπι-καθίζω**, *to sit upon*, Mat.
xxi. 7.*

1941 **ἐπι-καλέω**, ῶ, ἔσω, *to call upon,
to call by name, to invoke* in
prayer, Ac. vii. 59 (abs.);
Ro. x. 12, 14 (acc.); mid.,
to appeal to (acc.), Ac. xxv.
11; pass., *to be called* or *sur-
named*, Lu. xxii. 3; Ac. xv.
17.

1942 **ἐπι-κάλυμμα**, ατος, τό, *a covering, a cloak, a pretext*, 1 Pet.
ii. 16.*

1943 **ἐπι-καλύπτω**, *to cover over*, of
sins, *i.e.*, to pardon, Ro. iv.
7 (from S.).*

1944 **ἐπι-κατ-άρατος**, ον, *accursed,
doomed to punishment* or *destruction*, Jn. vii. 49 (W. H.
ἐπάρατος); Gal. iii. 10, 13
(from S.).*

1945 **ἐπί-κειμαι**, *to lie upon* (dat.),
Jn. xi. 38, xxi. 9; so *to press
upon*, as the multitude upon
Christ, Lu. v. 1; as a tempest on a ship, Ac. xxvii. 20;
fig., *to be laid on*, as necessity,
1 Cor. ix. 16; *to be laid* or
imposed upon, as by a law,
Heb. ix. 10; *to be urgent with
entreaties*, Lu. xxiii. 23.*

1946 **Ἐπικούρειος**, ου, ὁ, *an Epicu-
rean*, a follower of Epicurus,
Ac. xvii. 18.*

58

1947 ἐπι-κουρία, ας, ἡ (κοῦρος, *help*),
help, *aid*, Ac. xxvi. 22.*

1948 ἐπι-κρίνω, *to decree, to give sentence* (acc. and inf.), Lu.
xxiii. 24.*

1949 ἐπι-λαμβάνω, N. T. mid., *to
take hold of* (gen.), in kindness, as Lu. ix. 47; Ac. ix.
27; Heb. ii. 16; *to seize*, as a
prisoner, Ac. xxi. 30, 33;
met., *to lay hold of*, so as to
possess, 1 Tim. vi. 12, 19.

1950 ἐπι-λανθάνομαι, dep., *to forget,
neglect* (inf., gen. or acc.),
Mat. xvi. 5; Heb. vi. 10;
part. perf. pass., ἐπιλελησμένος, *forgotten*, Lu. xii. 6.

1951 ἐπι-λέγω, in pass., *to be named*,
Jn. v. 2; mid., *to choose*, Ac.
xv. 40.*

1952 ἐπι-λείπω, λείψω, *not to suffice,
to fail*, Heb. xi. 32.*

see 621 ἐπι-λείχω, *to lick over*, Lu. xvi.
21 (W. H.). (N. T.)*

1953 ἐπι-λησμονή, ῆς, ἡ, *forgetfulness*, Ja. i. 25; see Gr. § 257.
(Ap.)*

1954 ἐπί-λοιπος, ον, *remaining over*,
1 Pet. iv. 2.*

1955 ἐπί-λυσις, εως, ἡ, *an unloosing,
interpretation*, 2 Pet. i. 20.
(See ἴδιος.)*

1956 ἐπι-λύω, *to explain, interpret*,
Mar. iv. 34; *to decide*, as a debated question, Ac. xix. 39.*

1957 ἐπι-μαρτυρέω, ῶ, *to testify earnestly*, 1 Pet. v. 12.*

1958 ἐπι-μέλεια, ας, ἡ, *care, attention*,
Ac. xxvii. 3.*

1959 ἐπι-μέλομαι and ἔομαι, οῦμαι,
fut. ήσομαι, *to take care of*
(gen.), Lu. x. 34, 35; 1 Tim.
iii. 5.*

1960 ἐπι-μελῶς, adv., *carefully, diligently*, Lu. xv. 8.*

1961 ἐπι-μένω, μενῶ, (1) *to remain,
continue*, 1 Cor. xvi. 8; Gal.
i. 18; (2) met., *to be constant,
to persevere* (dat.), Ro. vi. 1;
1 Tim. iv. 16.

1962 ἐπι-νεύω, *to nod to, to assent*,
Ac. xviii. 20.*

1963 ἐπί-νοια, ας, ἡ, *thought, purpose*,
Ac. viii. 22.*

1964 ἐπι-ορκέω, ῶ, ήσω, *to swear
falsely*, Mat. v. 33.*

1965 ἐπί-ορκος, ον, *perjured*, 1 Tim.
i. 10.*

*
1967 ἐπιούσιος, ον, probably from
ἐπιοῦσα (ἔπειμι), *for the morrow, i.e., necessary* or *sufficient*, Mat. vi. 11; Lu. xi. 3.
(N. T.)*

1968 ἐπι-πίπτω, *to fall upon* (ἐπί,
acc.), *rush upon*, Mar. iii. 10
(dat.); fig., *to come upon* (dat.,
or ἐπί, acc. or dat.), as an
emotion, etc., Lu. i. 12; Ac.
viii. 16.

1969 ἐπι-πλήσσω, *to rebuke, to chide*,
** 1 Tim. v. 1.*

1971 ἐπι-ποθέω, ῶ, *to desire earnestly, to long for* or *after* (inf.
or acc.), as 2 Cor v. 2; *to
lust*, abs., Ja. iv. 5.

1972 ἐπι-πόθησις, εως, ἡ, *longing*, 2
Cor. vii. 7, 11. (N. T.)*

1973 ἐπι-πόθητος, ον, *longed for*,
Phil. iv. 1. (N. T.)*

1974 ἐπι-ποθία, ας, ἡ, like ἐπιπόθησις,
longing, Ro. xv. 23. (N. T.)*

1975 ἐπι-πορεύομαι, dep., mid., *to
journey to* (πρός), Lu. viii.
4.*

1976 ἐπι-ρράπτω, *to sew to*, or *upon*,
Mar. ii. 21 (ἐπί, dat.). (N.
T.)*

1977 ἐπι-ρρίπτω, *to cast*, or *throw
upon*, Lu. xix. 35; of care
cast upon God, 1 Pet. v. 7
(ἐπί, acc.).*

1978 ἐπί-σημος, ον, *remarkable, distinguished*, in either a bad
or good sense, Mat. xxvii.
16; Ro. xvi. 7.*

1979 ἐπι-σιτισμός, οῦ, ὁ, *food, provisions*, Lu. ix. 12.*

1980 ἐπι-σκέπτομαι, σκέψομαι, dep.,
to look upon, to visit, as Ac.
vii. 23; Mat. xxv. 36, 43; of
God, Ac. xv. 14; *to look out,
to select*, Ac. vi. 3.

see 643 ἐπι-σκευάζομαι, see ἀποσκ-.

1981 ἐπι-σκηνόω, ῶ, *to fix a tent
upon, to dwell*, or *remain on*
(ἐπί, acc.), 2 Cor. xii. 9.*

1982 ἐπι-σκιάζω, άσω, *to overshadow*
(acc. or dat.), Mat. xvii. 5;
Mar. ix. 7; Lu. i. 35, ix. 34;
Ac. v. 15.*

1983 ἐπι-σκοπέω, ῶ, *to act as* ἐπίσκοπος, *to oversee, to care for*,
1 Pet. v. 2 (W. H. omit); μή,
lest, Heb. xii. 15.*

1984 ἐπι-σκοπή, ῆς, ἡ, (1) *visitation*
for kind and gracious purposes, Lu. xix. 44; 1 Pet. ii.
12; (2) *office, charge*, Ac. i. 20
(from S.); (3) *the office of a
bishop*, 1 Tim. iii. 1. (S.)*

1985 ἐπί-σκοπος, ον, ὁ, (1) *one who
inspects*, or *superintends*, of
Christ, 1 Pet. ii. 25; (2) *an
overseer of a church*, bishop,
Ac. xx. 28; Phil. i. 1; 1 Tim.
iii. 2; Tit. i. 7.*

*For 1966 see Strong.

** For 1970 see Strong.

1986	ἐπι-σπάω, ῶ, to become uncircumcised, 1 Cor. vii. 18.*
see 4687	ἐπι-σπείρω, to sow in addition, Mat. xiii. 25 (W. H.).*
1987	ἐπ-ίσταμαι, dep., to know well, to understand (acc.), to know, with ὅτι, ὡς, etc.
see 1999	ἐπί-στασις, εως, ἡ (W. H.), approach, onset, Ac. xxiv. 12; 2 Cor. xi. 28.*
1988	ἐπι-στάτης, ου, ὁ, superintendent, master; only in Lu., in voc., ἐπιστάτα, addressed to Jesus, Master, v. 5, viii. 24, 45, ix. 33, 49, xvii. 13.*
1989	ἐπι-στέλλω, to send by letter to, to write, Ac. xv. 20, xxi. 25 (W. H. ἀποστ-); Heb. xiii. 22.*
1990	ἐπι-στήμων, ον, skillful, experienced, Ja. iii. 13.*
1991	ἐπι-στηρίζω, to establish besides, confirm, Ac. xiv. 22, xv. 32, 41, xviii. 23 (not W. H.).*
1992	ἐπι-στολή, ῆς, ἡ, an epistle, a letter, Ac. xv. 30; 2 Cor. x. 10.
1993	ἐπι-στομίζω, to stop the mouth of, Tit. i. 11.*
1994	ἐπι-στρέφω, ψω, (1) trans., to cause to turn (acc. and ἐπί), as to God, or to the worship of God, Ac. ix. 35; (2) intrans., to return, to turn back, either to good or evil, Ac. xxvi. 18; 2 Pet. ii. 21; to return upon, as a refused salutation, Mat. x. 13 (ἐπί, εἰς, πρός).
1995	ἐπι-στροφή, ῆς, ἡ, a turning, conversion, Ac. xv. 3.*
1996	ἐπι-συν-άγω, άξω, to gather together, into one place, as Mat. xxiii. 37.
1997	ἐπι-συν-αγωγή, ῆς, ἡ, a gathering together, in one place, 2 Th. ii. 1; Heb. x. 25. (Ap.)*
1998	ἐπι-συν-τρέχω, to run together besides, Mar. ix. 25. (N. T.)*
1999	ἐπι-σύ-στασις, εως, ἡ (W H. ἐπίστασις), (1) a seditious concourse, Ac. xxiv. 12; (2) a troublesome throng, 2 Cor. xi. 28. (S.)*
2000	ἐπι-σφαλής, ές, likely to fall, dangerous, Ac. xxvii. 9.*
2001	ἐπ-ισχύω, to be more urgent, Lu. xxiii. 5.*
2002	ἐπι-σωρεύω, εύσω, to heap up, to obtain a multitude of, 2 Tim. iv. 3.*
2003	ἐπι-ταγή, ῆς, ἡ, a command, an
	injunction, 2 Cor. viii. 8; Tit. ii. 15.
2004	ἐπι-τάσσω, ξω, to command (abs.), Lu. xiv. 22; enjoin upon (dat. of pers., thing in acc. or inf.), Mar. ix. 25.
2005	ἐπι-τελέω, ῶ, έσω, to bring to an end, to perform, as a service, Heb. ix. 6; mid., to come to an end, to leave off, Gal. iii. 3; pass., of sufferings, to be imposed upon, 1 Pet. v. 9.
2006	ἐπιτήδειος, α, ον, fit, needful, Ja. ii. 16.*
2007	ἐπι-τίθημι, θήσω, to put, place, or lay upon (with acc. and dat., or ἐπί, acc. or gen.), as the hands (to heal), as stripes, etc.; of gifts, to load with, Ac. xxviii. 10; mid., to rush upon in hostility, to oppose, Ac. xviii. 10.
2008	ἐπι-τιμάω, ῶ, to rebuke (dat.), Lu. xvii. 3; to admonish (ἵνα), Mat. xii. 16.
2009	ἐπι-τιμία, ας, ἡ, punishment, 2 Cor. ii. 6.*
2010	ἐπι-τρέπω, to allow, permit, Mat. viii. 21; Heb. vi. 3.
2011	ἐπι-τροπή, ῆς, ἡ, commission, full power, Ac. xxvi. 12.*
2012	ἐπί-τροπος, ου, ὁ, one who is intrusted with; (1) a steward, Mat. xx. 8; Lu. viii. 3; (2) a tutor, Gal. iv. 2.*
2013	ἐπι-τυγχάνω, to attain, acquire, (gen. or acc.), Ro. xi. 7; Heb. vi. 15, xi. 33; Ja. iv. 2.*
2014	ἐπι-φαίνω, 1st aor. inf. ἐπιφᾶναι, 2d aor. pass. ἐπεφάνην, (1) to appear, as stars, Ac. xxvii. 20; (2) to shine upon (dat.), Lu. i. 79; (3) met., to be clearly known, Tit. ii. 11, iii. 4.*
2015; see 602	ἐπιφάνεια, ας, ἡ, appearance, the advent of Christ, past and future, 1 Tim. vi. 14; 2 Tim. i. 10, iv. 1, 8; Tit. ii. 13; manifestation, 2 Th. ii. 8.* Syn.: see ἀποκάλυψις.
2016	ἐπιφανής, ές, glorious, illustrious, Ac. ii. 20.*
2017	ἐπι-φαύω, or -φαύσκω, fut. σω, to shine upon, give light to (dat.), Ep. v. 14. (S.)*
2018	ἐπι-φέρω (see Gr. § 103, 6), to bring to (ἐπί, acc.), Ac. xix. 12 (not W. H.); to superadd, Phil. i. 16; to bring upon, inflict, as punishment, Ro. iii. 5; to bring against, as an ac-

cusation, Ac. xxv. 18 (not W. H.) ; Ju. 9.*

2019 ἐπι-φωνέω, ῶ, *to cry out, to shout*, Lu. xxiii. 21 ; Ac. xii. 22, xxi. 34, xxii. 24 (W. H.).*

2020 ἐπι-φώσκω, *to grow light, to dawn*, Mat. xxviii. 1 ; Lu. xxiii. 54.*

2021 ἐπι-χειρέω, ῶ, *to take in hand, undertake*, Lu. i. 1 ; Ac. ix. 29, xix. 13.*

2022 ἐπι-χέω, *to pour upon*, Lu. x. 34.*

2023 ἐπι-χορηγέω, ῶ, *to supply*, 2 Pet. i. 5 ; 2 Cor. ix. 10 ; Gal. iii. 5 ; pass., *to be furnished or supplied*, Col. ii. 19 ; 2 Pet. i. 11.*

2024 ἐπι-χορηγία, ας, ἡ, *a supply*, Phil. i. 19 ; Ep. iv. 16. (N. T.)*

2025 ἐπι-χρίω, *to spread on, anoint* (ἐπί, acc.), Jn. ix. 6 (not W. H.), 11.*

2026 ἐπ-οικοδομέω, ῶ, *to build upon* (ἐπί, acc. or dat.), 1 Cor. iii. 10–14 ; Ep. ii. 20 ; *to build up, edify*, Ac. xx. 32 (not W. H.) ; Col. ii. 7 ; Ju. 20.*

2027 ἐπ-οκέλλω, *to force forward, to run* (a ship) *aground*, Ac. xxvii. 41 (ἐπικέλλω, W. H.).*

2028 ἐπ-ονομάζω, *to name*, or *call by a name of honor*, pass. only, Ro. ii. 17.*

2029 ἐπ-οπτεύω, *to look upon, view attentively*, 1 Pet. ii. 12, iii. 2.*

2030 ἐπ-όπτης, ου, ὁ, *an eye-witness*, 2 Pet. i. 16.*

2031 ἔπος, ους, τό, *a word; ὡς ἔπος εἰπεῖν, so to speak*, Heb. vii. 9.*

2032 ἐπ-ουράνιος, ον, *heavenly, celestial*, of God, Mat. xviii. 35 (W. H. οὐράνιος) ; of intelligent beings, Phil. ii. 10; of the starry bodies, 1 Cor. xv. 40; so of kingdom, country, etc. ; neut. plur., τὰ ἐπουράνια, *heavenly things*, or *places*, Jn. iii. 12 ; Ep. i. 3, 20, ii. 6, iii. 10 ; Heb. viii. 5, ix. 23.

2033 ἑπτά, οἱ, αἱ, τά, card. num., *seven*, Lu. ii. 36 ; Ac. vi. 3 ; often symbol. in Revelation; οἱ ἑπτά, *the seven* deacons, Ac. xxi. 8.

2034 ἑπτάκις, num. adv., *seven times*, Mat. xviii. 21, 22 ; Lu. xvii. 4.*

2035 ἑπτακισ-χίλιοι, αι, α, card. num., *seven thousand*, Ro. xi. 4.*

2036;
see Strong. ἔπω, see εἶπον.

2037 Ἔραστος, ου, ὁ, *Erastus*, (1) Ac. xix. 22 ; (2) Ro. xvi. 23. Which is meant in 2 Tim. iv. 20 is uncertain.*

2038 ἐργάζομαι, σομαι, dep., perf. in pass. sense, εἴργασμαι ; (1) abs., *to work, to trade*, Lu. xiii. 14 ; Mat. xxv. 16 ; (2) *to perform, do*, Col. iii. 23 ; Jn. vi. 28 ; (3) *to practice*, as virtues, *to commit*, as sin, Ac. x. 35 ; Ja. ii. 9 ; (4) *to acquire by labor*, Jn. vi. 27.

2039 ἐργασία, ας, ἡ, (1) *a working, performing*, Ep. iv. 9 ; (2) *effort, diligent labor*, Lu. xii. 58 ; (3) *work, gain by work*, Ac. xvi. 16, 19 ; Ac. xix. 24 ; (4) *occupation, business*, Ac. xix. 25.*

2040 ἐργάτης, ου, ὁ, *a worker, laborer*, Mat. ix. 37 ; applied to workers in the church, 2 Tim. ii. 15 ; *a doer*, of iniquity, Lu. xiii. 27.

2041 ἔργον, ου, τό, *work, employment*, Mat. xiii. 34 ; Jn. xvii. 4 ; 1 Cor. xv. 58 ; *anything accomplished*, Ac. vii. 41 ; Heb. i. 10 ; *an act, deed*, in various senses, Jn. ix. 3 ; Rev. ii. 6 ; Ja. ii. 14 ; 1 Pet. i. 17.

2042 ἐρεθίζω, *to stimulate, to provoke*, 2 Cor. ix. 2 ; Col. iii. 21.*

2043 ἐρείδω, σω, *to stick fast*, Ac. xxvii. 41.*

2044 ἐρεύγομαι, ξομαι, *to utter*, Mat. xiii. 35.*

2045 ἐρευνάω, ῶ, ήσω (W. H. ἐραυνάω), *to search diligently*, Jn. v. 39 ; Ro. viii. 27 ; Rev. ii. 23.

2046 ἐρέω, obsolete, see φημί and εἶπον.

2047 ἐρημία, ας, ἡ, *a solitude, a wilderness*, Mat. xv. 33 ; Mar. viii. 4 ; Heb. xi. 38 ; 2 Cor. xi. 26.*

2048 ἔρημος, ον, *deserted, desolate, waste*, Ac. i. 20 ; Gal. iv. 27 ; used in the fem., as a subst., for a *wilderness*, Lu. i. 80 · ἔρημος τῆς Ἰουδαίας, *the wilderness of Judæa*, the tract west of the Dead Sea, Mat. iii. 1 ; ἡ ἔρημος, the wilderness in which the Israelites wandered, Ac. vii. 30, 36, 38.

2049 ἐρημόω, ῶ, *to make desolate*, Mat. xii. 25 ; Lu. xi. 17 ; *to* *reduce to naught*, Rev. xviL 16, xviii. 17, 19.*

2050   **ἐρήμωσις**, εως, ἡ, *desolation*, Mat. xxiv. 15; Lu. xxi. 20; Mar. xiii. 14. (S.)*

2051   **ἐρίζω**, ίσω (ἔρις), *to contend, dispute*, Mat. xii. 19.*

2052   **ἐριθεία**, ας, ἡ (W. H. ἐριθία), *self-seeking, a partisan and factious spirit*, Ro. ii. 8; Phil. i. 16, ii. 3; Ja. iii. 14, 16; plur. in 2 Cor. xii. 20; Gal. v. 20.*

2053   **ἔριον**, ου, τό, *wool*, Heb. ix. 19; Rev. i. 14.*

2054   **ἔρις**, ιδος, ἡ, *contention, strife*, Ro. i. 29; Gal. v. 20.

2055   **ἐρίφιον**, ου, τό, and ἔριφος, ου, ὁ,
2056   *a goat, kid*, Mat. xxv. 32, 33; Lu. xv. 29.*

2057   **Ἑρμᾶς**, ᾶ, ὁ, Doric for Ἑρμῆς, *Hermas*, Ro. xvi. 14.*

2058   **ἑρμηνεία**, ας, ἡ, *interpretation* 1 Cor. xii. 10, xiv. 26.*

2059   **ἑρμηνεύω**, *to interpret, translate*, Jn. i. 38 (not W. H.), 42, ix. 7; Heb. vii. 2.*

2060   **Ἑρμῆς**, οῦ, ὁ, (1) the Greek deity *Hermes* (in Latin, *Mercury*), Ac. xiv. 12; (2) *Hermes*, Ro. xvi. 14.*

2061   **Ἑρμογένης**, ους, ὁ, *Hermogenes*, 2 Tim. i. 15.*

2062   **ἑρπετόν**, οῦ, τό, *a creeping creature, a reptile*, Ac. x. 12, xi. 6; Ro. i. 23; Ja. iii. 7.

2063   **ἐρυθρός**, ά, όν, *red; ἡ ἐρυθρὰ θάλασσα, the Red Sea*, Ac. vii. 36; Heb. xi. 29.*

2064   **ἔρχομαι**, ἐλεύσομαι (see Gr. § 103, 2, Wi. § 15, Bu. 58), *to come, to go*, of persons or of things; ὁ ἐρχόμενος, *the coming one, i.e.*, the Messiah, Mat. xi. 3; Heb. x. 37; Rev. i. 4, 8, iv. 8; *to come*, after, before, to, against, etc., as determined by the preposition which follows; *to come forth*, as from the grave, 1 Cor. xv. 35; *to come back*, as the prodigal, Lu. xv. 30.

2065   **ἐρωτάω**, ῶ, ήσω, *to question*, Mat. xxi. 24; *to ask, to beseech*, Lu. vii. 36; Phil. iv. 3. *Syn.:* see αἰτέω.

2066   **ἐσθής**, ῆτος, ἡ (ἔννυμι, 1st aor. ἔσθην), *clothing, raiment*, Lu. xxiii. 11; Ac. xii. 21.

2067   **ἔσθησις**, εως, ἡ, *clothing*, Lu. xxiv. 4 (ἐσθής, W. H.).*

2068   **ἐσθίω**, 2d aor. ἔφαγον (see Gr. § 103, 3, Wi. § 15, Bu. 58),

to eat, to partake of food, used abs. or with acc. of food, or ἐκ, a word like *some* being understood; with μετά, gen., *to eat with;* with dat. (as Ro. xiv. 6), *to eat to the honor of;* met., *to devour, to consume*, as rust does, Ja. v. 3; or fire, Heb. x. 27.

see 2068   **ἔσθω** (W. H.) = ἐσθίω, Mar. i. 6; Lu. xxii. 30.

2069   **Ἐσλί** (W. H. -εί), ὁ, *Esli*, Lu. ★   iii. 25.*

2072   **ἔσ-οπτρον**, ου, τό, *a mirror* (of polished metal), Ja. i. 23; 1 Cor. xiii. 12.*

2073   **ἑσπέρα**, ας, ἡ (prop. adj. with ὥρα), *evening*, Lu. xxiv. 29; Ac. iv. 3, xxviii. 23.*

2074   **Ἐσρώμ**, ὁ, *Esrom*, Mat. i. 3; ★   Lu. iii. 33.*

2078   **ἔσχατος**, η, ον, (1) *the last, remotest*, in situation, dignity, or time, τὸ ἔσχατον, τὰ ἔσχατα, as subst., *the extremity, last state;* (2) used predicatively as an adverb, Mar. xii. 6, 22; absolutely, 1 Cor. xv. 8; (3) *the end* of what is spoken of, *e.g.*, the feast, Jn. vii. 37; the world, Jn. vi. 39, 40; (4) spec. of the Christian dispensation as *the last*, or *latter* (days), Heb. i. 2; (5) *the last* (day), *i.e.*, the day of judgment; (6) the phrase ὁ πρῶτος καὶ ὁ ἔσχατος, Rev. i. 11, 17, ii. 8, *the first and the last*, describes the *eternity* of God.

2079   **ἐσχάτως**, adv., *extremely*, ἐσχάτως ἔχει, *is at the last extremity*, Mar. v. 23.*

2080   **ἔσω**, adv. of place, *within*, abs., Mat. xxvi. 58; with gen., Mar. xv. 16; with an article preced., *the inner*, Ro. vii. 22; οἱ ἔσω, *those within* the Christian fold, opp. to οἱ ἔξω, 1 Cor. v. 12.

2081   **ἔσωθεν**, adv. of place, *from within, within*, Lu. xi. 7; Rev. iv. 8; τὸ ἔσωθεν, *the interior, i.e.*, the mind or soul, Lu. xi. 39.

2082   **ἐσώτερος**, α, ον (comp. of ἔσω), *inner*, Ac. xvi. 24; Heb. vi. 19.*

2083   **ἑταῖρος**, ου, ὁ, *a companion, comrade*, Mat. xi. 16 (ἕτερος, W. H.); ἑταῖρε, voc., *friend*, Mat. xx. 13, xxii. 12, xxvi. 50.*

★ **For 2070, 2071 & 2075-2077 see Strong.**

2084 ἑτερό-γλωσσος, ου, ὁ, *one of another tongue* or *language,* 1 Cor. xiv. 21.*

2085 ἑτερο-διδασκαλέω, ῶ, *to teach a different doctrine,* 1 Tim. i. 3, vi. 3. (N. T.)*

2086 ἑτερο-ζυγέω, ῶ, *to be unequally yoked,* fig., 2 Cor. vi. 14. (N. T.)*

2087; see 243 ἕτερος, α, ον, *other, another;* indefinitely, *any other;* definitely, *the other; diverse, different from. Syn.:* see ἄλλος.

2088 ἑτέρως, adv., *otherwise, differently,* Phil. iii. 15.*

2089 ἔτι, adv., *yet, still, even,* Lu. i. 15; *also,* Heb. xi. 36; implying accession or addition, *besides.*

2090 ἑτοιμάζω, άσω, *to prepare, make ready,* Lu. xii. 47; Rev. xix. 7.

2091 ἑτοιμασία, as, ἡ, *preparation, readiness,* Ep. vi. 15.*

2092 ἕτοιμος, η, ον, and -ος, ον, *prepared, ready,* of things or persons, Mat. xxii. 4, 8; Lu. xii. 40; ἐν ἑτοίμῳ ἔχειν, *to be in readiness,* 2 Cor. x. 6.

2093 ἑτοίμως, adv., *readily, in readiness,* usually with ἔχω, Ac. xxi. 13; 2 Cor. xii. 14; 1 Pet. iv. 5.*

2094 ἔτος, ους, τό, *a year,* Lu. iv. 25; κάτ᾽ ἔτος, *yearly,* Lu. ii. 41.

2095 εὖ, adv. (old neuter from εὖς), *well,* Ep. vi. 3; εὖ ποιεῖν (acc.), Mar. xiv. 7, *to do good to;* εὖ πράσσειν, *to fare well, to prosper,* Ac. xv. 29; used in commendation, *well! well done!* Mat. xxv. 21, 23; Lu. xix. 17.*

2096 Εὕα, as, ἡ, *Eve,* 2 Cor. xi. 3; 1 Tim. ii. 13.*

2097 εὐ-αγγελίζω, σω, εὐηγγέλισα, εὐηγγέλισμαι, (1) act., *to bring glad tidings to* (acc. or dat.), Rev. x. 7, xiv. 6; (2) mid., *to announce, to publish* (acc. of message), *to announce the gospel* (abs.), *to preach to, evangelize* (acc. pers.); pass., *to be announced, to have glad tidings announced to* one. See Mat. xi. 5; Heb. iv. 2.

2098 εὐαγγέλιον, ου, τό, *good tidings, the gospel,* Mar. i. 15; Ac. xv. 7; Ep. i. 13.

2099 εὐαγγελιστής, οῦ, ὁ, *a messenger of good tidings, an evangelist,* Ac. xxi. 8; Ep. iv. 11; 2 Tim. iv. 5. (N. T.)*

2100 εὐ-αρεστέω, ῶ, *to be well-pleasing to* (dat.), Heb. xi. 5, 6; pass., *to be pleased with,* Heb. xiii. 16.*

2101 εὐ-άρεστος, ον, *acceptable, well-pleasing,* Ro. xii. 12. (Ap.)

2102 εὐαρέστως, adv., *acceptably,* Heb. xii. 28.*

2103 Εὔβουλος, ου, ὁ, *Eubulus,* 2 Tim. iv. 21.*

see 2095 εὖ-γε, *well done!* Lu. xix. 17 (W. H.).*

2104 εὐγενής, ές, *well-born, noble, noble-minded,* Lu. xix. 12; Ac. xvii. 11; 1 Cor. i. 26.*

2105 εὐδία, as, ἡ (from εὖ and Ζεύς, gen. Διός), *fair weather,* Mat. xvi. 2.*

2106 εὐ-δοκέω, ῶ, ήσω, εὐδόκησα and ηὐδόκησα, *to think it good, decide,* Lu. xii. 32; 1 Th. iii. 1; *to be well pleased with,* Mat. xvii. 5; 2 Pet. i. 17.

2107 εὐδοκία, as, ἡ, *pleasure, goodwill,* Phil. ii. 13; 2 Th. i. 11; Mat. xi. 26.

2108 εὐεργεσία, as, ἡ, *a good deed to* (gen.), *a benefit,* Ac. iv. 9; 1 Tim. vi. 2.*

2109 εὐεργετέω, ῶ, *to do good, to bestow benefits,* Ac. x. 38.*

2110 εὐ-εργέτης, ου, ὁ, *a benefactor,* Lu. xxii. 25.*

2111 εὔ-θετος, ον, *well-placed, fit, useful,* Lu. ix. 62, xiv. 35; Heb. vi. 7.*

2112 εὐθέως, adv., *immediately, soon,* Mat. iv. 20; Gal. i. 16; 3 Jn. 14.

2113 εὐθυ-δρομέω, ῶ, *to run in a straight course,* Ac. xvi. 11, xxi. 1.*

2114 εὐ-θυμέω, ῶ, *to be cheerful,* Ac. xxvii. 22, 25; Ja. v. 13.*

2115 εὔ-θυμος, ον, *cheerful, having good courage,* Ac. xxiv. 10 (Rec.), xxvii. 36.*

see 2115 εὐθύμως, *cheerfully,* Ac. xxiv. 10 (W. H.).*

2116 εὐθύνω, *to make straight,* Jn. i. 23; *to guide, to steer,* as a ship, Ja. iii. 4.*

2117 εὐθύς, εῖα, ύ, *straight;* met., *right, true;* also adv., of time, *straight, i.e., immediately, forthwith,* as εὐθέως (W. H. often εὐθύς for Rec. εὐθέως).

2118 εὐθύτης, τητος, ἡ, *rectitude, uprightness,* Heb. i. 8 (from S.).*

2119 εὐ-καιρέω, ῶ, *to have leisure* or *opportunity,* Mar. vi. 31; Ac. xvii. 21; 1 Cor. xvi. 12.*

2120   **εὐκαιρία,** as, ἡ, *convenient time, opportunity,* Mat. xxvi. 16; Lu. xxii. 6.*

2121   **εὔ-καιρος,** ον, *well-timed, opportune,* Mar. vi. 21; Heb. iv. 16.*

2122   **εὐκαίρως,** adv., *opportunely,* Mar. xiv. 11; opposed to ἀκαίρως, 2 Tim. iv. 2.*

2123   **εὔ-κοπος,** ον, *easy,* neut. comp. only, εὐκοπώτερον, *easier,* as Mat. ix. 5. (N. T.)

2124; see   **εὐ-λάβεια,** as, ἡ, *reverence, fear*
1167   *of God, piety,* Heb. v. 7, xii. 28.* *Syn.:* see δειλία.

2125   **εὐ-λαβέομαι,** οῦμαι, dep. pass., *to fear,* Ac. xxiii. 10 (W. H. φοβέω); with μή, *to take precaution,* Heb. xi. 7.*

2126   **εὐ-λαβής,** ές, *cautious, God-fearing, religious,* Lu. ii. 25; Ac. ii. 5, viii. 2, xxii. 12 (W. H.).* *Syn.:* see δεισιδαίμων.

2127   **εὐ-λογέω,** ῶ, ήσω, *to praise, i.e.,* God, Lu. i. 64; *to invoke blessings on, i.e.,* men, Ro. xii. 14; *to bless* or *to ask blessing on, i.e.,* food, Lu. ix. 16; so of the Lord's Supper, Mat. xxvi. 26; 1 Cor. x. 16; *used of what God does, to bless, to cause to prosper,* Ac. iii. 26; hence, perf. pass. part. εὐλογημένος, *blessed, favored of God,* Mat. xxv. 34.

2128   **εὐλογητός,** όν (verbal adj. from preced.), *worthy of praise, of blessing,* used only of God, Mar. xiv. 61; Lu. i. 68; Ro. i. 25, ix. 5; 2 Cor. i. 3, xi. 31; Ep. i. 3; 1 Pet. i. 3. (S.)*

2129   **εὐ-λογία,** as, ἡ, *adulation, flattery,* Ro. xvi. 18; *blessing, praise,* to God, Rev. vii. 12; *an invocation of blessings, benediction,* Heb. xii. 17; *blessing, benefit,* 2 Cor. ix. 5; 1 Pet. iii. 9.

2130   **εὐ-μετά-δοτος,** ον, *ready to give, liberal,* 1 Tim. vi. 18. (N. T.)*

2131   **Εὐνίκη,** ης, ἡ, *Eunice,* 2 Tim. i. 5.*

2132   **εὐ-νοέω,** ῶ, *to be well disposed to,* Mat. v. 25.*

2133   **εὔ-νοια,** as, ἡ, *good-will,* 1 Cor. vii. 3 (not W. H.); Ep. vi. 7.*

2134   **εὐνουχίζω,** σω, εὐνουχίσθην, *to emasculate, make a eunuch,* pass., Mat. xix. 12.*

2135   **εὐνοῦχος,** ον, ὁ, *a eunuch,* Mat. xix. 12; Ac. viii. 27–39.*

2136   **Εὐοδία,** as, ἡ, *Euodia,* Phil. iv. 2.*

2137   **εὐ-οδόω,** ῶ, in N. T. pass. only, *to be led in a good way, to prosper,* Ro. i. 10; 1 Cor. xvi. 2; 3 Jn. 2.*

see 2145   **εὐ-πάρεδρος,** ον, see εὐπρόσεδρος. (N. T.)

2138   **εὐ-πειθής,** ές, *easily obeying, compliant,* Ja. iii. 17.*

2139   **εὐ-περί-στατος,** ον, *skillfully surrounding, i.e., besetting,* Heb. xii. 1.*

2140   **εὐ-ποιία,** as, ἡ, *well-doing, beneficence,* Heb. xiii. 16.*

2141   **εὐ-πορέω,** ῶ, mid., *to have means, to be prosperous,* Ac. xi. 29.*

2142   **εὐ-πορία,** as, ἡ, *wealth,* Ac. xix. 25.*

2143   **εὐ-πρέπεια,** as, ἡ, *beauty, gracefulness,* Ja. i. 11.*

2144   **εὐ-πρόσ-δεκτος,** ον, *acceptable,* Ro. xv. 16, 31; 2 Cor. vi. 2, viii. 12; 1 Pet. ii. 5.*

2145   **εὐ-πρόσ-εδρος,** ον, *assiduous, constantly attending on,* 1 Cor. vii. 35 (εὐπάρεδρος, W. H.). (N. T.)*

2146   **εὐ-προσωπέω,** ῶ, *to make a fair appearance,* Gal. vi. 12. (N. T.)*

see 2148   **εὐρ-ακύλων,** ωνος, ὁ, *the Euraquilo, a N.E. wind,* Ac. xxvii. 14 (W. H.). (N. T.)*

2147   **εὑρίσκω,** εὑρήσω, εὕρηκα, εὗρον, εὑρέθην, (1) *to find, to discover,* Lu. ii. 45; (2) *to ascertain, to find by computation,* or *by examination,* as a judge, Ac. xiii. 28; (3) *to obtain,* Heb. ix. 12; (4) *to contrive, find out how,* Lu. xix. 48.

2148   **εὐρο-κλύδων,** ωνος, ὁ (from εὖρος, *the S.E. wind,* and κλύδων, *wave),* *Euroclydon, a stormy wind, a hurricane,* Ac. xxvii. 14. (N. T.)*

2149   **εὐρύ-χωρος,** ον, *broad, spacious,* Mat. vii. 13.*

2150   **εὐσέβεια,** as, ἡ, *piety, godliness,* Ac. iii. 12; 2 Tim. iii. 5.

2151   **εὐσεβέω,** ῶ, *to show piety, to worship,* Ac. xvii. 23; 1 Tim. v. 4.*

2152   **εὐ-σεβής,** ές, *religious, pious,* Ac. x. 2, 7, xxii. 12 (W. H. εὐλαβής); 2 Pet. ii. 9.* *Syn.:* see δεισιδαίμων.

2153   **εὐσεβῶς,** adv., *piously, religiously,* 2 Tim. iii. 12; Tit. ii. 12.*

2154   **εὔ-σημος,** ον, *distinct, intelligible,* 1 Cor. xiv. 9.*

2155   **εὔ-σπλαγχνος,** ον, *full of pity,*

tender-hearted, Ep. iv. 32;
1 Pet. iii. 8.*

2156 **εὐ-σχημόνως,** adv., *in a seemly manner, decently,* Ro. xiii. 13; 1 Cor. xiv. 40; 1 Th. iv. 12.*

2157 **εὐ-σχημοσύνη,** ης, ἡ, *decorum, becomingness,* 1 Cor. ii. 23.*

2158 **εὐ-σχήμων,** ον, *reputable, decorous,* Mar. xv. 43; Ac. xiii. 50, xvii. 12; τὸ εὐσχῆμον, *seemliness,* 1 Cor. vii. 35, xii. 24.*

2159 **εὐ-τόνως,** adv., *vehemently, forcibly,* Lu. xxiii. 10; Ac. xviii. 28.*

2160 **εὐ-τραπελία,** ας, ἡ, *low jesting, ribaldry,* Ep. v. 4.*

2161 **Εὔτυχος,** ου, ὁ, *Eutychus,* Ac. xx. 9.*

2162 **εὐ-φημία,** ας, ἡ, *commendation, good report,* 2 Cor. vi. 8.*

2163 **εὔ-φημος,** ον, *sounding well, spoken in a kindly spirit,* Phil. iv. 8.*

2164 **εὐ-φορέω,** ῶ, *to bear plentifully,* Lu. xii. 16.*

2165 **εὐ-φραίνω,** νῶ, εὐφράνθην and ηὐφράνθην, act., *to make glad,* 2 Cor. ii. 2; pass., *to be glad, to rejoice,* Lu. xii. 19; Ac. ii. 26; Rev. xviii. 20.

2166 **Εὐφράτης,** ου, ὁ, *the Euphrates,* Rev. ix. 14, xvi. 12.*

2167 **εὐφροσύνη,** ης, ἡ, *joy, gladness,* Ac. ii. 28, xiv. 17.*

2168 **εὐ-χαριστέω,** ῶ, *to thank, give thanks,* Ac. xxvii. 35; Ro. i. 8.

2169 **εὐχαριστία,** ας, ἡ, *gratitude, thanksgiving,* as 2 Cor. ix. 11, 12. *Syn.:* see αἴτημα.

2170 **εὐ-χάριστος,** ον, *thankful, grateful,* Col. iii. 15.*

2171 **εὐχή,** ῆς, ἡ, (1) *prayer,* Ja. v. 15; (2) *a vow,* Ac. xviii. 18, xxi. 23.* *Syn.:* see αἴτημα.

2172 **εὔχομαι,** *to pray,* Ac. xxvi. 29; 2 Cor. xiii. 7; Ja. v. 16 (*for* with ὑπέρ or περί, gen.); *to wish,* Ac. xxvii. 29; Ro. ix. 3; 2 Cor. xiii. 9; 3 Jn. 2.*

2173 **εὔ-χρηστος,** ον, *useful,* 2 Tim. ii. 21, iv. 11; Philem. 11.*

2174 **εὐ-ψυχέω,** ῶ, *to be in good spirits, to be cheerful,* Phil. ii. 19.*

2175 **εὐ-ωδία,** ας, ἡ, *fragrance, good odor,* 2 Cor. ii. 15; Ep. v. 2; Phil. iv. 18.*

2176 **εὐώνυμος,** ον, *left,* hand, Ac. xxi. 3; foot, Rev. x. 2; ἐξ εὐωνύμων (neut. plur.), *on the left,* Mat. xx. 21, 23.

2177 **ἐφ-άλλομαι,** *to leap upon, ἐπί,* acc., Ac. xix. 16.*

2178 **ἐφ-άπαξ,** adv., *once for all,* Ro. vi. 10; Heb. vii. 27, ix. 12, x. 10; *at once,* 1 Cor. xv. 6.*

2179 **Ἐφεσῖνος,** η, ον, *Ephesian, i.e.,* church, Rev. ii. 1 (not W. H.).*

2180 **Ἐφέσιος,** α, ον, *Ephesian, belonging to Ephesus,* Ac. xix. 28, 34, 35, xxi. 29.*

2181 **Ἔφεσος,** ου, ἡ, *Ephesus,* Ac. xviii. 19, 21, 24.

2182 **ἐφ-ευρετής,** οῦ, ὁ, *an inventor, contriver,* Ro. i. 30.*

2183 **ἐφ-ημερία,** ας, ἡ, *a course,* a division of priests for interchange of service, Lu. i. 5, 8. (S.)*

2184 **ἐφ-ήμερος,** ον, *daily,* Ja. ii. 15.*

2185 **ἐφ-ικνέομαι,** dep., 2d aor. inf. ἐφικέσθαι, *to come to, reach,* ἄχρι or εἰς, 2 Cor. x. 13, 14.*

2186 **ἐφ-ίστημι,** 2d aor. ἐπέστην; perf. part. ἐφεστώς; always intrans. or mid. in N. T.; (1) *to stand by,* Lu. ii. 38; Ac. xii. 7; (2) *to be urgent,* 2 Tim. iv. 2; (3) *to befall one,* as evil, Lu. xxi. 34; (4) *to be at hand, to impend,* 2 Tim. iv. 6.

see 160 **ἐφνίδιος,** see αἰφνίδιος.
see 1896 **ἐφ-οράω,** ῶ, 2d aor. ἐπεῖδον, *to look upon,* Lu. i. 25; Ac. iv. 29.*

2187 **Ἐφραΐμ,** ὁ, *Ephraim,* a city, Jn. xi. 54.*

2188 **ἐφφαθά,** an Aramaic verb, imperative, *be thou opened,* Mar. vii. 34. (N. T.)*

see 5504 **ἐχθές,** see χθές.

2189 **ἔχθρα,** ας, ἡ, *enmity,* Gal. v. 20; Ep. ii. 15, 16.

2190 **ἐχθρός,** ά, όν, *hated,* Ro. xi. 28; *hostile,* 1 Cor. xv. 25; used as subst., *an enemy,* Mat. x. 36; ὁ ἐχθρός, Lu. x. 19, *the enemy, i.e.,* Satan.

2191 **ἔχιδνα,** ης, ἡ, *a viper,* lit., Ac. xxviii. 3; fig., as Mat. iii. 7.

2192 **ἔχω,** ἕξω, impf. εἶχον, 2d aor. ἔσχον, perf. ἔσχηκα; (1) *to have* or *possess,* in general, physically or mentally, temporarily or permanently; μὴ ἔχειν, *to lack, to be poor,* Lu. viii. 6; 1 Cor. xi. 22; (2) *to be able,* Mar. xiv. 8; Heb. vi. 13; 2 Pet. i. 15; (3) with adverbs, or adverbial phrases, elliptically, "to have

(one's self) in any manner,"
to be, as κακῶς ἔχειν, to be ill ;
ἐσχάτως ἔχειν, to be at the
last extremity ; (4) to hold,
1 Tim. iii. 9 ; 2 Tim. i. 13 ;
to esteem, Mat. xiv. 5 ; Phil.
ii. 29 ; (5) mid., ἔχομαι, to be
near or next to, Mar. i. 38 ;
used of time, Ac. xxi. 26,
the day coming, the next day ;
τὰ ἐχόμενα σωτηρίας, things
joined to or pertaining to salvation, Heb. vi. 9.

2193 **ἕως,** conj. and adv., (1) of time,
till, until, used also as prep.
with gen. ἕως οὗ, or ἕως ὅτου,
until when, Lu. xiii. 8 ; (2)
of place, up to, or as far as,
also with gen., sometimes
with εἰς or πρός (acc.), Mat.
xxvi. 58 ; Lu. xxiv. 50 ; Ac.
xxvi. 11 ; (3) spoken of a
limit or term to anything,
up to the point of, Mat. xxvi.
38 ; Lu. xxii. 51 ; Ro. ii. 12 ;
(4) with particles, ἕως ἄρτι,
ἕως τοῦ νῦν, until now ; ἕως
ὧδε, to this place ; ἕως πότε ;
how long? ; ἕως ἑπτάκις, until
seven times ; ἕως ἄνω, up to
the brim, etc.

Z

Z, ζ, ζῆτα, zeta, z, the sixth
letter, orig. of a mixed or
compound sound, as if δs,
now generally pronounced z
or ts. As a numeral, ζ´ = 7 ;
͵ζ = 7000.

2194 **Ζαβουλών,** ὁ (Heb.), Zebulon,
Mat. iv. 13, 15 ; Rev. vii. 8.*

2195 **Ζακχαῖος,** ου, ὁ, Zacchæus, Lu.
xix. 2, 5, 8.*

2196 **Ζαρά,** ὁ (Heb.), Zara or Zerah,
Mat. i. 3.*

2197 **Ζαχαρίας,** ου, ὁ, Zacharias or
Zachariah, (1) the father of
John the Baptist, Lu. i. ; (2)
the son of Barachiah, slain
in the temple, Mat. xxiii. 35 ;
Lu. xi. 51 (in 2 Chron. xxiv.
20 the son of Jehoiada).*

2198 **ζάω,** ῶ, ζῇς, ζῇ, inf. ζῆν (W. H.
ζῆν), fut. ζήσω or -ομαι, 1st
aor. ἔζησα, to live, as (1) to
be alive ; part. ὁ ζῶν, the Living One, a description of
God, as Mat. xvi. 16 ; (2) to
receive or regain life, Jn. iv.
50 ; Mar. xvi. 11 ; (3) to spend
life in any way, Gal. ii. 14 ;
2 Tim. iii. 12 ; (4) to live, in

the highest sense, to possess
spiritual and eternal life, Lu.
x. 28 ; Heb. x. 38 ; (5) met.,
as of water, living or fresh,
opposed to stagnant, as Jn.
iv. 10.

2199 **Ζεβεδαῖος,** ου, ὁ, Zebedee, Mat.
iv. 21, x. 2.

2200 **ζεστός, ή, όν** (ζέω), boiling, hot,
fig., Rev. iii. 15, 16.*

2201 **ζεῦγος, ους, τό,** (1) a yoke
(ζεύγνυμι, to join), Lu. xiv.
19 ; (2) a pair, Lu. ii. 24.*

2202 **ζευκτηρία, ας, ἡ,** a band, a fast-
ening, Ac. xxvii. 40. (N.T.)*

2203 **Ζεύς, Διός,** acc. Δία, Zeus (Lat.
Jupiter), the chief of the
heathen deities, Ac. xiv. 12,
13.*

2204 **ζέω,** part. ζέων, to boil ; fig., to
be fervent, Ac. xviii. 25 ; Ro.
xii. 11.*

see 2206 **ζηλεύω,** to be zealous, Rev. iii.
19 (W. H.).*

2205 **ζῆλος, ου, ὁ,** (1) fervor, zeal, Jn.
ii. 17 ; (2) rivalry, jealousy,
Ac. v. 17, xiii. 45 ; fierceness,
Heb. x. 27.

2206 **ζηλόω, ῶ, ώσω,** (1) to have zeal
for, to desire earnestly (acc.),
1 Cor. xii. 31 ; 2 Cor. xi. 2 ;
Gal. iv. 17 ; (2) to be envious
or jealous, Ac. vii. 9 ; 1 Cor.
xiii. 4 ; Ja. iv. 2.

2207, 2208 **ζηλωτής, οῦ, ὁ,** (1) one very zealous for (gen.), Ac. xxi. 20 ;
(2) a Zealot, one of a class
of Jews very zealous for the
Mosaic law, only Lu. vi. 15 ;
Ac. i. 13. See Κανανίτης.

2209 **ζημία, ας, ἡ,** damage, loss, Ac.
xxvii. 10, 21 ; Phil. iii. 7, 8.*

2210 **ζημιόω, ῶ,** pass., to be damaged,
to suffer loss of (acc.), Mat.
xvi. 26 ; Phil. iii. 8.

2211 **Ζηνᾶς, ᾶ, ὁ,** Zenas, Tit. iii.
13.*

2212 **ζητέω, ῶ, ήσω,** (1) to seek, absolutely, as Mat. vii. 7 ; (2)
to seek for (acc.), Mat. vi. 33 ;
Jn. v. 30 ; (3) to desire, to
wish for, Mat. xii. 46 ; Col.
iii. 1 ; to inquire into, Lu. xii.
29 ; Jn. xvi. 19.

2213 **ζήτημα, ατος, τό,** a question,
dispute (gen., or περί, gen.) ;
Ac. xv. 2, xviii. 15, xxiii. 29,
xxv. 19, xxvi. 3.*

2214 **ζήτησις, εως, ἡ,** question, debate,
controversy, Jn. iii. 25 ; Ac.
xxv. 20.

2215 **ζιζάνιον, ου, τό** (perh. Syriac),
zizanium, darnel, a kind of

bastard wheat, Mat. xiii. 25–
40. (N. T.)*

2216 **Ζοροβάβελ**, ὁ (Heb.), *Zerub-
babel*, Mat. i. 12, 13; Lu. iii.
27.*

2217 **ζόφος**, ου, ὁ, *darkness, thick
gloom*, 2 Pet. ii. 4, 17; Ju. 6,
13; Heb. xii. 18 (W. H.).*

2218 **ζυγός**, οῦ, ὁ, *a yoke*, (1) met.,
of servitude, 1 Tim. vi. 1;
(2) fig., of any imposition
by authority, Mat. xi. 29, 30;
Ac. xv. 10; Gal. v. 1; (3) *a
balance, pair of scales*, Rev.
vi. 5.*

2219 **ζύμη**, ης, ἡ, *leaven*, Mat. xvi. 6;
fig., *corruptness*, 1 Cor. v. 6,
7, 8.

2220 **ζυμόω**, ῶ, *to ferment, to leaven*,
Mat. xiii. 33; Lu. xiii. 21;
1 Cor. v. 6; Gal. v. 9.*

2221 **ζωγρέω**, ῶ (ζωός, ἀγρέω), *to take
alive, to catch, capture*, Lu.
v. 10; 2 Tim. ii. 26.*

2222; see **ζωή**, ῆς, ἡ (ζάω), *life*, literal,
979   spiritual, eternal; *ζωὴ αἰώ-
νιος, eternal life*, used of
Christ, as *the source of life*,
Jn. v. 26. *Syn.:* see βίος.

2223 **ζώνη**, ης, ἡ, *a girdle*, Ac. xxi.
11; used as *a purse*, Mar.
vi. 8.

2224 **ζώννυμι** or *-νύω*, see Gr. § 114,
Bu. 45, *to gird*, Jn. xxi. 18;
Ac. xii. 8 (W. H.).*

2225 **ζωο-γονέω**, ῶ, ήσω, *to preserve
alive*, Lu. xvii. 33; Ac. vii.
19; *to give life to*, 1 Tim. vi.
13 (W. H.).*

2226 **ζῶον**, ου, τό, *a living creature,
animal*, Heb. xiii. 11; 2 Pet.
ii. 12.

2227 **ζωο-ποιέω**, ῶ, ήσω, *to make alive,
to give life to*, Jn. v. 21, vi.
63; 1 Cor. xv. 22, 36, 45;
2 Cor. iii. 6; Gal. iii. 21;
Ro. iv. 17, viii. 11; 1 Pet.
iii. 18.*

H

H, η, ῆτα, *eta, e*, the seventh
letter. As a numeral, η′ = 8;
,η = 8000.

2228 **ἤ,** a particle, disjunctive, *or;*
interrogative, *whether* (see
Gr. § 405, Wi. § 57, 1 b, Bu.
249); or comparative, *than*
(see Gr. § 320, Wi. § 35, 1,
2, Bu. 360). With other particles, ἀλλ᾽ ἤ, *except;* ἤ καὶ,
or else; ἤπερ, *than at all*, Jn.
xii. 43; ἤτοι . . . ἤ, *whether*

. . . *or* (excluding any other
alternative), Ro. vi. 16.

2229 **ἦ,** affirmative particle with μήν,
surely, Heb. vi. 14 (W. H.
el).*

2230 **ἡγεμονεύω,** *to be governor*, as
proconsul, Lu. ii. 2; pro-
curator, Lu. iii. 1.*

2231 **ἡγεμονία,** ας, ἡ, *rule*, as of an
emperor, Lu. iii. 1.*

2232 **ἡγεμών,** όνος, ὁ, *governor*, as the
head of a district, Mat. x.
18; especially the procurator
of Judæa, as Pilate, Felix,
Festus, Lu. xx. 20; *a chief
town*, Mat. ii. 6.

2233 **ἡγέομαι,** οῦμαι, dep. mid., (1) *to
be leader*, in N. T. only part.,
ὁ ἡγούμενος, *the leader* or
chief (gen.), as Ac. xiv. 12;
Heb. xiii. 7, 17, 24; (2) *to
consider, reckon, count*, as
Phil. iii. 7, 8.

2234 **ἡδέως,** adv. (ἡδύς, *sweet*), *gladly*,
Mar. vi. 20, xii. 37; 2 Cor.
xi. 19.*

2235 **ἤδη,** adv. of time, *now, already*,
as Mat. iii. 10; of the im-
mediate future, Ro. i. 10.

2236 **ἥδιστα,** adv., *most gladly*, 2
Cor. xii. 9, 15.*

2237 **ἡδονή,** ῆς, ἡ, *pleasure, i.e.*, sensual, *lust, strong desire*, Lu.
viii. 14; Tit. iii. 3; Ja. iv. 3;
2 Pet. ii. 13; *lust*, Ja. iv. 1.*

2238 **ἡδύ-οσμον,** ου, τό (ἡδύς, ὀσμή),
mint, Mat. xxiii. 23; Lu. xi.
42.*

2239 **ἦθος,** ους, τό, as ἔθος, *manner,
custom;* plur. ἤθη, *morals*,
1 Cor. xv. 33.*

2240 **ἥκω,** ξω (perf. ἧκα, only Mar.
viii. 3), *to have come, to be
present* (see Gr. § 361 d, note,
Wi § 40, 4 b, Bu. 203).

•2242 **Ἡλί,** ὁ (Heb.), *Heli*, Lu. iii. 23.*
2241 **ἠλί** (W. H. ἐλωί), (Heb.), *my
God*, Mat. xxvii. 46 (from
Ps. xxii. 2). (N. T.)*

2243 **Ἡλίας,** ου, ὁ, *Elias, i.e., Elijah*,
Mat. xi. 14, xvi. 14.

2244 **ἡλικία,** ας, ἡ, (1) *age, adult age;*
ἡλικίαν ἔχει, *he is of age*, Jn.
ix. 21; so, prob., Mat. vi. 27
(R. V. mrg.); (2) *stature,
size*, Lu. xix. 3.

2245 **ἡλίκος,** η, ον, *how great, how
small*, Col. ii. 1; Ja. iii. 5.*

2246 **ἥλιος,** ου, ὁ, *the sun, the light of
the sun*, Mat. v. 45; Ac. xiii.
11.

2247 **ἧλος,** ου, ὁ, *a nail*, Jn. xx.
25.*

●**2249, 2248** ἡμεῖς, gen. ἡμῶν, dat. ἡμῖν, acc. ἡμᾶς, plur. of ἐγώ.

2250 ἡμέρα, ας, ἡ, a day, i.e., from sunrise to sunset, Lu. xviii. 7; Ac. ix. 24; a day of twenty-four hours, Mat. vi. 34; fig. in various senses.

2251 ἡμέτερος, α, ον, our, our own, ★ Ac. ii. 11, xxvi. 5.

2253 ἡμιθανής, ές, half dead, Lu. x. ★ 30.*

2255 ἥμισυς, εια, υ, gen., ἡμίσους, half; in neut. only, half of, (gen.) plur. (ἡμίση, W. H. ἡμίσια), Lu. xix. 8; sing., Mar. vi. 23; Rev. xi. 9, 11, xii. 14.*

2256 ἡμιώριον, ον, τό, a half-hour, ★ Rev. viii. 1.*

2259 ἡνίκα, adv., when, whenever, 2 Cor. iii. 15, 16.*

2260 ἤπερ, see ἤ.

2261 ἤπιος, α, ον, placid, gentle, 1 Th. ii. 7 (W. H. νήπιος); 2 Tim. ii. 24.*

2262 Ἤρ, ὁ (Heb.), Er, Lu. iii. 28.*

2263 ἤρεμος, ον, quiet, tranquil, 1 Tim. ii. 2.*

2264 Ἡρώδης (W. H. -ῴ-), ου, ὁ, Herod. Four of the name are mentioned: (1) Herod the Great, Mat. ii. 1; (2) Herod Antipas, or H. the tetrarch, Mat. xiv. 1, 3, 6; Lu. xxiii.; (3) H. Agrippa, Ac. xii.; (4) H. Agrippa the younger, called only Agrippa, Ac. xxv.

2265 Ἡρωδιανοί (W. H. -ῴ-), ῶν, οἱ, Herodians, partisans of Herod Antipas, Mat. xxii. 16; Mar. iii. 6, xii. 13.*

2266 Ἡρωδιάς (W. H. -ῴ-), άδος, ἡ, Herodias, Mat. xiv. 3, 6.

2267 Ἡρωδίων (W. H. -ῴ-), ωνος, ὁ, Herodion, Ro. xvi. 11.*

2268 Ἡσαΐας, ου, ὁ, Esaias, i.e., Isaiah, Mat. iii. 3, iv. 14.

2269 Ἠσαῦ, ὁ, Esau, Ro. ix. 13; Heb. xi. 20, xii. 16.*

2270 ἡσυχάζω, σω, (1) to rest from work, Lu. xxiii. 56; (2) to cease from altercation, to be silent, Lu. xiv. 4; Ac. xi. 18, xxi. 4; (3) to live quietly, 1 Th. iv. 11.*

2271 ἡσυχία, ας, ἡ, (1) silence, Ac. xxii. 2; 1 Tim. ii. 11; (2) tranquillity, quietness, 2 Th. iii. 12.*

2272 ἡσύχιος, α, ον, quiet, tranquil 1 Tim. ii. 2; 1 Pet. iii. 4.*

2273; see ἤτοι, see ἤ.
Strong.

★For **2252, 2254, 2257 & 2258 see Strong.**

2274 ἡττάομαι, pass., (1) to be made inferior (abs.), 2 Cor. xii. 13; (2) to be overcome by (dat.), 2 Pet. ii. 19, 20.*

2275 ἥττημα, ατος, τό, inferiority, diminution, Ro. xi. 12; loss, 1 Cor. vi. 7. (S.)* Syn.: see ἀγνόημα.

2276 ἥττων or ἥσσων (W. H.), ον, compar. of κακός, inferior, ★ ★ neut. as adv., 2 Cor. xii. 15; τὸ ἧττον, as subst., the worse, 1 Cor. xi. 17.*

2278 ἠχέω, ῶ, to sound, as the sea, Lu. xxi. 25 (not W. H.); as brass, 1 Cor. xiii. 1.*

2279 ἦχος, ου, ὁ, and ους, τό, sound, noise, Lu. xxi. 25 (W. H.); Heb. xii. 19; Ac. ii. 2; rumor, report, Lu. iv. 37.*

Θ

Θ, θ, θῆτα, theta, th, the eighth letter. As a numeral, θ′ = 9; ϑ = 9000.

2280 Θαδδαῖος, ου, ὁ, Thaddæus, a surname of the apostle Jude (also called Lebbæus), Mat. x. 3; Mar. iii. 18.*

2281 θάλασσα, ης, ἡ, (1) the sea, Ro. ix. 27; (2) sea, as the Mediterranean, the Red Sea, Ac. vii. 36, x. 6, 32; (3) Hebraistically, for the lake Gennesaret, Mat. viii. 24.

2282 θάλπω, to cherish, nourish, Ep. v. 29; 1 Th. ii. 7.*

2283 Θάμαρ, ἡ, Tamar, Mat. i. 3.*

2284 θαμβέω, ῶ, to be astonished, amazed, Ac. ix. 6 (W. H. omit); so pass., Mar. i. 27, x. 32; with ἐπί (dat.), Mar. x. 24.*

2285 θάμβος, ους, τό, amazement, Lu. iv. 36, v. 9; Ac. iii. 10.*

2286 θανάσιμος, ον, deadly, mortal, Mar. xvi. 18.*

2287 θανατη-φόρος, ον, death-bringing, Ja. iii. 8.*

2288 θάνατος, ου, ὁ, death, lit. or fig., Jn. xi. 4; 2 Cor. iii. 7; Ro. i. 32; the cause of death, Ro. vii. 13.

2289 θανατόω, ῶ, ώσω, to put to death, pass., to be in danger of death, Ro. viii. 36; fig., to destroy, subdue, as evil passions, Ro. viii. 13; pass., to become dead to (dat.), Ro. vii. 4.

2290 θάπτω, ψω, 2d aor. ἔταφον, to bury, Mat. viii. 21, 22.

2291 Θάρα, ὁ, Terah, Lu. iii. 34.*

★★For **2277 see Strong.**

2292 θαρρέω, ῶ, ήσω, *to be of good courage, to have confidence,* εἰς or ἐν, 2 Cor. v. 6, 8, x. 1.

2293 In imperative, forms from θαρσέω are used, θάρσει, θαρσεῖτε, *take courage.*

2294 θάρσος, ους, τό, *courage,* Ac. xxviii. 15.*

2295 θαῦμα, ατος, τό, *a wonder,* 2 Cor. xi. 14 (W. H.); *wonder, amazement,* Rev. xvii. 6.*

2296 θαυμάζω, σω, or σομαι, *to wonder,* abs., with διά, acc., ἐπί, dat., περί, gen., or ὅτι, εἰ; *to wonder at, admire,* acc.; pass., *to be admired* or *honored.*

2297 θαυμάσιος, α, ον, *wonderful,* Mat. xxi. 15.*

2298 θαυμαστός, ή, όν, *wonderful, marvelous,* Mat. xxi. 42; Mar. xii. 11; Jn. ix. 30; 2 Cor. xi. 14 (Rec.); 1 Pet. ii. 9; Rev. xv. 1, 3.*

2299 θεά, ᾶς, ή, *a goddess,* Ac. xix. 27, and Rec. in 35, 37.*

2300 θεάομαι, ῶμαι, dep., 1st aor. ἐθεασάμην, pass. ἐθεάθην, *to behold, to contemplate, to visit,* Mat. xi. 7; Ro. xv. 24.

2301 θεατρίζω, *to make a spectacle of, expose to contempt,* Heb. x. 33. (N. T.)*

2302 θέατρον, ου, τό, (1) *a place for public shows, a theatre,* Ac. xix. 29, 31; (2) *a spectacle,* 1 Cor. iv. 9.*

2303 θεῖον, ου, τό, *sulphur* (from the following, *a divine incense*), Rev. ix. 17, 18.

2304 θεῖος, εία, εῖον, *divine,* 2 Pet. i. 3, 4; τὸ θεῖον, *the deity,* Ac. xvii. 29.*

2305 θειότης, τητος, ή, *deity, divine nature,* Ro. i. 20.* *Syn.:* θειότης is deity, *abstractly;* θεότης, *personally.*

2306 θειώδης, ες, *sulphurous,* Rev. ix. 17. (N. T.)*

2307 θέλημα, ατος, τό, *will,* Lu. xii. 47; Ep. i. 9; plur., *commands,* Ac. xiii. 22; *desire,* Ep. ii. 3.

2308 θέλησις, εως, ή, *a willing, will,* Heb. ii. 4. (S.)*

2309 θέλω, impf. ἤθελον, 1st aor. ἠθέλησα (ἐθέλω is not found in N. T.), *to wish, delight in, prefer, to will,* in the sense of assent, determination, or requirement.

2310 θεμέλιος, ον, *belonging to a foundation;* hence, masc. (sc. λίθος), *a foundation,* or τὸ θεμέλιον (Lu.), in the same sense, 2 Tim. ii. 9; Lu. vi. 49; fig., for the elements of doctrine or life, 1 Cor. iii. 10, 12; Heb. vi. 1.

2311 θεμελιόω, ῶ, ώσω, *to lay a foundation, to found,* Heb. i. 10; fig., *to make stable,* Col. i. 23.

2312 θεο-δίδακτος, ον, *taught of God,* 1 Th. iv. 9. (N. T.)*

2312′ θεο-λόγος, ου, ὁ, *one who treats of divine things,* of the apostle John in the title to Rev. (W. H. omit).*

2313 θεο-μαχέω, ῶ, *to fight against God,* Ac. xxiii. 9 (W. H. omit).*

2314 θεο-μάχος, ου, ὁ, *a fighter against God,* Ac. v. 39.*

2315 θεό-πνευστος, ον (πνέω), *God-breathed, inspired by God,* 2 Tim. iii. 16.*

2316 θεός, οῦ, ὁ, voc. once θεέ, Mat. xxvii. 46; (1) *a god,* generically, Ac. vii. 43, xii. 22; 2 Cor. iv. 4; Phil. iii. 19; Jn. x. 34 (quoted from S.); (2) *God;* ὁ θεός, *the revealed God,* Jn. i. 1; Ac. xvii. 24, etc.; (3) applied to Christ, Jn. i. 1, xx. 28.

2317 θεο-σέβεια, ας, ή, *fear of God, piety,* 1 Tim. ii. 10.*

2318 θεο-σεβής, ές, *God-worshipping, pious,* Jn. ix. 31.* *Syn.:* see δεισιδαίμων.

2319 θεο-στυγής, ές, *hateful to God,* Ro. i. 30.*

2320: see 2305 θεότης, τητος, ή, *deity, Godhead,* Col. ii. 9.* *Syn.:* see θειότης.

2321 Θεό-φιλος, ου, ὁ, *Theophilus,* Lu. i. 3; Ac. i. 1.*

2322 θεραπεία, ας, ή, (1) *service;* hence (abs. for concrete), *servants, household,* Lu. xii. 42; Mat. xxiv. 45 (not W. H.); (2) *medical service, healing,* Lu. ix. 11; Rev. xxii. 2.*

2323 θεραπεύω, εύσω, (1) *to serve, minister to,* only Ac. xvii. 25; (2) *to heal,* acc. of pers., and ἀπό or acc. of disease, Mat. xii. 10; Mar. vi. 5.

2324 θεράπων, οντος, ὁ, *a servant, an attendant,* Heb. iii. 5.*

2325 θερίζω, ίσω, *to reap* or *gather,* as grain, lit. or fig., Mat. vi. 26; Jn. iv. 37, 38.

2326 θερισμός, οῦ, ὁ, *harvest,* lit. or fig., Jn. iv. 35; Lu. x. 2.

2327 θεριστής, οῦ, ὁ, *a reaper,* Mat. xiii. 30, 39.*

2328 θερμαίνω, ανῶ, only mid. in N. T., *to warm one's self,* Mar.

xiv. 54, 67; Jn. xviii. 18, 25;
Ja. ii. 16.*

2329 θέρμη, ης, ή, *heat*, Ac. xxviii.
3.*

2330 θέρος, ους, τό, *summer*, Mat.
xxiv. 32; Mar. xiii. 28; Lu.
xxi. 30.*

2331 Θεσσαλονικεύς, έως, ὁ, *a Thes-
salonian*, Ac. xx. 4.

2332 Θεσσαλονίκη, ης, ή, *Thessalo-
nica*, Ac. xvii. 1, 11, 13.

2333 Θευδᾶς, ᾶ, ὁ, *Theudas*, Ac. v.
36.*

2334 θεωρέω, ῶ, *to be a spectator of,
to behold, to see, to know by
seeing, to experience;* abs.,
or with acc. or obj. clause.

2335 θεωρία, ας, ή, *a sight, a spectacle*,
Lu. xxiii. 48.*

2336 θήκη, ης, ή (τίθημι), *a receptacle*,
as a scabbard, Jn. xviii. 11.*

2337 θηλάζω, (1) *to give suck*, Mat.
xxiv. 19; (2) *to suck*, Mat.
xxi. 16.

2338 θῆλυς, εια, υ, *female*, fem., Ro.
i. 26, 27; neut., Mat. xix. 4;
Mar. x. 6; Gal. iii. 28.*

2339 θήρα, ας, ή, *hunting*, hence, *a
trap*, Ro. xi. 9.*

2340 θηρεύω, σω, *to hunt, to catch*,
Lu. xi. 54.*

2341 θηριο-μαχέω, ῶ, *to fight with
wild beasts*, 1 Cor. xv. 32.*

2342 θηρίον, ου, τό (prop. *a little
beast*), *a wild beast*, as Ac.
xi. 6; freq. in Rev.

2343 θησαυρίζω, σω, *to store up, reserve*, lit. and fig., Lu. xii.
21; 2 Pet. iii. 7.

2344 θησαυρός, οῦ, ὁ, *a treasure receptacle, treasure*, Lu. xii. 33,
34.

**2345; see
680** θιγγάνω, 2d aor. ἔθιγον, *to touch,
handle*, abs., Col. ii. 21; with
gen., Heb. xii. 20; *to injure*,
Heb. xi. 28.* *Syn.:* see
ἅπτω.

2346 θλίβω, ψω, *to press upon*, Mar.
iii. 9; fig., *to afflict*, 2 Cor. i.
6; pass. perf. part. τεθλιμμέ-
νος, contracted, *narrow*, Mat.
vii. 14.

2347 θλῖψις, εως, ή, *pressure, affliction, tribulation*, Ac. vii. 11;
2 Th. i. 6.

2348 θνήσκω, 2d aor. ἔθανον, *to die;*
in N. T. only perf. τέθνηκα,
to be dead, Lu. viii. 49; 1 Tim.
v. 6.

2349 θνητός, ή, όν, *liable to death,
mortal*, Ro. vi. 12, viii. 11;
1 Cor. xv. 53, 54; 2 Cor. iv.
11, v. 4.*

see 5182 θορυβάζω, *to disturb, trouble*, Lu.
x. 41 (W. H.). (N. T.)*

2350 θορυβέω, ῶ, *to disturb*, Ac. xvii.
5; pass., *to be troubled, to
wail*, Mat. ix. 23; Mar. v. 39;
Ac. xx. 10.*

2351 θόρυβος, ου, ὁ, *noise, uproar*,
Mar. v. 38; Ac. xx. 1.

2352 θραύω, σω, *to break, shatter*, Lu.
iv. 18.*

2353 θρέμμα, ατος, το (τρέφω), *the
young of cattle, sheep*, etc.,
Jn. iv. 12.*

2354 θρηνέω, ῶ, ήσω, abs., *to wail, lament*, Mat. xi. 17; Lu. vii.
32; Jn. xvi. 20; *to bewail*,
acc., Lu. xxiii. 27.*

2355 θρῆνος, ου, ὁ, *a wailing*, Mat. ii.
18 (not W. H.).*

2356 θρησκεία, ας, ή, *external worship, religious worship*, Ac.
xxvi. 5; Col. ii. 18; Ja. i. 26,
27.*

2357 θρῆσκος, ου, ὁ (prop. adj.), *a
devotee, religious person*, Ja.
i. 26. (N. T.)* *Syn.:* see
δεισιδαίμων.

2358 θριαμβεύω, σω, *to triumph over,
to lead in triumph*, 2 Cor. ii.
14; Col. ii. 15.*

2359 θρίξ, τριχός, dat. plur. θριξί, ή,
a hair, human or animal, Jn.
xi. 2; Rev. ix. 8.

2360 θροέω, ῶ, *to disturb, terrify by
clamor;* only pass. in N. T.,
Mat. xxiv. 6; Mar. xiii. 7;
2 Th. ii. 2.*

2361 θρόμβος, ου, ὁ, *a clot, large drop*,
as of blood, Lu. xxii. 44.*

2362 θρόνος, ου, ὁ, *a seat*, as of judgment, Mat. xix. 28; *a throne*,
or seat of power, Rev. iii.
21; met., of *kingly power*,
Rev. xiii. 2; concrete, of the
ruler, or occupant of the
throne, Col. i. 16.

2363 Θυάτειρα, ων, τά, *Thyatira*, Ac.
xvi. 14; Rev. i. 11, ii. 18,
24.*

2364 θυγάτηρ, τρός, ή, *a daughter*,
Mat. ix. 18; *a female descendant*, Lu. xiii. 16; met.,
of the inhabitants of a place,
collectively, Mat. xxi. 5.

2365 θυγάτριον, ου, τό (dim. of θυγάτηρ), *a little daughter*, Mar.
v. 23, vii. 25.*

2366 θύελλα, ης, ή, *a tempest*, Heb.
xii. 18.*

2367 θύϊνος, η, ον, *made of the citrus
tree*, a strongly aromatic tree
of Africa, Rev. xviii. 12.*

2368 θυμίαμα, ατος, τό, *incense*, Lu.

i. 10, 11 ; Rev. v. 8, viii. 3, 4,
xviii. 13.*

2369 θυμιατήριον, ου, τό, *a censer,* or
an altar of incense, Heb. ix.
4.*

2370 θυμιάω, ῶ, *to burn incense,* Lu.
i. 9.*

2371 θυμομαχέω, ῶ, *to be very angry
with* (dat.), Ac. xii. 20.*

2372 θυμός, οῦ, ὁ, *passion, great anger,
wrath,* Lu. iv. 28; Rev. xiv. 19.
Syn.: θυμός is *impulsive, tur-
bulent* anger ; ὀργή is anger
as a *settled habit,* both may
be right or wrong; παρ⸢οργισ-
μός* is the bitterness of anger,
always wrong.

2373 θυμόω, ῶ, *to provoke to great
anger;* pass., *to be very angry
with,* Mat. ii. 16.*

2374 θύρα, ας, ἡ, *a door,* Lu. xi. 7 ;
Mat. xxvii. 60; met., Jn. x.
7, 9.

2375 θυρεός, οῦ, ὁ, *a large* (door
shaped) *shield,* Ep. vi. 16.*

2376 θυρίς, ίδος, ἡ (prop. *a little door*),
a window, Ac. xx. 9; 2 Cor.
xi. 33.*

2377 θυρωρός, οῦ, ὁ, ἡ, *a door-keeper,
porter,* Mar. xiii. 34; Jn. x.
3, xviii. 16, 17.*

2378 θυσία, ας, ἡ, *a sacrifice,* lit.
and fig., Ep. v. 2 ; 1 Pet.
ii. 5.

2379; see θυσιαστήριον, ου, τό, *an altar,*
1041 for sacrifices, Lu. i. 11, ii.
51; Ja. ii. 21. (S.) *Syn.:* see
βωμός.

2380 θύω, σω, (1) *to slay in sacrifice,*
Ac. xiv. 13; (2) *to kill ani-
mals,* for feasting, Mat. xxii.
4; (3) *to slay,* generally, Jn.
x. 10.

2381 Θωμᾶς, ᾶ, ὁ (from Heb. = δίδυμος), *Thomas,* Mat. x. 3.

2382 θώραξ, ακος, ὁ, *a breast-plate,*
Ep. vi. 14; 1 Th. v. 8; Rev.
ix. 9, 17.*

I

I, ι, ἰῶτα, *iota, i,* the ninth letter.
As a numeral, ι′ = 10; ͺι =
10,000.

2383 Ἰάειρος, ου, ὁ, *Jairus,* Mar. v.
22; Lu. viii. 41.*

2384 Ἰακώβ, ὁ (Heb.), *Jacob,* (1) the
patriarch, Ac. vii. 8; (2) the
father-in-law of Mary, Mat.
i. 15.

2385 Ἰάκωβος, ου, ὁ, Greek form of
preced., *James,* (1) the son
of Zebedee, Mat. iv. 21; (2)

the son of Alphæus, Mat. x.
3; (3) the Lord's brother,
Mat. xiii. 55. Some identify
(2) and (3).

2386 ἴαμα, ατος, τό, *healing, cure,*
plur., 1 Cor. xii. 9, 28, 30.*

2387 Ἰαμβρῆς, ὁ, *Jambres,* 2 Tim.
iii. 8.*

2388 Ἰαννά, ὁ (W. H. -αί), (Heb.),
Jannai, Lu. iii. 24.*

2389 Ἰαννῆς, ὁ, *Jannes,* 2 Tim. iii.
8.*

2390 ἰάομαι, ῶμαι, ἰάσομαι, dep., mid.
aor., but passive in aor.,
perf. and fut., *to heal, to
restore to health,* of body or
mind; with ἀπό, of malady,
Mar. v. 29; Jn. xii. 40.

2391 Ἰαρέδ, ὁ (Heb.), *Jared,* Lu. iii.
37.*

2392 ἴασις, εως, ἡ, *a cure, healing,*
Lu. xiii. 32; Ac. iv. 22, 30.*

2393 ἴασπις, ιδος; ἡ, *jasper,* a precious stone, Rev. iv. 3, xxi.
11, 18, 19.*

2394 Ἰάσων, ονος, ὁ, *Jason,* Ac. xvii.
5, 6, 7, 9; Ro. xvi. 21; per-
haps two persons.*

2395 ἰατρός, οῦ, ὁ, *a physician,* Lu.
iv. 23; Col. iv. 14.

2396 ἴδε, or ἰδέ (εἶδον), imper. act.
as interj., *behold!* often followed by nominative.

2397 ἰδέα (W. H. εἰ-), ας, ἡ, *form,
outward appearance,* Mat.
xxviii. 3.* *Syn.:* see Trench,
§ lxx.

2398 ἴδιος, α, ον, (1) *one's own,* denoting ownership, Mat. xxii.
5; Jn. x. 12; also what is
peculiar to, Ac. i. 19 (W. H.
omit); hence, τὰ ἴδια, *one's
own things, home, nation*
or *people, business* or *duty;*
οἱ ἴδιοι, *one's own people,
friends, companions,* neut.
and masc. contrasted in Jn.
i. 11; (2) *that which specially
pertains to, and is proper for,*
as 1 Cor. iii. 8; Gal. vi. 9;
(3) adverbially, κατ' ἰδίαν,
privately; ἰδίᾳ, *individually.*

2399; see ἰδιώτης, ου, ὁ, *a private person,*
62 *one unskilled in anything,*
Ac. iv. 13; 1 Cor. xiv. 16, 23,
24; 2 Cor. xi. 6.* *Syn.:* see
ἀγράμματος.

2400 ἰδού (see ἴδε), imper. mid. as
interj., *lo! behold!* used to
call attention not only to
that which may be seen, but
also heard, or apprehended
in any way.

2401 Ἰδουμαία, ας, ἡ, *Idumæa*, the O. T. Edom, Mar. iii. 8.*

2402 ἱδρώς, ῶτος, ὁ, *sweat*, Lu. xxii. 44.*

2403 Ἰεζαβήλ, ἡ (Heb.), *Jezebel*, symbolically used, Rev. ii. 20.*

2404 Ἱεράπολις, -εως, ἡ, *Hierapolis*, in Phrygia, Col. iv. 13.*

2405 ἱερατεία (W. H. -τία), ας, ἡ, *the office of a priest, priesthood*, Lu. i. 9; Heb. vii. 5.*

2406 ἱεράτευμα, ατος, τό, *the order of priests, priesthood*, applied to Christians, 1 Pet. ii. 5, 9. (S.)*

2407 ἱερατεύω, σω, *to officiate as a priest*, Lu. i. 8.*

2408 Ἰερεμίας, ου, ὁ, *Jeremiah*, Mat. ii. 17, xvi. 14. xxvii. 9 (this quotation is from *Zechariah*).*

2409 ἱερεύς, έως, ὁ, *a priest*, Mat. viii. 4; sometimes *the High Priest*, Ac. v. 24 (not W. H.); of Christ, Heb. v. 6 (Ps. cx. 4); of Christians generally, Rev. i. 6, v. 10.

2410 Ἰεριχώ, ἡ (Heb.), *Jericho*, Lu. x. 30.

see 1494 ἱερόθυτος, ον, *offered in sacrifice*, 1 Cor. x. 28 (W. H.).*

2411 ἱερόν, οῦ, τό (prop. neut. of ἱερός), *a temple*, used of a heathen temple, as Ac. xix. 27; of the temple at Jerusalem, as Mat. xxiv. 1; and of parts of the temple, as Mat. xii. 5. *Syn.:* ἱερόν is the whole sacred enclosure; ναός, the *shrine* itself, the holy place and the holy of holies.

2412 ἱερο-πρεπής, ές, *suitable to a sacred character* (*reverent*, R. V.), Tit. ii. 3.*

2413 ἱερός, ά, όν, *sacred, holy*, of the Scriptures, 2 Tim. iii. 15; τὰ ἱερά, *sacred things*, 1 Cor. ix. 13.* *Syn.:* see ἅγιος.

2414 Ἱεροσόλυμα (W. H. Ἰ-), ων, τά, the usual form in Mat., Mar., and Jn.; see Ἱερουσαλήμ.

2415 Ἱεροσολυμίτης, ου, ὁ, *one of Jerusalem*, Mar. i. 5; Jn. vii. 25.*

2416 ἱερο-συλέω, ῶ, *to commit sacrilege*, Ro. ii. 22.*

2417 ἱερό-συλος, ον, *robbing temples, sacrilegious*, Ac. xix. 37.*

2418 ἱερουργέω, ῶ (ἱερός, ἔργον), *to minister in holy things*, Ro. xv. 16.*

2419 Ἱερουσαλήμ (W. H. Ἰ-), ἡ (Heb.), (for form, see Gr. § 156, Wi. § 10, 2, Bu. 6, 16, 18, 21), *Jerusalem*, (1) the city; (2) the inhabitants. In Gal. iv. 25, 26, ἡ νῦν Ἰ. is the *Jewish dispensation*, and is contrasted with ἡ ἄνω Ἰ., the ideal *Christian community;* also called Ἰ. ἐπουράνιος, Heb. xii. 22; ἡ καινὴ Ἰ., Rev. iii. 12, xxi. 2.

2420 ἱερωσύνη, ης, ἡ, *the priestly office*, Heb. vii. 11, 12, 14 (not W. H.), 24.*

2421 Ἰεσσαί, ὁ (Heb.), *Jesse*, Mat. i. 5, 6.

2422 Ἰεφθάε, ὁ (Heb.), *Jephthah*, Heb. xi. 32.*

2423 Ἰεχονίας, ου, ὁ, *Jechoniah*, or *Jehoiachin*, Mat. i. 11, 12.*

2424 Ἰησοῦς, οῦ, ὁ (Heb.), (see Gr. § 25, Wi. § 10, 1, Bu. 21), (1) *Jesus*, the Savior, Mat. i. 21, 25; (2) *Joshua*, Ac. vii. 45; Heb. iv. 8; (3) *a fellow-laborer of Paul*, so named, Col. iv. 11; (4) *Barabbas* is so named in some early MSS., Mat. xxvii. 16; (5) *an ancestor of Joseph*, Lu. iii. 29 (W. H.).

2425 ἱκανός, ή, όν, (1) *sufficient, competent* to, inf., πρός (acc.) or ἵνα; (2) *many, much*, of number or time.

2426 ἱκανότης, τητος, ἡ, *sufficiency, ability*, 2 Cor. iii. 5.*

2427 ἱκανόω, ῶ, *to make competent*, 2 Cor. iii. 6; Col. i. 12. (S.)*

2428 ἱκετηρία, ας, ἡ, *supplication*, Heb. v. 7.* *Syn.:* see αἴτημα.

2429 ἱκμάς, άδος, ἡ, *moisture*, Lu. viii. 6.*

2430 Ἰκόνιον, ου, τό, *Iconium*, Ac. xiv. 1, 19, 21.

2431 ἱλαρός, ά, όν, *joyous, cheerful*, 2 Cor. ix. 7.*

2432 ἱλαρότης, τητος, ἡ, *cheerfulness*, Ro. xii. 8. (S.)*

2433 ἱλάσκομαι, άσομαι, 1st aor. ἱλάσθην, (1) *to be propitious to*, dat., Lu. xviii. 13; (2) *to make atonement for, expiate*, acc., Heb. ii. 17.*

2434 ἱλασμός, οῦ, ὁ, *a propitiation, atoning sacrifice*, 1 Jn. ii. 2, iv. 10. (S.)* *Syn.:* see ἀπολύτρωσις.

2435 ἱλαστήριος, α, ον, *atoning*, neut., *propitiation*, Ro. iii. 25; (sc. ἐπίθεμα, *covering*), *the mercy seat*, Heb. ix. 5. (S.)*

2436   ἵλεως, ων (Attic for ἵλαος), *propitious, merciful,* Heb. viii. 12; ἵλεώς σοι, (God be) merciful to thee! *God forbid!* Mat. xvi. 22.*

2437   Ἰλλυρικόν, οῦ, τό, *Illyricum,* Ro. xv. 19.*

2438   ἱμάς, άντος, ὁ, a *thong* for scourging, Ac. xxii. 25; *thong, latchet* of a shoe, Mar. i. 7; Lu. iii. 16; Jn. i. 27.*

2439   ἱματίζω, perf. pass. part. ἱματισμένος, *to clothe,* Mar. v. 15; Lu. viii. 35. (N. T.)*

2440   ἱμάτιον, ου, τό (dim. of ἷμα = εἷμα, from ἕννυμι), (1) *clothing,* Mat. ix. 16; (2) *the outer garment,* worn over the χιτών, Jn. xix. 2. *Syn.:* see Trench, § 1.

2441   ἱματισμός, οῦ, ὁ, *clothing, raiment,* Lu. vii. 25. *Syn.:* see ἱμάτιον.

2442   ἱμείρομαι, *to long for, to love earnestly,* 1 Th. ii. 8 (W. H. ὁμείρομαι).*

2443   ἵνα, conj., *that, to the end that; ἵνα μή, that not, lest.* See Gr. § 384, Wi. § 53, 9, Bu. 229 sq.

2444   ἱνα-τί, or ἵνα τί (W. H.), conj., *in order that what* (may happen? sc. γένηται), *to what end?*

2445   Ἰόππη, ης, ἡ, *Joppa,* Ac. xi. 5, 13.

2446   Ἰορδάνης, ου, ὁ, *the Jordan,* Mar. i. 5, 9.

2447   ἰός, οῦ, ὁ, (1) *poison,* Ro. iii. 13; Ja. iii. 8; (2) *rust,* Ja. v. 3.*

•2449   Ἰουδαία, ας, ἡ (really adj., fem., sc. γῆ), *Judæa,* Mat. ii. 1; including all Palestine, Lu. vii. 17.

•2450   Ἰουδαΐζω (from Heb.), *to conform to Jewish practice,* to "Judaize," in life or ritual, Gal. ii. 14. (S.)*

•2451   Ἰουδαϊκός, ή, όν (from Heb.), *Jewish,* or *Judaical,* Tit. i. 14.*

•2452   Ἰουδαϊκῶς, adv., *Jewishly,* in Jewish style, Gal. ii. 14.*

•2453; see 1445   Ἰουδαῖος, αία, αῖον, *Jewish,* Jn. iv. 9; Ac. x. 28. Often in plur., with subst. understood, οἱ Ἰουδαῖοι, *the Jews. Syn.:* see Ἑβραῖος.

•2454   Ἰουδαισμός, οῦ, ὁ (from Heb.), *Judaism,* the religion of the Jews, Gal. i. 13, 14. (Ap.)*

2448, 2455   Ἰούδας, α, ὁ, and Ἰούδα, ὁ,

indecl., *Judah,* (1) son of Jacob; (2, 3) other unknown ancestors of Christ, Lu. iii. 26, 30; (4) *Jude,* an apostle; (5) *Judas* Iscariot; (6) *Judas* Barsabas, Ac. xv. 22; (7) *Judas,* a Jew living in Damascus, Ac. ix. 11; (8) *Judas,* a leader of sedition, Ac. v. 37; (9) *Judas,* a brother of our Lord, Mat. xiii. 55. See Ἰάκωβος.

2456   Ἰουλία, ας, ἡ, *Julia,* Ro. xvi. 15.*

2457   Ἰούλιος, ου, ὁ, *Julius,* Ac. xxvii. 1, 3.*

2458   Ἰουνίας, α, ὁ, *Junias,* Ro. xvi. 7.*

2459   Ἰοῦστος, ου, ὁ, *Justus.* Three of the name are mentioned, Ac. i. 23, xviii. 7; Col. iv. 11.*

2460   ἱππεύς, έως, ὁ, a *horseman,* Ac. xxiii. 23, 32.*

2461   ἱππικόν (prop. neut. adj.), οῦ, τό, *cavalry,* Rev. ix. 16.*

2462 2463   ἵππος, ου, ὁ, a *horse,* Ja. iii. 3. ἶρις, ἶδος, ἡ, a *rainbow,* Rev. iv. 3, x. 1.*

2464   Ἰσαάκ, ὁ (Heb.), *Isaac,* Ro. ix. 7, 10.

2465   ἰσ-άγγελος, ον, *like angels,* Lu. xx. 36. (N. T.)*

see 1492   ἴσασι, see οἶδα.

2466   Ἰσαχάρ, or Ἰσασχάρ, or Ἰσσαχάρ (W.H.), (Heb.), *Issachar,* Rev. vii. 7.*

2469   Ἰσκαριώτης, ου, ὁ, a man *of Kerioth,* Mat. xxvi. 14, 25. See Josh. xv. 25.

2470   ἴσος, η, ον (or ἴσος), *equal* (dat.), Mat. xx. 12; Lu. vi. 34; Jn. v. 18; Ac. xi. 17; *alike, consistent,* as truthful witnesses, Mar. xiv. 56, 59; ἴσα, adverbially, *on an equality* Phil. ii. 6; Rev. xxi. 16.*

2471   ἰσότης, τητος, ἡ, *equality,* 2 Cor. viii. 13, 14; *equity,* Col. iv. 1.*

2472   ἰσό-τιμος, ον, *equally precious,* 2 Pet. i. 1.*

2473   ἰσό-ψυχος, ον, *like-minded,* Phil. ii. 20.*

2474   Ἰσραήλ, ὁ (Heb.), *Israel,* Ac. vii. 42, met., for the whole nation of the Israelites, Ro. xi. 2, 7, 26.

2475; see 1445 see 1492   Ἰσραηλίτης, ου, ὁ, an *Israelite,* Ro. ix. 4. *Syn.:* see Ἑβραῖος. ἴστε, see οἶδα.

2476   ἵστημι (in Ro. iii. 31, Rec. has ἱστάω, W. H. ἱστάνω, see

*For 2467 & 2468 **see** Strong.

Gr. § 107, Wi. § 15, Bu. 44), trans. in pres., imperf., fut., 1st aor. ; *to cause to stand, to set up, to place, to fix* a time, *to confirm, to establish, to put in the balance, to weigh ;* intrans. in perf., plup., and 2d aor., *to stand, to stand still* or *firm, to endure, to be confirmed* or *established, to come to a stand, to cease.*

2477 ἱστορέω, ῶ, *to become personally acquainted with*, Gal. i. 18.*

2478 ἰσχυρός, ά, όν, *strong, mighty, powerful, vehement*, Mar. iii. 27; 1 Cor. i. 25; Rev. xix. 6.

2479 ἰσχύς, ύος, ἡ, *strength, power*, 2 Pet. ii. 11; Ep. i. 19.

2480 ἰσχύω, ύσω, *to be strong, sound to prevail, to be able* (inf.), *to have ability* for (acc.), Mar. ii. 17; Rev. xii. 8.

2481 ἴσως (ἴσος), adv., *perhaps*, Lu. xx. 13.*

2482 Ἰταλία, ας, ἡ, *Italy*, Ac. xviii. 2.
2483 Ἰταλικός, ή, όν, *Italian*, Ac. x. 1.*

2484 Ἰτουραία, ας, ἡ, *Ituræa*, Lu. iii. 1.*

2485 ἰχθύδιον, ου, τό (dim. of ἰχθύς), *a little fish*, Mat. xv. 34; Mar. viii. 7.*

2486 ἰχθύς, ύος, ὁ, *a fish*, Lu. v. 6; Jn. xxi. 11.

2487 ἴχνος, ους, τό, *a footstep*, fig., Ro. iv. 12; 2 Cor. xii. 18; 1 Pet. ii. 21.*

2488 Ἰωάθαμ, ὁ (Heb.), *Jotham*, Mat. i. 9.*

2489 Ἰωάννα, ης, ἡ, *Joanna*, Lu. viii. 3, xxiv. 10.*

2490 Ἰωαννᾶς, ᾶ, ὁ, *Joannas*, Lu. iii. 27.*

2491 Ἰωάννης, ου, ὁ, *John*, (1) the Baptist; (2) the apostle; (3) a member of the Sanhedrin, Ac. iv. 6; (4) John Mark, Ac. xii. 12.

2492 Ἰώβ, ὁ (Heb.), *Job*, Ja. v. 11.*
2493 see 5601 Ἰωβήδ, see Ὠβήδ.
Ἰωήλ, ὁ (Heb.), *Joel*, the prophet, Ac. ii. 16.*

2494 Ἰωνάν, ὁ (Heb.), *Jonan*, Lu. iii. 30.*

2495 Ἰωνᾶς, ᾶ, ὁ, *Jonas*, or *Jonah*, (1) the prophet, Mat. xii. 39–41; (2) the father of Peter, Jn. i. 42.

2496 Ἰωράμ, ὁ (Heb.), *Joram*, or *Jehoram*, son of Jehoshaphat, Mat. i. 8.*

2497 Ἰωρείμ, ὁ (Heb.), *Jorim*, Lu. iii. 29.*

2498 Ἰωσαφάτ, ὁ (Heb.), *Jehoshaphat*, Mat. i. 8.*

●2500. 2499 Ἰωσῆς, ῆ (or ῆτος, W. H.), ὁ, *Joses*. Four are mentioned: (1) Lu. iii. 29 (W. H. Ἰησοῦ); (2) Mar. vi. 3; Mat. xiii. 55 (W. H. Ἰωσήφ); (3) Mat. xxvii. 56 (W. H. mrg.), Mar. xv. 40, 47; (4) Ac. iv. 36 (W. H. Ἰωσήφ). Some think (2) and (3) identical.*

2501 Ἰωσήφ, ὁ (Heb.), *Joseph*, (1) the patriarch, Jn. iv. 5; (2, 3, 4) three among the ancestors of Jesus, Lu. iii. 24, 26 (W. H. Ἰωσήχ), 30; (5) the husband of Mary, the mother of Jesus, Mat. ii. 13, 19; (6) Joseph of Arimathæa, Mar. xv. 43, 45; (7) Joseph, called also Barsabas, Ac. i. 23. See also under Ἰωσῆς.

2502 Ἰωσίας, ου, ὁ, *Josiah*, Mat. i. 10, 11.*

2503 ἰῶτα, τό, *iota, yod*, the smallest letter of the Hebrew alphabet, Mat. v. 18.*

Κ

Κ, κ, κάππα, *kappa, k*, the tenth letter. As a numeral, κ´ = 20; ͵κ = 20,000.

2504 κἀγώ (κἄμοί, κἄμέ), contr. for καὶ ἐγώ (καὶ ἐμοί, καὶ ἐμέ), *and I, I also, even I*.

2505 καθά, adv., contr. from καθ᾽ ἅ, *according as*, Mat. xxvii. 10.*

2506 καθ-αίρεσις, εως, ἡ, *demolition, destruction* (opp. to οἰκοδομή, which see), 2 Cor. x. 4, 8, xiii. 10.*

2507 καθ-αιρέω, καθελῶ, καθεῖλον, (1) *to take down*, Ac. xiii. 29; (2) *to demolish, destroy*, lit., Lu. xii. 18, or fig., 2 Cor. x. 5.

2508 καθαίρω, αρῶ, *to cleanse, to prune*, Jn. xv. 2; Heb. x. 2 (W. H. καθαρίζω).*

2509 καθ-άπερ, adv., *even as, just as*, 1 Th. ii. 11.

2510 καθ-άπτω, άψω, *to fasten on*, intrans., Ac. xxviii. 3 (gen.).*

2511 καθαρίζω, att. fut. καθαριῶ, *to cleanse*, lit., Lu. xi. 39; a leper, by healing his disease, Mat. viii. 2, 3; from moral pollution, Heb. ix. 22, 23; *to declare clean, i.e.*, from ceremonial pollution, Ac. x. 15.

2512   καθαρισμός, οῦ, ὁ, *cleansing*, physical, moral, or ceremonial, Mar. i. 44; Lu. ii. 22, v. 14; Jn. ii. 6, iii. 25; Heb. i. 3; 2 Pet. i. 9. (S.)*

2513   καθαρός, ά, όν, *clean, pure*, physically, morally, or ceremonially, Mat. xxiii. 26; Tit. i. 15; Ro. xiv. 20.

2514   καθαρότης, τητος, ἡ, *purity, i.e.*, ceremonial, Heb. ix. 13.*

2515   καθ-έδρα, as, ἡ, *a seat*, lit., Mat. xxi. 12; Mar. xi. 15; met., *a chair* of authority, Mat. xxiii. 2.*

2516   καθ-έζομαι, *to sit down*, ἐν or ἐπί, dat., Lu. ii. 46; Jn. iv. 6.

see 1520   καθ-εῖς (W. H. καθ' εἷς), adv. (see Gr. § 300β, 4, Wi. § 37, 3, Bu. 30), *one by one*, Jn. viii. 9.

2517   καθ-εξῆς, adv. (see Gr. § 126 d), *in orderly succession*, Lu. i. 3; Ac. xi. 4, xviii. 23. With art., Lu. viii. 1, ἐν τῷ κ., *soon afterwards*; Ac. iii. 24, οἱ κ., *those that come after.*

2518   καθ-εύδω, *to sleep*, lit., Mat. viii. 24; fig., 1 Th. v. 6.

2519   καθηγητής, οῦ, ὁ, *a guide, master*, Mat. xxiii. 8 (not W. H.), 10.*

2520   καθ-ήκω, used only impers., *it is fit, it is becoming* (acc., inf.), Ac. xxii. 22; τὸ καθῆκον, *the becoming*, Ro. i. 28.*

2521   κάθ-ημαι, 2d pers. κάθῃ for κάθησαι, imper., κάθου (see Gr. § 367, Wi. § 15, 4, Bu. 49), *to be seated, to sit down, to sit, to be settled, to abide*; with εἰς, ἐν, ἐπί (gen., dat., acc.).

2522   καθ-ημερινός, ή, όν, *daily*, Ac. vi. 1.*

2523   καθ-ίζω, ίσω, (1) trans., *to cause to sit down, to set*; (2) intrans., *to seat one's self*, preps. as κάθημαι; *to sit down, to be sitting, to tarry*; mid. in Mat. xix. 28; Lu. xxii. 30.

2524   καθ-ίημι, 1st aor. καθῆκα (see Gr. § 112, Bu. 46), *to send* or *let down*, Lu. v. 19; Ac. ix. 25, x. 11, xi. 5.*

2525   καθ-ίστημι (and καθιστάω or -ανω), *to appoint, constitute, make, ordain, to conduct*, Ac. xvii. 15; *to appoint as ruler over* (ἐπί, gen., dat., acc.).

2526   καθ-ό, adv. (for καθ' ὅ), *as, according as*, Ro. viii. 26; 2

Cor. viii. 12; 1 Pet. iv. 13.*

2526'   καθολικός, ή, όν, *general, universal* (found in the inscriptions of the seven Epistles of James, Peter, John and Jude, but omitted by W. H.).*

2527   καθ-όλου, adv., *entirely; καθόλου μή*, Ac. iv. 18, *not at all.**

2528   καθ-οπλίσω, *to arm fully*, pass., Lu. xi. 21.*

2529   καθ-οράω, ῶ, *to see clearly*, pass., Ro. i. 20.*

2530   καθ-ότι, adv., *as, according as*, Ac. ii. 45, iv. 35; *because that, for*, Lu. i. 7, xix. 9; Ac. ii. 24, xvii. 31 (W. H.).*

2531   καθ-ώς, adv., *according as, even as*.

see 2509   καθώσ-περ, adv., *just as*, Heb. v. 4 (W. H.).*

2532   καί, conj., *and, also, even*. For the various uses of this conjunction, see Gr. § 403, Wi. § 53, 1–4, Bu. 360 sq.

2533   Καϊάφας, α, ὁ, *Caiaphas*, Jn. xi. 49.

2535   Κάϊν, ὁ (Heb.), *Cain*, Heb. xi. 4.

2536   Καϊνάν, ὁ (Heb.), *Cainan*. Two are mentioned, Lu. iii. 36, 37.*

2537   καινός, ή, όν, *new*, Lu. v. 38; Ac. xvii. 19. *Syn.: νέος* is new under the aspect of *time*; καινός, new in quality, of different character.

2538   καινότης, τητος, ἡ, *newness* (moral and spiritual), Ro. vi. 4, vii. 6.*

2539   καί-περ, conj., *although*, Phil. iii. 4; Heb. v. 8.

2540   καιρός, οῦ, *a fixed time, season, opportunity*, Lu. viii. 13; Heb. xi. 15; Ac. xiv. 17; Ro. viii. 18. *Syn.: χρόνος* is time in general, viewed simply as such; καιρός, definite, suitable time, the time of some decisive event, *crisis, opportunity*.

2541   Καῖσαρ, αρος, ὁ, *Cæsar*, a title assumed by Roman emperors, after Julius Cæsar, as Lu. ii. 1, xx. 22; Ac. xvii. 7; Phil. iv. 22.

2542   Καισάρεια, ας, ἡ, *Cæsarea*. Two cities of Palestine, one in Galilee (*Cæsarea Philippi*), Mat. xvi. 13; the other on the coast of the Mediterranean, Ac. viii. 40.

*For 2534 see Strong.

2543   καί-τοι, conj., *and yet, although*,
★   Heb. iv. 3; so καίτοιγε.

2545   καίω, perf. pass. κέκαυμαι, *to
kindle, light*, Mat. v. 15;
pass., *to burn*, Lu. xii. 35;
to burn, consume, Jn. xv. 6;
fig., Lu. xxiv. 32.

2546   κἀκεῖ (καὶ ἐκεῖ), *and there*, Ac.
xiv. 7.

2547   κἀκεῖθεν (καὶ ἐκεῖθεν), *and thence*,
Ac. vii. 4, xx. 15.

2548   κἀκεῖνος, η, ο (καὶ ἐκεῖνος), *and
he, she, it*, Lu. xi. 7; Ac. xv.
11.

2549   κακία, ας, ἡ, *badness*, (1) of
character, *wickedness*, Ac.
viii. 22; (2) of disposition,
malice, ill-will, Col. iii. 8;
(3) of condition, *affliction,
evil*, Mat. vi. 34.

2550   κακο-ήθεια, ας, ἡ, *malignity*,
Ro. i. 29.*

2551   κακο-λογέω, ῶ, *to speak evil of*
(acc.), Mar. ix. 39; Ac. xix.
9; *to curse*, Mat. xv. 4; Mar.
vii. 10.*

2552   κακο-πάθεια, ας, ἡ, *a suffering of evil, affliction*, Ja. v.
10.*

2553   κακο-παθέω, ῶ, *to suffer evil, to
endure affliction*, 2 Tim. ii. 3
(W. H. συνκακ-), 9, iv. 5; Ja.
v. 13.*

2554   κακοποιέω, ῶ, abs., *to do harm*,
Mar. iii. 4; Lu. vi. 9; *to do
wrong*, 1 Pet. iii. 17; 3 Jn.
11.*

2555   κακο-ποιός, όν, as subst., *an
evil-doer*, Jn. xviii. 30 (not
W. H.); 1 Pet. ii. 12, 14, iii.
16 (W. H. omit), iv. 15.*

2556   κακός, ή, όν, *evil, wicked; τὸ
κακόν, wickedness*, Mat. xxvii.
23: also *affliction*, Lu. xvi.
35.

2557   κακ-οῦργος, ον, as subst., *a male-
factor*, Lu. xxiii. 32, 33, 39;
2 Tim. ii. 9.*

2558   κακ-ουχέω, ῶ, only in pass.,
part., *treated ill, harassed*,
Heb. xi. 37, xiii. 3.*

2559   κακόω, ῶ, ώσω, *to ill-treat, oppress*, Ac. vii. 6, 19, xii. 1,
xviii. 10; 1 Pet. iii. 13; *to
embitter*, Ac. xiv. 2.*

2560   κακῶς, adv., *badly, wickedly*,
Jn. xviii. 23; κακῶς ἔχειν, *to
be sick*, or *in trouble*, Mat.
iv. 24; Lu. v. 31.

2561   κάκωσις, εως, ἡ, *affliction, ill-
treatment*, Ac. vii. 34.*

2562   καλάμη, ης, ἡ, *stubble*, 1 Cor.
iii. 12.*

2563   κάλαμος, ου, ὁ, *a stalk*, as (1) *a
reed*, growing, Mat. xi. 7;
(2) *a reed*, as a mock sceptre,
Mat. xxvii. 29; (3) *a pen*, 3
Jn. 13; (4) *a measuring-rod*,
Rev. xxi. 15.

2564   καλέω, ῶ, έσω, κέκληκα, *to call;*
hence, (1) *to summon*, Lu.
xix. 13; (2) *to name*, Mat. i.
21, x. 25; (3) *to invite*, Jn.
ii. 2; (4) *to appoint*, or *select*,
for an office, Heb. v. 4; (5)
pass., *to be called*, or *account-
ed*, *i.e.*, *to be*, Mat. v. 9, 19;
Ja. ii. 23.

2565   καλλι-έλαιος, ου, ἡ, *a cultivated
olive tree*, Ro. xi. 24.*

2566   καλλίων (compar. of καλός),
better; adv., κάλλιον, Ac. xxv.
10.*

2567   καλο-διδάσκαλος, ου, ὁ, ἡ, *a
teacher of what is good*, Tit.
ii. 3. (N. T.)*

2568   Καλοὶ Λιμένες, *Fair Havens*, a
harbor in the island of Crete,
Ac. xxvii. 8.*

2569   καλο-ποιέω, ῶ, *to act uprightly*,
2 Th. iii. 13. (S.)*

2570   καλός, ή, όν, *beautiful;* (1) physically, Lu. xxi. 25; (2) mor-
ally beautiful, *good, noble*,
Mat. v. 16; Heb. xiii. 18;
(3) *excellent, advantageous*,
Lu. vi. 43; 1 Cor. vii. 1.

2571   κάλυμμα, ατος, τό, *a covering,
veil*, 2 Cor. iii. 13–16.*

2572   καλύπτω, ψω, *to cover, veil*, Lu.
xxiii. 30; 2 Cor. iv. 3.

2573   καλῶς, adv., *well, rightly, nobly*,
Jn. iv. 17; 1 Cor. xiv. 17.

see 2504   κἀμέ, see κἀγώ.
2574   κάμηλος, ου, ὁ, ἡ, *a camel*, Mar.
i. 6, x. 25.

2575   κάμινος, ου, ἡ, *a furnace*, Mat.
xiii. 42, 50; Rev. i. 15, ix. 2.*

2576   καμ-μύω (κατά and μύω), *to shut*,
close the eyes, Mat. xiii. 15;
Ac. xxviii. 27.*

2577   κάμνω, καμῶ, perf. κέκμηκα, *to
be weary, to be sick*, Heb. xii.
3; Ja. v. 15; Rev. ii. 3 (W.
H. omit).*

see 2504   κἀμοί, see κἀγώ.
2578   κάμπτω, ψω, *to bend* the knee,
bow, Ro. xi. 4, xiv. 11; Ep.
iii. 14; Phil. ii. 10.*

2579   κἄν (καὶ ἐάν), *and if*, Lu. xiii.
9; *even if, though*, Mat. xxvi.
35; *if even*, Heb. xii. 20;
elliptically, *if only*, Mar. v.
28; Ac. v. 15.

2580   Κανᾶ, ἡ, *Cana*, Jn. ii. 1, 11.

2581   Κανανίτης, ου, ὁ, *a Zealot* (from

★For 2544 see Strong.

the Aramaic, meaning the same as ζηλωτής), Mat. x. 4; Mar. iii. 18 (W. H. read Καναναῖος, which has the same meaning). (N. T.)*

2582 Κανδάκη, ης, ἡ, Candace, Ac. viii. 27.*

2583 κανών, όνος, ὁ, prop. a rod; hence (1) a rule of conduct, Gal. v. 16; Phil. iii. 16 (W. H. or it); (2) a limit or sphere of duty, province (R. V.), 2 Cor. x. 13, 15, 16.*

2584 Καπερ-ναούμ, or Καφαρ-ναούμ (W. H.), ἡ (Heb.), Capernaum, Jn. vi. 17, 24.

2585 καπηλεύω, to be a petty trader; hence (with acc.), to make merchandise of, or adulterate, corrupt, 2 Cor. ii. 17.*

2586 καπνός, οῦ, ὁ, smoke, Ac. ii. 19; Rev. viii. 4.

2587 Καππαδοκία, ας, ἡ, Cappadocia, Ac. ii. 9; 1 Pet. i. 1.*

2588 καρδία, ας, ἡ, the heart, met., as the seat of the affections, but chiefly of the understanding; fig., the heart of the earth, Mat. xii. 40.

2589 καρδιο-γνώστης, ου, ὁ, a knower of hearts, Ac. i. 24, xv. 8. (N. T.)*

2590 καρπός, οῦ, ὁ, fruit, produce, Lu. xii. 17; met., for children, Ac. ii. 30; deeds, conduct, the fruit of the hands, Mat. iii. 8; effect, result, Ro. vi. 21. Praise is called the fruit of the lips, Heb. xiii. 15.

2591 Κάρπος, ου, ὁ, Carpus, 2 Tim. iv. 13.*

2592 καρποφορέω, ῶ, ήσω, to bring forth fruit, Mar. iv. 28; mid., to bear fruit of one's self, Col. i. 6.

2593 καρπο-φόρος, ον, fruitful, Ac. xiv. 17.*

2594 καρτερέω, ῶ, ήσω, to be strong, steadfast, Heb. xi. 27.*

2595 κάρφος, ους, τό, a dry twig, a straw, Mat. vii. 3, 4, 5; Lu. vi. 41, 42.*

2596 κατά, prep., gov. the gen. and acc. cases, down; hence, gen., down from, against, etc.; acc., according to, against, etc. (see Gr. §§ 124, 147 a, Wi. §§ 47 k, 49 d, Bu. 334 sq.). In composition, κατά may import descent, subjection, opposition, distribution, and with certain verbs (as of destruction, diminu-

tion, and the like) is intensive = "utterly."

2597 κατα-βαίνω, βήσομαι, βέβηκα, 2d aor. κατέβην, to go or come down, descend, used of persons and of things, as gifts from heaven, of the clouds, storms, lightnings; also of anything that falls, Lu. xxii. 44; Rev. xvi. 21.

2598 κατα-βάλλω, 1st aor. pass. κατεβλήθην, to cast down, Rev. xii. 10 (W. H. βάλλω); 2 Cor. iv. 9 mid., to lay, as a foundation, Heb. vi. 1.*

2599 κατα-βαρέω, ῶ, to weigh down, to burden, 2 Cor. xii. 16.*

see 916 κατα-βαρύνω = καταβαρέω, Mar. xiv. 40 (W. H.).*

2600 κατά-βασις, εως, ἡ, descent, place of descent, Lu. xix. 37.*

2601 κατα-βιβάζω, to bring down, cast down, Mat. xi. 23 (W. H. καταβαίνω), Lu. x. 15 (Rec., W. H. mrg.).*

2602 κατα-βολή, ῆς, ἡ, a founding, laying the foundation of, Mat. xiii. 35; Heb. xi. 11.

2603 κατα-βραβεύω, to give judgment against as umpire of the games, to deprive of reward, Col. ii. 18.*

2604 κατ-αγγελεύς, έως, ὁ, a proclaimer, a herald, Ac. xvii. 18. (N. T.)*

2605 κατ-αγγέλλω, to declare openly, to proclaim, to preach, Ac. xiii. 5, xv. 36.

2606 κατα-γελάω, ῶ, to laugh at, deride, gen., Mat. ix. 24; Mar. v. 40; Lu. viii. 53.*

2607 κατα-γινώσκω, to condemn, blame, gen. of persons, Gal. ii. 11; 1 Jn. iii. 20, 21.*

2608 κατ-άγνυμι, fut. κατεάξω, to break down, to break in pieces, Mat. xii. 20; Jn. xix. 31–33.*

2609 κατ-άγω, to bring down, as Ac. ix. 30; Ro. x. 6; as a nautical term, to bring to land, Lu. v. 11; pass., to come to land, Ac. xxvii. 3, xxviii. 12.

2610 κατ-αγωνίζομαι, dep., to contend against, subdue (acc.), Heb. xi. 33.*

2611 κατα-δέω, ῶ, to bind up, as wounds, Lu. x. 34.*

2612 κατά-δηλος, ον, thoroughly evident, Heb. vii. 15.*

2613 κατα-δικάζω, to condemn, to pronounce sentence against, Mat. xii. 7, 37; Lu. vi. 37; Ja. v. 6.*

see 1349
& 2613

κατα-δίκη, ης, ή, *a sentence of condemnation,* Ac. xxv. 15 (W. H.).*

2614 **κατα-διώκω,** *to follow closely,* Mar. i. 36.*

2615 **κατα-δουλόω, ῶ, ώσω,** *to enslave,* 2 Cor. xi. 20; Gal. ii. 4.*

2616 **κατα-δυναστεύω,** *to exercise power over, to oppress,* Ac. x. 38; Ja. ii. 6.*

see 2652 **κατά-θεμα,** W. H. for *καταναθεμα,* Rev. xxii. 3. (N T.)*

see 2653 **κατα-θεματίζω,** W. H. for *καταναθ-,* Mat. xxvi. 74. (N. T.)*

2617 **κατ-αισχύνω,** *to make ashamed,* 1 Cor. i. 27; *to dishonor,* 1 Cor. xi. 4, 5; *to shame,* as with disappointed expectation, 1 Pet. ii. 6; pass., *to be ashamed,* as Lu. xiii. 17.

2618 **κατα-καίω, αύσω,** *to burn up, to consume entirely,* as Mat. iii. 12; Heb. xiii. 11.

2619 **κατα-καλύπτω,** in mid., *to wear a veil,* 1 Cor. xi. 6, 7.*

2620 **κατα-καυχάομαι, ῶμαι,** *to rejoice against, to glory over* (gen.), Ro. xi. 18; Ja. ii. 13, iii. 14. (S.)*

2621 **κατά-κειμαι,** *to lie down,* as the sick, Mar. i. 30; *to recline* at table, Mar. xiv. 3.

2622 **κατα-κλάω, ῶ,** *to break in pieces,* Mar. vi. 41; Lu. ix. 16.*

2623 **κατα-κλείω,** *to shut up, confine,* Lu. iii. 20; Ac. xxvi. 10.*

2624 **κατα-κληρο-δοτέω, ῶ,** *to distribute by lot,* Ac. xiii. 19 (W. H. read the following). (S.)*

see 2624 **κατα-κληρο-νομέω, ῶ,** *to distribute by lot,* Ac. xiii. 19 (W. H.). (S.)*

2625 **κατα-κλίνω, νῶ,** *to cause to recline* at table, Lu. ix. 14, 15 (W. H.); mid., *to recline* at table, Lu. vii. 36 (W. H.), xiv. 8, xxiv. 30.*

2626 **κατα-κλύζω, σω,** *to inundate, deluge,* pass., 2 Pet. iii. 6.*

2627 **κατα-κλυσμός, οῦ, ό,** *a deluge, flood,* Mat. xxiv. 38, 39; Lu. xvii. 27; 2 Pet. ii. 5.*

2628 **κατ-ακολουθέω, ῶ,** *to follow after* (abs. or dat.), Lu. xxiii. 55; Ac. xvi. 17.*

2629 **κατα-κόπτω, ψω,** *to wound,* Mar. v. 5.*

2630 **κατα-κρημνίζω, σω,** *to cast down headlong,* Lu. iv. 29.*

2631 **κατά-κριμα, ατος, τό,** *con-*

---

demnation, Ro. v. 16, 18, viii. 1.*

2632 **κατα-κρίνω, νῶ,** *to judge worthy of punishment* (gen. and dat.), *to condemn,* as Mat. xx. 18; Ro. ii. 1, viii. 3; in a more general sense, Lu. xi. 31, 32.

2633 **κατά-κρισις, εως, ή,** *the act of condemnation,* 2 Cor. iii. 9, vii. 3. (N. T.)*

2634 **κατα-κυριεύω,** *to exercise authority over,* Mat. xx. 25; Mar. x. 42; 1 Pet. v. 3; *to get the mastery of,* Ac. xix. 16 (gen.).

2635 **κατα-λαλέω, ῶ,** *to speak against* (gen.), Ja. iv. 11; 1 Pet. ii. 12, iii. 16.*

2636 **κατα-λαλιά, ᾶς, ή,** *evil-speaking, defamation,* 2 Cor. xii. 20, 1 Pet. ii. 1. (N. T.)*

2637 **κατά-λαλος, ον, ό, ή,** *an evil-speaker, a defamer,* Ro. i. 30. (N. T.)*

2638 **κατα-λαμβάνω, λήψομαι,** *to seize* or *lay hold of,* as Mar. ix. 18; *to grasp, to obtain,* as the prize in public games, Phil. iii. 12, 13; *to overtake,* 1 Th. v. 4; mid., *to comprehend, to perceive,* ὅτι, or acc. and inf., Ep. iii. 18.

2639 **κατα-λέγω,** *to register, to enrol,* pass., 1 Tim. v. 9.*

2640 **κατά-λειμμα, ατος, τό,** *a remnant, a residue,* Ro. ix. 27 (W. H. ὑπόλιμμα). (S.)*

2641 **κατα-λείπω, ψω,** *to leave utterly, to forsake,* Mar. x. 7; *to depart from,* Heb. xi. 27; *to leave remaining, to reserve,* Ro. xi. 4.

2642 **κατα-λιθάζω, σω,** *to stone, to destroy by stoning,* Lu. xx. 6. (N. T.)*

2643; see **καταλλαγή, ῆς, ή,** *reconciliation,*
629 Ro. v. 11, xi. 15; 2 Cor. v. 18, 19.* *Syn.:* see *ἀπολύτρωσις.*

2644 **κατ-αλλάσσω, ξω,** *to reconcile* (acc. and dat.), Ro. v. 10; 1 Cor. vii. 11; 2 Cor. v. 18, 19, 20.*

2645 **κατά-λοιπος, ον,** plur., *the rest, the residue,* Ac. xv. 17.*

2646 **κατάλυμα, ατος, τό,** *a lodging-place, an inn,* Lu. ii. 7; *a guest-chamber,* Mar. xiv. 14; Lu. xxii. 11.*

2647 **κατα-λύω, ύσω,** *to unloose,* (1) lit., of a building, *to destroy,* Mar. xiv. 58; (2) fig., of law or command, *to render* *void*, Mat. v. 17; (3) *to pass the night, to lodge*, Lu. ix. 12, xix. 7.

2648 κατα-μανθάνω, 2d aor. κατέμαθον, *to consider carefully*, Mat. vi. 28.*

2649 κατα-μαρτυρέω, ῶ, *to bear testimony against* (acc. of thing, gen. of pers.), Mat. xxvi. 62, xxvii. 13; Mar. xiv. 60, xv. 4 (not W. H.).*

2650 κατα-μένω, *to remain, abide*, Ac. i. 13.*

2651 κατα-μόνας (W. H. κατὰ μόνας), adv., *privately, alone*, Mar. iv. 10; Lu. ix. 18.*

2652 κατ-ανά-θεμα, ατος, τό, *a curse*, Rev. xxii. 3; see κατάθεμα. (N. T.)*

2653 κατ-ανα-θεματίζω, *to curse, devote to destruction*, Mat. xxvi. 74; see καταθεματίζω. (N. T.)*

2654 κατ-αν-αλίσκω, *to consume*, as fire, Heb. xii. 29.*

2655 κατα-ναρκάω, ῶ, ήσω, *to be burdensome to* (gen.), 2 Cor. xi. 9, xii. 13, 14.*

2656 κατα-νεύω, *to nod, to make signs to*, dat., Lu. v. 7.*

2657 κατα-νοέω, ῶ, (1) *to observe carefully, perceive*, Lu. vi. 41; (2) *to consider* (acc.), Ac. xi. 6.

2658 κατ-αντάω, ῶ, *to come to, to arrive at*, with εἰς, as Ac. xvi. 1; once with ἀντικρύ, Ac. xx. 15; met., *to attain to*, Phil. iii. 11.

2659 κατάνυξις, εως, ἡ, *stupor*, Ro. xi. 8. (S.)*

2660 κατα-νύσσω, ξω, 2d aor., pass. κατενύγην, *to prick through, to agitate greatly*, pass., Ac. ii. 37. (S.)*

2661 κατ-αξιόω, ῶ, ώσω, *to judge worthy of* (gen.), pass., Lu. xx. 35, xxi. 36; Ac. v. 41; 2 Th. i. 5.*

2662 κατα-πατέω, ῶ, *to trample on, to tread under foot* (acc.), as Lu. viii. 5.

2663 κατάπαυσις, εως, ἡ, *a resting, rest*, Ac. vii. 49; Heb. iii. 11, 18, iv. 1, 3, 5, 10, 11.*

2664 κατα-παύω, (1) trans., *to restrain*, acc. (also τοῦ μή, and inf.), Ac. xiv. 18; *to give rest*, Heb. iv. 8; (2) intrans., *to rest*, ἀπό, Heb. iv. 4, 10.*

2665 κατα-πέτασμα(πετάννυμι),ατος, τό, *a veil, curtain*, separating the holy place and the

holy of holies, as Lu. xxiii. 45. (S.)

2666 κατα-πίνω, 2d aor. κατέπιον, 1st aor. pass. κατεπόθην, *to drink down, swallow*, Mat. xxiii. 24; Rev. xii. 16; fig., *to devour, destroy*, 1 Cor. xv. 54; 2 Cor. ii. 7, v. 4; Heb. xi. 29; 1 Pet. v. 8.*

2667 κατα-πίπτω, 2d aor. κατέπεσον, *to fall down*, Lu. viii. 6 (W. H.); Ac. xxvi. 14, xxviii. 6.*

2668 κατα-πλέω, εύσομαι, 1st aor. κατέπλευσα, *to sail* to land, Lu. viii. 26.*

2669 κατα-πονέω, ῶ, in pass., *to be oppressed, distressed*, Ac. vii. 24; 2 Pet. ii. 7.*

2670 κατα-ποντίζω, pass., *to sink down*, Mat. xiv. 30; *to be drowned*, Mat. xviii. 6.*

2671 κατ-άρα, ας, ἡ, *a curse, cursing*, Gal. iii. 10, 13; Heb. vi. 8; 2 Pet. ii. 14; Ja. iii. 10.*

2672 κατ-αράομαι, ῶμαι, *to curse*, Mat. v. 44 (W. H. omit); Mar. xi. 21; Lu. vi. 28; Ro. xii. 14; Ja. iii. 9; pass., perf. part., *accursed*, Mat. xxv. 41.*

2673 κατ-αργέω, ῶ, ήσω, *to render useless*, Lu. xiii. 7; *to cause to cease, abolish*, as Ro. iii. 3, 31, and frequently in Paul; *to sever* from (ἀπό), Ro. vii. 2; Gal. v. 4.

2674 κατ-αριθμέω, ῶ, *to number among*, Ac. i. 17.*

2675 κατ-αρτίζω, ίσω, *to refit, to repair*, Mat. iv. 21; *to restore from error or sin*, Gal. vi. 1; *to perfect, to complete*, 1 Th. iii. 10; 1 Pet. v. 10; pass., *to be restored* to harmony, 1 Cor. i. 10.

2676 κατάρτισις, εως, ἡ, *a perfecting*, 2 Cor. xiii. 9.*

2677 καταρτισμός, οῦ, ὁ, *a perfecting*, Ep. iv. 12. (N. T.)*

2678 κατα-σείω, σω, *to shake* the hand, *to beckon*, Ac. xii. 17, xiii. 16, xix. 33, xxi. 40.*

2679 κατα-σκάπτω, ψω, *to dig under, to demolish*, Ro. xi. 3; perf. part., pass., *ruins*, Ac. xv. 16 (not W. H.).*

2680 κατα-σκευάζω, άσω, *to prepare, to build, to equip*, as Mat. xi. 10; Lu. i. 17; Heb. iii. 3, 4.

2681 κατα-σκηνόω, ῶ, ώσω, *to pitch one's tent, to dwell*, Mat. xiii.

32; Mar. iv. 32; **Lu. xiii.** 19;
Ac. ii. 26.*

2682   **κατα-σκήνωσις,** εως, ἡ, *a dwell-*
ing-place, a haunt, as of
birds, Mat. viii. 20; Lu. ix.
58.*

2683   **κατα-σκιάζω,** σω, *to overshadow,*
Heb. ix. 5.*

2684   **κατα-σκοπέω,** ῶ, *to spy out, to*
plot against, Gal. ii. 4.*

2685   **κατά-σκοπος,** ου, ὁ, *a spy,* Heb.
xi. 31.*

2686   **κατα-σοφίζομαι,** σομαι, *to deal*
deceitfully with, Ac. vii. 19.*

2687   **κατα-στέλλω,** λῶ, 1st aor. κατέ-
στειλα, *to appease, restrain,*
Ac. xix. 35, 36.*

2688   **κατά-στημα,** ατος, τό, *behavior,*
conduct, Tit. ii. 3.*

2689   **κατα-στολή,** ῆς, ἡ, *dress, attire,*
1 Tim. ii. 9.*

2690   **κατα-στρέφω,** ψω, *to overthrow,*
Mat. xxi. 12; Mar. xi. 15;
Ac. xv. 16 (W. H.).*

2691   .**κατα-στρηνιάω,** ῶ, άσω, *to grow*
wanton to the loss of (gen.),
1 Tim. v. 11. (N. T.)*

2692   **κατα-στροφή,** ῆς, ἡ, *overthrow,*
destruction, 2 Tim. ii. 14;
2 Pet. ii. 6 (W. H. omit).*

2693   **κατα-στρώννυμι,** στρώσω, *to*
prostrate, slay, 1 Cor. x. 5 *

2694   **κατα-σύρω,** *to drag along* by
force, Lu. xii. 58.*

2695   **κατα-σφάζω,** ξω, *to slay,* Lu.
xix. 27.*

2696   **κατα-σφραγίζω,** σω, *to seal up,*
as a book, Rev. v. 1.*

2697   **κατά-σχεσις,** εως, ἡ, *a posses-*
sion, Ac. vii. 5, 45. (S.)*

2698   **κατα-τίθημι,** θήσω, 1st aor. κα-
τέθηκα, *to deposit,* as a body
in a tomb, Mar. xv. 46
(W. H. τίθημι); mid. κατα-
τίθεσθαι χάριν, *to gain favor*
with (dat.), Ac. xxiv. 27
xxv. 9.*

2699   **κατα-τομή,** ῆς, ἡ, *mutilation*
paronomasia with περιτομή
Phil. iii. 2.*

2700   **κατα-τοξεύω,** *to transfix,* Heb.
xii. 20 (W. H. omit).*

2701   **κατα-τρέχω,** 2d aor. κατέδραμον,
to run down (ἐπί, acc.), Ac.
xxi. 32.*

see 2719   **κατα-φάγω,** see κατεσθίω.

2702   **κατα-φέρω,** κατοίσω, 1st aor.
κατήνεγκα, pass. κατηνέχθην,
to cast down, as an adverse
vote, Ac. xxv. 7, xxvi. 10
(W. H.); pass., *to be borne*
down, to be overcome, Ac. xx.
9.*

2703   **κατα-φεύγω,** 2d aor. κατέφυγον,
to flee for refuge, with εἰς,
Ac. xiv. 6; with inf., Heb.
vi. 18.*

2704   **κατα-φθείρω,** pass., perf. κατέ-
φθαρμαι, 2d aor. κατεφθάρην,
to corrupt, 2 Tim. iii. 8; *to*
destroy, 2 Pet. ii. 12 (W. H.
φθείρω).*

2705   **κατα-φιλέω,** ῶ, *to kiss affection-*
ately, or *repeatedly* (acc.), as
Mat. xxvi. 49; Lu. xv. 20.

2706   **κατα-φρονέω,** ῶ, ήσω, *to despise*
(gen.), as Mat. vi. 24.

2707   **καταφρονητής,** οῦ, ὁ, *a despiser,*
Ac. xiii. 41. (S.)*

2708   **κατα-χέω,** εύσω, 1st aor. κατέ-
χεα, *to pour down upon,* Mat.
xxvi. 7; Mar. xiv. 3.*

2709   **κατα-χθόνιος,** ον, *subterranean,*
Phil. ii. 10.*

2710   **κατα-χράομαι,** ῶμαι, *to use ful-*
ly, 1 Cor. vii. 31, ix. 18 (dat.).*

2711   **κατα-ψύχω,** *to cool, to refresh,*
Lu. xvi. 24.*

2712   **κατ-είδωλος,** ον, *full of idols*
(R. V.), Ac. xvii. 16. (N.T.)*

2713   **κατ-έναντι,** adv., or as prep.
with gen., *over against, be-*
fore, in presence or *in sight*
of.

2714   **κατ-ενώπιον,** adv., *in the pres-*
ence of (gen.). (S.)

2715   **κατ-εξουσιάζω,** *to exercise au-*
thority over (gen.), Mat. xx.
25; Mar. x. 42. (N. T.)*

2716   **κατ-εργάζομαι,** άσομαι, (with
mid. and pass. aor. (augm.
εἰ-), *to accomplish, achieve,*
Ro. xv. 18; Ep. vi. 13; *to*
*   work out, result in,* Ro. iv.
15, vii. 8.

2718   **κατ-έρχομαι,** 2d aor. κατῆλθον,
to come down, Lu. iv. 31, ix.
37.

2719   **κατ-εσθίω** and -ἔσθω (Mar. xii.
40, W. H.), fut. καταφάγομαι
(Jn. ii. 17, W. H.), 2d aor.
κατέφαγον, *to eat up, to de-*
vour entirely, lit. or fig., Mat.
xiii. 4; Jn. ii. 17; Gal. v.
15.

2720   **κατ-ευθύνω,** νῶ, *to direct, to*
guide, Lu. i. 79; 1 Th. iii. 11;
2 Th. iii. 5.*

see 2127   **κατ-ευλογέω,** *to bless greatly,*
Mar. x. 16 (W. H.).*

2721   **κατ-εφ-ίστημι,** 2d aor. κατεπέ-
στην, *to rise up against,* Ac.
xviii. 12. (N. T.)*

2722   **κατ-έχω,** κατασχήσω, *to seize*
on, to hold fast, to retain,
possess, to prevent from doing

✻ Strong mistakenly omitted
2717.

a thing (τοῦ μή, with inf.),
to repress, Ro. i. 18; τὸ κα-
τέχον, the hindrance, 2 Th.
ii. 6; κατεῖχον εἰς τὸν αἰγια-
λόν, they held for the shore,
Ac. xxvii. 40.

2723 κατ-ηγορέω, ῶ, ήσω, to accuse,
to speak against, abs., or with
person in gen.; charge in
gen. alone or after περί or
κατά; pass., to be accused;
with ὑπό or παρά, of the accuser.

2724 κατηγορία, as, ή, an accusation,
a charge, pers. in gen. alone,
or after κατά; charge also
in gen., 1 Tim. v. 19; Tit.
i. 6.

2725 κατήγορος, ου, ὁ, an accuser,
Ac. xxiii. 30, 35.

see 2725 κατήγωρ, ὁ (Heb.?), an accuser,
Rev. xii. 10 (W. H.). (N.T.)*

2726 κατήφεια, as, ή, dejection, gloom,
Ja. iv. 9.*

2727 κατ-ηχέω, ῶ, ήσω, perf., pass.
κατήχημαι (ῆχος), to instruct
orally, to teach, inform, Lu.
i. 4; Ac. xviii. 25, xxi. 21,
24; Ro. ii. 18; 1 Cor. xiv.
19; Gal. vi. 6.*

see 2398 κατ᾽ ἰδίαν, separately, privately,
by one's self (see ἴδιος).

2728 κατ-ιόω, ῶ (ἰός), to cover with
rust, Ja. v. 3. (Ap.)*

2729 κατ-ισχύω, to prevail against,
overpower (gen.), Mat. xvi.
18; Lu. xxi. 36 (W. H.), xxiii.
23.*

2730 κατ-οικέω, ῶ, (1) intrans., to
dwell, with ἐν, εἰς (const.
præg.), ἐπί, gen., or adverbs
of place, Ac. i. 20, vii. 4;
fig., of qualities or attributes,
to abide, Col. ii. 9; (2) trans.,
to dwell in, to inhabit (acc.),
Mat. xxiii. 21; Ac. i. 19.

2731 κατοίκησις, εως, ή, a dwelling,
habitation, Mar. v. 3.*

2732 κατοικητήριον, ου, τό, a dwelling-place, Ep. ii. 22; Rev.
xviii. 2. (S.)*

2733 κατοικία, as, ή, a dwelling, habitation, Ac. xvii. 26.*

see 2730 κατ-οικίζω, to cause to dwell,
Ja. iv. 5 (W. H.).*

2734 κατοπτρίζω, mid., to behold,
as in a mirror, 2 Cor. iii.
18.*

2735 κατ-όρθωμα, ατος, τό, an honorable or successful achieve-
ment, Ac. xxiv. 2 (W. H.
διόρθωμα).*

2736 κάτω, adv., downwards, down,

Mat. iv. 6, beneath, Mar.
xiv. 66; of age, comp., κατω-
τέρω, under, Mat. ii. 16.

2737 κατώτερος, a, ον (κάτω), lower,
Ep. iv. 9 (on which see Gr.
§ 259, Wi. § 11, 2 c, Bu. 28).*

2738 καῦμα, ατος, τό (καίω), heat,
scorching heat, Rev. vii. 16,
xvi. 9.*

2739 καυματίζω, σω, to scorch, burn,
Mat. xiii. 6; Mar. iv. 6; Rev.
xvi. 8, 9.*

2740 καῦσις, εως, ή, a burning, burning up, Heb. vi. 8.*

2741 καυσόω, ῶ, to burn up, pass.,
2 Pet. iii. 10, 12. (N. T.)*

2742 καύσων, ωνος, ὁ, scorching heat;
perhaps a hot wind from the
E., Mat. xx. 12; Lu. xii. 55;
Ja. i. 11 (see Hos. xii. 1, etc.).
(S.)*

2743 καυτηριάζω (W. H. καυστ-), to
brand, as with a hot iron;
fig., pass., 1 Tim. iv. 2.*

2744 καυχάομαι, ῶμαι, 2d pers. καυ-
χᾶσαι, fut. ήσομαι, to glory,
to boast, both in a good sense
and in a bad, 1 Cor. i. 29;
Ep. ii. 9; followed with prep.,
ἐν, περί, gen.; ὑπέρ, gen.; ἐπί,
dat.

2745 καύχημα, ατος, τό, the ground
of glorying, as Ro. iv. 2;
a glorying, 1 Cor. v. 6.

2746 καύχησις, εως, ή, the act of
boasting, glorying, Ro. xv. 17;
Ja. iv. 16. (S.)

see 2584 Καφαρναούμ (see Καπερναούμ),
Capernaum.

2747 Κεγχρεαί, ῶν, αἱ, Cenchreæ, a
port of Corinth, Ac. xviii.
18; Ro. xvi. 1.*

see 2748 κέδρος, ου, ή, a cedar, Jn. xviii.
1; perhaps a mistaken read-
ing for following.*

2748 Κεδρών, ὁ (Heb. dark or turbid),
Cedron, a turbid brook be-
tween the Mount of Olives
and Jerusalem, a variant
reading in Jn. xviii. 1.*

2749 κεῖμαι, σαι, ται; impf. ἐκείμην,
σο, το; to lie, to recline, to be
laid, Lu. xxiii. 53; 1 Jn. v.
19; met., to be enacted, as
laws, 1 Tim. i. 9.

2750 κειρία, as, ή, a band or bandage
of linen, Jn. xi. 44.*

2751 κείρω, κερῶ, to shear, as sheep,
Ac. viii. 32; mid., to have
the head shorn, Ac. xviii. 18;
1 Cor. xi. 6.*

2752 κέλευσμα, ατος, τό, a command,
a loud cry, 1 Th. iv. 16.*

2753 κελεύω, σω, *to command, to order,* Ac. iv. 15, v. 34.

2754 κενοδοξία, as, ἡ, *vainglory, empty pride,* Phil. ii. 3.*

2755 κενό-δοξος, ον, *vainglorious,* Gal. v. 26.*

2756 κενός, ή, όν, *empty, vain,* Ep. v. 6; Col. ii. 8; *empty-handed,* Lu. i. 53; Ja. ii. 20; *fruitless, ineffectual,* 1 Cor. xv. 10, 58. *Syn.* : κενός, *empty,* refers to the contents; μάταιος, *aimless, purposeless,* to the result.

2757 κενο-φωνία, ας, ἡ, *empty disputing, useless babbling,* 1 Tim. vi. 20; 2 Tim. ii. 16. (N. T.)*

2758 κενόω, ῶ, ώσω, with ἑαυτόν, *to empty* one's self, *divest* one's self *of rightful dignity,* Phil. ii. 7; *to make useless* or *false,* Ro. iv. 14; 1 Cor. i. 17, ix. 15; 2 Cor. ix. 3.*

2759 κέντρον, ου, τό, *a sting,* Rev. ix. 10; 1 Cor. xv. 55, 56; *a goad,* Ac. ix. 5 (W. H. omit), xxvi. 14.*

2760 κεντυρίων, ωνος, ὁ, Latin (see Gr. § 154 c), *a centurion,* the commander of a hundred foot-soldiers, Mar. xv. 39, 44, 45.*

2761 κενῶς, adv., *in vain,* Ja. iv. 5.*

2762 κεραία, or κερέα (W. H.), ας, ἡ, *a little horn* (the small projecting stroke by which certain similar Hebrew letters are distinguished, as ר and ד); met., *the minutest part,* Mat. v. 18; Lu. xvi. 17.*

2763 κεραμεύς, έως, ὁ, *a potter,* Mat. xxvii. 7, 10; Ro. ix. 21.*

2764 κεραμικός, ή, όν, *made of clay, earthen,* Rev ii. 27.*

2765 κεράμιον, ου, τό, *an earthen vessel, a pitcher,* Mar. xiv. 13; Lu. xxii. 10.*

2766 κέραμος, ου, ὁ, *a roofing tile,* Lu. v. 19.*

2767 κεράννυμι (see Gr. §§ 113, 114, Wi. § 15, Bu. 60), *to mix, to pour out for drinking,* Rev. xiv. 10, xviii. 6.*

2768 κέρας, ατος, τό, *a horn,* as Rev. v. 6; fig., for *strength,* only Lu. i. 69; *a projecting point, horn* of the altar, only Rev. ix. 13.

2769 κεράτιον, ου, τό, *a little horn,* the name of the fruit of the *carob tree,* Lu. xv. 16.*

2770 κερδαίνω, ανῶ, 1st aor. ἐκέρδησα,

to gain, acquire, Mat. xxv. 16 (W. H.), 22; Ja. iv. 13; *to gain, win,* Phil. iii. 8; *to gain over* to a cause, 1 Cor. ix. 19–22.

2771 κέρδος, ους, τό, *gain, advantage,* Phil. i. 21, iii. 7; Tit. i. 11.*

2772 κέρμα, ατος, τό (κείρω), *a small piece of money,* Jn. ii. 15.*

2773 κερματιστής, οῦ, ὁ, *a money-changer,* Jn. ii. 14.*

2774 κεφάλαιον, ου, τό, *a sum of money,* Ac. xxii. 28; *the sum, main point* of an argument, Heb. viii. 1 (see R. V. and mrg.).*

2775 κεφαλαιόω (W. H. -λιόω), ῶ, ώσω, *to smite on the head,* Mar. xii. 4.*

2776 κεφαλή, ῆς, ἡ, *the head,* of human beings or animals; for the whole person, Ac. xviii. 6; *the head* of a corner (with γωνία), *corner-stone,* Lu. xx. 17; met., implying authority, *head, lord,* 1 Cor. xi. 3; Ep. i. 22; Col. i. 18.

2777 κεφαλίς, ίδος, ἡ (prop. *top*), *a roll, a volume,* Heb. x. 7.*

see 5392 κημόω, *to muzzle,* 1 Cor. ix. 9 (W. H. mrg.).*

2778 κῆνσος, ου, ὁ, Latin (Gr. § 154 d, Bu. 16), *a tax, a poll-tax,* Mat. xvii. 25, xxii. 17, 19; Mar. xii. 14.*

2779 κῆπος, ου, ὁ, *a garden,* Lu. xiii. 19; Jn. xviii. 1, 26, xix. 41.*

2780 κηπ-ουρός, οῦ, ὁ, *a gardener,* Jn. xx. 15.*

2781 κηρίον, ου, τό, *a honeycomb,* Lu. xxiv. 42 (W. H. omit).*

2782 κήρυγμα, ατος, τό, *a proclaiming, preaching,* as Mat. xii. 41; 1 Cor. i. 21; 2 Tim. iv. 17.

2783 κῆρυξ, υκος, ὁ, *a herald, a preacher,* 1 Tim. ii. 7; 2 Tim. i. 11; 2 Pet. ii. 5.*

2784 κηρύσσω, ξω, (1) *to proclaim, to publish,* Mar. vii. 36; (2) specially, *to preach* the Gospel, abs., or acc. and dat., Mar. i. 38; Lu. xii. 3; 1 Pet. iii. 19.

2785 κῆτος, ους, τό, *a sea monster, a whale,* Mat. xii. 40.*

2786 Κηφᾶς, ᾶ, ὁ (Aramaic, *a rock*), *Cephas, i.e.,* Peter, 1 Cor. i. 12, iii. 22.

2787 κιβωτός, οῦ, ἡ, *a wooden chest,* used of the ark of the covenant, Heb. ix. 4; Rev. xi. 19;

of Noah's ark, Lu. xvii. 27 ;
Heb. xi. 7.

2788 κιθάρα, ας, ἡ, a harp, 1 Cor.
xiv. 7 ; Rev. xv. 2.

2789 κιθαρίζω, to play upon a harp,
1 Cor. xiv. 7 ; Rev. xiv. 2.*

2790 κιθαρ-ῳδός, οῦ, ὁ, a harper,
singer to the harp, Rev. xiv.
2, xviii. 22.*

2791 Κιλικία, ας, ἡ, Cilicia, Ac. vi.
9, xxi. 39.

2792 κινάμωμον (W. H. κιννά-), ου,
τό, cinnamon, Rev. xviii. 13.*

2793 κινδυνεύω, σω, to be in danger,
Lu. viii. 23; Ac. xix. 27, 40;
1 Cor. xv. 30.*

2794 κίνδυνος, ου, ὁ, danger, peril,
Ro. viii. 35; 2 Cor. xi. 26.*

2795 κινέω, ῶ, ήσω, to move, to stir,
Mat. xxiii. 4; Ac. xvii. 28;
to shake the head in mockery,
Mat. xxvii. 39; Mar. xv. 29;
to remove, Rev. ii. 5, vi. 14;
to excite, Ac. xvii. 28, xxi. 30,
xxiv. 5.*

2796 κίνησις, εως, ἡ, a moving, agita-
tion, Jn. v. 3 (W. H. omit).*

2797 Κίς (W. H. Κείς), ὁ (Heb.),
Kish, father of Saul, Ac. xiii.
21.*

see 5531 κίχρημι, to lend, Lu. xi. 5.*

2798 κλάδος, ου, ὁ, a branch, as Mat.
xiii. 32; met., Ro. xi. 16-19.

2799 κλαίω, αύσω, (1) abs., to wail,
to lament, Lu. xix. 41 ; (2)
trans., to weep for (acc.),
Mat. ii. 18.

2800 κλάσις, εως, ἡ, a breaking, Lu.
xxiv. 35; Ac. ii. 42.*

2801 κλάσμα, ατος, τό, a broken
piece, a fragment, as Mat.
xiv. 20

2802 Κλαύδη (W. H. Καῦδα), ης, ἡ,
Clauda or Cauda, a small
island near Crete, Ac. xxvii.
16.*

2803 Κλαυδία, ας, ἡ, Claudia, 2 Tim.
iv. 21.*

2804 Κλαύδιος, ου, ὁ, Claudius, the
Roman emperor, Ac. xi. 28,
xviii. 2 ; a military tribune
(Lysias), Ac. xxiii. 26.*

2805 κλαυθμός, οῦ, ὁ (κλαίω), weeping, lamentation, as Mat. ii.
18.

2806 κλάω, άσω, only with ἄρτον,
to break bread, in the ordinary meal, Mat. xiv. 19 ; or
in the Lord's Supper, xxvi.
26; fig., of the body of
Christ, 1 Cor. xi. 24 (W. H.
omit).

2807 κλείς, κλειδός, acc. sing. κλεῖδα

or κλεῖν, acc. plur. κλεῖδας or
κλεῖς, ἡ, a key, as a symbol
of power and authority, Mat.
xvi. 19; Rev. i. 18, iii. 7, ix.
1, xx. 1; met., Lu. xi. 52.*

2808 κλείω, σω, to shut, shut up, Mat.
vi. 6; Lu. iv. 25.

2809 κλέμμα, ατος, τό (κλέπτω), theft,
Rev. xi. 21.*

2810 Κλεόπας, α, ὁ, Cleopas, Lu.
xxiv. 18.*

2811 κλέος, ους, τό, glory, praise, 1
Pet. ii. 20.*

2812 κλέπτης, ου, ὁ, a thief, as Mat.
vi. 19; met., of false teach-
ers, Jn. x. 8. Syn.: κλέπτης,
a thief, who steals secretly ;
λῃστής, a robber, who plun-
ders openly, by violence.

2813 κλέπτω, ψω, to steal, abs., Mat.
xix. 18; or trans. (acc.), Mat.
xxvii. 64.

2814 κλῆμα, ατος, τό (κλάω), a tender
branch, a shoot, of a vine,
etc., Jn. xv. 2, 4, 5, 6.*

2815 Κλήμης, εντος, ὁ, Clement, Phil.
iv. 3.*

2816 κληρονομέω, ῶ, ήσω, to inherit,
Gal. iv. 30; to obtain, generally, Lu. x. 25.

2817 κληρονομία, ας, ἡ, an inherit-
ance, Lu. xii. 13; a posses-
sion, Gal. iii. 18.

2818 κληρο-νόμος, ου, ὁ, an heir,
Mat. xxi. 38; applied to
Christ, Heb. i. 2 ; in general,
one who obtains a possession,
Heb. vi. 17.

2819 κλῆρος, ου, ὁ, (1) a lot, Mat.
xxvii. 35; hence, (2) that
which is allotted, a portion,
Ac. i. 17, 25, viii. 21, xxvi.
18; Col. i. 12; plur., persons
assigned to one's care, 1 Pet.
v. 3.*

2820 κληρόω, ῶ, to make a heritage,
Ep. i. 11.*

2821 κλῆσις, εως, ἡ, a calling, invita-
tion, in N. T. always of the
divine call, as Ro. xi. 29;
Ep. iv. 4.

2822 κλητός, ή, όν, verb. adj. (καλέω),
called, invited, Mat. xxii. 14;
of Christians, the called, Ro.
i. 6, 7, viii. 28; called to
an office, Ro. i. 1 ; 1 Cor.
i. 1.

2823 κλίβανος, ου, ὁ, an oven, a furnace, Mat. vi. 30; Lu. xii.
28.*

2824 κλίμα, ατος, τό, a tract of country, a region, Ro. xv. 23;
2 Cor. xi. 10; Gal. i. 21.*

see 2825   κλινάριον, ου, τό, a small bed,
Ac. v. 15 (W. H.).*

2825   κλίνη, ης, ἡ, a bed, Mar. vii. 30;
a portable bed, Mat. ix. 2,
6; a couch for reclining at
meals, Mar. iv. 21.

2826   κλινίδιον, ου, τό (dim.), a small
bed, a couch, Lu. v. 19, 24.*

2827   κλίνω, νῶ, perf. κέκλικα, (1)
trans., to bow, in reverence,
Lu. xxiv. 5; in death, Jn.
xix. 30; to recline the head
for rest, Mat. viii. 20; to
turn to flight, Heb. xi. 34;
(2) intrans., to decline, as the
day, Lu. ix. 12.

2828   κλισία, ας, ἡ, a company reclining at a meal, Lu. ix. 14.*

2829   κλοπή, ῆς, ἡ, theft, Mat. xv. 19;
Mar. vii. 21.*

2830   κλύδων, ωνος, ὁ, a violent agita-
tion of the sea, a wave, Lu.
viii. 24; Ja. i. 6.*

2831   κλυδωνίζομαι, to be agitated, as
waves by the wind, Ep. iv.
14. (S.)*

2832   Κλωπᾶς, ᾶ, ὁ, Clopas, Jn. xix.
25.*

2833   κνήθω, to tickle; pass., to be
tickled, to itch, 2 Tim. iv. 3.*

2834   Κνίδος, ου, ἡ, Cnidus, Ac. xxvii.
7.*

2835   κοδράντης, ου, ὁ, Lat. (see Gr.
§ 154a, Bu. 17), a quadrans,
farthing, the fourth part of
the Roman as, Mat. v. 26;
Mar. xii. 42. (N. T.)*

2836   κοιλία, ας, ἡ, (1) the belly, Mat.
xv. 17; (2) the womb, Mat.
xix. 12; (3) fig., the inner
man, the heart, Jn. vii. 38.

2837   κοιμάω, ῶ, pass., to fall asleep,
Lu. xxii. 45; met., to die, Jn.
xi. 12.

2838   κοίμησις, εως, ἡ, repose, taking
rest, Jn. xi. 13.*

2839   κοινός, ἡ, όν, common, i.e.,
shared by many, Ac. iv. 32;
unclean, ceremonially, Ac. x.
15; Heb. x. 29.

2840   κοινόω, ῶσω, to make common
or unclean, to profane, Mat.
xv. 11; Ac. xxi. 28.

2841   κοινωνέω, ῶ, ήσω, to have common share in, to partake in,
Ro. xv. 27; to be associated
in, Gal. vi. 6.

2842   κοινωνία, ας, ἡ, participation,
communion, fellowship, as 1
Cor. x. 16; 2 Cor. xiii. 13;
1 Jn. i. 3, 6, 7; a contribu-
tion, Ro. xv. 26; Heb. xiii.
16.

2843   κοινωνικός, ἡ, όν, ready to communicate, liberal, 1 Tim. vi.
18.*

2844   κοινωνός, ἡ, όν, as subst., a
partner, Lu. v. 10; a sharer
with, gen. obj., 2 Cor. i. 7.

2845   κοίτη, ης, ἡ, a bed, Lu. xi. 7;
met., marriage bed, Heb. xiii.
4; sexual intercourse (as il-
licit), Ro. xiii. 13; κοίτην
ἔχειν, to conceive, Ro. ix.
10.*

2846   κοιτών, ῶνος, ὁ, a bed-chamber,
Ac. xii. 20.*

2847   κόκκινος, η, ον, dyed from the
κόκκος, crimson, Heb. ix. 19;
Rev. xvii. 4. (S.)

2848   κόκκος, ου, ὁ, a kernel, a grain,
Lu. xiii. 19, xvii. 6.

2849   κολάζω, σω, mid., to chastise, to
punish, Ac. iv. 21; pass., 2
Pet. ii. 9.*

2850   κολακεία (W. H. -κία), ας, ἡ,
flattery, 1 Th. ii. 5.*

2851   κόλασις, εως, ἡ, chastisement,
punishment, Mat. xxv. 46;
1 Jn. iv. 18.*

see 2857   Κολασσαί, ῶν, αἱ, see Κολοσσαί.

2852   κολαφίζω, σω, to strike with the
fist, to maltreat, Mar. xiv. 65.
(N. T.)

2853   κολλάω, ῶ, ήσω, pass., to cleave
to, to join one's self to, Lu. x.
11; Ac. viii. 29.

2854   κολλούριον, or κολλύριον, ου, τό,
collyrium, eye-salve, Rev. iii.
18.*

2855   κολλυβιστής, οῦ, ὁ (κόλλυβος,
small coin), a money-changer,
Mat. xxi. 12; Mar. xi. 15;
Jn. ii. 15.*

2856   κολοβόω, ῶ, ώσω, to cut off, to
shorten, Mat. xxiv. 22; Mar.
xiii. 20.*

●2858   Κολοσσαεύς, έως, ὁ, plur. Κολοσσαεῖς (W. H. Κολοσσαεῖς),
Colossians, only in the head-
ing and subscription (Rec.)
to the Epistle.

2857   Κολοσσαί, or Κολασσαί, ῶν, αἱ,
Colossæ, Col. i. 2.*

2859   κόλπος, ου, ὁ, the bosom, the
chest, (1) of the body; ἐν τῷ
κόλπῳ (or τοῖς κόλποις) εἶναι,
ἀνακεῖσθαι, to be in the bosom
of, i.e., recline next to, at
table; Lu. xvi. 22, 23 (of the
heavenly banquet); Jn. xiii.
23; the phrase in Jn. i. 18
implies a still closer fellowship; (2) of the dress, used
as a bag or pocket, Lu. vi.

38; (3) *a bay, a gulf of the sea,* Ac. xxvii. 39.*

2860 κολυμβάω, ῶ, ήσω, *to swim,* Ac. xxvii. 43.*

2861 κολυμβήθρα, ας, ἡ, *a swimming-place, a pool,* Jn. v. 2, 4 (Rec.), 7, ix. 7, 11 (Rec.).*

2862 κολώνια, or κολωνία (W. H.), ας, ἡ (Lat.), *a colony;* Philippi is so called, Ac. xvi. 12. (N. T.)*

2863 κομάω, ῶ, *to wear the hair long,* 1 Cor. xi. 14, 15.*

2864 κόμη, ης, ἡ, *hair of the head,* 1 Cor. xi. 15.*

2865 κομίζω, σω, mid. fut. κομίσομαι or κομιοῦμαι, *to bear, to bring,* Lu. vii. 37; mid., *to bring for one's self, i.e., to obtain,* Heb. x. 36; *to receive again, to recover,* Heb. xi. 19.

2866 κομψότερον (comp. of κομψός), *better,* of convalescence, adverbially with ἔχω, Jn. iv. 52.*

2867 κονιάω, ῶ, *to whitewash,* Mat. xxiii. 27; pass., Ac. xxiii. 3.*

2868 κονι-ορτός, οῦ, ὁ (ὄρνυμι), *dust,* Mat. x. 14.

2869 κοπάζω, σω, *to grow weary, to cease,* of the wind, Mat. xiv. 32; Mar. iv. 39, vi. 51.*

2870 κοπετός, οῦ, ὁ (κόπτω), *vehement lamentation,* Ac. viii. 2.*

2871 κοπή, ῆς, ἡ, *cutting, slaughter,* Heb. vii. 1.*

2872 κοπιάω, ῶ, άσω, *to be weary,* Mat. xi. 28; *to labor, to toil,* Lu. v. 5; in the Gospel, Ro. xvi. 6, 12; 1 Cor. xv. 10.

2873 κόπος, ου, ὁ, *labor, toil, trouble,* Lu. xi. 7; 2 Th. iii. 8.

2874 κοπρία, ας, ἡ, *dung, manure,* Lu. xiii. 8 (not W. H.), xiv. 35.*

see 2874 κόπριον, ου, τό, *dung,* Lu. xiii. 8 (W. H.).*

2875 κόπτω, mid. fut. κόψομαι, *to cut off,* as branches, trees, etc., Mat. xxi. 8; mid., *to beat or cut one's self in grief, to bewail,* as Mat. xi. 17.

2876 κόραξ, ακος, ὁ, *a raven,* Lu. xii. 24.*

2877 κοράσιον, ου, τό (prop. dim. from κόρη), *a girl,* as Mar. vi. 22, 28.

2878 κορβᾶν (W. H. κορβάν), (indecl.), and κορβανᾶς, ᾶ, ὁ (from Heb.), (1) *a gift, an offering* to God, Mar. vii. 11; (2) *the sacred treasury,* Mat. xxvii. 6.*

2879 Κορέ, ὁ (Heb.), *Korah,* Ju. 11.*

2880 κορέννυμι, ἐσω, pass. perf. κεκόρεσμαι, *to satiate, satisfy,* Ac. xxvii. 38; 1 Cor. iv. 8.*

2881 Κορίνθιος, ου, ὁ, *a Corinthian,* Ac. xviii. 8; 2 Cor. vi. 11.*

2882 Κόρινθος, ου, ἡ, *Corinth,* Ac. xviii. 1, xix. 1.

2883 Κορνήλιος, ου, ὁ, *Cornelius,* Ac. x.*

2884 κόρος, ου, ὁ (from Heb.), *a cor,* the largest dry measure, equal to ten βάτοι, or ten Attic medimni, Lu. xvi. 7. (S.)*

2885 κοσμέω, ῶ, ήσω, *to put in order, to prepare,* Mat. xxv. 7; *to adorn,* Mat. xxiii. 29; 1 Tim. ii. 9; met., with honor, Tit. ii. 10; 1 Pet. iii. 5.

2886 κοσμικός, ή, όν, (1) *earthly,* opp. to ἐπουράνιος, Heb. ix. 1; (2) *worldly, i.e., corrupt,* Tit. ii. 12.*

2887 κόσμιος, ον, *orderly, modest,* 1 Tim. ii. 9, iii. 2.*

2888 κοσμο-κράτωρ, ορος, ὁ, *lord of this world, world-ruler* (R. V.), Ep. vi. 12.*

2889 κόσμος, ου, ὁ, (1) *ornament, decoration,* only 1 Pet. iii. 3; hence, (2) *the material universe,* Lu. xi. 50, as well ordered and beautiful; (3) *the world,* Jn. xi. 9; *worldly affairs,* Gal. vi. 14; (4) *the inhabitants of the world,* 1 Cor. iv. 9; as opposed to God, Jn. viii. 23; (5) *a vast collection,* of anything, Ja. iii. 6. *Syn.:* see αἰών.

2890 Κούαρτος, ου, ὁ (Latin, see Gr. § 159), *Quartus,* Ro. xvi. 23.*

2891 κούμι (a Hebrew imperative fem.), *arise,* Mar. v. 41 (W. H. read κούμ, the masculine form). (N. T.)*

2892 κουστωδία, ας, ἡ (Latin, see Gr. § 154c, Bu. 17), *a guard,* Mat. xxvii. 65, 66, xxviii. 11. (N. T.)*

2893 κουφίζω, *to lighten,* as a ship, Ac. xxvii. 38.*

2894 κόφινος, ου, ὁ, *a basket,* as Mat. xiv. 20.

2895 κράββατος (W. H. κράβαττος), ου, ὁ, *a couch, a light bed,* as Mar. ii. 12.

2896 κράζω, ξω, *to cry out,* hoarsely, or urgently, or in anguish, Mar. v. 5; Ac. xix. 32.

2897 κραιπάλη, ης, ἡ, *surfeiting,*

85

caused by excessive drinking, Lu. xxi. 34.*

2898 **κρανίον**, ου, τό, *a skull*, Lu.
xxiii. 33; Κρανίου Τόπος,
Greek for Γολγοθά, which
see, Mat. xxvii. 33; Mar. xv.
22; Jn. xix. 17.*

2899 **κράσπεδον**, ου, τό, *the fringe,
tassel*, of a garment, as Mat.
xxiii. 5.

2900 **κραταιός**, ά, όν, *strong, mighty*,
1 Pet. v. 6.*

2901 **κραταιόω**, ῶ, in pass. only, *to
be strong, to grow strong*, Lu.
i. 80, ii. 40; 1 Cor. xvi. 13;
Ep. iii. 16. (S.)*

2902 **κρατέω**, ῶ, ήσω, with acc., or
gen., or acc. and gen. (see
Gr. § 264, Wi. § 30, 8 *d*, Bu.
161), *to get possession of, obtain*, Ac. xxvii. 13; *to take
hold of*, Mar. i. 31; Ac. iii.
11; *to seize*, Mat. xiv. 3; *to
hold*, Rev. ii. 1; *to hold fast*,
Rev. ii. 25, iii. 11; *to retain*,
of sins, Jn. xx. 23.

2903 **κράτιστος**, η, ον (prop. superlative of κρατύς, see κράτος),
most excellent, most noble, a
title of honor, Lu. i. 3; Ac.
xxiii. 26, xxiv. 3, xxvi. 25.*

2904 **κράτος**, ους, τό, *strength, power,
dominion*, Ep. i. 19; 1 Pet.
iv. 11; Heb. ii. 14; κατὰ
κράτος, Ac. xix. 20, *greatly,
mightily*.

2905 **κραυγάζω**, σω, *to cry out, to
shout*, as Mat. xii. 19.

2906 **κραυγή**, ῆς, ἡ, *a crying, outcry*,
as Heb. v. 7.

2907 **κρέας** (ατος, aos, contr. κρέως),
τό, plur. κρέατα, κρέα, *flesh,
flesh-meat*, Ro. xiv. 21; 1 Cor.
viii. 13.*

2908, 2909; **κρείσσων** (or -ττ-), ον (prop.
see Strong. compar. of κρατύς, see κράτος), *stronger, more excellent*,
as Heb. vii. 7, xii. 24.

2910 **κρεμάννυμι**, or κρεμάω, ῶ, fut.
άσω, *to hang up*, trans., Ac.
v. 30; mid., *to be suspended,
to hang*, Mat. xxii. 40; Ac.
xxviii. 4.

2911 **κρημνός**, οῦ, ὁ (κρεμάννυμι), *a
precipice*, from its overhang-
ing, Mat. viii. 32; Mar. v. 13;
Lu. viii. 33.*

2912 **Κρής**, ητός, ὁ, *a Cretan*, Ac. ii.
11; Tit. i. 12.*

2913 **Κρήσκης**, ὁ (Latin), *Crescens*,
2 Tim. iv. 10.*

2914 **Κρήτη**, ης, ἡ, *Crete*, now Can-
dia, Ac. xxvii. 7.

2915 **κριθή**, ῆς, ἡ, *barley*, Rev. vi.
6.*

2916 **κρίθινος**, η, ον, *made of barley;*
ἄρτοι κρίθινοι, *barley loaves*,
Jn. vi. 9, 13.*

2917 **κρίμα**, ατος, τό, *a judgment, a
sentence, condemnation*, as 1
Cor. xi. 29.

2918 **κρίνον**, ου, τό, *a lily*, Mat. vi.
28; Lu. xii. 27.*

2919 **κρίνω**, νῶ, κέκρικα, 1st aor. pass.
ἐκρίθην, (1) *to have an opinion,
to think*, Ac. xiii. 46, xv. 19;
(2) *to approve, prefer*, Ro.
xiv. 5; (3) *to resolve, determine*, 1 Cor. vii. 37; Tit. iii.
12; (4) *to try, to sit in judgment on*, Jn. xviii. 31; pass.
and mid., *to appeal to trial,
i.e., to have a lawsuit*, 1 Cor.
vi. 6.

2920 **κρίσις**, εως, ἡ, (1) *opinion*,
formed and expressed, Jn.
viii. 16; Ju. 9; (2) *judgment*,
the act or result of, Ja. ii.
13; Lu. x. 14; (3) *condemnation and punishment*, Heb. x.
27; Rev. xviii. 10; (4) *a tribunal*, Mat. v. 21, 22; (5)
justice, Mat. xxiii. 23.

2921 **Κρίσπος**, ου, ὁ, *Crispus*, Ac.
xviii. 8; 1 Cor. i. 14.*

2922 **κριτήριον**, ου, τό, (1) *a tribunal,
a court of justice*, 1 Cor. vi.
2, 4 (see R. V.); Ja. ii. 6.*

2923 **κριτής**, οῦ, ὁ, *a judge*, Mat. v.
25; Ac. xviii. 15; of the
O. T. "Judges," Ac. xiii.
20.

2924 **κριτικός**, ή, όν, *skilled in judging*, gen. obj., Heb. iv. 12.*

2925 **κρούω**, σω, *to knock* at a door,
Lu. xiii. 25.

2926 **κρύπτη**, ης, ἡ, *a cellar, a vault*,
Lu. xi. 33.*

2927 **κρυπτός**, ή, όν, verbal adj.
(κρύπτω), *hidden, secret*, Mat.
x. 26; Ro. ii. 16.

2928 **κρύπτω**, ψω, 2d aor. pass. ἐκρύ-
βην, *to hide, conceal, to lay up*,
as Col. iii. 3.

2929 **κρυσταλλίζω**, *to be clear*, like
crystal, Rev. xxi. 11. (N.T.)*

2930 **κρύσταλλος**, ου, ὁ, *crystal*, Rev.
iv. 6, xxii. 1.*

see 2927 **κρυφαῖος**, α, ον, *hidden, secret*,
Mat. vi. 18 (W. H.).*

2931 **κρυφῇ** (W. H. -ῇ), adv., *in
secret, secretly*, Ep. v. 12.*

2932 **κτάομαι**, ῶμαι, fut. ήσομαι, ἐκ-
τησάμην, dep., *to acquire,
procure* (price, gen., or ἐκ),
(see Gr. § 273, Wi. §§ 38, 7,

2933 40, 4*b*), Mat. x. 9; Lu. xviii. 12, xxi. 19; Ac. i. 18, viii. 20, xxii. 28; 1 Th. iv. 4.*

2933 κτῆμα, ατος, τό, *anything acquired, a possession,* Mat. xix. 22; Mar. x. 22; Ac. ii. 45, v. 1.

2934 κτῆνος, ους, τό, *a beast of burden* (as representing property), Lu. x. 34; Ac. xxiii. 24; 1 Cor. xv. 39; Rev. xviii. 13.*

2935 κτήτωρ, ορος, ὁ, *a possessor,* Ac. iv. 34.*

2936 κτίζω, σω, perf. pass. ἔκτισμαι, *to create, form, shape,* physically or spiritually, as Ro. i. 25; Ep. ii. 10.

2937 κτίσις, εως, ἡ, *creation,* (1) the act, Ro. i. 20; (2) the thing created, *creature,* Ro. i. 25; *creation,* generally, Ro. viii. 19–22; (3) met., *an ordinance,* 1 Pet. ii. 13.

2938 κτίσμα, ατος, τό, *a thing created, a creature,* 1 Tim. iv. 4; Ja. i. 18; Rev. v. 13, viii. 9.*

2939 κτίστης, ου, ὁ, *a founder; a creator,* 1 Pet. iv. 19.*

2940 κυβεία, ας, ἡ, *dice-playing, fraud,* Ep. iv. 14.*

2941 κυβέρνησις, εως, ἡ, *governing, direction,* 1 Cor. xii. 28.*

2942 κυβερνήτης, ου, ὁ, *a steersman, a pilot,* Ac. xxvii. 11; Rev. xviii. 17.*

see 2944 κυκλεύω, *to encircle, surround,* Rev. xx. 9 (W. H.).*

2943 κυκλόθεν, adv. (κύκλος), *round about,* gen., Rev. iv. 3, 4, 8, v. 11 (not W. H.).*

●2945 κύκλος, ου, ὁ, *a circle;* only in dat., κύκλῳ, as adv., abs., or with gen., *round about, around,* Mar. iii. 34; vi. 6.

2944 κυκλόω, ῶ, *to encircle, surround, besiege,* Lu. xxi. 20; Jn. x. 24; Ac. xiv. 20; Heb. xi. 30; Rev. xx. 9 (Rec.).*

2946 κύλισμα, ατος, τό, *a place for wallowing,* 2 Pet. ii. 22 (not W. H.). (N. T.)*

see 2946 κυλισμός, οῦ, ὁ, *a rolling, wallowing,* 2 Pet. ii. 22 (W. H.).*

2947; see Strong κυλίω (for κυλίνδω), pass., *to be rolled, to wallow,* Mar. ix. 20.*

2948 κυλλός, ή, όν, *crippled, lame,* especially in the hands, Mat. xv. 30 (not W. H.), 31 (not W. H.), xviii. 8; Mar. ix. 43.*

2949 κῦμα, ατος, τό, *a wave,* as Mat. viii. 24; Mar. iv. 37; Ju. 13.

2950 κύμβαλον, ου, τό (κύμβος, *hollow*), *a cymbal,* 1 Cor. xiii. 1.*

2951 κύμινον, ου, τό (from Heb.), *cumin,* Mat. xxiii. 23.*

2952 κυνάριον, ου, τό (dim. of κύων), *a little dog,* Mat. xv. 26, 27; Mar. vii. 27, 28.*

2953 Κύπριος, ου, ὁ, *a Cyprian* or *Cypriote,* Ac. iv. 36.

2954 Κύπρος, ου, ἡ, *Cyprus,* Ac. xi. 19, xiii. 4.

2955 κύπτω, ψω, *to bend, to stoop down,* Mar. i. 7; Jn. viii. 6, 8 (W. H. omit).

2956 Κυρηναῖος, ου, ὁ, *a Cyrenæan,* Ac. vi. 9, xi. 20.

2957 Κυρήνη, ης, ἡ, *Cyrene,* a city of Africa, Ac. ii. 10.*

2958 Κυρήνιος, ου, ὁ, *Cyrenius* or *Quirinius,* Lu. ii. 2.*

2959 κυρία, ας, ἡ, *a lady,* 2 Jn. i. 5 (some read Κυρία, *Cyria,* a proper name).*

2960 κυριακός, ή, όν, *of* or *pertaining to the Lord,* as the supper, 1 Cor. xi. 20; the day, Rev. i. 10.*

2961 κυριεύω, εύσω, *to have authority,* abs., 1 Tim. vi. 15; *to rule over* (gen.), Lu. xxii. 25.

2962; see 1203 κύριος, ου, ὁ, (1) *lord, master,* Lu. xx. 15; Ac. xvi. 16; a title of honor, Mat. xiii. 27, xvi. 22; (2) *the Lord,* applied to God, Mar. v. 19; Ac. vii. 33; (3) *the Lord,* employed in the Epp. constantly of Christ (see Gr. § 217 *b,* Wi. § 19, 1 *a,* p. 124, Bu. 89), Ac. ix. 1; Ro. xiv. 8. *Syn.;* see δεσπότης.

2963 κυριότης, τητος, ἡ, *lordship, dominion;* collective concr., *lords,* Ep. i. 21; Col. i. 16; 2 Pet. ii. 10; Ju. 8. (N. T.)*

2964 κυρόω, ῶ, *to confirm, ratify,* 2 Cor. ii. 8; Gal. iii. 15.*

2965 κύων, κυνός, ὁ, ἡ, *a dog,* Lu. xvi. 21; fig., of *shameless persons,* Phil. iii. 2.

2966 κῶλον, ου, τό, *a limb, a carcase,* N T. plur. only, Heb. iii. 17.*

2967 κωλύω, σω, *to restrain, forbid, hinder,* Mar. ix. 38.

2968 κώμη, ης, ἡ, *a village,* unwalled, Mat. ix. 35.

2969 κωμό-πολις, εως, ἡ, *a large, city-like village,* without walls, Mar. i. 38.*

2970 κῶμος, ου, ὁ, *a feasting, revel-*

ing, Ro. xiii. 13; Gal. v. 21; 1 Pet. iv. 3.*

2971 κώνωψ, ωπος, ὁ, *a gnat*, Mat. xxiii. 24.*

2972 Κῶς, ῶ, ἡ, *Cos*, Ac. xxi. 1.*

2973 Κωσάμ, ὁ (Heb.), *Cosam*, Lu. iii. 28.*

2974 κωφός, ή, όν (κόπτω, lit., *blunted*), *dumb*, Mat. ix. 32, 33; *deaf*, Mat. xi. 5.

Λ

Λ, λ, λάμβδα, *lambda, l*, the eleventh letter. As a numeral, λ' = 30; ‚λ = 30,000.

2975 λαγχάνω, 2d aor. ἔλαχον, trans., *to obtain by lot, to obtain*, acc. or gen., Lu. i. 9; Ac. i. 17; 2 Pet. i. 1; abs., *to cast lots*, περί, gen., Jn. xix. 24.*

2976 Λάζαρος, ου, ὁ, *Lazarus*, (1) of Bethany, Jn. xi. 1, 2; (2) in the parable, Lu. xvi. 20–25.

2977 λάθρα (W. H. λάθρᾳ), (λανθάνω), adv., *secretly*, Jn. xi. 28.

2978 λαῖλαψ, απος, ἡ, *a whirlwind, a violent storm*, Mar. iv. 37; Lu. viii. 23; 2 Pet. ii. 17.*

2979 λακτίζω (λάξ, adv., *with the heel*), *to kick*, Ac. ix. 5 (W. H. omit), xxvi. 14.*

2980 λαλέω, ῶ, ήσω, (1) *to utter a sound, to speak*, absolutely, Rev. x. 4; Heb. xii. 24; Ja. ii. 12; (2) *to speak, to talk*, with acc. of thing spoken, also with modal dat. and dat. of person addressed. Hence, according to the nature of the case, met., *to declare*, by other methods than *vivâ voce*, as Ro. vii. 1; *to preach, to publish, to announce. Syn.:* λέγω has reference to the *thought* uttered; λαλέω simply to the *fact* of utterance.

2981 λαλιά, ᾶς, ἡ, (1) *speech, report*, Jn. iv. 42; (2) *manner of speech, dialect*, Mat. xxvi. 73; Mar. xiv. 70 (W. H. omit); Jn. viii. 43.*

2982 λαμά, or λαμμᾶ (perh. Heb.), and λεμά (Aram.), *why*, Mat. xxvii. 46; Mar. xv. 34 (Ps. xxii. 1). (N. T.)*

2983 λαμβάνω, λήψομαι (W. H. λήμψομαι), εἴληφα, ἔλαβον, (1) *to take*, as in the hand, Mat. xiv. 19; hence, (2) *to claim, procure*, Lu. xix. 12; (3) *to*

take by force, seize, Mat. xxi. 35; (4) *to take away*, by violence or fraud, Mat. v. 40; (5) *to choose*, Ac. xv. 14; (6) *to receive, accept, obtain*, Jn. xvi. 24; Ja. iii. 1; Rev. xviii. 4; (7) in certain periphrastic expressions — λαμβάνειν ἀρχήν, *to begin;* λ. λήθην, *to forget;* λ. ὑπόμνησιν, *to remember;* λ. πεῖραν, *to experience;* λ. πρόσωπον, "*to accept the person*," *i.e., to be partial.* The preposition "*from*," after this verb, is expressed by ἐκ, ἀπό, παρά (ὑπό, 2 Cor. xi. 24).

2984 Λάμεχ, ὁ (Heb.), *Lamech*, Lu. iii. 36.*

2985 λαμπάς, άδος, ἡ, prop. *a torch*, Rev. iv. 5, viii. 10; also *a lamp*, Jn. xviii. 3. *Syn.:* φῶς is light in general; φέγγος, radiance; φωστήρ, a heavenly body, luminary; λαμπάς, a torch; λύχνος, a lamp.

2986 λαμπρός, ά, όν, *shining, magnificent*, Rev. xxii. 16; Lu. xxiii. 11.

2987 λαμπρότης, τητος, ἡ, *splendor, brightness*, Ac. xxvi. 13.*

2988 λαμπρῶς, adv., *magnificently*, Lu. xvi. 19.*

2989 λάμπω, ψω, *to shine*, Mat. v. 15, 16, xvii. 2.

2990 λανθάνω, 2d aor. ἔλαθον, (1) *to be hidden*, abs., Mar. vii. 24; Lu. viii. 47; (2) *to be hidden from* (acc.), Ac. xxvi. 26; 2 Pet. iii. 5, 8; (3) for part. constr., see Gr. § 394, 2, Wi. § 54, 4, Bu. 299; Heb. xiii. 2.*

2991 λαξευτός, ή, όν, *hewn out of a rock*, Lu. xxiii. 53. (S.)*

●2993 Λαοδικεία, ας, ἡ, *Laodicea*, Col. ii. 1, iv. 13.

●2994 Λαοδικεύς, έως, ὁ, *a Laodicean*, Col. iv. 16; Rev. iii. 14 (not W. H.).*

2992 λαός, οῦ, ὁ, (1) *a people*, spec. of *the people* of God, Lu. ii. 31; Ac. iv. 10; (2) *the common people*, Mat. xxvi. 5.

2995 λάρυγξ, υγγος, ὁ, *the throat*, Ro. iii. 13.*

2996 Λασαία (W. H. Λασέα), ας, ἡ, *Lasæa*, Ac. xxvii. 8.*

2997 λάσκω, 1st aor. ἐλάκησα, *to burst asunder*, Ac. i. 18.*

2998 λατομέω, ῶ, *to hew stones, to cut stones*, Mat. xxvii. 60; Mar. xv. 46. (S.)*

2999 λατρεία, ας, ἡ, *worship, service rendered to God*, Jn. xvi. 2; Ro. ix. 4, xii. 1; Heb. ix. 1, 6.*

3000 λατρεύω, σω, (1) *to worship, to serve*, Ac. vii. 7; (2) *to officiate as a priest*, Heb. xiii. 10. *Syn.:* λατρεύω is to worship God, as any one may do; λειτουργέω, to serve him in a special office or ministry.

3001 λάχανον, ου, τό, *an herb, a garden plant*, Mat. xiii. 32.

3002 Λεββαῖος, ου, ὁ, *Lebbæus*, Mat. x. 3 (not W. H.). See Θαδδαῖος.*

3003 λεγεών (W. H. λεγιών), ῶνος, ὁ (Lat., see Gr. § 154 c, Bu. 16), *a legion*, Mat. xxvi. 53; Mar. v. 9, 15; Lu. viii. 30; in N.T. times containing probably 6826 men. (N. T.)*

3004; see λέγω, only pres. and impf. in
2980 N. T., (1) *to speak, to say*, Ac. xiii. 15; Jn. i. 29; used also of writings, as Jn. xix. 37; (2) *to relate, to tell*, Lu. ix. 31, xviii. 1; (3) *to call*, pass., *to be called* or *named;* (4) pass., *to be chosen* or *appointed*. Dat. of person addressed. *Syn.:* see λαλέω.

3005 λεῖμμα, ατος, τό (λείπω), *a remnant*, Ro. xi. 5.*

3006 λεῖος, εία, εῖον, *smooth, level*, Lu. iii. 5 (from S.).*

3007 λείπω, ψω, *to leave, to be wanting*, Lu. xviii. 22; Tit. i. 5, iii. 13; pass., *to be lacking, to be destitute of*, Ja. i. 4, 5, ii. 15.*

3008; see λειτουργέω, ῶ, (1) *to serve pub-*
3000 *licly in sacred things*, Ac. xiii. 2, Heb. x. 11; (2) *to minister to charitably*, Ro. xv. 27.* *Syn.:* see λατρεύω.

3009 λειτουργία, ας, ἡ, (1) *a public ministration* or *service*, Lu. i. 23; Phil. ii. 17; Heb. viii. 6, ix. 21; (2) *a charitable gift*, Phil. ii. 30; 2 Cor. ix. 12.*

3010 λειτουργικός, ή, όν, *employed in ministering*, Heb. i. 14 (S.)*

3011 λειτουργός, οῦ, ὁ, *a minister* or *servant* to, gen. obj., Ro. xiii. 6, xv. 16; Phil. ii. 25; Heb. i. 7, viii. 2.*

3012 λέντιον, ου, τό (Lat., see Gr. § 154 e), *a towel, apron*, Jn. xiii. 4, 5. (N. T.)*

3013 λεπίς, ίδος, ἡ, *a scale*, Ac. ix. 18.*

3014 λέπρα, ας, ἡ, *the leprosy*, Mat. viii. 3; Mar. i. 42; Lu. v. 12, 13.*

3015 λεπρός, οῦ, ὁ, *a leper*, Lu. iv. 27, vii. 22.

3016 λεπτόν, οῦ, τό, prop. verb. adj. (sc. νόμισμα), from λέπω (*ta strip off, pare down*), *a mite*, a small brass coin, one eighth of an *as*, the smallest Jewish coin, Mar. xii. 42; Lu. xii. 59, xxi. 2.*

3017, 3018 Λευΐ, or Λευΐς (W. H. Λευείς), gen. Λευΐ, ὁ, *Levi*. Four are mentioned: (1) son of Jacob, ancestor of the priestly tribe; (2, 3) ancestors of Jesus, Lu. iii. 24, 29; (4) the apostle, also called *Matthew*, Lu. v. 27, 29.

3019 Λευΐτης, ου, ὁ, *a Levite*, Lu. x. 32; Jn. i. 19; Ac. iv. 36.*

3020 Λευϊτικός, ή, όν, *Levitical*, Heb. vii. 11.*

3021 λευκαίνω, ανῶ, 1st aor. ἐλεύκανα, *to make white*, Mar. ix. 3; Rev. vii. 14.*

3022 λευκός, ή, όν, (1) *white*, as Mat. v. 36; Jn. iv. 35; (2) *bright*, as Mat. xvii. 2.

3023 λέων, οντος, ὁ, *a lion*, Heb. xi. 33; fig., 2 Tim. iv. 17; of Christ, Rev. v. 5.

3024 λήθη, ης, ἡ, *forgetfulness*, 2 Pet. i. 9.*

3025 ληνός, οῦ, ὁ, ἡ, *a wine-press*, Mat. xxi. 33; fig. in Rev. xiv. 19, 20, xix. 15.*

3026 λῆρος, ου, ὁ, *idle talk*, Lu. xxiv. 11.*

3027; see ληστής, οῦ, ὁ, *a robber*, Mar. xi.
2812 17; Jn. x. 1, 8. *Syn.:* see κλέπτης.

3028 λῆψις (W. H. λῆμψις), εως, ἡ (λαμβάνω), *a receiving*, Phil. iv. 15.*

3029 λίαν, adv., *very much;* with adj. or adv., *very*, Mat. iv. 8; Mar. xvi. 2.

3030 λίβανος, ου, ὁ, *frankincense*, Mat. ii. 11; Rev. xviii. 13.*

3031 λιβανωτός, οῦ, ὁ, *a censer for burning frankincense*, Rev. viii. 3, 5.*

3032 λιβερτῖνος, ου, ὁ (Lat. *libertinus*), *a freedman*, Ac. vi. 9. Probably Jews who had been slaves at Rome under Pompey, and afterwards freed.*

3033 Λιβύη, ης, ἡ, *Libya*, Ac. ii. 10.*

3034 λιθάζω, σω, *to stone*, Jn. xi. 8; Ac. xiv. 19.

3035 λίθινος, η, ον, *made of stone*, Jn. ii. 6; 2 Cor. iii. 3; Rev. ix. 20.*

3036 λιθο-βολέω, ῶ, ήσω, *to throw stones at, to stone*, Mat. xxiii. 37; Mar. xii. 4 (W. H. omit). (S.)

3037 λίθος, ου, ὁ, *a stone, i.e.*, (1) loose and lying about, Mat. iv. 3, 6; (2) built into a wall, etc., Mar. xiii. 2; (3) *a precious stone*, Rev. iv. 3, xvii. 4; (4) *a statue* or *idol of stone*, Ac. xvii. 29.

3038 λιθό-στρωτον, ου, τό (prop. adj., *spread with stones*), *a mosaic pavement*, as name of a place near the prætorium or palace at Jerusalem, Jn. xix. 13.*

3039 λικμάω, ῶ, ήσω, *to scatter*, as grain in winnowing, *to grind to powder* that may be scattered, Mat. xxi. 44; Lu. xx. 18.*

3040 λιμήν, ένος, ὁ, *a harbor*, Ac. xxvii. 8, 12.*

3041 λίμνη, ης, ἡ, *a lake, e.g.*, Gennesaret, Lu. v. 1.

3042 λιμός, οῦ, ὁ, (1) *hunger*, 2 Cor. xi. 27; (2) *a famine*, Mat. xxiv. 7.

3043 λίνον, ου, τό, *flax, linen made of flax*, Rev. xv. 6 (W. H. λίθος); *a lamp-wick*, Mat. xii. 20.*

3044 Λῖνος (W. H. Λίνος), ου, ὁ, *Linus*, 2 Tim. iv. 21.*

3045 λιπαρός, ά, όν, *fat, dainty*, Rev. xviii. 14.*

3046 λίτρα, ας, ἡ, *a pound*, a weight of twelve ounces, Jn. xii. 3, xix. 39.*

3047 λίψ, λιβός, ὁ, *the S.W. wind;* used for the S.W. quarter of the heavens, Ac. xxvii. 12.*

3048 λογία, ας, ἡ, *a collection, i.e.*, of money, 1 Cor. xvi. 1, 2. (N. T.)*

3049 λογίζομαι, σομαι, dep. with mid. and pass., (1) *to reckon;* (2) *to place to the account of, to charge with*, acc. and dat., or with εἰς (see Gr. § 298, 6, Wi. § 32, 4 b, Bu. 151); (3) *to reason, argue, to infer, conclude*, from reasoning; (4) *to think, suppose*.

3050 λογικός, ή, όν, *rational, i.e.*, belonging to the sphere of

the reason, Ro. xii. 1; 1 Pet. ii. 2.*

3051 λόγιον, ου, τό, *something spoken*, in N. T., *a divine communication, e.g.*, the Old Testament, Ac. vii. 38; Ro. iii. 2; and the doctrines of Christ, Heb. v. 12; 1 Pet. iv. 11.*

3052 λόγιος, ον, *eloquent*, Ac. xviii. 24.*

3053 λογισμός, οῦ, ὁ, *a reasoning, decision*, Ro. ii. 15; 2 Cor. x. 5.*

3054 λογο-μαχέω, ῶ, *to contend about words*, 2 Tim. ii. 14. (N.T.)*

3055 λογομαχία, ας, ἡ, *contention about words*, 1 Tim. vi. 4. (N. T.)*

3056 λόγος, ου, ὁ, (1) *a speaking, a saying, a word*, as the expression of thought (whereas ἔπος, ὄνομα, ῥῆμα refer to words in their outward form, as parts of speech), Mat. viii. 8; (2) the thing spoken, Mat. vii. 24, 26 — whether *doctrine*, 1 Tim. iv. 6; *prophecy*, 2 Pet. i. 19; *question*, Mat. xxi. 24; *a common saying* or *proverb*, Jn. iv. 37; *a precept, a command*, Jn. viii. 55; *the truth*, Mar. viii. 38; *conversation*, Lu. xxiv. 17; *teaching*, 1 Cor. ii. 4; *a narrative*, Ac. i. 1; *a public rumor*, Mat. xxviii. 15; *an argument*, Ac. ii. 40; *a charge* or *accusation*, Ac. xix. 38; (3) *reason*, Ac. xviii. 14; (4) *account, reckoning*, Heb. iv. 13; Ac. xx. 24; Mat. xviii. 23; Ac. x. 29; λόγος is used by John as a name of Christ, the Word of God, *i.e.*, the expression or manifestation of his thoughts to man, Jn. i. 1, etc.

3057 λόγχη, ης, ἡ, *a lance, a spear*, Jn. xix. 34.*

3058 λοιδορέω, ῶ, *to rail at, revile*, Jn. ix. 28; Ac. xxiii. 4; 1 Cor. iv. 12; 1 Pet. ii. 23.*

3059 λοιδορία, ας, ἡ, *reviling*, 1 Tim. v. 14; 1 Pet. iii. 9.*

3060 λοίδορος, ου, ὁ, *a reviler*, 1 Cor. v. 11, vi. 10.*

3061 λοιμός, οῦ, ὁ, *a pestilence*, Mat. xxiv. 7 (W. H. omit), Lu. xxi. 11; Paul so called, Ac. xxiv. 5.*

3062, 3063 λοιπός, ή, όν, *remaining, the rest*, Mat. xxv. 11; adv. τὸ λοιπόν, *as for the rest, more-*

3064
over, finally, henceforth, 1 Cor. i. 16; Heb. x. 13; τοῦ λοιποῦ, from henceforth, Gal. vi. 17.

3065 Λουκᾶς, ᾶ, ὁ (from Λουκανός, see Gr. § 159 d, Wi. § 16, 4, note 1, Bu. 20), Luke, Ac. xvi. 10, xx. 5.

3066 Λούκιος, ου, ὁ (Lat.), Lucius, Ac. xiii. 1; Ro. xvi. 21.*

3067 λουτρόν, οῦ, τό, a bath; in N.T. baptism, Ep. v. 26; Tit. iii. 5.*

3068 λούω, σω, to bathe, to wash, Ac. ix. 37, xvi. 33; to cleanse, to purify, Rev. i. 5 (W. H. λύω). Syn.: πλύνω is to wash inanimate things; λούω, to bathe the whole body; νίπτω, to wash a part of the body.

3069 Λύδδα, ης, ἡ, also Λύδδα, ων, τά (W. H.), Lydda, Ac. ix. 32, 35, 38.*

3070 Λυδία, ας, ἡ, Lydia, Ac. xvi. 14, 40.*

3071 Λυκαονία, ας, ἡ, Lycaonia, Ac. xiv. 6.*

3072 Λυκαονιστί, adv., in the speech of Lycaonia, Ac. xiv. 11.*

3073 Λυκία, ας, ἡ, Lycia, Ac. xxvii. 5.*

3074 λύκος, ου, ὁ, a wolf, Jn. x. 12; fig., Ac. xx. 29.

3075 λυμαίνομαι, to ravage, to devastate, Ac. viii. 3.*

3076 λυπέω, ῶ, to grieve, a general word, 2 Cor. ii. 2, 5; pass., to be grieved, saddened, Mat. xxvi. 22, 37; 1 Pet. i. 6; to aggrieve or offend, Ro. xiv. 15; Ep. iv. 30.

3077 λύπη, ης, ἡ, grief, sorrow, 2 Cor. ix. 7; cause of grief, annoyance, 1 Pet. ii. 19.

3078 Λυσανίας, ου, ὁ, Lysanias, Lu. iii. 1.*

3079 Λυσίας, ου, ὁ, Lysias, Ac. xxiii. 26.

3080 λύσις, εως, ἡ, a loosing, divorce, 1 Cor. vii. 27.*

3081 λυσι-τελέω, ῶ (lit., to pay taxes), impers., -εῖ, it is profitable or preferable (dat. and ῇ), Lu. xvii. 2.*

3082 Λύστρα, ας, ἡ, or ων, τά, Lystra, Ac. xiv. 6, 8.

3083 λύτρον, ου, τό, a ransom. Mat. xx. 28; Mar. x. 45.*

3084 λυτρόω, ῶ, ώσω, in N. T. only mid. and pass., to ransom, to deliver by paying a ransom, Lu. xxiv. 21; Tit. ii. 14; 1 Pet. i. 18 (acc., pers.; dat., price, and ἀπό or ἐκ).*

3085 λύτρωσις, εως, ἡ, deliverance, redemption, Lu. i. 68, ii. 38; Heb. ix. 12.*

3086 λυτρωτής, οῦ, ὁ, a redeemer, a deliverer, Ac. vii. 35.*

3087 λυχνία, ας, ἡ, a lampstand, Mat. v. 15; fig., of a church, Rev. ii. 1, 5; of a Christian teacher, Rev. xi. 4.

3088; see 2985 λύχνος, ου, ὁ, a lamp, Mat. v. 15, vi. 22; used of John the Baptist, Jn. v. 35; of Christ, Rev. xxi. 23. Syn.: see λαμπάς.

3089 λύω, σω, to loose, as (1) lit., to unbind, Mar. i. 7; Rev. v. 2; (2) to set at liberty, Jn. xi. 44; Ac. xxii. 30; (3) to pronounce not binding, e.g., a law, Mat. xviii. 18; (4) to disobey or nullify the divine word, Jn. vii. 23, x. 35; (5) to destroy, e.g., the temple, Jn. ii. 19; (6) to dismiss, i.e., an assembly, Ac. xiii. 43.

3090 Λωΐς, ΐδος, ἡ, Lois, 2 Tim. i. 5.*

3091 Λώτ, ὁ (Heb.), Lot, Lu. xvii. 28–32; 2 Pet. ii. 7.*

M

M, μ, μῦ, mu, m, the twelfth letter. As a numeral, μ′ = 40; ͵μ = 40,000.

3092 Μαάθ, ὁ (Heb.), Maath, Lu. iii. 26.*

3093 Μαγδαλά, ἡ (Heb.), Magdala, Mat. xv. 39 (W. H. and R.V. Μαγαδάν).*

3094 Μαγδαληνή, ῆς, ἡ, Magdalene, i.e., a woman of Magdala, as Mat. xxvii. 56, 61.

3095 μαγεία (W. H. μαγία), ας, ἡ, magic, plur., magical arts, Ac. viii. 11.*

3096 μαγεύω, σω, to practice magical arts, Ac. viii. 9.*

3097 μάγος, ου, ὁ, (1) a magus, a Persian astrologer, Mat. ii. 1, 7, 16; (2) a sorcerer, Ac. xiii. 6, 8.*

3098 Μαγώγ, ὁ (Heb.), Magog, Rev. xx. 8; see Γώγ.*

3099 Μαδιάμ, ἡ (Heb.), Midian, Ac. vii. 29.*

3100 μαθητεύω, σω, (1) trans., to make a disciple of (acc.), to instruct, Mat. xiii. 52, xxviii. 19; Ac. xiv. 21; (2) intrans., to be a disciple, Mat. xxvii. 57 (Rec., W. H. read pass., W. H. with active in mrg.).*

3101 μαθητής, οῦ, ὁ (μανθάνω), a disciple, Mat. ix. 14, x. 24, xxii. 16; οἱ μαθηταί, specially, the twelve, Mat. ix. 19.

3102 μαθήτρια, ας, ἡ, a female disciple, Ac. ix. 36.*

3103 Μαθουσάλα, ὁ (Heb.), Methuselah, Lu. iii. 37.*

3104 Μαϊνάν, ὁ (W. H. Μεννά). (Heb.), Mainan or Menna, Lu. iii. 31.*

3105 μαίνομαι, dep., to be mad, to rave, Jn. x. 20; Ac. xii. 15, xxvi. 24, 25; 1 Cor. xiv. 23.*

3106 μακαρίζω, fut. ιῶ, to pronounce happy or blessed, Lu. i. 48; Ja. v. 11.*

3107 μακάριος, α, ον, happy, blessed, Mat. v. 3–11; Lu. i. 45, vi. 20; 1 Cor. vii. 40.

3108 μακαρισμός, οῦ, ὁ, a declaring blessed, a pronouncing happy, Ro. iv. 6, 9; Gal. iv. 15.*

3109 Μακεδονία, ας, ἡ, Macedonia, Ac. xvi. 9, 10, 12.

3110 Μακεδών, όνος, ὁ, a Macedonian, Ac. xix. 29, xxvii. 2.

3111 μάκελλον, ου, τό (Lat.), a meat-market, 1 Cor. x. 25.*

3112 μακράν, adv. (acc. of μακρός, sc. ὁδόν), afar, afar off, Lu. xv. 20; εἰς preceding, Ac. ii. 39; ἀπό following, Ac. xvii. 27.

3113 μακρόθεν, adv., from afar, Mar. viii. 3; with ἀπό, as Mat. xxvii. 55.

3114 μακρο-θυμέω, ῶ, ήσω, to suffer long, to have patience, to be forbearing, 1 Cor. xiii. 4; to delay, Lu. xviii. 7; to wait patiently, Heb. vi. 15. (S.)

3115; see 463 μακρο-θυμία, ας, ἡ, forbearance, long-suffering, patience, Ro. ii. 4, ix. 22. Syn.: see ἀνοχή.

3116 μακρο-θύμως, adv., patiently. Ac. xxvi. 3. (N. T.)*

3117 μακρός, ά, όν, long; of place, distant, Lu. xv. 13, xix. 12; of time, long, only in the phrase μακρὰ προσεύχεσθαι, to make long prayers, Mat. xxiii. 14 (W. H. omit); Mar. xii. 40; Lu. xx. 47.*

3118 μακρο-χρόνιος, ον, long-lived, Ep. vi. 3.*

3119 μαλακία, ας, ἡ, weakness, infirmity, Mat. iv. 23, ix. 35 x. 1.*

3120 μαλακός, ή, όν, soft, of garments, Mat. xi. 8; Lu. vii.

25; disgracefully effeminate, 1 Cor. vi. 9.*

3121 Μαλελεήλ, ὁ (Heb.), Maleleel or Mahalaleel, Lu. iii. 37.*

3122 μάλιστα, adv. (superl. of μάλα, very), most of all, especially, Gal. vi. 10; 2 Tim. iv. 13.

3123 μᾶλλον, adv. (comp. of μάλα), more, rather; πολλῷ μᾶλλον, much more, Mat. vi. 30; πόσῳ μᾶλλον, how much more, Mat. vii. 11; μᾶλλον ἤ, more than, Mat. xviii. 13; μᾶλλον is often of intensive force, e.g., Mat. xxvii. 24; Ro. viii. 34. See Gr. § 321, Wi. §§ 35, 1, 65, 2, Bu. 83.

3124 Μάλχος, ου, ὁ (Heb.), Malchus, Jn. xviii. 10.*

3125 μάμμη, ης, ἡ, a grandmother, 2 Tim. i. 5.*

3126 μαμμωνᾶς (W. H. μαμωνᾶς), ᾶ, ὁ (Aram.), mammon, gain, wealth, Mat. vi. 24; Lu. xvi. 9, 11, 13. (N. T.)*

3127 Μαναήν, ὁ (Heb.), Manaen, Ac. xiii. 1.*

3128 Μανασσῆς, gen. and acc. ῆ, ὁ, Manasseh, (1) son of Joseph, Rev. vii. 6; (2) Mat. i. 10.*

3129 μανθάνω, μαθήσομαι, 2d aor. ἔμαθον, perf. μεμάθηκα, to learn, to understand, to know, to be informed, to comprehend. Used abs., or with acc. (ἀπό or παρά with gen. of the teacher, ἐν with example, 1 Cor. iv. 6).

3130 μανία, ας, ἡ, madness, Ac. xxvi. 24.*

3131 μάννα, τό (Heb., deriv. uncertain), manna, the food of the Israelites in the desert, Jn. vi. 31, 49; Heb. ix. 4. (S.)

3132 μαντεύομαι, dep., to utter responses, practice divination, Ac. xvi. 16.*

3133 μαραίνω, ανῶ, fut. pass. μαρανθήσομαι, to wither, to fade away, Ja. i. 11.*

3134 μαρὰν ἀθά (two Aram. words), our Lord cometh (R.V. mrg.), 1 Cor. xvi. 22. (N. T.)*

3135 μαργαρίτης, ου, ὁ, a pearl, Mat. xiii. 45, 46.

3136 Μάρθα, ας, ἡ, Martha, Lu. x. 38, 40, 41.

3137 Μαρία, ας, or Μαριάμ, indecl. (Heb. Miriam), ἡ, Mary. Six of the name are mentioned: (1) the mother of Jesus, Lu. i. 27; (2) the Magdalene, Mar. xv. 40, 47;

(3) the sister of Martha and
Lazarus, Lu. x. 39, 42; (4)
the wife of Cleopas, Mat.
xxvii. 56, 61; (5) the mother
of John Mark, Ac. xii. 12;
(6) a Christian woman in
Rome, Ro. χvi. 6.

3138   Μάρκος, ου, ὁ, *Mark*, Ac. xii.
12, 25.

3139   μάρμαρος, ου, ὁ, ἡ, *marble*, Rev.
xviii. 12.*

3140   μαρτυρέω, ῶ, ἡσω, *to be a witness*, abs., *to testify* (περί,
gen.), *to give testimony* (*to*,
dat. of pers. or thing), *to
commend; pass., to be at-
tested, i.e.*, honorably, *to be
of good report.*

3141   μαρτυρία, ας, ἡ, *testimony, i.e.*,
legal, Mar. xiv. 56, 59; or
general, Jn. v. 34; with obj.
gen., as Rev. xix. 10.

3142   μαρτύριον, ου, τό, *testimony*,
Mat. viii. 4 (*to*, dat.; *against*,
ἐπί, acc.).

3143   μαρτύρομαι, dep., *to call to
witness*, Ac. xx. 26; Gal. v.
3; *to exhort solemnly*, Ac.
xxvi. 22 (W. H.); Ep. iv. 17;
1 Th. ii. 11 (W. H.).*

3144   μάρτυς, υρος, dat. plur. μάρτυσι,
ὁ, *a witness, i.e.*, judicially,
Mat. xviii. 16; *one who tes-
tifies* from what he has seen
or experienced, 1 Th. ii. 10,
Lu. xxiv. 48; *a martyr*, wit-
nessing by his death, Ac.
xxii. 20; Rev. ii. 13, xvii. 6.

3145   μασσάομαι (W. H. -ασά-), ῶμαι,
to bite, to gnaw, Rev. xvi. 10.*

3146   μαστιγόω, ῶ, ὡσω, *to scourge*,
Mat. x. 17; fig., Heb. xii. 6.

3147   μαστίζω, *to scourge*, Ac. xxii.
25.*

3148   μάστιξ, ιγος, ἡ, *a whip, a
scourge*, Ac. xxii. 24; Heb.
xi. 36; fig., *calamity, disease*,
Mar. iii. 10, v. 29, 34; Lu.
vii. 21.*

3149   μαστός, οῦ, ὁ, *the breast*, pl.,
Lu. xi. 27, xxiii. 29; Rev. i.
13.*

3150   ματαιολογία, ας, ἡ, *vain, fruitless talk*, 1 Tim. i. 6.*

3151   ματαιο-λόγος, ου, ὁ, *a vain,
empty talker*, Tit. i. 10.*

3152;   see   μάταιος (αία), αιον, *vain, useless, empty*, 1 Cor. xv. 17;
2756   Ja. i. 26; τὰ μάταια, *vanities*,
spec. of heathen deities, Ac.
xiv. 15 (and O. T.). *Syn.:* see
κενός.

3153   ματαιότης, τητος, ἡ, (1) *vanity*,

2 Pet. ii. 18; (2) *perverseness*, Ep. iv. 17; (3) *frailty*,
Ro. viii. 20.*

3154   ματαιόω, ῶ, *to make vain* or
foolish; pass., Ro. i. 21.
(S.)*

3155   μάτην, adv., *in vain, fruitless-
ly*, Mat. xv. 9; Mar. vii. 7.*

3156   Ματθαῖος (W. H. Μαθθαῖος), ου,
ὁ, *Matthew*, the apostle and
evangelist, Mat. ix. 9, 10;
also called Λευΐ.

3157   Ματθάν (W. H. Μαθθάν), ὁ
(Heb.), *Matthan*, Mat. i. 15.*

3158   Ματθάτ, ὁ (Heb.), *Matthat*, Lu.
iii. 24, 29 (W. H. Μαθθάτ).*

3159   Ματθίας (W. H. Μαθθίας), α, ὁ,
Matthias, Ac. i. 23, 26.*

3160   Ματταθά, ὁ (Heb.), *Mattatha*,
Lu. iii. 31.*

3161   Ματταθίας, ου, ὁ, *Mattathias*,
Lu. iii. 25, 26.*

3162   μάχαιρα, ας and ης, ἡ, *a sword*,
Jn. xviii. 10, 11; met., for
strife, Mat. x. 34; fig., of
spiritual weapons, Ep. vi. 17.

3163   μάχη, ης, ἡ, *battle; contention,
strife*, 2 Cor. vii. 5; 2 Tim.
ii. 23; Tit. iii. 9; Ja. iv. 1.*

3164   μάχομαι, *to fight, contend, dis-
★   pute*, Jn. vi. 52; Ac. vii. 26;
2 Tim. ii. 24; Ja. iv. 2.*

3166   μεγαλ-αυχέω, ῶ, *to boast great
things, to be arrogant*, Ja. iii.
5 (W. H. μεγάλα αὐχεῖ).*

3167   μεγαλεῖος, εία, εῖον, *grand, magnificent*, Lu. i. 49 (W. H. με-
γάλα); Ac. ii. 11.*

3168   μεγαλειότης, τητος, ἡ, *majesty,
magnificence*, Lu. ix. 43; Ac.
xix. 27; 2 Pet. i. 16.*

3169   μεγαλο-πρεπής, ές, gen. οῦς, *fitting for a great man, magnif-
icent, majestic*, 2 Pet. i. 17.*

3170   μεγαλύνω, νῶ, (1) *to make great*,
Mat. xxiii. 5; (2) *to magnify,
extol, celebrate with praise*,
Lu. i. 46; Ac. v. 13.

3171   μεγάλως, adv., *greatly*, Phil. iv.
10.*

3172   μεγαλωσύνη, ης, ἡ, *majesty*,
Heb. i. 3, viii. 1; Ju. 25.
(S.)*

3173,●3176 μέγας, μεγάλη, μέγα (see Gr.
§ 39), comp. μείζων, sup. μέ-
γιστος, *great*, in size, *full-
grown, intense*, Mat. ii. 10,
xxviii. 8; *wonderful*, 2 Cor.
xi. 15; *noble, of high rank*,
Rev. xi. 18, xiii. 16; applied
to age, ὁ μείζων, *the elder*,
Ro. ix. 12; μέγας indicates
the *size* of things, their *meas-*

ure, number, cost, and estimation; μεγάλη ἡμέρα, a
solemn, sacred day, Jn. xix.
31.

3174 μέγεθος, ους, τό, greatness, Ep.
i. 19.*

3175 μεγιστᾶνες, άνων, οἱ (sing. μεγι-
στάν, only in Ap., Sirach iv.
7), princes, great men, nobles,
Mar. vi. 21; Rev. vi. 15, xviii.
23. (S.)*

3177 μεθ-ερμηνεύω, to translate, to
interpret, pass. only, Mar. v.
41; Jn. i. 41.

3178 μέθη, ης, ἡ, drunkenness, Lu.
xxi. 34; Ro. xiii. 13; Gal. v.
21.*

3179 μεθ-ίστημι (and μεθιστάνω, 1
Cor. xiii. 2), μεταστήσω,
1st aor., pass., μετεστάθην,
lit., to change the place of;
hence, to remove, 1 Cor.
xiii. 2; Col. i. 13; to lead
astray, Ac. xix. 26; to remove from life, Ac. xiii. 22;
to remove from office, Lu.
xvi. 4.*

3180 μεθ-οδεία (-οδία, W. H.), as, ἡ,
a fraudulent artifice, a trick,
Ep. iv. 14, vi. 11. (N.T.)*

3181 μεθ-όριος, α, ον, bordering on;
τὰ μεθόρια, borders, frontiers,
Mar. vii. 24 (W. H. ὅρια).*

3182 μεθύσκω, to make drunk; pass.,
to be drunk, Lu. xii. 45; Jn.
ii. 10; Ep. v. 18; 1 Th. v.
7.*

3183 μέθυσος, ου, ὁ (prop. adj.), a
drunkard, 1 Cor. v. 11, vi.
10.*

3184 μεθύω, to be drunken, Mat. xxiv.
49; Ac. ii. 15; met., Rev.
xvii. 6.

3185, 3186, μείζων, comp. of μέγας, which
3187; see see. It has itself a com-
Strong. parative, μειζότερος, 3 Jn. 4
(see Gr. § 47, Wi. § 11, 2 b,
Bu. 28).

3188 μέλαν, ανος, τό (μέλας), ink, 2
Cor. iii. 3; 2 Jn. 12; 3 Jn.
13.*

3189 μέλας, αινα, αν, black, Mat. v.
36; Rev. vi. 5, 12.*

3190 Μελεᾶς, ᾶ, ὁ, Melea, Lu. iii.
31.*

see 3199 μέλει, impers. (see Gr. § 101,
Wi. § 30, 10d, Bu. 164), it
concerns, dat. of pers., with
gen. of object, as 1 Cor. ix.
9; or περί, as Jn. x. 13; or
ὅτι, as Mar. iv. 38.

3191 μελετάω, ῶ, ἥσω, to practice, 1
Tim. iv. 15; to devise, Ac. iv.

25; to meditate, Mar. xiii. 11
(not W. H.).*

3192 μέλι, ιτος, τό, honey, Mat. iii.
4; Mar. i. 6; Rev. x. 9, 10.*

3193 μελίσσιος, α, ον, made by bees,
Lu. xxiv. 42 (W. H. omit).
(N. T.)*

3194 Μελίτη, ης, ἡ, Melita, now
Malta, Ac. xxviii. 1 (W. H.
Μελιτήνη).*

3195 μέλλω, ἥσω, to be about to do, to
be on the point of doing, with
infin., generally the present
infin., rarely aor.; the fut.
infin. (the regular classical
use) occurs only in the
phrase μέλλειν ἔσεσθαι (only
in Ac.); the verb may often
be adequately rendered by
our auxiliaries, will, shall,
must; to delay, only Ac. xxii.
16. The participle is used
absolutely: τὸ μέλλον, the
future, Lu. xiii. 9; τὰ μέλλοντα, things to come, Ro.
viii. 38. See Gr. § 363f,
Wi. § 44, 7 c, Bu. 259.

3196 μέλος, ους, τό, a member of the
body, a limb, as Mat. v. 29,
30; Ro. xii. 4; fig., 1 Cor. vi.
15.

3197 Μελχί (W. H. -εί), ὁ (Heb.),
Melchi. Two are mentioned,
Lu. iii. 24, 28.*

3198 Μελχισεδέκ, ὁ (Heb. king of
★★ righteousness), Melchizedek,
Heb. v., vi., vii.*

3200 μεμβράνα, ης, ἡ (Lat.), parch-
ment, 2 Tim. iv. 13. (N.T.)*

3201 μέμφομαι, ψομαι, dep., to blame,
to censure, abs., Mar. vii. 2
(W. H. omit); Ro. ix. 19;
abs. or dat., Heb. viii. 8 (W.
H. acc., with dat. mrg.).*

3202 μεμψί-μοιρος, ον, discontented,
★★ complaining, Ju. 16.*

3303 μέν, antithetic particle, truly,
indeed (see Gr. § 136, Wi.
§ 53, 7 b), Bu. 364 sq.).

see 3303 μεν-οῦν, conj., moreover, therefore, but.

3304 μεν-οῦν-γε, conj., nay rather,
nay truly, Lu. xi. 28 (W. H.
μενοῦν); Ro. ix. 20, x. 18;
Phil. iii. 8 (W. H. μὲν οὖν γε).
See Gr. § 406, Wi. § 61, 6,
Bu. 370 sq.*

3305 μέν-τοι, conj., yet truly, nevertheless, however, Jn. iv. 27.

3306 μένω, μενῶ, ἔμεινα, (1) intrans.,
to remain, to abide; so (a) of
place, to dwell, Mat. x. 11;
to lodge, Lu. xix. 5; (b) of

* For 3176 see 3173.

★★ **For 3199 see Strong. James
Strong inadvertently skipped
numbers 3203-3302 in
numbering his entries.**

state, as Ac. v. 4; *to continue firm* and *constant in*, Jn. xv. 4; *to endure, to last, to be permanent*, 1 Cor. iii. 14; (2) trans., *to await, wait for*, only Ac. xx. 5, 23.

3307 μερίζω, σω, (1) *to divide, separate*, mid., *to share* (μετά, gen.), Lu. xii. 13; pass., *to be divided, to be at variance*, Mat. xii. 25, 26; 1 Cor. i. 13; (2) *to distribute*, Mar. vi. 41, acc. and dat.

3308 μέριμνα, ης, ἡ, *care, anxiety*, as dividing, distracting the mind, Mat. xiii. 22; Lu. viii. 14.

3309 μεριμνάω, ῶ, ήσω, *to be anxious, distracted, to care for*; abs., with dat., περί (gen.), acc. The various constructions may be illustrated from Mat. vi.: abs., vers. 27, 31; acc., ver. 34 (Rec.; see also 1 Cor. vii. 32–34); gen., ver. 34 (W. H.); dat., ver. 25; εἰς, ver. 34; περί, ver. 28.

3310 μερίς, ίδος, ἡ, *a part* or *division* of a country, Ac. xvi. 12; *a share, portion*, Lu. x. 42; Ac. viii. 21, 2 Cor. vi. 15; Col. i. 12.*

3311 μερισμός, οῦ, ὁ, *a dividing* or *division*, Heb. iv. 12; *distribution, gifts distributed*, Heb. ii. 4.*

3312 μεριστής, οῦ, ὁ, *a divider*, Lu. xii. 14. (N. T.)*

3313 μέρος, ους, τό, *a part*; hence, (1) *a share*, Rev. xxii. 19; *fellowship*, Jn. xiii. 8; *a business* or *calling*, Ac. xix. 27; (2) *a part*, as the result of division, Jn. xix. 23. In adverbial phrases, μέρος τι, *partly, in some part*; ἀνὰ μέρος, *alternately*; ἀπὸ μέρους, *partly*; ἐκ μέρους, *individually*, of persons, *partially, imperfectly*, of things; κατὰ μέρος, *particularly, in detail*, Heb. ix. 5.

3314 μεσημβρία, ας, ἡ, *midday, noon*, Ac. xxii. 6; *the south*, Ac. viii. 26.

3315 μεσιτεύω, σω, *to mediate, to give surety*, Heb. vi. 17.*

3316 μεσίτης, ου, ὁ, *a mediator, i.e.*, one who interposes between parties and reconciles them, Gal. iii. 19, 20; 1 Tim. ii. 5; in the phrase μεσίτης διαθήκης, *mediator of a covenant*, Heb. viii. 6, ix. 15, xii. 24.*

3317 μεσο-νύκτιον, ου, τό, *midnight*, as Lu. xi. 5.

3318 Μεσο-ποταμία, ας, ἡ, *Mesopotamia*, the region between the Euphrates and the Tigris, Ac. ii. 9, vii. 2.*

3319 μέσος, η, ον, *middle*, of time or place, *in the midst* of (gen.), as Mat. xxv. 6; Jn. i. 26, xix. 18; Ac. i. 18, xxvi. 13; neut., τὸ μέσον, *the middle part*, used chiefly in adverbial phrases, with prepositions (art. generally omit.), ἐκ μέσου, *from among, away*; ἐν μέσῳ, *among*; ἀνὰ μέσον, *through the midst, among, between*; also with διά and εἰς.

3320 μεσό-τοιχον, ου, τό, *a partition-wall*, Ep. ii. 14. (N. T.)*

3321 μεσ-ουράνημα, ατος, τό, *mid-heaven*, Rev. viii. 13, xiv. 6, xix. 17.*

3322 μεσόω, ῶ, *to be in the middle*, Jn. vii. 14.*

3323 Μεσσίας, ου, ὁ (from Heb. *anointed*), *Messiah*, the same as Greek Χριστός, Jn. i. 41, iv. 25. (N. T.)*

3324 μεστός, ή, όν, *full*, gen., Jn. xix. 29; Ro. i. 29.

3325 μεστόω, ῶ, *to fill*, gen., Ac. ii. 13.*

3326 μετά (akin to μέσος), prep., gov. the gen. and acc.; gen., *with, among*; acc., *after* (see Gr. § 301, Wi. §§ 47 *h*, 49 *f*, 52, 4, 10), Bu. 338 sq.). In composition, μετά denotes *participation, nearness, change*, or *succession* (often like the Latin prefix *trans-*, as in the words *transfer, translate*).

3327 μετα-βαίνω, βήσομαι, *to pass over, to depart*, Lu. x. 7; Mat. xi. 1.

3328 μετα-βάλλω, in mid., *to change one's mind*, Ac. xxviii. 6.*

3329 μετ-άγω, *to turn about, to direct*, as horses, ships, Ja. iii. 3, 4.*

3330 μετα-δίδωμι, *to share with, to impart*, Lu. iii. 11; Ro. i. 11; 1 Th. ii. 8; Ep. iv. 28; ὁ μεταδιδούς, *a distributor* of alms, Ro. xii. 8.*

3331 μετά-θεσις, εως, ἡ, (1) *a transfer, a translation*, Heb. xi. 5; *a removal*, Heb. xii. 27; (2) *a change*, Heb. vii. 12.*

3332 μετ-αίρω, *to remove*, intrans., *to depart*, Mat. xiii. 53, xix. 1.*

3333 μετα-καλέω, ῶ, in mid., *to call to one's self, to send for*, Ac. vii. 14, x. 32, xx. 17, xxiv. 25.*

3334 μετα-κινέω, ῶ, *to move away*, pass., *to be moved away*, Col. i. 23.*

3335 μετα-λαμβάνω, *to take a share of*, Ac. ii. 46; *partake*, gen., 2 Tim. ii. 6; *to obtain* (acc.), Ac. xxiv. 25.

3336 μετά-ληψις (W. H.-λημψις), εως, ἡ, *participation; εἰς μ.*, *to be received*, 1 Tim. iv. 3.*

3337 μετ-αλλάσσω, *to change* one thing (acc.) for (ἐν, εἰς) another, Ro. i. 25, 26.*

3338 μετα-μέλομαι, μελήσομαι, 1st aor. μετεμελήθην, dep., pass., *to change one's mind*, Mat. xxi. 30, 32; Heb. vii. 21; *to repent, to feel sorrow for, regret*, Mat. xxvii. 3, 2 Cor. vii. 8. *Syn.:* μετανοέω is the nobler word, the regular expression for thorough repentance; μεταμέλομαι is more loosely used, generally expressing sorrow, regret or remorse.

3339 μετα-μορφόω, ῶ, *to change the form, to transform*, Mat. xvii. 2; Mar. ix. 2; 2 Cor. iii. 18; Ro. xii. 2.*

3340; see 3338 μετα-νοέω, ῶ, ήσω, *to change one's views* and *purpose, to repent*, as Mat. iii. 2; Ac. viii. 22. *Syn.:* see μεταμέλομαι.

3341 μετάνοια, ας, ἡ, *change of mind, repentance*, as Mat. iii. 8, 11.

3342 μετα-ξύ (σύν or ξύν), adv. of time, *meanwhile*, Jn. iv. 31; *afterwards*, perh., Ac. xiii. 42 (see Gr. § 298, 7 b); as prep. with gen., *between*, of place, Mat. xxiii. 35.

3343 μετα-πέμπω, in mid., *to send for to one's self, to summon*, Ac. x. 5, 22, 29, xi. 13, xxiv. 24, 26, xxv. 3; pass., x. 29.*

3344 μετα-στρέφω (with 2d fut. and 2d aor. pass.), *to turn about, to change*, Ja. iv. 9; Ac. ii. 20; *to pervert, to corrupt*, Gal. i. 7.*

3345 μετα-σχηματίζω, ἴσω, *to change the figure of, transfigure*, Phil. iii. 21; mid., *to assume the appearance of any one*, 2 Cor. xi. 13, 14, 15; fig., *to transfer, i.e., to speak by way of illustration*, 1 Cor. iv. 6.*

3346 μετα-τίθημι, *to transpose, to transfer*, Ac. vii. 16; Heb. xi. 5; *to change*, Heb. vii. 12; mid., *to transfer one's self, i.e., to fall away, to desert*, Gal. i. 6; *to pervert*, Ju. 4.*

3347 μετ-έπειτα, adv., *afterwards*, Heb. xii. 17.*

3348 μετ-έχω, μετασχήσω, 2d aor. μετέσχον, *to be partaker of, to share in*, 1 Cor. ix. 10, 12, x. 17, 21, 30; Heb. ii. 14. v. 13, vii. 13.*

3349 μετεωρίζω, in pass., *to be troubled with anxiety, to be in suspense*, Lu. xii. 29.*

3350 μετ-οικεσία, ας, ἡ, *change of abode, migration* (of the Babylonian exile), Mat. i. 11, 12, 17.*

3351 μετ-οικίζω, ιῶ, *to cause to change one's habitation, to cause to migrate*, Ac. vii. 4, 43.*

3352 μετοχή, ῆς, ἡ, *a sharing, a fellowship*, 2 Cor. vi. 14.*

3353 μέτοχος, ον, ὁ (prop. adj.), *a partaker*, Heb. iii. 1, 14, vi. 4, xii. 8; *a partner, an associate*, Heb. i. 9; Lu. v. 7.*

3354 μετρέω, ῶ, *to measure*, Rev. xi. 2; Lu. vi. 38; met., *to estimate, to judge of*, 2 Cor. x. 12.

3355 μετρητής, οῦ, ὁ, prop. *a measurer; an amphora*, a liquid measure containing 72 sextarii, or somewhat less than 9 English gallons, Jn. ii. 6.*

3356 μετριο-παθέω, ῶ, *to treat with moderation, bear gently with* (R. V.), Heb. v. 2.*

3357 μετρίως, adv., *moderately*, Ac. xx. 12.*

3358 μέτρον, ον, τό, *a measure*, Mat. xxiii. 32; Mar. iv. 24; *a measuring-rod*, Rev. xxi. 15; *a definite portion* or *measure*, Ro. xii. 3; Ep. iv. 16; adv. phrases, ἐκ μέτρου, *by measure, sparingly*, Jn. iii. 34; ἐν μέτρῳ, *in due measure*, Ep. iv. 16.

3359 μέτωπον, ον, τό (ὤψ), *the forehead*, Rev. vii. 3, ix. 4 (only in Rev.).

3360 μέχρι, or μέχρις, adv., as prep. with gen., *unto*, time, Mat. xiii 30; Mar. xiii. 30; place, Ro. xv. 19; degree, 2 Tim. ii. 9; Heb. xii. 4; as conj., *until*, Ep. iv. 13.

3361 μή, a negative particle, *not;* for

distinction between μή and
οὐ, see Gr. § 401, Wi. § 55,
1, Bu. 351 ; elliptically, *lest,*
see Gr. § 384, Wi. § 56, 2 *b,*
Bu. 241 sq.; interrogatively,
*   see Gr. § 369, Wi. § 57, 3 *b,*
Bu. 248 ; for the combina-
tion οὐ μή, see Gr. § 377,
Wi. § 57, 3 *b,* Bu. 211 sq.

see 1065   μή-γε, in the phrase εἰ δὲ μήγε,
but if not, emphatic.

3365   μηδαμῶς, adv., *by no means,*
Ac. x. 14, xi. 8.*

3366   μηδέ, compare οὐδέ, and see
Gr. § 401, Wi. § 55, 6, Bu.
366 sq.; *not even,* Mar. ii. 2 ;
1 Cor. v. 11 ; generally used
after a preceding μή, *and
not, neither, but not, nor yet,*
as Mat. vi. 25, vii. 6.

3367   μηδείς, μηδεμία, μηδέν (εἷς), differing from οὐδείς as μή from
οὐ (see Gr. § 401, Wi. § 55,
1, Bu. 351) ; *not one, no one,
no person* or *thing, nothing,*
Mat. viii. 4 ; Mar. v. 26 ; Gal.
vi. 3.

3368   μηδέ-ποτε, adv., *never,* 2 Tim.
iii. 7.*

3369   μηδέ-πω, adv., *not yet,* Heb.
xi. 7.*

3370   Μῆδος, ου, ὁ, *a Mede,* Ac. ii. 9.*

3371   μηκέτι, adv. (ἔτι) *no more, no
longer,* Mar. ix. 25, xi. 14 ;
Ac. iv. 17.

3372   μῆκος, ους, τό, *length,* Ep. iii.
18 ; Rev. xxi. 16.*

3373   μηκύνω, *to make long,* pass., *to
grow up,* as plants, Mar. iv.
27.*

3374   μηλωτή, ῆς, ἡ, *a sheepskin,* Heb.
xi. 37.*

3375   μήν, a part. of strong affirma-
tion, N. T. only in the com-
bination ἦ μήν, *assuredly,
certainly,* Heb. vi. 14 (W. H.
εἰ μήν).*

3376   μήν, μηνός, ὁ, (1) *a month,* as
Ac. vii. 20; (2) *the new moon,*
as a festival, Gal. iv. 10.

3377   μηνύω, *to show, declare,* Lu. xx.
37 ; Jn. xi. 57 ; Ac. xxiii. 30 ;
1 Cor. x. 28.*

3378   μὴ οὐκ, an interrogative formula, expecting the answer
"yes," Ro. x. 18, 19 ; 1 Cor.
ix. 4, 5.

3379   μή-ποτε, adv., *never,* Heb. ix.
17 ; as conj., *lest ever, lest
perhaps, lest at any time,* Lu.
xii. 58 ; Ac. v. 39 ; interrog.
part., *whether indeed,* Jn. vii.
26 ; Lu. iii. 15.

see 3381   μή που, *lest anywhere,* Ac.
xxvii. 29 (W. H., for Rec.
μήπως).

3380   μή-πω, adv., *not yet,* Ro. ix. 11 ;
Heb. ix. 8.*

3381   μή-πως, conj., *lest in any way,
lest perhaps,* as Ac. xxvii.
29 (W. H. μή που), 1 Th.
iii. 5.

3382   μηρός, οῦ, ὁ, *the thigh,* Rev. xix.
16.*

3383   μήτε, conj., differing from οὔτε
as μή from οὐ (see Gr. § 401) ;
and not, used after a preceding μή or μήτε, *neither . . .
nor;* in Mar. iii. 20, *not even,*
W. H. read μηδέ.

3384   μήτηρ, τρός, ἡ, *a mother,* Mat.
i. 18, ii. 11 ; met., *a mother
city,* Gal. iv. 26.

3385, 3386   μήτι, adv., interrogatively used,
is it? whether at all? gener-
ally expecting a negative
answer ; μήτιγε (W. H., Rec.
μήτι γε), *not to say then?* 1
Cor. vi. 3.

3387   μήτις (W. H. μή τις), pron.
interrcg., *has* or *is any one?
whether any one?* Jn. iv. 33.*

3388   μήτρα, ας, ἡ, *the womb,* Lu. ii.
23 ; Ro. iv. 19.*

3389   μητρ-αλῴας (W. H. -ολῴας), ου,
ὁ, *a matricide,* 1 Tim. i. 9.*

3391   μία, fem. of εἷς, *one.*

3392   μιαίνω, ανῶ, perf. pass. μεμί-
ασμαι, *to stain, pollute, defile,*
Jn. xviii. 28; Tit. i. 15, Heb.
xii. 15 ; Ju. 8.*

3393   μίασμα, ατος, τό, *pollution, defilement,* 2 Pet. ii. 20.*

3394   μιασμός, οῦ, ὁ, *the act of defilement, pollution,* 2 Pet. ii.
10.*

3395   μίγμα, ατος, τό, *a mixture,* Jn.
xix. 39 (W. H. text ἔλιγμα).*

3396   μίγνυμι, μίξω, ἔμιξα, perf. pass.
μέμιγμαι, *to mix, to mingle,*
Mat. xxvii. 34 ; Lu. xiii. 1 ;
Rev. viii. 7, xv. 2.*

3397, 3398   μικρός, ά, όν, *little, small, i.e.,*
in size, Mat. xiii. 32 ; quan-
tity, 1 Cor. v. 6; number, Lu.
xii. 32 ; time, Jn. vii. 33 ;
dignity, Mat x. 42 ; age,
Mat. xviii. 6, 10, 14.

3399   Μίλητος, ου, ἡ, *Miletus,* Ac. xx.
15, 17 ; 2 Tim. iv. 20.*

3400   μίλιον, ου, τό (Lat. *miliarium*),
a mile (somewhat less than
our mile), Mat. v. 41.*

3401   μιμέομαι, οῦμαι, dep. mid., *to
imitate,* 2 Th. iii. 7, 9 ; Heb.
xiii. 7 ; 3 Jn. 11.*

97

3402 μιμητής, οῦ, ὁ, *an imitator*, as 1 Cor. iv. 16.

3403 μιμνήσκω (μνα-), mid., with fut. in pass. form μνησθήσομαι, 1st aor. ἐμνήσθην, perf. μέμνημαι, *to call to mind, to remember*, gen. pers. or thing, Mat. xxvi. 75; Lu. xxiii. 42; pass., *to be remembered, to be had in mind*, only Ac. x. 31; Rev. xvi. 16.

3404 μισέω, ῶ, ήσω, *to hate, to detest*, Mat. v. 43; Jn. vii. 7; Ro. ix. 13.

3405 μισθ-απο-δοσία, ας, ἡ, *recompense*, as (1) *reward*, Heb. x. 35, xi. 26; (2) *punishment*, Heb. ii. 2. (N. T.)*

3406 μισθ-απο-δότης, ου, ὁ, *a rewarder*, Heb. xi. 6. (N. T.)*

3407 μίσθιος, α, ον, *hired*, as subst., *a hired servant*, Lu. xv. 17, 19, 21 (W. H. in br.).*

3408 μισθός, οῦ, ὁ, *hire, wages, recompense*, Mat. xx. 8; used of *reward*, Mat. v. 12, 46; of *punishment*, 2 Pet. ii. 13.

3409 μισθόω, ῶ, ώσω, mid., *to hire*, Mat. xx. 1, 7.*

3410 μίσθωμα, ατος, τό, *hire, rent; anything rented*, as a house, Ac. xxviii. 30.*

3411 μισθωτός, οῦ, ὁ, *a hired servant*, Mar. i. 20; Jn. x. 12, 13.*

3412 Μιτυλήνη, ης, ἡ, *Mitylene*, the capital of Lesbos, Ac. xx. 14.*

3413 Μιχαήλ, ὁ (Heb. *who is like God?*), *Michael*, an archangel, Ju. 9; Rev. xii. 7.*

3414 μνᾶ, ᾶς, ἡ, *a mina*, silver money = 100 δραχμαί, or about sixteen or seventeen dollars, Lu. xix. 13–25.*

3415 μνάομαι, see μιμνήσκω.

3416 Μνάσων, ωνος, ὁ, *Mnason*, Ac. xxi. 16.*

3417 μνεία, ας, ἡ, *remembrance, recollection*, Phil. i. 3; 1 Th. iii. 6; μνείαν ποιεῖσθαι, *to mention*, Ro. i. 9.

3418 μνῆμα, ατος, τό, *a monument, a tomb*, Mar. v. 5; Lu. xxiii. 53; less frequent than the following.

3419 μνημεῖον, ου, τό, *a tomb, a sepulchre*, Mat. viii. 28; Jn. xi. 31.

3420 μνήμη, ης, ἡ, *remembrance, mention*; μνήμην ποιεῖσθαι, *to make mention*, 2 Pet. i. 15.*

3421 μνημονεύω, *to remember* (ὅτι),

recollect, *call to mind* (gen. or acc.), Mat. xvi. 9; Ac. xx. 31; *to be mindful of*, Heb. xi. 15; *to make mention of* (περί, gen.), Heb. xi. 22.

3422 μνημόσυνον, ου, τό, *a memorial, honorable remembrance*, Mat. xxvi. 13; Mar. xiv. 9; Ac. x. 4.*

3423 μνηστεύω, *to ask in marriage;* pass., *to be betrothed*, Mat. i. 18; Lu. i. 27, ii. 5.*

3424 μογι-λάλος, ου, ὁ (prop. adj.), *one speaking with difficulty, a stammerer*, Mar. vii. 32.*

3425 μόγις, adv., *with difficulty, hardly*, Lu. ix. 39 (W. H. μόλις).*

3426 μόδιος, ου, ὁ (Lat.), *a dry measure* (16 sextarii), containing about a peck; *a modius*, Mat. v. 15; Mar. iv. 21; Lu. xi. 33. (N. T.)*

3428 μοιχαλίς, ίδος, ἡ, *an adulteress*, Ro. vii. 3; fig., for departure from God, Mat. xvi. 4; Ja. iv. 4. (S.)

3429 μοιχάομαι, ῶμαι, *to commit adultery*, Mat. v. 32.

3430 μοιχεία, ας, ἡ, *adultery*, Mat. xv. 19.

3431 μοιχεύω, σω, *to commit adultery*, abs. (acc., Mat. v. 28); fig., of forsaking God, Rev. ii. 22.

3432 μοιχός, οῦ, ὁ, *an adulterer*, Lu. xviii. 11; 1 Cor. vi. 9; Heb. xiii. 4; Ja. iv. 4 (not W. H.).*

3433 μόλις, adv., *with difficulty, hardly*, Lu. ix. 39 (W. H.); Ac. xiv. 18, xxvii. 7, 8, 16; Ro. v. 7; 1 Pet. iv. 18.*

3434 Μολόχ, ὁ (Heb.), *Moloch*, Ac. vii. 43 (from S.).*

3435 μολύνω, υνῶ, *to pollute, to defile*, 1 Cor. viii. 7; Rev. iii. 4, xiv. 4.*

3436 μολυσμός, οῦ, ὁ, *pollution, defilement*, 2 Cor. vii. 1. (S.)*

3437 μομφή, ῆς, ἡ, *complaint, ground of complaint*, Col. iii. 13.*

3438 μονή, ῆς, ἡ, *an abode, a dwelling-place*, Jn. xiv. 2, 23.*

3439 μονο-γενής, ές, gen. οῦς, *only begotten*, Lu. vii. 12, viii. 42, ix. 38; Heb. xi. 17; of Christ, Jn. i. 14, 18, iii. 16, 18; 1 Jn. iv. 9.*

3440, 3441 μόνος, η, ον, *only, alone, single*, Lu. xxiv. 18; *solitary, without company*, Mar. vi. 47; *forsaken, desolate*, Jn. viii. 29; adv., μόνον, *only*.

* For 3427 see 1698.

3442 μον-όφθαλμος, ον, *having but one eye*, Mat. xviii. 9; Mar. ix. 47.*

3443 μονόω, ῶ, *to leave alone ;* pass., *to be left alone* or *desolate*, 1 Tim. v. 5.*

3444 μορφή, ῆς, ἡ, *outward appearance, form, shape*, Mar. xvi. 12; Phil. ii. 6, 7.* *Syn.:* see ἰδέα.

3445 μορφόω, ῶ, ὡσω, *to form, to fashion*, Gal. iv. 19.*

3446 μόρφωσις, εως, ἡ, *form, semblance*, 2 Tim. iii. 5; *form, system*, Ro. ii. 20.*

3447 μοσχο-ποιέω, ῶ, *to make an image of a calf*, Ac. vii. 41. (N. T.)*

3448 μόσχος, ου, ὁ, ἡ, *a calf, a young bullock*, Lu. xv. 23, 27, 30; Heb. ix. 12, 19; Rev. iv. 7.*

●3451 μουσικός, ή, όν, *skilled in music, a musician*, Rev. xviii. 22.*

3449 μόχθος, ου, ὁ, *wearisome labor, toil*, 2 Cor. xi. 27; 1 Th. ii. 9; 2 Th. iii. 8.*

*

3452 μυελός, οῦ, ὁ, *marrow*, Heb. iv. 12.*

3453 μυέω, ῶ, *to initiate into, to instruct*, Phil. iv. 12.*

3454 μῦθος, ου, ὁ, *a word ;* hence, *a fiction, a fable, a falsehood*, 1 Tim. i. 4, iv. 7; 2 Tim. iv. 4; Tit. i. 14; 2 Pet. i. 16.*

3455 μυκάομαι, ῶμαι, *to bellow, to roar*, as a lion, Rev. x. 3.*

3456 μυκτηρίζω, *to turn up the nose ; to mock, deride*, Gal. vi. 7.*

3457 μυλικός, ή, όν, *pertaining to a mill ;* with λίθος, *millstone*, Mar. ix. 42 (not W. H.); Lu. xvii. 2 (W. H.). (N. T.)*

see 3457 μύλινος, η, ον, in sense of foregoing, Rev. xviii. 21 (W. H.).*

3458 μύλος, ου, ὁ, *a millstone*, as Mat. xviii. 6.

3459 μυλών, ῶνος, ὁ, *a mill-house*, the place where grain was ground, Mat. xxiv. 41 (W. H. μύλος).*

3460 Μύρα (W. H. Μύρρα), ων, τά, *Myra*, a city near the coast of Lycia, Ac. xxvii. 5.*

3461 μυριάς, άδος, ἡ, *a myriad, ten thousand*, Ac. xix. 19; *a vast multitude*, Lu. xii. 1; Ac. xxi. 20; Heb. xii. 22; Ju. 14; Rev. v. 11, ix. 16.*

3462 μυρίζω, σω, *to anoint*, Mar. xiv. 8.*

3463 μυρίοι, ιαι, ια, *innumerable*, 1 Cor. iv. 15, xiv. 19; μύριοι,

ιαι, ια, *ten thousand*, Mat. xviii. 24.*

3464 μύρον, ου, τό, *ointment*, Mat. xxvi. 7.

3465 Μυσία, ας, ἡ, *Mysia*, Ac. xvi. 7, 8.*

3466 μυστήριον, ου, τό, *a mystery, anything hidden, a secret*, Mat. xiii. 11; Ro. xi. 25. In classical Greek, τὰ μυστήρια are *hidden religious rites and knowledge*, revealed only to the initiated; hence, the word is used in N. T. of the truths of the Gospel as *mysteries* partly hidden, partly revealed, Ep. iii. 9; Col. i. 26, iv. 3; 1 Tim. iii. 16; *a hidden meaning*, Ep. v. 32; Rev. i. 20.

3467 μυωπάζω, *to see dimly*, 2 Pet. i. 9.*

3468 μώλωψ, ωπος, ὁ, *a bruise, a stripe*, 1 Pet. ii. 24.*

3469 μωμάομαι, ῶμαι, dep., aor. mid. and pass., *to blame, to find fault with*, 2 Cor. vi. 3, viii. 20.*

3470 μῶμος, ου, ὁ, *a blemish ;* met., *disgrace*, 2 Pet. ii. 13.*

3471 μωραίνω, ανῶ, *to make foolish*, 1 Cor. i. 20; pass., *to become foolish*, Ro. i. 22; *to become insipid, tasteless*, like spoiled salt, Mat. v. 13; Lu. xiv. 34.*

3472 μωρία, ας, ἡ, *folly, absurdity*, 1 Cor. i. 18, 21, 23, ii. 14, iii. 19.*

3473 μωρο-λογία, ας, ἡ, *foolish talking*, Ep. v. 4.*

3474 μωρός, ά, όν, *stupid, foolish*, Mat. vii. 26, xxiii. 17, 19, (on Mat. v. 22, acc Gr. § 153, ii.); τὸ μωρόν, *foolishness*, 1 Cor. i. 25, 27.

3475 Μωσῆς (W. H. Μωυσῆς), έως, dat. εῖ or ῇ; acc. ῆν (once ἐα, Lu. xvi. 29), ὁ, *Moses*, met., the books of Moses, *the Pentateuch*, Lu. xvi. 29; 2 Cor. iii. 15.

N

N, ν, νῦ, *nu, n*, the thirteenth letter. As a numeral, ν' = 50; ͵ν = 50,000.

3476 Ναασσών, ὁ (Heb.), *Naasson*, Mat. i. 4; Lu. iii. 32.*

3477 Ναγγαί, ὁ (Heb.), *Naggai*, Lu. iii. 25.*

3478 Ναζαρέτ, -ρέθ or -ρά (W. H.

* For 3450 see 1700.

have all the forms), ἡ, *Naza-reth*, Mat. ii. 23; Lu. ii. 4, 39, 51.

3479 Ναζαρηνός, οῦ, ὁ, *a Nazarene*, as Mar. i. 24.

3480 Ναζωραῖος, ον, ὁ, *a Nazarene*, an appellation of Christ, Mat. ii. 23, xxvi. 71; Christians are called οἱ Ναζωραῖοι, Ac. xxiv. 5.

3481 Ναθάν (W. H. -άμ), ὁ (Heb.), *Nathan*, Lu. iii. 31.*

3482 Ναθαναήλ, ὁ, *Nathanael*, perhaps the same as *Bartholomew*, Jn. i. 45–49, xxi. 2.*

3483 ναί, adv., affirming, *yes*, Mat. ix. 28; *even so*, Mat. xi. 26; Lu. x. 21; Rev. xxii. 20; *yea*, strongly affirming, Lu. vii. 26.

3484 Ναΐν, ἡ, *Nain*, Lu. vii. 11.*

3485; see ναός, οῦ, ὁ (ναίω), *a temple, a*
2411 *shrine*, in general, Ac. xix. 24; *the temple*, Mat. xxiii.16; met., used of Jesus Christ, Jn. ii. 19, 20; of Christians generally, 1 Cor. iii. 16; 2 Cor. vi. 16. *Syn.:* see ἱερόν.

3486 Ναούμ, ὁ (Heb.), *Nahum*, Lu. iii. 25 (not the prophet).*

3487 νάρδος, ου, ἡ, *nard, oil* or *ointment*, Mar. xiv. 3; Jn. xii. 3.*

3488 Νάρκισσος, ου, ὁ, *Narcissus*, Ro. xvi. 11.*

3489 ναυαγέω, ῶ (ἄγνυμι), *to suffer shipwreck*, 2 Cor. xi. 25; fig., 1 Tim. i. 19.*

3490 ναύ-κληρος, ου, ὁ, *a ship-master*, or *owner*, Ac. xxvii. 11.*

3491 ναῦς, acc. ναῦν, ἡ, *a ship*, Ac. xxvii. 41.*

3492 ναύτης, ου, ὁ, *a sailor*, Ac. xxvii. 27, 30; Rev. xviii. 17.*

3493 Ναχώρ, ὁ (Heb.), *Nachor*, Lu. iii. 34.*

3494 νεανίας, ου, ὁ, *a young man, a youth*, Ac. vii. 58, xx. 9, xxiii. 17, 18, 22 (not W. H.).*

3495 νεανίσκος, ου, ὁ, *a young man*, Mat. xix. 20; plur., of soldiers, Mar. xiv. 51; 1 Jn. ii. 13, 14; *an attendant*, Ac. v. 10.

3496 Νεάπολις, εως, ἡ, *Neapolis*, Ac. xvi. 11.*

3497 Νεεμάν (W. H. Ναιμάν), ὁ (Heb.), *Naaman*, Lu. iv. 27.*

3498 νεκρός, ά, όν, *dead*, (1) lit., as Mat. xi. 5; οἱ νεκροί, *the dead*, generally, 1 Pet. iv. 6; (2) fig., *dead*, spiritually, Ep. ii. 1; *dead* to (dat.), Ro. vi. 11;

inactive, inoperative, Ro. vii. 8.

3499 νεκρόω, ῶ, *to put to death;* fig., *to deprive of power, to render weak* and *impotent*, Ro. iv. 19; Col. iii. 5; Heb. xi. 12.*

3500 νέκρωσις, εως, ἡ, *death, a being put to death*, 2 Cor. iv. 10; *deadness, impotency*, Ro. iv. 19.*

see 3561 νεο-μηνία, see νουμηνία.

3501□; see νέος, α, ον, (1) *new, fresh*, Mat.
2537 ix. 17; 1 Cor. v. 7; Col. iii. 10; (2) *young*, of persons, Tit. ii. 4. *Syn.:* see καινός.

3502 νεοσσός (W. H. νοσσός), οῦ, ὁ, *a young bird*, Lu. ii. 24.*

3503 νεότης, τητος, ἡ, *youth*, Lu. xviii. 21; 1 Tim. iv. 12.

3504 νεό-φυτος, ον, *newly planted;* fig., *a recent convert*, 1 Tim. iii. 6.*

3505 Νέρων, ωνος, ὁ, *Nero*, the Roman emperor, 2 Tim. iv. 23 (Rec.).*

3506 νεύω, σω, *to nod;* so, *to beckon, to signify*, Jn. xiii. 24; Ac. xxiv. 10.*

3507 νεφέλη, ης, ἡ, *a cloud*, Mar. ix. 7, xiii. 26.

3508 Νεφθαλείμ, ὁ (Heb.), *Naphtali*, Mat. iv. 13, 15; Rev. vii. 6.*

3509 νέφος, ους, τό, *a cloud;* met., *a multitude, a great company*, Heb. xii. 1.*

3510 νεφρός, οῦ, ὁ, *a kidney*, plur., *the kidneys, the loins*, used (as Heb.) for the secret thoughts, desires, and purposes, Rev. ii. 23.*

3511 νεω-κόρος, ου, ἡ (ναός and κορέω, *to sweep*), *a temple-keeper*, a designation of the people of Ephesus, Ac. xix. 35.*

3512 νεωτερικός, ή, όν, *youthful, juvenile*, 2 Tim. ii. 22.*

3501□ νεώτερος, α, ον (comp. of νέος, which see), *younger, inferior in rank*, Lu. xv. 12, 13, xxii. 26; 1 Tim. v. 11, 14.

3513 νή, adv., of affirmative swearing, *by*, with acc., 1 Cor. xv. 31.*

3514 νήθω, *to spin*, Mat. vi. 28; Lu. xii. 27.*

3515 νηπιάζω, *to be an infant*, 1 Cor. xiv. 20.*

3516 νήπιος, α, ον, *infantile;* as subst., *an infant, a babe*, Mat. xxi. 16; 1 Cor. xiii. 11; used of an age below manhood, Gal. iv. 1; fig., of *un-*

learned, unenlightened persons, Mat. xi. 25; Ro. ii. 20; 1 Th. ii. 7 (W. H.).

3517 Νηρεύς, έως, ὁ, Nereus, Ro. xvi. 15.*

3518 Νηρί, ὁ (Heb.), Neri, Lu. iii. 27.*

3519 νησίον, ου, τό (dim. of νῆσος), a small island, Ac. xxvii. 16.*

3520 νῆσος, ου, ἡ (νέω, to swim), an island, Ac. xiii. 6, xxvii. 26.

3521 νηστεία, ας, ἡ, a fasting, a fast, Mat. xvii. 21 (W. H. omit); Ac. xiv. 23; the day of atonement, the chief Jewish fastday, Ac. xxvii. 9; want of food, 2 Cor. vi. 5, xi. 27.

3522 νηστεύω, σω, to abstain from food, to fast, Mat. iv. 2, vi. 16-18.

3523 νῆστις, ιος, plur. νήστεις, ὁ, ἡ, fasting, Mat. xv. 32; Mar. viii. 3.*

3524 νηφάλιος or -λεος, ον, sober, temperate, 1 Tim. iii. 2, 11; Tit. ii. 2.*

3525 νήφω, ψω, to be sober, temperate, fig., 1 Th. v. 6, 8.

3526 Νίγερ, ὁ (Lat.), Niger, Ac. xiii. 1.*

3527 Νικάνωρ, ορος, ὁ, Nicanor, Ac. vi. 5.*

3528 νικάω, ῶ, ήσω, to be victorious, abs., Rev. iii. 21; to conquer, overcome (acc.), Lu. xi. 22; Jn. xvi. 33.

3529 νίκη, ης, ἡ, victory, 1 Jn. v. 4.*
3530 Νικό-δημος, ου, ὁ, Nicodemus, Jn. iii. 1.

3531 Νικολαΐτης, ου, ὁ, a follower of Nicolaus (probably a Greek equivalent for Balaam), a Nicolaitan, Rev. ii. 6, 15.*

3532 Νικό-λαος, ου, ὁ, Nicolaus, Ac. vi. 5 (not to be confounded with preced.).*

3533 Νικό-πολις, εως, ἡ, Nicopolis, Tit. iii. 12. Several cities of the name existed; this was probably on the promontory of Epirus.*

3534 νῖκος, ους, τό, victory, 1 Cor. xv. 55, 57; εἰς νῖκος, from S., to a victorious consummation, utterly, Mat. xii. 20; 1 Cor. xv. 54.*

3535 Νινευΐ, ἡ (Heb.), Nineveh, Lu. xi. 32 (W. H. read following).*

3536 Νινευΐτης (W. H. -είτης), ου, ὁ, a Ninevite, Mat. xii. 41; Lu. xi. 30, 32 (W. H.).*

3537 νιπτήρ, ῆρος, ὁ, a basin, for washing hands and feet, Jn. xiii. 5. (N. T.)*

3538; **3068** **see** νίπτω, ψω, to wash (acc.), Jn. xiii. 8; mid., to wash one's self, acc. of part, as Mar. vii. 3. Syn. · see λούω.

3539 νοέω, ῶ, ήσω, to understand, to consider, abs., or with acc., or ὅτι, Jn. xii. 40; Ep. iii. 4; Mar. xiii. 14.

3540 νόημα, ατος, τό, (1) a thought, purpose, device, 2 Cor. ii. 11, x. 5; Phil. iv. 7; (2) the mind, i.e., the understanding or intellect, 2 Cor. iii. 14, iv. 4, xi. 3.*

3541 νόθος, η, ον, illegitimate, bastard, Heb. xii. 8.*

3542 νομή, ῆς, ἡ (νέμω, to pasture), (1) pasturage, Jn. x. 9; (2) met., growth, increase, as of a gangrene, 2 Tim. ii. 17.*

3543 νομίζω, σω (νόμος), (1) to think, to suppose, to expect, as the result of thinking, Mat. v. 17, xx. 10; (2) pass., to be customary, only Ac. xvi. 13 (but see W. H. and R. V.).

3544 νομικός, ή, όν, pertaining to (the) law, Tit. iii. 9; as subst., a person learned in or teacher of the Mosaic law, Mat. xxii. 35; Tit. iii. 13.

3545 νομίμως, adv., lawfully, 1 Tim. i. 8; 2 Tim. ii. 5.*

3546 νόμισμα, ατος, τό, (lawful) money, coin, Mat. xxii. 19.*

3547 νομο-διδάσκαλος, ου, ὁ, a teacher and interpreter of the Mosaic law, Lu v. 17; Ac. v. 34; 1 Tim. i. 7. (N. T.)*

3548 νομο-θεσία, ας, ἡ, lawgiving, legislation, Ro. ix. 4.*

3549 νομο-θετέω, ῶ, to enact laws; pass., to be enacted, Heb. viii. 6; to be furnished with laws, Heb. vii. 11.*

3550 νομο-θέτης, ου, ὁ (τίθημι), a lawgiver, legislator, Ja. iv. 12.*

3551 νόμος, ου, ὁ (νέμω, to apportion), a law, an edict, a statute, Lu. ii. 22; a standard of acting or judging, Ro. iii. 27; a written law, Ro. ii. 14; the Mosaic economy, Mat. v. 18; Ro. x. 4; the Christian dispensation or doctrines, Gal. vi. 2; Ro. xiii. 8; met., for the books containing the Mosaic law, i.e., the five books of Moses, Mat. xii. 5;

and for the Old Testament generally, Jn. x. 34. On the article with νόμος, see Gr. § 234, Wi. § 19, 1 a, Bu. 89.

see 3563 νόος, see νοῦς.

3552 νοσέω, ῶ, *to be sick;* fig., *to have a diseased appetite* or *craving for,* περί (acc.), 1 Tim. vi. 4.*

3553 νόσημα, ατος, τό, *disease, sickness,* Jn. v. 4 (W. H. omit).*

3554 νόσος, ου, ἡ, *disease, sickness,* Mat. iv. 23, 24.

3555 νοσσιά, ᾶς, ἡ, *a brood of young birds,* Lu. xiii. 34. (S.)*

3556 νοσσίον, ου, τό, *a brood of young birds,* Mat. xxiii. 37.*

see 3502 νοσσός, see νεοσσός.

3557 νοσφίζω, in mid., *to remove for one's self, to purloin,* Ac. v. 2, 3; Tit. ii. 10.*

3558 νότος, ου, ὁ, *the south wind,* Lu. xii. 55; *the South,* Lu. xi. 31.

3559 νου-θεσία, ας, ἡ, *admonition, counsel,* 1 Cor. x. 11; Ep. vi. 4; Tit. iii. 10.*

3560 νου-θετέω, ῶ, *to admonish, to counsel,* Ac. xx. 31.

3561 νου-μηνία (W. H. νεο-), ας, ἡ, *the new moon,* as a festival, Col. ii. 16.*

3562 νουν-εχῶς, adv., *wisely, judiciously,* Mar. xii. 34.*

3563 νοῦς (orig. νόος), νοός, νοΐ, νοῦν, ὁ, *the mind, i.e., the understanding* or *intellect,* Lu.xxiv. 45; Phil. iv. 7; *the reason,* Ro. vii. 25, xii. 2; hence, *any affection of the mind* — as modes of thought — *inclinations* or *dispositions,* Ro. xiv. 5; 1 Cor. i. 10.

3564 Νυμφᾶς, ᾶ, ὁ, *Nymphas,* Col. iv. 15.*

3565 νύμφη, ης, ἡ, *a betrothed woman, a bride,* Rev. xviii. 23; *a daughter-in-law,* Mat. x. 35.

3566 νυμφίος, ου, ὁ, *a bridegroom,* Jn. iii. 29.

3567 νυμφών, ῶνος, ὁ, *a bridal chamber;* οἱ υἱοὶ τοῦ νυμφῶνος, *the sons of the bridal chamber,* friends of the bridegroom, Mat. ix. 15; Mar. ii. 19; Lu. v. 34; *a room in which the marriage ceremonies were held,* Mat. xxii. 10 (W. H.). (Ap.)*

3568, ●3570 νῦν and νυνί, adv., (1) of time, *now, i.e.,* the actually present; *now,* in relation to time

just past, *just now, even now; now,* in relation to future time, *just at hand, even now, immediately;* ὁ, ἡ, τὸ νῦν, *the present,* with subst. or (neut.) without; (2) of logical connection, *now,* 2 Cor. vii. 9; *now then, i.e.,* implying the rise of one thing from another, 1 Cor. xiv. 6; (3) in commands and appeals, νῦν is emphatic, *at this instant,* Mat. xxvii. 42; Ja. iv. 13.

3571 νύξ, νυκτός, ἡ, *the night, nighttime,* lit., Ac. xvi. 33; often fig., *a time of darkness and ignorance,* Ro. xiii. 12; 1 Th. v. 5; *death,* Jn. ix. 4.

3572 νύσσω, ξω, *to stab, to pierce,* Jn. xix. 34.*

3573 νυστάζω, ξω, *to nod* in sleep, *to be drowsy,* Mat. xxv. 5; fig., *to delay,* 2 Pet. ii. 3.*

3574 νυχθ-ήμερον, ου, τό, *a night and a day, twenty-four hours,* 2 Cor. xi. 25.*

3575 Νῶε, ὁ (Heb.), *Noah,* Lu. iii. 36, xvii. 26, 27.

3576 νωθρός, ά, όν, *sluggish, dull, stupid,* Heb. v. 11, vi. 12.*

3577 νῶτος, ου, ὁ, *the back* of men or animals, Ro. xi. 10.*

Ξ

Ξ, ξ, ξῖ, *xi,* the double letter *x* (= γς, κς, or χς), the fourteenth letter of the alphabet. As numeral, ξʹ = 60; ͵ξ = 60,000.

3578 ξενία, ας, ἡ, *hospitality; a lodging,* Ac. xxviii. 23; Philem. 22.*

3579 ξενίζω, σω, (1) *to receive as a guest* (acc.), Ac. x. 23, xxviii. 7; Heb. xiii. 2; pass., *to be entertained, to lodge,* Ac. x. 6, 18, 32, xxi. 16; (2) *to astonish by strangeness,* Ac. xvii. 20; pass., *to think strangely of, to be surprised at* (dat.), 1 Pet. iv. 4, 12.*

3580 ξενο-δοχέω, ῶ, *to entertain guests, to practice hospitality,* 1 Tim. v. 10.*

3581 ξένος, η, ον, masc., *a guestfriend;* as subst.. *a stranger, foreigner,* Mat. xxv. 35, 38, 43, 44; *a host,* Ro. xvi. 23; *alien,* Ep. ii. 12; *new, novel,* Heb. xiii. 9; 1 Pet. iv. 12.

3582 ξέστης, ου, ὁ (the Latin *sextarius*), *a sextarius,* a vessel

*For 3569 see Strong.

for measuring liquids, holding about a pint; *a pitcher,*
of any size, Mar. vii. 4, 8
(W. H. omit).*

3583 ξηραίνω, ανῶ, 1st aor., act.,
ἐξήρανα, 1st aor., pass., ἐξη-
ράνθην, perf., pass., ἐξήραμ-
μαι (3 s., ἐξήρανται, Mar. xi.
21), *to make dry, to wither,*
Ja. i. 11; pass., *to become dry,
be withered,* Mat. xiii. 6; *to
be dried up,* Rev. xvi. 12; *to
be ripened,* as corn, Rev. xiv.
15; *to pine away,* Mar. ix.
18.

3584 ξηρός, ά, όν, *dry, withered,* of
a tree, Lu. xxiii. 31; of a
useless limb, Mat. xii. 10;
Mar. iii. 3 (W. H.); Lu.
vi. 6, 8; Jn. v. 3; of land,
Heb. xi. 29; ἡ ξηρά (sc. γῆ),
dry land, Mat. xxiii. 15.*

3585 ξύλινος, ίνη, ινον, *wooden,* 2 Tim.
ii. 20; Rev. ix. 20.*

3586 ξύλον, ου, τό, *wood, e.g., timber*
in building, 1 Cor. iii. 12;
*anything made of wood, e.g.,
the stocks,* Ac. xvi. 24; *a staff,*
Mat. xxvi. 47, 55; *a cross,*
Ac. xiii. 29; Gal. iii. 13; *a
living tree,* Rev. ii. 7.

3587 ξυράω, ῶ, ήσω, perf. pass. ἐξύ-
ρημαι, *to shave,* Ac. xxi. 24;
1 Cor. xi. 5, 6.*

O

Ο, ο, ὁ μικρόν, *omicron,* short *o,*
the fifteenth letter. As a
numeral, ο΄= 70; ‚ο =70,000.

3588 ὁ, ἡ, τό, the definite article,
the, originally demonstrative.
For its uses, see Gr. §§ 193–
234, Wi. §§ 17–20, Bu. 85–
103.

3589 ὀγδοήκοντα, num., indeclin.,
eighty, Lu. ii. 37, xvi. 7.*

3590 ὄγδοος, η, ον, ord., *eighth;* on
2 Pet. ii. 5, see Gr. § 331,
Wi. § 37, 2, Bu. 30.

3591 ὄγκος, ου, ὁ, *a weight, an en-
cumbrance,* Heb. xii. 1.*

3592 ὅδε, ἥδε, τόδε, demon. pron.,
this, that (here).   See Gr.
§ 339, Wi. § 23, 5, Bu. 103.

3593 ὁδεύω, *to pass along a way, to
journey,* Lu. x. 33.*

3594 ὁδηγέω, ῶ, ήσω, *to lead along a
way, to conduct, to guide,*
Mat. xv. 14; Lu. vi. 39; Jn.
xvi. 13; Ac. viii. 31; Rev.
vii. 17.*

3595 ὁδ-ηγός, οῦ, ὁ, *a leader, a guide,*

Ac. i. 16; fig., of instructors,
Mat. xv. 14, xxiii. 16, 24;
Ro. ii. 19.*

3596 ὁδοι-πορέω, ῶ, *to travel, to pursue a way,* Ac. x. 9.*

3597 ὁδοι-πορία, ας, ἡ, *a journey, a
journeying,* Jn. iv. 6; 2 Cor.
xi. 26.*

3598 ὁδός, οῦ, ἡ, (1) *a way, a road,*
Mat. ii. 12; (2) *a going, a
progress,* Mar. vi. 8; (3) *a
journey,* a day's or a Sabbath day's, Lu. ii. 44; Ac.
i. 12; (4) fig., *manner of
action, method of proceeding,*
Ac. xiii. 10; Mat. xxi. 32;
especially (5) *the Christian
way,* Ac. ix. 2; 2 Pet. ii. 2;
(6) used of Christ himself,
the Way, Jn. xiv. 6.

3599 ὀδούς, ὀδόντος, ὁ, *a tooth,* Mat.
v. 38.

3600 ὀδυνάω, ῶ, in mid. and pass.,
*to be tormented, to be greatly
distressed,* Lu. ii. 48, xvi. 24,
25; Ac. xx. 38.*

3601 ὀδύνη, ης, ἡ, *pain, distress,* of
body or mind, Ro. ix. 2; 1
Tim. vi. 10.*

3602 ὀδυρμός, οῦ, ὁ, *lamentation,
wailing,* Mat. ii. 18; 2 Cor.
*   vii. 7.*

3604 Οζίας, ου, ὁ, *Uzziah,* Mat. i.
8, 9.*

3605 ὄζω, *to stink, be offensive,* Jn. xi.
39.*

3606 ὅθεν, adv., *whence,* of place,
source, or cause, Mat. xii.
44; 1 Jn. ii. 18; Heb. ii. 17.

3607 ὀθόνη, ης, ἡ, *a linen cloth;*
hence, *a sheet,* Ac. x. 11, xi.
5.*

3608 ὀθόνιον, ου, τό (dim. of ὀθόνη),
a linen bandage, Jn. xix. 40.

see 1492 οἶδα, plur. οἴδαμεν (for Attic
ἴσμεν), οἴδατε (and Attic ἴστε,
Heb. xii. 17), οἴδασι (and
Attic ἴσασι, only Ac. xxvi.
4), *I know* (see Gr. § 103, 4,
Wi. § 40, 4 b).

see 3615 οἰκειακός, ἡ, όν, see οἰκιακός.

3609 οἰκεῖος, α, ον, *domestic, belonging to a household,* Gal. vi.
10; Ep. ii. 19; 1 Tim. v. 8.*

see 3610 οἰκέτεια, ας, ἡ, *household, body
of servants,* Mat. xxiv. 45
(W. H.).*

3610 οἰκέτης, ου, ὁ, *a domestic, a
household servant,* Lu. xvi.
13; Ac. x. 7; Ro. xiv. 4; 1
Pet. ii. 18.

3611 οἰκέω, ῶ, ήσω, trans., *to inhabit,*
1 Tim. vi. 16; intrans., *to*

* For 3603 **see Strong.**

dwell, Ro. viii. 9; 1 Cor. vii. 12, 13.

3612 οἴκημα, ατος, τό, *a dwelling,* used of *a prison,* Ac xii. 7.*

3613 οἰκητήριον, ου, τό, *a dwelling-place, a habitation,* 2 Cor. v. 2; Ju. 6.*

3614 οἰκία, ας, ἡ, (1) *a house,* Lu. xv. 8; (2) met., *a household, a family, goods, i.e.,* a house and all that is in it, Jn. iv. 53; Mar. xii. 40.

3615 οἰκιακός, οῦ, ὁ, *one of a family,* whether child, or servant, Mat. x. 25, 36.*

3616 οἰκοδεσποτέω, ῶ, *to manage a household,* 1 Tim. v. 14.*

3617 οἰκο-δεσπότης, ου, ὁ, *a house-holder, a master of a house,* Mat. x. 25.

3618 οἰκοδομέω, ῶ, *to erect a build-ing, build,* Lu. xiv. 30; fig., of the building up of char-acter, *to build up, edify,* 1 Cor. x. 23; *to encourage,* 1 Cor. viii. 10.

3619 οἰκο-δομή, ῆς, ἡ (δέμω), *the act of building; a building,* lit., Mat. xxiv. 1; of the spiritual body, 2 Cor. v. 1; of the church, Ep. ii. 21; met., *edification, spiritual advance-ment,* Ro. xiv. 19, xv. 2.

3620 οἰκοδομία, ας, ἡ, *edification,* 1 Tim. i. 4 (W. H. οἰκονομία).*

see 3618 οἰκο-δόμος, ου, ὁ, *a builder,* Ac. iv. 11 (W. H.).*

3621 οἰκονομέω, ῶ, *to be a steward,* Lu. xvi. 2.*

3622 οἰκονομία, ας, ἡ, *management of household affairs, steward-ship,* Lu. xvi. 2–4; *a dis-pensation,* 1 Cor. x. 17.

3623 οἰκο-νόμος, ου, ὁ (νέμω), *a house-manager, a steward,* Lu. xvi. 1, 3, 8; of the Christian stewardship, 1 Cor. iv. 1; 1 Pet. iv. 10; Tit. i. 7.

3624 οἶκος, ου, ὁ, *a house, a building,* for any purpose (gen.); met., *a family* resident in one house, *a family* perpetuated by succession; *the house* of God, *i.e.,* the temple; *the family* of God, *i.e.,* the church.

3625 οἰκουμένη, ης, ἡ, pres. part. pass. fem. of οἰκέω (sc. γῆ), *the inhabited land,* or *world;* (1) *the Roman empire,* Lu. ii. 1; (2) *the world at large,* Lu. iv. 5, xxi. 26; (3) met., *the inhabitants of the world*

Ac. xvii. 6, 31; (4) *the uni-verse,* Heb. ii. 5.

3626 οἰκ-ουρός, οῦ, ὁ, ἡ (οὖρος, *keeper*), *attending to household affairs, domestic,* Tit. ii. 5 (W. H. οἰκουργός, with same mean-ing).*

3627 οἰκτείρω, ήσω, *to pity, to have compassion on,* Ro. ix. 15 (from S.).*

3628 οἰκτιρμός, οῦ, ὁ, *compassion, pity,* Ro. xii. 1; 2 Cor. i. 3; Phil. ii. 1; Col. iii. 12; Heb. x. 28.*

3629 οἰκτίρμων, ον, *pitiful, merciful,* Lu. vi. 36; Ja. v. 11.*

see 3633 οἶμαι, see οἴομαι.

3630 οἰνο-πότης, ου, ὁ, *one given to wine-drinking,* Mat. xi. 19; Lu. vii. 34.*

3631 οἶνος, ου, ὁ, *wine,* Mar. ii. 22; met., *a vine,* Rev. vi. 6; fig., of that which excites or in-flames, Rev. xiv. 10, xvii. 2.

3632 οἰνο-φλυγία, ας, ἡ (φλύω, *to overflow*), *drunkenness,* 1 Pet. iv. 3.*

3633 οἴομαι and οἶμαι, *to think, to suppose,* acc. and inf., or ὅτι, Jn. xxi. 25; Phil. i. 16; Ja. i. 7.*

3634 οἷος, α, ον, rel. pron., correl. to τοιοῦτος, *of what kind, such as.*

see 5342 οἴσω, see φέρω.

3635 ὀκνέω, ῶ, ήσω, *to be slothful, to delay, to hesitate,* Ac. ix. 38.*

3636 ὀκνηρός, ά, όν, *slothful, back-ward,* Mat. xxv. 26; Ro. xii. 11; Phil. iii. 1.*

3637 ὀκτα-ήμερος, ον, *of* or *belonging to the eighth day,* Phil. iii. 5.*

3638 ὀκτώ, num., indecl., *eight,* Lu. ii. 21.

3639 ὄλεθρος, ου, ὁ, *destruction, per-dition,* 1 Cor. v. 5; 1 Th. v. 3; 2 Th. i. 9; 1 Tim. vi. 9.*

see 3640 ὀλιγο-πιστία, ας, ἡ, *little faith,* Mat. xvii. 20 (W. H.). (N. T.)*

3640 ὀλιγό-πιστος, ον, *of little faith,* Mat. vi. 30. (N. T.)

3641 ὀλίγος, η, ον, (1) *little, small, brief,* Lu. x. 2; Ac. xiv. 28; (2) in plur., *few,* sometimes with gen., Mat. vii. 14; Ac. xvii. 4; (3) neut. as adv., ὀλίγον, of time, *soon,* Lu. v. 3; of space, *a little way,* Mar. vi. 31; (4) with prepositions preced. in various phrases, as ἐν ὀλίγῳ, with little trouble, Ac. xxvi. 28.

3642 ὀλιγό-ψυχος, ον, faint-hearted, 1 Th. v. 14. (S.)*

3643 ὀλιγωρέω, ῶ, to care little for, to despise (gen.), Heb. xii. 5 (from S.).*

see 3641 ὀλίγως, adv., a little, scarcely, 2 Pet. ii. 18 (W. H.).*

3644 ὀλοθρευτής, οῦ, ὁ, a destroyer, 1 Cor. x. 10. (N. T.)*

3645 ὀλοθρεύω, to destroy, Heb. xi. 28.*

3646 ὀλο-καύτωμα, ατος, τό (καίω), a whole burnt-offering, the whole being consumed, Mar. xii. 33; Heb. x. 6, 8. (S.)*

3647 ὀλοκληρία, ας, ἡ, perfect soundness, Ac. iii. 16. (S.)*

3648; see 739 ὀλό-κληρος, ον, complete in every part, sound, perfect, 1 Th. v. 23; Ja. i. 4. Syn.: see ἄρτιος.

3649 ὀλολύζω, as from the cry ολ-ολ, to howl, to lament aloud, Ja. v. 1.*

3650 ὅλος, η, ον, all, the whole (see Gr. § 225, Wi. § 20, 1 b, a, Bu. 94), Jn. vii. 23; Ja. iii. 2; 1 Jn. v. 19.

3651 ὁλο-τελής, ές, perfect, complete, 1 Th. v. 23.*

3652 Ὀλυμπᾶς, ᾶ, ὁ, Olympas, Ro. xvi. 15.*

3653 ὄλυνθος, ου, ὁ, an unripe fig, one which, not ripening in due time, grows through the winter and falls off in the spring, Rev. vi. 13.*

3654 ὅλως (ὅλος), adv., wholly, altogether, 1 Cor. v. 1, vi. 7; with neg., not at all, Mat. v. 34; 1 Cor. xv. 29.*

3655 ὄμβρος, ου, ὁ, a violent rain, Lu. xii. 54.*

see 2442 ὀμείρομαι, to long for, 1 Th. ii. 8 (W. H., Rec. ἱμείρομαι).*

3656 ὁμιλέω, ῶ, ἥσω, to associate with (dat.), to talk with (πρός, acc.), Lu. xxiv. 14, 15; Ac. xx. 11, xxiv. 26.*

3657 ὁμιλία, ας, ἡ, intercourse, companionship, 1 Cor. xv. 33.*

3658 ὅμιλος, ου, ὁ, a crowd, company, Rev. xviii. 17 (not W. H.).*

see 3509 ὁμίχλη, ης, ἡ, a mist, 2 Pet. ii. 17 (W. H.).*

3659 ὄμμα, ατος, τό, an eye, Mat. xx. 34 (W. H.); Mar. viii. 23.*

3660 ὄμνυμι and ὀμνύω, ὀμόσω (see Gr. § 116, 3, Wi. § 15, Bu.

45), to swear, to take an oath, Mar. xiv. 71; to promise with an oath, Mar. vi. 23.

3661 ὁμο-θυμαδόν, adv., with one mind, unanimously, only in Ac. and Ro. xv. 6.

3662 ὁμοιάζω, σω, to be like, Mat. xxiii. 27 (W. H. mrg.); Mar. xiv. 70 (not W. H.). (N. T.)*

3663 ὁμοιο-παθής, ές, being affected like another (dat.), having like passions or feelings, Ac. xiv. 15; Ja. v. 17.*

3664 ὅμοιος, οία, οιον, like, similar to, resembling (dat.), Jn. ix. 9; Rev. iv. 3; of equal rank, Mat. xxii. 39.

3665 ὁμοιότης, τητος, ἡ, likeness, Heb. iv. 15, vii. 15.*

3666 ὁμοιόω, ῶ, ὥσω, (1) to make like; pass., to be like, or to resemble, Mat. vi. 8, xiii. 24; Ac. xiv. 11; (2) to liken, to compare, Mat. vii. 24; Mar. iv. 30; with acc. and dat.

3667; see 1504 ὁμοίωμα, ατος, τό, likeness, similitude, Ro. i. 23, v. 14, vi. 5, viii. 3; Phil. ii. 7; Rev. ix. 7.* Syn.: see εἰκών.

3668 ὁμοίως, adv., in like manner, Lu. iii. 11; Jn. v. 19.

3669; see 1504 ὁμοίωσις, εως, ἡ, likeness, Ja. iii. 9.* Syn.: see εἰκών.

3670 ὁμο-λογέω, ῶ, ἥσω, 1st aor. ὡμολόγησα, to speak the same thing; hence, (1) to confess, in the sense of conceding or admitting, generally with ὅτι, Mat. xiv. 7; Heb. xi. 13; (2) to profess, or acknowledge openly, acc., or with ἐν, Mat. x. 32; Lu. xii. 8; Jn. ix. 22; (3) as ἐξομολογέω, to praise (dat.), Heb. xiii. 15.

3671 ὁμολογία, ας, ἡ, a profession, or a confession, 2 Cor. ix. 13; 1 Tim. vi. 12, 13; Heb. iii. 1, iv. 14, x. 23.*

3672 ὁμολογουμένως, adv., confessedly, by assent of all, 1 Tim. iii. 16.*

3673 ὁμό-τεχνος, ον, of the same trade or craft, Ac. xviii. 3.*

3674 ὁμοῦ, adv., together, at the same place or time, Jn. iv. 36.

3675 ὁμό-φρων, ον (φρήν), of one mind, 1 Pet. iii. 8.*

see 3660 ὀμόω, see ὄμνυμι.

3676 ὅμως, adv., yet, 1 Cor. xiv. 7; Gal. iii. 15; with μέντοι, nevertheless, Jn. xii. 42.*

3677　ὄναρ, τό, indecl., *a dream;* κατ᾽ ὄναρ, *in a dream,* Mat. i. 20, ii. 12, 13, 19, 22, xxvii. 19.*

3678　ὀνάριον, ου, τό (dim. of ὄνος), *a young ass,* Jn. xii. 14.*

3679　ὀνειδίζω, σω, *to reproach, revile, upbraid,* Mat. xi. 20; Mar. xvi. 14; Lu. vi. 22.

3680　ὀνειδισμός, οῦ, ὁ, *reproach, reviling,* Ro. xv. 3; 1 Tim. iii. 7; Heb. x. 33, xi. 26, xiii. 13. (S.)*

3681　ὄνειδος, ους, τό, *reproach, disgrace,* Lu. i. 25.*

3682　Ὀνήσιμος, ου, ὁ (*profitable*), *Onesimus,* Col. iv. 9; Philem. 10.*

3683　Ὀνησί-φορος, ου, ὁ, *Onesiphorus,* 2 Tim. i. 16, iv. 19.*

3684　ὀνικός, ή, όν, *pertaining to an ass;* μύλος ὀνικός, *a millstone turned by an ass, i.e.,* the large upper millstone, Mat. xviii. 6; Lu. xvii. 2 (not W. H.); Mar. ix. 42 (W. H.). (N. T.)*

3685　ὀνίνημι, *to be useful, to help;* mid. aor., opt., ὀναίμην, *may I have help* or *joy from,* Philem. 20.*

3686　ὄνομα, ατος, τό, *a name,* almost always of persons; in N. T., as in O. T., the *name* of a person is a mark of what he himself is, the name expresses the character, Mat. i. 21; Mar. iii. 16, v. 9; Lu. i. 31; hence the expressions ποιεῖν τι ἐπὶ τῷ ὀνόματι, ἐν τῷ ὀνόματι, διὰ τοῦ ὀνόματος; the name is often introduced by ὀνόματι, *by name,* once by τοὔνομα (τὸ ὄνομα), Mat. xxvii. 57; *fame, reputation,* Ep. i. 21; Phil. ii. 9.

3687　ὀνομάζω, σω, *to give a name to,* Lu. vi. 13, 14; *to mention,* Ep. v. 3; *to call upon the name of,* 2 Tim. ii. 19.

3688　ὄνος, ου, ὁ, ἡ, *an ass,* Mat. xxi. 2, 7; Lu. xiii. 15.

3689　ὄντως, adv. (ὄν, neut. part. of εἰμί), *really, truly,* 1 Cor. xiv. 25; 1 Tim. v. 3, 5.

3690　ὄξος, ους, τό, *vinegar;* in N. T., *sour wine,* mixed with water, a common drink of Roman soldiers, Jn. xix. 29, 30.

3691　ὀξύς, εῖα, ύ, (1) *sharp,* as a weapon, Rev. i. 16, ii. 12; (2) *swift, eager,* Ro. iii. 15.

3692　ὀπή, ῆς, ἡ, *an opening, a cavern,* Ja. iii. 11; Heb. xi. 38.*

3693　ὄπισθεν, adv. of place, *from behind, after,* Mat. ix. 20, xv. 23.

3694　ὀπίσω, adv., *behind, after,* of place, Lu. vii. 38; of time, Mat. iii. 11; abs., or with gen.; τὰ ὀπίσω, *those things that are behind,* Phil. iii. 14; εἰς τὰ ὀπίσω, *backward,* Jn. xviii. 6.

3695　ὁπλίζω, σω, N. T., mid., *to arm one's self* with, acc., fig., 1 Pet. iv. 1.*

3696　ὅπλον, ου, τό, *an instrument,* Ro. vi. 13; hence, plur., *arms, weapons,* Jn. xviii. 3; Ro. xiii. 12; 2 Cor. vi. 7, x. 4.*

3697　ὁποῖος, οἵα, οἷον, relat. pron., *of what kind* or *manner,* correl. to τοιοῦτος, Ac. xxvi. 29; 1 Cor. iii. 13; Gal. ii. 6; 1 Th. i. 9; Ja. i. 24.*

3698　ὁπότε, adv. of time, *when,* Lu. vi. 3 (W. H. ὅτε).*

3699　ὅπου, adv. of place, *where, whither; where,* referring to state, Col. iii. 11; *in case that,* 1 Cor. iii. 3.

3700　ὀπτάνω, *to behold;* in pass., *to appear,* Ac. i. 3; see ὁράω. (S.)*

3701　ὀπτασία, ας, ἡ, *a vision, a supernatural appearance,* Lu. i. 22, xxiv. 23; Ac. xxvi. 19; 2 Cor. xii. 1.*

3702　ὀπτός, ή, όν, *roasted, broiled,* Lu. xxiv. 42.*

see 3708　ὄπτω, ὄπτομαι, see ὁράω.

3703　ὀπώρα, ας, ἡ, *autumn, autumnal fruits,* Rev. xviii. 14.*

3704　ὅπως, rel. adv., *how,* Lu. xxiv. 20; as conj., *in order that, so that;* with ἄν, Ac. iii. 19 (see Gr. § 384, 2, Wi. § 42, 6, Bu. 234); after verbs of *beseeching,* and the like, *that,* Mat. ix. 38; Mar. iii. 6.

3705　ὅραμα, ατος, τό, (1) *a spectacle,* Ac. vii. 31; (2) *a vision,* Ac. ix. 10, 12.

3706　ὅρασις, εως, ἡ, *appearance,* Rev. iv. 3; *a vision,* Ac. ii. 17; Rev. ix. 17.

3707　ὁρατός, ή, όν, *visible,* plur., neut., Col. i. 16.*

3708　ὁράω, ῶ, ὄψομαι, ἑώρακα, εἶδον (see Gr. § 103, 4, Wi. § 15, Bu. 64), (1) *to see,* generally; (2) *to look upon* or *contemplate;* (3) *to see,* and so *to*

participate in, Lu. xvii. 22 ;
Jn. iii. 36 ; (4) *to take heed*,
Heb. viii. 5 ; Mat. viii. 4 ;
with μή or equiv., *to beware*,
Mat. xvi. 6 ; (5) pass., *to be
seen, to appear to, to present
one's self to* (dat.).

**3709; see
2372**   ὀργή, ῆς, ἡ, *anger, indignation*,
Ep. iv. 31 ; often of the
wrath of God, and its manifestation, Ro. i. 18. *Syn.:*
see θυμός.

3710   ὀργίζω, σω, *to irritate, to provoke;* pass., *to be angry*, abs.,
Mat. xviii. 34 ; *to be enraged
with*, dat., or ἐπί, dat., Mat.
v. 22 ; Rev. xii. 17.

3711   ὀργίλος, η, ον, *prone to anger*,
Tit. i. 7.*

3712   ὀργυιά, ᾶς, ἡ, *a fathom*, about
five or six feet, Ac. xxvii.
28.*

3713   ὀρέγω, *to stretch forth;* mid., *to
reach after, to desire* or *long
eagerly for*, gen., 1 Tim. iii.
1, vi. 10 ; Heb. xi. 16.*

3714   ὀρεινός, ή, όν, *mountainous,
hilly* (sc. χώρα), I.u. i. 39,65.*

3715   ὄρεξις, εως, ἡ, *strong desire, lust*,
Ro. i. 27.*

3716   ὀρθο-ποδέω, ῶ, *to walk in a
straight course*, fig., *to act
uprightly*, Gal. ii. 14. (N.T.)*

3717   ὀρθός, ή, όν, *upright*, Ac. xiv.
10 ; *straight*, Heb. xii. 13.*

3718   ὀρθο-τομέω, ῶ (τέμνω), *to cut
straight;* met., *to handle
rightly, i.e., to teach correctly*,
2 Tim. ii. 15. (S.)*

3719   ὀρθρίζω, *to rise early in the
morning, to come early in
the morning*, Lu. xxi. 38.
(S.)*

3720   ὀρθρινός, ή, όν, *early in the
morning*, Lu. xxiv. 22 (W.
H.) ; Rev. xxii. 16 (not W.
H.).*

3721   ὄρθριος, α, ον, *early in the
morning*, Lu. xxiv. 22 (W.
H. read preceding).*

3722   ὄρθρος, ου, ὁ, *early dawn, day-
break*, Lu. xxiv. 1 ; Jn. viii
2 (W. H. omit) ; Ac. v. 21.*

3723   ὀρθῶς, adv., *rightly*, Mar. vii.
35 ; Lu. vii. 43, x. 28, xx.
21.*

3724   ὁρίζω, σω, *to define; to determine*,
Ac. xvii. 26 ; Heb. iv. 7 ; *to
appoint, to decree*, Ac. x. 42,
xi. 29 ; pass., perf. part.,
ὡρισμένος, *decreed*, Ac. ii. 23 ;
neut., *decree*, Lu. xxii. 22.

3725   ὅριον, ου, τό, plur., *the bound-*

aries of a place ; hence, *districts, territory*, Mat. ii. 6, iv.
13.

3726   ὁρκίζω, *to adjure by, to charge
solemnly by*, with double
acc., Mar. v. 7 ; Ac. xix. 13 ;
1 Th. v. 27 (W. H. ἐνορκίζω).*

3727   ὅρκος, ου, ὁ, *an oath*, Mat. xiv.
7, 9 ; *a promise with an oath,
a vow*, Mat. v. 33.

3728   ὁρκ-ωμοσία, ας, ἡ, *the taking of
an oath, an oath*, Heb. vii.
20, 21, 28. (S.)*

3729   ὁρμάω, ῶ, ήσω, N. T., intrans.,
to rush, Mat. viii. 32 ; Ac.
vii. 57 (εἰς, or ἐπί, acc.).

3730   ὁρμή, ῆς, ἡ, *a rush, a violent
assault*, Ac. xiv. 5 ; Ja. iii.
4.*

3731   ὅρμημα, ατος, τό, *a rushing on,
impulse*, Rev. xviii. 21.*

3732   ὄρνεον, ου, τό, *a bird*, Rev. xviii.
2, xix. 17, 21.*

3733   ὄρνις, ιθος, ἡ, *a bird, a hen*,
Mat. xxiii. 37 ; Lu. xiii.
34.*

3734   ὁρο-θεσία, ας, ἡ, *a setting of
boundaries, a definite limit*,
Ac. xvii. 26. (N.T.)*

3735   ὄρος, ους, τό, *a mountain*, Lu.
iii. 5, ix. 28.

3736   ὀρύσσω, ξω, *to dig, to dig out*,
Mat. xxi. 33, xxv. 18 ; Mar.
xii. 1.*

3737   ὀρφανός, ή, όν, *bereaved, an
orphan*, Jn. xiv. 18 ; as subst.,
Ja. i. 27.*

3738   ὀρχέομαι, οῦμαι, ήσομαι, dep.,
mid., *to dance*, Mat. xi. 17,
xiv. 6 ; Mar. vi. 22 ; Lu. vii.
32.*

3739   ὅς, ἥ, ὅ, relative pronoun, *who,
which* (see Gr. §§ 58, 343–
348, Wi. § 24, Bu. 281 sq. ;
for ὅς ἄν, ὅς ἐάν, *whoever*,
see Gr. § 380, Wi. § 42, 3,
Bu. 288) ; as demonst. in the
phrase, ὅς μέν ... ὅς δέ, *that
one ... this one*, as 2 Cor. ii.
16.

3740   ὁσάκις, rel. adv., *as often as*,
always with ἄν or ἐάν, 1 Cor.
xi. 25, 26 ; Rev. xi. 6.*

3741   ὅσιος (α), ον, *holy, pious*, of
human beings, of Christ,
and of God ; τὰ ὅσια, *the
holy promises*, Ac. xiii. 34.
Syn.: see ἅγιος.

3742   ὁσιότης, τητος, ἡ, *holiness, godliness*, Lu. i. 75 ; Ep. iv.
24.*

3743   ὁσίως, adv., *holily*, 1 Th. ii.
10.*

3744 ὀσμή, ῆς, ἡ, a smell, an odor, lit., Jn. xii. 3; fig., 2 Cor. ii. 14, 16; Ep. v. 2; Phil. iv. 18.*

3745 ὅσος, η, ον, relat. pron., how much, how great, (1) of time, how long, as long as, Ro. vii. 1; repeated, the meaning is intensified, Heb. x. 37: ἔτι μικρὸν ὅσον ὅσον, yet a little, a very, very little; (2) of quantity, of number, how much, plur., how many, Mar. iii. 8; Jn. vi. 11; Ac. ix. 13; as many as, Mat. xiv. 36; with ἄν, ἐάν, as many as, whatsoever, Mat. vii. 12, xxi. 22; (3) of measure, degree, Heb. vii. 20.

3746 ὅσ-περ, ἥ-περ, ὅ-περ, the very one who, Mar. xv. 6 (not W. H.).*

3747 ὀστέον, contr. ὀστοῦν, οῦ, τό, a bone, Jn. xix. 36.

3748 ὅσ-τις, ἥ-τις, ὅ, τι, compound relat., whosoever, whichsoever, whatsoever (see Gr. §§ 58 c, 349, Wi. § 42, 3, Bu. 115); the addition of ἄν, ἐάν, gives indefiniteness.

3749 ὀστράκινος, η, ον, made of earth, earthen, 2 Cor. iv. 7; 2 Tim. ii. 20.*

3750 ὄσφρησις, εως, ἡ, the sense of smell, smelling, 1 Cor. xii. 17.*

3751 ὀσφύς, ύος, ἡ, the loins, Mat. iii. 4; Lu. xii. 35; Ac. ii. 30; 1 Pet. i. 13.

3752 ὅταν (ὅτε, ἄν), rel. adv., when, whensoever; always with subj. except Mar. iii. 11, xi. 19 (W. H.), 25 (W. H.); Rev. iv. 9, viii. 1 (W. H.).

3753 ὅτε, rel. adv., when, Mar. xiv. 12.

3754 ὅτι, conj., (1) that, after verbs of declaring, etc., introducing the object-sentence; sometimes as a mere quotation mark, Mat. ii. 23; (2) because (see Gr. § 136, 6, Wi. § 53, 8 b, Bu. 357 sq.).

3755 ὅτου (gen. of ὅστις), ἕως ὅτου, until, Lu. xxii. 16.

●3757 οὗ, adv. (gen. of ὅς), where, whither; οὗ ἐάν, whithersoever; also used of time, when, in the phrases, ἀφ' οὗ, since, ἄχρις, ἕως, μέχρις οὗ, until.

3756 οὐ (οὐκ before a vowel, οὐχ if the vowel is aspirated), no,

not (see Gr. §§ 134, 401, Wi. §§ 55, 56, Bu. 344 sq.).

3758 οὐά, interj., ah! aha! derisive, Mar. xv. 29. (N. T.)*

3759 οὐαί, interj., woe! alas! uttered in grief or denunciation, Mat. xi. 21; 1 Cor. ix. 16; ἡ οὐαί, as subst., Rev. ix. 12, the woe, the calamity. (S.)

3760 οὐδαμῶς, adv., by no means, Mat. ii. 6.*

3761 οὐ-δέ, conj., disj. neg., but not, nor yet (cf. μηδέ), neither, nor, not even (see Gr. § 401, Wi. § 55, 6, Bu. 366 sq.).

3762 οὐδ-είς, οὐδεμία, οὐδέν (οὐδὲ εἷς), neg. adj., not one, no one, none, nothing, of no moment, of no value, vain.

3763 οὐδέ-ποτε, adv., never, 1 Cor. xiii. 8; Mat. vii. 23.

3764 οὐδέ-πω, adv., not yet, never, Jn. xix. 41.

see 3762 οὐθείς, οὐθέν (οὔτε εἷς), no one, nothing, Ac. xxvi. 26 (W. H.); 1 Cor. xiii. 2, 2 Cor. xi. 8 (W. H.).*

3765 οὐκ-έτι, adv., no further, no more, no longer.

3766 οὐκ-οῦν, adv., not therefore; hence, in ordinary classic usage, an affirmative adverb, therefore (whereas οὔκουν retains its negative force, not therefore), Jn. xviii. 37.*

●3364; see Strong. οὐ μή, an emphatic negative (see Gr. § 377, Wi. § 56, 3, Bu. 211 sq.).

3767 οὖν, conj., therefore, then, Mat. xii. 12; employed espec. (1) in arguing, 1 Cor. iv. 16; (2) in exhortation, Mat. xxii. 9, 17, 21; (3) in interrogation, Mat. xiii. 27; Gal. iii. 19, 21; (4) to resume an interrupted subject, Mar. iii. 31; Jn. xi. 6; (5) to indicate mere transition from one point to another, most frequently in John, as viii. 13.

3768 οὔ-πω, adv., not yet.

3769 οὐρά, ᾶς, ἡ, a tail of an animal, Rev. ix. 10, 19, xii. 4.*

3770 οὐράνιος, ον, heavenly, in or pertaining to heaven, as Lu. ii. 13; Ac. xxvi. 19.

3771 οὐρανόθεν, adv., from heaven, Ac. xiv. 17, xxvi. 13.*

3772 οὐρανός, οῦ, ὁ, heaven, (1) the visible heavens (both sing. and plural), through their whole extent, the atmosphere, the sky, the starry heavens:

(2) *the spiritual heavens*, the abode of God and holy beings, Mat. vi. 10; 2 Cor. xii. 2; "the third heaven," above the atmospheric and the sidereal; met., for the inhabitants of heaven, Rev. xviii. 20; especially for God, Lu. xv. 18.

3773 Οὐρβανός, οῦ, ὁ, *Urbanus*, Ro. xvi. 9.*

3774 Οὐρίας, ου, ὁ, *Uriah*, Mat. i. 6.*

3775 οὖς, ὠτός, τό, (1) *the ear*, Mat. x. 27; (2) met., *the faculty of perception*, Mat. xi. 15.

3776 οὐσία, ας, ἡ (ὤν, part. εἰμί), *property, wealth*, Lu. xv. 12, 13.*

3777 οὔ-τε, conj., *and not; neither, nor*, with a negative preced.; οὔτε ... οὔτε, *neither ... nor*. (The readings often vary between οὔτε and οὐδέ.)

3778 οὗτος, αὕτη, τοῦτο, demonstr. pron., *this* (near), appl. to persons and things, sometimes emphatic, Mat. v. 19; sometimes comtemptuous, *this fellow*, Mat. xiii. 55 (see Gr. §§ 338–342, Wi. § 23, Bu. 103 sq.; also ἐκεῖνος and ὅδε).

3779 οὕτως (and before a consonant sometimes οὕτω), adv., *thus, in this wise, so*, (1) in reference to antecedent or following statement; (2) correlative with ὡς or καθώς, *so* ... *as*; (3) qualifying adjectives, adverbs, or verbs, *so*, Heb. xii. 21; Mat. ix. 33; οὕτως ... οὕτως, 1 Cor. vii. 7, *in this manner ... in that.*

3780 οὐχί, adv., (1) an intensive form of οὐ, Jn. xiii. 10, *by no means, not at all*, (2) mostly interrog., as Mat. v. 46, expecting an affirmative answer.

3781 ὀφειλέτης, ου, ὁ, *a debtor*, Mat. xviii. 24; *one bound to some duty, e.g.*, obedience to the law, Gal. v. 3; *a delinquent, sinner*, Lu. xiii. 4.

3782 ὀφειλή, ῆς, ἡ, *a debt, a duty*, Mat. xviii. 32; Ro. xiii. 7; 1 Cor. vii. 3 (W. H.). (N. T.)*

3783 ὀφείλημα, ατος, τό, *a debt, what is justly due*, Ro. iv. 4; fig., *an offense, a sin*, Mat. vi. 12.*

3784 ὀφείλω, (1) *to owe money* (acc.

and dat.), Mat. xviii. 28; τὸ ὀφειλόμενον, *the due*, Mat. xviii. 30; (2) *to be under obligation*, Mat. xxiii. 16; *to sin against*, Lu. xi. 4.

3785 ὄφελον (see Gr. § 378, Wi. § 41 *b*, 5, note 2, Bu. 214 sq.), interjection, *O that! I wish! would that!* followed by indicative, 1 Cor. iv. 8; 2 Cor. xi. 1; Gal. v. 12; Rev. iii. 15.*

3786 ὄφελος, ους, τό (ὀφέλλω, *to increase*), *profit, advantage*, 1 Cor. xv. 32; Ja. ii. 14, 16.*

3787 ὀφθαλμο-δουλεία, ας, ἡ, *eye-service*, Ep. vi. 6; Col. iii. 22. (N. T.)*

3788 ὀφθαλμός, οῦ, ὁ, *an eye;* fig., of the eye as the receptive channel into mind and heart, Mat. vi. 23 (see Mar. vii. 22; Mat. xx. 15); fig., *the eye of the mind, i.e., the understanding*, Ac. xxvi. 18.

3789 ὄφις, εως, ὁ, *a serpent*, Mat. vii. 10; an emblem of wisdom, Mat. x. 16; of cunning, Mat. xxiii. 33; used symbol. for Satan, Rev. xii. 9, 14.

3790 ὀφρύς, ύος, ἡ, *the eyebrow; the brow* of a mountain or hill, Lu. iv. 29.*

3791 ὀχλέω, ῶ, *to disturb, to vex*, only in pass., Lu. vi. 18 (W. H. ἐνοχλέω), Ac. v. 16.*

3792 ὀχλο-ποιέω, ῶ, *to gather a crowd*, Ac. xvii. 5. (N. T.)*

3793 ὄχλος, ου, ὁ, *a crowd, an unorganized multitude*, Mat. ix. 23, 25; *the multitude, the common people*, Mar. xii. 12.

3794 ὀχύρωμα, ατος, τό, *a fortress, a strong defense*, 2 Cor. x. 4.*

3795 ὀψάριον, ου, τό (a relish with bread), *a little fish*, Jn. vi. 9, 11, xxi. 9, 10, 13. (N. T.)*

3796 ὀψέ, adv., *late, in the evening*, Mar. xi. 11 (W. H.), 19, xiii. 35; *late in*, gen., Mat. xxviii. 1.*

3797 ὄψιμος, ον, *latter*, of the rain, Ja. v. 7.*

3798 ὄψιος, α, ον, *late*, Mar. xi. 11 (not W. H., see mrg.); as subst., ἡ ὀψία, *evening*, either the former of the two evenings reckoned among the Jews, Mat. viii. 16; or the latter, Mat. xiv. 23; see ver. 15.

3799 ὄψις, εως, ἡ, *sight; the countenance*, Jn. xi. 44; Rev. i.

16; *external appearance*, Jn. vii. 24.*

3800 ὀψώνιον, ου, τό, lit., *relish, sauce*, like ὀψάριον, (1) plur., the *rations* of soldiers, their *wages*, Lu. iii. 14; 1 Cor. ix. 7; hence, (2) *wages*, generally, Ro. vi. 23; 2 Cor. xi. 8.*

Π

Π, π, πῖ, *pi, p*, the sixteenth letter. As a numeral, π' = 80; ,π = 80,000.

3802 παγιδεύω, σω, *to ensnare, to entrap*, fig., Mat. xxii. 15. (S.)*

3803 παγίς, ίδος, ἡ, *a snare, a trap*, Lu. xxi. 35; fig., Ro. xi. 9; 1 Tim. iii. 7, vi. 9; 2 Tim. ii. 26.*

see 697 πάγος, ου, ὁ, *a hill;* only with the adj. Ἄρειος, *Mars' Hill, Areopagus*, Ac. xvii. 19, 22.*

3804 πάθημα, ατος, τό, (1) *suffering, affliction*, Ro. viii. 18; (2) *affection of mind, passion*, Ro. vii. 5; Gal. v. 24; (3) *an undergoing, an enduring*, Heb. ii. 9.

3805 παθητός, ή, όν, *destined to suffer*, Ac. xxvi. 23.*

3806 πάθος, ους, τό, *suffering, emotion*, in N.T., of an evil kind, *depraved passion, lust*, Ro. i. 26; 1 Th. iv. 5; Col. iii. 5.*

3807 παιδ-αγωγός, οῦ, ὁ, *a boys' guardian* or *tutor*, "pædagogue," a slave who had the charge of the life and morals of the boys of a family, not strictly a teacher, 1 Cor. iv. 15; Gal. iii. 24, 25.*

3808 παιδάριον, ου, τό (dim. of παῖς), *a little boy, a lad*, Mat. xi. 16 (W. H. παιδίον); Jn. vi. 9.*

3809 παιδεία, ας, ἡ, *training and education* of children, Ep. vi. 4; hence, *instruction*, 2 Tim. iii. 16; *chastisement, correction*, Heb. xii. 5–11.*

3810 παιδευτής, οῦ, ὁ, (1) *an instructor*, Ro. ii. 20; (2) *a chastiser*, Heb. xii. 9.*

3811 παιδεύω, σω, *to train a child*, Ac. xxii. 3; hence, (1) *to instruct*, 1 Tim. i. 20, (2) *to correct, to chasten*, 2 Tim. ii. 25; Heb. xii. 7.

3812 παιδιόθεν, adv., *from childhood*, Mar. ix. 21. (N. T.)*

3813 παιδίον, ου, τό (dim. of παῖς),

a little child, an infant, Mat. ii. 8; *a child* more advanced, Mat. xiv. 21; fig., 1 Cor. xiv. 20.

3814 παιδίσκη, ης, ἡ (fem. dim. of παῖς), *a young girl; a young female slave*, Lu. xii. 45, xxii. 56.

3815 παίζω, *to play*, as a child, *to sport, to jest*, 1 Cor. x. 7.*

3816 παῖς, παιδός, ὁ, ἡ, (1) *a child, a boy* or *girl*, Lu. ii. 43, viii. 51, 54; (2) *a servant, a slave*, as Mat. viii. 6, 8; ὁ παῖς τοῦ θεοῦ, *the servant of God*, used of any servant, Lu. i. 69; *of the Messiah*, Mat. xii. 18.

3817 παίω, σω, *to strike, to smite*, with the fist, Mat. xxvi. 68; Lu. xxii. 64; with a sword, Mar. xiv. 47; Jn. xviii. 10; as a scorpion with its sting, Rev. ix. 5.*

3818 Πακατιανή, ῆς, ἡ, *Pacatiana*, a part of Phrygia, 1 Tim. vi. 22 (Rec.).*

3819 πάλαι, adv., *of old*, Heb. i. 1; *long ago*, Mat. xi. 21.

3820 παλαιός, ά, όν, (1) *old, ancient*, 2 Cor. iii. 14; ὁ παλαιὸς ἄνθρωπος, *the old* or *former man*, i.e., man in his old, unrenewed nature, Ro. vi. 6; (2) *worn out*, as a garment, Mat. ix. 16.

3821 παλαιότης, τητος, ἡ, *oldness, obsoleteness*, Ro. vii. 6.*

3822 παλαιόω, ῶ, *to make old, to declare obsolete*, Heb. viii. 13; pass., *to grow old, to become obsolete*, Lu. xii. 33; Heb. i. 11, viii. 13.*

3823 πάλη, ης, ἡ, *a wrestling*, Ep. vi. 12.*

3824 παλιγ-γενεσία (W. H. παλινγ-), ας, ἡ, *a new birth, regeneration*, Tit. iii. 5; *a renovation* of all things, Mat. xix. 28.* *Syn.:* see ἀνακαίνωσις.

3825 πάλιν, adv., *again, back*, used of place or of time; a particle of continuation, *again, once more, further;* and of antithesis, as 2 Cor. x. 7, *on the other hand*.

3826 παμ-πληθεί, adv., *all at once, all together*, Lu. xxiii. 18. (N. T.)*

3827 πάμ-πολυς, παμπόλλη, πάμπολυ, *very great*, Mar. viii. 1 (not W. H.).*

3828 Παμφυλία, ας, ἡ, *Pamphylia*, Ac. xiii. 13.

3829   παν-δοχεῖον, ου, τό, *a khan*, or
3830   Eastern *inn*, Lu. x. 34.*
παν-δοχεύς, έως, ὁ (δέχομαι), *the keeper of a khan, a host*, Lu. x. 35.*

3831   παν-ήγυρις, εως, ἡ (ἀγείρω), *a general festal assembly*, Heb. xii. 23.* *Syn.:* see ἐκκλησία.

3832   παν-οικί, adv., *with one's whole household* or *family*, Ac. xvi. 34.*

3833   παν-οπλία, as, ἡ, *complete armor*, Lu. xi. 22; Ep. vi. 11, 13.*

3834   πανουργία, as, ἡ, *shrewdness, skill;* hence, *cunning, craftiness*, Lu. xx. 23, 1 Cor. iii. 19; 2 Cor. iv. 2, xi. 3; Ep. iv. 14.*

3835   παν-οῦργος, ον (ἔργον), *doing everything; cunning, crafty*, 2 Cor. xii. 16.*

see 3837   πανταχῇ, adv., *everywhere*, Ac. xxi. 28 (W. H.).*

3836   πανταχόθεν, adv., *from all sides*, Mar. i. 45 (W. H. πάντοθεν).*

3837   πανταχοῦ, adv., *everywhere*, Mar. xvi. 20; Lu. ix. 6.

3838   παντελής, ές, *complete;* εἰς τὸ παντελές, *completely, perfectly*, Heb. vii. 25; the same phrase, with μή, *not at all*, Lu. xiii. 11.*

3839   πάντῃ, adv., *in every way*, Ac. xxiv. 3.*

3840   πάντοθεν, adv., *from all sides*, Mar. i. 45 (W. H.); Lu. xix. 43; Heb. ix. 4.*

3841   παντο-κράτωρ, ορος, ὁ, *the almighty*, used of God, Rev. i. 8, iv. 8.

3842   πάντοτε, adv., *always, at all times*, Mat. xxvi. 11.

3843   πάντως, adv., *wholly, entirely*, 1 Cor. v. 10; *in every way, by all means*, Ro. iii. 9; *assuredly, certainly*, Ac. xxi. 22.

3844   παρά, prep., gov. the gen., the dat., and accus., *beside;* with a gen. (of person), it indicates *source* or *origin;* with a dat., it denotes *presence with;* with an accus., it indicates motion *towards*, or *alongside*, and is employed in comparisons, *beyond;* for details see Gr. § 306, Wi. §§ 47 *b*, 48 *d*, 49*g*, Bu. 339 sq. In composition, παρά retains its general meaning, *besides*, sometimes denoting *nearness.* sometimes *motion by* or

past, so as to miss or fail; occasionally also *stealthiness (by the way)*, as in παρεισάγω.

3845   παρα-βαίνω, 2d aor. παρέβην, *to transgress*, Mat. xv. 2, 3; 2 Jn. 9 (W. H. προάγω); *to depart, desert*, Ac. i. 25.*

3846   παρα-βάλλω, (1) *to compare*, Mar. iv. 30 (not W. H.); (2) *to betake one's self, arrive*, Ac. xx. 15.*

3847   παρά-βασις, εως, ἡ, *a transgression*, Ro. ii. 23. *Syn.:* see ἀγνόημα.

3848   παρα-βάτης, ου, ὁ, *a transgressor*, Ro. ii. 25, 27; Gal. ii. 18; Ja. ii. 9, 11.*

3849   παρα-βιάζομαι, *to constrain by entreaties*, Lu. xxiv. 29; Ac. xvi. 15.*

see 3851   παρα-βολεύομαι, *to expose one's self to peril, to be venturesome*, Phil. ii. 30 (W. H.). (N. T.)*

3850   παρα-βολή, ῆς, ἡ, (1) *a comparison*, Heb. ix. 9; (2) *a parable*, often of those uttered by our Lord, Mar. iv. 2, 10; (3) *a proverb, an adage*, Lu. iv. 23; (4) perhaps in Heb. xi. 19, *a venture, a risk* (see παραβολεύομαι).

3851   παραβουλεύομαι, *to consult amiss, be reckless*, Phil. ii. 30 (Rec.). (N. T.)*

3852   παραγγελία, as, ἡ, *a command, a charge*, Ac. v. 28, xvi. 24; 1 Th. iv. 2; 1 Tim. i. 5, 18.*

3853   παρ-αγγέλλω, *to notify, to command, to charge*, Lu. viii. 29; 2 Th. iii. 4; dat. of person, acc. of thing, or ὅτι, ἵνα or inf., 1 Tim. vi. 13.

3854   παρα-γίνομαι, *to come near, come forth, come against* (ἐπί, πρός), Lu. xii. 51, xxii. 52; Jn. iii. 23; Heb. ix. 11.

3855   παρ-άγω, *to pass by*, Mat. xx. 30; *to depart*, Mat. ix. 27; *to pass away*, act., 1 Cor. vii. 31; pass., only 1 Jn. ii. 8, 17.

3856   παρα-δειγματίζω, *to make a public example of, to expose to disgrace*, Mat. i. 19 (W. H. δειγματίζω); Heb. vi. 6.*

3857   παράδεισος, ου, ὁ (probably a Persian word, "garden," "park"), *Paradise*, Lu. xxiii. 43; 2 Cor. xii. 4; Rev. ii. 7.*

3858   παρα-δέχομαι, dep., mid., *to receive, accept, acknowledge*, Mar. iv. 20; Ac. xv. 4 (W.

H.), xvi. 21, xxii. 18; 1 Tim.
v. 19; Heb. xii. 6.*

3859 παρα-δια-τριβή, ῆς, ἡ, *useless
occupation*, 1 Tim. vi. 5 (W.
H. διαπαρατριβή). (N. T.)*

3860 παρα-δίδωμι, acc. and dat., (1)
to deliver over, as to prison,
judgment, or punishment,
Mat. iv. 12; *to betray*, spec.
of the betrayal by Judas;
(2) *to surrender, abandon*
one's self, Ep. iv. 19; (3) *to
hand over, entrust, commit,
deliver*, as Mat. xxv. 14; Lu.
i. 2; Ac. vi. 14; (4) *to commend* to kindness, Ac. xiv.
26; (5) *to give* or *prescribe*,
as laws, etc., Ac. vi. 14; (6)
prob. *to permit*, in Mar. iv.
29, *when the fruit permits*
or *allows*.

3861 παρά-δοξος, ον, *strange, wonderful*, Lu. v. 26.*

3862 παρά-δοσις, εως, ἡ, *an instruction*, or *tradition*, Mat. xv. 2;
1 Cor. xi. 2; 2 Th. ii. 15,
iii. 6.

3863 παρα-ζηλόω, ῶ, ώσω, *to provoke to rivalry*, Ro. xi. 11,
14; *to jealousy*, Ro. x. 19; *to
anger*, 1 Cor. x. 22. (S.)*

3864 παρα-θαλάσσιος, a, ον, *by the
sea*, Mat. iv. 13.*

3865 παρα-θεωρέω, ῶ, *to overlook,
neglect*, Ac. vi. 1.*

3866 παρα-θήκη, ης, ἡ, *a deposit,
anything committed to one's
charge*, 1 Tim. vi. 20 (W.H.);
2 Tim. i. 12, 14 (W. H.).*

3867 παρ-αινέω, ῶ, *to exhort, admonish*, Ac. xxvii. 9, 22.*

3868 παρ-αιτέομαι, οῦμαι, dep., mid.,
*to entreat for, to beg off,
make excuse, refuse, reject*,
Mar. xv. 6 (W. H.); Lu.
xiv. 18, 19; Ac. xxv. 11;
1 Tim. iv. 7, v. 11; 2 Tim.
ii. 23; Tit. iii. 10; Heb. xii.
19, 25.*

see 3869 παρα-καθέζομαι, *to seat one's
self*, Lu. x. 39 (W. H.).*

3869 παρα-καθίζω, intrans., *to sit
down beside*, Lu. x. 39 (Rec.).*

3870 παρα-καλέω, ῶ, έσω, (1) *to send
for, summon*, Ac. xxviii. 20;
(2) *to beseech, entreat*, Mar.
i. 40; (3) *to exhort, admonish*,
Ac. xv. 32; 1 Tim. vi. 2;
(4) *to comfort*, 2 Cor. i. 4;
pass., *to be comforted*, Lu.
xvi. 25.

3871 παρα-καλύπτω, *to hide, to conceal*, Lu. ix. 45.*

3872 παρα-κατα-θήκη, ης, ἡ, *a trust,
a deposit*, 1 Tim. vi. 20; 2
Tim. i. 14 (in both passages
W. H. read παραθήκη).*

3873 παρά-κειμαι, *to be at hand, be
present with* (dat.), Ro. vii.
18, 21.*

3874 παρά-κλησις, εως, ἡ, *a calling
for, a summons;* hence, (1)
exhortation, Heb. xii. 5; (2)
entreaty, 2 Cor. viii. 4; (3) *encouragement*, Phil. ii. 1; (4)
consolation, comfort, Ro. xv.
4; met., of the Consoler, Lu.
ii. 25; (5) generally, of the
power of imparting all these,
Ac. iv. 36.

3875 παρά-κλητος, ον, ὁ, (1) *an ad-
vocate, intercessor*, 1 Jn. ii.
1; (2) *a consoler, comforter,
helper*, of the Holy Spirit,
Jn. xiv. 16, 26, xv. 26, xvi.
7.*

3876 παρ-ακοή, ῆς, ἡ, *disobedience*,
Ro. v. 19; 2 Cor. x. 6; Heb.
ii. 2.* *Syn.* : see ἀγνόημα.

3877 παρ-ακολουθέω, ῶ, ήσω, *to follow closely, to accompany*
(dat.), Mar. xvi. 17 (not W.
H., see mrg.); *to follow so
as to trace out, to examine*,
Lu. i. 3; *to follow teaching*,
1 Tim. iv. 6; 2 Tim. iii. 10.*

3878 παρ-ακούω, *to hear negligently,
to disregard*, Mat. xviii. 17;
Mar. v. 36 (W. H.).*

3879 παρα-κύπτω, ψω, *to stoop*, Lu.
xxiv. 12; Jn. xx. 5, 11; fig.,
with εἰς, *to search into*, Ja. i.
25; 1 Pet. i. 12.*

3880 παρα-λαμβάνω, λήψομαι (W. H.
-λήμψ-), (1) *to take to one's self,
to take with one*, Lu. ix. 10,
28, xi. 26; *to lead off* a prisoner, Jn. xix. 16; Ac. xxiii.
18; (2) *to receive by trans-
mission*, Col. iv. 17; Heb.
xii. 28; fig., *to receive by instruction*, Mar. vii. 4.

3881 παρα-λέγω, N.T. in mid., *to lay
one's course near*, in sailing,
to coast along, Ac. xxvii. 8,
13.*

3882 παρ-άλιος, ον, *adjacent to the
sea, on the coast*, Lu. vi.
17.*

3883 παρ-αλλαγή, ῆς, ἡ, *change, variation*, Ja. i. 17.*

3884 παρα-λογίζομαι, dep., *to impose
upon, to delude*, acc., Col. ii.
4; Ja. i. 22.*

3885 παρα-λυτικός, ἡ, όν, *afflicted
with paralysis*, in the whole

3886 or a part of the body, Mat. iv. 24, viii. 6. (N. T.)

3886 παρα-λύω, to relax, to enfeeble, only perf. part., pass., παραλελυμένος, paralyzed, enfeebled.

3887 παρα-μένω, μενῶ, to remain by (dat., or πρός, acc.), to abide with, 1 Cor. xvi. 6 (W. H. καταμένω); Phil. i. 25 (W. H.); to continue, Ja. i. 25; Heb. vii. 23.*

3888 παρα-μυθέομαι, οῦμαι, to speak to, to cheer, to comfort, Jn. xi. 19, 31; 1 Th. ii. 11, v. 14.*

3889 παρα-μυθία, ας, ἡ, encouragement, comfort, 1 Cor. xiv. 3.*

3890 παρα-μύθιον, ου, τό, comfort, Phil. ii. 1.*

3891 παρα-νομέω, ῶ, to act contrary to law, Ac. xxiii. 3.*

3892 παρα-νομία, ας, ἡ, violation of law, transgression, 2 Pet. ii. 16.* Syn.: see ἀγνόημα.

3893 παρα-πικραίνω, ανῶ, 1st aor. παρεπίκρανα, to provoke God to anger, Heb. iii. 16. (S.)*

3894 παρα-πικρασμός, οῦ, ὁ, provocation of God, Heb. iii. 8, 15. (S.)*

3895 παρα-πίπτω, 2d aor. παρέπεσον, to fall away, Heb. vi. 6.*

3896 παρα-πλέω, ῶ, εύσομαι, to sail past, acc., Ac. xx. 16.*

3897 παρα-πλήσιον, adv., near to (gen.), Phil. ii. 27.*

3898 παραπλησίως, adv., similarly, in like manner, Heb. ii. 14.*

3899 παρα-πορεύομαι, dep., mid., to pass by, to pass along by, Mar. xi. 20, xv. 29.

3900 παρά-πτωμα, ατος, τό (παραπίπτω), a falling away or aside, a sin, Ep. i. 7, ii. 1, 5. Syn.: see ἀγνόημα.

3901 παρα-ρρέω, 2d aor., pass., παρερρύην, pass., to be carried past, to lose, Heb. ii. 1.*

3902 παρά-σημος, ον, marked with (dat.), Ac. xxviii. 11.*

3903 παρα-σκευάζω, σω, to prepare, Ac. x. 10; mid., to prepare one's self, 1 Cor. xiv. 8; pass., to be in readiness, 2 Cor. ix. 2, 3.*

3904 παρα-σκευή, ῆς, ἡ, a preparation, i.e., the day immediately before a sabbath or other festival, Mat. xxvii. 62; Mar. xv. 42; Lu. xxiii 54; Jn. xix. 14, 31, 42.*

3905 παρα-τείνω, to extend, to prolong, Ac. xx. 7.*

3906 παρα-τηρέω, ῶ, ήσω, (1) to watch, Mar. iii. 2; (2) to observe scrupulously, Gal. iv. 10.

3907 παρα-τήρησις, εως, ἡ, observation, Lu. xvii. 20.*

3908 παρα-τίθημι, θήσω (see Gr. § 107), (1) to place near or by the side of, as food, Lu. xi. 6; (2) to set or lay before, as instruction, used of a parable, Mat. xiii. 24; mid., to give in charge to, to entrust, Lu. xii. 48· to commend, to recommend (acc. and dat., or εἰς), Ac. xiv. 23.

3909 παρα-τυγχάνω, to fall in with, chance to meet, Ac. xvii. 17.*

3910 παρ-αυτίκα, adv., for the moment, 2 Cor. iv. 17.*

3911 παρα-φέρω (see Gr. § 103, 6, Wi. § 52, 4, 11)), to remove (acc. and ἀπό), Mar. xiv. 36; Lu. xxii. 42; pass., to be led aside, carried away, Heb. xiii. 9 (W. H.); Ju. 12 (W. H.).*

3912 παρα-φρονέω, ῶ, to be beside one's self, 2 Cor. xi. 23.*

3913 παρα-φρονία, ας, ἡ, being beside one's self, madness, folly, 2 Pet. ii. 16. (N. T.)*

3914 παρα-χειμάζω, άσω, to pass the winter, Ac. xxvii. 12, xxviii. 11; 1 Cor. xvi. 6; Tit. iii. 12.*

3915 παρα-χειμασία, ας, ἡ, a passing the winter, Ac. xxvii. 12.*

3916 παρα-χρῆμα, adv., instantly, immediately, Lu. i. 64, iv. 39.

3917 πάρδαλις, εως, ἡ, a leopard, a panther, Rev. xiii. 2.*

see 4332 παρ-εδρεύω, to wait upon, to attend to (dat.), 1 Cor. ix. 13 (W. H.).*

3918 πάρ-ειμι (εἰμί), to be near, to be present; part., παρών, present; τὸ παρόν, the present time; τὰ παρόντα, possessions.

3919 παρ-εισ-άγω, ξω, to bring in secretly, 2 Pet. ii. 1.*

3920 παρ-είσ-ακτος, ον, brought in secretly, surreptitious, Gal. ii. 4.*

3921 παρ-εισ-δύω, or -ύνω, ύσω, to come in by stealth, to enter secretly, Ju. 4.*

3922 παρ-εισ-έρχομαι (see Gr. § 103, 2), (1) to enter secretly, Gal.

ii. 4; (2) *to enter in addition,*
Ro. v. 20.*

3923   **παρ-εισ-φέρω,** *to contribute be-sides,* 2 Pet. i. 5.*

3924   **παρ-εκτός,** adv., *besides;* τὰ παρεκτός, *the things that oc-cur besides,* 2 Cor. xi. 28 (see R.V. mrg.); prep. with gen., *except,* Mat. v. 32; Ac. xxvi. 29; also Mat. xix. 9, W. H. mrg.*

see 4016   **παρ-εμ-βάλλω,** βαλῶ, *to cast up* a bank about a city, Lu. xix. 43 (W. H.).*

3925   **παρ-εμ-βολή,** ῆς, ἡ, (1) *a camp,* Heb. xiii. 11, 13; (2) *soldiers' barracks,* Ac. xxi. 34, 37; (3) *an army in battle array,* Heb. xi. 34.

3926   **παρ-εν-οχλέω,** ῶ, *to cause dis-turbance to, to disquiet* (dat.), Ac. xv. 19.*

3927   **παρ-επί-δημος,** ον, *residing in a strange country;* as subst., *a stranger, foreigner,* Heb. xi. 13; 1 Pet. i. 1, ii. 11.*

3928   **παρ-έρχομαι,** ελεύσομαι (see Gr. § 103, 2, Wi. § 52, 4, 11)), (1) *to pass by,* with acc. of person or place; (2) *to pass, elapse,* as time; (3) *to pass away* or *perish;* (4) *to pass from* any one; (5) *to pass carelessly, i.e., to disregard, neglect.*

3929; see 859   **πάρ-εσις,** εως, ἡ (ἵημι), *passing over, prætermission,* Ro. iii. 25.* *Syn.:* see ἄφεσις.

3930   **παρ-έχω,** έξω, 2d aor. παρέσχον (dat. and acc.), (1) *to offer, to supply,* Lu. vi. 29; Ac. xxii. 2; espec. the phrase παρέχω κόπους, *to cause trouble,* Mat. xxvi. 10; (2) in mid., *to pre-sent, manifest,* Tit. ii. 7; *to bestow,* Col. iv. 1.

3931   **παρ-ηγορία,** ας, ἡ, *solace,* Col. iv. 11.*

3932   **παρθενία,** ας, ἡ, *virginity,* Lu. ii. 36.*

3933   **παρθένος,** ου, ἡ, *a virgin, a maid,* Mat. xxv. 1, 7, 11; hence one who is *chaste,* Rev. xiv. 4, applied to the male sex.

3934   **Πάρθος,** ου, ὁ, *a Parthian,* Ac. ii. 9.*

3935   **παρ-ίημι,** *to pass by* or *over, to relax;* pass., perf. part., παρειμένος, *weary,* Heb. xii. 12.*

3936   **παρ-ίστημι,** or παριστάνω (Ro. vi. 13, 16; see Gr. § 107),

στήσω, (1) trans. in act., pres., imp., fut., and 1st aor., *to place near* or *at hand, to provide,* Ac. xxiii. 24; *to pre-sent, to offer,* Ro. vi. 13, 16; specially, *to dedicate, to con-secrate,* Lu. ii. 22; *to cause to appear, to demonstrate,* Ac. xxiv. 13; (2) intrans., perf., plup., 2d aor., and mid., *to stand by,* Mar. xiv. 47, 69, 70; Lu. xix. 24; *to have come,* Mar. iv. 29; *to stand by, i.e.,* for aid or support, Ro. xvi. 2; *to stand in hostile array,* Ac. iv. 26.

3937   **Παρμενᾶς,** acc. ᾶν, ὁ, *Parmenas,* Ac. vi. 5.*

3938   **πάρ-οδος,** ου, ἡ, *a passing by* or *through,* 1 Cor. xvi. 7.*

3939   **παρ-οικέω,** ῶ, *to dwell in* (ἐν or εἰς, const. præg.) *as a stranger,* Lu. xxiv. 18; Heb. xi. 9.*

3940   **παρ-οικία,** ας, ἡ, *a sojourning, a dwelling in a strange land,* Ac. xiii. 17; 1 Pet. i. 17. (S.)*

3941   **πάρ-οικος,** ον, generally as sub-stantive, *a stranger, a for-eigner,* Ac. vii. 6, 29; Ep. ii. 19; 1 Pet. ii. 11.*

3942   **παρ-οιμία,** ας, ἡ (οἶμος, *a way*), (1) *a current* or *trite saying, a proverb,* 2 Pet. ii. 22; (2) *an obscure saying, a symbolic saying,* Jn. xvi. 25, 29; (3) *a comparative discourse, an al-legory,* Jn. x. 6.

3943   **πάρ-οινος,** ον, *given to wine, drunken,* 1 Tim. iii. 3; Tit. i. 7.*

3944   **παρ-οίχομαι,** *to pass away,* of time, Ac. xiv. 16.*

3945   **παρ-ομοιάζω,** *to resemble,* Mat. xxiii. 27. (N. T.)*

3946   **παρ-όμοιος,** ον, *similar,* Mar. vii. 8 (W. H. omit), 13.*

3947   **παρ-οξύνω,** *to provoke, tc irri-tate,* in pass., Ac. xvii. 16; 1 Cor. xiii. 5.*

3948   **παρ-οξυσμός,** οῦ, ὁ, (1) *incite-ment,* Heb. x. 24; (2) *con-tention, irritation,* Ac. xv. 39.*

3949   **παρ-οργίζω,** ιῶ, *to provoke great-ly, exasperate,* Ro. x. 19; Ep. vi. 4.*

3950; see 2372   **παρ-οργισμός,** οῦ, ὁ, *exaspera-tion, wrath,* Ep. iv. 26. (S.)* *Syn.:* see θυμός.

3951   **παρ-οτρύνω,** *to stir up, to incite,* Ac. xiii. 50.*

3952 παρ-ουσία, ας, ἡ (εἰμί), (1) *presence*, 2 Cor. x. 10; Phil. ii. 20; (2) *a coming, an arrival, advent,* often of the second coming of Christ, 2 Cor. vii. 6, 7; 1 Th. iii. 13.

3953 παρ-οψίς, ίδος, ἡ, *a dish for delicacies*, Mat. xxiii. 25, 26.*

3954 παρρησία, ας, ἡ, *freedom, openness,* especially in speaking, *boldness, confidence,* Ac. iv. 13; Heb. x. 19; παρρησίᾳ, ἐν παρρησίᾳ, or μετὰ παρρησίας, *boldly, openly.*

3955 παρρησιάζομαι, dep., mid., 1st aor. ἐπαρρησιασάμην, *to speak freely, boldly, to be confident,* Ac. xviii. 26, xxvi. 26.

3956 πᾶς, πᾶσα, πᾶν (see Gr. § 37), *all, the whole, every kind of* (see Gr. § 224, Wi. § 18, 4, Bu. 119 sq., and for negative in phrases, Gr. § 328, iii., Wi. § 26, 1, Bu. 121 sq.); adverbial phrases are διαπαντός (which see), *always; ἐν παντί, ἐν πᾶσιν, in everything;* and πάντα (neut. plur. acc.), *altogether.*

3957 πάσχα, τό (Aram.), *the paschal lamb,* Mar. xiv. 12; applied to Christ, 1 Cor. v. 7; *the paschal supper,* Mar. xiv. 16; *the passover feast,* Mat. xxvi. 2. (S.)

3958 πάσχω (παθ-, see Gr. § 94, i. 7), *to be affected with* anything, good or bad; so, *to enjoy good,* Gal. iii. 4; more commonly, *to endure suffering,* Mat. xvii. 15; *to suffer* (acc. of that suffered, ἀπό or ὑπό, gen., of person inflicting).

3959 Πάταρα, άρων, τά, *Patara,* Ac. xxi. 1.*

3960 πατάσσω, ξω, *to smite, to strike, to smite to death, to afflict,* Mat. xxvi. 31; Ac. xii. 23.

3961 πατέω, ῶ, ήσω, *to tread upon,* Lu. x. 19; *to press by treading,* as grapes, Rev. xiv. 20, xix. 15; fig., *to tread down, to trample upon,* Lu. xxi. 24; Rev. xi. 2.*

3962 πατήρ, τρός, ὁ (see Gr. § 30, ii., Wi. §§ 19, 1 a, 30, 3, Bu. 94), *a father;* often of God as the father of men, Mat. v. 16, 45; as the father of the Lord Jesus Christ, Mat. vii. 21; as the first person in the Trinity, Mat. xxviii. 19; as the source of manifold bless-

mgs, 2 Cor. i. 3. Secondary meanings are: (1) *a founder of a race, an ancestor;* (2) *a senior, a father in age,* 1 Jn. ii. 13, 14; (3) *the author,* or *cause,* or *source of anything,* Jn. viii. 44; Heb. xii. 9; (4) *a spiritual father,* or means of converting any one to Christ, 1 Cor. iv. 15; (5) *one to whom resemblance is borne,* Jn. viii. 38, 41, 44.

3963 Πάτμος, ου, ἡ, *Patmos,* Rev. i. 9.*

3964 πατρ-αλῴας (W. H. -ολῴας), ου, ὁ, *a parricide,* 1 Tim. i. 9.*

3965 πατριά, ᾶς, ἡ, *a family* (in O. T. a division between the tribe and the household), Lu. ii. 4; Ac. iii. 25; Ep. iii. 15 (on which see Gr. § 224).*

3966 πατρι-άρχης, ου, ὁ, *head* or *founder of a family, a patriarch,* Ac. ii. 29, vii. 8, 9; Heb. vii. 4. (S.)*

3967 πατρικός, ή, όν, *paternal, ancestral,* Gal. i. 14.*

3968 πατρίς, ίδος, ἡ, *one's native place, fatherland,* Heb. xi. 14; *one's native place, i.e., city,* Mat. xiii. 54, 57.

3969 Πατρόβας, acc. αν, ὁ, *Patrobas,* Ro. xvi. 14.*

3970 πατρο-παρά-δοτος, ον, *handed down from ancestors,* 1 Pet. i. 18.*

3971 πατρῷος, α, ον, *received from the fathers, hereditary,* Ac. xxii. 3, xxiv. 14, xxviii. 17.*

3972 Παῦλος, ου, ὁ, *Paul,* (1) Sergius Paulus, Ac. xiii. 7; (2) the apostle of the Gentiles, Ac. xxi. 40 (see Gr. § 159c, Wi § 18, 6).

3973 παύω, σω, *to cause to cease, to restrain,* 1 Pet. iii. 10; generally mid., *to cease, desist,* Lu. v. 4, viii. 24.

3974 Πάφος, ου, ἡ, *Paphos,* Ac. xiii. 6, 13.*

3975 παχύνω (παχύς), *to make fat, to fatten;* pass., fig., *to become stupid,* Mat. xiii. 15; Ac. xxviii. 27.*

3976 πέδη, ης, ἡ, *a shackle, a fetter for the feet,* Mar. v. 4; Lu. viii. 29.*

3977 πεδινός, ή, όν, *level,* Lu. vi. 17.*

3978 πεζεύω (πεζός), *to travel on foot* or *by land,* Ac. xx. 13.*

3979 πεζῇ, adv., *on foot,* or *by land,* Mat. xiv. 13; Mar. vi. 33.*

3980 πειθ-αρχέω, ῶ, (1) *to obey a ruler* or *one in authority*, Ac. v. 29, 32; Tit. iii. 1; (2) *to obey*, or *conform to advice*, Ac. xxvii. 21.*

3981 πειθός (W. H. πιθός), ή, όν, *persuasive*, 1 Cor. ii. 4. (N.T.)*

3982 πείθω, πείσω, *to persuade*, Ac. xviii. 4; *to influence by persuasion*, Mat. xxvii. 20; *to seek to please, to conciliate*, Ac. xiv. 29; 2 Cor. v. 11; *to appease, to render tranquil*, 1 Jn. iii. 19; *to conciliate, to aspire to the favor of*, Gal. i. 10; pass., *to yield to persuasion, to assent, to listen to, to obey*, Ac. v. 36, 37; the 2d perf., πέποιθα, is intrans., *to trust, to rely on, to have confidence in*, Mat. xxvii. 43; Ro. ii. 19.

3983 πεινάω, ῶ, inf. πεινᾶν, ἄσω, (1) *to be hungry*, Mat. iv. 2, xii. 1, 3; hence, (2) *to be needy*, Lu. i. 53; (3) *to desire earnestly, to long for*, acc., Mat. v. 6.

3984 πεῖρα, as, ή, *trial, experiment*; with λαμβάνω, *to make trial of, to experience*, Heb. xi. 29, 36.*

3985; see 1381 πειράζω, σω, (1) *to attempt* (inf.), Ac. xvi. 7; (2) *to make trial of, to test* (acc.), Jn. vi. 6; (3) *to tempt to sin*, Ja. i. 13, 14; ὁ πειράζων, *the tempter*, *i.e., the devil*, Mat. iv. 3. *Syn.:* see δοκιμάζω.

3986 πειρασμός, οῦ, ὁ, *a trying, proving*, 1 Pet. iv. 12; Heb. iii. 8; *a tempting to sin*, Mat. vi. 13; *calamity, adversity*, as trying men, Ac. xx. 19. (S.)

3987 πειράω, ῶ, only in mid., *to attempt*, Ac. ix. 26 (W. H. πειράζω), xxvi. 21.*

3988 πεισμονή, ῆς, ή, *persuasion, conviction*, Gal. v. 8. (N.T.)*

3989 πέλαγος, ους, τό, *the sea, the deep*, Mat. xviii. 6; Ac. xxvii. 5.*

3990 πελεκίζω (πέλεκυς, *an axe*), *to behead*, Rev. xx. 4.*

3991 πέμπτος, η, ον, ord. num., *the fifth*, Rev. vi. 9.

3992 πέμπω, ψω, (1) *to send*, of persons, *to send forth*, spoken of teachers, as John Baptist, Jn. i. 33; of Jesus, Jn. iv. 34; of the Spirit, Jn. xiv. 26; of apostles, Jn. xiii. 20; (2) *to send*, of things, *to transmit*, Rev. xi. 10; *to send among* or *upon*, 2 Th. ii. 11; *to thrust in* the sickle, Rev. xiv. 15, 18.

3993 πένης, ητος, ὁ, *poor*, 2 Cor. ix. 9.* *Syn.:* πτωχός implies utter destitution, usually beggary; πένης, simply poverty, scanty livelihood.

3994 πενθερά, ᾶς, ή, *a mother-in-law*, a wife's mother, Mar. i. 30.

3995 πενθερός, οῦ, ὁ, *a father-in-law*, a wife's father, Jn. xviii. 13.*

3996 πενθέω, ῶ, ήσω, (1) *to mourn*, intrans., Ja. iv. 9; (2) *to mourn passionately for, to lament*, trans., 2 Cor. xii. 21.

3997 πένθος, ους, τό, *mourning*, Ja. iv. 9; Rev. xviii. 7, 8, xxi. 4.*

3998 πενιχρός, ά, όν, *poor, needy*, Lu. xxi. 2.*

3999 πεντάκις, num. adv., *five times*, 2 Cor. xi. 24.*

4000 πεντακισ-χίλιοι, αι, α, num., *five thousand*, Mat. xiv. 21.

4001 πεντακόσιοι, αι, α, num., *five hundred*, Lu. vii. 41; 1 Cor. xv. 6.*

4002 πέντε, οἱ, αἱ, τά, num. indecl., *five*, Mat. xiv. 17.

4003 πεντε-και-δέκατος, η, ον, ord. num., *fifteenth*, Lu. iii. 1. (S.)*

4004 πεντήκοντα, οἱ, αἱ, τά, num. indecl., *fifty*, Lu. vii. 41.

4005 πεντηκοστή, ῆς, ή (lit. *fiftieth*), *Pentecost*, the feast beginning the fiftieth day after the second day of the Passover, *i.e.*, from the sixteenth day of the month Nisan, Ac. ii. 1, xx. 16; 1 Cor. xvi. 8.*

see 3982 πέποιθα, see πείθω.

4006 πεποίθησις, εως, ή, *trust, confidence*, with εἰς or ἐν, 2 Cor. viii. 22; Phil. iii. 4. (S.)

4007 πέρ, an enclitic particle, cognate with περί, only found joined to pronouns or particles for intensity of meaning, as ἐάνπερ, εἴπερ, *if indeed*; ἐπείπερ, *since indeed*; καίπερ, *and really*; ὅσπερ, *the very one who*.

see 4012 & 2087 περαιτέρω (πέρα), adv., *further, besides*, Ac. xix. 39 (W.H.).*

4008 πέραν, adv., *over, on the other side, beyond*, with article prefixed or genitive following, Mat. viii. 18, 28, xix. 1.

4009 πέρας, ατος. τό, *a limit, the ex-*

4010

4011

4012

4013

4014

see 681

4015

4016

4017

4018

4019

see 4063
4020

4021

4022

tremity, in space, as Mat.
xii. 42; or time, Heb. vi. 16.
Πέργαμος, ου, ἡ, *Pergamus* or
Pergamum, Rev. i. 11, ii.
12.*

Πέργη, ης, ἡ, *Perga*, Ac. xiii.
13.

περί, a prep., governing the
gen. and acc.; with gen.,
about, *i.e.*, concerning or re-
specting a thing; with acc.,
about, around, in reference
to (see Gr. § 302, Wi. §§ 47 *e*,
49 *i*, Bu. 335). In composition, περί denotes *round
about, on account of, above,
beyond.*

περι-άγω, trans., *to lead* or
take about, 1 Cor. ix. 5; intrans., *to go about* (acc. of
place), Mat. iv. 23, ix. 35,
xxiii. 15; Mar. vi. 6; Ac.
xiii. 11.*

περι-αιρέω, ῶ (see Gr. § 103, 2,
Wi. § 15, Bu. 53), *to take
from around, take entirely
away*, lit., Ac. xxvii. 40 (*to
cast off* anchors, R. V.); fig.,
of the removal of sin, Heb.
x. 11.

περι-άπτω, *to kindle*, Lu. xxii.
55 (W. H.).*

περι-αστράπτω, *to lighten a-
round, to flash around* (acc.,
or περί, acc.), Ac. ix. 3, xxii.
6. (Ap.)*

περι-βάλλω, βαλῶ, βέβληκα, *to
cast around* (acc. and dat.),
Lu. xix. 43; *to clothe*, Mat.
xxv. 36; for const., see Gr.
§ 284, Wi. § 53, 4, 12), Bu.
149; mid., *to clothe one's self,
to be clothed*, Mat. vi. 29.

περι-βλέπω, N. T., in mid., *to
look around*, abs., Mar. v. 32,
ix. 8, x. 23; *to look round
upon*, acc., Mar. iii. 5, 34, xi.
11; Lu. vi. 10.*

περι-βόλαιον, ου, τό, (1) *a man-
tle*, Heb. i. 12; (2) *a veil*, 1
Cor. xi. 15.*

περι-δέω, *to bind round about*,
pass., plup., Jn. xi. 44.*

περι-δρέμω, see περιτρέχω.

περι-εργάζομαι, *to overdo, to be
a busybody*, 2 Th. iii. 11.*

περί-εργος, ου, act., *overdoing,
intermeddling*, 1 Tim. v. 13;
pass., τὰ περίεργα, *super-
fluous arts, sorcery*, Ac. xix.
19.*

περι-έρχομαι (see Gr. § 103, 2,
Wi. § 53, 4, 12)), *to go about,*

4023

4024

4025

4026

4027

4028

4029

4030

4031

4032

4033

4034

4035

4036

4037

4038

4039

Ac. xix. 13; 1 Tim. v. 13;
Heb. xi. 37; *to tack*, as a
ship, Ac. xxviii. 13 (not W.
H.).*

περι-έχω, *to encompass; so, to
contain*, as a writing, Ac.
xxiii. 25 (W. H. ἔχω); intrans., *to be contained*, 1 Pet.
ii. 6; *to seize*, as astonish-
ment, Lu. v. 9.*

περι-ζώννυμι, or -ζωννύω (see
Gr. § 114, Wi. § 53, 4, 12),
Bu. 191), *to gird one's self
around*, mid. or pass., Ep.
vi. 14; Lu. xii. 35, 37.

περί-θεσις, εως, ἡ, *a putting
around*, as ornaments, 1 Pet.
iii. 3. (N. T.)*

περι-ίστημι (see Gr. § 107, Wi.
§ 14, 1), in intrans. tenses of
act., *to stand around*, Jn. xi.
42; Ac. xxv. 7; mid., *to
avoid, shun* (acc.), 2 Tim. ii.
16; Tit. iii. 9.*

περι-κάθαρμα, ατος, τό, *refuse,
offscouring*, 1 Cor. iv. 13.
(S.)*

περι-καλύπτω, *to cover round
about, to cover up*, as the face,
Mar. xiv. 65; Lu. xxii. 64;
Heb. ix. 4.*

περί-κειμαι, *to lie about, surround*, dat., or περί, acc.,
Mar. ix. 42; Lu. xvii. 2;
Heb. xii. 1; *to be encom-
passed* or *surrounded with*,
acc., Ac. xxviii. 20; Heb.
v. 2.*

περι-κεφαλαία, ας, ἡ, *a helmet*,
Ep. vi. 17; 1 Th. v. 8.*

περι-κρατής, ές, *having full
power over* (gen.), Ac. xxvii.
16. (Ap.)*

περι-κρύπτω, *to hide entirely*,
Lu. i. 24. (N. T.)*

περι-κυκλόω, ῶ, ώσω, *to encircle,
surround*, Lu. xix. 43.*

περι-λάμπω, *to shine around*,
Lu. ii. 9; Ac. xxvi. 13.*

περι-λείπω, *to leave remaining;*
pass., *to be left*, 1 Th. iv. 15,
17.*

περί-λυπος, ου, *very sorrowful*,
Mat. xxvi. 38; Mar. vi. 26,
xiv. 34; Lu. xviii. 23, 24
(W. H. omit).*

περι-μένω, *to wait for* (acc.), Ac.
i. 4.*

πέριξ, adv., *round about*, Ac. v.
16.*

περι-οικέω, ῶ, *to dwell around,
to be neighboring to* (acc.), Lu.
i. 65.*

4040 περί-οικος, ον, *dwelling around, a neighbor,* Lu. i. 58.*

4041 περι-ούσιος, ον, *costly, treasured, select;* hence, *specially chosen,* Tit. ii. 14 (S.). (S.)*

4042 περι-οχή, ῆς, ἡ (περιέχω), *a section* or *passage* of Scripture, Ac. viii. 32.*

4043 περι-πατέω, ῶ, ἤσω, *to walk, to walk about;* fig., as Hebrew, *to pass one's life, to conduct one's self* (adv. or nom. pred.), *to live according to* (ἐν, dat.; κατά, acc.).

4044 περι-πείρω, *to pierce through,* fig., 1 Tim. vi. 10.*

4045 περι-πίπτω, *to fall into the midst of* (dat.), robbers, Lu. x. 30; temptations, Ja. i. 2; *to happen upon* a place, Ac. xxvii. 41.*

4046 περι-ποιέω, ῶ, N. T. in mid., *to preserve for one's self,* Lu. xvii. 33 (W. H.); *to get for one's self, purchase,* Ac. xx. 28; 1 Tim. iii. 13.*

4047 περι-ποίησις, εως, ἡ, (1) *a preserving,* Heb. x. 39; (2) *an obtaining, a possessing,* 1 Th. v. 9; 2 Th. ii. 14; (3) *a possession,* Ep. i. 14; 1 Pet. ii. 9.

4048 περι-ρρήγνυμι, *to tear off,* as garments, Ac. xvi. 22.*

4049 περι-σπάω, ῶ, *to drag around;* hence, fig., pass., *to be distracted in mind,* Lu. x. 40.*

4050 περισσεία, ας, ἡ, *abundance, superfluity,* Ro. v. 17; 2 Cor. viii. 2; Ja. i. 21; εἰς περισσείαν, as adv., *abundantly,* 2 Cor. x. 15.*

4051 περίσσευμα, ατος, τό, *abundance,* Mat. xii. 34; Lu. vi. 45; 2 Cor. viii. 14; pl. *a residue,* Mar. viii. 8.*

4052 περισσεύω, εύσω, *to be more than enough, to remain over, to be in abundance,* Lu. xii. 15; Jn. vi. 12; τὸ περισσεῦον, *the residue,* Mat. xiv. 20; *to redound to,* εἰς, 2 Cor. viii. 2; *to make to abound,* Mat. xiii. 12; 2 Cor. iv. 15.

4053 περισσός, ή, όν, *abundant, more than is necessary,* Mat. v. 37; Mar. vii. 36; *superior,* Mat. v. 47; τὸ περισσόν, *excellence, pre-eminence,* Ro. iii. 1.

★

4056 περισσοτέρως, adv. (compar. of περισσῶς), *more abundantly, more earnestly,* 2 Cor. vii. 13, 15.

4057 περισσῶς, adv., *greatly, exceedingly,* Mar. x. 26.

4058 περιστερά, ᾶς, ἡ, *a dove,* Mat. iii. 16, x. 16.

4059 περι-τέμνω, *to cut around, to circumcise,* Lu. i. 59; pass. and mid., *to undergo circumcision, to cause one's self to be circumcised,* 1 Cor. vii. 18.

4060 περι-τίθημι, *to place,* or *put about* or *around* (dat. and acc.), Mat. xxi. 33; fig., *to bestow, to confer,* 1 Cor. xii. 23.

4061 περι-τομή, ῆς, ἡ, *circumcision,* the act, the custom, or state, Jn. v. 22, 23; Gal. v. 6; with art., *the circumcision, i.e.,* the Jews, Ro. iii. 30, iv. 9, 12; fig., for *spiritual purity,* Ro. ii. 29; Col. ii. 11. (S.)

4062 περι-τρέπω, *to turn about, to turn* into (εἰς) madness, Ac. xxvi. 24.*

4063 περι-τρέχω, 2d aor. περιέδραμον, *to run around* (acc.), Mar. vi. 55.*

4064 περι-φέρω, *to bear* or *carry around,* Mar. vi. 55; 2 Cor. iv. 10; pass., fig., *to be carried about, carried away* by false teaching, Ep. iv. 14; Heb. xiii. 9; Ju. 12 (W. H., in last two, παραφέρω).*

4065 περι-φρονέω, ῶ, *to look down upon, to despise,* Tit. ii. 15.*

4066 περί-χωρος, ον, *lying round about;* only as subst., ἡ περίχωρος (sc. γῆ), *the region round about,* Lu. iii. 3, iv. 14; *the inhabitants of such a region,* Mat. iii. 5.

4067 περί-ψημα, ατος, τό, *scrapings, offscourings,* 1 Cor. iv. 13.*

4068 περπερεύομαι, dep., intrans., *to boast,* 1 Cor. xiii. 4.*

4069 Περσίς, ίδος, ἡ, *Persis,* Ro. xvi. 12.*

4070 πέρυσι, adv., *last year;* ἀπὸ πέρυσι, *a year ago,* 2 Cor. viii. 10, ix. 2.*

●4072▫ πετάομαι, ῶμαι, or πέτομαι (W. H.), *to fly,* as a bird, Rev.*

4071 πετεινόν, οῦ, τό, *a bird;* only in plur., *birds,* Mat. vi. 26, xiii. 4.

4072▫ πέτομαι, see πετάομαι.

4073 πέτρα, ας, ἡ, *a rock, a ledge, cliff,* Mat. vii. 24, 25, xxvii. 51; with art., *the rock, i.e.,* the rocky substratum of the soil, Lu. viii. 6, 13; *a large*

★ **For 4054 & 4055 see Strong.**

4074 detached *rock*, fig., Ro. ix. 33; see also Mat. xvi. 18.
Πέτρος, ου, ὁ, *Peter* (prop., a rock = Κηφᾶς), Lu. iv. 38; Jn. i. 42.

4075 πετρώδης, ες, *rocky, stony*, Mat. xiii. 5, 20; Mar. iv. 5, 16.*

4076 πήγανον, ου, τό, *rue*, Lu. xi. 42.*

4077 πηγή, ῆς, ἡ, *a fountain, spring*, Jn. iv. 14; Ja. iii. 11; fig., Rev. vii. 17; *a flow* of blood, Mar. v. 29.

4078 πήγνυμι, πήξω, *to fasten, to pitch* a tent, Heb. viii. 2.*

4079 πηδάλιον, ου, τό, *the rudder* of a ship, Ac. xxvii. 40; Ja. iii. 4.*

4080 πηλίκος, η, ον, *how large*, Gal. vi. 11 (see γράμμα); *how distinguished*, Heb. vii. 4.*

4081 πηλός, οῦ, ὁ, *clay, mud*, Jn. ix. 6-15; Ro. ix. 21.*

4082 πήρα, ας, ἡ, *a sack, a wallet*, for carrying provisions, Mat. x. 10; Mar. vi. 8; Lu. ix. 3, x. 4, xxii. 35, 36.*

4083 πῆχυς, εως, ὁ, *a cubit*, the length from the elbow to the tip of the middle finger, *about a foot and a half*, Mat. vi. 27; Lu. xii. 25; Jn. xxi. 8; Rev. xxi. 17.*

4084 πιάζω, σω, *to lay hold of*, Ac. iii. 7; *to take*, as in fishing or in hunting, Jn. xxi. 3, 10; Rev. xix. 20; *to arrest*, Jn. vii. 30.

4085 πιέζω, *to press together*, as in a measure, Lu. vi. 38.*

4086 πιθανο-λογία, ας, ἡ, *persuasive* or *plausible speech*, Col. ii. 4.*

4087 πικραίνω, ανῶ, *to render bitter*, lit., Rev. viii. 11, x. 9, 10; *to embitter*, fig., Col. iii. 19.*

4088 πικρία, ας, ἡ, *bitterness*, fig., Ac. viii. 23; Ro. iii. 14; Ep. iv. 31; Heb. xii. 15.*

4089 πικρός, ά, όν, *bitter, acrid, malignant*, Ja. iii. 11, 14.*

4090 πικρῶς, adv., *bitterly*, of weeping, Mat. xxvi. 75; Lu. xxii. 12.*

4091 Πιλᾶτος, or Πιλάτος (W. H Πειλᾶτος), ου, ὁ (Lat. *pilatus*, "armed with a javelin"), *Pilate*, Mar. xv. 1, 2.

•4130; see Strong πίμπλημι, πλήσω, 1st aorist pass., ἐπλήσθην, (1) *to fill* with (gen.), Mat. xxvii. 48; fig., of emotions, Lu. iv. 28; or of the Holy Spirit, Ac. ii.

4; (2) pass., *to be fulfilled* or *completed*, of time, Lu. i. 23, 57.

4092 πίμπρημι (πρα-), and πιμπράω, pass., inf., πίμπρασθαι, *to be inflamed, to swell*, Ac. xxviii. 6.*

4093 πινακίδιον, ου, τό (dim. of πίναξ), *a tablet for writing*, Lu. i. 63.*

4094 πίναξ, ακος, ὁ, *a plate, platter*, Lu. xi. 39.

4095 πίνω, fut. πίομαι, perf. πέπωκα, 2d aor. ἔπιον (inf. πεῖν, W. H.), *to drink*, abs., or with acc. of thing drunk (sometimes ἐκ or ἀπό), Lu. xii. 19, 29; *to imbibe*, as the earth imbibes rain, Heb. vi. 7; fig., *to receive into the soul, to partake of*, Jn. vii. 37.

4096 πιότης, τητος, ἡ, *fatness*, as of the olive, Ro. xi. 17.*

4097 πιπράσκω (πρα-), perf. πέπρακα, 1st aor. pass. ἐπράθην, perf. pass. πέπραμαι, *to sell*, Mat. xiii. 46; pass., with ὑπό, *to be sold under*, *to be a slave to*, Ro. vii. 14.

4098 πίπτω (πετ-, see Gr. § 94, i. 8 *d*, Wi. § 13, 1 *a*, Bu. 167), πεσοῦμαι, (1) *to fall* (whence, by ἀπό or ἐκ; whither, by ἐπί or εἰς, acc.), Mat. xv. 27; Mar. iv. 5, 7, 8; hence, (2) *to fall prostrate*, as of persons, *to die, to perish*, Jn. xviii. 6; Rev. i. 17; of structures, *to fall in ruins*, Mat. vii. 25, 27; of institutions, *to fail*; (3) *to fall to*, as a lot, Ac. i. 26; (4) *to fall into* or *under*, as condemnation.

4099 Πισιδία, ας, ἡ, *Pisidia*, Ac. xiv. 24, xiii 14, where W. H. have adj. form.*

4100 πιστεύω (see Gr. § 74, Wi. §§ 31, 5, 32, 5, 33 *d*, 39, 1 *a*, Bu. 173 sq., 337), εύσω, *to believe, be persuaded* of a thing (acc. or ὅτι); *to give credit to*, dat.; *to have confidence in, to trust, believe*, dat., εἰς, ἐν, ἐπί (dat.) or ἐπί (acc.), often of Christian faith, in God, in Christ; *to entrust* something (acc.) to any one (dat.); pass., *to be entrusted with* (acc.).

4101 πιστικός, ή, όν, *genuine, pure*, of ointment, Mar. xiv. 3; Jn. xii. 3.*

4102 πίστις, εως, ἡ, (1) *faith*, generally, as 2 Th. ii. 13; Heb. xi.

119

1 ; the object of the faith is expressed by obj. gen., or by εἰς, ἐν, πρός (acc.) ; (2) *fidelity, good faith*, Ro. iii. 3; 2 Tim. ii. 22; (3) *a pledge, a promise given*, 2 Tim. iv. 7 ; (4) met., for the whole of the *Christian character*, and (generally with art.) for the *Christian religion*.

4103 πιστός, ή, όν, (1) *trustworthy, faithful*, in any relation or to any promise, of things or (generally) persons ; (2) *believing*, abs., as οἱ πιστοί, *the followers of Christ*, or with dat.

4104 πιστόω, ῶ, *to make faithful;* N. T., only in pass., *to be assured of*, 2 Tim. iii. 14.*

4105 πλανάω, ῶ, ήσω, *to lead astray, to cause to wander*, Heb. xi. 38; fig., *to deceive*, Jn. vii.12; pass., *to be misled, to err*, Mar. xii. 24, 27 ; Lu. xxi. 8.

4106 πλάνη, ης, ή, *a wandering;* only fig., *deceit, delusion, error*, Mat. xxvii. 64 ; Ep. iv. 14.

4107 πλανήτης, ου, ὁ, *a wanderer; ἀστὴρ πλανήτης, a wandering star*, Ju. 13.*

4108 πλάνος, ον, *causing to wander, misleading*, 1 Tim. iv. 1 ; as subst., *a deceiver*, Mat. xxvii. 63 ; 2 Cor. vi. 8; 2 Jn. 7.*

4109 πλάξ, ακός, ή, *a tablet* to write on, 2 Cor. iii. 3 ; Heb. ix. 4.*

4110 πλάσμα, ατος, τό, *a thing formed* or *fashioned*, Ro. ix. 20.*

4111 πλάσσω, άσω, *to form, mould*, as a potter his clay, Ro. ix. 20; 1 Tim. ii. 13.*

4112 πλαστός, ή, όν, *formed, moulded;* fig., *feigned*, 2 Pet. ii. 3.*

4113 πλατεῖα, ας, ή (fem. of πλατύς, *broad*, sc. ὁδός), *a street*, Mat. vi. 5, xii. 19.

4114 πλάτος, ους, τό, *breadth*, Ep. iii. 18 ; Rev. xx. 9, xxi. 16.*

4115 πλατύνω, *to make broad, to enlarge*, Mat. xxiii. 5 ; pass., fig., *to be enlarged*, in mind or heart, 2 Cor. vi. 11, 13.*

4116 πλατύς, εῖα, ύ, *broad*, Mat. vii. 13.*

4117 πλέγμα, ατος, τό (πλέκω), *anything interwoven, braided hair*, 1 Tim. ii. 9.*

4118 πλεῖστος, η, ον, superl. of πολύς,

the greatest, the most, very great; τὸ πλεῖστον, adv., mostly, at most, 1 Cor. xiv. 27.

4119 πλείων, εῖον (for declension see Gr. § 44, Bu. 127), compar. of πολύς, *more, greater*, in number, magnitude, comparison ; *οἱ πλείονες, οἱ πλείους, the more, the most, the many, majority*, 2 Cor. ii. 6; πλεῖον οἱ πλέον, as adv., *more*, Jn. xxi. 15; *ἐπὶ πλεῖον, further, longer*, Ac. iv. 17.

4120 πλέκω, ξω, *to weave together, to plait*, Mat. xxvii. 29; Mar. xv. 17; Jn. xix. 2.*

see 4119 πλέον, see πλείων.

4121 πλεονάζω, σω, intrans., *to have more than enough*, 2 Cor. viii. 15 ; *to abound, to increase*, Ro. v. 20; 2 Cor. iv. 15 ; trans., *to cause to increase*, 1 Th. iii. 12.

4122 πλεονεκτέω, ῶ, *to have more than another; hence, to overreach, take advantage of* (R. V.), 2 Cor. vii. 2, xii. 17, 18; 1 Th. iv. 6; pass., 2 Cor. ii. 11.*

4123 πλεον-έκτης, ου, ὁ, *a covetous* or *avaricious person*, 1 Cor. v. 10, 11, vi. 10; Ep. v. 5.*

4124 πλεονεξία, ας, ή, *covetousness, avarice*, Lu. xii. 15; 2 Pet. ii. 3. *Syn.:* πλεονεξία is more active, seeking to grasp the things it has not ; φιλαργυρία, more passive, seeking to retain and multiply what it has.

4125 πλευρά, ᾶς, ή, *the side* of the body, Jn. xix. 34.

see 4130 πλέω, see πίμπλημι.

4126 πλέω, impf. ἔπλεον, *to sail*, Lu. viii. 23 ; Ac. xxi. 3, xxvii. 6, 24; Rev. xviii. 17 (W. H.) ; with acc. of direction, Ac. xxvii. 2 (but W. H. read εἰς).*

4127 πληγή, ῆς, ή (πλήσσω), *a blow, a stripe, a wound*, Ac. xvi. 33; Rev. xiii. 14 ; *an affliction*, Rev. ix. 20.

4128 πλῆθος, ους, τό, *a multitude, a great number*, Mar. iii. 7, 8; Heb. xi. 12; with art., *the multitude, the whole number, the assemblage*, Ac. xiv. 4 ; *a quantity*, Ac. xxviii. 3.

4129 πληθύνω, νῶ, (1) intrans., *to increase*, Ac. vi. 1 ; (2) trans., *to multiply, augment*, 2 Cor.

4130 · ix. 10; pass., *to be increased*,
see on Mat. xxiv. 12.
p. 119 πλήθω, see πίμπλημι.
4131 πλήκτης, ου, ὁ, *a striker, a contentious person*, 1 Tim. iii. 3;
Tit. i. 7.*
4132 πλημμύρα, ας (W. H. ης), ἡ, *a flood*, Lu. vi. 48.*
4133 πλήν, adv. (akin to πλέον, hence it *adds* a thought, generally adversative, sometimes partly confirmatory), *besides, but, nevertheless, of a truth*, Mat. xi. 22, xviii. 7, xxvi. 39, 64; πλὴν ὅτι, *except that*, Ac. xx. 23; as prep. with gen., *besides, excepting*, Mar. xii. 32; Ac. viii. 1.
4134 πλήρης, ες, (1) *full*, abs., Mar. iv. 28; (2) *full of* (gen.), *abounding in*, Mar. viii. 19; Lu. iv. 1.
4135 πληρο-φορέω, ῶ (φέρω), *to bring to the full, to fulfill*, 2 Tim. iv. 5, 17; pass., of things, *to be fully accomplished*, Lu. i. 1; of persons, *to be fully convinced*, Ro. iv. 21, xiv. 5; Col. iv. 12 (W. H.).*
4136 πληρο-φορία, ας, ἡ, *fullness, entire possession, full assurance*, Col. ii. 2; 1 Th. i. 5; Heb. vi. 11, x. 22. (N. T.)*
4137 πληρόω, ῶ, ώσω, *to fill* with (gen.), *to fill up, to pervade, to complete*, either time or number; *to bestow abundantly, to furnish liberally*, Phil. iv. 18; Ep. iii. 19; *to accomplish, to perform fully*, as prophecies, etc.; pass., *to be full of*, 2 Cor. vii. 4; Ep. v. 18; *to be made full, complete*, or *perfect*, Jn. iii. 29; Col. iv. 12 (W. H. read πληρο-φορέω).
4138 πλήρωμα, ατος, τό, *fullness, plenitude, i.e.*, that which fills, 1 Cor. x. 26, 28; so, *the full number*, Ro. xi. 25; *the completion, i.e.*, that which makes full, *the fulfillment*, Mat. ix. 16; Ro. xiii. 10; *the fullness of time*, Gal. iv. 4, is the completion of an era; *the fullness of Christ*, Ep. i. 23, that which is filled by Christ, *i.e.*, the Church; *the fullness of the Godhead*, Col. ii. 9, all divine attributes.
4139 πλησίον, adv., *near, near by*, with gen., Jn. iv. 5; with the art., ὁ πλησίον, *a neighbor*, Ac. vii. 27.
4140 πλησμονή, ῆς, ἡ, *full satisfying, indulgence*, Col. ii. 23.*
4141 πλήσσω, 2d aor. pass. ἐπλήγην, *to smite*, Rev. viii. 12.*
4142 πλοιάριον, ου, τό (dim. of πλοῖον), *a small vessel, a boat*, Mar. iii. 9; Jn. xxi. 8.
4143 πλοῖον, ου, τό, *a ship, a vessel*, Mat. iv. 21, 22; Mar. i. 19.
4144 πλόος, οῦς, gen. οῦ or οός, ὁ, *a voyage*, Ac. xxi. 7, xxvii. 9, 10.*
4145 πλούσιος, α, ον, *rich, abounding in* (ἐν), Lu. xii. 16; Ep. ii. 4.
4146 πλουσίως, adv., *richly, abundantly*, Col. iii. 16.
4147 πλουτέω, ῶ, ήσω, *to become rich, to be rich, to abound in*, Lu. i. 53; Ro. x. 12; Rev. xviii. 15.
4148 πλουτίζω, *to make rich, to cause to abound in*, 1 Cor. i. 5; 2 Cor. vi. 10, ix. 11.*
4149 πλοῦτος, ου, ὁ (see Gr. § 32 a, Wi. § 9 e, note 2, Bu. 22), *riches, wealth, abundance*, Ja. v. 2; Col. i. 27; spiritually, *enrichment*, Ro. xi. 12.
4150; see πλύνω, νῶ, *to wash*, Lu. v. 2
3068 (W. H.); Rev. vii. 14, xxii. 14 (W. H.). *Syn.*: see λούω.
4151 πνεῦμα, ατος, τό, (1) properly, *the wind*, or *the air in motion*, Jn. iii. 8; hence, (2) *the human spirit*, dist. from σῶμα and ψυχή, 1 Th. v. 23; (3) *a temper* or *disposition* of the soul, Lu. ix. 55; Ro. viii. 15; (4) *any intelligent, incorporeal being*, as (a) *the human spirit*, separated from the body, *the undying soul;* (b) *angels*, good and bad; (c) *God*, Jn. iv. 24; (d) *the Holy Spirit*, the third person of the Trinity (see Gr. § 217 f, Wi. § 19, 1 a, Bu. 89), in relation to Jesus, Lu. iv. 1; Ac. x. 38; in relation to prophets and apostles, Ac. xxi. 11; Jn. xx. 22; and in relation to saints generally, Gal. iii. 2.
4152 πνευματικός, ή, όν, *spiritual*, relating to the human spirit, or belonging to a spirit, or imparted by the divine Spirit, 1 Cor. ii. 13 (see Gr. § 316, Wi. § 64, 5), 15, xv. 44; τὰ πνευματικά, *spiritual things*, Ro. xv. 27; *spiritual gifts*, 1 Cor. xii. 1.

4153 πνευματικῶς, adv., *spiritually*, *i.e.*, by the aid of the Holy Spirit, 1 Cor. ii. 14; in a mystical sense, Rev. xi. 8. (N. T.)*

4154 πνέω, εύσω, *to blow*, as the wind, Mat. vii. 25, 27.

4155 πνίγω, *to choke, to seize by the throat*, Mat. xviii. 28; Mar. v. 13.*

4156 πνικτός, ή, όν, *strangled*, Ac. xv. 20, 29; xxi. 25.

4157 πνοή, ῆς, ἡ, (1) *breath*, Ac. xvii. 25; (2) *wind*, Ac. ii. 2.*

4158 ποδήρης, ες, *reaching to the feet;* as subst. (sc. χιτών or ἐσθής), *a long robe*, Rev. i. 13.* *Syn.*. see ἱμάτιον.

4159 πόθεν, adv., interrog., *whence?* of place, Mat. xv. 33; *from what source?* Mat. xiii. 27; of cause, *how?* Lu. i. 43; Mar. xii. 37.

see 4169 ποία, ας, ἡ, *grass, herbage*, according to some, in Ja. iv. 14; but more probably the word here is the fem. of ποῖος, *of what sort?* *

4160 ποιέω, ῶ, ἡσω, (1) *to make, i.e., to form, to bring about, to cause;* spoken of religious festivals, etc., *to observe, to celebrate;* of trees and plants, *to germinate, to produce; to cause to be* or *to become*, Mat. xxi. 13; *to declare to be*, Jn. viii. 53; *to assume*, Mat. xii. 33; (2) *to do*, generally; *to do, i.e.*, habitually, *to perform, to execute, to exercise, to practice, i.e., to pursue a course of action, to be active, to work, to spend, to pass, i.e.*, time or life, Ac. xv. 33. *Syn.*: see Trench, § xcvi.

4161 ποίημα, ατος, τό, *a thing made, a work*, Ro. i. 20; Ep. ii. 10.*

4162 ποίησις, εως, ἡ, *a doing*, Ja. i. 25.*

4163 ποιητής, οῦ, ὁ, (1) *a doer, performer*, Ro. ii. 13; Ja. i. 22, 23, 25, iv. 11; (2) *a poet*, Ac. xvii. 28.*

4164 ποικίλος, η, ον, *various, of different colors, diverse*, Lu. iv. 40.

4165: see 1006 ποιμαίνω, ανῶ, (1) *to feed a flock*, Lu. xvii. 7; 1 Cor. ix. 7; hence, fig., (2) *to be shepherd of, to tend, to cherish*. Mat. ii. 6; Jn. xxi. 16; Ac. xx. 28; 1 Pet. v. 2; Ju. 12;

Rev. vii. 17; (3) *to rule, govern*, Rev. ii. 27, xii. 5, xix. 15.* *Syn.*: see βόσκω.

4166 ποιμήν, ένος, ὁ, (1) *a shepherd*, Mat. ix. 36, xxv. 32; (2) fig., of Christ as the *Shepherd*, Heb. xiii. 20; 1 Pet. ii. 25; and of his ministers as *pastors*, Ep. iv. 11

4167 ποίμνη, ης, ἡ, (1) *a flock* of sheep or goats, Lu. ii. 8; 1 Cor. ix. 7; (2) fig., of Christ's followers, Mat. xxvi. 31; Jn. x. 16.*

4168 ποίμνιον, ου, τό (= ποίμνη), *a flock;* only fig., Lu. xii. 32; Ac. xx. 28, 29; 1 Pet. v. 2, 3.*

4169 ποῖος, ποία, ποῖον, an interrog. pronoun corresponding to οἷος and τοῖος, *of what kind, sort, species? what? what one?* In Lu. v. 19, sc. ὁδοῦ.

4170 πολεμέω, ῶ, ἡσω, *to make war, to contend* with (μετά, gen.), Rev. ii. 16, xiii. 4.

4171 πόλεμος, ου, ὁ, (1) *war, a war*, Lu. xiv. 31; (2) *a battle*, Rev. ix. 7, 9; (3) *strife*, Ja. iv. 1.

4172 πόλις, εως, ἡ, *a city*, Ac. v. 16; met., *the inhabitants of a city*, Mar. i. 33; with art., *the city Jerusalem, the heavenly city*, of which Jerusalem was a symbol, Heb. xiii. 14; Rev. iii. 12.

4173 πολιτ-άρχης, ου, ὁ, *a ruler of a city, a city magistrate*, Ac. xvii. 6, 8.*

4174 πολιτεία, ας, ἡ, (1) *citizenship*, Ac. xxii. 28; (2) *a state, commonwealth*, Ep. ii. 12.*

4175 πολίτευμα, ατος, τό, *a state, a commonwealth*, Phil. iii. 20.*

4176 πολιτεύω, in mid., *to behave as a citizen;* hence, *to live, i.e., to order one's life*, Ac. xxiii. 1; Phil. i. 27.*

4177 πολίτης, ου, ὁ, *a citizen*, Lu. xv. 15; Ac. xxi. 39; with gen., αὐτοῦ, *a fellow-citizen*, Lu. xix. 14; Heb. viii. 11 (W. H.).*

4178 πολλάκις, adv., *many times, often*, Mar. v. 4, ix. 22.

4179 πολλα-πλασίων, ον, gen. ονος, *manifold, many times more*, Mat. xix. 29 (W. H.); Lu. xviii. 30.*

4180 πολυ-λογία, ας, ἡ, *much speaking*, Mat. vi. 7.*

4181 πολυ-μερῶς, adv., *in many*

parts, by many portions, Heb. i. 1.*

4182 πολυ-ποίκιλος, ον, much varied, manifold, Ep. iii. 10.*

4183 πολύς, πολλή, πολύ (see Gr. § 39, 2), many, numerous; πολύ, much, greatly, as adv.; πολλοί, many, often with partitive genitive, or ἐκ; οἱ πολλοί, the many (see Gr. § 227, Wi. § 18, 3); πολλά, in like manner, much, very much, often, many times; πολλῷ, by much, joined with comparatives; ἐπὶ πολύ, for a great while, Ac. xxviii. 6; ἐν πολλῷ, altogether, Ac.xxvi. 29 (not W. H.).

4184 πολύ-σπλαγχνος, ον, very compassionate, of great mercy, Ja. v. 11. (N. T.)*

4185 πολυ-τελής, ές, very costly, very precious, Mar. xiv. 3; 1 Tim. ii. 9; 1 Pet. iii. 4.*

4186 πολύ-τιμος, ον, of great value, very costly, Mat. xiii. 46; Jn. xii. 3; compar., 1 Pet. i. 7 (W. H.).*

4187 πολυ-τρόπως, adv., in many ways, Heb. i. 1.*

4188 πόμα, ατος, τό, drink, 1 Cor. x. 4; Heb. ix. 10.*

4189 πονηρία, ας, ἡ, evil disposition, wickedness, Mat. xxii. 18; Lu. xi. 39; Ro. i. 29; 1 Cor. v. 8; Ep. vi. 12; plur., malignant passions, iniquities, Mar. vii. 22; Ac. iii. 26.*

4190 πονηρός, ά, όν (πόνος), evil, bad, actively, of things or persons; wicked, depraved, spec. malignant, opp. to ἀγαθός; ὁ πονηρός, the wicked one, i.e., Satan; τὸ πονηρόν, evil.

★

4192 πόνος, ου, ὁ, (1) labor, Col. iv. 13 (W. H.); (2) pain, anguish, Rev. xvi. 10, 11, xxi. 4.*

4193 Ποντικός, ή, όν, belonging to Pontus, Ac. xviii. 2.*

4194 Πόντιος, ου, ὁ, Pontius, the prænomen of Pilate, Lu. iii. 1.

4195 Πόντος, ου, ὁ, Pontus, Ac. ii. 9; 1 Pet. i. 1.*

4196 Πόπλιος, ου, ὁ, Publius, Ac. xxviii. 7, 8.*

4197 πορεία, ας, ἡ, a journey, Lu. xiii. 22; a pursuit, undertaking, Ja. i. 11.*

4198 πορεύομαι, σομαι, dep., with pass. aor., ἐπορεύθην, to go, to go away, to depart, to journey,

to travel, often (as Hebrew) to take a course in life.

4199 πορθέω, ήσω, to lay waste, to destroy, Ac. ix. 21; Gal. i. 13, 23.*

4200 πορισμός, οῦ, ὁ, a source of gain, 1 Tim. vi. 5, 6.*

4201 Πόρκιος, ου, ὁ, Porcius, the prænomen of Festus, Ac. xxiv. 27.*

4202 πορνεία, ας, ἡ, fornication, Ac. xv. 20, 29; fig. in Rev., idolatry, xiv. 8, xvii. 2, 4.

4203 πορνεύω, σω, to commit fornication, 1 Cor. vi. 18; fig. in Rev., to worship idols, xviii. 3, 9.

4204 πόρνη, ης, ἡ, a harlot, a prostitute, Mat. xxi. 31, 32; fig. in Rev., an idolatrous community, xvii. 1, 5.

4205 πόρνος, ου, ὁ, a man who prostitutes himself; a fornicator, Ep. v. 5.

4206 •**4208** πόρρω, adv., far, far off, Mat. xv. 8; Mar. vii. 6; Lu. xiv. 32; comp., πορρωτέρω (or -τερον, W. H.), Lu. xxiv. 28.*

4207 πόρρωθεν, adv., from afar, far off, Lu. xvii. 12; Heb. xi. 13.*

4209 πορφύρα, ας, ἡ, a purple garment, indicating wealth or rank, Mar. xv. 17, 20; Lu. xvi. 19; Rev. xvii. 4 (W. H. read following), xviii. 12.*

4210 πορφύρεος, οῦς, ᾶ, οῦν, purple, Jn. xix. 2, 5; Rev. xvii. 4 (W. H.), xviii. 16.*

4211 πορφυρό-πωλις, ιδος, ἡ, a female seller of purple cloth, Ac. xvi. 14. (N. T.)*

4212 ποσάκις, interrog. adv., how often? Mat. xviii. 21, xxiii. 37; Lu. xiii. 34.*

4213 πόσις, εως, ἡ, drink, Jn. vi. 55; Ro. xiv. 17; Col. ii. 16.*

4214 πόσος, η, ον, how much? how great? plur., how many? πόσῳ, as adv. with comparatives, by how much?

4215 ποταμός, οῦ, ὁ, a river, a torrent, Mar. i. 5; Lu. vi. 48, 49.

4216 ποταμο-φόρητος, ον, carried away by a stream, Rev. xii. 15. (N. T.)*

4217 ποταπός, ή, όν, interrog. adj., of what kind? of what manner? Lu. i. 29, vii. 39.

•4219 πότε, interrog. adv., when? at what time? with ἕως, how long?

4218 ποτέ, enclitic particle, at some

123

time, at one time or other
(see Gr. § 129, Wi. § 57, 2).

4220 πότερος, a, ον, *which of two?*
N. T. neut. as adv., *whether,*
correlating with ἤ, *or,* Jn. vii.
17.*

4221 ποτήριον, ου, τό, *a drinking-*
cup, Mar. vii. 4, xiv. 23; *the*
contents of the cup, 1 Cor. xi.
25; fig., *the portion which*
God allots, whether of good
or ill, commonly of the latter, Mat. xx. 22, 23, xxvi. 39.

4222 ποτίζω, σω, *to cause to drink*
(two accs.); *to give drink to*
(acc.); fig., 1 Cor. iii. 2; *to*
water or *irrigate,* as plants,
1 Cor. iii. 6–8.

4223 Ποτίολοι, ων, οἱ, *Puteoli,* Ac.
xxviii. 13.*

4224 πότος, ου, ὁ (πίνω), *a drinking,*
carousing, 1 Pet. iv. 3.*

•4226 ποῦ, interrog. adv., *where?*
whither? Mat. ii. 4; Jn. vii.
35.

4225 πού, an enclitic particle of
place or degree, *somewhere,*
somewhere about, Heb. ii. 6,
16 (W. H., see δήπου), iv. 4;
Ro. iv. 19 (see Gr. § 129, Bu.
71).*

4227 Πούδης, δεντος, ὁ, *Pudens,* 2
Tim. iv. 21.*

4228 πούς, ποδός, ὁ, *the foot,* Lu. i.
79; ὑπὸ τοὺς πόδας, *under*
the feet, i.e., entirely subdued,
as Ro. xvi. 20.

4229 πρᾶγμα, ατος, τό, *a thing done,*
a fact, a thing, a business, a
suit, as at law, Lu. i. 1; 1 Th.
iv. 6; Ro. xvi. 2; Heb. x. 1.

4230 πραγματεία (W. H. -τία), ας, ἡ,
a business, occupation, 2 Tim.
ii. 4.*

4231 πραγματεύομαι, σομαι, dep., *to*
transact business, to trade,
Lu. xix. 13.*

4232 πραιτώριον, ου, τό (Lat. *præ-*
torium), *the palace* at Jerusalem occupied by the Ro-
man governor, Mat. xxvii.
27; Mar. xv. 16; Jn. xviii.
28, 33, xix. 9; so at Cæsarea,
Ac. xxiii. 35; *the quarters of*
the prætorian army in Rome,
Phil. i. 13.*

4233 πράκτωρ, ορος, ὁ, *an officer em-*
ployed to execute judicial sen-
tences, Lu. xii. 58.*

4234 πρᾶξις, εως, ἡ, (1) *a doing,*
action, mode of action, Mat.
xvi. 27; Lu. xxiii. 51; plur.,
deeds, acts, Ac. xix. 18; Ro.

viii. 13; Col. iii. 9; and in
inscription to the Acts of
the Apostles; (2) *function,*
business, Ro. xii. 4.*

4235; see πρᾷος, a, ον, Rec. in Mat. xi.
4239 29 for πραΰς (W. H.).*

4236 πρᾳότης, τητος, ἡ, Rec. for
πραΰτης (W. H.) in 1 Cor.
iv. 21; 2 Cor. x. 1; Gal. v.
23, vi. 1; Ep. iv. 2; Col. iii.
12; 1 Tim. vi. 11 (W. H.
πραϋπάθια); 2 Tim. ii. 25;
Tit. iii. 2.*

4237 πρασιά, ᾶς, ἡ, *a company*
formed into divisions like
garden-beds, Mar. vi. 40.*
For constr., see Gr. § 242,
Wi. § 37, 3, Bu. 30, 139.

4238 πράσσω, or πράττω, ξω, pf.
πέπραχα, πέπραγμαι, (1) *to*
do, perform, accomplish, with
acc., 1 Th. iv. 11; 2 Cor. v.
10; (2) with advs., *to be in*
any condition, i.e., to fare,
Ac. xv. 29; Ep. vi. 21; (3) *to*
exact, to require, Lu. iii. 13.
Syn.: see ποιέω.

see 4236 πραϋ-παθεία (or ία), ας, ἡ (W.
H.), *mildness,* 1 Tim. vi. 11.*

4239 πραΰς, εῖα, ύ, gen. έος or έως
(W. H.), pl. εῖς, *mild, gentle,*
Mat. v. 5, xi. 29 (see πρᾷος),
xxi. 5; 1 Pet. iii. 4.*

4240 πραΰτης, τητος, ἡ, *mildness,*
gentleness, Ja. i. 21, iii. 13;
1 Pet. iii. 15; and W. H.
(πραΰτης) in the passages
quoted under πρᾳότης.*

4241 πρέπω, *to become, be fitting to*
(dat.), 1 Tim. ii. 10; Tit. ii.
1; Heb. vii. 26; impers. (see
Gr. § 101, Bu. 278), *it be-*
comes, it is fitting to, Mat. iii.
15; 1 Cor. xi. 13; Ep. v. 3;
Heb. ii. 10.*

4242 πρεσβεία, ας, ἡ, *an embassy,*
ambassadors, Lu. xiv. 32,
xix. 14.*

4243 πρεσβεύω, from πρέσβυς (lit.,
to be aged, old men being
usually chosen for the office), *to act as ambassador,*
2 Cor. v. 20; Ep. vi. 20.*

4244 πρεσβυτέριον, ου, τό, *an assem-*
bly of elders, the Sanhedrin,
Lu. xxii. 66; Ac. xxii. 5;
officers of the church assem-
bled, presbytery, 1 Tim. iv.
14.*

4245 πρεσβύτερος, τέρα, τερον (compar. of πρέσβυς, *old*), generally used as subst., *elder,*
(1) in age, Ac. ii. 17; 1 Tim.

v. 1 ; plur., often, *ancestors,*
as Heb. xi. 2 ; (2) as subst.,
an elder, in dignity and office, *a member of the Jewish
Sanhedrin,* Mat. xvi. 21 ; *an
elder* of a Christian church,
Ac. xx. 17, 28 ; in Rev., of
the twenty-four *members of
the heavenly Sanhedrin,* iv.
4, 10

4246 πρεσβύτης, ου, ὁ, *an old man,*
Lu. i. 8 ; Tit. ii. 2 ; Philem.
9.*

4247 πρεσβῦτις, ιδος, ἡ, *an old woman,*
Tit. ii. 3.*

4248 πρηνής, ές, *falling headlong,*
Ac i. 18.*

4249 πρίζω, or πρίω, 1st aor. pass.
ἐπρίσθην, *to saw, to saw
asunder,* Heb. xi. 37.*

4250 πρίν, adv., of time, *formerly ;*
as conj. in N. T., with or
without ἤ, *before that ;* generally with acc. and inf.,
Mat. xxvi. 34 ; but after a
negative we find πρὶν ἄν
with subj. where the principal verb is in a primary
tense, Lu. ii. 26 ; πρίν with
opt. where it is in a histor-
ical tense, Ac. xxv. 16.

4251
4252 Πρίσκα, ης, ἡ, and dim. Πρισ-
κίλλα, ης, ἡ, a proper name,
Prisca or *Priscilla,* Ro. xvi.
3 ; 2 Tim. iv. 19.

4253 πρό, prep. with gen., *before, i.e.,*
of place, time, or superiority
(see Gr. § 294, Wi. § 47 d,
Bu. 153). In composition,
it retains the same mean-
ings.

4254 προ-άγω, άξω, *to bring out,* Ac
xvi. 30 ; gen. intrans., *to go
before, to lead the way, to
precede,* in place, Mat. ii. 9 ;
in time, Mar. vi. 45 ; part.
προάγων, *preceding, previous,*
1 Tim. i. 18 ; Heb. vii. 18.

4255 προ-αιρέω, ῶ, N. T., in mid., *to
propose to one's self, to pur-
pose,* 2 Cor. ix. 7.*

4256 προ-αιτιάομαι, ῶμαι, *to lay to
one's charge beforehand,* Ro.
iii. 9. (N. T.)*

4257 προ-ακούω, *to hear before,* Col.
i. 5.*

4258 προ-αμαρτάνω, *to sin before,* 2
Cor xii. 21, xiii. 2. (N. T.)*

4259 προ-αύλιον, ου, τό, *a court before a building, a porch,* Mar.
xiv. 68.*

4260 προ-βαίνω, *to go forward,* Mat.
iv. 21 ; Mar. i. 19 ; pf. part

προβεβηκὼς ἐν ἡμέραις, *advanced in age,* Lu. i. 7, 18, ii.
36.*

4261 προ-βάλλω, *to put forth,* as
trees their leaves, Lu. xxi.
30 ; *to thrust forward,* Ac.
xix. 33.*

4262 προβατικός, ή, όν, *pertaining to
sheep,* Jn. v. 2.*

see 4263 προβάτιον, ου, τό, dim. of following, *a little sheep, a lamb,*
Jn. xxi. 16, 17 (W. H.).*

4263 πρόβατον, ου, τό (προβαίνω), *a
sheep,* Mat. vii. 15 ; fig., *a
follower of Christ,* Jn. x.
7, 8.

4264 προ-βιβάζω, σω, *to drag forward, to urge forward,* Mat.
xiv. 8 ; Ac. xix. 33 (not W.
H.).*

4265 προ-βλέπω, N. T., in mid., *to
foresee* or *provide,* Heb. xi.
40. (S.)*

4266 προ-γίνομαι, *to happen before,*
Ro. iii. 25.*

4267 προ-γινώσκω, *to know beforehand,* Ac. xxvi. 5 ; 2 Pet. iii.
17 ; of the divine foreknowl-
edge, Ro. viii. 29, xi. 2 ; 1
Pet. i. 20.*

4268 πρόγνωσις, εως, ἡ, *foreknowl-
edge,* Ac. ii. 23 ; 1 Pet. i. 2.*

4269 πρό-γονος, ου, ὁ, *a progenitor,*
plur., *ancestors,* 1 Tim. v. 4 ;
2 Tim. i. 3.*

4270 προ-γράφω, ψω, *to write before,*
in time, Ro. xv. 4 ; Ep. iii.
3 ; *to depict* or *portray openly,*
Gal. iii. 1 ; *to designate beforehand,* Ju. 4.*

4271 πρό-δηλος, ον, *manifest to all,
evident,* 1 Tim. v. 24, 25 ;
Heb. vii. 14.*

4272 προ-δίδωμι, (1) *to give before,*
Ro. xi. 35 ; (2) *to give forth,
betray ;* see following word.*

4273 προδότης, ου, ὁ, *a betrayer,* Lu.
vi. 16 ; Ac. vii. 52 ; 2 Tim.
iii. 4.*

4274 πρό-δρομος, ου, ὁ, ἡ (προτρέχω),
a precursor, a forerunner,
Heb. vi. 20.*

see 4275St προ-εῖδον, 2d aor. of προοράω.

see 4253 προ-εῖπον, 2d aor. of πρόφημι,
& 2036St perf. προείρηκα.

4276 προ-ελπίζω, *to hope before,* Ep.
★ i. 12.*

4278 προ-εν-άρχομαι, *to begin before,*
2 Cor. viii. 6, 10. (N. T.)*

4279 προ-επ-αγγέλλω, in mid., *to pro-
★ mise before,* Ro. i. 2 ; 2 Cor.
ix. 5 (W. H.). (N. T.)*

4281 προ-έρχομαι (see Gr. § 103, 2,

★ For 4277 & 4280 see Strong.

Bu. 144), (1) *to go forward,
advance*, Ac. xii. 10; (2) *to
go before, precede*, in time or
place (gen. or acc.), Lu. xxii.
47; 2 Cor. ix. 5.

4282 προ-ετοιμάζω, σω, *to prepare
beforehand, to predestine*, Ro.
ix. 23; Ep. ii. 10.*

4283 προ-ευ-αγγελίζομαι, *to foretell
good tidings, preach the gos-
pel beforehand*, Gal. iii. 8.*

4284 προ-έχω, in mid., *to hold one's
self before, to be superior*,
Ro. iii. 9 (see Gr. § 358, Wi.
§ 39, 3, note 3).*

4285 προ-ηγέομαι, οῦμαι, *to lead on-
ward by example*, Ro. xii.
10.*

4286 πρόθεσις, εως, ἡ (προτίθημι), (1)
a setting forth; οἱ ἄρτοι τῆς
προθέσεως, *the loaves of the
presentation*, or *the show-
bread*, Mat. xii. 4, compare
Heb. ix. 2; (2) *a predetermi-
nation, purpose*, Ac. xi. 23.

4287 προ-θέσμιος, α, ον, *set beforehand, appointed before*, Gal.
iv. 2.*

4288 προ-θυμία, ας, ἡ, *inclination,
readiness*, Ac. xvii. 11; 2 Cor.
viii. 11, 12, 19, ix. 2.*

4289 πρό-θυμος, ον, *eager, ready, willing*, Mat. xxvi. 41; Mar. xiv.
38; τὸ πρόθυμον, *readiness*,
Ro. i. 15.*

4290 προθύμως, adv., *readily, with
alacrity*, 1 Pet. v. 2.*

see 4406 πρόϊμος, W. H., for πρώϊμος.

4291 προ-ίστημι, N.T. only intrans.,
act., 2d aor. and perf., and
mid., (1) *to preside over, to
rule*, gen., Ro. xii. 8; 1 Th.
v. 12; 1 Tim. iii. 4, 5, 12, v.
17; (2) *to give attention to*,
gen., Tit. iii. 8.*

4292 προ-καλέω, ῶ, in mid., *to provoke, stimulate*, Gal. v. 26.*

4293 προ-κατ-αγγέλλω, *to announce
beforehand, to promise*, Ac.
iii. 18, 24 (not W. H.), vii. 52;
2 Cor. ix. 5 (not W. H.).*

4294 προ-κατ-αρτίζω, *to prepare beforehand*, 2 Cor. ix. 5.*

4295 πρό-κειμαι, *to lie or be placed
before, to be appointed*, as
duty, example, reward, etc.,
Heb. vi. 18, xii. 1, 2; Ju. 7;
to be at hand, to be present, 2
Cor. viii. 12.*

4296 προ-κηρύσσω, ξω, *to announce
or preach beforehand*, Ac. iii.
20 (not W. H.), xiii. 24.*

4297 προ-κοπή, ῆς, ἡ, *progress, ad-*

vancement, Phil. i. 12, 25;
1 Tim. iv. 15.*

4298 προ-κόπτω, *to make progress in*
(dat. or ἐν), Lu. ii. 52; *to advance to* (ἐπί, acc.), 2 Tim.
iii. 9; of time, *to be advanced*
or *far spent*, Ro. xiii. 12.

4299 πρό-κριμα, ατος, τό, *a prejudg-
ment, a prejudice*, 1 Tim. v
21. (N. T.)*

4300 προ-κυρόω, ῶ, *to establish* or
ratify before, Gal. iii. 17.
(N. T.)*

4301 προ-λαμβάνω, *to take before,
anticipate*, Mar. xiv. 8 ("she
hath anticipated the anointing," *i.e.*, hath anointed beforehand); 1 Cor. xi. 21;
pass., *to be overtaken* or
caught, Gal. vi. 1.*

4302 προ-λέγω, *to tell beforehand,
forewarn*, 2 Cor. xiii. 2;
Gal. v. 21; 1 Th. iii. 4.*

4303 προ-μαρτύρομαι, *to testify beforehand, to predict*, 1 Pet. i.
11. (N. T.)*

4304 προ-μελετάω, ῶ, *to meditate beforehand*, Lu. xxi. 14.*

4305 προ-μεριμνάω, ῶ, *to be anxious
beforehand*, Mar. xiii. 11.
(N. T.)*

4306 προ-νοέω, ῶ, *to perceive beforehand, to provide for*, gen.,
1 Tim. v. 8; in mid., *to take
thought for*, acc., Ro. xii. 17;
2 Cor. viii. 21.*

4307 πρό-νοια, ας, ἡ, *forethought*, Ac.
xxiv. 3; *provision for* (gen.),
Ro. xiii. 14.*

4308 προ-οράω, ῶ, 2d aor. προεῖδον,
to see beforehand, Ac. ii. 31,
xxi. 29; Gal. iii. 8; mid., *to
have before one's eyes*, Ac. ii.
25 (S.).*

4309 προ-ορίζω, *to predetermine, to
foreordain*, Ac. iv. 28; Ro.
viii. 29, 30; 1 Cor. ii. 7; Ep.
i. 5, 11. (N. T.)*

4310 προ-πάσχω, *to suffer beforehand*, 1 Th. ii. 2.*

see 3962 προ-πάτωρ, ορος, ὁ, *a fore-
father*, Ro. iv. 1 (W. H.).*

4311 προ-πέμπω, *to send forward, to
accompany*, Ro. xv. 24; *to
equip for a journey*, Tit. iii.
13.

4312 προ-πετής, ές (πίπτω), *precipi-
tate, rash*, Ac. xix. 36; 2 Tim.
iii. 4.*

4313 προ-πορεύομαι, σομαι, in mid.,
to precede, to pass on before
(gen.), Lu. i. 76; Ac. vii. 40.*

4314 πρός (see Gr. § 307, Wi. §§ 47 f,

48 e, 49 h, Bu. 340), prep., gov. gen., dat., and accus. cases, general signif., towards. In composition, it denotes motion, direction, reference, nearness, addition.

4315 προ-σάββατον, ου, τό, the day before the sabbath, Mar. xv. 42. (S.)*

4316 προσ-αγορεύω, to address by name, to designate, Heb. v. 10.*

4317 προσ-άγω, (1) trans., to bring to, to bring near, Mat. xviii. 24 (W. H.); Lu. ix. 41; Ac. xii 6 (W. H.), xvi. 20; 1 Pet. iii. 18; (2) intrans., to come to or towards, to approach, Ac. xxvii. 27.*

4318 προσ-αγωγή, ῆς, ἡ, approach, access (εἰς, πρός, acc.), Ro. v. 2; Ep. ii. 18, iii. 12.*

4319 προσ-αιτέω, ῶ, to beg, to ask earnestly, Mar. x. 46 (not W. H.); Lu. xviii. 35 (not W. H.); Jn. ix. 8.*

see 4319 προσαίτης, ου, ὁ, a beggar, Mar. x. 46 (W. H.); Jn. ix. 8 (W. H.).*

4320 προσ-ανα-βαίνω, to go up farther, Lu. xiv. 10.*

4321 προσ-αναλίσκω, to spend in addition, Lu. viii. 43 (W. H. omit).*

4322 προσ-ανα-πληρόω, ῶ, to fill up by adding to, to supply, 2 Cor. ix. 12, xi. 9.*

4323 προσ-ανα-τίθημι, to lay up in addition; in mid., (1) to communicate or impart (acc. and dat.), Gal. ii. 6; (2) to consult with (dat.), Gal. i. 16.*

4324 προσ-απειλέω, ῶ, to utter additional threats, Ac. iv. 21.*

4325 προσ-δαπανάω, ῶ, ἥσω, to spend in addition, Lu. x. 35.*

4326 προσ-δέομαι, to want more, to need in addition (gen.), Ac. xvii. 25.*

4327 προσ-δέχομαι, dep. mid., (1) to receive to companionship, Lu. xv. 2; (2) to admit, accept, Heb. xi. 35; (3) to await, to expect (acc.), Mar. xv. 43.

4328 προσ-δοκάω, ῶ, to look for, expect, anticipate, whether with hope or fear, Lu. iii. 15, vii. 19, 20.

4329 προσδοκία, ας, ἡ, a looking for, expectation, Lu. xxi. 26; Ac. xii. 11.*

4330 προσ-εάω, ῶ, to permit one to approach, Ac. xxvii. 7. (N. T.)*

4331 προσ-εγγίζω, to approach, to come near to (dat.), Mar. ii. 4 (not W. H.).*

4332 προσεδρεύω, to wait upon, to minister to (dat.), 1 Cor. ix. 13 (W. H. παρεδρεύω).*

4333 προσ-εργάζομαι, dep. mid., to gain by labor in addition, Lu. xix. 16.*

4334 προσ-έρχομαι (see Gr. § 103, 2, Wi. § 52, 3, 4, 14)), (1) generally, to come or to go to, to approach, abs., or dat. of place or person, Mat. iv. 11, ix. 20, xxiv. 1; (2) specially, to approach, to draw near to, God or Christ, Heb. vii. 25; (3) to assent to, concur in, 1 Tim. vi. 3.

4335 προσ-ευχή, ῆς, ἡ, (1) prayer to God, 1 Cor. vii. 5; Col. iv. 2; (2) a place where prayer is offered, only Ac. xvi. 13, 16 (see Gr. § 268, note). Syn.: see αἴτημα.

4336 προσ-εύχομαι, dep. mid., to pray to God (dat.), to offer prayer, to pray for (acc. of thing, ὑπέρ or περί, of person, ἵνα or ὅπως, of object, occasionally inf.).

4337 προσ-έχω, ῶ, to apply, with νοῦν expressed or understood, to apply the mind, to attend to, dat.; with ἀπό, to beware of; also, to give heed to, inf. with μή.

4338 προσ-ηλόω, ῶ, to fasten with nails, nail to, Col. ii. 14.*

4339 προσ-ήλυτος, ου, ὁ (from προσ-έρχομαι, orig. adj.), a newcomer; a convert to Judaism, a proselyte, Mat. xxiii. 15; Ac. ii. 10, vi. 5, xiii. 43. (S.)*

4340 πρόσ-καιρος, ον, for a season, temporary, Mat. xiii. 21; Mar. iv. 17; 2 Cor. iv. 18; Heb. xi. 25.*

4341 προσ-καλέω, ῶ, N. T., mid., to call to one's self, to call for, to summon, Mar. iii. 13, 23, vi. 7; fig., to call to an office, to call to the Christian faith, Ac. ii. 39, xiii. 2.

4342 προσ-καρτερέω, ῶ, ἥσω, to persevere in, to continue steadfast in (dat.), Ac. i. 14, ii. 42; to wait upon (dat.), Mar. iii. 9; Ac. x. 7.

4343 προσ-καρτέρησις, εως, ἡ, per-

severance, Ep. vi. 18. (N. T.)*

4344 προσ-κεφάλαιον, ου, τό, *a cushion for the head, a pillow*, Mar. iv. 38.*

4345 προσ-κληρόω, ῶ, *to assign by lot, to allot ;* pass. (dat.), Ac. xvii. 4.*

see4347 προσ-κλίνω, *to incline towards*, Ac. v. 36 (W. H.).*

4346 πρόσκλισις, εως, ἡ, *an inclination towards, partiality*, 1 Tim. v. 21.*

4347 προσ-κολλάω, ῶ, pass., *to join one's self to* (dat.), as a companion, Ac. v. 36 (W. H. προσκλίνω); *to cleave to* (πρός, acc.), as husband to wife, Mat. xix. 5 (W. H. κολλάω); Mar. x. 7 ; Ep. v. 31.*

4348 πρόσ-κομμα, ατος, τό, *a stumbling-block, an occasion of falling*, Ro. xiv. 13, 20 ; 1 Cor. viii. 9 ; with λίθος, *a stone of stumbling* (R. V.), 1 Pet. ii. 8 ; Ro. ix. 32, 33 (S.)*

4349 προσ-κοπή, ῆς, ἡ, *an occasion of stumbling*, 2 Cor. vi. 3.*

4350 προσ-κόπτω, *to strike the foot against*, Mat. iv. 6 ; so, *to stumble*, 1 Pet. ii. 8.

4351 προσ-κυλίω, *to roll to* (dat., or ἐπί, acc.), Mat. xxvii. 60 ; Mar. xv. 46.*

4352 προσ-κυνέω, ῶ, *to bow down, to prostrate one's self to, to worship*, God or inferior beings, *to adore* (dat. or acc.).

4353 προσ-κυνητής, οῦ, ὁ, *a worshipper*, Jn. iv. 23.*

4354 προσ-λαλέω, ῶ, *to speak to* (dat.), Ac. xiii. 43, xxviii. 20.*

4355 προσ-λαμβάνω, N. T., mid., *to take to one's self, i.e.*, food, companions, Ac. xxvii. 33, xxviii. 2 ; *to receive to fellowship*, Ro. xiv. 1.

4356 πρόσ-ληψις (W. H. -λημψις), εως, ἡ, *a taking to one's self, a receiving*, Ro. xi. 15.*

4357 προσ-μένω, *to continue with or in, to adhere to* (dat.), *to stay in* (ἐν) *a place*, Mat. xv. 32 ; 1 Tim. i. 3, v. 5.

4358 προσ-ορμίζω (ὅρμος), mid., *to come to anchor*, Mar. vi. 53.

4359 προσ-οφείλω, *to owe besides*, Philem. 19.*

4360 προσ-οχθίζω (ὀχθέω or ὀχθίζω), *to be displeased or offended*

with (dat.), Heb. iii. 10, 17 (S.).*

4361 πρόσ-πεινος, ον (πεῖνα), *very hungry*, Ac. x. 10. (N. T.)*

4362 προσ-πήγνυμι, *to fasten to*, applied to Christ's being fastened to the cross, Ac. ii. 23.*

4363 προσ-πίπτω, (1) *to fall down before* (dat., or πρός, acc.), Mar. vii. 25 ; Lu. v. 8 ; (2) *to beat against* (dat.), Mat. vii. 25.

4364 προσ-ποιέω, ῶ, in mid., *to conform one's self to ;* hence, *to pretend* (inf.), Lu. xxiv. 28 ; in Jn. viii. 6, perhaps, *to regard* (W. H. omit).*

4365 προσ-πορεύομαι, *to come to, approach* (dat.), Mar. x. 35.*

4366 προσ-ρήγνυμι, *to dash against*, as waves, Lu. vi. 48, 49.*

4367 προσ-τάσσω, ξω, abs., or acc. and inf., *to enjoin* (acc.) *upon* (dat.), Lu. v. 14 ; Ac. x. 33.

4368 προ-στάτις, ιδος, ἡ, *a female guardian, a protector*, Ro. xvi. 2.*

4369 προσ-τίθημι, *to place near or by the side of, to add to* (dat., or ἐπί, dat. or acc.), Lu. iii. 20 ; Ac. xi. 24 ; mid., with inf., *to go on to do* a thing, *i.e., to do again*, Ac. xii. 3 ; Lu. xx. 11, 12 ; so 1st aor. pass., part., Lu. xix. 11, προσθεὶς εἶπεν, *he spoke again* (see Gr. § 399 *d*, Wi. § 54, 5, Bu. 299 sq.).

4370 προσ-τρέχω, 2d aor. προσέδραμον, *to run to*, Mar. ix. 15, x. 17 ; Ac. viii. 30.*

4371 προσ-φάγιον, ου, τό, *anything eaten with bread*, as fish, meat, etc., Jn. xxi. 5.*

4372 πρό-σφατος, ον (from σφάζω, *to slaughter, just slaughtered*), *recent, new*, Heb. x. 20.*

4373 προσφάτως, adv., *recently*, Ac. xviii. 2.*

4374 προσ-φέρω, *to bring to*, dat., Mat. iv. 24, viii. 16 ; *to offer, to present*, as money, Ac. viii. 18 ; specially, *to offer sacrifice*, Ac. vii. 42 ; pass., *to bear one's self towards, to deal with*, Heb. xii. 7.

4375 προσ-φιλής, ές, *pleasing, acceptable*, Phil. iv. 8.*

4376 προσ-φορά, ᾶς, ἡ, *an offering, a sacrifice*, Ac. xxi. 26 ; Heb. x. 18.

4377 προσ-φωνέω, ῶ, *to call to* (dat.),

4378 Mat. xi. 16; *to call to one's self* (acc.), Lu. vi. 13.

4378 πρόσ-χυσις, εως, ἡ (προσχέω), *an affusion, a sprinkling,* Heb. xi. 28. (N. T.)*

4379 προσ-ψαύω, *to touch lightly,* Lu. xi. 46.*

4380 προσωπολημπτέω (W. H. προσωπολημπτέω), ῶ, *to respect the person of any one, to show partiality,* Ja. ii. 9. (N. T.)*

4381 προσωπο-λήπτης (W. H. προσωπολήμπτης), ου, ὁ, *a respecter of persons, a partial one,* Ac. x. 34. (N. T.)*

4382 προσωπολημψία (W. H. -λημψ-), ας, ἡ, *respect of persons, partiality,* Ro. ii. 11; Ep. vi. 9; Col. iii. 25; Ja. ii. 1. (N. T.)*

4383 πρόσωπον, ου, τό (ὤψ), (1) *the face, the countenance,* Ja. i. 23; in antithesis with καρδία, *mere appearance,* 2 Cor. v. 12; (2) *the surface,* as of the earth, Lu. xxi. 35; of the heaven, Lu. xii. 56.

4384 προ-τάσσω, *to appoint before,* Ac. xvii. 26 (W. H. προστάσσω).*

4385 προ-τείνω, *to stretch out, to tie up* for scourging, Ac. xxii. 25.*

4386, 4387 πρότερος, έρα, ερον (comparative of πρό), *former,* Ep. iv. 22; πρότερον or τὸ πρότερον, as adv., *before, formerly,* Heb. iv. 6.

4388 προ-τίθημι, N. T. mid., *to set forth,* Ro. iii. 25; *to purpose, to design beforehand,* Ro. i. 13; Ep. i. 9.*

4389 προ-τρέπω, in mid., *to exhort,* Ac. xviii. 27.*

4390 προ-τρέχω, 2d aor. προέδραμον, *to run before, to outrun,* Lu. xix. 4; Jn. xx. 4.*

4391 προ-ϋπ-άρχω, *to be previously,* with participle, Lu. xxiii. 12; Ac. viii. 9.*

4392 πρό-φασις, εως, ἡ, *a pretext, an excuse,* 1 Th. ii. 5; dat. adverbially, *in appearance, ostensibly,* Mar. xii. 40.

4393 προ-φέρω, *to bring forth,* Lu. vi. 45.*

see 4253 & 2036 St πρό-φημι, fut. προερῶ, perf. προείρηκα, 2d aor. προεῖπον, *to say before, i.e.,* at an earlier time, Gal. i. 9; in an earlier part of the discourse, 2 Cor. vii. 3; or prophetically, Mar. xiii. 23.

4394 προ-φητεία, ας, ἡ, *prophecy,* as a gift, or in exercise, Ro. xii. 6; Rev. xix. 10; plur., *prophecies,* 1 Cor. xiii. 8.

4395 προ-φητεύω, σω, *to be a prophet, to prophesy, to forth-tell,* or speak of divine things (the meaning *foretell* is secondary and incidental), Lu. i. 67; Ac. ii. 17, 18; of false prophets, Mat. vii. 22; *to divine,* used in mockery, Mat. xxvi. 68.

4396 προ-φήτης, ου, ὁ, (1) *a prophet, i.e.,* one who has insight into divine things and speaks them forth to others, Mat. v. 12, xxi. 46; plur., *the prophetic books of the O. T.,* Lu. xxiv. 27, 44; (2) *a poet,* Tit. i. 12.

4397 προ-φητικός, ή, όν, *prophetic, uttered by a prophet,* Ro. xvi. 26; 2 Pet. i. 19.*

4398 προ-φῆτις, ιδος, ἡ, *a prophetess,* Lu. ii. 36; Rev. ii. 20.*

4399 προ-φθάνω, *to anticipate, to be beforehand,* with participle, Mat. xvii. 25.*

4400 προ-χειρίζομαι, *to appoint, to choose,* Ac. iii. 20 (W. H.), xxii. 14, xxvi. 16.*

4401 προ-χειρο-τονέω, ῶ, *to designate beforehand,* Ac. x. 41.*

4402 Πρόχορος, ου, ὁ, *Prochorus,* Ac. vi. 5.*

4403 πρύμνα, ης, ἡ, *the hindmost part of a ship, the stern,* Mar. iv. 38; Ac. xxvii. 29, 41.*

4404, 4405 πρωΐ, adv., *early in the morning, at dawn,* Mar. i. 35, xi. 20; with advs., ἅμα πρωΐ, λίαν πρωΐ, *very early in the morning,* Mat. xx. 1; Mar. xvi. 2.

4406 πρώϊμος (W. H. πρό-), η, ον, *early, of the early rain,* Ja. v. 7.*

4407 πρωϊνός, ή, όν, *belonging to the morning,* of the morning star, Rev. ii. 28, xxii. 16. (S.)*

see 4404 πρωΐος, α, ον, *of the morning;* fem. (sc. ὥρα), *morning,* Mat. xxi. 18 (W. H. πρωΐ), xxvii. 1; Jn. xviii. 28 (W. H. πρωΐ), xxi. 4.*

4408 πρώρα, ας, ἡ, *the forward part of a ship, the prow,* Ac. xxvii. 30, 41.*

4409 πρωτεύω, *to have pre-eminence, to be chief,* Col. i. 18.*

4410 πρωτο-καθεδρία, ας, ἡ, *a chief seat*, Lu. xi. 43. (N. T.)

4411 πρωτο-κλισία, ας, ἡ, *the chief place at a banquet*, Mar. xii. 39. (Ap.)

4412, 4413 πρῶτος, η, ον (superlative of πρό), *first*, in place, time, or order; like πρότερος with following gen., *before*, only Jn. i. 15, 30; πρῶτον, as adverb, *first*, Mar. iv. 28; with gen., *before*, Jn. xv. 18; τὸ πρῶτον, *at the first*, Jn. x. 40.

4414 πρωτο-στάτης, ου, ὁ, *a leader, a chief*, Ac. xxiv. 5.*

4415 πρωτοτόκια, ων, τά, *the right of the first-born, the birthright*, Heb. xii. 16. (S.)*

4416 πρωτό-τοκος, ον, *first-born;* ὁ πρωτότοκος, specially a title of Christ, Lu. ii. 7; plur., *the first-born*, Heb. xii. 23, of saints already dead.

see 4413 πρώτως, adv., *first*, Ac. xi. 26 (W. H.).*

4417 πταίω, σω, *to stumble, to fall, to sin*, Ro. xi. 11; 2 Pet. i. 10; Ja. ii. 10, iii. 2.*

4418 πτέρνα, ης, ἡ, *the heel*, Jn. xiii. 18.*

4419 πτερύγιον, ου, τό (dim. of πτέρυξ), *an extremity*, as a *battlement* or *parapet*, Mat. iv. 5; Lu. iv. 9.*

4420 πτέρυξ, υγος, ἡ, *a wing*, Rev. iv. 8, xii. 14.

4421 πτηνός, ή, όν (πέτομαι), *winged*, τὰ πτηνά, *birds*, 1 Cor. xv. 39.*

4422 πτοέω, ῶ, *to terrify*, Lu. xxi. 9, xxiv. 37.*

4423 πτόησις, εως, ἡ, *terror, consternation*, 1 Pet. iii. 6.*

4424 Πτολεμαῖς, ΐδος, ἡ, *Ptolemais*, Ac. xxi. 7.*

4425 πτύον, ου, τό, *a winnowing-shovel*, Mat. iii. 12; Lu. iii. 17.*

4426 πτύρω, *to frighten*, Phil. i. 28.*
4427 πτύσμα, ατος, τό, *spittle*, Jn. ix. 6.*

4428 πτύσσω, ξω, *to fold, to roll up*, as a scroll, Lu. iv. 20.*

4429 πτύω, σω, *to spit*, Mar. vii. 33, viii. 23; Jn. ix. 6.*

4430 πτῶμα, ατος, τό (πίπτω), *a body fallen in death, a carcase*, Mat. xxiv. 28.

4431 πτῶσις, εως, ἡ, *a falling, a fall*, lit. or fig., Mat. vii. 27; Lu. ii. 34.*

4432 πτωχεία, ας, ἡ, *beggary, poverty*, 2 Cor. viii. 2, 9; Rev. ii. 9.*

4433 πτωχεύω, σω, *to be in poverty*, 2 Cor. viii. 9.*

4434; see 3993 πτωχός, ἡ, όν, *reduced to beggary, poor, destitute*, Lu. xiv. 13, 21, xviii. 22; Ja. ii. 5; *spiritually poor*, in a good sense, Mat. v. 3; in a bad sense, Rev. iii. 17. *Syn.:* see πένης.

4435 πυγμή, ῆς, ἡ (πύξ), *the fist*, Mar. vii. 3 (see R. V. and mrg.).*

4436 Πύθων, ωνος, ὁ, *Python;* in N.T. *a divining spirit;* called after the Pythian serpent said to have guarded the oracle at Delphi and been slain by Apollo, Ac. xvi. 16 (see R. V.).*

4437 πυκνός, ή, όν, *frequent*, 1 Tim. v. 23; neut. plur. πυκνά, as adverb, *often*, Lu. v. 33; so πυκνότερον, *more frequently*, Ac. xxiv. 26.*

4438 πυκτεύω (πύκτης), *to be a boxer, to box*, 1 Cor. ix. 26.*

4439 πύλη, ης, ἡ, *a door* or *gate;* πύλαι ᾅδου, *the gates of Hades*, *i.e.*, the powers of the unseen world, Mat. xvi. 18.

4440 πυλών, ῶνος, ὁ, *a large gate*, Ac. x. 17; *a gateway, porch*, Mat. xxvi. 71.

4441 πυνθάνομαι, 2d aor. ἐπυθόμην, (1) *to ask, ask* from (παρά, gen.), *to inquire*, Mat. ii. 4; Lu. xv. 26; (2) *to ascertain by inquiry*, only Ac. xxiii. 34.

4442 πῦρ, πυρός, τό, *fire* generally; of *the heat of the sun*, Rev. xvi. 8; of *lightning*, Lu. ix. 54; God is so called, Heb. xii. 29; fig. for *strife*, Lu. xii. 49; *trials*, 1 Cor. iii. 13; of *the eternal fire*, or future punishment, Mat. xviii. 8.

4443 πυρά, ᾶς, ἡ, *a fire*, a pile of burning fuel, Ac. xxviii. 2, 3.*

4444 πύργος, ου, ὁ, *a tower, fortified structure*, Lu. xiii. 4, xiv. 28.

4445 πυρέσσω, *to be sick with a fever*, Mat. viii. 14; Mar. i. 30.*

4446 πυρετός, οῦ, ὁ, *a fever*, Lu. iv. 38, 39.

4447 πύρινος, η, ον, *fiery, glittering*, Rev. ix. 17.*

4448 πυρόω, ῶ, N. T., pass., *to be set on fire, to burn, to be inflamed*, 2 Pet. iii. 12; 1 Cor. vii. 9; *to glow with heat*, as metal in a furnace, *to be purified by fire*, Rev. iii. 18.

4449 πυρράζω, *to be fire-colored, to be red*, Mat. xvi. 2, 3 (W. H. omit both). (S. πυρρίζω.)*

4450 πυρρός, ά, όν, *fire-colored, red*, Rev. vi. 4, xii. 3.*

see 4450 Πύρρος, ου, ὁ, *Pyrrhus*, Ac. xx. 4 (W. H.).*

4451 πύρωσις, εως, ἡ, *a burning, a conflagration*, Rev. xviii. 9, 18; *severe trial*, as by fire, 1 Pet. iv. 12.*

4452 πώ, *an enclitic particle, even, yet*, used only in composition; see μήπω, μηδέπω, οὔπω, οὐδέπω.

4453 πωλέω, ῶ, ἤσω, *to sell*, Mat. xxi. 12.

4454 πῶλος, ου, ὁ, *a colt, a young ass*, as Mat. xxi. 2.

4455 πώ-ποτε, adv., *at any time*, used only after a negative, *not at any time, never*, Jn. i. 18, v. 37.

4456 πωρόω, ῶ, *to harden, to render callous*, fig., Jn. xii. 40; Ro. xi. 7.

4457 πώρωσις, εως, ἡ, *hardness* of heart, *obtuseness*, Mar. iii. 5; Ro. xi. 25; Ep. iv. 18.*

•4459 πῶς, adv., interrog., *how? in what manner? by what means?* Also in exclamations, as Lu. xii. 50; Jn. xi. 36; with subj. or opt. (ἄν), implying a strong negative, Mat. xxvi. 54; Ac. viii. 31; often (N. T.) in indirect interrogations (classical ὅπως), Mat. vi. 28, etc.

4458 πώς, *an enclitic particle, in a manner, by any means*.

P

P, ρ, ῥῶ, *rho, r*, and as an initial always ῥ, *rh*, the seventeenth letter. As a numeral, ρ´ = 100 ; ͵ρ = 100,000.

4460 Ῥαάβ, or Ῥαχάβ, ἡ (Heb.), *Rahab*, Heb. xi. 31.

4461 ῥαββί (W. H. ῥαββεί), (Heb.), *Rabbi, my master*, a title of respect in Jewish schools of learning, often applied to Christ, Jn. iii. 26, iv. 31. (N. T.)

4462 ῥαββονί, or ῥαββουνί (W. H. ῥαββουνεί), (Aram.), similar to ῥαββί, *my master*, Mar. x. 51 ; Jn. xx. 16. (N. T.)*

4463 ῥαβδίζω, ίσω, *to scourge, to beat*

with rods, Ac. xvi. 22 ; 2 Cor. xi. 25.*

4464 ῥάβδος, ου, ἡ, *a rod, staff*, Mat. x. 10 ; 1 Cor. iv. 21 ; Rev. xi. 1 ; *a rod of authority, a sceptre*, Heb. i. 8.

4465 ῥαβδ-οῦχος, ου, ὁ (ἔχω), *a holder of the rods, a lictor*, a Roman officer, Ac. xvi. 35, 38.*

4466 Ῥαγαῦ, ὁ (Heb.), *Ragau*, Lu. iii. 35.*

4467 ῥᾳδι-ούργημα, ατος, τό, *a careless action, an act of villainy*, Ac. xviii. 14.*

4468 ῥᾳδι-ουργία, ας, ἡ, *craftiness, villainy*, Ac. xiii. 10.*

4469 ῥακά (Aram.), *an empty, i.e., senseless man*, Mat. v. 22 (see Gr. § 153, ii.). (N. T.)*

4470 ῥάκος, ους, τό (ῥήγνυμι), *a remnant torn off, a piece of cloth*, Mat. ix. 16; Mar. ii. 21.*

4471 Ῥαμᾶ, ἡ (Heb.), *Ramah*, Mat. ii. 18.*

4472 ῥαντίζω, ίσω, *to sprinkle, to cleanse ceremonially* (acc.) *by sprinkling, to purify from* (ἀπό), Mar. vii. 4 (W. H.) ; Heb. ix. 13, 19, 21, x. 22. (S.)*

4473 ῥαντισμός, οῦ, ὁ, *sprinkling, purification*, Heb. xii. 24; 1 Pet. i. 2. (S.)*

4474 ῥαπίζω, ίσω, *to smite with the hand*, Mat. v. 39, xxvi. 67.*

4475 ῥάπισμα, ατος, τό, *a blow with the open hand*, Mar. xiv. 65; Jn. xviii. 22, xix. 3.*

4476 ῥαφίς, ίδος, ἡ, *a needle*, Mat. xix. 24; Mar. x. 25; Lu. xviii. 25 (W. H. βελόνη).*

4477; see 4460 Ῥαχάβ, see Ῥαάβ.

4478 Ῥαχήλ, ἡ (Heb.), *Rachel*, Mat. ii. 18.*

4479 Ῥεβέκκα, ης, ἡ, *Rebecca*, Ro. ix. 10.*

4480 ῥέδα, or ῥέδη, ης, ἡ (Gallic), *a chariot*, Rev. xviii. 13. (N. T.)*

4481 Ῥεμφάν, or Ῥεφάν (W. H. Ῥομφά), ὁ (prob. Coptic), *Remphan*, the *Saturn* of later mythology, Ac. vii. 43 (Heb., Chiun, Amos v. 26).*

4482 ῥέω, ῥεύσω, *to flow*, Jn. vii. 38.*

4483 ῥέω (see φημί, εἶπον). From this obs. root, *to say*, are derived : act. perf., εἴρηκα ; pass., εἴρημαι ; 1st aor. pass., ἐρρέθην or ἐρρήθην ; part., ῥηθείς ; espec. the neut. τὸ ῥηθέν, *that which was spoken by* (ὑπό, gen.).

4484 'Ρήγιον, ου, τό, *Rhegium*, now Reggio, Ac. xxviii. 13.*

4485 ῥῆγμα, ατος, τό (ῥήγνυμι), *what is broken, a ruin*, Lu. vi. 49.*

4486 ῥήγνυμι (or ῥήσσω, as Mar. ix. 18), ῥήξω, *to break, to rend, to burst, to dash down, to break forth*, as into praise, Mat. vii. 6, ix. 17; Mar. ii. 22, ix. 18; Lu. v. 37, ix. 42; Gal. iv. 27.*

4487 ῥῆμα, ατος, τό, *a thing spoken;* (1) *a word* or *saying* of any kind, as *command, report, promise*, Lu. vii. 1, ix. 45; Ro. x. 8; (2) *a thing, a matter, a business*, Lu. ii. 15; 2 Cor. xiii. 1.

4488 'Ρησά, ὁ (Heb.), *Rhesa*, Lu. iii. 27.*

see 4486 ῥήσσω, see ῥήγνυμι.

4489 ῥήτωρ, ορος, ὁ, *an orator*, Ac. xxiv. 1.*

4490 ῥητῶς, adv., *expressly, in so many words*, 1 Tim. iv. 1.*

4491 ῥίζα, ης, ἡ, (1) *a root of a tree* or *a plant*, Mar. xi. 20; met., *the origin* or *source of anything*, 1 Tim. vi. 10; fig., *constancy, perseverance*, Mat. xiii. 21; (2) that which comes from the root, *a descendant*, Ro. xv. 12; Rev. v. 5.

4492 ῥιζόω, ῶ, *to root; perf. pass.*, participle, ἐρριζωμένος, *firmly rooted*, fig., Ep. iii. 17; Col. ii. 7.*

4493 ῥιπή, ῆς, ἡ (ῥίπτω), *a stroke, a twinkle*, as of the eye, 1 Cor. xv. 52.*

4494 ῥιπίζω, *to toss to and fro*, as waves by the wind, Ja. i. 6.*

4495 ῥιπτέω, ῶ, *to throw off* or *away*, Ac. xxii. 23.*

4496 ῥίπτω, ψω, 1st aor. ἔρριψα; part ῥίψας; *to throw, throw down, throw out, prostrate*, Mat. ix. 36, xv. 30, xxvii. 5; Lu. iv. 35, xvii. 2; Ac. xxvii. 19, 29.*

4497 'Ροβοάμ, ὁ (Heb.), *Rehoboam*, Mat. i. 7.*

4498 'Ρόδη, ης, ἡ (*rose*), *Rhoda*, Ac. xii. 13.*

4499 'Ρόδος, ου, ἡ, *Rhodes*, Ac. xxi. 1.*

4500 ῥοιζηδόν, adv. (ῥοιζέω), *with a great noise*, 2 Pet. iii. 10.*

4501 ῥομφαία, ας, η, *a large sword*, as Rev. i. 16; fig., *piercing grief*, Lu. ii. 35.

4502 'Ρουβήν, ὁ (Heb.), *Reuben*, Rev. vii. 5.*

4503 'Ρούθ, ἡ (Heb.), *Ruth*, Mar. i. 5.*

4504 'Ροῦφος, ου, ὁ (Lat.), *Rufus*, Mar. xv. 21; Ro. xvi. 13.*

4505 ῥύμη, ης, ἡ, *a street, a lane*, Mat. vi. 2; Lu. xiv. 21; Ac. ix. 11, xii. 10.*

4506 ῥύομαι, σομαι, dep. mid., 1st aor., pass., ἐρρύσθην, *to draw* or *snatch from danger, to deliver*, 2 Pet. ii. 7; ὁ ῥυόμενος, *the deliverer*, Ro. xi. 26.

see 4510 ῥυπαίνω, *to defile*, Rev. xxii. 11 (W. H.).*

see 4510 ῥυπαρεύομαι, *to be filthy*, Rev. xxii. 11 (W. H. mrg.). (N. T.)*

4507 ῥυπαρία, ας, ἡ, *filth, pollution*, Ja. i. 21.*

4508 ῥυπαρός, ά, όν, *filthy, defiled*, Ja. ii. 2; Rev. xxii. 11 (W. H.).*

4509 ῥύπος, ου, ὁ, *filth, filthiness*, 1 Pet. iii. 21.*

4510 ῥυπόω, ῶ, *to be filthy*, Rev. xxii. 11 (not W. H.).*

4511 ῥύσις, εως, ἡ (ῥέω), *a flowing, an issue*, Mar. v. 25; Lu. viii. 43, 44.*

4512 ῥυτίς, ίδος, ἡ, *a wrinkle;* fig., *a spiritual defect*, Ep. v. 27.*

4513 'Ρωμαϊκός, ή, όν, *Roman*, Lu. xxiii. 38 (W. H. omit).*

4514 'Ρωμαῖος, ου, ὁ, *a Roman*, Jn. xi. 48.

4515 'Ρωμαϊστί, adv., *in the Latin language*, Jn. xix. 10.*

4516 'Ρώμη, ης, ἡ, *Rome*, Ac. xviii. 2; 2 Tim. i. 17.

4517 ῥώννυμι, *to strengthen;* only perf., pass., impv., ἔρρωσο, ἔρρωσθε, *farewell*, Ac. xv. 29, xxiii. 30 (W. H. omit).*

Σ

Σ, σ, final ς, *sigma*, *s*, the eighteenth letter. As a numeral, σ′=200; ͵σ=200,000.

4518 σαβαχθανί (W. H. -εί), (Aram.), *sabachthani, thou hast forsaken me*, Mat. xxvii. 46; Mar. xv. 34; from the Aramaic rendering of Ps. xxii. 1. (N. T.)*

4519 σαβαώθ (Heb.), *sabaoth, hosts, armies*, Ro. ix. 29; Ja. v. 4. (S.)*

4520 σαββατισμός, οῦ, ὁ, *a keeping of sabbath, a sabbath rest* (R. V.), Heb. iv. 9.*

4521 σάββατον, ου, τό (from Heb.),

dat. plur. σάββασι(ν), (1) *the sabbath*, Mat. xii. 8, xxviii. 1; (2) *a period of seven days, a week*, Mar. xvi. 2, 9; in both senses the plural is also used. (S.)

4522; see 293   σαγήνη, ης, ἡ, *a drag-net*, Mat. xiii. 47. (S.)* *Syn.:* see ἀμφίβληστρον.

4523   Σαδδουκαῖος, ου, ὁ, *a Sadducee;* plur., of the sect in general; prob. derived from the Heb. name Zadok.

4524   Σαδώκ, ὁ (Heb.), *Sadok*, Mat. i. 13.*

4525   σαίνω, *to move, disturb*, pass., 1 Th. iii. 3.*

4526   σάκκος, ου, ὁ, *hair-cloth, sack-cloth*, a sign of mourning, Mat. xi. 21; Lu. x. 13; Rev. vi. 12, xi. 3.*

4527   Σαλά, ὁ (Heb.), *Sala*, Lu. iii. 35.*

4528   Σαλαθιήλ, ὁ (Heb.), *Salathiel*, Mat. i. 12; Lu. iii. 27.*

4529   Σαλαμίς, ῖνος, ἡ, *Salamis*, Ac. xiii. 5.*

4530   Σαλείμ, τό, *Salim*, Jn. iii. 23.*

4531   σαλεύω, σω, *to shake, to cause to shake*, as Mat. xi. 7; Heb. xii. 27; so, *to excite*, as the populace, Ac. xvii. 13; *to disturb in mind*, 2 Th. ii. 2.

4532   Σαλήμ, ἡ (Heb.), *Salem*, Heb. vii. 1.*

4533   Σαλμών, ὁ (Heb.), *Salmon*, Mat. i. 4, 5, Lu. iii. 32 (W. H. Σαλά).*

4534   Σαλμώνη, ης, ἡ, *Salmone*, Ac. xxvii. 7.*

4535   σάλος, ου, ὁ, *the tossing of the sea in a tempest*, Lu. xxi. 25.*

4536   σάλπιγξ, ιγγος, ἡ, *a trumpet*, 1 Cor. xiv. 8; 1 Th. iv. 16.

4537   σαλπίζω, ίσω (class. ίγξω), *to sound a trumpet*, Rev. ix. 1, 13; for impers. use, 1 Cor. xv. 52 (see Gr. § 171, Wi. § 58, 9 b, β), Bu. 134).

4538   σαλπιστής, οῦ, ὁ (class. -ιγκτής), *a trumpeter*, Rev. xviii. 22.*

4539   Σαλώμη, ης, ἡ, *Salome*, wife of Zebedee, Mar. xv. 40, xvi. 1.*

4540   Σαμάρεια, ας, ἡ, *Samaria*, either (1) *the district*, Lu. xvii. 11; Jn. iv. 4; or (2) *the city*, afterwards called *Sebaste*, only Ac. viii. 5 (W. H.).

4541   Σαμαρείτης, ου, ὁ, *a Samaritan*, Mat. x. 5; Lu. ix. 52.

4542   Σαμαρεῖτις, ιδος, ἡ, *a Samaritan woman*, Jn. iv. 9.*

4543   Σαμο-θρᾴκη, ης, ἡ, *Samothrace*, Ac. xvi. 11.*

4544   Σάμος, ου, ἡ, *Samos*, Ac. xx. 15.*

4545   Σαμουήλ, ὁ (Heb.), *Samuel*, Ac. iii. 24.

4546   Σαμψών, ὁ (Heb.), *Samson*, Heb. xi. 32.*

4547   σανδάλιον, ου, τό, *a sandal*, Mar. vi. 9; Ac. xii. 8.*

4548   σανίς, ίδος, ἡ, *a plank, a board*, Ac. xxvii. 44.*

4549   Σαούλ, ὁ (Heb.), *Saul*, (1) the king of Israel, Ac. xiii. 21; (2) the apostle, only in direct address (elsewhere Σαῦλος), Ac. ix. 4, 17.

4550   σαπρός, ά, όν, *rotten*, hence, *useless*, Mat. vii. 17, 18; fig., *corrupt*, Ep. iv. 29.

4551   Σαπφείρη, ης, ἡ, *Sapphira*, Ac. v. 1.*

4552   σάπφειρος, ου, ἡ, *a sapphire*, Rev. xxi. 19.*

4553   σαργάνη, ης, ἡ, *a basket*, generally of twisted cords, 2 Cor. xi. 33.*

4554   Σάρδεις, ων, dat. εσι(ν), αί, *Sardis*, Rev. i. 11, iii. 1, 4.*

4555   σάρδινος, ου, ὁ (Rec. in Rev. iv. 3 for following). (N. T.)*

4556   σάρδιον, ου, τό, *a precious stone, sardius* or *carnelian*, Rev. iv. 3 (W. H.), xxi. 20.*

4557   σαρδ-όνυξ, υχος, ὁ, *a sardonyx*, a precious stone, white streaked with red, Rev. xxi. 20.*

4558   Σάρεπτα, ων, τά, *Sarepta*, Lu. iv. 26.*

4559   σαρκικός, ή, όν, *fleshly, carnal*, whether (1) belonging to human nature in its bodily manifestation, or (2) belonging to human nature as sinful, Ro. xv. 27; 1 Cor. iii. 3, ix. 11; 2 Cor. i. 12, x. 4; 1 Pet. ii. 11; for Rec. σαρκικός, W. H. substitute σάρκινος, in Ro. vii. 14; 1 Cor. iii. 1; Heb. vii. 16; and ἄνθρωπος in 1 Cor. iii. 4.*

4560   σάρκινος, η, ον, (1) *fleshly, consisting of flesh*, opp. to λίθινος, 2 Cor. iii. 3; (2) *fleshy, carnal* (W.H. in the passages quoted under σαρκικός).*

4561   σάρξ, σαρκός, ἡ, *flesh*, sing., Lu. xxiv. 39; plur., Ja. v. 3; *the human body, man;* the *human nature* of man as distinguished from his divine nature (πνεῦμα); *human nature*, as sinful; πᾶσα σάρξ, *every man. all men*; κατὰ σάρκα, *as a man*; σὰρξ καὶ αἷμα, *flesh and blood, i.e,* man as frail and fallible; ζῆν, περιπατεῖν κατὰ σάρκα, *to live, to walk after flesh*, cf a carnal, unspiritual life. The word also denotes *kinship*, Ro. xi. 14.

4562 Σαρούχ, ὁ (Heb.), (W. H. Σερούχ), *Saruch* or *Serug*, Lu. iii. 35.*

4563 σαρόω, ῶ, *to sweep, to cleanse by sweeping*, Mat. xii. 44. Lu. xi. 25, xv. 8.*

4564 Σάρρα, ας, ἡ, *Sarah*, Ro. iv. 19, ix. 9.

4565 Σάρων, ωνος, ὁ, *Sharon*, Ac. ix. 35.*

4566, 4567 σατᾶν, ὁ (Heb.), and σατανᾶς, ᾶ, ὁ, *an adversary, i.e.*, *Satan*, the Heb. proper name for the devil, διάβολος, Mat. iv. 10, 15; Ac. xxvi. 18; met., for one who does the work of Satan, Mat. xvi. 23; Mar. viii. 33. (S.)

4568 σάτον, ου, τό (Aram.), *a seah*, a measure equal to about a peck and a half, Mat. xiii. 33; Lu. xiii. 21. (S.)*

4569 Σαῦλος, ου, ὁ, *Saul*, the apostle, generally in this form (see Σαούλ), Ac. vii. 58, viii. 1, 3.

4570 σβέννυμι, σβέσω, (1) *to extinguish, to quench*, Ep. vi. 16; (2) fig., *to suppress*, 1 Th. v. 19.
★

4572 σεαυτοῦ, ῆς, οῦ (only masc. in N. T.), a reflex. pron., *of thyself*; dat., σεαυτῷ, *to thyself*; acc., σεαυτόν, *thyself*.

4573 σεβάζομαι, dep., pass., *to stand in awe of, to worship*, Ro. i. 25.*

4574 σέβασμα, ατος, τό, *an object of religious worship*, Ac. xvii. 23; 2 Th. ii. 4.*

4575 σεβαστός, ή, όν, *venerated, august*, a title of the Roman emperors (= Lat. *augustus*), Ac. xxv. 21, 25. Hence, secondarily, *Augustan, imperial*, Ac. xxvii. 1.*

4576 σέβομαι, dep., *to reverence, to worship* God, Mar. vii. 7; οἱ σεββόμενοι, *the devout, i.e,* proselytes of the gate, Ac. xvii. 17.

4577 σειρά, ᾶς, ἡ, *a chain*, 2 Pet. ii. 4 (W. H. read following).*

see 4577 σειρός, οῦ, ὁ, *a pit*, 2 Pet. ii. 4 (W. H.).*

4578 σεισμός, οῦ, ὁ, *a shaking*, as an *earthquake*, Mat. xxiv. 7; *a storm* at sea, Mat. viii. 24.

4579 σείω, σω, *to shake*, Heb. xii. 26; fig., *to agitate*, Mat. xxi. 10.

4580 Σεκοῦνδος, ου, ὁ (Lat.), *Secundus*, Ac. xx. 4.*

4581 Σελεύκεια, ας, ἡ, *Seleucia*, Ac. xiii. 4.*

4582 σελήνη, ης, ἡ, *the moon*, Mar. xiii. 24.

4583 σεληνιάζομαι, *io be epileptic*, Mat. iv. 24, xvii. 15. (N. T.)*

4584 Σεμεΐ, ὁ (Heb.), (W. H. Σεμεείν), *Semei* or *Semein*, Lu. iii. 26.*

4585 σεμίδαλις, acc. ιν, ἡ, *the finest wheaten flour*, Rev. xviii. 13.*

4586 σεμνός, ή, όν, *venerable, honorable*, of men, 1 Tim. iii. 8, 11; Tit. ii. 2; of acts, Phil. iv. 8.*

4587 σεμνότης, τητος, ἡ, *dignity, honor*, 1 Tim. ii. 2, iii. 4; Tit. ii. 7.*

4588 Σέργιος, ου, ὁ, *Sergius*, Ac. xiii. 7.*

4589 Σήθ, ὁ (Heb.), *Seth*, Lu. iii. 38.*

4590 Σήμ, ὁ (Heb.), *Shem*, Lu. iii. 36.*

4591 σημαίνω, 1st aor. ἐσήμανα, *to signify, indicate*, Jn. xii. 33; Ac. xxv. 27.

4592; see 1411 σημεῖον, ου, τό, *a sign, that by which a thing is known, a token, an indication*, of divine presence and power, 1 Cor. xiv. 22; Lu. xxi. 7, 11; hence, especially, *a miracle*, whether real or unreal, Lu. xi. 16, 29; 2 Th. ii. 9. *Syn.*: see δύναμις.

4593 σημειόω, ῶ, in mid., *to mark for one's self, to note*, 2 Th. iii. 14.*

4594 σήμερον, adv., *to-day, at this time, now*, Mat. vi. 11; Lu. ii. 11; ἡ σήμερον (ἡμέρα), *this very day*, Ac. xix. 40.

4595 σήπω, *to make rotten*; 2d perf. σέσηπα, *to become rotten, perish*, Ja. v. 2.*

4596 σηρικός, ή, όν (W. H. σιρικός), *silken*; neut. as subst., *silk*, Rev. xviii. 12.*

4597 σής, σητός, ὁ, *a moth*, Mat. vi. 19, 20; Lu. xii. 33.*

★For **4571** see **Strong.**

4598 σητό-βρωτος, ον, moth-eaten, Ja. v. 2.*

4599 σθενόω, ῶ, to strengthen, 1 Pet. v. 10. (N. T.)*

4600 σιαγών, όνος, ἡ, the jawbone, Mat. v. 39; Lu. vi. 29.*

4601 σιγάω, ῶ, to keep silence, Lu. ix. 36; pass., to be concealed, Ro. xvi. 25.

4602 σιγή, ῆς, ἡ, silence, Ac. xxi. 40; Rev. viii. 1.*

4603 σιδήρεος, έα, εον, contr., οῦς, ᾶ, οῦν, made of iron, Ac. xii. 10; Rev. ii. 27.

4604 σίδηρος, ου, ὁ, iron, Rev. xviii. 12.*

4605 Σιδών, ῶνος, ἡ, Sidon, Mat. xi. 21, 22.

4606 Σιδώνιος, α, ον, Sidonian, inhabitant of Sidon, Lu. iv. 26 (W. H.); Ac. xii. 20.

4607 σικάριος, ου, ὁ (Lat.), an assassin, Ac. xxi. 38.*

4608 σίκερα, τό (Aram.), intoxicating drink, Lu. i. 15. (S.)*

4609 Σίλας, dat. ᾳ, acc. αν, ὁ, Silas, contr. from Σιλουανός, Ac. xv. 22, 27.

4610 Σιλουανός, οῦ, ὁ, Silvanus, 2 Cor. i. 9.

4611 Σιλωάμ, ὁ, Siloam, Lu. xiii. 4; Jn. ix. 7, 11.*

4612 σιμικίνθιον, ου, τό (Lat. semicinctium), an apron, worn by artisans, Ac. xix. 12. (N. T.)*

4613 Σίμων, ωνος, ὁ, Simon; nine persons of the name are mentioned: (1) Peter, the apostle, Mat. xvii. 25; (2) the Zealot, an apostle, Lu. vi. 15; (3) a brother of Jesus, Mar. vi. 3; (4) a certain Cyrenian, Mar. xv. 21; (5) the father of Judas Iscariot, Jn. vi. 71; (6) a certain Pharisee, Lu. vii. 40; (7) a leper, Mat. xxvi. 6; (8) Simon Magus, Ac. viii. 9; (9) a certain tanner, Ac. ix. 43.

4614 Σινᾶ, τό (Heb.), Sinai, Ac. vii. 30, 38; Gal. iv. 24, 25.*

4615 σίναπι, εως, τό, mustard, Lu. xiii. 19, xvii. 6.

4616 σινδών, όνος, ἡ, fine linen, a linen cloth, Mar. xiv. 51, 52, xv. 46.

4617 σινιάζω, to sift, as grain, to prove by trials, Lu. xxii. 31. (N. T.)*

see 4596 σιρικός, see σηρικός.

4618 σιτευτός, ή, όν, fattened, fatted, Lu. xv. 23, 27, 30.*

see 4621 σιτίον, ου, τό, grain, Ac. vii. 12 (W. H.).*

4619 σιτιστός, ή, όν, fattened; τὰ σιτιστά, fatlings, Mat. xxii. 4.*

4620 σιτο-μέτριον, ου, τό, a measured portion of grain or food, Lu. xii. 42. (N. T.)*

4621 σῖτος, ου, ὁ, wheat, grain, Jn. xii. 24; 1 Cor. xv. 37.

see 4965 Σιχάρ, see Συχάρ.

4622 Σιών, ἡ, τῷ, Zion, the hill; used for the city of Jerusalem, Ro. xi. 26; fig., for heaven, the spiritual Jerusalem, Heb. xii. 22; Rev. xiv. 1.

4623 σιωπάω, ῶ, ήσω, to be silent, whether voluntarily or from dumbness, Mar. iii. 4; Lu. i. 20; to become still, as the sea, Mar. iv. 39.

4624 σκανδαλίζω, ίσω, to cause to stumble; met., to entice to sin, Mat. xviii. 6, 8, 9; to cause to fall away, Jn. vi. 61; pass., to be indignant, Mat. xv. 12.

4625 σκάνδαλον, ου, τό, a snare, a stumbling-block; fig., a cause of error or sin, Mat. xiii. 41; Ro. xiv. 13. (S.)

4626 σκάπτω, ψω, to dig, Lu. vi. 48, xiii. 8, xvi. 3.*

4627 σκάφη, ης, ἡ, any hollow vessel; a boat, Ac. xxvii. 16, 30, 32.*

4628 σκέλος, ους, τό, the leg, Jn. xix. 31, 32, 33.*

4629 σκέπασμα, ατος, τό, clothing, 1 Tim. vi. 8.*

4630 Σκευᾶς, ᾶ, ὁ, Sceva, Ac. xix. 14.*

4631 σκευή, ῆς. ἡ, furniture, fittings, Ac. xxvii. 19.*

4632 σκεῦος, ους, τό, (1) a vessel, to contain a liquid, or for any other purpose, Heb. ix. 21; 2 Tim. ii. 20; fig., of recipients generally, a vessel of mercy, of wrath, Ro. ix. 22, 23; an instrument by which anything is done; household utensils, plur., Mat. xii. 29; of a ship, the tackling, Ac. xxvii. 17; fig., of God's servants, Ac. ix. 15; 2 Cor. iv. 7.

4633 σκηνή, ῆς, ἡ, a tent, a tabernacle, an abode or dwelling, Mat. xvii. 4; Ac. vii. 43, xv. 16; Heb. viii. 5, xiii. 10.

4634 σκηνο-πηγία, ας, ἡ, the feast of tabernacles, Jn. vii. 2.*

4635 σκηνο-ποιός, οῦ, ὁ, a tent-maker, Ac. xviii. 3. (N. T.)*

4636 σκῆνος, ους, τό, a tent; fig., of

the human body, 2 Cor. v.
1, 4.*

4637 σκηνόω, ῶ, ώσω, to spread a
tent, Rev. vii. 15; met., to
dwell, Jn. i. 14; Rev. xii. 12,
xiii. 6, xxi. 3.*

4638 σκήνωμα, ατος, τό, a tent
pitched, a dwelling, Ac. vii.
46; fig., of the body, 2 Pet.
i. 13, 14.*

4639 σκιά, ᾶς, ἡ, (1) a shadow, a
thick darkness, Mat. iv. 16
(S.); (2) a shadow, an outline, Col. ii. 17.

4640 σκιρτάω, ῶ, ήσω, to leap for
joy, Lu. i. 41, 44, vi. 23.*

4641 σκληρο-καρδία, ας, ἡ, hardness
of heart, perverseness, Mat.
xix. 8; Mar. x. 5, xvi. 14.
(S.)*

4642 σκληρός, ά, όν, hard, violent,
as the wind, Ja. iii. 4; fig.,
grievous, painful, Ac. ix. 5
(W. H. omit), xxvi. 14; Ju.
15; harsh, stern, Mat. xxv.
24; Jn. vi. 60.*

4643 σκληρότης, τητος, ἡ, fig., hardness of heart, obstinacy, Ro.
ii. 5.*

4644 σκληρο-τράχηλος, ον, stiff-
necked; fig., obstinate, Ac.
vii. 51. (S.)*

4645 σκληρύνω, fig., to make hard,
to harden, as the heart, Ro.
ix. 18; Heb. iii. 8, 15, iv. 7;
pass., to be hardened, to become obstinate, Ac. xix. 9;
Heb. iii. 13.*

4646 σκολιός, ά, όν, crooked, Lu. iii.
5; fig., perverse, Ac. ii. 40;
Phil. ii. 15; unfair, 1 Pet. ii.
18.*

4647 σκόλοψ, οπος, ὁ, a stake or
thorn; fig., a sharp infliction,
2 Cor. xii. 7.*

4648 σκοπέω, ῶ, (1) to look at, to regard attentively, Ro. xvi. 17;
(2) to take heed (acc.), beware
(μή), Gal. vi. 1.

4649 σκοπός, οῦ, ὁ, a mark aimed at,
a goal; κατὰ σκοπόν, towards
the goal, i.e., aiming straight
at it, Phil. iii. 14.*

4650 σκορπίζω, σω, to disperse, to
scatter abroad, as frightened
sheep, Jn. x. 12; to distribute
alms, 2 Cor. ix. 9.

4651 σκορπίος, ου, ὁ, a scorpion, Lu.
x. 19.

4652 σκοτεινός· ή, όν, full of darkness, dark, Mar. vi. 23; Lu.
xi. 34, 36.*

4653 σκοτία, ας, ἡ, darkness, Mat. x.

27; fig., spiritual darkness,
Jn. i. 5, vi. 17.

4654 σκοτίζω, σω, in pass., to be
darkened, as the sun, Mar.
xiii. 24; fig., as the mind,
Ro. i. 21.

4655 σκότος, ους, τό (σκότος, ου, ὁ,
only in Heb. xii. 18, where
W. H. read ζόφος), darkness,
physical, Mat. xxvii. 45;
moral, Jn. iii. 19.

4656 σκοτόω, ῶ, pass. only, to be
darkened, Ep. iv. 18 (W.H.);
Rev. ix. 2 (W. H.), xvi. 10.*

4657 σκύβαλον, ου, τό, refuse, dregs,
Phil. iii. 8.*

4658 Σκύθης, ου, ὁ, a Scythian, as
typical of the uncivilized,
Col. iii. 11.*

4659 σκυθρ-ωπός, όν, sad-counte-
nanced, gloomy, Mat. vi. 16;
Lu. xxiv. 17.*

4660 σκύλλω, pass. perf. part. ἐσκυλ-
μένος, to flay; to trouble, an-
noy, Mat. ix. 36 (W. H.);
Mar. v. 35; Lu. vii. 6, viii.
29.*

4661 σκῦλον, ου, τό, spoil taken from
a foe, Lu. xi. 22.*

4662 σκωληκό-βρωτος, ον, eaten by
worms, Ac. xii. 23.*

4663 σκώληξ, ηκος, ὁ, a gnawing
worm, Mar. ix. 44 (W. H.
omit)· 46 (W. H. omit),
48.*

4664 σμαράγδινος, η, ον, made of
emerald, Rev. iv. 3. (N.T.)*

4665 σμάραγδος, ου, ὁ, an emerald,
Rev. xxi. 19.*

4666 σμύρνα, ης, ἡ, myrrh, Mat. ii.
11; Jn. xix. 39.*

4667 Σμύρνα, ns. ἡ, Smyrna. Rev. i.
11, ii. 8 (W. H.).*

4668 Σμυρναῖος, ου, ἡ, one of
Smyrna, a Smyrnæan, Rev.
ii. 8 (not W. H.).*

4669 σμυρνίζω, to mingle with myrrh,
Mar. xv. 23. (N. T.)*

4670 Σόδομα, ων, τά, Sodom, Mat.
★ x. 15, xi. 23, 24.

4672 Σολομών or -μῶν, ῶντος or
ῶνος, ὁ, Solomon, Mat. vi. 29,
xii. 42.

4673 σορός, οῦ, ἡ, a bier, an open
coffin, Lu. vii. 14.*

4674 σός, σή, σόν, poss. pron., thy,
★ thine (see Gr. §§ 56, 255, Bu.
115).

4676 σουδάριον, ου, τό (Lat.), a hand-
kerchief, Lu. xix. 20; Jn. xi.
44. (N. T.)

4677 Σουσάννα, ης, ἡ, Susanna, Lu.
viii. 3.*

★ For 4671 & 4675 see Strong.

4678 σοφία, as, ἡ, wisdom, insight, skill, human, Lu. xi. 31; or divine, 1 Cor. i. 21, 24. Syn.: see γνῶσις.

4679 σοφίζω, to make wise, 2 Tim. iii. 15; pass., to be devised skillfully, 2 Pet. i. 16.*

4680 σοφός, ή, όν, wise, either (1) in action, expert, Ro. xvi. 19; (2) in acquirement, learned, cultivated, 1 Cor. i. 19, 20; (3) philosophically, profound, Ju. 25; (4) practically, Ep. v. 15.

4681 Σπανία, as, ἡ, Spain, Ro. xv. 24, 28.*

4682 σπαράσσω, ξω, to convulse, to throw into spasms, Mar. i. 26, ix. 20 (not W. H.), 26; Lu. ix. 39.*

4683 σπαργανόω, ῶ, perf. pass. part. ἐσπαργανωμένος, to swathe, to wrap in swaddling clothes, Lu. ii. 7, 12.*

4684 σπαταλάω, ῶ, ήσω, to live extravagantly or luxuriously, 1 Tim. v. 6; Ja. v. 5.* Syn.: The fundamental thought of στρηνιάω is of insolence and voluptuousness which spring from abundance; of τρυφάω, effeminate self-indulgence; of σπαταλάω, is effeminacy and wasteful extravagance.

4685 σπάω, ῶ, mid., to draw, as a sword, Mar. xiv. 47; Ac. xvi. 27.*

4686 σπεῖρα, ης, ἡ, (1) a cohort of soldiers, the tenth part of a legion, Ac. x. 1; (2) a military guard, Jn. xviii. 3, 12.

4687 σπείρω, σπερῶ, 1st aor. ἔσπειρα, perf. pass. part. ἐσπαρμένος, 2d aor. pass. ἐσπάρην, to sow or scatter, as seed, Lu. xii. 24; to spread or scatter, as the word of God, Mat. xiii. 19; applied to giving alms, 2 Cor. ix. 6; to burial, 1 Cor. xv. 42, 43; and to spiritual effort generally, Gal. vi. 8.

4688 σπεκουλάτωρ, ορος, ὁ (Lat.), a body-guardsman, a soldier in attendance upon royalty, Mar. vi. 27 (see Gr. § 154 c). (N. T.)*

4689 σπένδω, to pour out, as a libation, fig., Phil. ii. 17; 2 Tim. iv. 6.*

4690 σπέρμα, ατος, τό, seed, produce, Mat. xiii. 24–38; children, offspring, posterity, Jn. vii. 42; a remnant, Ro. ix. 29.

4691 σπερμο-λόγος, ου, ὁ, a babbler, i.e., one who picks up trifles, as birds do seed, Ac. xvii. 18.*

4692 σπεύδω, σω, (1) to hasten, intrans., usually adding to another verb the notion of speed, Lu. xix. 5, 6; (2) to desire earnestly (acc.), 2 Pet. iii. 12.

4693 σπήλαιον, ου, τό, a cave, a den, Heb. xi. 38.*

4694 σπιλάς, άδος, ἡ, a rock in the sea, a reef; fig., of false teachers, a hidden rock (R. V.), Ju. 12.*

●4696 σπῖλος, ου, ὁ, a spot; fig., a fault, Ep. v. 27; 2 Pet. ii. 13.*

4695 σπιλόω, ῶ, to defile, to spot, Ja. iii. 6; Ju. 23.*

●4698 σπλάγχνα, ων, τά, bowels, only Ac. i. 18; elsewhere, fig., the affections, compassion, the heart, as Col. iii. 12; 1 Jn. iii. 17.

4697 σπλαγχνίζομαι, dep., with 1st aor. pass. ἐσπλαγχνίσθην, to feel compassion, to have pity on (gen., or ἐπί, dat. or acc., once περί, Mat. ix. 36).

4699 σπόγγος, ου, ὁ, a sponge, Mat. xxvii. 48; Mar. xv. 36; Jn. xix. 29.*

4700 σποδός, οῦ, ἡ, ashes, Mat. xi. 21; Lu. x. 13; Heb. ix. 13.*

4701 σπορά, ᾶς, ἡ, seed, 1 Pet. i. 23.*

4702 σπόριμος, όν, sown; neut. plur. τὰ σπόριμα, sown fields, Mat. xii. 1; Mar. ii. 23; Lu. vi. 1.*

4703 σπόρος, ου, ὁ, seed, for sowing, Lu. viii. 5, 11.

4704 σπουδάζω, άσω, to hasten, to give, diligence (with inf.), Heb. iv. 11; 2 Tim. iv. 9, 21.

4705, 4706, 4707 σπουδαῖος, αία, αῖον, diligent, earnest, 2 Cor. viii. 17, 22; compar. neut. as adv., σπουδαιότερον, 2 Tim. i. 17 (not W. H.).*

4708, 4709 σπουδαίως, adv., diligently, earnestly, Lu. vii. 4; 2 Tim. i. 17 (W. H.); Tit. iii. 13; hastily, compar., Phil. ii. 28.*

4710 σπουδή, ῆς, ἡ, (1) speed, haste, Mar. vi. 25; (2) diligence, earnestness, Ro. xii. 11.

4711 σπυρίς (W. H. σφυρίς), ίδος, ἡ, a plaited basket, Mar. viii. 8, 20.

4712 στάδιον, ου, τό, plur. οἱ στάδιοι, (1) a stadium, one eighth of

a Roman mile, Jn. xi. 18;
(2) *a race-course,* for public
games, 1 Cor. ix. 24.

4713 στάμνος, ου, ὁ, ἡ, *a jar* or *vase,*
for the manna, Heb. ix. 4.*

see 4955 στασιαστής, οῦ, ὁ, *an insurgent,*
Mar. xv. 7 (W. H.).*

4714 στάσις, εως, ἡ (ἵστημι), *a stand-
ing,* lit. only Heb. ix. 8; *an
insurrection,* Mar. xv. 7; *dissension,* Ac. xv. 2.

4715 στατήρ, ῆρος, ὁ, *a stater,* a silver
coin equal to two of the
δίδραχμον (which see), a
Jewish shekel, Mat. xvii.
27.*

4716 σταυρός, οῦ, ὁ, *a cross,* Mat.
xxvii. 32, 40; met., often of
Christ's death, Gal. vi. 14;
Ep. ii. 16.

4717 σταυρόω, ῶ, ώσω, *to fix to the
cross, to crucify,* Lu. xxiii.
21, 23; fig., *to destroy,* the
corrupt nature, Gal. v. 24.

4718 σταφυλή, ῆς, ἡ, *a grape, a
cluster of grapes,* Mat. vii.
16; Lu. vi. 44; Rev. xiv.
18.*

4719 στάχυς, υος, ὁ, *an ear of corn,*
Mat. xii. 1; Mar. ii. 23, iv.
28; Lu. vi. 1.*

4720 Στάχυς, υος, ὁ, *Stachys,* Ro. xvi.
9.*

4721 στέγη, ης, ἡ (lit. *a cover*), *a* flat
roof of a house, Mat. viii. 8;
Mar. ii. 4; Lu. vii. 6.*

4722 στέγω, *to cover, to conceal, to
bear with,* 1 Cor. ix. 12, xiii.
7; 1 Th. iii. 1, 5.*

4723 στεῖρος, α, ον, *barren,* Lu. i. 7,
36, xxiii. 29; Gal. iv. 27.*

4724 στέλλω, *to set, arrange;* in mid.,
to provide for, take care, 2
Cor. viii. 20; *to withdraw
from* (ἀπό), 2 Th. iii. 6.*

4725 στέμμα, ατος, τό, *a garland,* Ac.
xiv. 13.*

4726 στεναγμός, οῦ, ὁ, *a groaning,*
Ac. vii. 34; Ro. viii. 26.*

4727 στενάζω, ξω, *to groan,* expressing grief, anger, or desire,
Mar. vii. 34; Heb. xiii.
17.

4728 στενός, ή, όν, *narrow,* Mat. vii.
13, 14; Lu. xiii. 24.*

4729 στενο-χωρέω, ῶ, *to be narrow;*
in pass., *to be distressed,* 2
Cor. iv. 8, vi. 12.*

4730 στενο-χωρία, ας, ἡ, *a narrow
space; great distress,* Ro. ii.
9, viii. 35; 2 Cor. vi. 4, xii.
10.*

4731 στερεός, ά, όν, *solid,* as food,

4732 στερεόω, ῶ, ώσω, *to strengthen,
confirm, establish,* Ac. iii. 7,
16, xvi. 5.*

4733 στερέωμα, ατος, τό, *firmness,*
steadfastness, Col. ii. 5.*

4734 Στεφανᾶς, ᾶ, ὁ, *Stephanas,* 1
Cor. i. 16, xvi. 15, 17.

**4735; see
1238** στέφανος, ου, ὁ, *a crown, a
garland,* of royalty, of victory in the games, of festal
joy, Jn. xix. 2, 5; 1 Cor. ix.
25; often used fig., 2 Tim.
iv. 8; Rev. ii. 10. *Syn.:* see
διάδημα.

4736 Στέφανος, ου, ὁ, *Stephen,* Ac.
vi., vii.

4737 στεφανόω, ῶ, ώσω, *to crown, to
adorn,* 2 Tim. ii. 5; Heb. ii.
7, 9.*

4738 στῆθος, ους, τό, *the breast,* Lu.
xviii. 13.

4739 στήκω (ἵστημι, ἕστηκα), *to stand,*
in the attitude of prayer,
Mar. xi. 25; generally, *to
stand firm, persevere,* as Ro.
xiv. 4; 1 Cor. xvi. 13; Gal.
v. 1. (S.)

4740 στηριγμός, οῦ, ὁ, *firmness,
steadfastness,* 2 Pet. iii. 17.*

4741 στηρίζω, ξω or ίσω, pass. perf.
ἐστήριγμαι, (1) *to fix, to set
firmly,* Lu. ix. 51, xvi. 26;
(2) *to strengthen, to confirm,
to support,* as Lu. xxii. 32;
Ro. i. 11.

see 4746 στιβάς, see στοιβάς.

4742 στίγμα, ατος, τό, *a mark* or
brand, used of the traces of
the apostle's sufferings for
Christ, Gal. vi. 17.*

4743 στιγμή, ῆς, ἡ, *a point of time,
an instant,* Lu. iv. 5.*

4744 στίλβω, *to shine, to glisten,* Mar.
ix. 3.*

4745 στοά, ᾶς, ἡ, *a colonnade, a
portico,* Jn. v. 2, x. 23; Ac.
iii. 11, v. 12.*

4746 στοιβάς, άδος, ἡ (W.H. στιβάς),
a bough, a branch of a tree.
Mar. xi. 8.*

4747 στοιχεῖα, ων, τά, *elements, ru-
diments,* Gal. iv. 3, 9; Col.
ii. 8, 20; Heb. v. 12; 2 Pet.
iii. 10, 12.*

4748 στοιχέω, ῶ, ήσω, *to walk,* always fig. of conduct; *to
walk* in (local dat.), Ac. xxi.
24; Ro. iv. 12; Gal. v. 25,
vi. 16; Phil. iii. 16.*

4749 στολή, ῆς, ἡ, *a robe, i.e.,* the

long outer garment which
was a mark of distinction,
Lu. xv. 22. *Syn.:* see ἱμάτιον.

4750   στόμα, ατος, τό, (1) *the mouth,*
generally; hence, (2) *speech,
speaking;* used of *testimony,*
Mat. xviii. 16; *eloquence* or
power in speaking, Lu. xxi.
15; (3) applied to an opening in the earth, Rev. xii.
16; (4) *the edge* or *point* of a
sword, Lu. xxi. 24.

4751   στόμαχος, ου, ὁ, *the stomach,* 1
Tim. v. 23.*

4752   στρατεία, ας, ἡ, *warfare, military service;* of Christian
warfare, 2 Cor. x. 4; 1 Tim.
i. 18.*

4753   στράτευμα, ατος, τό, (1) *an
army,* Rev. ix. 16; (2) *a de-
tachment of troops,* Ac. xxiii.
10, 27; plur., Lu. xxiii. 11.

4754   στρατεύομαι, dep. mid., *to wage
war, to fight,* Lu. iii. 14;
fig., of the warring of lusts
against the soul, Ja. iv. 1;
to serve as a soldier, of
Christian work, 1 Tim. i. 18;
2 Cor. x. 3.

4755   στρατ-ηγός, οῦ, ὁ (ἄγω), (1) *a
leader of an army, a general;*
(2) *a magistrate* or *governor,*
Ac. xvi. 20–38; (3) *the captain*
of the temple, Lu. xxii. 4,
52; Ac. iv. 1, v. 24, 26.*

4756   στρατιά, ᾶς, ἡ, *an army;* met.,
a host of angels, Lu. ii. 13;
the host of heaven, *i.e., the
stars,* Ac. vii. 42.*

4757   στρατιώτης, ου, ὁ, *a soldier,* as
Mat. viii. 9; fig., of a Chris-
tian, 2 Tim. ii. 3.

4758   στρατο-λογέω, ῶ, ήσω, *to collect
an army, to enlist troops,* 2
Tim. ii. 4.*

4759   στρατοπεδ-άρχης, ου, ὁ, *the prætorian prefect, i.e.,* command-
er of the Roman emperor's
body-guard, Ac. xxviii. 16
(W. H. omit).*

4760   στρατό-πεδον, ου, τό, *an en-
camped army,* Lu. xxi. 20.*

4761   στρεβλόω, ῶ, *to rack, to pervert, to twist,* as words from
their proper meaning, 2 Pet.
iii. 16.*

4762   στρέφω, ψω, 2d aor. pass. ἐστρά-
φην, *to turn,* trans., Mat. v.
39; Rev. xi. 6 (*to change* into,
εἰς); intrans., Ac. vii. 42;
mostly in pass., *to turn one's
self,* Jn. xx. 14; *to be con-*

verted, to be changed in mind
and conduct, Mat. xviii. 3.

**4763; see
4684**   στρηνιάω, ῶ, άσω, *to live volupt-
uously,* Rev. xviii. 7, 9.*
Syn.: see σπαταλάω.

4764   στρῆνος, ους, τό, *profligate luxury, voluptuousness,* Rev.
xviii. 3.*

4765   στρουθίον, ου, τό (dim. of στρου-
θός), *a small bird, a sparrow,*
Mat. x. 29, 31; Lu. xii. 6, 7.*

4766   στρωννύω, or -ώννυμι, στρώσω,
pass. perf. part. ἐστρωμένος
ἔστρωμαι, *to spread,* Mat.
xxi. 8; *to make a bed,* Ac. ix.
34; pass., *to be spread with
couches,* ἀνάγαιον ἐστρωμέ-
νον, *an upper room fur-
nished,* Mar. xiv. 15; Lu.
xxii. 12.

4767   στυγητός, όν, *hateful, detest-
able,* Tit. iii. 3.*

4768   στυγνάζω, άσω, *to be gloomy,*
Mar. x. 22; of the sky, Mat.
xvi. 3.*

4769   στύλος, ου, ὁ, *a pillar,* Gal. ii.
9; 1 Tim. iii. 15; Rev. iii.
12, x. 1.*

4770   Στωϊκός, ή, όν (στοά, *portico*),
Stoic, Ac. xvii. 18.*

4771   σύ, σοῦ, σοί, σέ, plur. ὑμεῖς,
thou, ye, the pers. pron. of
second person (see Gr. § 53).

συγγ-.   In some words commencing thus, W. H. pre-
fer the unassimilated form
συνγ-.

4772   συγ-γένεια, ας, ἡ, *kindred, family,* Lu. i. 61; Ac. vii. 3,
14.*

4773   συγ-γενής, ές, *akin,* as subst.,
a relative, Mar. vi. 4; Lu.
xiv. 12; *a fellow-country-
man,* Ro. ix. 3.

see 4773   συγ-γενίς, ίδος, ἡ, *a kinswoman,*
Lu. i. 36 (W. H.).*

4774   συγ-γνώμη, ης, ἡ, *permission,
indulgence,* 1 Cor. vii. 6.*

συγκ-.   In words commencing
thus, W. H. prefer the unassimilated form συνκ-.

4775   συγ-κάθημαι, *to sit with* (dat.
or μετά, gen.), Mar. xiv. 54;
Ac. xxvi. 30.*

4776   συγ-καθίζω, σω, (1) *to cause to
sit down with,* Ep. ii. 6; (2)
to sit down together, Lu. xxii.
55.*

4777   συγ-κακο-παθέω, ῶ, *to suffer
hardships together with,* 2
Tim. i. 8, ii. 3 (W. H.). (N.
T.)*

4778   συγ-κακουχέω, ῶ, pass., *to suffer*

ill-treatment with, Heb. xi.
25. (N. T.)*

4779   **συγ-καλέω**, ῶ, ἔσω, *to call together*, Lu. xv. 6; mid., *to call together to one's self*, Lu. ix. 1.

4780   **συγ-καλύπτω**, *to conceal closely, to cover up wholly*, Lu. xii. 2.*

4781   **συγ-κάμπτω**, ψω, *to bend together; to oppress*, Ro. xi. 10 (S.)*

4782   **συγ-κατα-βαίνω**, *to go down with* any one, Ac. xxv. 5.*

4783   **συγ-κατά-θεσις**, εως, ἡ, *assent, agreement*, 2 Cor. vi. 16.*

4784   **συγ-κατα-τίθημι**, in mid., *to give a vote with, to assent to* (dat.), Lu. xxiii. 51.*

4785   **συγ-κατα-ψηφίζω**, in pass., *to be voted* or *classed with* (μετά), Ac. i. 26.*

4786   **συγ-κεράννυμι**, 1st aor. συνεκέρασα, pass. perf. συγκέκραμαι, *to mix with, to unite*, 1 Cor. xii. 24; pass., *to be united with*, Heb. iv. 2.*

4787   **συγ-κινέω**, ῶ, ήσω, *to move together, stir up*, Ac. vi. 12.*

4788   **συγ-κλείω**, σω, *to inclose, to shut in*, as fishes in a net, Lu. v. 6; *to shut* one *up* into (εἰς) or under (ὑπό, acc.) something, *to make subject to*, Ro. xi. 32; Gal. iii. 22, 23.*

4789   **συγ-κληρο-νόμος**, ου, ὁ, ἡ, *a joint heir, a joint participant*, Ro. viii. 17; Ep. iii. 6; Heb. xi. 9; 1 Pet. iii. 7.*

4790   **συγ-κοινωνέω**, ῶ, *to be a partaker with, have fellowship with*, Ep. v. 11; Phil. iv. 14; Rev. xviii. 4.*

4791   **συγ-κοινωνός**, οῦ, ὁ, ἡ, *a partaker with, a co-partner*, Ro. xi. 17. (N. T.)

4792   **συγ-κομίζω**, *to bear away together*, as in burying a corpse, Ac. viii. 2.*

4793   **συγ-κρίνω**, *to join together, to combine*, 1 Cor. ii. 13; *to compare* (acc., dat.), 2 Cor. x. 12.*

4794   **συγ-κύπτω**, *to be bowed together* or *bent double*, Lu. xiii. 11.*

4795   **συγ-κυρία**, ας, ἡ, *a coincidence, an accident; κατὰ συγκυρίαν, by chance*, Lu. x. 31.*

4796   **συγ-χαίρω**, 2d aor. in pass. form συνεχάρην, *to rejoice with* (dat.), Lu. i. 58, xv. 6, 9; 1 Cor. xii. 26, xiii. 6; Phil. ii. 17, 18.*

4797   **συγ-χέω**, also συγχύνω and

4798   **συγχύννω**, perf. pass. συγκέχυμαι, *to mingle together;* (1) *to bewilder*, Ac. ii. 6, ix. 22; (2) *to stir up, to throw into confusion*, Ac. xix. 32, xxi. 27, 31.*

4799   **συγ-χράομαι**, ῶμαι, *to have dealings with* (dat.), Jn. iv. 9.*

4800   **σύγ-χυσις**, εως, ἡ, *confusion, disturbance*, Ac. xix. 29.*

4801   **συ-ζάω** (W. H. συνζ-), ῶ, ήσω, *to live together with* (dat.), Ro. vi. 8; 2 Cor. vii. 3; 2 Tim. ii. 11.*

4802   **συ-ζεύγνυμι**, 1st aor. συνέζευξα, *to yoke together; to unite* (acc.), as man and wife, Mat. xix. 6; Mar. x. 9.*

4803   **συ-ζητέω**, ῶ, *to seek together, to discuss, dispute*, with dat., or πρός, acc., Mar. viii. 11, ix. 16.

4804   **συ-ζήτησις**, εως, ἡ, *mutual questioning, disputation*, Ac. xv. 2 (W. H. ζήτησις), 7 (W. H. ζήτησις), xxviii. 29 (W. H. omit).*

4805   **συ-ζητητής**, οῦ, ὁ, *a disputer*, as the Greek sophists, 1 Cor. i. 20. (N. T.)*

4806   **σύ-ζυγος**, ου, ὁ, *a yoke-fellow, a colleague*, Phil. iv. 3 (prob. a proper name, *Syzygus*).*

  συ-ζωο-ποιέω, ῶ, 1st aor. συνεζωοποίησα, *to make alive together with*, Ep. ii. 5; Col. ii. 13. (N. T.)*

4807   **συκάμινος**, ου, ἡ, *a sycamine-tree*, Lu. xvii. 6.*

4808   **συκῆ**, ῆς, ἡ (contr. from -έα), *a fig-tree*, Mar. xi. 13, 20, 21.

4809   **συκο-μωραία**, ας, ἡ (W. H. -μορέα), *a sycamore-tree*, Lu. xix. 4.*

4810   **σῦκον**, ου, τό, *a fig*, Ja. iii. 12.

4811   **συκο-φαντέω**, ῶ, ήσω, *to accuse falsely, to defraud*, Lu. iii. 14, xix. 8 (gen. person, acc. thing).*

4812   **συλ-αγωγέω**, ῶ, *to plunder*, Col. ii. 8. (N. T.)*

4813   **συλάω**, ῶ, *to rob, to plunder*, 2 Cor. xi. 8.*

  συλλ-. In words commencing thus, W. H. prefer the unassimilated form συνλ-.

4814   **συλ-λαλέω**, 1st aor. συνελάλησα, *to talk with* (dat.), μετά (gen.), πρός (acc.), Mat. xvii. 3; Mar. ix. 4; Lu. iv. 36, ix. 30, xxii. 4; Ac. xxv. 12.*

4815   **συλ-λαμβάνω**, συλλήψομαι, συν-

νείληφα, συνέλαβον, (1) *to take
together, to seize,* Mat. xxvi.
55; (2) *to conceive,* of a
woman, Lu. i. 24, 31; (3)
mid., *to apprehend* (acc.), *to
help* (dat.), Ac. xxvi. 21;
Phil. iv. 3.

4816 συλ-λέγω, ξω, *to collect, to
gather,* Mat. xiii. 28, 29, 30.

4817 συλ-λογίζομαι, σομαι, *to reckon
with one's self, to reason,* Lu.
xx. 5.*

4818 συλ-λυπέομαι, οῦμαι, pass., *to
be grieved* (ἐπί, dat.), Mar.
iii. 5.*

συμβ-, συμμ-, συμπ-, συμφ-.
In some words commencing
thus, W. H. prefer the unassimilated form συνβ-, συνμ-,
συνπ-, συνφ-.

4819 συμ-βαίνω, 2d aor. συνέβην, *to
happen, to occur,* Mar. x. 32;
Ac. xx. 19; perf. part. τὸ
συμβεβηκὸς *an event,* Lu.
xxiv. 14.

4820 συμ-βάλλω, 2d aor. συνέβαλον,
to throw together, hence, *to
ponder,* Lu. ii. 19; *to come
up with, to encounter,* with
or without hostile intent
(dat.), Lu. xiv. 31; Ac. xx.
14; *to dispute with,* Ac. xvii.
18; mid., *to confer, consult
with,* Ac. iv. 15; *to contribute*
(dat.), Ac. xviii. 27.*

4821 συμ-βασιλεύω, σω, *to reign together with,* 1 Cor. iv. 8; 2
Tim. ii. 12.*

4822 συμ-βιβάζω, άσω, (1) *to unite,*
or *knit together,* Col. ii. 2,
19; (2) *to put together in
reasoning,* and so, *to conclude, prove,* Ac. ix. 22; (3)
to teach, instruct, 1 Cor. ii.
16.

4823 συμ-βουλεύω, *to give advice*
(dat.), Jn. xviii. 14; Rev. iii.
18; mid., *to take counsel together* (ἵνα or inf.), Mat. xxvi.
4; Jn. xi. 53 (W. H. βουλεύ-
ομαι); Ac. ix. 23.*

4824 συμ-βούλιον, ου, τό, (1) *mutual
consultation, counsel;* λαμ-
βάνω, ποιέω συμβούλιον, *to
take counsel together,* Mat.
xii. 14, xxii. 15, xxvii. 1, 7,
xxviii. 12; Mar. iii. 6, xv.
1; (2) *a council, a gathering of counselors,* Ac. xxv.
12.*

4825 σύμ-βουλος, ου, ὁ, *an adviser, a
counselor,* Ro. xi. 34.*

4826 Συμεών, ὁ (Heb.), *Simeon* or

Simon (see Σίμων); the
apostle Peter is so called,
Ac. xv. 14; 2 Pet. i. 1; and
four others are mentioned:
(1) Lu. ii. 25, 34; (2) Lu. iii.
30; (3) Ac. xiii. 1; (4) Rev.
vii. 7.*

4827 συμ-μαθητής, οῦ, ὁ, *a fellow-
disciple,* Jn. xi. 16.*

4828 συμ-μαρτυρέω, ῶ, *to bear witness together with,* Ro. ii. 15,
viii. 16, ix. 1; Rev. xxii. 18
(not W. H.).*

4829 συμ-μερίζω, in mid., *to divide
together with, partake with*
(dat.), 1 Cor. ix. 13.*

4830 συμ-μέτοχος, ον, *jointly partak-
ing,* Ep. iii. 6, v. 7.*

4831 συμ-μιμητής, οῦ, ὁ, *a joint-
imitator,* Phil. iii. 17. (N.
T.)*

see **4833** συμ-μορφίζω, see συμμορφόω.
(N. T.)

4832 σύμ-μορφος, ον, *similar, con-
formed to,* gen., Ro. viii. 29;
dat., Phil. iii. 21.*

4833 συμ-μορφόω, ῶ, *to bring to the
same form with* (dat.), Phil.
iii. 10 (W. H. συμμορφίζω, in
same sense). (N. T.)*

4834 συμ-παθέω, ῶ, *to sympathize
with, to have compassion on*
(dat.), Heb. iv. 15, x. 34.*

4835 συμ-παθής, ές, *sympathizing,
compassionate,* 1 Pet. iii. 8.*

4836 συμ-παρα-γίνομαι, *to come together to* (ἐπί, acc.), Lu. xxiii.
48; *to stand by one, to help*
(dat.), 2 Tim. iv. 16 (W. H.
παραγίνομαι).*

4837 συμ-παρα-καλέω, ῶ, in pass., *to
be strengthened together,* Ro.
i. 12.*

4838 συμ-παρα-λαμβάνω, 2d aor. συμ-
παρέλαβον, *to take with one's
self,* as companion, Ac. xii.
25, xv. 37, 38; Gal. ii. 1.*

4839 συμ-παρα-μένω, μενῶ, *to remain*
or *continue together with*
(dat.), Phil. i. 25 (W. H. παρα-
μένω).*

4840 συμ-πάρειμι, *to be present together with,* Ac. xxv. 24.*

4841 συμ-πάσχω, *to suffer together
with,* Ro. viii. 17; 1 Cor. xii.
26.*

4842 συμ-πέμπω, *to send together
with,* 2 Cor. viii. 18, 22.*

4843 συμ-περι-λαμβάνω, *to embrace
completely,* Ac. xx. 10.*

4844 συμ-πίνω, 2d aor. συνέπιον, *to
drink together with,* Ac. x.
41.*

see 4098 συμ-πίπτω, *to fall together*, Lu. vi. 49 (W. H.).*

4845 συμ-πληρόω, ῶ, *to fill complete-ly*, Lu. viii. 23; pass., *to be completed, to be fully come*, Lu. ix. 51; Ac. ii. 1.*

4846 συμ-πνίγω, *to choke utterly*, as weeds do plants, Mat. xiii. 22; Mar. iv. 7, 19; Lu. viii. 14; *to crowd upon* (acc.), Lu. viii. 42.*

4847 συμ-πολίτης, ου, ὁ, *a fellow-citizen*, Ep. ii. 19.*

4848 συμ-πορεύομαι, (1) *to journey together with* (dat.), Lu. vii. 11, xiv. 25, xxiv. 15; (2) in-trans., *to come together, to as-semble*, Mar. x. 1.*

4849 συμπόσιον, ου, τό (συμπίνω), *a drinking party, a festive com-pany*, συμπόσια συμπόσια, *by companies*, Mar. vi. 39.*

4850 συμ-πρεσβύτερος, ου, ὁ, *a fellow-elder*, 1 Pet. v. 1. (N. T.)*

see 4906 συμ-φάγω, see συνεσθίω.

4851 συμ-φέρω, 1st aor. συνήνεγκα, *to bring together, to collect*, only Ac. xix. 19; generally intrans., and often impers., *to conduce to, to be profitable to*, 1 Cor. x. 23; 2 Cor. xii. 1; part. τὸ συμφέρον, *profit, ad-vantage*, 1 Cor. vii. 35.

4852 σύμ-φημι, *to assent to*, Ro. vii. 16.*

see 4851 σύμ-φορος, ον, *profitable*, 1 Cor. vii. 35, x. 33 (W. H. for Rec. συμφέρον).*

4853 συμ-φυλέτης, ου, ὁ, *one of the same tribe, a fellow-country-man*, 1 Th. ii. 14. (N. T.)*

4854 σύμ-φυτος, ον, *grown together, united with* (R. V.), Ro. vi. 5.*

4855 συμ-φύω, 2d aor. pass. part. συμφυείς, pass., *to grow at the same time*, Lu. viii. 7.*

4856 συμ-φωνέω, ῶ, ήσω, *to agree with, agree together, arrange with* (dat., or μετά, gen.), of persons, Mat. xviii. 19, xx. 2, 13; Ac. v. 9; of things, *to be in accord with*, Lu. v. 36; Ac. xv. 15.*

4857 συμ-φώνησις, εως, ἡ, *concord, agreement*, 2 Cor. vi. 15. (N. T.)*

4858 συμ-φωνία, ας, ἡ, *harmony*, of instruments, *music*, Lu. xv. 25.* —

4859 σύμ-φωνος, ον, *harmonious, agreeing with; ἐκ συμφώνου, by agreement*, 1 Cor. vii. 5.*

4860 συμ-ψηφίζω, *to compute, reckon up*, Ac. xix. 19.*

4861 σύμ-ψυχος, ον, *of one accord*, Phil. ii. 2. (N. T.)*

4862 σύν, a prep. gov. dative, *with* (see Gr. § 296; Wi. § 48b, Bu. 331). In composition, σύν denotes association with, or is intensive. The final ν changes to γ, λ, or μ, or is dropped, according to the initial letter of the word with which it is compounded (see Gr. § 4d, 5, Bu. 8); but W. H. usually prefer the un-assimilated forms.

4863 συν-άγω, άξω, (1) *to bring to-gether, to gather, to assemble*, Lu. xv. 13; Jn. xi. 47; pass., *to be assembled, to come to-gether*, Ac. iv. 5, xiii. 44; (2) *to receive hospitably*, only Mat. xxv. 35, 38, 43.

4864 συναγωγή, ῆς, ἡ, *an assembly, a congregation, synagogue*, either the place, or the people gathered in the place, Lu. xii. 11, xxi. 12. *Syn.:* see ἐκκλησία.

4865 συν-αγωνίζομαι, *to strive to-gether with* another, *to aid* (dat.), Ro. xv. 30.*

4866 συν-αθλέω, ῶ, ήσω, *to strive to-gether for* (dat. of thing), Phil. i. 27; or *with*, (dat. of person), Phil. iv. 3.*

4867 συν-αθροίζω, σω, *to gather or collect together*, Ac. xix. 25; pass., *to be assembled together*, Lu. xxiv. 33 (W. H. ἀθροίζω); Ac. xii. 12.*

4868 συν-αίρω, *to reckon together, to make a reckoning with*, Mat. xviii. 23, 24, xxv. 19.*

4869 συν-αιχμάλωτος, ου, ὁ, *a fellow-captive* or *prisoner*, Ro. xvi. 7; Col. iv. 10; Philem. 23. (N. T.)*

4870 συν-ακολουθέω, ῶ, ήσω, *to follow together with, to accompany*, Mar. v. 37, xiv. 51 (W. H.); Lu. xxiii. 49.*

4871 συν-αλίζω, in pass., *to be as-sembled together with* (dat.), Ac. i. 4.*

see 4900 συν-αλλάσσω, *to reconcile*, see συνελαύνω.

4872 συν-ανα-βαίνω, *to go up together with* (dat.), Mar. xv. 41; Ac. xiii. 31.*

4873 συν-ανά-κειμαι, *to recline to-gether with*, as at a meal, *to* *feast with* (dat.), Mat. ix. 10; part. οἱ συνανακείμενοι, *the guests*, Mar. vi. 22, 26. (Ap.)

4874 συν-ανα-μίγνυμι, pass., *to mingle together with, to keep company with* (dat.), I Cor. v. 9, 11; 2 Th. iii. 14.*

4875 συν-ανα-παύομαι, σομαι, *to find rest* or *refreshment together with* (dat.), Ro. xv. 32. (S.)*

4876 συν-αντάω, ῶ, ήσω, (1) *to meet with* (dat.), Lu. ix. 37, xxii. 10; Ac. x. 25; Heb. vii. 1, 10; (2) *of things, to happen to, to befall;* τὰ συναντήσοντα, *the things that shall happen*, Ac. xx. 22.*

4877 συν-άντησις, εως, ἡ, *a meeting with*, Mat. viii. 34 (W. H. ὑπάντησις).*

4878 συν-αντι-λαμβάνω, mid., lit., *to take hold together with; to assist, help* (dat.), Lu. x. 40; Ro. viii. 26.*

4879 συν-απ-άγω, *to lead away along with;* in pass., *to be led* or *carried away in mind*, Ro. xii. 16 (see R. V. mrg.); Gal. ii. 13; 2 Pet. iii. 17.*

4880 συν-απο-θνήσκω, *to die together with* (dat.), Mar. xiv. 31; 2 Cor. vii. 3; 2 Tim. ii. 11.*

4881 συν-απ-όλλυμι, in mid., *to perish together with* (dat.), Heb. xi. 31.*

4882 συν-απο-στέλλω, *to send together with* (acc.), 2 Cor. xii. 18.*

4883 συν-αρμολογέω, ῶ, in pass., *to be framed together*, Ep. ii. 21, iv. 16. (N.T.)*

4884 συν-αρπάζω, σω, *to seize*, or *drag by force* (dat.), Lu. viii. 29; Ac. vi. 12, xix. 29, xxvii. 15.*

4885 συν-αυξάνω, in pass., *to grow together*, Mat. xiii. 30.*

4886 σύν-δεσμος, ου, ὁ, *that which binds together, a band, a bond*, Ac. viii. 23; Ep. iv. 3; Col. ii. 19, iii. 14.*

4887 συν-δέω, in pass., *to be bound together with* any one, as fellow-prisoners, Heb. xiii. 3.*

4888 συν-δοξάζω, *to glorify together with* (σύν), pass., Ro. viii. 17.*

4889 σύν-δουλος, ου, ὁ, *a fellow-slave, a fellow-servant*, Mat. xviii. 28–33; of Christians, *a fellow-worker, a colleague*, Col. i. 7.

4890 συν-δρομή, ῆς, ἡ, *a running together, a concourse*, Ac. xxi. 30.*

4891 συν-εγείρω, 1st aor. συνήγειρα, pass. συνηγέρθην; *to raise together, to raise with*, Ep. ii. 6; Col. ii. 12, iii. 1. (S.)*

4892 συνέδριον, ου, τό, *a council, a tribunal*, Mat. x. 17; specially, *the Sanhedrin*, the Jewish council of seventy-one members, usually presided over by the high priest, Mat. v. 22, xxvi. 59; *the council-hall*, where the Sanhedrin met, Ac. iv. 15.

4893 συν-είδησις, εως, ἡ, *consciousness*, Heb. x. 2; *the conscience*, Ro. ii. 15; 2 Cor. iv. 2, v. 11; I Pet. ii. 19.

4894 συν-εῖδον, 2d aor. of obs. pres., *to be conscious* or *aware of, to understand*, Ac. xii. 12, xiv. 6; perf. σύνοιδα, part. συνειδώς, *to be privy to* a design, Ac. v. 2; *to be conscious to one's self* (dat.) of guilt (acc.), I Cor. iv. 4.*

4895 σύν-ειμι, *to be with* (dat.), Lu. ix. 18; Ac. xxii. 11.*

4896 σύν-ειμι (εἶμι), part. συνιών, *to go* or *come with, to assemble*, Lu. viii. 4.*

4897 συν-εισ-έρχομαι, *to enter together with* (dat.), Jn. vi. 22, xviii. 15.*

4898 συν-έκδημος, ου, ὁ, ἡ, *a fellow-traveler*, Ac. xix. 29; 2 Cor. viii. 19.*

4899 συν-εκλεκτός, ή, όν, *elected together with*, I Pet. v. 13. (N. T.)*

4900 συν-ελαύνω, ελάσω, *to compel, to urge* (acc. and εἰς), Ac. vii. 26 (W. H. συναλλάσσω).*

4901 συν-επι-μαρτυρέω, ῶ, *to unite in bearing witness*, Heb. ii. 4.*

see 4934 συν-επι-τίθημι, mid., *to join in assailing*, Ac. xxiv. 9 (W. H. for συντίθημι).*

4902 συν-έπομαι, *to follow with, to accompany* (dat.), Ac. xx. 4.*

4903 συν-εργέω, ῶ, *to co-operate with* (dat.), *to work together*, I Cor. xvi. 16; Ro. viii. 28.

4904 συν-εργός, όν, *co-working, helping;* as a subst., *a companion in work, a fellow-worker*, gen. of person, obj. with εἰς, or dat., or (met.) gen., 2 Cor. i. 24.

4905 συν-έρχομαι (see Gr. § 103, 2, Wi. § 15, Bu. 58), *to come* or

go with, to accompany, Ac. i.
21; to come together, to as-
semble, Ac. i. 6, v. 16; used
also of conjugal intercourse,
to come or live together, Mat.
i. 18.

4906 συν-εσθίω, 2d aor. συνέφαγον,
to eat with (dat., or μετά,
gen.), Lu. xv. 2; Ac. x. 41,
xi. 3; 1 Cor. v. 11; Gal. ii.
12.*

4907 σύνεσις, εως, ἡ (συνίημι), a putting together, in mind; hence,
understanding, Lu. ii. 47;
the understanding, the source
of discernment, Mar. xii. 33.

4908 συνετός, ἡ, όν (συνίημι), intelligent, prudent, wise, Mat. xi.
25; Lu. x. 21; Ac. xiii. 7; 1
Cor. i. 19.*

4909 συν-ευδοκέω, ῶ, to be pleased together with, to approve to-
gether (dat.), Lu. xi. 48; Ac.
viii. 1, xxii. 20; to be of one
mind with (dat.), Ro. i. 32;
to consent, agree to (inf.), 1
Cor. vii. 12, 13.*

4910 συν-ευωχέω, ῶ, in pass., to feast
sumptuously with, 2 Pet. ii.
13; Ju. 12.*

4911 συν-εφ-ίστημι, to rise up together against (κατά), Ac.
xvi. 22.*

4912 συν-έχω, ξω, (1) to press together, to close, Ac. vii. 57;
(2) to press on every side,
to confine, Lu. viii. 45; (3) to
hold fast, Lu. xxii. 63; (4)
to urge, impel, Lu. xii. 50;
2 Cor. v. 14; (5) in pass., to
be afflicted with sickness, Lu.
iv. 38.

4913 συν-ήδομαι, to delight inwardly
in (dat.), Ro. vii. 22.*

4914 συν-ήθεια, ας, ἡ, a custom, Jn.
xviii. 39; 1 Cor. viii. 7 (W.
H.), xi. 16.*

4915 συν-ηλικιώτης, ου, ὁ, one of the
same age, Gal. i. 14.*

4916 συν-θάπτω, 2d aor. pass. συνε-
τάφην, in pass., to be buried
together with, Ro. vi. 4; Col.
ii. 12.*

4917 συν-θλάω, ῶ, fut. pass. συν-
θλασθήσομαι, to break, to
break in pieces, Mat. xxi. 44;
Lu. xx. 18.*

4918 συν-θλίβω, to press on all sides,
to crowd upon, Mar. v. 24,
31.*

4919 συν-θρύπτω, to break in pieces,
to crush, fig., Ac. xxi. 13.
(N. T.)*

4920 συν-ίημι, inf. συνιέναι, part.
συνιῶν or συνιείς, fut. συνήσω,
1st aor. συνῆκα, to put together, in mind; hence, to
consider, understand (acc.),
to be aware (ὅτι), to attend to
(ἐπί, dat.), Mat. xiii. 23, 51,
xvi. 12; Mar. vi. 52.

4921 συν-ίστημι, also συνιστάνω and
συνιστάω, to place together;
to commend, 2 Cor. iii. 1, vi.
4; to prove, exhibit, Gal. ii.
18; Ro. iii. 5, v. 8; perf. and
2d aor., intrans., to stand
with, Lu. ix. 32; to be composed of, to cohere, Col. i. 17;
2 Pet. iii. 5.

4922 συν-οδεύω, to journey with, to
accompany (dat.), Ac. ix.
7.*

4923 συν-οδία, ας, ἡ, a company
traveling together, a caravan,
Lu. ii. 44.*

4924 συν-οικέω, ῶ, to dwell together,
as in marriage, 1 Pet. iii. 7.*

4925 συν-οικοδομέω, ῶ, in pass., to
be built up together, Ep. ii.
22.*

4926 συν-ομιλέω, ῶ, to talk with
(dat.), Ac. x. 27.*

4927 συν-ομορέω, ῶ, to be contiguous
to (dat.), Ac. xviii. 7. (N. T.)*

4928 συν-οχή, ῆς, ἡ, constraint of
mind; hence, distress, an-
guish, Lu. xxi. 25; 2 Cor. ii.
4.*

4929 συν-τάσσω, ξω, to arrange with,
prescribe, appoint, Mat. xxi.
6 (W. H.), xxvi. 19, xxvii.
10.*

4930 συν-τέλεια, ας, ἡ, a completion, a
consummation, an end, Mat.
xiii. 39, 40, 49, xxiv. 3,
xxviii. 20; Heb. ix. 26.*

4931 συν-τελέω, ῶ, έσω, (1) to bring
completely to an end, Mat.
vii. 28 (W. H. τελέω); Lu.
iv. 2, 13; Ac. xxi. 27; (2) to
fulfill, to accomplish, Ro. ix.
28; Mar. xiii. 4; to make, to
conclude, Heb. viii. 8.*

4932 συν-τέμνω, to cut short, to bring
to swift accomplishment, Ro.
ix. 28.*

4933 συν-τηρέω, ῶ, (1) to preserve, to
keep safe, Mat. ix. 17; Mar.
vi. 20; Lu. v. 38 (W. H.
omit); (2) to keep in mind,
Lu. ii. 19.*

4934 συν-τίθημι, in mid., to place
together, to make an agree-
ment, Lu. xxii. 5; Jn. ix. 22;
Ac. xxiii. 20; to assent, Ac.

xxiv. 9 (W. H. συνεπιτί-
θημι).*

4935 συν-τόμως, adv., concisely, brief-
ly, Ac. xxiv. 4.*

4936 συν-τρέχω, 2d aor. συνέδραμον,
to run together, as a multi-
tude, Mar. vi. 33; Ac. iii.
11; to run with (fig.), 1 Pet.
iv. 4.*

4937 συν-τρίβω, ψω, to break by
crushing, to break in pieces,
Lu. ix. 39; Ro. xvi. 20; perf.
pass. part. συντετριμμένος,
bruised, Mat. xii. 20.

4938 σύν-τριμμα, ατος, τό, crushing;
fig., destruction, Ro. iii. 16.
(S.)*

4939 σύν-τροφος, ον, ὁ, one brought
up with, a foster-brother, Ac.
xiii. 1.*

4940 συν-τυγχάνω, 2d aor. inf. συν-
τυχεῖν, to meet with, come to
(dat.), Lu. viii. 19.*

4941 Συντύχη, acc. ην, ἡ, Syntyche,
Phil. iv. 2.*

4942 συν-υπο-κρίνομαι, dep. pass.,
1st aorist συνυπεκρίθην, to
dissemble with, Gal. ii.
13.*

4943 συν-υπουργέω, ῶ, to help together, 2 Cor. i. 11.*

4944 συν-ωδίνω, to be in travail together, Ro. viii. 22.*

4945 συν-ωμοσία, ας, ἡ, a swearing
together, a conspiracy, Ac.
xxiii. 13.*

4946 Συράκουσαι, ῶν, αἱ, Syracuse,
Ac. xxviii. 12.*

4947 Συρία, ας, ἡ, Syria, Lu. ii. 2.

4948 Σύρος, ον, ὁ, a Syrian, Lu. iv.
27.*

4949 Συρο-φοίνισσα (W. H. Συρο-
φοινίκισσα, mrg., Σύρα Φοινίκισσα), ης, ἡ, an appellative,
a Syrophenician woman, Mar.
vii. 26.*

4950 Σύρτις, εως, acc. ιν, ἡ, (a quick-
sand), the Syrtis major, Ac.
xxvii. 17.*

4951; see σύρω, to draw, to drag, Jn. xxi.
1670 8; Ac. viii. 3, xiv. 19, xvii.
6; Rev. xii. 4.* Syn.: see
ἕλκω.

συσ-. In some words com-
mencing thus, W. H. prefer
the uncontracted form συνσ-.

4952 συ-σπαράσσω, ξω, to convulse
completely (acc.), Mar. ix. 20
(W. H.); Lu. ix. 42.*

4953 σύσ-σημον, ον, τό, a concerted
signal, a sign agreed upon,
Mar. xiv. 44.*

4954 σύσ-σωμος (W. H. σύνσωμος),

ον, belonging to the same
body; fig., of Jews and Gentiles, in one church, Ep. iii.
6. (N. T.)*

4955 συ-στασιαστής, οῦ, ὁ, a fellow-
insurgent (W. H. στασιασ-
τής), Mar. xv. 7.*

4956 συ-στατικός, ἡ, όν, commenda-
tory, 2 Cor. iii. 1.*

4957 συ-σταυρόω, ῶ, to crucify together with (acc. and dat.);
lit., Mat. xxvii. 44; fig., Gal.
ii. 19. (N. T.)

4958 συ-στέλλω, (1) to contract, perf.
pass. part., contracted, short-
ened, 1 Cor. vii. 29; (2) to
wrap round, to swathe, as a
dead body, Ac. v. 6.*

4959 συ-στενάζω, to groan together,
Ro. viii. 22.*

4960 συ-στοιχέω, ῶ, to be in the same
rank with; to answer to, to
correspond to (dat.), Gal. iv.
25.*

4961 συ-στρατιώτης, ου, ὁ, a fellow-
soldier, i.e., in the Christian
service, Phil. ii. 25; Philem.
2.*

4962 συ-στρέφω, ψω, to roll or gather
together, Mat. xvii. 22 (W.
H.); Ac. xxviii. 3.*

4963 συ-στροφή, ῆς, ἡ, a gathering
together, a riotous concourse,
Ac. xix. 40; a conspiracy, Ac.
xxiii. 12.*

4964 συ-σχηματίζω, in pass., to conform one's self, to be assimilated to (dat.), Ro. xii. 2; 1
Pet. i. 14.*

4965 Συχάρ (W. H.), or Σιχάρ, ἡ,
Sychar, Jn. iv. 5.*

4966 Συχέμ, Shechem, (1) ὁ, the
prince, Ac. vii. 16 (Rec., W.
H. the city); (2) ἡ, the city,
Ac. vii. 16.*

4967 σφαγή, ῆς, ἡ, (1) slaughter, Ac.
viii. 32; Ro. viii. 36 (S.); Ja.
v. 5.*

4968 σφάγιον, ον, τό, a slaughtered
victim, Ac. vii. 42.*

4969 σφάζω, ξω, pass., perf. part.
ἐσφαγμένος, 2d aor. ἐσφάγην,
to kill by violence, to slay, 1
Jn. iii. 12; Rev. v. 9, vi. 4.

4970 σφόδρα, adv., exceedingly, greatly, Mat. ii. 10.

4971 σφοδρῶς, adv., exceedingly, Ac.
xxvii. 18.*

4972 σφραγίζω, ίσω, to seal, to set a
seal upon, (1) for security,
Mat. xxvii. 66; (2) for secrecy, Rev. xxii. 10; (3) for
designation, Ep. i. 13; or

(4) for authentication, Ro. xv. 28.

4973 σφραγίς, ῖδος, ἡ, (1) *a seal, a signet-ring*, Rev. vii. 2 ; (2) *the impression of a seal* whether for security and secrecy, as Rev. v. 1 ; or for designation, Rev. ix. 4 ; (3) *that which the seal attests, the proof*, 1 Cor. ix. 2.

see 4711 σφυρίς, see σπυρίς.

4974 σφυρόν (W. H. σφυδρόν), οῦ, τό, *the ankle-bone*, Ac. iii. 7.*

4975 σχεδόν, adv., *nearly, almost*, Ac. xiii. 44, xix. 26; Heb. ix. 22.*

4976 σχῆμα, ατος, τό, *fashion, habit*, 1 Cor. vii. 31 ; *form, appearance*, Phil. ii. 7.* *Syn.:* see ἰδέα.

4977 σχίζω, ίσω, *to rend, to divide asunder*, Mat. xxvii. 51 ; pass., *to be divided into factions*, Ac. xiv. 4.

4978 σχίσμα, ατος, τό, *a rent*, as in a garment, Mar. ii. 21 ; *a division, a dissension*, 1 Cor. i. 10.

4979 σχοινίον, ου, τό (dim. of σχοῖνος, *a rush*), *a cord, a rope*, Jn. ii. 15 ; Ac. xxvii. 32.*

4980 σχολάζω, άσω, *to be at leisure; to be empty* or *unoccupied*, Mat. xii. 44; *to have leisure for* (dat.), *give one's self to*, 1 Cor. vii. 5.*

4981 σχολή, ῆς, ἡ, *leisure; a place where there is leisure for anything, a school*, Ac. xix. 9.*

4982 σώζω, σώσω, perf. σέσωκα, pass. σέσωσμαι, 1st aor. pass. ἐσώθην; (1) *to save*, from evil or danger, Mat. viii. 25, xvi. 25 ; (2) *to heal*, Mat. ix. 21, 22 ; Jn. xi. 12 ; (3) *to save, i.e.*, from eternal death, 1 Tim. i. 15 ; part. pass. οἱ σωζόμενοι, *those who are being saved, i.e.*, who are in the way of salvation, Ac. ii. 47.

4983 σῶμα, ατος, τό, *a body, i.e.*, (1) *the living body* of an animal, Ja. iii. 3 ; or *of a man*, as 1 Cor. xii. 12, espec. as the medium of human life, and of human life as sinful; the *body* of Christ, as the medium and witness of his humanity; σώματα, Rev. xviii. 13, *slaves* ; (2) *a dead body, a corpse*, Ac. ix. 40 ; (3) fig.,

a community, the church, *the mystic body of Christ*, Col. i. 24; (4) *any material body*, plants, sun, moon, etc., 1 Cor. xv. 37, 38, 40; (5) *substance*, opp. to shadow, Col. ii. 17.

4984 σωματικός, ἡ, όν, *of* or *pertaining to the body*, 1 Tim. iv. 8 ; *bodily, corporeal*, Lu. iii. 22.*

4985 σωματικῶς, adv., *bodily, corporeally*, Col. ii. 9.*

4986 Σώπατρος, ου, ὁ, *Sopater*, Ac. xx. 4 ; (perh. = Σωσίπατρος, see Ro. xvi. 21).*

4987 σωρεύω, σω, *to heap up, to load*, Ro. xii. 20 ; 2 Tim. iii. 16.*

4988 Σωσθένης, ου, ὁ, *Sosthenes*, (1) Ac. xviii. 17; (2) 1 Cor. i. 1.*

4989 Σωσίπατρος, ου, ὁ, *Sosipater*, Ro. xvi. 21 (see Ac. xx. 4).*

4990 σωτήρ, ῆρος, ὁ, *a savior, deliverer, preserver;* a name given to God, Lu. i. 47 ; 1 Tim. i. 1, ii. 3, iv. 10; Tit. i. 3, ii. 10, iii. 4 ; Ju. 25 ; elsewhere always of Christ, Lu. ii. 11 ; Jn. iv. 42.

4991 σωτηρία, ας, ἡ, *welfare, prosperity, deliverance, preservation*, from temporal evils, Ac. vii. 25, xxvii. 34 ; Heb. xi. 7; 2 Pet. iii. 15; specially *salvation, i.e.*, deliverance from eternal death, viewed either as present or future, 2 Cor. i. 6; 1 Th. v. 9.

4992 σωτήριος, ον, *saving, bringing salvation*, Tit. ii. 11 ; neut. τὸ σωτήριον, *salvation*, Lu. ii. 30, iii. 6 ; Ac. xxviii. 28 ; Ep. vi. 17.*

4993 σωφρονέω, ῶ, ήσω, (1) *to be of sound mind*, Mar. v. 15 ; (2) *to be sober-minded*, Ro. xii. 3 ; (3) *to exercise self-control*, Tit. ii. 6.

4994 σωφρονίζω, *to make sober-minded, to admonish*, Tit. ii. 4.*

4995 σωφρονισμός, οῦ, ὁ, *self-control*, or *discipline*, 2 Tim. i. 7.*

4996 σωφρόνως, adv., *soberly, with moderation*, Tit. ii. 12.*

4997 σωφροσύνη, ης, ἡ, *soundness of mind, sanity*, Ac. xxvi. 25 ; *self-control, sobriety*, 1 Tim. ii. 9, 15.*

4998 σώ-φρων, ον (σάος, σῶς, *sound*, and φρήν), *of sound mind, self-controlled, temperate*, 1 Tim. iii. 2; Tit. i. 8, ii. 2, 5.*

T

T, τ, ταῦ, *tau, t,* the nineteenth letter. As a numeral, τ' = 300; ,τ = 300,000.

4999 **ταβέρναι, ῶν, αἱ** (Lat.), *taverns;* Ac. xxviii. 15, Τρεῖς Ταβέρναι, *Three Taverns,* a place on the Appian Way. (N. T.)*

5000 **Ταβιθά, ἡ** (Aram.), *Tabitha,* Ac. ix. 36, 40.*

5001 **τάγμα, ατος, τό,** *an order* or *series, a class,* 1 Cor. xv. 23.*

5002 **τακτός, ή, όν,** *appointed, fixed,* Ac. xii. 21.*

5003 **ταλαιπωρέω, ῶ, ήσω,** *to be distressed, to be miserable,* Ja. iv. 9.*

5004 **ταλαιπωρία, ας, ἡ,** *hardship, misery,* Ro. iii. 16; Ja. v. 1.*

5005 **ταλαί-πωρος, ον,** *afflicted, miserable,* Ro. vii. 24; Rev. iii. 17.*

5006 **ταλαντιαῖος, αία, αῖον,** *of the weight of a talent,* Rev. xvi. 21.*

5007 **τάλαντον, ον, τό,** *a talent,* of silver or gold, Mat. xviii. 24. The N. T. talent is probably the Syrian silver talent, worth about 237 dollars, rather than the Attic, worth about 1000 dollars.

5008 **ταλιθά, ἡ** (Aram.), *a damsel,* Mar. v. 41. (N. T.)*

5009 **ταμεῖον** (or -μιεῖ-), **ον, τό,** *a storechamber,* Lu. xii. 24; *a secret chamber,* Mat. vi. 6, xxiv. 26; Lu. xii. 3.*

•3569 **τανῦν,** adv. (τὰ νῦν, *the things that now are*), *as respects the present, at present, now,* only in Ac. (W. H. always write τὰ νῦν).

5010 **τάξις, εως, ἡ,** *order, i.e.,* (1) *regular arrangement,* Col. ii. 5; (2) *appointed succession,* Lu. i. 8; (3) *position, rank,* Heb. v. 6.

5011 **ταπεινός, ή, όν,** *humble, lowly,* in condition or in spirit; in N. T. in a good sense, Ja. i. 9, iv. 6.

5012 **ταπεινοφροσύνη, ης, ἡ,** *lowliness of mind, humility,* real, as Phil. ii. 3; or affected, as Col. ii. 18.

see 5391 **ταπεινό-φρων, ον,** *humble,* 1 Pet. iii. 8 (W. H. for φιλόφρων). (S.)*

5013 **ταπεινόω, ῶ, ώσω,** *to make or* *bring low,* Lu. iii. 5; *to humble, humiliate,* 2 Cor. xii. 21; pass., *to be humbled,* Lu. xviii. 14; pass., in mid. sense, *to humble one's self,* Ja. iv. 10.

5014 **ταπείνωσις, εως, ἡ,** *low condition,* in circumstances, Lu. i. 48; *abasement,* in spirit, Ja. i. 10.

5015 **ταράσσω, ξω,** *to agitate,* as water in a pool, Jn. v. 4 (W. H. omit), 7; *to stir up, to disturb in mind,* with fear, grief, anxiety, doubt, Ac. xviii. 8; 1 Pet. iii. 14.

5016 **ταραχή, ῆς, ἡ,** *a disturbance,* Jn. v. 4 (W. H. omit); *a tumult, sedition,* Mar. xiii. 8 (W. H. omit).*

5017 **τάραχος, ον, ὁ,** *a disturbance,* Ac. xix. 23; *commotion,* Ac. xii. 18.*

5018 **Ταρσεύς, έως, ὁ,** *one of Tarsus,* Ac. ix. 11, xxi. 39.*

5019 **Ταρσός, οῦ, ἡ,** *Tarsus,* Ac. ix. 30.

5020 **ταρταρόω, ῶ, ώσω,** *to thrust down to Tartarus (Gehenna),* 2 Pet. ii. 4. (N. T.)*

5021 **τάσσω, ξω,** (1) *to assign, arrange,* Ro. xiii. 1; (2) *to determine;* mid., *to appoint,* Mat. xxviii. 16.

5022 **ταῦρος, ον, ὁ,** *a bull,* Ac. xiv. 13.

•5024 **ταὐτά,** by crasis for τὰ αὐτά, *the same things.*

5023; see •3778 **ταῦτα,** see οὗτος.

5027 **ταφή, ῆς, ἡ** (θάπτω), *a burial,* Mat. xxvii. 7.*

5028 **τάφος, ον, ὁ,** *a burial-place, a sepulchre,* as Mat. xxiii. 27.

5029 **τάχα,** adv. *quickly, perhaps,* Ro. v. 7; Philem. 15.*

5030 **ταχέως,** adv. (ταχύς), *soon, quickly,* Gal. i. 6; *hastily,* 2 Th. ii. 2; 1 Tim. v. 22.

5031 **ταχινός, ή, όν,** *swift, quick,* 2 Pet. i. 14; ii. 1.*

•5034 **τάχος, ους, τό,** *quickness, speed,* only in the phrase ἐν τάχει, *quickly, speedily,* Lu. xviii. 8.

•5035, 5036, 5032 & 5033; see Strong **ταχύς, εῖα, ύ,** *quick, swift,* only Ja. i. 19; ταχύ, compar. τάχιον (W. H. τάχειον), superl. τάχιστα, adverbially, *swiftly; more, most quickly.*

5037 **τέ,** conj. *of annexation, and, both* (see Gr. § 403, Wi. § 53, 2, Bu. 360 sq.).

147

*For 5025 & 5026 see Strong.

5038　τεῖχος, ους, τό, *a wall* of a city, Ac. ix. 25.

5039　τεκμήριον, ου, τό, *a sign, a certain proof*, Ac. i. 3.*

5040　τεκνίον, ου, τό (dim. of τέκνον), *a little child*, Jn. xiii. 33; Gal. iv. 19; 1 Jn. ii. 1, 12, 28, iii. 7, 18, iv. 4, v. 21.*

5041　τεκνο-γονέω, ῶ, *to bear children*, 1 Tim. v. 14.*

5042　τεκνο-γονία, ας, ἡ, *child-bearing*, 1 Tim. ii. 15.*

5043　τέκνον, ου, τό (τίκτω), *a child, a descendant; an inhabitant*, Lu. xiii. 34; fig. of various forms of intimate union and relationship, *a disciple, a follower*, Philem. 10; hence, such phrases as τέκνα τῆς σοφίας, τέκνα ὑπακοῆς, τέκνα τοῦ φωτός, *children of wisdom, obedience, the light*, and espec. τέκνα τοῦ θεοῦ, *children of God*, Ro. viii. 16, 17, 21; 1 Jn.

5044　τεκνο-τροφέω, ῶ, *to bring up children*, 1 Tim. v. 10.*

5045　τέκτων, ονος, ὁ, *a carpenter*, Mat. xiii. 55; Mar. vi. 3.*

5046; see 739　τέλειος, α, ον, *perfect*, as (1) *complete* in all its parts, Ja. i. 4; (2) *full grown of full age*, Heb. v. 14; (3) specially of the completeness of Christian character, *perfect*, Mat. v. 48. *Syn.:* see ἄρτιος.

5047　τελειότης, τητος, ἡ, *perfectness, perfection*, Col. iii. 14; Heb. vi. 1.*

5048　τελειόω, ῶ, ώσω, (1) *to complete, to finish*, as a course, a race, or the like, Jn. iv. 34; (2) *to accomplish*, as time, or prediction, Lu. ii. 43; Jn. xix. 28; (3) *to make perfect*, Heb. vii. 19; pass., *to be perfected*, Lu. xiii. 32.

5049　τελείως (τέλειος), adv., *perfectly*, 1 Pet. i. 13.*

5050　τελείωσις, εως, ἡ, *completion, fulfillment*, Lu. i. 45; *perfection*, Heb. vii. 11.*

5051　τελειωτής, οῦ, ὁ, *a perfecter*, Heb. xii. 2. (N.T.)*

5052　τελεσ-φορέω, ῶ, *to bring to maturity*, Lu. viii. 14.*

5053　τελευτάω, ῶ, *to end, to finish, e.g.*, life; so, *to die*, Mat. ix. 18; Mar. vii. 10.

5054　τελευτή, ῆς, ἡ, *end* of life, *death*, Mat. ii. 15.*

5055　τελέω, ῶ, έσω, τετέλεκα, τετέλεσμαι, ἐτελέσθην, (1) *to end, to finish*, Rev. xx. 3, 5, 7; (2) *to fulfill, to accomplish*, Lu. ii. 39; Ja. ii. 8; (3) *to pay*, Mat. xvii. 24.

5056　τέλος, ους, τό, (1) *an end*, Lu. i. 33; (2) *event* or *issue*, Mat. xxvi. 58; (3) *the principal end, aim, purpose*, 1 Tim. i. 5; (4) *a tax*, Mat. xvii. 25; Ro. xiii. 7.

5057　τελώνης, ου, ὁ, *a collector of taxes*, Lu. iii. 12, v. 27.

5058　τελώνιον, ου, τό, *a toll-house, a tax-collector's office*, Mat. ix. 9; Mar. ii. 14; Lu. v. 27.*

5059; see 1411　τέρας, ατος, τό, *a wonder, a portent;* in N.T. only in plur., and joined with σημεῖα, *signs and wonders*, Ac. vii. 36; Jn. iv. 48. *Syn.:* see δύναμις.

5060　Τέρτιος, ου, ὁ (Lat.), *Tertius*, Ro. xvi. 22.*

5061　Τέρτυλλος, ου, ὁ, *Tertullus*, Ac. xxiv. 1, 2.*

5062　τεσσαράκοντα, *forty*, Mat. iv. 2; Mar. i. 13.

5063　τεσσαρακοντα-ετής, ές, *of forty years*, age or time, Ac. vii. 23, xiii. 18.*

5064　τέσσαρες, τέσσαρα, gen. ων, *four*, Lu. ii. 37; Jn. xi. 17.

5065　τεσσαρες-και-δέκατος, η, ον, ord. num., *fourteenth*, Ac. xxvii. 27, 33.*

5066　τεταρταῖος, αία, αῖον, *of the fourth* (day); τεταρταῖος ἐστιν, *he has been dead four days*, Jn. xi. 39.*

5067　τέταρτος, η, ον, ord. num., *fourth*, Mat. xiv. 25.

5068　τετρά-γωνος, ον, *four-cornered, square*, Rev. xxi. 16.*

5069　τετράδιον, ου, τό, *a quaternion*, or *guard of four soldiers*, Ac. xii. 4.*

5070　τετρακισ-χίλιοι, αι, α, *four thousand*, Mar. viii. 9, 20.

5071　τετρακόσιοι, αι, α, *four hundred*, Ac. v. 36.

5072　τετρά-μηνος, ον, *of four months;* sc. χρόνος, *a period of four months*, Jn. iv. 35.*

5073　τετρα-πλόος, οῦς, ῆ, οῦν, *four-fold*, Lu. xix. 8.*

5074　τετρά-πους, ουν, gen. οδος, *four-footed*, Ac. x. 12, xi. 6; Ro. i. 23.*

5075　τετρ-αρχέω (W.H. τετρααρχέω), ῶ, *to rule over as a tetrarch* (gen.), Lu. iii. 1.*

5076 τετρ-άρχης (W. H. τετραάρχης), ov, ὁ, *a ruler over a fourth part of a region, a tetrarch,* applied also to rulers over any small dominion, Mat. xiv. 1.

see 5177 τεύχω, see *τυγχάνω.*

5077 τεφρόω, ῶ, ώσω (τέφρα, *ashes*), *to reduce to ashes,* 2 Pet. ii. 6.*

5078 τέχνη, ης, ἡ, (1) *art, skill,* Ac. xvii. 29; (2) *an art, a trade,* Ac. xviii. 3; Rev. xviii. 22.*

5079; see τεχνίτης, ov, ὁ, *an artificer,*
1217   *craftsman,* Ac. xix. 24, 38; Rev. xviii. 22; used of God, Heb. xi. 10.* *Syn.:* see δημιουργός.

5080 τήκω, *to make liquid ;* pass., *to melt,* 2 Pet. iii. 12.*

5081 τηλ-αυγῶς, adv. (τῆλε, *afar,* αὐγή, *radiance*), *clearly, distinctly,* Mar. viii. 25.*

5082 τηλικ-οῦτος, αύτη, οῦτο, *so great,* 2 Cor. i. 10; Heb. ii. 3; Ja. iii. 4; Rev. xvi. 18.*

5083 τηρέω, ῶ, ήσω, *to watch carefully,* with good or evil design; (1) *to guard,* Mat. xxvii. 36, 54; (2) *to keep* or *reserve,* 1 Cor. vii. 37; (3) *to observe, keep,* enactments or ordinances, Jn. xiv. 15, 21.

5084 τήρησις, εως, ἡ, (1) *a prison,* Ac. iv. 3, v. 18; (2) *observance,* as of precepts, 1 Cor. vii. 19.*

5085 Τιβεριάς, άδος, ἡ, *Tiberias,* Jn. vi. 1, 23, xxi. 1.*

5086 Τιβέριος, ov, ὁ, *Tiberius,* Lu. iii. 1.*

5087 τίθημι, θήσω (see Gr. § 107, Wi. § 14, 1, Bu. 45 sq.), (1) *to place, set, lay, put forth, put down, put away, put aside ;* mid., *to cause to put,* or *to put for one's self;* (2) *to constitute, to make, to render;* mid., *to assign, determine.*

5088 τίκτω, τέξομαι, 2d aor. ἔτεκον, 1st aor. pass. ἐτέχθην, *to bear, to bring forth,* of women, Lu. i. 57, ii. 6, 7 ; *to produce,* of the earth, Heb. vi. 7.

5089 τίλλω, *to pluck, to pluck off,* Mat. xii. 1; Mar. ii. 23; Lu. vi. 1.*

5090 Τιμαῖος, ov, ὁ, *Timæus,* Mar. x. 46.*

5091 τιμάω, ῶ, ήσω, (1) *to estimate, to value at a price,* Mat. xxvii. 9; (2) *to honor, to reverence,* Mar. vii. 6, 10.

5092 τιμή, ῆς, ἡ, (1) *a price,* Mat. xxvii. 6, 9; (2) *honor,* Ro. ix. 21; Heb. v. 4; 2 Tim. ii. 20, 21; 1 Pet. ii. 7.

5093 τίμιος, a, ov, *of great price, precious, honored,* Rev. xvii. 4; Heb. xiii. 4.

5094 τιμιότης, τητος, ἡ, *preciousness, costliness,* Rev. xviii. 19.*

5095 Τιμό-θεος, ov, ὁ, *Timothy,* Ac. xvii. 14, 15.

5096 Τίμων, ωνος, ὁ, *Timon,* Ac. vi. 5.*

5097 τιμωρέω, ῶ, *to punish* (acc.), Ac. xxii. 5, xxvi. 11.*

5098 τιμωρία, ας, ἡ, *punishment, penalty,* Heb. x. 29.*

5099 τίνω, τίσω, *to pay ;* with δίκην, *to pay penalty, suffer punishment,* 2 Th. i. 9.*

5100 τὶς, τὶ, gen. τινός (enclitic), indef. pron., *any one, some one* (see Gr. § 352, Wi. § 25, 2, Bu. 85, 93).

5101 τίς, τί, gen. τίνος; interrogative pron., *who ? which ? what ?* (see Gr. § 350, Wi. § 25, 1, Bu. 115, 138).

see 5103 Τίτιος, ov, ὁ, *Titius,* Ac. xviii. 7 (W. H.).*

5102 τίτλος, ov, ὁ (Lat.), *a title, an inscription,* Jn. xix. 19, 20.*

5103 Τίτος, ov, ὁ, *Titus,* 2 Cor. vii. 6, 13, 14.

5104 τοι, an enclitic part., *truly, indeed ;* see καιτοίγε, μέντοι, τοιγαροῦν, τοίνυν.

5105 τοι-γαρ-οῦν, *consequently, therefore,* 1 Th. iv. 8; Heb. xii. 1.*

see 2544 τοί-γε, *although* (in καιτοίγε).

5106 τοί-νυν, *indeed now, therefore,* Lu. xx. 25; 1 Cor. ix. 26; Heb. xiii. 13; Ja. ii. 24 (not W. H.).*

5107 τοιόσ-δε, τοιάδε, τοιόνδε, do monst. pron., *of this kind, such,* 2 Pet. i. 17.*

5108 τοιοῦτος, τοιαύτη, τοιοῦτο, demonst. denoting quality (as τοσοῦτος denotes quantity, and οὗτος simply determines), *of such a kind, such, so,* used either with or without a noun, the corresponding relative is οἷος, as, only Mar. xiii. 19; 1 Cor. xv. 48; 2 Cor. x. 11; once ὁποῖος, Ac. xxvi. 29. For τοιοῦτος with the article, see Gr. § 220, Wi. § 18, 4, Bu. 87.

5109 τοῖχος, ov, ὁ, *a wall* of a house, Ac. xxiii. 3; disting. from τεῖχος, *a wall of a city.*

5110 **τόκος, ου, ὁ** (*a bringing forth*), *interest, usury*, Mat. xxv. 27; Lu. xix. 23.*

5111 **τολμάω, ῶ, ήσω,** (1) *to dare* (inf.), Mar. xi. 34; (2) *to endure*, Ro. v. 7; (3) *to be bold*, 2 Cor. xi. 21.

5112 **τολμηρότερον** (τολμηρός), neut. compar. as adv., *more boldly*, Ro. xv. 15 (W. H. τολμηρότέρως).*

5113 **τολμητής, οῦ, ὁ,** *a daring, presumptuous man*, 2 Pet. ii. 10.*

5114 **τομός, ή, όν,** *sharp, keen,* comp. τομώτερος, Heb. iv. 12.*

5115 **τόξον, ου, τό,** *a bow*, Rev. vi. 2.*

5116 **τοπάζιον, ου, τό,** *topaz*, Rev. xxi. 20. (N. T.)*

5117 **τόπος, ου, ὁ,** (1) *a place, i.e., a district* or *region,* or *a particular spot in a region;* (2) *the place one occupies, the room, an abode, a seat, a sheath for a sword;* (3) *a passage in a book;* (4) *state, condition;* (5) *opportunity.*

5118 **τοσοῦτος, τοσαύτη, τοσοῦτο,** demonst. pron. denoting quantity (see τοιοῦτος), *so great, so much, so long;* plur., *so many.*

5119 **τότε,** demonst. adv., *then.*

5121 **τοὐναντίον,** for τὸ ἐναντίον, *on the contrary*, 2 Cor. ii. 7; Gal. ii. 7; 1 Pet. iii. 9.*

5122 **τοὔνομα,** for τὸ ὄνομα, acc. absol., *by name*, Mat. xxvii. 57.*

5123 **τουτέστι,** for τοῦτ᾽ ἔστι (W. H. prefer the uncontracted form), *that is*, Ac. i. 19; Ro. x. 6, 7, 8.

5124 * **τοῦτο,** neut. of οὗτος, which see.

5131 **τράγος, ου, ὁ,** *a he-goat*, Heb. ix. 12, 13, 19, x. 4.*

5132 **τράπεζα, ης, ἡ,** *a table,* (1) *for food and banqueting*, Mat. xv. 27; met., *food*, Ac. xvi. 34; (2) *for money-changing* or *business*, Mar. xi. 15.

5133 **τραπεζίτης, ου, ὁ,** *a money-changer, a banker*, Mat. xxv. 27.*

5134 **τραῦμα, ατος, τό,** *a wound*, Lu. x. 34.*

5135 **τραυματίζω, ίσω,** *to wound*, Lu. xx. 12; Ac. xix. 16.*

5136 **τραχηλίζω,** in pass., *to be laid bare, to be laid open*, Heb. iv. 13.*

5137 **τράχηλος, ου, ὁ,** *the neck*, Lu. xv. 20; Ro. xvi. 4.

5138 **τραχύς, εῖα, ύ,** *rough,* as ways, Lu. iii. 5; as rocks in the sea, Ac. xxvii. 29.*

5139 **Τραχωνῖτις, ιδος, ἡ,** *Trachonitis,* the N.E. of the territory beyond Jordan, Lu. iii. 1.*

5140 **τρεῖς, τρία,** *three*, Mat. xii. 40.

5141 **τρέμω,** *to tremble*, Mar. v. 33; Lu. viii. 47; Ac. ix. 6 (W. H. omit); *to be afraid*, 2 Pet. ii. 10.*

5142 **τρέφω, θρέψω,** perf. pass. part. τεθραμμένος, *to feed, to nourish*, Mat. vi. 26; Ac. xii. 20; Ja. v. 5; *to bring up, rear*, Lu. iv. 16.

5143 **τρέχω,** 2d aor. ἔδραμον, (1) *to run,* in general, Lu. xv. 20; (2) *to exert one's self*, Ro. ix. 16; (3) *to make progress,* as doctrine, 2 Th. iii. 1.

see 5168 **τρῆμα, ατος, τό,** *a perforation, the eye* of a needle, Mat. xix. 24 (W. H.); Lu. xviii. 25 (W. H.).*

5144 **τριάκοντα, οἱ, αἱ, τά,** indecl., *thirty*, Mat. xiii. 8.

5145 **τριακόσιοι, αι, α,** *three hundred*, Mar. xiv. 5; Jn. xii. 5.*

5146 **τρίβολος, ου, ὁ,** *a thistle*, Mat. vii. 16; Heb. vi. 8.*

5147 **τρίβος, ου, ἡ,** *a worn path, a beaten way*, Mat. iii. 3; Mar. i. 3; Lu. iii. 4.*

5148 **τρι-ετία, ας, ἡ,** *a space of three years*, Ac. xx. 31.*

5149 **τρίζω,** *to grate, to gnash,* as the teeth, Mar. ix. 18.*

5150 **τρί-μηνος, ον,** *of three months,* neut. as subst., Heb. xi. 23.*

5151 **τρίς,** num. adv., *thrice*, Mat. xxvi. 34, 75.

5152 **τρί-στεγος, ον,** *having three stories;* neut., *the third story*, Ac. xx. 9.*

5153 **τρισ-χίλιοι, αι, α,** *three thousand*, Ac. ii. 41.*

5154 **τρίτος, η, ον,** ord. num., *third;* neut. τὸ τρίτον, *the third part*, Rev. viii. 7; *the third time*, Mar. xiv. 41; ἐκ τρίτου, *the third time*, Mat. xxvi. 44; τῇ τρίτῃ (sc. ἡμέρᾳ), *on the third day*, Lu. xiii. 32.

see 2359 **τρίχες,** plur. of θρίξ, which see.

5155 **τρίχινος, η, ον,** *made of hair*, Rev. vi. 12.*

*For 5120 & 5125-5130 see Strong.

5156   τρόμος, ου, ὁ, *a trembling*, from fear, Mar. xvi. 8.

5157   τροπή, ῆς, ἡ, *a turning,* Ja. i. 17 (see R.V.).*

5158   τρόπος, ου, ὁ, (1) *way, manner; ὃν τρόπον, in like manner as, as,* Mat. xxiii. 37; (2) *manner of life, character,* Heb. xiii. 5.

5159   τροπο-φορέω, ῶ, ήσω, *to bear with the disposition* or *character* of others, Ac. xiii. 18 (Rec. W. H., some read ἐτρο-φοφόρησεν, *he bore them as a nurse*). (S.)*

5160   τροφή, ῆς, ἡ, *food, nourishment,* Mat. iii. 4, vi. 25.

5161   Τρόφιμος, ου, ὁ, *Trophimus,* Ac. xx. 4, xxi. 29; 2 Tim. iv. 20.*

5162   τροφός, οῦ, ἡ, *a nurse,* 1 Th. ii. 7.*

see 5159   τροφο-φορέω, ῶ, see τροπο-φορέω.

5163   τροχιά, ᾶς, ἡ, *a track of a wheel, a path,* fig., Heb. xii. 13.*

5164   τροχός, οῦ, ὁ, *a wheel,* Ja. iii. 6.*

5165   τρύβλιον, ου, τό, *a deep dish, a platter,* Mat. xxvi. 23; Mar. xiv. 20.*

5166   τρυγάω, ῶ, ήσω, *to gather,* as the vintage, Lu. vi. 44; Rev. xiv. 18, 19.*

5167   τρυγών, όνος, ἡ (τρύζω), *a turtle-dove,* Lu. ii. 24.*

5168   τρυμαλιά, ᾶς, ἡ, *the eye* of a needle, Mar. x. 25; Lu. xviii. 25 (W. H. τρῆμα).*

5169   τρύπημα, ατος, τό, *a hole, the eye* of a needle, Mat. xix. 24 (W. H. text τρῆμα).*

5170   Τρύφαινα, ης, ἡ, *Tryphæna,* Ro. xvi. 12.*

5171; see 4684   τρυφάω, ῶ, ήσω, *to live luxuriously and effeminately,* Ja. v. 5.* *Syn.:* see σπαταλάω.

5172   τρυφή, ῆς, ἡ, *effeminate luxury,* Lu. vii. 25; 2 Pet. ii. 13.*

5173   Τρυφῶσα, ης, ἡ, *Tryphosa,* Ro. xvi. 12.*

5174   Τρωάς, άδος, ἡ, *Troas,* a city of Mysia, properly *Alexandria Troas,* Ac. xvi. 8, 11.

5175   Τρωγύλλιον, ου, τό, *Trogyllium,* Ac. xx. 15 (W. H. omit).*

5176   τρώγω, *to eat,* Mat. xxiv. 38; Jn. vi. 54–58, xiii. 18.*

5177   τυγχάνω, 2d aor. ἔτυχον, perf. τέτυχα, (1) *to obtain, to get possession of* (gen.), Lu. xx. 35; Ac. xxiv. 2; (2) *to fall out, to happen, to happen to be; εἰ τύχοι, if it should chance, it may be, perhaps,* 1 Cor. xiv. 10; 2d aor., part., *τυχών, ordinary, commonplace,* Ac. xix. 11; neut. *τυχόν, it may be, perhaps,* 1 Cor. xvi. 6.

5178   τυμπανίζω, *to beat to death when stretched on a wheel,* Heb. xi. 35.*

see 5179   τυπικῶς, adv., *typically, by way of example,* 1 Cor. x. 11 (W. H.). (N. T.)*

5179   τύπος, ου, ὁ, (1) *a mark, an impression,* produced by a blow, Jn. xx. 25; (2) *the figure of a thing, a pattern,* Ac. vii. 44; Heb. viii. 5; (3) *an emblem, an example,* 1 Cor. x. 6; Phil. iii. 17; (4) *the form* or *contents* of a letter, Ac. xxiii. 25; (5) *a type,* Ro. v. 14.

5180   τύπτω, ψω, *to beat, to strike,* as the breast in grief, Lu. xviii. 13; *to inflict punishment,* Ac. xxiii. 3; *to wound* or *disquiet* the conscience, 1 Cor. viii. 12.

5181   Τύραννος, ου, ὁ, *Tyrannus,* Ac. xix. 9.*

5182   τυρβάζω, *to agitate* or *disturb in mind,* Lu. x. 41 (W. H. θορυβάζω).*

5183   Τύριος, ου, ὁ, ἡ (prop. adj.), *a Tyrian,* an inhabitant of Tyre, Ac. xii. 20.*

5184   Τύρος, ου, ἡ, *Tyre,* a city of Phœnicia, Mat. xi. 21, 22.

5185   τυφλός, ἡ, όν, *blind,* (1) physically, Lu. xiv. 13, 21; (2) mentally, *i.e., stupid, dull of apprehension,* Ro. ii. 19; ? Pet. i. 9.

5186   τυφλόω, ῶ, ώσω, fig., *to make blind* or *dull of apprehension,* Jn. xii. 40; 2 Cor. iv. 4; 1 Jn. ii. 11.*

5187   τυφόω, ῶ, *to raise a smoke;* pass., fig., *to be proud, to be arrogant* and *conceited,* 1 Tim. iii. 6, vi. 4; 2 Tim. iii. 4.*

5188   τύφω, pres. pass. part. τυφό-μενος, *smoking,* Mat. xii. 20.*

5189   τυφωνικός, ἡ, όν, *violent, tempestuous,* Ac. xxvii. 14.*

5190   Τυχικός, or Τύχικος (W. H.), ου, ὁ, *Tychichus,* 2 Tim. iv. 12.

see 5177   τυχόν, see τυγχάνω.

Υ

Υ, υ, ὐψῖλον, upsilon, *u,* the twentieth letter. As a numeral, υ′ = 400; ͵υ = 400,000. At the commencement of a word, υ is always aspirated.

5191   **ὑακίνθινος, η, ον,** *of the color of hyacinth, dark purple,* Rev. ix. 17.*

5192   **ὑάκινθος, ου, ὁ,** a precious stone of the color of hyacinth, *jacinth,* Rev. xxi. 20.*

5193   **ὑάλινος, η, ον,** *glassy, transparent,* Rev. iv. 6, xv. 2.*

5194   **ὕαλος, ου, ὁ,** *glass,* Rev. xxi. 18, 21.*

5195   **ὑβρίζω, σω,** *to treat with insolence, to insult,* Mat. xxii. 6; Lu. xi. 45.

5196   **ὕβρις, εως, ἡ,** (1) *insolence, insult,* 2 Cor. xii. 10; (2) *damage, loss,* Ac. xxvii. 10, 21.*

5197   **ὑβριστής, οῦ, ὁ,** *an insolent, insulting man,* Ro. i. 30; 1 Tim. i. 13.*

5198   **ὑγιαίνω,** *to be well, to be in health,* Lu. v. 31, xv. 27; fig., *to be sound,* in (ἐν) faith, doctrine, etc., Tit. i. 13; part. *ὑγιαίνων, healthful, wholesome,* of instruction, 1 Tim. i. 10.

5199   **ὑγιής, ές,** (1) *sound, whole,* in health, Mat. xii. 13; Jn. v. 11, 15; (2) fig., *wholesome,* of teaching, Tit. ii. 8.

5200   **ὑγρός, ά, όν,** *moist, green, i.e.,* full of sap, Lu. xxiii. 31.*

5201   **ὑδρία, ας, ἡ,** *a water-pot,* Jn. ii. 6, 7, iv. 28.*

5202   **ὑδρο-ποτέω, ῶ,** *to be a water-drinker,* 1 Tim. v. 23.*

5203   **ὑδρωπικός, ή, όν,** *dropsical,* Lu. xiv. 2.*

5204   **ὕδωρ, ὕδατος, τό,** *water;* ὕδατα, *waters, streams,* Jn. iii. 23; also *a body of water,* as Mat. xiv. 28; ὕδωρ ζῶν, *living* or *running water;* fig., of spiritual truth, Jn. iv. 14.

5205   **ὑετός, οῦ, ὁ** (ὕω, *to rain*), *rain,* Heb. vi. 7.

5206   **υἱο-θεσία, ας, ἡ,** *adoption* as a son, into the divine family, Ro. viii. 15, 23, ix. 4: Gal. iv. 5; Ep. i. 5.*

5207   **υἱός, οῦ, ὁ,** *a son,* Mat. x. 37; *a descendant,* Lu. xx. 41, 44; *the offspring* or *young* of an animal, Mat. xxi. 5; *an adopted son,* Heb. xi. 24 · of various forms of close

union and relationship (see τέκνον); *a disciple* or *follower,* Mat. xii. 27; *one who resembles* (gen.), Mat. v. 45; *one who partakes of any quality* or *character,* Lu. x. 6; Jn. xii. 36; ὁ υἱὸς τοῦ ἀνθρώπου, *son of man* (once only without art., Jn. v. 27), very often used by our Lord of himself (only once by another of him, Ac. vii. 56); *sons of men* denote *men* generally, Mar. iii. 28; Ep. iii. 5; υἱὸς τοῦ θεοῦ, *son of God,* used of men, Lu. xx. 36; Heb. ii. 10; usually of Christ, Mat. viii. 29; Jn. ix. 35; see also Gr. § 217c.

5208 - - - -

5209 & 5210
see Strong

ὕλη, ης, ἡ, *wood, fuel,* Ja. iii. 5.*

ὑμεῖς, plur. of σύ, which see.

5211   **Ὑμέναιος, ου, ὁ,** *Hymenæus,* 1 Tim. i. 20; 2 Tim. ii. 17.*

5212   **ὑμέτερος, α, ον,** possess. pron., *your,* as belonging to, or as proceeding from; for the use of the article with the word, see Gr. § 223.

★

5214   **ὑμνέω, ῶ, ήσω,** *to sing hymns to* (acc.), Ac. xvi. 25; Heb. ii. 12; *to sing,* Mat. xxvi. 30; Mar. xiv. 26.*

5215   **ὕμνος, ου, ὁ,** *a hymn, a sacred song,* Ep. v. 19; Col. iii. 16.* Syn.: ψαλμός is used of the Psalms of the O. T.; ὕμνος designates a song of *praise to God;* ᾠδή is a general expression for a song.

★

5217   **ὑπ-άγω,** *to go away, to depart,* Mar. vi. 31; Jn. vi. 67; imperat., sometimes an expression of aversion, *begone,* Mat. iv. 10; sometimes a farewell only, Mat. viii. 13, 32; *to die,* Mat. xxvi. 24.

5218   **ὑπ-ακοή, ῆς, ἡ,** *obedience,* Ro. vi. 16. (S.)

5219   **ὑπ-ακούω, σω,** (1) *to listen,* as at a door, to find who seeks admission, only Ac. xii. 13; (2) *to hearken to;* hence, *to obey* (dat.), Mat. viii. 27; Heb. xi. 8.

5220   **ὕπ-ανδρος, ον,** *subject to a husband, married,* Ro. vii. 2.*

5221   **ὑπ-αντάω, ῶ, ήσω,** *to meet* (dat.), Mat. viii. 28.

5222   **ὑπ-άντησις, εως, ἡ,** *a meeting,* Mat. viii. 34 (W. H.), xxv. 1 (W. H.); Jn. xii. 13. (S.)*

5223   **ὕπαρξις, εως, ἡ,** *goods, substance,*

★ For 5213 & 5216 **see Strong.**

property, Ac. ii. 45; Heb. x. 34.*

●5225, 5224 ὑπ-άρχω, *to begin to be; to be originally, to subsist;* hence generally, *to be*, Lu. viii. 41; Ac. xxi. 20; with dat. of pers., *to have, to possess*, Ac. iii. 6, iv. 37; part., neut. pl., τὰ ὑπάρχοντα, *things which one possesses, goods, property*, Mat. xix. 21.

5226 ὑπ-είκω, *to yield, to submit to authority*, Heb. xiii. 17.*

5227 ὑπ-εναντίος, α, ον, *opposite to, adverse*, Col. ii. 14; as subst., *an adversary*, Heb. x. 27.*

5228 ὑπέρ, prep., gov. gen. and acc.: with gen., *over, for, on behalf of;* with acc., *above, superior to* (see Gr. § 303, Wi. § 47 *l*, Bu. 335); adverbially, *above, more*, 2 Cor. xi. 23. In composition, ὑπέρ denotes *superiority* (above), or *aid* (on behalf of).

5229 ὑπερ-αίρω, in mid., *to lift up one's self, to exalt one's self, to be arrogant*, 2 Cor. xii. 7; 2 Th. ii. 4.*

5230 ὑπέρ-ακμος, ον, *past the bloom of youth*, 1 Cor. vii. 36.*

5231 ὑπερ-άνω, adv. (gen.), *above*, Ep. i. 21, iv. 10; Heb. ix. 5.*

5232 ὑπερ-αυξάνω, *to increase exceedingly*, 2 Th. i. 3.*

5233 ὑπερ-βαίνω, *to go beyond, to overreach, defraud*, 1 Th. iv. 6.*

5234 ὑπερ-βαλλόντως, adv., *beyond measure*, 2 Cor. xi. 23.*

5235 ὑπερ-βάλλω, intrans., *to surpass;* N.T., only pres. part. ὑπερβάλλων, *surpassing, excelling*, 2 Cor. iii. 10, ix. 14; Ep. i. 19, ii. 7, iii. 19.*

5236 ὑπερ-βολή, ῆς, ἡ, *excess, surpassing excellence, pre-eminence*, 2 Cor. iv. 7, xii. 7; καθ' ὑπερβολήν, as adv., *exceedingly*, Ro. vii. 13; 1 Cor. xii. 31; 2 Cor. i. 8; Gal. i. 13; καθ' ὑπερβολὴν εἰς ὑπερβολήν, *more and more exceedingly* (R. V.), 2 Cor. iv. 17.*

5237 ὑπερ-είδον, *to overlook, to take no notice of*, Ac. xvii. 30.*

5238 ὑπερ-έκεινα, adv., *beyond*, 2 Cor. x. 16. (N. T.)*

see 5228, 1537 & 4053   ὑπερ-εκ-περισσοῦ, adv., *beyond all measure, in the highest degree*, Ep. iii. 20; 1 Th. iii. 10, v. 13.*

5239 ὑπερ-εκ-τείνω, *to stretch out beyond measure*, 2 Cor. x. 14.*

5240 ὑπερ-εκ-χύνω, pass., *to be poured out, to overflow*, Lu. vi. 38.*

5241 ὑπερ-εν-τυγχάνω, *to intercede for*, Ro. viii. 26. (N. T.)*

5242 ὑπερ-έχω, *to excel, to surpass* (gen.), *to be supreme;* N.T. only pres. part., Ro. xiii. 1; Phil. ii. 3, iv. 7; 1 Pet. ii. 13; part. neut. τὸ ὑπερέχον, *excellency, super-eminence*, Phil. iii. 8.*

5243 ὑπερηφανία, ας, ἡ, *pride, arrogance*, Mar. vii. 22.*

5244 ὑπερ-ήφανος, ον, *proud, arrogant*, Ja. iv. 6.

see 5228 & 3029   ὑπερ-λίαν, adv., *very much, pre-eminently*, 2 Cor. xi. 5, xii. 11.*

5245 ὑπερ-νικάω, ῶ, *to be more than conqueror*, Ro. viii. 37. (N. T.)*

5246 ὑπέρ-ογκος, ον, *immoderate, boastful*, of language, 2 Pet. ii. 18; Ju. 16.*

5247 ὑπερ-οχή, ῆς, ἡ, *superiority, excellence*, 1 Cor. ii. 1; 1 Tim. ii. 2.*

5248 ὑπερ-περισσεύω, *to superabound*, Ro. v. 20; pass., *to be very abundant in* (dat.), 2 Cor. vii. 4. (N. T.)*

5249 ὑπερ-περισσῶς, adv., *superabundantly, beyond measure*, Mar. vii. 37. (N. T.)*

5250 ὑπερ-πλεονάζω, *to be exceedingly abundant*, 1 Tim. i. 14.*

5251 ὑπερ-υψόω, ῶ, *to highly exalt*, Phil. ii. 9. (S.)*

5252 ὑπερ-φρονέω, ῶ, *to think too highly of one's self*, Ro. xii. 3.*

5253 ὑπερῷον, ου, τό, *the upper part of a house, an upper chamber*, Ac. i. 13, ix. 37, 39, xx. 8.*

5254 ὑπ-έχω, *to submit to, to undergo* (acc.), Ju. 7.*

5255 ὑπ-ήκοος, ον, *listening to, obedient*, Ac. vii. 39; 2 Cor. ii. 9; Phil. ii. 8.*

5256 ὑπηρετέω, ῶ, *to minister to, to serve* (dat.), Ac. xiii. 36, xx. 34, xxiv. 23.*

5257 ὑπ-ηρέτης, ου, ὁ (ἐρέτης, a rower), *a servant, attendant*, specially (1) *an officer, a lictor*, Mat. v. 25; (2) *an attendant in a synagogue*, Lu. iv. 20; (3) *a minister of the gospel*, Ac. xxvi. 16.

5258 ὕπνος, ου, ὁ, *sleep*, Lu. ix. 32;

fig., *spiritual sleep*, Ro. xiii.
11.

5259 ὑπό, prep., gov. gen. and acc.,
under : with gen., *by*, generally signifying the agent ;
with acc., *under, beneath*, of
place, of time, or of subjection to authority (see Gr.
§ 304, Wi. §§ 47 *b*, 49 *k*, Bu.
340 sq.). In composition,
ὑπό denotes *subjection, diminution, concealment.*

5260 ὑπο-βάλλω, *to suborn, to instruct privately*, Ac. vi. 11.*

5261 ὑπο-γραμμός, οῦ, ὁ, *a writing-
copy ; an example*, 1 Pet. ii.
21.*

5262 ὑπό-δειγμα, ατος, τό, (1) *a
figure, copy*, Heb. viii. 5, ix.
23 ; (2) *an example* for imi-
tation, or for warning, Jn.
xiii. 15 ; Heb. iv. 11 ; 2 Pet.
ii. 6 ; Ja. v. 10.*

5263 ὑπο-δείκνυμι, δείξω, *to show
plainly, to teach, to warn*,
Mat. iii. 7 ; Lu. iii. 7, vi. 47,
xii. 5 ; Ac. ix. 16, xx. 35.*

5264 ὑπο-δέχομαι, *to receive as a
guest* (acc.), Lu. x. 38, xix. 6 ;
Ac. xvii. 7, Ja. ii. 25.*

5265 ὑπο-δέω, ῶ, ήσω, in mid., *to
bind on one's sandals, be
shod with* (acc.), Mar. vi. 9 ;
Ac. xii. 8 ; Ep. vi. 15 (lit.,
shod as to your feet).*

5266 ὑπό-δημα, ατος, τό, *a sandal*,
Mat. iii. 11, x. 10.

5267 ὑπό-δικος, ον, *subject to judgment, under penalty to* (dat.),
Ro. iii. 19.*

5268 ὑπο-ζύγιον, ου, τό, *an animal
under yoke, an ass*, Mat. xxi.
5 ; 2 Pet. ii. 16.*

5269 ὑπο-ζώννυμι, *to under-gird*, as
a ship for strength against
the waves, Ac. xxvii. 17.*

5270 ὑπο-κάτω, adv., *underneath* (as
prep. with gen.), Rev. v. 3,
13.

5271 ὑπο-κρίνομαι, dep., *to act under
a mask, to personate, to feign*
(acc., inf.), Lu. xx. 20.*

5272 ὑπό-κρισις, εως, ἡ, lit., *stage
playing ; hypocrisy, dissem-
bling*, 1 Tim. iv. 2.

5273 ὑπο-κριτής, οῦ, ὁ, lit., *a stage
player ; a hypocrite, a dis-
sembler*, Mat. vi. 2, 5, 16.

5274 ὑπο-λαμβάνω, 2d aor. ὑπέλαβον,
(1) *to take from under, to
receive up*, Ac. i. 9 ; (2) *to
take up a discourse, to answer*,
Lu. x. 30 ; (3) *to think, to*

suppose, Lu. vii. 43 ; Ac. ii.
15 ; (4) *to receive, welcome*, 3
Jn. 8 (W. H.).*

see 2640 ὑπό-λειμμα (or -λιμμα), ατος, τό,
a remnant, Ro. ix. 27 (W.
H.).*

5275 ὑπο-λείπω, *to leave behind*,
pass., Ro. xi. 3.*

5276 ὑπο-λήνιον, ου, τό (ληνός), *a
wine-vat, a pit under the
wine-press*, dug in the
ground, Mar. xii. 1. (S.)*

5277 ὑπο-λιμπάνω, *to leave behind*,
1 Pet. ii. 21.*

5278 ὑπο-μένω, μενῶ, (1) *to remain,
tarry behind*, Lu. ii. 43 ; (2)
to bear up under, to endure
(acc.), 1 Pet. ii. 20 ; (3) *to
persevere, to remain constant*,
Mat. x. 22.

5279 ὑπο-μιμνήσκω, ὑπομνήσω, 1st
aor. pass. ὑπεμνήσθην, *to remind* (acc. of pers.), Jn. xiv.
26 ; mid., *to be reminded, to
remember*, only Lu. xxii. 61.

5280 ὑπό-μνησις, εως, ἡ, (1) *remembrance, recollection*, 2 Tim. i.
5 ; (2) *a putting in mind*, 2
Pet. i. 13, iii. 1.*

5281 ὑπο-μονή, ῆς, ἡ, *a bearing up
under, endurance, steadfast-
ness, patient waiting for*
(gen.), Lu. viii. 15 ; 2 Th. iii.
5. *Syn.:* see ἀνοχή.

5282 ὑπο-νοέω, ῶ, *to conjecture, to
suppose*, Ac. xiii. 25, xxv. 18,
xxvii. 27.*

5283 ὑπό-νοια, ας, ἡ, *a surmising,
suspicion*, 1 Tim. vi. 4.*

5284 ὑπο-πλέω, 1st aor. ὑπέπλευσα,
to sail under, i.e., to leeward
of (acc.), Ac. xxvii. 4, 7.*

5285 ὑπο-πνέω, 1st aor. ὑπέπνευσα,
to blow gently, of the wind,
Ac. xxvii. 13.*

5286 ὑπο-πόδιον, ου, τό, *a footstool*,
Lu. xx. 43 ; Ac. ii. 35.

5287 ὑπό-στασις, εως, ἡ, *that which
underlies ;* hence, (1) *the substance, the reality* underlying
mere appearance, Heb. i. 3 ;
(2) *confidence, assurance*, 2
Cor. ix. 4, xi. 17 ; Heb. iii.
14, xi. 1.*

5288 ὑπο-στέλλω, 1st aor. ὑπέστειλα,
to draw back, Gal. ii. 12 ; mid.,
*to shrink, to draw one's self
back*, Ac. xx. 27 ; Heb. x. 38 ;
to withhold, conceal (acc.),
Ac. xx. 20.*

5289 ὑπο-στολή, ῆς, ἡ, *a shrinking,
a drawing back*, Heb. x. 39.*

5290 ὑπο-στρέφω, ψω, *to turn back,*

to return, intrans., Lu. ii. 43,
viii. 37, 40.

5291 ὑπο-στρώννυμι, or -ωννύω, *to*
spread under, Lu. xix. 36.
(S.)*

5292 ὑπο-ταγή, ῆς, ἡ, *subjection, sub-*
mission, 2 Cor. ix. 13; Gal.
ii. 5; 1 Tim. ii. 11, iii. 4.*

5293 ὑπο-τάσσω, ξω, 2d aor. pass.
ὑπετάγην, *to place under, to*
subject, 1 Cor. xv. 27; mid.,
to submit one's self, to be obe-
dient, Ro. xiii. 5; Ep. v. 21.

5294 ὑπο-τίθημι, *to set* or *put under,*
to lay down, Ro. xvi. 4; mid.,
to suggest to, put in mind,
1 Tim. iv. 6.*

5295 ὑπο-τρέχω, 2d aor. ὑπέδραμον,
to run under lee or shelter
of, Ac. xxvii. 16.*

5296 ὑπο-τύπωσις, εως, ἡ, *pattern,*
example, 1 Tim. i. 16; 2 Tim.
i. 13.*

5297 ὑπο-φέρω, 1st aor. ὑπήνεγκα, *to*
bear up under, to sustain, to
endure, 1 Cor. x. 13; 2 Tim.
iii. 11; 1 Pet. ii. 19.*

5298 ὑπο-χωρέω, ῶ, ήσω, *to with-*
draw, to retire, Lu. v. 16, ix.
10.*

5299 ὑπωπιάζω, *to strike under the*
eye; hence, (1) *to bruise;* fig.,
to buffet, 1 Cor. ix. 27; (2) *to*
weary out, by repeated application, Lu. xviii. 5.*

5300 ὗς, ὑός, ὁ, ἡ, *a hog, boar* or *sow,*
2 Pet. ii. 22.*

5301 ὕσσωπος, ου, ἡ (from Heb.),
hyssop, a stalk or *stem of*
hyssop, Jn. xix. 29; *a bunch*
of hyssop for sprinkling.
Heb. ix. 19. (S.)*

5302 ὑστερέω, ῶ, ήσω, *to be behind;*
abs., *to be lacking, to fall*
short, Jn. ii. 3, with obj., *to*
be lacking in, acc., Mat. xix.
20; gen., Lu. xxii. 35; ἀπό,
Heb. xii. 15; *to be lacking,*
Mar. x. 21; pass., *to lack, to*
come short, 1 Cor i. 7, viii.
8; *to suffer need*, Lu. xv. 14.

5303 ὑστέρημα, ατος, τό, (1) *that*
which is lacking from (gen.),
Col. i. 24; 1 Th. iii. 10; (2)
poverty, destitution, Lu. xxi.
4. (S.)

5304 ὑστέρησις, εως, ἡ, *poverty, pen-*
ury, Mar. xii. 44; Phil. iv. 11.
(N. T.)*

5305, 5306 ὕστερος, α, ον, compar., *later,*
only 1 Tim. iv. 1 and Mat.
xxi. 31 (W. H.); neut. as
an adv., *lastly, afterward,*

with gen., Mat. xxii. 27; Lu.
xx. 32.

5307 ὑφαντός, ή, όν (ὑφαίνω, *to*
weave), *woven*, Jn. xix. 23.*

5308 ὑψηλός, ή, όν, *high, lofty*, lit.
or fig., τὰ ὑψηλά, *things that*
are high, Ro. xii. 16; ἐν
ὑψηλοῖς, *on high*, Heb. i. 3.

5309 ὑψηλο-φρονέω, ῶ, *to be high-*
minded, proud, Ro. xi. 20
(W. H. ὑψηλὰ φρόνει); 1 Tim.
vi. 17. (N. T.)*

5310 ὕψιστος, η, ον (superlat. of ὕψι,
highly), *highest, most high;*
neut., plur., *the highest places,*
the heights, i.e., heaven, Lu.
ii. 14; ὁ ὕψιστος, *the Most*
High, i.e., God, Ac. vii. 48,
xvi. 17; Lu. i. 32, 35, 76.

5311 ὕψος, ους, τό, *height*, opp. to
βάθος, Ep. iii. 18; Rev. xxi.
16; ἐξ ὕψους, *from on high,*
i.e., from heaven, Lu. i. 78,
xxiv. 49; so εἰς ὕψος, *to*
heaven, Ep. iv. 8; fig., *high*
station, Ja. i. 9.*

5312 ὑψόω, ῶ, ώσω, (1) *to raise on*
high, to lift up, as the brazen
serpent, and Jesus on the
cross, Jn. iii. 14, viii. 28;
(2) *to exalt, to set on high,*
Ac. ii. 33; Mat. xxiii. 12.

5313 ὕψωμα, ατος, τό, *height*, Ro.
viii. 39; *barrier, bulwark*
(fig.), 2 Cor. x. 5.*

Φ

Φ, φ, φῖ, *phi, ph*, the twenty-
first letter. As a numeral,
φʹ = 500; ͵φ = 500,000.

5314 φάγος, ου, ὁ, *a glutton*, Mat. xi.
19; Lu. vii. 34 (N. T.)*

5315 φάγω, only used in fut. φάγο-
μαι, and 2d aor. ἔφαγον; see
ἐσθίω.

5341; see Strong φαιλόνης, ου, ὁ (W. H. φελόνης),
(Lat. *pænula*), *a traveling-*
cloak, 2 Tim. iv. 13. (N.
T.)*

5316 φαίνω, φανῶ, 2d aor. pass. ἐφά-
νην, (1) trans., *to show*, in
N.T. only mid. or pass., *to*
appear, to be seen, to seem;
τὰ φαινόμενα, *things which*
can be seen, Heb. xi. 3; (2)
intrans., *to shine, to give*
light, Jn. i. 5, v. 35. *Syn..*
see δοκέω.

5317 Φάλεκ, ὁ (Heb.), *Peleg*, Lu. iii.
35.*

5318 φανερός, ά, όν, *apparent, mani-*
fest, Ac. iv. 16; Gal. v. 19;

ἐν τῷ φανερῷ, as adv., *manifestly, openly*, Ro. ii. 28.

5319 φανερόω, ῶ, ώσω, *to make apparent, to manifest, to disclose*, Jn. vii. 4, xxi. 11; pass., *to be manifested, made manifest*, 1 Tim. iii. 16; 2 Cor. v. 11.

5320 φανερῶς, adv., *clearly*, Ac. x. 3; *openly*, Mar. i. 45; Jn. vii. 10.*

5321 φανέρωσις, εως, ἡ, *a manifestation* (gen. obj.), 1 Cor. xii. 7; 2 Cor. iv. 2.* *Syn.:* see ἀποκάλυψις.

5322 φανός, οῦ, ὁ, *a torch, a lantern*, Jn. xviii. 3.*

5323 Φανουήλ, ὁ (Heb.), *Phanuel*, Lu. ii. 36.*

5324 φαντάζω, *to cause to appear;* pass. part. τὸ φανταζόμενον, *the appearance*, Heb. xii. 21.*

5325 φαντασία, ας, ἡ, *display, pomp*, Ac. xxv. 23.*

5326 φάντασμα, ατος, τό, *an apparition, a spectre*, Mat. xiv. 26; Mar. vi. 49.*

5327 φάραγξ, αγγος, ἡ, *a valley, ravine*, Lu. iii. 5.*

5328 Φαραώ, ὁ, *Pharaoh*, the title of ancient Egyptian kings, Ac. vii. 13, 21.

5329 Φαρές, ὁ (Heb.), *Phares*, Mat. i. 3; Lu. iii. 33.*

5330 Φαρισαῖος, ου, ὁ (from the Heb. verb, *to separate*), *a Pharisee*, one of the Jewish sect so called, Mar. ii. 16, 18, 24. (N. T.)

5331 φαρμακεία (W. H. -κία), ας, ἡ, *magic, sorcery, enchantment*, Gal. v. 20; Rev. ix. 21 (W. H. φάρμακον), xviii. 23.*

5332 φαρμακεύς, έως, ὁ, *a magician, sorcerer*, Rev. xxi. 8 (W. H. read following).*

see 5331 φάρμακον, ου, τό, *a drug; an enchantment*, Rev. ix. 21 (W. H.).*

5333 φαρμακός, οῦ, ὁ (prop. adj.), *a magician, sorcerer*, Rev. xxi. 8 (W. H.), xxii. 15.*

5334 φάσις, εως, ἡ, *report, tidings*, Ac. xxi. 31.*

5335 φάσκω (freq. of φημί), *to assert, to affirm, to profess*, Ac. xxiv. 9, xxv. 19; Ro. i. 22; Rev. ii. 2 (W. H. omit).*

5336 φάτνη, ης, ἡ, *a manger, a crib*, Lu. ii. 7, 12, 16, xiii. 15.*

5337 φαῦλος, η, ον, *good for nothing, wicked, base*, Jn. iii. 20, v. 29; Ro. ix. 11 (W. H.); 2

Cor. v. 10 (W. H.); Tit. ii. 8; Ja. iii. 16.*

5338; see 2985 φέγγος, ους, τό, *brightness, light*, Mat. xxiv. 29; Mar. xiii. 24; Lu. xi. 33 (W. H. φῶς). *Syn.:* see λαμπάς.

5339 φείδομαι, φείσομαι, dep., (1) *to spare* (gen.), Ac. xx. 29; (2) *to abstain* (inf.), 2 Cor. xii. 6.

5340 φειδομένως, adv., *sparingly*, 2 Cor. ix. 6.*

5341; see also on p. 155. φελόνης, see φαιλόνης.

5342 φέρω, οἴσω, ἤνεγκα, ἠνέχθην (see Gr. § 103, Wi. § 15, Bu. 68), *to bear*, as (1) *to carry*, as a burden, Lu. xxiii. 26; (2) *to produce* fruit, Jn. xii. 24; (3) *to bring*, Ac. v. 16; (4) *to endure, to bear with*, Ro. ix. 22; (5) *to bring forward*, as charges, Jn. xviii. 29; (6) *to uphold*, Heb. i. 3; (7) pass., as nautical term, *to be borne along*, Ac. xxvii. 15, 17; (8) mid., *to rush* (bear itself on), Ac. ii. 2; *to go on* or *advance*, in learning, Heb. vi. 1. *Syn.:* φορέω means to bear something continually, while in φέρω it is temporary bearing, and on special occasions.

5343 φεύγω, ξομαι, ἔφυγον, *to flee, to escape, to shun* (acc. or ἀπό), Mat. viii. 33; 1 Cor. vi. 18; Heb. xii. 34; Rev. xvi. 20.

5344 Φῆλιξ, ικος, ὁ, *Felix*, Ac. xxv. 14.

5345 φήμη, ης, ἡ, *a report, fame*, Mat. ix. 26; Lu. iv. 14.*

5346 φημί, impf. ἔφην (for other tenses, see εἶπον), *to say*, with ὅτι, dat. of pers., πρός (acc.), with pers., acc. of thing (once acc., inf., Ro. iii. 8).

5347 Φῆστος, ου, ὁ, *Festus*, Ac. xxv. 1, 4, 9.

5348 φθάνω, φθάσω, perf. ἔφθακα, (1) *to be before, to precede*, 1 Th. iv. 15; (2) *to arrive, attain to* (εἰς, ἄχρι, ἐπί), Mat. xii. 28; Lu. xi. 20; Ro. ix. 31; 2 Cor. x. 14; Phil. iii. 16; 1 Th. ii. 16.*

5349 φθαρτός, ή, όν (φθείρω), *corruptible, perishable*, Ro. i. 23; 1 Cor. ix. 25, xv. 53, 54; 1 Pet. i. 18, 23.*

5350 φθέγγομαι, γξομαι, dep., *to speak aloud, to utter*, Ac. iv. 18; 2 Pet. ii. 16, 18.*

5351 φθείρω, φθερῶ, 2d aor. pass. ἐφθάρην, *to corrupt*, physically or morally, *to spoil, to destroy*, 2 Cor. vii. 2; Rev. xix. 2.

5352 φθιν-οπωρινός, ή, όν, *autumnal*, Ju. 12.*

5353 φθόγγος, ου, ὁ (φθέγγομαι), *a sound*, Ro. x. 18; 1 Cor. xiv. 7.*

5354 φθονέω, ῶ, *to envy* (dat.), Gal. v. 26.*

5355 φθόνος, ου, ὁ, *envy*, Phil. i. 15; Tit. iii. 3.

5356 φθορά, ᾶς, ἡ (φθείρω), *corruption, destruction*, physical or moral, 1 Cor. xv. 42, 2 Pet. i. 4.

5357 φιάλη, ης, ἡ, *a bowl*, broad and flat, Rev. v. 8, xv. 7.

5358 φιλ-άγαθος, ον, *loving goodness*, Tit. i. 8.*

5359 Φιλαδέλφεια, ας, ἡ, *Philadelphia*, Rev. i. 11, iii. 7.*

5360 φιλαδελφία, ας, ἡ, *brotherly love, love of Christian brethren*, Ro. xii. 10; 1 Pet. i. 22; 2 Pet. i. 7.*

5361 φιλ-άδελφος, ον, *loving the brethren*, 1 Pet. iii. 8.*

5362 φίλ-ανδρος, ον, *loving one's husband*, Tit. ii. 4.*

5363 φιλ-ανθρωπία, ας, ἡ, *love of mankind, benevolence*, Ac. xxviii. 2; Tit. iii. 4.*

5364 φιλ-ανθρώπως, adv., *humanely, kindly*, Ac. xxvii. 3.*

5365; see 4124 φιλαργυρία, ας, ἡ, *love of money, avarice*, 1 Tim. vi. 10.* *Syn.*: see πλεονεξία.

5366 φιλ-άργυρος, ον, *money-loving, avaricious*, Lu. xvi. 14; 2 Tim. iii. 2.*

5367 φίλ-αυτος, ον, *self-loving, selfish*, 2 Tim. iii. 2.*

5368 φιλέω, ῶ, ἥσω, (1) *to love*, Mat. vi. 5, x. 37; Lu. xx. 46; (2) *to kiss*, Mat. xxvi. 48. *Syn.*: see ἀγαπάω.

see 5384 φίλη, ἡ, see φίλος.

5369 φιλ-ήδονος, ον, *pleasure-loving*, 2 Tim. iii. 4.*

5370 φίλημα, ατος, τό, *a kiss*, Lu. vii. 45; Ro. xvi. 16.

5371 Φιλήμων, ονος, ὁ, *Philemon*, Philem. 1.*

5372 Φίλητος, or Φιλητός, ου, ὁ, *Philetus*, 2 Tim. ii. 17.*

5373 φιλία, ας, ἡ, *friendship*, Ja. iv. 4 (gen. obj.).*

5374 Φιλιππήσιος, ου, ὁ, *a Philippian*, Phil. iv. 15.*

5375 Φίλιπποι, ων, οἱ, *Philippi*, Ac. xvi. 12, xx. 6.

5376 Φίλιππος, ου, ὁ, *Philip*. Four of the name are mentioned: (1) Jn. i. 44–47 · (2) Ac. vi. 5; (3) Lu. iii. 1; (4) Mat. xiv. 3.

5377 Φιλό-θεος, ον, *loving God*, 2 Tim. iii. 4.*

5378 Φιλό-λογος, ου, ὁ, *Philologus*, Ro. xvi. 15.*

5379 φιλονεικία, ας, ἡ, *love of dispute, contention*, Lu. xxii. 24.*

5380 φιλό-νεικος, ον, *strife-loving, contentious*, 1 Cor. xi. 16.*

5381 φιλοξενία, ας, ἡ, *love to strangers, hospitality*, Ro. xii. 13; Heb. xiii. 2.*

5382 φιλό-ξενος, ον, *hospitable*, 1 Tim. iii. 2; Tit. i. 8; 1 Pet. iv. 9.*

5383 φιλο-πρωτεύω, *to love the first place, to desire pre-eminence*, 3 Jn. 9. (N. T.)*

5384 φίλος, η, ον, *friendly; ὁ φίλος*, as subst., *a friend*, Lu. vii. 6, xi. 5; *an associate*, Mat. xi. 19; *ἡ φίλη*, *a female friend*, only Lu. xv. 9.

5385 φιλοσοφία, ας, ἡ, *love of wisdom, philosophy*, in N. T. of the Jewish traditional theology, Col. ii. 8.*

5386 φιλό-σοφος, ου, ὁ (prop. adj., *wisdom-loving*),*a philosopher*, in N. T. of Greek philosophers, Ac. xvii. 18.*

5387 φιλό-στοργος, ον, *tenderly loving, kindly affectionate to* (εἰς), Ro. xii. 10.*

5388 φιλό-τεκνος, ον, *loving one's children*, Tit. ii. 4.*

5389 φιλο-τιμέομαι, οῦμαι, dep., *to make a thing one's ambition, to desire very strongly* (inf.), Ro. xv. 20; 2 Cor. v. 9; 1 Th. iv. 11.*

5390 φιλοφρόνως, adv., *in a friendly manner, kindly*, Ac. xxviii. 7.*

5391 φιλό-φρων, ον, *friendly, kindly*, 1 Pet. iii. 8 (W. H. ταπεινόφρων).*

5392 φιμόω, ῶ, ώσω, *to muzzle*, 1 Cor. ix. 9; *to reduce to silence*, Mat. xxii. 34; pass., *to be reduced to silence, to be silent*, Mat. xxii. 12; *of a storm*, Mar. iv. 39.

5393 Φλέγων, οντος, ὁ, *Phlegon*, Ro. xvi. 14.*

5394 φλογίζω, *to inflame, to fire with passion*, Ja. iii. 6.*

5395 φλόξ, φλογός, ἡ, *a flame*, Lu. xvi. 24.

5396 φλυαρέω, ῶ, *to talk idly, to make empty charges* against any one (acc.), 3 Jn. 10.*

5397 φλύαρος, ον, *prating; talking foolishly*, 1 Tim. v. 13.*

5398 φοβερός, ά, όν, *fearful, dreadful*, Heb. x. 27, 31, xii. 21.*

5399 φοβέω, ῶ, ήσω, *to make afraid, to terrify;* in N.T. only passive, *to be afraid, to be terrified*, sometimes with cognate acc., Mar. iv. 41 ; *to fear* (acc.), Mat. x. 26; *to reverence*, Mar. vi. 20; Lu. i. 50.

5400 φόβητρον (W. H. -θρον), ου, τό, *a terrible sight, a cause of terror*, Lu. xxi 11.*

5401; see 1167 φόβος, ου, ὁ, (1) *fear, terror, alarm*, Mat. xiv. 26 ; (2) *the object* or *cause of fear*, Ro. xiii. 3 ; (3) *reverence, respect*, 1 Pet. ii. 18; *towards God*, Ro. iii. 18; 1 Pet. i. 17. *Syn.:* see δειλία.

5402 Φοίβη, ης, ἡ, *Phœbe*, Ro. xvi. 1.*
5403 Φοινίκη, ης, ἡ, *Phœnice* or *Phœnicia*, Ac. xi. 19, xv. 3, xxi. 2.

5404 φοίνιξ, ικος, ὁ, *a palm-tree, a palm branch*, Jn. xii. 13 ; Rev. vii. 9.*

5405 Φοίνιξ, ικος, ὁ, a proper name, *Phœnice*, a city of Crete, Ac. xxvii. 12.*

5406 φονεύς, έως, ὁ, *a murderer*, Ac. vii. 52, xxviii. 4.

5407 φονεύω, σω, *to murder*, Mat. xxiii. 31, 35; Ja. iv. 2.

5408 φόνος, ου, ὁ, *murder, slaughter*, Heb. xi. 37 ; Rev. ix. 21.

5409; see 5342 φορέω, ῶ, έσω, *to bear about, to wear*, Mat. xi. 8; Jn. xix. 5; Ro. xiii. 4 ; 1 Cor. xv. 49 ; Ja. ii. 3.* *Syn.:* see φέρω.

5410 φόρον, ου, τό (Lat.), *forum* (see ˝Αππιος), Ac. xxviii. 15. (N. T.)*

5411 φόρος, ου, ὁ (φέρω), *a tax*, especially on persons, Lu. xx. 22, xxiii. 2 ; Ro. xiii. 6, 7.*

5412 φορτίζω, perf. pass. part. πεφορτισμένος, *to load, to burden*, Mat. xi. 28 ; Lu. xi. 46.*

5413 φορτίον, ου, τό, *a burden*, Mat. xi. 30; *the freight* of a ship, Ac. xxvii. 10 (W. H.) ; *the burden* of ceremonial observances, Mat. xxiii. 4 ; Lu. xi. 46; *the burden* of faults, Gal. vi. 5.*

5414 φόρτος, ου, ὁ, *load, a ship's cargo*, Ac. xxvii. 10 (W. H. read φορτίον).*

5415 Φορτουνάτος, ου, ὁ (Lat.), *Fortunatus*, 1 Cor. xvi. 17.*

5416 φραγέλλιον, ου, τό (Lat.), *a scourge*, Jn. ii. 15. (N. T.)*

5417 φραγελλόω, ῶ (Lat.), *to flagellate, to scourge*, Mat. xxvii. 26 ; Mar. xv. 15. (N. T.)*

5418 φραγμός, οῦ, ὁ, *a hedge*, Mat. xxi. 33; Mar. xii. 1 ; Lu. xiv. 23; fig., *partition*, Ep. ii. 14.*

5419 φράζω, άσω, *to declare, explain, interpret*, Mat. xiii. 36 (not W. H.), xv. 15.*

5420 φράσσω, ξω, *to stop, to close up*, Ro. iii. 19; 2 Cor. xi. 10; Heb. xi. 33.*

5421 φρέαρ, φρέατος, τό, *a pit, a well*, Jn. iv. 11, 12.

5422 φρεναπατάω, ῶ, *to deceive the mind, to impose upon* (acc.), Gal. vi. 3. (N. T.)*

5423 φρεν-απάτης, ου, ὁ, *a mind-deceiver*, Tit. i. 10. (N. T.)*

5424 φρήν, φρενός, ἡ (lit. *diaphragm*), plur. αἱ φρένες, *the mind, the intellect*, 1 Cor. xiv. 20.

5425 φρίσσω, *to shudder*, Ja. ii. 19.*
5426 φρονέω, ῶ, ήσω (φρήν), (1) *to think* (abs.), 1 Cor. xiii. 11 ; (2) *to think, judge* (acc.), Gal. v. 10; (3) *to direct the mind to, to seek for* (acc.), Ro. viii. 5; (4) *to observe*, a time as sacred, Ro. xiv. 6; (5) with ὑπέρ, *to care for*, Phil. iv. 10.

5427 φρόνημα, ατος, τό, *thought, purpose*, Ro. viii. 6, 7, 27.*

5428 φρόνησις, εως, ἡ, *understanding*, Lu. i. 17 ; Ep. i. 8.* *Syn.:* see γνῶσις.

5429 φρόνιμος, ον, *intelligent, prudent*, Lu. xii. 42 ; 1 Cor. x. 15.

5430 φρονίμως, adv., *prudently*, Lu. xvi. 8.*

5431 φροντίζω, *to be thoughtful, to be careful*, inf., Tit. iii. 8.*

5432 φρουρέω, ῶ, *to guard, to keep*, as by a military guard, lit., 2 Cor. xi. 32; fig., Gal. iii. 23 (as if in custody); Phil. iv. 7 (in security) ; 1 Pet. i. 5 (in reserve).*

5433 φρυάσσω, ξω, *to rage*, Ac. iv. 25. (S.)*

5434 φρύγανον, ου, τό, *a dry stick*, for burning, Ac. xxviii. 3.*

5435 Φρυγία, ας, ἡ, *Phrygia*, Ac. ii. 10, xvi. 6, xviii. 23.

5436 Φύγελλος (W. H. -ελος), ου, ὁ, *Phygellus*, 2 Tim. i. 15.*

5437 **φυγή,** ῆς, ἡ, *flight*, Mat. xxiv.
20; Mar. xiii. 18 (W. H.
omit).*

5438 **φυλακή,** ῆς, ἡ, (1) *a keeping
guard, a watching*, Lu. ii. 8;
espec. of the four *watches*
into which the night was
divided, Mat. xiv. 25, Lu.
xii. 38; (2) *a guard, i.e.*, men
on guard, *a watch*, Ac. xii.
10; (3) *a prison*, Mat. v. 25;
(4) *an imprisonment*, 2 Cor.
vi. 5.

5439 **φυλακίζω,** *to imprison*, Ac. xxii.
19. (S.)*

5440 **φυλακτήρια,** ων, τά (plur. of
adj.), *a safeguard, an amulet,
a phylactery*, a slip of parch-
ment, with Scripture words
thereon, worn by the Jews,
Mat. xxiii. 5.*

5441 **φύλαξ,** ακος, ὁ, *a keeper, sen-
tinel*, Ac. v. 23, xii. 6, 19.*

5442 **φυλάσσω,** ξω, (1) *to keep guard*,
or *watch over*, Ac. xii. 4; (2)
to keep in safety, Lu. xi. 21;
(3) *to observe*, as a precept,
Gal. vi. 13; (4) mid., *to keep
one's self from* (acc. or ἀπό),
Lu. xii. 15; Ac. xxi. 25.

5443 **φυλή,** ῆς, ἡ, (1) *a tribe*, of Israel,
Heb. vii. 13, 14; (2) *a race*,
or *people*, Rev. xiii. 7, xiv. 6.

5444 **φύλλον,** ου, τό, *a leaf*, Mar. xi.
13.

5445 **φύραμα,** ατος, τό, *a mass
kneaded, a lump*, as of
dough or clay, Ro. ix. 21,
xi. 16; 1 Cor. v. 6, 7; Gal.
v. 9.*

5446 **φυσικός,** ἡ, όν, *natural*, as (1)
according to nature, Ro. i.
26, 27; (2) *merely animal*, 2
Pet. ii. 12.*

5447 **φυσικῶς,** adv., *by nature*, Ju.
10.*

5448 **φυσιόω,** ῶ, *to inflate, to puff up*,
1 Cor. viii. 1; pass., *to be
inflated, arrogant*, 1 Cor. iv.
6, 18, 19, v. 2, xiii. 4; Col. ii.
18.*

5449 **φύσις,** εως, ἡ, generally, *nature*;
specially, (1) *natural birth*,
Gal. ii. 15; (2) *natural disposition, propensity*, Ep. ii.
3; (3) *native qualities*, or
properties, Ja. iii. 7; 2 Pet.
i. 4.

5450 **φυσίωσις,** εως, ἡ, *a puffing
up, pride*, 2 Cor. xii. 20.
(N. T.)*

5451 **φυτεία,** ας, ἡ, *a plant*, Mat. xv.
13.*

5452 **φυτεύω,** σω, *to plant*, abs., or
with acc., Mat. xxi. 33; 1 Cor.
iii. 6, 8.

5453 **φύω,** σω, 2d aor. pass. ἐφύην,
part. φυείς, *to produce ;* pass.,
to grow, Lu. viii. 6, 8; intrans., *to spring up*, Heb. xii.
15.*

5454 **φωλεός,** οῦ, ὁ, *a burrow, a
hole*, Mat. viii. 20; Lu. ix.
58.*

5455 **φωνέω,** ῶ, ήσω, (1) *to sound, to
utter a sound* or *cry*, Lu. viii.
8; espec. of cocks, *to crow*,
Mar. xiv. 30; (2) *to call to, to
invite* (acc.), Mat. xx. 32;
Lu. xiv. 12; (3) *to address,
to name*, acc. (nom. of title),
Jn. xiii. 13.

5456 **φωνή,** ῆς, ἡ, (1) *a sound*, mu-
sical or otherwise, 1 Cor.
xiv. 7, 8; Rev. vi. 1, xiv. 2,
xix. 1, 6; (2) *an articulate
sound, a voice, a cry*, Lu.
xvii. 13; Ac. iv. 24; (3) *a
language*, 1 Cor. xiv. 10.

**5457; see
2985** **φῶς,** φωτός, τό (contr. from
φάος, from φάω, *to shine*),
(1) lit., *light*, Mat. xvii. 2;
Jn. xi. 9; *a source of light*,
Lu. xxii. 56; Ja. i. 17; *brightness*, Rev. xxii. 5; ἐν τῷ
φωτί, *publicly*, Mat. x. 27;
(2) fig., *light*, as an appellation of God, 1 Jn. i. 5; as a
symbol of truth and purity,
espec. the truth of Christ,
Jn. iii. 19, 20, 21; used of
Christ, Jn. i. 7, 8. *Syn.*: see
λαμπάς.

**5458; see
2985** **φωστήρ,** ῆρος, ὁ, (1) *a luminary*,
Phil. ii. 15; (2) *brightness,
splendor*, Rev. xxi. 11.* *Syn.*:
see λαμπάς.

5459 **φωσ-φόρος,** ον, *light-bearing,
radiant*, the name of the
morning star (Lat. *Lucifer*),
the planet Venus, 2 Pet. i.
19.*

5460 **φωτεινός** (W. H. -τινός), ή, όν,
bright, luminous, full of light,
lit., Mat. xvii. 5; fig., Mat.
vi. 22; Lu. xi. 34, 36.*

5461 **φωτίζω,** ίσω, pass. perf. πεφώ-
τισμαι, 1st aor. ἐφωτίσθην;
(1) *to light up, illumine*, lit.
or fig. (acc., but ἐπί in Rev.
xxii. 5), Lu. xi. 36; (2) *to
bring to light, make evident*,
1 Cor. iv. 5.

5462 **φωτισμός,** οῦ, ὁ, *light, lustre,
illumination*, 2 Cor. iv. 4, 6.
(S.)*

X

X, χ, χί, *chi, ch,* guttural, the twenty-second letter. As a numeral, χ' = 600; ͵χ = 600,000.

5463 **χαίρω,** χαρήσομαι, 2d aor. pass. as act. ἐχάρην, *to rejoice, to be glad,* Lu. xv. 5, 32; Jn. iii. 29; impv. χαῖρε, χαίρετε, *hail!* Mat. xxvi. 49; inf. χαίρειν, *greeting,* Ac. xv. 23.

5464 **χάλαζα,** ης, ἡ, *hail,* Rev. viii. 7, xi. 19, xvi. 21.*

5465 **χαλάω,** ῶ, άσω, 1st aor. pass. ἐχαλάσθην, *to let down, to lower,* Mar. ii. 4; Lu. v. 4, 5; Ac. ix. 25, xxvii. 17, 30; 2 Cor. xi. 33.*

5466 **Χαλδαῖος,** ου, ὁ, *a Chaldæan,* Ac. vii. 4.*

5467 **χαλεπός,** ή, όν, (1) *hard, troublesome,* 2 Tim. iii. 1; (2) *harsh, fierce,* Mat. viii. 28.*

5468 **χαλιν-αγωγέω,** ῶ, *to bridle, to curb,* Ja. i. 26, iii. 2. (N.T.)*

5469 **χαλινός,** οῦ, ὁ, *a bridle, a curb,* Ja. iii. 3; Rev. xiv. 20.*

5470 **χάλκεος,** οῦς, ῆ, οῦν, *brazen,* Rev. ix. 20.*

5471 **χαλκεύς,** έως, ὁ, *a worker in brass* or *copper,* 2 Tim. iv. 14.*

5472 **χαλκηδών,** όνος, ὁ, *chalcedony,* a precious stone, Rev. xxi. 19.*

5473 **χαλκίον,** ου, τό, *a brazen vessel,* Mar. vii. 4.*

5474 **χαλκο-λίβανον,** ου, τό (or -νος, ου, ἡ), meaning uncertain, either *some precious metal,* or *frankincense* (λίβανος) *of a yellow color,* Rev. i. 15, ii. 8. (N.T.)*

5475 **χαλκός,** οῦ, ὁ, *copper, brass, money,* Mar. vi. 8, 1 Cor. xiii. 1.

5476 **χαμαί,** adv., *on* or *to the ground,* Jn. ix. 6, xviii. 6.*

5477 **Χαναάν,** ἡ, *Canaan,* Ac. vii. 11, xiii. 19.*

5478 **Χαναναῖος,** αία, αῖον, *Canaanite, i.e.,* Phœnician, Mat. xv. 22.*

5479 **χαρά,** ᾶς, ἡ, *joy, gladness,* Gal. v. 22; Col. i. 11; *a source of joy,* 1 Th. ii. 19, 20.

5480 **χάραγμα,** ατος, τό, *sculpture,* Ac. xvii. 29; *engraving, a stamp, a sign,* Rev. xiv. 9, 11, xvi. 2.

5481 **χαρακτήρ,** ῆρος, ὁ, *an impres-*

sion, an exact reproduction, Heb. i. 3.*

5482 **χάραξ,** ακος, ὁ, *a palisade, a mound for besieging,* Lu. xix. 43.*

5483 **χαρίζομαι,** ίσομαι, dep. mid., fut. pass. χαρισθήσομαι, (1) *to show favor to* (dat.), Gal. iii. 18; (2) *to forgive* (dat. pers., acc. thing), 2 Cor. xii. 10; Ep. iv. 32; Col. ii. 13; (3) *to give freely, bestow,* Lu. vii. 21; 1 Cor. ii. 12.

•5485, 5484 **χάρις,** ιτος, acc. χάριν and χάριτα (W. H. in Ac. xxiv. 27; Ju. 4), ἡ, (1) objectively, *agreeableness, charm,* Lu. iv. 22; (2) subjectively, *inclination towards, favor, kindness, liberality, thanks,* Lu. i. 30, ii. 40, 52; Ac. ii. 47, xxiv. 27; χάριν ἔχειν, *to thank;* χάριν ἔχειν πρός, *to be in favor with;* especially of the undeserved favor of God or Christ, 2 Cor. iv. 15, xii. 9; χάριν, used as prep. with gen. (lit., *with inclination towards*), *for the sake of, on account of,* Ep. iii. 14; 1 Tim. v. 14; Tit. i. 11.

5486 **χάρισμα,** ατος, τό, *a gift of grace, an undeserved favor* from God to man, Ro. i. 11, v. 15, 16, vi. 23, xi. 29, xii. 6; 1 Cor. i. 7, vii. 7, xii. 4, 9, 28, 30, 31; 2 Cor. i. 11; 1 Tim. iv. 14; 2 Tim. i. 6; 1 Pet. iv. 10.*

5487 **χαριτόω,** ῶ, *to favor, bestow freely on* (acc.), Ep. i. 6; pass., *to be favored,* Lu. i. 28. (Ap.)*

5488 **Χαρράν,** ἡ (Heb.), *Charran* or *Haran,* Ac. vii. 2, 4.*

5489 **χάρτης,** ου, ὁ, *paper,* 2 Jn. 12.*

5490 **χάσμα,** ατος, τό, *a gap, a gulf,* Lu. xvi. 26.*

5491 **χεῖλος,** ους, τό, *a lip;* plur., *mouth,* Mat. xv. 8; 1 Cor. xiv. 21; fig., *shore,* Heb. xi. 12.

5492 **χειμάζω,** in pass., *to be stormbeaten,* or *tempest-tossed,* Ac. xxvii. 18.*

5493 **χείμαρρος,** ου, ὁ, *a storm-brook, a wintry torrent,* Jn. xviii. 1.*

5494 **χειμών,** ῶνος, ὁ, (1) *a storm, a tempest,* Ac. xxvii. 20; (2) *winter, the rainy season,* Mat. xxiv. 20.

5495 χείρ, χειρός, ἡ, *a hand,* Lu. vi. 6; 1 Tim. ii. 8; met., for any exertion of *power,* Mat. xvii. 22; Lu. ix. 44; espec. in the phrases *the hand* of God, *the hand* of the Lord, for help, Ac. iv. 30, xi. 21; for punishment, Heb. x. 31.

5496 χειραγωγέω, ῶ, *to lead by the hand,* Ac. ix. 8, xxii. 11.*

5497 χειρ-αγωγός, όν, *leading* one *by the hand,* Ac. xiii. 11.*

5498 χειρό-γραφον, ου, τό, *a handwriting, a bond;* fig., of the Mosaic law, Col. ii. 14.*

5499 χειρο-ποίητος, ον, *done* or *made with hands,* Mar. xiv. 58; Ac. vii. 48, xvii. 24; Ep. ii. 11; Heb. ix. 11, 24.*

5500 χειρο-τονέω, ῶ, *to vote by stretching out the hand, to choose by vote,* 2 Cor. viii. 19; *to appoint,* Ac. xiv. 23.*

5501 χείρων, ον, compar. of κακός (which see), *worse,* Mat. xii. 45; *worse, more severe,* Heb. x. 29; εἰς τὸ χεῖρον, *worse,* Mar. v. 26; ἐπὶ τὸ χεῖρον, *worse and worse,* 2 Tim. iii. 13.

5502 χερουβίμ (W. H. Χερουβείν), τά, *cherubim,* the Heb. plural of cherub, the golden figures on the mercy-seat, Heb. ix. 5. (S.)*

5503 χήρα, ας, ἡ, *a widow,* Ac. vi. 1, ix. 39, 41; Ja. i. 27.

5504 χθές (W. H. ἐχθές), adv., *yesterday,* Jn. iv. 52; Ac. vii. 28; Heb. xiii. 8.*

● 5506 χιλί-αρχος, ου, ὁ, *a commander of a thousand men, a military tribune,* Ac. xxi–xxv.

5505 χιλιάς, άδος, ἡ, *a thousand,* Lu. xiv. 31; 1 Cor. x. 8.

5507 χίλιοι, αι, α, *a thousand,* 2 Pet. iii. 8; Rev. xi. 3.

5508 Χίος, ου, ἡ, *Chios,* Ac. xx. 15.*

5509 χιτών, ῶνος, ὁ, *a tunic,* an under-garment, Lu. iii. 11, vi. 29; *a garment,* Mar. xiv. 63. *Syn.:* see ἱμάτιον.

5510 χιών, όνος, ἡ, *snow,* Mat. xxviii. 3; Mar. ix. 3 (W. H. omit); Rev. i. 14.*

5511 χλαμύς, ύδος, ἡ, *a short cloak* worn by Roman officers and magistrates, Mat. xxvii. 28, 31.* *Syn.:* see ἱμάτιον.

5512 χλευάζω, *to mock, scoff* (abs.), Ac. ii. 13 (W. H. διαχλευάζω), xvii. 32.*

5513 χλιαρός, ά, όν, *lukewarm,* Rev. iii. 16.*

5514 Χλόη, ης, ἡ, *Chloe,* 1 Cor. i. 11.*

5515 χλωρός, ά, όν, (1) *green,* Mar. vi. 39; Rev. viii. 7, ix. 4; (2) *pale,* Rev. vi. 8.*

5516 χξϛ΄, *six hundred and sixty-six,* Rev. xiii. 18 (W. H. write the numbers in full).*

5517 χοϊκός, ή, όν, *earthy, made of earth,* 1 Cor. xv. 47–49. (N. T.)*

5518 χοῖνιξ, ικος, ἡ, *a chœnix,* a measure containing two sextarii (see ξέστης), Rev. vi. 6.*

5519 χοῖρος, ου, ὁ, plur., *swine,* Lu. viii. 32, 33, xv. 15, 16.

5520 χολάω, ῶ, *to be angry* (dat.), Jn. vii. 23.*

5521 χολή, ῆς, ἡ, (1) *gall,* fig., Ac. viii. 23; (2) perh. *bitter herbs,* such as wormwood, Mat. xxvii. 34.*

5522□ χόος, see χοῦς.

5523 Χοραζίν (W. H. Χοραζείν), ἡ, *Chorazin,* Mat. xi. 21; Lu. x. 13.*

5524 χορ-ηγέω, ῶ, *to lead* or *furnish a chorus;* hence, *to furnish abundantly, to supply,* 2 Cor. ix. 10; 1 Pet. iv. 11.*

5525 χορός, οῦ, ὁ, *a dance, dancing,* plur., Lu. xv. 25.*

5526 χορτάζω, *to feed, to satisfy* with (gen. or ἀπό), Mat. v. 6, xv. 33; Mar. viii. 4; Lu. xvi. 21.

5527 χόρτασμα, ατος, τό, *food, sustenance,* Ac. vii. 11.*

5528 χόρτος, ου, ὁ, *grass, herbage,* Mat. vi. 30; *growing grain,* Mat. xiii. 26; *hay,* 1 Cor. iii. 12.

5529 Χουζᾶς, ᾶ, ὁ, *Chuzas,* Lu. viii. 3.*

● 5522□ χοῦς, οός, acc. οῦν, ὁ, *dust,* Mar. vi. 11; Rev. xviii. 19.*

5530 χράομαι, ῶμαι, dep. (prop. mid. of χράω), *to use* (dat.), *to make use of,* 1 Cor. ix. 12, 15; 2 Cor. xiii. 10 (dat. om.); *to deal with,* Ac. xxvii. 3.

5531; see Strong χράω, see κίχρημι.

5532 χρεία, ας, ἡ, (1) *need, necessity,* plur., *necessities,* Mar. xi. 3; Tit. iii. 14; ἔχω χρείαν, *to need,* Jn. xiii. 10; (2) *business,* Ac. vi. 3.

5533 **χρεωφειλέτης** (W. H. χρεοφιλέτης), ου, ὁ, *a debtor*, Lu. vii. 41, xvi. 5.*

5534 **χρή**, impers. (from χράω), *it is necessary, it is proper* (acc. and inf.), Ja. iii. 10.*

5535 **χρῄζω**, *to have need of, to need* (gen.), Lu. xi. 8, xii. 30.

5536 **χρῆμα**, ατος, τό, *a thing* of use; *money*, sing., only Ac. iv. 37; plur., *riches, money*, Mar. x. 23; Ac. viii. 18, 20.

5537 **χρηματίζω**, ίσω, *to transact business;* hence, (1) *to utter an oracle, to give a divine warning*, Lu. ii. 26; Heb. xii. 25; pass., *to receive a divine response, be warned of God*, Mat. ii. 12, 22; Ac. x. 22; Heb. viii. 5, xi. 7; (2) *to receive a name, to be called*, Ac. xi. 26; Ro. vii. 3.*

5538 **χρηματισμός**, οῦ, ὁ, *an oracle*, Ro. xi. 4.*

5539 **χρήσιμος**, η, ον, *useful, profitable*, 2 Tim. ii. 14.*

5540 **χρῆσις**, εως, ἡ, *use*, Ro. i. 26, 27.*

5541 **χρηστεύομαι**, dep., *to be kind*, 1 Cor. xiii. 4. (N. T.)*

5542 **χρηστο-λογία**, ας, ἡ, *a kind address;* in a bad sense, *plausible speaking*, Ro. xvi. 18. (N. T.)*

5543 **χρηστός**, ή, όν, *useful, good*, 1 Cor. xv. 33; *gentle, pleasant*, Lu. v. 39; *kind*, 1 Pet. ii. 3; τὸ χρηστόν, *kindness*, Ro. ii. 4.

5544 **χρηστότης**, τητος, ἡ, (1) *goodness*, generally, Ro. iii. 12; (2) specially, *benignity, kindness*, Col. iii. 12. *Syn.:* see ἀγαθωσύνη.

5545 **χρίσμα**, ατος, τό, *an anointing*, 1 Jn. ii. 20, 27.*

5546 **Χριστιανός**, οῦ, ὁ, *a Christian*, Ac. xi. 26, xxvi. 28; 1 Pet. iv. 16.*

5547 **Χριστός**, οῦ, ὁ (verbal adj. from χρίω), *anointed;* as a proper name, *the Messiah, the Christ* (see Gr. § 217 e, Wi. § 18, 9, note 1, Bu. 89), Mat. xxiii. 10, etc.

5548 **χρίω**, σω, *to anoint, to consecrate by anointing*, as Jesus, the Christ, Lu. iv. 18; Ac. iv. 27, x. 38; Heb. i. 9; applied also to Christians, 2 Cor. i. 21. *Syn.:* see ἀλείφω.

5549 **χρονίζω**, *to delay, to tarry*, Mat.

xxiv. 48, xxv. 5; Lu. i. 21, xii. 45; Heb. x. 37.*

5550 **χρόνος**, ου, ὁ, (1) *time*, generally, Lu. iv. 5; Gal. iv. 4; (2) *a particular time*, or *season*, Mat. ii. 7; Ac. i. 7. *Syn.:* see καιρός.

5551 **χρονο-τριβέω**, ῶ, *to wear away time, to spend time*, Ac. xx. 16.*

5552 **χρύσεος**, οῦς, ῆ, οῦν, *golden*, 2 Tim. ii. 20; Heb. ix. 4.

5553 **χρυσίον**, ου, τό (dim. of χρυσός), *a piece of gold, a golden ornament*, Ac. iii. 6; 1 Pet. iii. 3.

5554 **χρυσο-δακτύλιος**, ον, *adorned with a gold ring*, Ja. ii. 2. (N. T.)*

5555 **χρυσό-λιθος**, ου, ὁ (*a golden stone*), a gem of a bright yellow color, *a topaz*, Rev. xxi. 20. (S.)*

5556 **χρυσό-πρασος**, ου, ὁ, a gem of a greenish-golden color, *a chrysoprase*, Rev. xxi. 20. (N. T.)*

5557 **χρυσός**, οῦ, ὁ, *gold, anything made of gold, gold coin*, Mat. ii. 11, x. 9; Ja. v. 3.

5558 **χρυσόω**, ῶ, *to adorn with gold, to gild*, Rev. xvii. 4, xviii. 16.*

5559 **χρώς**, χρωτός, ὁ, *the skin*, Ac. xix. 12.*

5560 **χωλός**, ή, όν, *lame*, Ac. iii. 2; *deprived of a foot*, Mar. ix. 45.

5561 **χώρα**, ας, ἡ, (1) *a country*, or *region*, Jn. xi. 54; (2) *the land*, opposed to the sea, Ac. xxvii. 27; (3) *the country*, dist. from town, Lu. ii. 8; (4) plur., *fields*, Jn. iv. 35.

5562 **χωρέω**, ῶ, ήσω, lit., *to make room;* hence, (1) *to have room for, receive, contain*, Mat. xix. 11, 12; Jn. ii. 6, xxi. 25; 2 Cor. vii. 2; impers., *to be room for*, Mar. ii. 2; (2) *to make room by departing, to go*, Mat. xv. 17; *to make progress*, Jn. viii. 37; *to turn one's self*, 2 Pet. iii. 9.*

5563 **χωρίζω**, ίσω, *to put apart, to separate*, Mat. xix. 6; mid. (1st aor. pass.), *to separate one's self*, of divorce, 1 Cor. vii. 11, 15; *to depart, to go away* (ἀπό or ἐκ), Ac. i. 4, xviii. 1.

5564 **χωρίον**, ου, τό, *a place, a field*

Mar. xiv. 32; plur., *lands*, Ac. iv. 34; *a farm, estate*, Ac. xxviii. 7.

5565 **χωρίς,** adv., *separately, by itself*, only Jn. xx. 7; as prep. gov. gen., *apart from, without*, Jn. xv. 5; Ro. iii. 21; *besides, exclusive of*, Mat. xiv. 21.

5566 **χῶρος,** ου, ὁ (Lat. *Caurus*), *the N.W. wind;* used for the N.W. quarter of the heavens, Ac. xxvii. 12. (N. T.)*

Ψ

Ψ, ψ, ψῖ, *psi, ps,* the twenty-third letter. As a numeral, ψ´ = 700; ͵ψ = 700,000.

5567 **ψάλλω,** ψαλῶ, *to sing*, accompanied with instruments, *to sing psalms*, Ro. xv. 9; 1 Cor. xiv. 15; Ep. v. 19; Ja. v. 13.*

5568: see **ψαλμός,** οῦ, ὁ, *a psalm, a song of*
5215 *praise*, Ep. v. 19; Col. iii. 16; plur., *the book of Psalms* in the O. T., Lu. xxiv. 44. *Syn.:* see ὕμνος.

5569 **ψευδ-άδελφος,** ου, ὁ, *a false brother, a pretended Christian*, 2 Cor. xi. 26; Gal. ii. 4. (N. T.)*

5570 **ψευδ-απόστολος,** ου, ὁ, *a false* or *pretended apostle*, 2 Cor. xi. 13. (N. T.)*

5571 **ψευδής,** ές, *false, deceitful, lying*, Ac. vi. 13; Rev. ii. 2, xxi. 8.*

5572 **ψευδο-διδάσκαλος,** ου, ὁ, *a false teacher, a teacher of false doctrines*, 2 Pet. ii. 1. (N. T.)*

5573 **ψευδο-λόγος,** ον, *false speaking, speaking lies*, 1 Tim. iv. 2.*

5574 **ψεύδομαι,** dep., 1st aor. ἐψευσάμην, *to deceive, to lie, to speak falsely*, Heb. vi. 18; Rev. iii. 9; *to lie to* (acc.), Ac. v. 3.

5575 **ψευδο-μάρτυρ,** or -υς, υρος, ὁ, *a false witness*, Mat. xxvi. 60; 1 Cor. xv. 15.*

5576 **ψευδο-μαρτυρέω,** ῶ, ήσω, *to testify falsely*, Lu. xviii. 20.

5577 **ψευδο-μαρτυρία,** ας, ἡ, *false testimony*, Mat. xv. 19, xxvi. 59.*

5578 **ψευδο-προφήτης,** ου, ὁ, *a false prophet*, one who in God's name teaches what is false, Mar. xiii. 22; 2 Pet. ii. 1. (S.)

5579 **ψεῦδος,** ους, τό, *a falsehood, a lie*, Jn. viii. 44; 2 Th. ii. 11.

5580 **ψευδό-χριστος,** ου, ὁ, *a false Christ, a pretended Messiah*, Mat. xxiv. 24; Mar. xiii. 22. (N. T.)*

5581 **ψευδ-ώνυμος,** ον, *falsely named*, 1 Tim. vi. 20.*

5582 **ψεῦσμα,** ατος, τό, *falsehood, perfidy*, Ro. iii. 7.*

5583 **ψεύστης,** ου, ὁ, *a liar, a deceiver*, Jn. viii. 44, 55; Ro. iii. 4.

5584: see **ψηλαφάω,** ῶ, *to feel, to touch,*
680 *to handle* (acc.), Lu. xxiv. 39; Heb. xii. 18; 1 Jn. i. 1; *to feel after, grope for*, fig., Ac. xvii. 27.* *Syn.:* see ἅπτω.

5585 **ψηφίζω,** ίσω, *to reckon, to compute*, Lu. xiv. 28; Rev. xiii. 18.*

5586 **ψῆφος,** ου, ἡ, *a small stone, a pebble*, Rev. ii. 17; used for voting, hence, *a vote*, Ac. xxvi. 10.*

5587 **ψιθυρισμός,** οῦ, ὁ, *a whispering, a secret slandering*, 2 Cor. xii. 20. (S.)*

5588 **ψιθυριστής,** οῦ, ὁ, *a whisperer, a secret slanderer*, Ro. i. 30.*

5589 **ψιχίον,** ου, τό, *a crumb*, Mat. xv. 27; Mar. vii. 28; Lu. xvi. 21 (W. H. omit). (N. T.)*

5590 **ψυχή,** ῆς, ἡ, (1) *the vital breath, the animal life*, of animals, Rev. viii. 9, xvi. 3, elsewhere only of man, Mat. vi. 25; (2) *the human soul*, as distinguished from the body, Mat. x. 28; (3) *the soul* as the seat of the affections, the will, etc., Ac. xiv. 2, 22; (4) *the self* (like Heb.), Mat. x. 39; (5) *a human person, an individual*, Ro. xiii. 1.

5591 **ψυχικός,** ή, όν, *animal, natural, sensuous*, 1 Cor. ii. 14, xv. 44, 46; Ja. iii. 15; Ju. 19.*

5592 **ψῦχος,** ους, τό, *cold*, Jn. xviii. 18.

5593 **ψυχρός,** ά, όν, *cold*, Mat. x. 42 (sc. ὕδατος); fig., *cold-hearted*, Rev. iii. 15, 16.*

5594 **ψύχω,** 2d fut. pass. ψυγήσομαι, *to cool;* pass., fig., *to be cooled, to grow cold*, Mat. xxiv. 12.*

5595 **ψωμίζω,** *to feed*, Ro. xii. 20; *to spend in feeding*, 1 Cor. xiii. 3.*

5596   ψωμίον, ου, τό, *a bit, a morsel,* Jn. xiii. 26, 27, 30. (S.)*

5597   ψώχω, *to rub, to rub to pieces,* as ears of corn, Lu. vi. 1.*

Ω

5598   Ω, ω, ὦ μέγα, *omega, o,* the twenty-fourth letter. As a numeral, ω′ = 800 ; ͵ω = 800,000. τὸ ʼΩ, a name ot God and Christ (see under A), Rev. i. 8, 11 (W. H. omit), xxi. 6, xxii. 13.*

5599   ὦ, interj., *O,* used before the vocative in address, Ac. i. 1, xviii. 14; in exclamation, Mat. xv. 28; Ro. xi. 33; or of reproof, Lu. xxiv. 25.

★

5601   ʼΩβήδ, ὁ, *Obed,* Mat. i. 5 (W. H. ʼΙωβήδ); Lu. iii. 32 (W. H. ʼΙωβήλ).*

5602   ὧδε, adv., of place, *hither, here ;* so, *in this life,* Heb. xiii. 14; *herein, in this matter,* Rev. xiii. 10; ὧδε ἢ ὧδε, *here or there,* Mat. xxiv. 23.

5603; see 5215   ᾠδή, ῆς, ἡ, *an ode, a song,* Rev. v. 9, xv. 3. *Syn.:* see ὕμνος.

5604   ὠδίν, ῖνος, ἡ, *the pain of childbirth, acute pain, severe anguish,* Mat. xxiv. 8; Mar. xiii. 8; Ac. ii. 24; 1 Th. v. 3.*

5605   ὠδίνω, *to feel the pains of childbirth, to travail,* Gal. iv. 27; Rev. xii. 2; fig., Gal. iv. 19.*

5606   ὦμος, ου, ὁ, *a shoulder,* Mat. xxiii. 4; Lu. xv. 5.*
★

5608   ὠνέομαι, οῦμαι, ήσομαι, *to buy* (gen. of price), Ac. vii. 16.*

5609   ᾠόν (W. H. ᾠόν), οῦ, τό, *an egg,* Lu. xii. 12.*

5610   ὥρα, ας, ἡ, (1) *a definite space of time, a season;* (2) *an hour,* Mar. xiii. 32; Ac. xvi. 33; (3) *the particular time for anything,* Lu. xiv. 17; Mat. xxvi. 45.

5611   ὡραῖος, αία, αῖον, *fair, beautiful,* Mat. xxiii. 27; Ac. iii. 2, 10; Ro. x. 15.*

5612   ὠρύομαι, dep. mid., *to roar, to*

howl, as a beast, 1 Pet. v. 8.*

5613   ὡς, an adv. of comparison, *as, like as, about, as it were, according as,* 2 Pet. i. 3; *how,* Lu. viii. 47; *how!* Ro. x. 15; as particle of time, *when, while, as soon as,* Lu. i. 23, xx. 37; Ro. xv. 24; as consecutive particle, *so that* (inf.), Ac. xx. 24; ὡς ἔπος εἰπεῖν, *so to speak,* Heb. vii. 9.

5614   ὡσαννά, interj., *hosanna!* (Heb., Ps. cxviii. 25, *save now!*), Mat. xxi. 9, 15; Mar. xi. 9, 10; Jn. xii. 13. (N. T.)*

5615   ὡσ-αύτως, adv., *in like manner, likewise,* Mat. xx. 5, 1 Tim. ii. 9.

5616   ὡσ-εί, adv., *as if, as though, like as,* with numerals, *about,* Ac. ii. 3, 41.

5617   ʼΩσηέ, ὁ, *Hosea,* Ro. ix. 25.*
5618   ὥσ-περ, adv., *just as, as,* Mat. xii. 40; 1 Cor. viii. 5.

5619   ὡσ-περ-εί, adv., *just as if, as it were,* 1 Cor. xv. 8.*

5620   ὥσ-τε, conj., *so that* (inf., see Gr. § 391, Wi. §§ 41*b*, 5, note 1, 44, 1, Bu. 244), *therefore,* Mat. viii. 24; Gal. iii. 9, 24.

see 5621   ὠτάριον, ου, τό (dim. of οὖς, see παιδάριον), *an ear,* Mar. xiv. 47 (W. H.); Jn. xviii. 10 (W. H.).*

5621   ὠτίον, ου, τό (dim. of οὖς, *an ear), an ear,* Mat. xxvi. 51; Lu. xxii. 51; Jn. xviii. 26; also in the passages under ὠτάριον (Rec.).*

5622   ὠφέλεια, ας, ἡ, *usefulness, profit, advantage,* Ro. iii. 1; Ju. 16.*

5623   ὠφελέω, ῶ, ήσω, *to be useful, to profit, to benefit, to help* (acc., also acc. of definition), Ro. ii. 25; 1 Cor. xiv. 6; pass., *to be profited, to be helped,* Mat. xvi. 26.

5624   ὠφέλιμος, ον, *profitable, beneficial,* dat. of pers., Tit. iii. 8; πρός (acc.), of obj., 1 Tim. iv. 8; 2 Tim. iii. 16.*

164

NEW TESTAMENT SYNONYMS

INTRODUCTION

A *careful* discrimination between synonyms in the study of any language is a matter of the utmost importance, and also consequently of considerable difficulty. But there are some considerations which make a treatment of the synonyms of the New Testament especially difficult and especially necessary. The Greek language in classical times was one which was admirably adapted for expressing fine shades of meaning, and therefore one which abounded in synonyms. In later Greek, outside of the New Testament, some of these distinctions were changed or modified. The writers of the New Testament were men of Semitic habits of thought and expression. They also had theological and ethical teachings to impart which were far more profound and spiritual than had been conveyed by the Greek language previous to that time. These and other facts affecting the New Testament Greek necessarily modify the meaning of many of the synonyms there used, in some cases effecting a complete transformation.

The object in the present treatment is to consider the New Testament usage. Hence, the distinctions of classical Greek are stated only so far as they are also found in New Testament usage, or are of importance for determining the latter. For a discrimination of the distinctive meanings of New Testament synonyms, three things must usually be considered :

> First, the etymological meaning of the words ;
> Second, the relations in which the words are found in classical Greek ;
> Third, the relations in which they are found in New Testament Greek, the last being often the chief factor.

The use of the words in the Septuagint is also important, for their connection with the Hebrew words which they are used to translate often throws light on their meaning.

The discussions here given aim to be brief, but yet to outline clearly the important and fundamental differences of meaning. Some words which are often given in works on this subject have been omitted, for the reason that the definitions as given in the Lexicon sufficiently indicate the important distinctions. There has been added, however, a consideration of some other words which are not so commonly included.

The chief works from which material and suggestions have been drawn are mentioned in the Introduction to the Lexicon.

The reason is stated in the Introduction to the Lexicon why in some cases the same word is treated both in the synonyms of the Lexicon itself, and also in this place. In every such instance the treatment here is to be regarded as supplementary to that in the Lexicon proper.

The synonyms here discussed do not belong exclusively nor chiefly to any one class of words. Both theological and non-theological terms are included. The aim has been to consider all the synonyms most likely to be confounded with one another, *i.e.*, all those most important, for practical use, to the average student of the New Testament.

INDEX TO SYNONYMS

This Index includes all the synonyms discussed in any way, even those indicated by simply giving references to literature concerning them, both in the Lexicon itself and in this separate chapter. Where the same word is discussed in both, the treatment in this separate chapter, as previously stated, is to be considered as supplementary to that in the Lexicon proper.

The references **BY PAGES** *are in every case to the Lexicon itself;*
BY SECTIONS, *to this separate chapter.*

§ 1. Holy, sacred, pure.

2413 ἱερός, 3741 ὅσιος, 40 ἅγιος, 53 ἁγνός, 4586 σεμνός.

None of these words in classical Greek has necessarily any moral significance. Those which now have such a meaning have developed it in Biblical Greek. 2413 ἱερός means *sacred*, implying some special relation to God, so that it may not be violated. It refers, however, to formal relation rather than to character. It designates an external relation, which ordinarily is not an internal relation as well. It is used to describe persons or things. This is the commonest word for *holy* in classical Greek, and expresses their usual conception of holiness, but it is rare in the N.T. because it fails to express the fullness of the N.T. conception. 3741 ὅσιος, used of persons or things, describes that which is in harmony with the divine constitution of the moral universe. Hence, it is that which is in accordance with the general and instinctively felt idea of right, "what is consecrated and sanctioned by universal law and consent" (Passow), rather than what is in accordance with any system of revealed truth. As contrary to 3741 ὅσιος, *i.e.*, as ἀνοσία (see L-S, p. 148A), the Greeks regarded, *e.g.*, a marriage between brother and sister such as was common in Egypt, or the omission of the rites of sepulture in connection with a relative. 40 ἅγιος has probably as its fundamental meaning *separation*, *i.e.*, from the world to God's service. If not the original meaning, this at any rate is a meaning early in use. This separation, however, is not chiefly external, it is rather a separation from evil and defilement. The moral signification of the word is therefore the prominent one. This word, rare and of neutral meaning in classical Greek, has been developed in meaning, so that it expresses the full N.T. conception of holiness as no other does. 53 ἁγνός is probably related to 40 ἅγιος. It means specifically *pure*. But this may be only in a ceremonial sense, or it may have a moral signification. It sometimes describes freedom from impurities of the flesh. 4586 σεμνός is that which inspires *reverence* or *awe*. In classical Greek it was often applied to the gods. But frequently it has the lower idea of that which is humanly venerable, or even refers simply to externals, as to that which is magnificent, grand, or impressive.

§ 2. Sin.

266 ἁμαρτία, 265 ἁμάρτημα, 763 ἀσέβεια, 3876 παρακοή, 458 ἀνομία, 3892 παρανομία, 3847 παράβασις, 3900 παράπτωμα, 51 ἀγνόημα, 2275 ἥττημα.

266 ἁμαρτία meant originally *the missing of a mark*. When applied to moral things the idea is similar, it is missing the true end of life, and so

it is used as a general term for *sin*. It means both the act of sinning and the result, the sin itself. 265 ἁμάρτημα means only the sin itself, not the act, in its particular manifestations as separate deeds of disobedience to a divine law. 763 ἀσέβεια is *ungodliness*, positive and active irreligion, a condition of direct opposition to God. 3876 παρακοή is strictly *failing to hear*, or hearing carelessly and inattentively. The sin is in this failure to hear when God speaks, and also in the active disobedience which ordinarily follows. 458 ἀνομία is *lawlessness*, contempt of law, a condition or action not simply without law, as the etymology might indicate, but contrary to law. The law is usually by implication the Mosaic law. 3892 παρονομία occurs only once, 2 Pet. ii. 16, and is practically equivalent to 458 ἀνομία. 3847 παράβασις is *transgression*, the passing beyond some assigned limit. It is the breaking of a distinctly recognized commandment. It consequently means more than 266 ἁμαρτία. 3900 παράπτωμα is used in different senses, sometimes in a milder sense, denoting an error, a mistake, a fault; and sometimes meaning a trespass, a willful sin. 51 ἀγνόημα occurs only once, Heb. ix. 7. It indicates *error*, sin which to a certain extent is the result of ignorance. 2275 ἥττημα denotes *being worsted, defeated*. In an ethical sense it means *a failure in duty, a fault*.—All these different words may occasionally but not usually be used simply to describe the same act from different points of view. The fundamental meanings of these words may well be summed up in the language of Trench: Sin "may be regarded as the missing of a mark or aim: it is then [266] ἁμαρτία or [265] ἁμάρτημα; the overpassing or transgressing of a line: it is then [3847] παράβασις; the disobedience to a voice: in which case it is [3876] παρακοή; the falling where one should have stood upright: this will be [3900] παράπτωμα; ignorance of what one ought to have known: this will be [51] ἀγνόημα; diminishing of that which should have been rendered in full measure, which is [2275] ἥττημα; non-observance of a law, which is [458] ἀνομία or [3892] παρανομία."

§ 3. Sincere.

573 ἁπλοῦς, 185 ἀκέραιος, 172 ἄκακος, 97 ἄδολος.

573 ἁπλοῦς is literally *spread out without folds*, and hence means single, simple, without complexity of character and motive. In the N.T. this idea of simplicity is always favorable; in classical Greek the word is also occasionally used in an unfavorable sense, denoting foolish simplicity. 185 ἀκέραιος also means *simple*, literally *free from any foreign admixture, unadulterated, free from disturbing elements*. 172 ἄκακος in Heb. vii. 26

means one in whom exists absence of all evil, and so by implication the presence of all good. It passes also through the merely negative meaning of absence of evil, found in S., to the unfavorable meaning of simple, easily deceived, credulous, which is found in Ro. xvi. 18. 97 ἄδολος, occurring only in I Pet. ii. 2, means *sincere, unmixed, without guile*.

§ 4. Sins of the tongue.

3473 μωρολογία, 148 αἰσχρολογία, 2160 εὐτραπελία.

3473 μωρολογία, used only once in the N.T., is *foolish talking*, but this in the Biblical sense of the word foolish, which implies that it is also sinful. It is conversation which is first insipid, then corrupt. It is random talk, which naturally reveals the vanity and sin of the heart. 148 αἰσχρολογία, also used once, means any kind of disgraceful language, especially abuse of others. In classical Greek it sometimes means distinctively language which leads to lewdness. 2160 εὐτραπελία, occurring once, originally meant *versatility in conversation*. It acquires, however, an unfavorable meaning, since polished, refined conversation has a tendency to become evil in many ways. The word denotes, then, a subtle form of evil-speaking, sinful conversation without the coarseness which frequently accompanies it, but not without its malignity.

§ 5. Shame, disgrace.

127 αἰδώς, 152 αἰσχύνη, 1791 ἐντροπή (4997 σωφροσύνη).

127 αἰδώς is the feeling of *innate moral repugnance* to doing a dishonorable act. This moral repugnance is not found in 152 αἰσχύνη, which is rather the feeling of *disgrace* which results from doing an unworthy thing, or the fear of such disgrace which serves to prevent its being done. 127 αἰδώς is thus the nobler word, 152 αἰσχύνη having regard chiefly to the opinions of others. 127 αἰδώς is the fear of doing a shameful thing, 152 αἰσχύνη is chiefly the fear of being found out. "[127] αἰδώς would always restrain a good man from an unworthy act, while [152] αἰσχύνη might sometimes restrain a bad one" (Trench). 1791 ἐντροπή stands somewhat between the other two words in meaning, but in the N.T. leans to the nobler side, indicating that *wholesome shame* which leads a man to consideration of his condition if it is unworthy, and to a change of conduct for the better. 4997 σωφροσύνη, *self-command*, may not seem to have much in common with these three words. As a matter of fact, however, it expresses positively that which 127 αἰδώς expresses negatively.

§ 6. Prayer.

2171 εὐχή, 4335 προσευχή, 1162 δέησις, 1783 ἔντευξις, 2169 εὐχαριστία, 155 αἴτημα, 2428 ἱκετηρία.

2171 εὐχή, when it means *prayer*, has apparently a general significa-tion. 4335 προσευχή and 1162 δέησις are often used together. 4335 προσευχή is restricted to prayer to God, while 1162 δέησις has no such restriction. 1162 δέησις also refers chiefly to prayer *for particular benefits*, while 4335 προσευχή is more general. The prominent thought in 1783 ἔντευξις is that of boldness and freedom in approach to God. 2169 εὐχαριστία is *thanksgiving*, the grateful acknowledgment of God's mercies, chiefly in prayer. 155 αἴτημα, much like 1162 δέησις, denotes a specific petition for a particular thing. In 2428 ἱκετηρία the attitude of humility and deprecation in prayer is specially emphasized. All these words may indicate at times not different kinds of prayer, but the same prayer viewed from different stand-points.

§ 7. To rebuke; rebuke, accusation.

2008 ἐπιτιμάω, 1651 ἐλέγχω; 156 αἰτία, 1650 ἔλεγχος.

2008 ἐπιτιμάω means simply *to rebuke*, in any sense. It may be justly or unjustly, and, if justly, the rebuke may be heeded or it may not. 1651 ἐλέγχω, on the other hand, means to rebuke with sufficient cause, and also effectually, so as to bring the one rebuked to a confession or at least a conviction of sin. In other words, it means *to convince*. A similar distinction exists between the nouns 156 αἰτία and 1650 ἔλεγχος. 156 αἰτία is an accusation, whether false or true. 1650 ἔλεγχος is a charge which is shown to be true, and often is so confessed by the accused. It has both a judicial and a moral meaning.

§ 8. Boaster, proud, insolent.

213 ἀλαζών, 5244 ὑπερήφανος, 5197 ὑβριστής.

213 ἀλαζών is properly *a boaster*, who tells great things concerning his own prowess and achievements, with the implied idea that many of his claims are false. This word naturally describes a trait which manifests itself in contact with one's fellow-men, not one which exists simply within the heart. 5244 ὑπερήφανος describes one who thinks too highly of himself, describing a trait which is simply internal, not referring primarily to external manifestation, although this is implied. It means

one who is *proud*, the external manifestation when it appears being in the form of *arrogance* in dealing with others. 5197 ὑβριστής describes one who delights in *insolent wrong-doing* towards others, finds pleasure in such acts. Cruelty and lust are two of the many forms which this quality assumes. These three words occur together in Ro. i. 30. They are never used in a good sense. They may be said to move in a certain sense in an ascending scale of guilt, designating respectively "the boastful *in words*, the proud and overbearing *in thoughts*, the insolent and injurious *in acts*" (Cremer).

§ 9. Incorruptible, unfading.

862 ἄφθαρτος, 263 ἀμάραντος, 262 ἀμαράντινος.

862 ἄφθαρτος is properly *incorruptible*, unaffected by corruption and decay. It is applied to God, and to that which is connected with him. 263 ἀμάραντος expresses the same idea in another way. It means *unfading*, the root idea being that it is unaffected by the withering which is common in the case of flowers. 262 ἀμαράντινος, derived from 263 ἀμάραντος, means *composed of amaranths*, *i.e.*, of unfading flowers.

§ 10. Faultless, unblamed.

299 ἄμωμος, 273 ἄμεμπτος, 410 ἀνέγκλητος, 423 ἀνεπίληπτος.

299 ἄμωμος is *faultless, without blemish, free from imperfections*. It refers especially to character. 273 ἄμεμπτος is strictly *unblamed*, one with whom no fault is found. This of course refers particularly to the verdict of others upon one. 410 ἀνέγκλητος designates one against whom there is no accusation, implying not acquittal of a charge, but that no charge has been made. 423 ἀνεπίληπτος means *irreprehensible*, designating one who affords nothing upon which an adversary might seize, in order to make a charge against him.

§ 11. Regeneration, renovation.

3824 παλιγγενεσία, 342 ἀνακαίνωσις.

3824 παλιγγενεσία means *new birth*. In classical Greek it was used in a weakened sense to denote a recovery, restoration, revival. In the N.T. it is used only twice, but in a higher sense. In Tit. iii. 5 it means *new birth, regeneration*, referring to God's act of causing the sinner to pass from the death of sin into spiritual life in Christ. It has a wider meaning in Mat. xix. 28, where it is used of the change which is ultimately to take place in all the universe, its regeneration, which is the full working out of the change involved in the regeneration of the individual. 342 ἀνακαίνωσις is *renewal* or *renovation*, denoting a continuous process through which man becomes more fully Christ-like, in which process he is a worker together with God. Some, as *e.g.* Cremer, without sufficient reason, have thought that the early use of 3824 παλιγγενεσία as a somewhat technical term, to denote the Pythagorean doctrine of transmigration, gave to the word a permanent eschatological coloring, so that in the N.T. it has the meaning *resurrection*, especially in Mat. xix. 28.

§ 12. Murderer.

5406 φονεύς, 443 ἀνθρωποκτόνος, 4607 σικάριος.

Both in derivation and usage, 5406 φονεύς and 443 ἀνθρωποκτόνος are distinguished from each other just as the English *murderer* from *manslayer* or *homocide*. 4607 σικάριος, used only in Ac. xxi. 38, is the Latin *sicarius*, and means *an assassin*, usually hired for the work, who furtively stabbed his enemy with a short sword, the Latin *sica*. 5406 φονεύς is a generic word and may denote a murderer of any kind, 4607 σικάριος being one of the specific varieties which it includes.

§ 13. Anti-Christ, false Christ.

5580 ψευδόχριστος, 500 ἀντίχριστος.

5580 ψευδόχριστος means *a false Christ, a pretended Messiah,* who sets himself up instead of Christ, proclaiming that he is Christ. Some have given about the same meaning to 500 ἀντίχριστος. But it is much more probable that it means one diametrically opposed to Christ, one who sets himself up against Christ, proclaiming that there is no Christ.

§ 14. Profligacy.

810 ἀσωτία, 766 ἀσέλγεια.

The fundamental idea of 810 ἀσωτία is "wastefulness and riotous excess; of [766] ἀσέλγεια, lawless insolence and wanton caprice" (Trench). 810 ἀσωτία means reckless and extravagant expenditure, chiefly for the gratification of one's sensual desires. It denotes a dissolute, profligate course of life. In 766 ἀσέλγεια also there is included the idea of profligacy, often of lasciviousness, but the fundamental thought is the acknowledging of no restraints, the insolent doing of whatever one's caprice may suggest.

§ 15. Covenant-breaker, implacable.

802 ἀσύνθετος, 786 ἄσπονδος.

These words are quite similar in their effects, but opposite in their conception. 802 ἀσύνθετος, occurring only in Ro. i. 31, is *covenant-breaker*, one who interrupts a state of peace and brings on war by disregarding an agreement by which peace is maintained. 786 ἄσπονδος is *implacable*, one who refuses to agree to any terms or suggestions of peace. It implies a state of war, and a refusal of covenant or even of armistice to end it permanently or temporarily. In the N.T. use both words probably refer not to war in the strict sense so much as to discord and strife.

§ 16. Beautiful, graceful.

791 ἀστεῖος, 5611 ὡραῖος, 2570 καλός.

791 ἀστεῖος is properly one living in a city, urban. It soon acquires the meaning *urbane, polite, elegant*. Then it obtains to a limited extent the meaning *beautiful*, although never in the highest degree. 5611 ὡραῖος, from 5610 ὥρα, hour, period, means properly *timely*. From that comes the idea of being beautiful, since nearly everything is beautiful in its hour of fullest perfection. 2570 καλός is a much higher word. It means *beautiful*, physically or morally. It is, however, distinctly the beauty which comes from harmony, the beauty which arises from a symmetrical adjustment in right proportion, in other words, from the harmonious completeness of the object concerned.

§ 17. Wisdom, knowledge.

4678 σοφία, 5428 φρόνησις, 1108 γνῶσις, 1922 ἐπίγνωσις.

4678 σοφία is certainly the highest word of all these. It is properly *wisdom*. It denotes mental excellence in the highest and fullest sense, expressing an *attitude* as well as an *act* of the mind. It comprehends knowledge and implies goodness, including the striving after the highest ends, as well as the using of the best means for their attainment. It is never ascribed to any one but God and good men, except in a plainly ironical sense. 5428 φρόνησις is a middle term, sometimes having a meaning nearly as high as 4678 σοφία, sometimes much lower. It means *prudence, intelligence,* a skillful adaptation of the means to the end desired, the end, however, not being necessarily a good one. 1108 γνῶσις is *knowledge, cognition,* the understanding of facts or truths, or else *insight, discernment.* 1922 ἐπίγνωσις has an intensive meaning as compared with 1108 γνῶσις; it is a fuller, clearer, more thorough knowledge. The verb 1921 ἐπιγινώσκω has the same intensive force as compared with 1097 γινώσκω.

§ 18. Religious.

2318 θεοσεβής, 2152 εὐσεβής, 2126 εὐλαβής,
2357 θρῆσκος, δεισιδαίμων (cf 1174St).

2318 θεοσεβής, according to derivation and usage, means *worship of God* (or of the gods), a fulfillment of one's duty towards God. It is a general term, meaning *religious* in a good sense. 2152 εὐσεβής is distinguished from 2318 θεοσεβής in two ways. It is used to include the fulfillment of obligations of all kinds, both towards God and man. It is thus applied to the fulfillment of the duties involved in human relations, as towards one's parents. Furthermore, when used in the higher sense, it means not any kind of worship, but, as the etymology indicates, the worshipping of God *aright.* 2126 εὐλαβής, meaning originally *careful in handling,* in its religious application means careful in handling divine things. It characterizes the anxious and scrupulous worshipper, careful not to change anything that should be observed in worship, and fearful of offending. It means *devout,* and may be applied to an adherent of any religion, being especially appropriate to describe the best of the Jewish worshippers. 2357 θρῆσκος is one who is diligent in the performance of the *outward* service of God. It applies especially to ceremonial worship. δεισιδαίμων (cf 1174St), in accordance with its derivation, makes prominent the element of *fear.* It emphasizes strongly the ideas of dependence and of anxiety for divine favor. It may be used as practically equivalent to 2318 θεοσεβής. Often, however, it implies that the fear which it makes prominent is an unworthy fear, so that it comes to have the meaning *superstitious.* In the N.T. it is used, as is also the noun 1175 δεισιδαιμονία, in a purposely neutral sense, meaning simply *religious,* neither conveying the highest meaning, nor plainly implying a lower meaning.

§ 19. Pure.

1506 εἰλικρινής, 2513 καθαρός, 283 ἀμίαντος.

1506 εἰλικρινής denotes chiefly that which is pure as being *sincere*, free from foreign admixture. 2513 καθαρός is that which is pure as being *clean*, free from soil or stain. The meaning of both in the N.T. is distinctly ethical. 283 ἀμίαντος is *unspotted*, describing that which is far removed from every kind of contamination.

§ 20. Assembly, church.

4864 συναγωγή, 1577 ἐκκλησία, 3831 πανήγυρις.

According to their derivation, 4864 συναγωγή is simply *an assembly*, a mass of people gathered together; 1577 ἐκκλησία is a narrower word, also *an assembly*, but including only those specially *called together out of* a larger multitude, for the transaction of business. 1577 ἐκκλησία usually denotes a somewhat more select company than 4864 συναγωγή. A significant use of 1577 ἐκκλησία in strict harmony with its derivation was common among the Greeks. It was their common word for the lawful assembly in a free Greek city of all those possessing the rights of citizenship, for the transaction of public affairs. They were *summoned out of* the whole population, "a select portion of it, including neither the populace, nor strangers, nor yet those who had forfeited their civic rights" (Trench). 4864 συναγωγή had been, before N.T. times, appropriated to designate *a synagogue*, a Jewish assembly for worship, distinct from the Temple, in which sense it is used in the N.T. Probably for that reason, and also for its greater inherent etymological fitness, 1577 ἐκκλησία is the word taken to designate *a Christian church*, a company of believers who meet for worship. Both these words, however, are some times used in the N.T. in a non-technical sense. 3831 πανήγυρις, occurring only in Heb. xii. 23, differs from both, denoting a solemn assembly for festal rejoicing.

§ 21. Humility, gentleness.

5012 ταπεινοφροσύνη, 4236 πραότης.

5012 ταπεινοφροσύνη is *humility*, not the making of one's self small when he is really great, but thinking little of one's self, because this is in a sense the right estimate for any human being, however great. 4236 πραότης is founded upon this idea, and goes beyond it. It is the attitude of mind and behavior which, arising from humility, disposes one to receive with *gentleness* and *meekness* whatever may come to him from others or from God.

§ 22. Gentleness.

4236 πραότης, 1932 ἐπιείκεια.

Both words may be translated *gentleness*, yet there are marked differences in meaning. 4236 πραότης is rather passive, denoting, as has been said above, see § 21, one's attitude toward others in view of their acts, bad or good. 1932 ἐπιείκεια is distinctly active; it is seen in one's deeds toward others, and it usually implies the relation of superior to inferior. It is fundamentally a relaxing of strict legal requirements concerning others, yet doing this in order more fully to carry out the real spirit of the law. It is *clemency* in which there is no element of weakness or injustice.

§ 23. Desire, lust.

1939 ἐπιθυμία, 3806 πάθος, 3730 ὁρμή, 3715 ὄρεξις.

1939 ἐπιθυμία is the broadest of these words. Its meaning may be good, but it is usually bad. It denotes any natural desire or appetite, usually with the implication that it is a depraved desire. 3806 πάθος has not as broad a meaning as in classical Greek, but denotes evil desire, chiefly, however, as a condition of the soul rather than in active operation. 3730 ὁρμή indicates *hostile* motion toward an object, either for seizing or repelling. 3715 ὄρεξις is a desire or appetite, especially seeking the object of gratification in order to make it one's own.

§ 24. Affliction.

2347 θλῖψις, 4730 στενοχωρία.

2347 θλῖψις according to its derivation means *pressure*. In its figurative sense it is that which presses upon the spirit, *affliction*. 4730 στενοχωρία meant originally *a narrow, confined space*. It denotes affliction as arising from cramping circumstances. In use it cannot always be distinguished from 2347 θλῖψις, but it is ordinarily a stronger word.

§ 25. Bad, evil.

2556 κακός, 4190 πονηρός, 5337 φαῦλος.

These words may be used with very little distinction of meaning, but often the difference is marked. 2556 κακός frequently means *evil* rather negatively, referring to the absence of the qualities which constitute a person or thing what it should be or what it claims to be. It is also used meaning *evil* in a moral sense. It is a general antithesis to 18 ἀγαθός. 4190 πονηρός is a word at once stronger and more active, it means *mischief-making*, delighting in injury, doing evil to others, dangerous, destructive. 2556 κακός describes the quality according to its nature, 4190 πονηρός, according to its effects. 5337 φαῦλος is the bad chiefly as the *worthless*, the good for nothing.

§ 26. Punishment.

5098 τιμωρία, 2851 κόλασις.

5098 τιμωρία in classical and N.T. usage denotes especially the vindicative character of punishment; it is the punishment in relation to the *punisher*. 2851 κόλασις in classical Greek meant usually punishment which aimed at the reformation of the offender. But sometimes in later Greek, and always in the N.T., the idea of reformation seems to disappear, so that there remains simply the idea of punishment, but viewed in relation to the *punished*.

§ 27. To pollute.

3392 μιαίνω, 3435 μολύνω.

3392 μιαίνω meant originally *to stain*, as with color. 3435 μολύνω meant originally *to smear over*, as with mud or filth, always having a bad meaning, while the meaning of 3392 μιαίνω might be either good or bad. According to classical Greek, 3392 μιαίνω has a religious meaning, *to profane*, while 3435 μολύνω is simply *to spoil, disgrace*. As ethically applied in the N.T. they have both practically the same meaning, *to pollute, defile*. It is, however, true that 3392 μιαίνω, to judge from classical usage, refers chiefly to the effect of the act not on the individual, but on others, on the community.

§ 28. To do.

4160 ποιέω, 4238 πράσσω.

These words are often used interchangeably, but in many cases a distinction can be drawn. 4160 ποιέω refers more to the object and end of an act; 4238 πράσσω rather to the means by which the object is attained. Hence, while 4160 ποιέω means *to accomplish*, 4238 πράσσω may mean nothing more than merely *to busy one's self about.* 4160 ποιέω often means to do a thing once for all, 4238 πράσσω, to do continually or repeatedly. From these distinctions it follows that 4160 ποιέω, being on the whole the higher word, is more often used of doing good, 4238 πράσσω more frequently of doing evil.

§ 29. Fleshly, fleshy, sensual.

4559 σαρκικός, 4560 σάρκινος, 5591 ψυχικός.

4559 σαρκικός means *fleshly*, that which is controlled by the wrong desires which rule in the flesh, flesh often being understood in its broad sense (see 4561 σάρξ). It describes a man who gives the flesh the dominion in his life, a place which does not belong to it by right. It means distinctly opposed to the Spirit of God, anti-spiritual. 4560 σάρκινος properly means *fleshy*, made of flesh, flesh being the material of which it is composed. When given a bad meaning, however, it is plainly similar to 4559 σαρκικός, but according to Trench not so strong, denoting one as unspiritual, undeveloped, rather than anti-spiritual. Others, as Cremer and Thayer, with more probability make 4560 σάρκινος the stronger; it describes one who is flesh, wholly given up to the flesh, rooted in the flesh, rather than one who simply acts according to the flesh (4559 σαρκικός). There is much confusion between the two in the N.T. manuscripts. 5591 ψυχικός has a meaning somewhat similar to 4559 σαρκικός. Both are used in contrast with 4152 πνευματικός. But 5591 ψυχικός has really a distinct meaning, describing the life which is controlled by the 5590 ψυχή. It denotes, therefore, that which belongs to the animal life, or that which is controlled simply by the appetites and passions of the sensuous nature.

§ 30. Mercy, compassion.

1656 ἔλεος, 3628 οἰκτιρμός.

Both words denote sympathy, fellow-feeling with misery, mercy, compassion. 1656 ἔλεος, however, manifests itself chiefly in acts rather than words, while 3628 οἰκτιρμός is used rather of the inward feeling of compassion which abides in the heart. A criminal might ask for 1656 ἔλεος, *mercy*, from his judge; but hopeless suffering may be the object of 3628 οἰκτιρμός, *compassion*.

§ 31. To love.

25 ἀγαπάω, 5368 φιλέω.

25 ἀγαπάω, and not 5368 φιλέω, is the word used of God's love to men; 5363 φιλανθροπία is, however, once used with this meaning, Tit. iii.4. 25 ἀγαπάω is also the word ordinarily used of men's love to God, but 5368 φιλέω is once so used, I Cor. xvi.22. 25 ἀγαπάω is the word used of love to one's enemies. The interchange of the words in Jn. xxi. 15–17 is very interesting and instructive.

§ 32. To will, to wish.

1014 βούλομαι, 2309 θέλω.

In many cases these two words are used without appreciable distinction, meaning *conscious willing, purpose*. But frequently it is evident that a difference is intended, although there is much difference of opinion as to the exact distinction. Thayer says that 1014 βούλομαι "seems to designate the will which follows deliberation," 2309 θέλω, "the will which proceeds from inclination." Grimm, on the other hand, says that 2309 θέλω gives prominence to the emotive element, 1014 βούλομαι to the rational and volitive; 2309 θέλω signifies the choice, while 1014 βούλομαι marks the choice as deliberate and intelligent. The view of Cremer on the whole seems preferable to any other. According to this view, 1014 βούλομαι has the wider range of meaning, but 2309 θέλω is the stronger word; 2309 θέλω denotes the active resolution, the will urging on to action, see Ro. vii. 15, while 1014 βούλομαι is rather to have in thought, to intend, to be determined. 1014 βούλομαι sometimes means no more than to have an inclination, see Ac. xxiii. 15. Instructive examples of the use of the two words in close proximity are found in Mar. xv. 9, 15, and especially Mat. i. 19.

§ 33. Schism.

4978 σχίσμα, 139 αἵρεσις.

4978 σχίσμα is *actual division, separation*. 139 αἵρεσις is rather *the separating tendency*, so it is really more fundamental than 4978 σχίσμα.

§ 34. Mind, understanding.

3563 νοῦς, 1271 διάνοια.

3563 νοῦς is distinctly *the reflective consciousness*, "the organ of moral thinking and knowing, the intellectual organ of moral sentiment" (Cremer). 1271 διάνοια meant originally *activity of thinking*, but has borrowed from 3563 νοῦς its common meaning of *faculty of thought*. It is more common than 3563 νοῦς, and has largely replaced it in its usual meanings.

§ 35. Law.

3551 νόμος, θεσμός (L-S, p. 795A), 1785 ἐντολή, 1378 δόγμα.

3551 νόμος is the common word meaning *law*. It may mean law in general. In the N.T., however, it usually means the law of God, and most frequently the Mosaic law. θεσμός (L-S, p. 795A) is law considered with special reference to the authority on which it rests. 1785 ἐντολή is more specific, being used of a particular command. 1378 δόγμα is an authoritative conclusion, a proposition which it is expected that all will recognize as universally binding.

§ 36. Type, image.

5179 τύπος, 499 ἀντίτυπος.

5179 τύπος has many meanings, among the most common being *image*, *pattern* or *model*, and *type*. In the last sense it means a person or thing prefiguring a future person or thing, *e.g.*, Adam as a type of Christ, Ro. v. 14. 499 ἀντίτυπος, as used in I Pet. iii. 21, is by Thayer and many others thought to correspond to 5179 τύπος as its counterpart, in the sense which the English word antitype suggests. By Cremer it is rather given the meaning *image*.

§ 37. To ask.

154 αἰτέω, 2065 ἐρωτάω.

Thayer, as opposed to Trench and others, would make the distinction between these two words to be this: "[154] αἰτέω signifies to ask for something to be given, not done, giving prominence to the thing asked for rather than the person, and hence is rarely used in exhortation. [2065] ἐρωτάω, on the other hand, is to request a person to do (rarely to give) something; referring more directly to the person, it is naturally used in exhortation, etc."

§ 38. World, age.

165 αἰών, 2889 κόσμος.

It is only in a part of their meanings that these two words are in any real sense synonymous, and it is that part which is here considered. Both A.V. and R.V. often translate 165 αἰών by *world*, thus obscuring the distinction between it and 2889 κόσμος. 165 αἰών is usually better expressed by *age;* it is the world at a given time, a particular period in the world's history. 2889 κόσμος has very frequently an unfavorable meaning, denoting the inhabitants of the world, mankind in general, as opposed to God. A similar meaning is often attached to 165 αἰών; it means the spirit of the age, often in an unfavorable sense. See Ep. ii. 2, where both words occur together. An exceptional meaning for the plural of 165 αἰών is found in Heb. i. 2 and xi. 3, where it denotes the worlds, apparently in reference to space rather than time.

§ 39. Rest.

372 ἀνάπαυσις, 425 ἄνεσις.

Both words in a certain sense mean *rest,* but from different standpoints. 372 ἀνάπαυσις is rest which comes by cessation from labor, which may be simply temporary. 425 ἄνεσις means literally the relaxation of strings which have been drawn tight. Hence, it is used to designate ease, especially that which comes by relaxation of unfavorable conditions of any kind, such as affliction.

§ 40. Wind.

4151 πνεῦμα, 4157 πνοή, 417 ἄνεμος, 2978 λαῖλαψ, 2366 θύελλα.

4151 πνεῦμα when used in its lower meaning to denote wind means simply *an ordinary wind,* a regularly blowing current of air of considerable force. 4157 πνοή is distinguished from it as being a gentler motion of the air. 417 ἄνεμος, on the other hand, is more forcible than 4151 πνεῦμα; it is the strong, often the tempestuous, wind. 2978 λαῖλαψ is the violent fitful wind which accompanies a heavy shower. 2366 θύελλα is more violent than any of the others, and often implies a conflict of opposing winds.

§ 41. Old.

3820 παλαιός, 744 ἀρχαῖος.

According to their derivation, 3820 παλαιός is that which has been in existence for a long time, 774 ἀρχαῖος that which has been from the beginning. In use, at times no distinction can be drawn. Often, however, 744 ἀρχαῖος does denote distinctively that which has been from the beginning, and so it reaches back to a point of time beyond 3820 παλαιός. 3820 παλαιός has often the secondary meaning of that which is old and so worn out, having suffered more or less from the injuries and ravages of time, its opposite in this sense being 2537 καινός.

§ 42. Harsh, austere.

840 αὐστηρός, 4642 σκληρός.

840 αὐστηρός has not necessarily an unfavorable meaning. It is well represented by the word *austere;* it means one who is earnest and severe, strict in his ways, opposed to all levity. By implication it may have the unfavorable meaning of harshness or moroseness. 4642 σκληρός has always an unfavorable meaning. It indicates one who is uncivil, intractable, rough and harsh. There is in it the implication of inhumanity.

§ 43. Darkness.

4655 σκότος, 1105 γνόφος, 2217 ζόφος, 887 ἀχλύς.

4655 σκότος is a general word, meaning *darkness* in any sense. 1105 γνόφος usually refers to darkness that accompanies a storm. 2217 ζόφος meant originally *the gloom* of twilight. It was then applied in classical Greek to the darkness of the underworld, the gloom of a sunless region. The latter meaning seems to be practically the one which the word has in the N.T. 887 ἀχλύς is specifically a misty darkness.

§ 44. People, nation.

2992 λαός, 1484 ἔθνος, 1218 δῆμος, 3793 ὄχλος.

2992 λαός is a word which is usually limited in use to the chosen people, Israel. 1484 ἔθνος in the singular is a general term for nation, applied to any nation, even to the Jews. In the plural it ordinarily denotes all mankind aside from the Jews and in contrast with them, the

Gentiles. 1218 δῆμος is a people, especially organized and convened together, and exercising their rights as citizens. 3793 ὄχλος is a *crowd*, an unorganized multitude, especially composed of those who have not the rights and privileges of free citizens.

§ 45. Servant, slave.

1401 δοῦλος, 2324 θεράπων, 1249 διάκονος, 3610 οἰκέτης, 5257 ὑπηρέτης.

1401 δοῦλος is the usual word for *slave*, one who is permanently in servitude, in subjection to a master. 2324 θεράπων is simply one who renders service at a particular time, sometimes as a slave, more often as a freeman, who renders voluntary service prompted by duty or love. It denotes one who serves, *in his relation to a person*. 1249 διάκονος also may designate either a slave or a freeman; it denotes a servant viewed *in relation to his work*. 3610 οἰκέτης designates a slave, sometimes being practically equivalent to 1401 δοῦλος. Usually, however, as the etymology of the term indicates, it means a slave as a member of the household, not emphasizing the servile idea, but rather the relation which would tend to mitigate the severity of his condition. 5257 ὑπηρέτης means literally *an under-rower*, and was used to describe an ordinary rower on a war-galley. It is then used, as in the N.T., to indicate any man, not a slave, who served in a subordinate position under a superior.

§ 46. To adulterate.

2585 καπηλεύω, 1389 δολόω.

Both these words mean *to adulterate*, and some maintain that they are practically identical. But it is more probable that 1389 δολόω means simply to adulterate, while 2585 καπηλεύω conveys the idea of adulterating for the sake of making an unjust profit by the process.

§ 47. Animal.

2226 ζῶον, 2342 θηρίον.

2226 ζῶον is a general term, meaning *living creature*, which may include all living beings, in classical Greek even including man. In the N.T. it means ordinarily *animal*. 2342 θηρίον is *beast*, usually wild beast. It implies perhaps not necessarily wildness and ferocity, but at least a certain amount of brutality which is wanting in 2226 ζῶον. 2226 ζῶον emphasizes the qualities in which animals are akin to man, 2342 θηρίον, those in which they are inferior.

§ 48. Sea.

2281 θάλασσα, 3989 πέλαγος.

2281 θάλασσα is the more general word, indicating *the sea* or *ocean* as contrasted with the land or shore. It may be applied to small bodies of water. 3989 πέλαγος is *the open sea*, the uninterrupted expanse of water, in contrast with the portions broken by islands or with partly inclosed bays. The prominent thought is said by Trench to be breadth rather than depth. Noteworthy is the distinction between the two words in Mat. xviii.6.

§ 49. To grieve.

3076 λυπέομαι, 3996 πενθέω, 2354 θρηνέω, 2875 κόπτομαι.

3076 λυπέομαι is the most general word, meaning simply *to grieve*, outwardly or inwardly. 3996 πενθέω means properly *to lament for the dead*. It is also applied to passionate lamentation of any kind, so great that it cannot be hid. 2354 θρηνέω is *to give utterance to a dirge* over the dead, either in unstudied words, or in a more elaborate poem. This word is used by S. in describing David's lament over Saul and Jonathan. 2875 κόπτομαι is *to beat the breast in grief*, ordinarily for the dead.

§ 50. Form, appearance.

2397 ἰδέα, 3444 μορφή, 4976 σχῆμα.

2397 ἰδέα denotes merely *outward appearance*. Both 3444 μορφή and 4976 σχῆμα express something more than that. They too denote outward form, but as including one's habits, activities and modes of action in general. In 3444 μορφή it is also implied that the outward form expresses the inner essence, an idea which is absent from 4976 σχῆμα. 3444 μορφή expresses the form as that which is intrinsic and essential; 4976 σχῆμα signifies the figure, shape, as that which is more outward and accidental. Both 4976 σχῆμα and 2397 ἰδέα therefore deal with externals, 4976 σχῆμα being more comprehensive than 2397 ἰδέα, while 3444 μορφή deals with externals as expressing that which is internal.

§ 51. Clothing.

2440 ἱμάτιον, 5509 χιτών, 2441 ἱματισμός, 5511 χλαμύς, 4749 στολή, 4158 ποδήρης.

2440 ἱμάτιον is used in a general sense to mean *clothing*, and may thus be applied to any garment when it is not desired to express its exact nature. In a more specific use, however, it denotes the large loose outer garment, *a cloak*, which ordinarily was worn, but in working was laid aside. 5509 χιτών is best expressed by the word *tunic*. It was a closely fitting under-garment, usually worn next the skin. At times, especially in working, it was the only garment worn. A person clothed only in the 5509 χιτών was often called 1131 γυμνός (Jn. xxi. 7). 2440 ἱμάτιον and 5509 χιτών are often found associated as the upper and under garment respectively. 2441 ἱματισμός does not denote a specific garment, but means *clothing*, being used, however, ordinarily only of garments more or less stately or costly. 5511 χλαμύς is *a robe* or *cloak;* it is a technical expression for a garment of dignity or office. 4749 στολή is any stately robe, ordinarily long, reaching to the feet or sweeping the ground, often worn by women. 4158 ποδήρης was originally an adjective meaning *reaching to the feet*. It can hardly be distinguished in use from 4749 στολή. It occurs only in Rev. i. 13.

§ 52. New.

3501 νέος, 2537 καινός.

3501 νέος is *the new* as contemplated under the aspect of time, that which has recently come into existence. 2537 καινός is *the new* under the aspect of quality, that which has not seen service. 2537 καινός therefore often means new as contrasted with that which has decayed with age, or is worn out, its opposite then being 3820 παλαιός. It sometimes suggests that which is unusual. It often implies praise, the new as superior to the old. Occasionally, on the other hand, it implies the opposite, the new as inferior to that which is old, because the old is familiar or because it has improved with age. Of course it is evident that both 3501 νέος and 2537 καινός may sometimes be applied to the same object, but from different points of view.

§ 53. Labor.

3449 μόχθος, 4192 πόνος, 2873 κόπος.

3449 μόχθος is *labor*, hard and often painful. It is the ordinary word for common labor which is the usual lot of humanity. 4192 πόνος is *labor* which demands one's whole strength. It is therefore applied to labors of an unusual kind, specially wearing or painful. In classical Greek it was the usual word employed to describe the labors of Hercules. 2873 κόπος denotes *the weariness* which results from labor, or labor considered from the stand-point of the resulting weariness.

§ 54. Drunkenness, drinking.

3178 μέθη, 4224 πότος, 3632 οἰνοφλυγία, 2970 κῶμος, 2897 κραιπάλη.

3178 μέθη is the ordinary word for *drunkenness*. 4224 πότος is rather concrete, *a drinking, carousing*. 3632 οἰνοφλυγία is a prolonged condition of drunkenness, *a debauch*. 2970 κῶμος includes *riot* and *revelry*, usually as arising from drunkenness. 2897 κραιπάλη denotes *the sickness* and *discomfort* resulting from drunkenness.

§ 55. War, battle.

4171 πόλεμος, 3163 μάχη.

4171 πόλεμος ordinarily means *war, i.e.*, the whole course of hostilities; 3163 μάχη, *battle*, a single engagement. It is also true that 3163 μάχη has often the weaker force of *strife* or *contention*, which is very seldom found in 4171 πόλεμος.

§ 56. Basket.

4711 σπυρίς, 2894 κόφινος.

These words in the N.T. are used with an evident purpose to discriminate between them. The distinction, however, does not seem to have been chiefly one of size, as some have thought, but of use. 4711 σπυρίς is usually a basket for food, *a lunch-basket, a hamper*, while 2894 κόφινος is a more general term for *basket*. The descriptions of the two miracles of feeding the multitude use always different words in the two cases, see *e.g.* Mar. viii. 19, 20.

§57. It is necessary.

1163 δεῖ, 3784 ὀφείλει.

1163 δεῖ, the third person of δέω (L-S, p. 383A), is commonly used impersonally in classical Greek. This usage is less common, but frequent, in the N.T. 1163 δεῖ indicates a necessity in the nature of things rather than a personal obligation; it describes that which *must* be done. 3784 ὀφείλει indicates rather the personal obligation; it is that which is proper, something that *ought* to be done.

§ 58. Tax.

5411 φόρος, 5056 τέλος, 2778 κῆνσος, 1323 δίδραχμον.

5411 φόρος indicates *a direct tax* which was levied annually on houses, lands, and persons, and paid usually in produce. 5056 τέλος is *an indirect tax* on merchandise, which was collected at piers, harbors, and gates of cities. It was similar to modern import duties. 2778 κῆνσος, originally an enrollment of property and persons, came to mean *a poll-tax*, levied annually on individuals by the Roman government. 1323 δίδραχμον was the coin used to pay an annual tax levied by the religious leaders of Israel for the purpose of defraying the general expenses of the Temple.

§ 59. Tax-collector.

5057 τελώνης, 754 ἀρχιτελώνης.

The Roman system of collecting taxes, especially the 5056 τέλοι, in their provinces, included ordinarily three grades of officials. There was the highest, called in Latin *publicanus*, who paid a sum of money for the taxes of a certain province, and then exacted that and as much more as he could from the province. This man lived in Rome. Then there were the *submagistri*, who had charge each of a certain portion of territory, and who lived in the provinces. Then there were the *portitores*, the actual custom-house officers, who did the real work of collecting the taxes. The N. T. word 5057 τελώνης is used to describe one of the *portitores*; it is the lowest of these three grades. It does not correspond to the Latin *publicanus*, and the word *publican* used to translate it in A. V. and R. V. is apt to be misleading; *tax-collector* would be better. 754 ἀρχιτελώνης, only occurring in Lu. xix. 2, evidently describes a higher official than 5057 τελώνης, and is probably one of the *submagistri*, the next higher grade.

§ 60. Child.

5043 τέκνον, 5207 υἱός, 3816 παῖς, 3813 παιδίον, 3808 παιδάριον, 3814 παιδίσκη.

5043 τέκνον and 5207 υἱός both point to parentage. 5043 τέκνον, however, emphasizes the idea of descent, giving prominence to the physical and outward aspects; while 5207 υἱός emphasizes the idea of relationship, and considers especially the inward, ethical, and legal aspects. 3816 παῖς as well as 5043 τέκνον emphasizes the idea of descent, but gives especial prominence to age, denoting a child as one who is young. 3816 παῖς is also often used of a servant. The number of years covered by the term 3816 παῖς is quite indefinite. Its diminutives 3813 παιδίον and 3808 παιδάριον are used without appreciable difference to denote a young child. (παιδίσκος [L-S, p. 1287B] in classical Greek and) 3814 παιδίσκη, in which the diminutive force is largely lost, cover the years of late childhood and early youth.

§ 61. Tribe, family, household.

5443 φυλή, 3965 πατριά, 3624 οἶκος.

These words form a series. 5443 φυλή is sometimes *a race, nation*, but usually *a tribe*, such as one of the twelve tribes of Israel, descended from the twelve sons of Jacob. 3965 πατριά is a smaller division within the tribe; it is an association of families closely related, in the N.T. generally used of those descended from a particular one of the sons of Jacob's sons. 3624 οἶκος is yet narrower, *household*, including all the inmates of a single house, being the unit of organization.